Buying Right

John Schaub

Edited By
Valerie Davis Schaub

Published by
Pro Serve Corp. of Sarasota, Inc.
1938 Ringling Boulevard
Sarasota, Florida 33577

Library of Congress Cataloging In Publication Data
Schaub, John W. III, 1948 -
Buying right
1. Negotiation I. Title

BF637.N4C55 158.5
ISBN 0-936177-00-4

The ideas and suggestions contained in this book have been researched and applied in actual cases by the Author. Any information concerning taxes or specific legal or technical situations should be referred to those competent and authorized to render such advice.

The Author and Publisher specifically disclaim any liability, loss, or risk, personal or otherwise, incurred as a consequence directly or indirectly of the use and application of any of the contents of this book.

Buying Right

TABLE OF CONTENTS

DEDICATION

To my best friend and partner in life,
Valerie Davis Schaub

ACKNOWLEDGMENTS

Many people have given freely of their time and experiences, which have made this book possible. I am especially grateful to Mrs. Hazel Auldridge, my secretary for thirteen years, who has been my loyal right hand in good years - and bad; to my friend Warren G. Harding, whose teaching and idealism have inspired me to a better and better life; and to my friends Jack Miller and Jim Napier for all the good times that we had buying right.

INTRODUCTION

This is a book for buyers of all kinds. I have made my living and accumulated the assets I have by buying real estate below the market price. The same principles I use in buying real estate are applicable in most buying situations.

I am not a compulsive buyer, but I really enjoy getting a good deal on almost anything. When you consider how hard you have to work to earn a dollar, it makes sense to try to get the most value from that dollar when you buy. The old saying that a penny saved is a penny earned was true before income taxes. Now, a penny saved may be worth two pennies earned, in the event you are in a high tax bracket.

Regardless of your tax situation, it is easier to save money by learning how to BUY RIGHT than it is to earn it. BUYING RIGHT is a skill you will have for life and will save you tens of thousands of dollars.

BUYING RIGHT means getting a better price or better terms than are available to most buyers. Many people pay the asking price on everything they purchase. Better prices are available to those with skill and the energy to use that skill.

You will become a better buyer only with practice. Reading this book can give you techniques. For them to work for you, and save you money as you buy, you must practice them until they become your good habits.

While formulas, checklists and guidelines are helpful, you alone are the key ingredient in the program. Your ability to identify "good" deals, negotiate purchases, and close deals is the very personal aspect of this system. I can give you suggestions, but you must do the work yourself.

The case studies and techniques taught in this book, are from real experiences. The names in many cases have been changed to protect those who are innocent, and otherwise.

The principles in the book, when applied, can save you thousands of dollars. Unapplied they cost you nothing, but, perhaps, a better lifestyle for you and your family.

CHAPTER ONE

WHEN "BUYING RIGHT" WILL WORK BEST FOR YOU

Buying right, or getting a better price or better terms, than is offered to the general public, works better in some markets than others. In a "perfect" market, where all buyers have access to all sellers you have little advantage over anyone else.

In a perfect market each seller could offer his product to all buyers at once. The buyers as a group would set the price by their bidding. When the bidding reached a price where the seller was willing, he then should sell all the goods he has at that price.

The New York Stock Exchange is a fair example of a perfect market. Buyers and sellers have access to each other, and one buyer has little advantage over another, even if he is the world's best negotiator.

The real estate market is at the other end of the spectrum. Buyers and sellers have a horrible time finding each other. A seller, with a house priced below what it is worth, sometimes cannot find an interested buyer. A seller who wants to sell quickly, must often take far less than what his property is actually worth in order to dispose of the property.

A good negotiator can do quite well buying real estate, and will often purchase properties for ten, twenty, and occasionally thirty percent less than what they are worth. Purchases are made by professional buyers at even greater discounts than thirty percent, but not very frequently. As there are more houses for sale in most areas, than other types of improved real estate, I suggest that you practice the techniques in this book on houses.

When negotiating for a house, you are less likely to run into a professional negotiator on the selling end. This makes it more likely that you can make a good buy. Also, there are a lot of houses around, and thousands are for sale; therefore, you can practice as much as you want to, and not run out of buying situations. Educators know that you learn through repetition, and experience.

With Whom Are You More Likely To Buy Right?

There are many markets which fall between the real estate market and the stock markets in degrees of "perfection". Owner/sellers are typically easier to deal with than agents or employees of the sellers. This is true in any market for a number of reasons.

First, agents or employees rarely know all of the factors influencing the seller. The owner of the business may have just been notified by the IRS that he owes an additional $100,000 in taxes, and would be delighted to sell for a little less, if the buyer will buy today.

The agent/employee is not as positively or adversely effected financially by the sale. He may receive a commission, or a bonus, or his job may depend on making an occasional sale, but the bulk of the proceeds will go into the seller's account, not his.

As the agent is generally paid a commission, in the event you can deal directly with an owner, he can avoid paying that commission, and therefore make you a little better deal.

Because the owner is receiving the lion's share of the proceeds, he is more likely to get excited about the prospects of receiving that money. That excitement, perceived by an astute negotiator, can be translated into a better deal, a lower price. When dealing with an agent, his excitement can sometimes be used to negotiate a lesser fee, therefore a lower price.

As you can only give back what is yours in any negotiation, it is foolish to spend much time negotiating with a salesclerk at Sears over a ten dollar item; his commission may be only fifty cents. First, he could probably care less about losing the fifty cents, and secondly, that's all you have to gain.

Also, the salesclerk at this level usually doesn't have the authority to make any decision. A real estate broker who has the listing on a ninety thousand dollar house, has much more to give. He also has the authority to make a decision about his commission, in the event that you can show him how he'll benefit from the total transaction.

A clerk at Sears may be able to help you by telling you the same item will be on sale begining tomorrow for thirty percent off. With that information, you can try to talk him into accepting the sale price today. Again, the clerk has little to gain, so the odds are against you. Company policy is probably against you too, although for a large item a department manager might decide to start the sale early.

What Products Are Likely To Be Bought Best

Whatever you are buying, it never hurts to ask for a little discount. Certain items are more likely to be discounted than others. A perishable product, such as fresh vegetables or flowers, have a limited life and can often be purchased for less than the asking price at the end of a day.

Other goods which are less perishable still have a short life in the eyes of the seller. Christmas ornaments, cards and candy are in demand before the holiday, but are dead inventory after the event. Many items of clothing and footwear have little value when the style or the season changes.

All of the above items are marked-up substantially, to compensate the seller for the risk he takes when buying a product which will have little value in a short time.

Items which are being sold for a large profit are items which can potentially be purchased for far less than the asking price. Conversely, items which are being sold at only a small profit, or none at all, are unlikely to be purchased below the asking price.

When buying a real estate investment, the same rules apply. The seller with the largest profit is likely to make you the best deal. Before I make an offer on a property, I always find out what the seller paid for it and how long they have owned it.

These facts will tell me who is most likely to give me the best price. The price they paid has little bearing on what they may sell it for today, but it will tell me which seller I should spend more time pursuing.

What, Where and With Whom: A Buying Right Summary

The ideal circumstances for buying right then would be: 1) when you are dealing directly with an owner, 2) who is anxious to sell something 3) in which he has a large profit.

You are dealing at the other end of the spectrum, 1) with an employee; 2) who has nothing to gain if you buy; 3) and there is little profit in the sales price. You should not be disappointed if you don't make the deal of your lives.

As a confession, I will state that I have never made a good deal when buying a gallon of milk and a loaf of bread in our local supermarket. It does not bother me to pay the same as everyone else for those items. I find comfort in the fact that when I make a larger purchase, like the new glasses I bought yesterday, that I will save several dollars.

When buying an investment property, like a house, the savings will be in the thousands of dollars in the event you combine the three factors above, with the rest of the techniques in this book.

Whatever you buy, you will like it more when you buy it right.

CHAPTER TWO

GETTING RICHER IS A GOOD HABIT

There are many differences between those who have, and those who have not. One major difference is the habits they develop. Study any wealthy person who has made it on their own. You are likely to find he or she has developed the following good habits during their lifetime.

Thrift

Wealthy people tend to be thrifty. Thrift is defined as "wise economy in the management of money". However much money you have, it is efficient to spend it as wisely as possible. Thrifty people can enjoy the best life has to offer. They get even more satisfaction knowing that they bought the object of their enjoyment at a good price.

Some carry a good idea to the extreme and become cheap. Cheap people hoard money and assets, and work very hard not to spend their money at all. In my estimation, they seem to miss many of the good things in life, although those I know personally swear this gives them pleasure.

I have a friend who has more money than he will ever spend, but he never tips. No matter how good the service is, he leaves the table penniless. Just eating at the same table makes me nervous.

I don't suggest that you live like my cheap friend, but wisely spend and invest your assets, whatever they might be.

Patience

Impulse buying condemns you to paying too much, or buying things that you do not need - or even want. The opposite of impulse buying is patient buying. A patient buyer will wait for the right opportunity, and will not buy the wrong item just because that is all there is in stock or "today is the day to buy".

Being effective or efficient in what you buy is as important as knowing how to get a good deal when you finally make a purchase. You shouldn't buy an item you don't need personally, or an investment that you can't turn a sure profit on, even if it's on sale. Who among us has not bought a sweater or record or gadget because it was on sale and looked good at the time, only to have never used it?

In the investment world an impulse buy is called a "hot tip". In the event I could recover the money I've spent on hot tips, I could buy sweaters for everybody and have change left over.

Hot tips are the downfall of many otherwise successful investors. A hot tip is generally a secret shared by a friend about a deal that "can't miss". It is the grown up version of a friendly dare.

When your buddy calls you up and is willing to share the opportunity of a lifetime with you, it is easier - and more fun - to say "count me in", than to pass. If you pass, you run the risk that your buddy might not call you again for a while. You also dramatically increase your chances of financial success. I can't recall a single success when I acted on emotion, and on the sketchy details which accompany these deals. My policy today is not to buy anything for an investment that I don't thoroughly understand and see a clear profit in the day I buy.

The houses we buy for investment fit those parameters. I can recognize a bargain, and know that I can make a profit renting the property. Stock tips, tips on new businesses, and tips on "hot areas" are long shots, and you don't get rich betting on long shots.

Persistence

Worthwhile accomplishments and good buys rarely come quickly or easily. Those who make buying right look easy have probably spent hours studying the situation before making their offer.

As I mentioned in the introduction, this is no magic course. You will need to practice these skills in order for them to work for you. You just can't give up the first time someone rejects your offer.

One of the first houses I purchased for investment was owned by a retired couple. These people were tired of managing a house which they held for investment. Another investor had been trying to buy the house for some time, with no luck.

The first time I visited with them, I stayed three hours. It was two weeks and several visits later that I purchased the house. The sellers knew the neighbors, and wanted to know the person buying the house.

I invested at least a dozen hours talking with the sellers before they signed, But I was rewarded by buying the house about ten thousand dollars below the market price.

Being persistent pays when negotiating with people who have pride in what they are selling. By listening to their stories, and being a peer, you begin to establish a relationship of trust which is necessary before serious negotiations can begin.

Persistence also means pursuing a good idea to its conclusion. There are many great idea people in the world, but only a few rich ones. The rich ones are not only thinkers, but implementers. Most of us have had great ideas, which we later saw others bring to life.

My friend Jimmy Napier says "Everybody should have one good idea, just one". Have yours, and show us all what it is.

Discipline

Great athletes have it, great institutions have it, and you must have it, to some degree, to be successful. Discipline is controlled behavior which is learned through training. Discipline is learned, not inherited.

A disciplined buyer will have a set of rules, call them policies if you will, that he has learned from experience. These will guide him to a successful purchase.

An undisciplined buyer will enter into each new situation, unprepared, hoping that his good looks and wishful thinking will again win the day. An undisciplined buyer learns little from his past experiences and will probably repeat the same mistakes.

A disciplined buyer will review each purchase, learn from his mistakes, and change his policies to reflect his new knowledge. As you read this book, establish your own set of buying policies. Make these part of your buying system by practicing and being determined to use them.

Enthusiasm

Thrift, patience, and persistence are building blocks of success, but the real key is enthusiasm. Picture the thriftiest, most patient and persistent person in the world. Without a smile on his face, and a sparkle in his eye, he is doomed to a life of mediocrity.

Enthusiasm is directed excitement. When you are excited about something you will lie awake nights thinking about it. The more you think about something, and the more you work at it, the more likely you are to achieve your goal.

Motivational speakers have told us for years that attitude is more important than skill when it comes to making a success out of a venture. There are many highly trained people who, because they lack a positive attitude toward their work or their life, will never know the thrill of enthusiasm.

It Doesn't Cost Any More To Go First Class

The above line is right out of a class taught by my good friend Warren Harding. Warren makes the point, and it's a good one, that you're probably going to spend all your money before you leave this world anyway, so why not enjoy the best that the world has to offer.

Before I give further explanation, let me anticipate your reservations, and state that first you have to BUY RIGHT, so you can afford to go first class at all!

When you buy the best and highest quality product on the market, you will often pay a premium price the day you buy. However, in addition to the enjoyment that the top of the line may bring you, there is a practical aspect to buying the best. This product will last longer, require less maintenance and give more utility. And so, it is typically cheaper - in the long run - to buy the best and keep it longer than to buy the inferior item and replace it at regular intervals.

If you study the wealthy people in this world, you will find they have several things in common. They often drive the best cars but keep them for years and years. They might be driving a ten year old Mercedes or Rolls or Jaguar, which is in excellent condition. Because the car is still stylish and runs well, there is no need to trade it every year for a newer model.

Notice how seldom your top-of-the-line car companies, like Mercedes and Rolls Royce, radically change their models. They know that their buyers would rather pay more for a car that will be dependable, comfortable, and hold its value. Since these buyers are not as likely to trade on a yearly basis, there is no need to change the model annually to appeal to that market.

The same principles apply to all purchases from real estate to shoes. With boats, cars, clothes, appliances, and nearly every product line - you get what you pay for.

In real estate there is a great difference in quality of construction. Those that choose to invest in the more cheaply constructed properties will spend much more on maintenance than those who buy well constructed property to start with.

Likewise, those who do not choose the location of their purchase carefully the first time around will be more likely to trade up to different properties. While there can be profits made in this progress, the act of buying and selling itself is inefficient.

Of course, even the best and highest priced goods can be purchased at considerable discount. And, typically, the higher the price of the product, the more the mark-up, and the greater the available discount.

Whenever you are buying, try to buy something you can be happy with for a long period of time. If you're buying a car, get a size that will be right for several years. Try to choose colors that aren't so wild or bright that you tire of them quickly. When buying clothes, try to buy things that aren't so faddish that they go out of style overnight. This is not to say you can't spice up your wardrobe with some flashy items, but plan your major purchases so that they give you several years of use.

CHAPTER THREE

BEFORE YOU BUY

Now, you're ready! You have patient persistence and disciplined enthusiasm; you want to go first class and plan to enjoy it.

But BUYING RIGHT is more than philosophy and platitudes. It includes preparation and research before you even decide what to buy. After you know what you want to buy you have to find it - if it is not in a retail setting. And, finally, you need to have some self-restraint to keep yourself on the path to better purchasing.

Research

Preparation and research is the dull side of making good deals. The more expensive the item you are planning on buying, the more time you should spend on research.

Fortunately, there is an abundance of information available on just about any consumer item you could hope to purchase. Take some time and read consumer reports, trade journals and magazine articles about the item you want to buy. There are public libraries available to everyone in this country, and they are staffed by people who can help you find the information you need.

Determine if it matters to you that the article was approved by the Underwriters Lab, has the Good Housekeeping Seal of Approval, or won the Car of the Year Award. If you are shopping around to find a local company or tradesman to do business with, check with the local Better Business Bureau. Ask for references, and check them out. See if there is a warranty, and read it!

Let your fingers do the walking, and use the telephone to do some research. Call ahead to see if a certain item is in stock; ask if there are any sales planned. Too many times research is cut short because the researcher tries to cover too much ground and, in exhaustion, just buys the next item he sees.

In the event it is real estate you are researching, a wealth of information is available in the public records of the county in which the property is located. As discussed in the next chapter, our country has a system of recording that puts a wealth of information before you - if you only bother to go and look at it.

Overresearching has diminishing returns. You know people who will shop at four different stores for a three dollar item, trying to save seventy-five cents. There is a time to complete the research and buy. If you are so uncertain of the purchase that you can't commit yourself, then it would be better not to buy at all.

List What You Will Buy - Be Specific

For major purchases it is important to have definite goals written down before you buy. This is not a grocery list that merely lists items to buy, but a list of features that you have determined are important to you.

With most items, you will have several objectives in mind, and you should write out what is important to you. After you make the list, try to set some priorities by deciding which features are critical to you, and which you could do without or modify.

For example, when buying a car your list could look like this:

Four door model

A split front seat

A large trunk

At least 18 miles to a gallon

A good safety record

A light color that won't fade

Automatic transmission

Power windows

Cruise control

The above list certainly does not cover all of the options or limit you to one or two models. It does give you some definite guidelines and will keep you from buying a fire engine red fastback coupe on impulse. You may love that coupe for a week or two, but then you would start wishing for all of the features you failed to acquire.

Give your list of goals plenty of thought, and then stick with it. It is easy to get excited when buying a car, or house, and lose sight of your original purpose.

When we found the house we now live in, we first wrote down all of the things we really wanted in a house. By doing this we could remain objective as we started searching through all of the possibilities. Our list looked like this:

At least two bedrooms and two baths

At least a double car garage

Location within a ten minute drive of the office

Large rooms suitable for entertaining

Fireplace

Waterfront location with good dockage

A family area, good for raising children

While this list gave us some latitude, it also helped us narrow the field considerably. It saved us lots time traipsing through strangers' houses, mumbling compliments. Many people finally agree to buy a house just so they don't have to look at anymore.

Using our list we found a house that was OK, but definitely not the house of our dreams. It met all our requirements, but also had some drawbacks that would have been on our "do not get" list. It was an older home and needed considerable cosmetic improvement and maintenance.

The list helped us to be more objective, because it made us note that all the features we wanted were present. On the other hand, the fact that we did not love this house actually gave us a tremendous edge when it came time to negotiate the rental terms. Because we did not care that much whether we got the house, I was able to ask for a fabulous rent and extra benefits (weekly lawn care). The list took some of the emotional reactions out of my responses.

Beware Of Impulsive Buying

Writing the details of your purchase, and doing some research will put you in a position to make the best deal possible. Remember now, that patience pays, and there is no substitute for self-restraint. Needless to say, purchases made in a hurry or on a whim will not be the ones where you get the most value for your money.

The manner in which goods are sold in this country truly encourages impulsive, emotional buying. Just buying things can be fun, and doubtless there are times when buying for pleasure meets some deep inner need. But this book wants to help you get more for your money; psychological buying tips you'll have to get elsewhere.

Once you've determined what you want to buy, and at what price, it's a good idea to decide in advance how far you may vary from your specific purchase plan. Is the name-brand item the only one you will buy, or will a generic suit you as well? Should you buy accessories right now for the major purchase, or wait and use it alone for a while?

Last Christmas, my two sisters and I decided to buy a VCR for our parents. After several hours of research we decided on a certain brand and model. A timely newspaper ad showed that a local discount merchant had this very item at a good price. We sent my younger sister on the buying trip armed with this information and explicit instructions.

She returned from her shopping trip, not only with a different brand, but with a set that had many different functions and at a far higher price than we had planned to spend. The salesman had told her that although they could get the model she wanted, they weren't sure it would be available before Christmas. Besides, he said, this other model was superior to the one she wanted and at only a slightly higher cost. About 30% higher.

I returned the set to the store, and after a discussion of bait and switch with the manager, he found the set in another store that I could take delivery on that very afternoon.

Bait and switch, of course, is the unsavory tactic of advertising an unavailable or nonexistent item in order to get the customer into the sales arena to be sold a more expensive item. Don't be a victim of this procedure. If you have taken the time and effort to select a good purchase, go to a person with authority and demand that they make good on their advertisement.

"Selling up" on the other hand is what you may encounter with any red-blooded commissioned salesperson. They are paid more when they sell a higher- priced item; it is part of their job to interest you in the more expensive version of whatever you wanted.

Be firm. Keep in mind the research you've done, what you really want, and how much you want to spend. If you know you will only use the microwave to heat baby food and pop popcorn, there is no need to buy a model that can prepare an entire Thanksgiving dinner.

Further, to protect yourself from an enthusiastic salesman or a rush of excitement from within, develop a system of counting. This works much like counting before you lose your temper.

Drop by any household with children and you will likely find one or both parents counting to ten. This technique is designed to insure the continued well being of certain small people.

A similar system will work when about to make an impulsive purchase. *Rather than counting to ten, think of ten other ways you could spend the same amount of money*. By considering alternate purchases, you bring into perspective the value you are getting for the money spent.

If after reviewing your research and reasons, and considering what else you could buy with the money, you decide to buy - consider this a successful purchase.

Timing

Timing is one more factor that can make a difference when you try to maximize your buying power.

First, you need to allow enough time to work through the steps listed above. To go grocery shopping you probably won't need any research, but a moment to write out a list - and the resolve to use it - will make you an effective buyer, and save you money every week.

To buy a larger item, a car for example, will take more of your time. You need to do some consumer research, calculate what you can afford to spend, think about the features you need in a vehicle and list them, speak with car owners in your price range, visit some car lots and take some test drives. If you decide one morning that you need to purchase a car before noon, you will probably sacrifice efficiency and economy because you haven't allowed much time.

When you can plan your purchases and wait before buying, your patience and foresight will be rewarded. Some items go on sale regularly, and to get the best bargain it is wise to buy these things during the sale. White sales, appliance sales, after-Christmas sales; you can use time to buy right.

This brings us to the topic of deadlines, and how to plan your purchases around them. Some deadlines are real, like a foreclosure sale. Others are invented to make the buyer act.

I worked at Sears when I was in college, and it was easy to notice that the same items were put on sale at the same prices time after time. If you missed a sale at Sears, all you had to do was wait a few weeks, and the sale would be repeated. These sales were not deadlines for Sears, only ploys to get the customer to buy today.

Other retail sales, like end-of-the-year sales in the auto trade, do represent more of a deadline. The dealers want to move out this year's models, so they have the money and space to stock the newer, faster-selling cars. For a buyer to use a deadline to his advantage, you must determine if the seller will suffer a loss.

Sears, or even the commissioned salesman at Sears, has little to lose the last day of a sale. Can you tell this year's model wrench or battery or refrigerator from last year's? That is no accident.

With other commissioned salespeople, the best time to buy is toward the end of their accounting period. This is typically on a monthly basis. Whether you are buying a car, a typewriter, or television set, shop towards the end of the month and make sure you deal with a commissioned salesman who is anxious to make a quota.

With that in mind, it's often best to deal with the best and highest paid salesman who, because of their volume, can afford to make you a better deal than the struggling salesman.

CHAPTER FOUR

BUYING RIGHT: THE REAL ESTATE MARKET

The suggestions discussed above were presented to reflect buying in the retail arena. But I have found and commend to you, the buying of houses as both an investment and an excellent way to practice BUYING RIGHT skills.

The suggestions above apply, and in some cases are even more important. In addition, you will actually have to find the item you want to buy and determine its value.

This discussion is directed towards house buying, but most of it will also be applicable to all unique items, being purchased from a non-commercial owner.

Researching Real Estate

The importance of researching a real estate purchase before you make an offer cannot be overemphasized. You will be able to learn a great deal about the house, the financing, the neighborhood, and perhaps the owners by delving into the public records. As the name implies, these public records are open to all, and are located in the courthouse or hall of records in that county.

No need to be shy; this information has been compiled for everyone to use. The staff of this area are usually very helpful in showing you how to use the machines or find the information, but they won't do your research for you.

The price that the present owners paid for the property, and the prices that all their neighbors paid, is on record. Any loans and other liens of record can be reviewed. The purchase prices reported and the terms of these loans can give the researching buyer insight as to the history of the property, sales price in the past, and motivation of the sellers.

There is some skill involved, and if you have never done this work before you will have to take some time and educate yourself as to what you are looking for and how to find it. I mentioned that the staff of the public records room is usually helpful as far as showing you how the machines work and where records are kept. You will need to know, however, what a legal description is, what documents you should look for, and what this information means to you.

If you have never read a mortgage or trust deed, you will have to read one. Then decide if you understand what it means or if you need some education or tutoring in order to decipher what it can tell you. If you are not experienced in financial matters you may need some education in order to understand the relationship of interest rates, principal, balloon notes and the value of the property.

I have purchased property from sellers who appeared to be nonchalant about their debt, but have found terms in their loans which would force them to sell or refinance. Such terms as a balloon clause, which calls for a large payment on one date, can often put pressure on a seller to sell by that date.

Also, notices of any law suits pending against the owners or the property are available to the public. In the event the seller is being sued, that may be the motivation for selling. It will help you make a wise purchase to know this.

The tax assessor's and collector's offices can tell you at what value the county has assessed the property for taxing purposes. They also keep records on any improvements to a property which required a building permit. In the event the owners proudly advertised an addition, this is one way to tell if they had a permit and had the work inspected when it was completed.

Knowing what someone paid for a property or what they owe on it, does not necessarily have much bearing on what the property is worth today. They may have purchased the property before substantial improvements were made in the neighborhood. The owners may have paid too much when they purchased. However, it will give you an indication of how much profit, if any, the sellers have.

List What You Want In An Investment House

The listing process can be very valuable in locating a house for investment. It can also help you plan your offer, determine the financing you want or need, and perhaps keep your feet on the ground. Falling in love with an investment property can be fatal to BUYING RIGHT.

If you remember, we used such a list when searching for a house we wanted to rent. When buying a house for investment your list may look like this:

Three or four bedrooms

At least two full baths

Good storage, either in garage or basement

Good neighborhood without other noticeable rentals

Good school district

An assumable loan, or an owner willing to finance

A maximum down payment of $5,000

Monthly payments less than the probable monthly rent

A purchase price of at least 10% below market

No balloons or personal guarantees in the loan

There are hundreds of properties which fit within these parameters. A list will help you eliminate the thousands of properties which are not what you want to buy.

Incidently, if you can't believe that there are houses available to you that meet the requirements on the list above, keep reading for practical suggestions. And when you practice your skills, remember the need for patience and persistence.

Hazards Of Impulsive Buying

After you research and write your list it's time to go out into the market and look for a bargain.

I hope you remember the previous section on the hazards of impulsive purchases. This is also true for houses you buy - only more so.

Many investors of real estate break even or even lose a little because they buy impulsively. Unfortunately, the property purchased without due care is often the one which is hard to manage or has poor financing. The investor can be forced to sell before there is a profit.

You can buy nearly any real estate, hold it 20 years, and make a profit. But many times the investor just can't hold onto the property because it is hard to manage or has unbearable cash flow due to bad financing. You may have to sell a property during a low period in the economic cycle, or just too soon for that property to have appreciated and shown a profit.

CHAPTER FIVE

FINDING THE DEAL

An important item to consider when you are buying a house, a piece of art from a private collection, or any item outside the retail setting: first you have to find it. You need to find a seller that has the item for sale that you want; how do you find that seller?

Finding Deals In The Newspaper

Using the classified ads in the newspaper is a good place to start. One day a week read the classified ads for a local area advertising "houses for sale". At least in the beginning of your investment work you may want to concentrate on calling "for sale by owner" ads, since working directly with the owner without an agent is usually more efficient.

Circle all the ads that you think have some promise; be sure to concentrate on a neighborhood that would be comfortable and safe for a typical family. Probably a house with three bedrooms and two bathrooms is best.

Finding Deals - Other Sources

There are, of course, other ways to find people who are interested in selling their house. You can check the public records to see who has filed for divorce. Or, read the obituaries to contact a representative of an estate to see if the house will be sold. If you contact a loan company they might be willing to tell you about people who are behind on their loans, if the company thinks you might bring the loan current if you buy it. If you drive through a neighborhood you think has potential, look for houses that look as though no one is living there. Then try to contact the owners.

There are countless ways, but if you are a beginner just checking the newspaper ads should keep you busy. Circle all the ads that might be within the parameters of your list, and use your telephone to efficiently narrow the field.

Identifying The Good Deals Using Your Phone

In buying real estate, I spend at least ten hours on the phone for every hour in the field looking at property and making offers. The ratio of good deals to property for sale in the single family house market is about one out of a hundred. You could go out and look at fifty houses without ever getting close to a seller who will make you a good deal. You can maximize your effort by using the telephone to scout for good deals.

In the seminar I teach, class members learn to use the telephone to locate sellers who are likely to sell their property at a below market price and at better than market terms. Learning to use the phone effectively is critical to buying good deals in the house market.

There are thousands of houses on the market in an average town at any one time; only a few are "good deals". A typical buyer would begin by making a few short phone calls to obtain some addresses, and then proceed to tour the town to check out the properties.

Most sellers will give you a pitch over the phone to get you out to their house. Even the overpriced houses will sound good over the phone to a novice who does not take the time to dig in and get the facts.

If you have a system of asking pointed questions, and recording the factual answers, then you can objectively rank the motivation of the sellers over the phone. To be objective, you need to be consistent about the questions you ask, so it is better to work from a list than to ad lib each phone call.

The list used in the seminar contains sixty-one questions. That's right, 61 questions. Each question is designed to determine the motivation and flexibility of the seller as well as the physical aspects of the property. Once you are familiar with the questions it takes about 15 minutes to go through all 61 assuming the questionee lasts that long.

Obviously, there are many sellers whom you won't want to talk to that long. The first few questions are designed to categorically weed out those with whom you wish to waste no time. The first question is, "Are you the owner?". Talking to a neighbor, brother-in-law, or agent representing the owner is generally a complete waste of time. Either they do not know why the owner is selling, or will not tell you out of loyalty to the owner.

If the answer is "No", call back when you can speak with the owner.

When you have the owner on the phone talk to the person about:

Why are they selling the house? It does make a difference in terms of timing and flexibility.

How much money do they want? How did they decide on the purchase price?

How much of the purchase price must be paid in cash? Why do they need this much in cash?

When do they want to close the deal? Is there any time pressure, or will they wait to get their price and terms?

What are the features of the house: bedrooms, bathrooms, garage, family room, nice neighborhood....

What are the problems with the house: roof leaks, kitchen appliances 12 years old, no insulation, out-dated windows

Ask any other questions that you would need to know in order to decide whether this house could hold any possibly for you. Use your list; is it meeting the features you thought you wanted? If not, thank the person and move on to the next call.

The last question I ask is, "If I buy your house this weekend, will you make me a good deal?". This one is designed to find someone to whom time is important, and who would rather liquidate at a lower price than continue to be an owner. It is important to convey to the owner that you are able and willing to buy this weekend, but are looking for a "deal".

While a "good deal" is a rather fluid concept, in the event a seller asks me to define it, I respond by stating, "let me ask you a few questions about your property, and I'll tell you if we are close". The next few questions deal with the location, age, and existing financing.

CHAPTER SIX

TALKING ABOUT MONEY

Now a word about squeamishness when talking to strangers about money. When I give the directions for talking to sellers on the telephone, people tell me flatly that, "you can't ask someone that intimate a question" and further, that "no one would ever answer that question." In the United States there is definitely a perceived prohibition about discussing these things.

First of all, the answers to some of these questions is recorded in the public records, which certainly defeats the argument that such a matter is too delicate to discuss. Intimacy is not a factor in knowing how much you paid for the house, when you bought it, who financed the purchase or what the terms of the loan are. It is more a matter of convenience to ask this, and to double check to see if the owner tells you the truth.

Also, if I buy this house then it is actually *my* money we are discussing. How did they arrive at the price that will be paid with *my* money? How much of *my* money will be required at closing? With this outlook you may feel more comfortable. You really do need this kind of information to make any preliminary decision about your future with this house.

Regarding the type of questions people will answer: if you talk to a "motivated" seller, you will not believe how much they will tell you. These people want to sell their house. Most of them will answer your questions as long as they feel you are a potential buyer and not just using them for practice.

Of course, there will be people who won't answer your questions, and will even be rude. That is also one of the reasons that it is helpful to scout for property on the telephone. No one can see you blush, no one can physically intimidate you, and you can end the call whenever it appears that it won't serve any purpose. Go on to the next call, which may be just the situation you've been waiting for.

Know The Value Of What You Are Buying

When you consider a purchase in a retail setting, there is a fixed price for that item. Of course you can often improve the deal, but the price listed can give you a starting point in determining the value of whatever you're inspecting. Also, there are often other stores or companies selling the same item, or a similiar one, and you can price shop in that manner.

Sometimes half price sales are not bargains at all, because the sale items are out of style or obsolete. Is a Nehru jacket a bargain at any price? How about a house in Times Beach, Missouri? That is the town which was condemed by the Federal Government because of toxic waste.

Buying outside the retail setting can be much more exciting. You may be buying a one-of-a-kind item and have no way to verify its value. As in houses, there may be thousands to compare, but the value varies depending on the location, quality or age. And the price usually varies depending on the seller and financing.

When you begin your search for an investment house to purchase, you need to have some ability to decide what that house is worth. The same applies if you are dealing with a used car, custom furniture or any other item being sold by the owner. When buying a ten dollar item on sale at K Mart for five dollars, in the worst case you are making a five dollar mistake. When buying real estate you can easily make a mistake 1000 times that costly.

Most items purchased in a retail store are sold originally for at least twice what it cost to manufacture the item. When a house is built, the markup is far less. However, it is easy to pay more for the raw materials in a real estate deal than the end product will be worth.

Look around any moderately priced neighborhood and you will find a house which has been overimproved for the area. Adding a pool to an inexpensive house will do the trick. The ten thousand dollars it cost to build the pool and deck area may only add a fraction of that cost to the value of the property.

Often sellers of properties like to point out all of the improvements they have made to the house. The shag carpeting on the walls and ceilings may be beautiful in their eyes, but probably detracts from the value. It will cost money to remove it and refinish the walls and ceiling.

Similiarly, poorly constructed room additions and garage enclosures do little to improve the value of the house. The cost of the improvements of a parcel of real estate does not necessarily relate to what the property is worth.

How then do you determine what a property is worth, in the event you want to buy a parcel of real estate? Once again, when making a purchase this expensive you really need to research the market. Also, you will become well versed in the values of a particular market over time if you systematically talk to sellers and make offers on property.

Using Professional Appraisals

One way to get a professional opinion of value is to hire a competent appraiser to appraise the property. Typically, an appraiser will charge about one hundred dollars, plus or minus fifty, for a standard house appraisal.

The appraiser will use different methods depending on the type of property being appraised. The method given the most weight in appraising residential property is the market value approach. This value is determined by researching what other houses of comparable size, and location have recently sold for. Minor adjustments are then made for superior or inferior construction, the difference in value of the lot, and amenities such as a pool or outbuilding.

The fee paid for an appraisal is well worth it, in the event you think you are about to make a good deal, but are nervous about the value.

Suppose you found a seller of a home, who was willing to take $70,000 for a house they paid $80,000 for two years ago. They claim that the house is now worth nearly $90,000, but want to sell this week, and are willing to take a loss to sell quickly.

You calculate a potential twenty thousand dollar profit, but then start thinking, why are they selling so cheaply? You find yourself wondering if the house is really worth $90,000, or if the sellers are pulling your leg.

If you are going to buy, you will have to buy quickly. If the house is really worth $90,000, someone else will come along and take it. Sign a contract at the $70,000 price with one contingency. You reserve the right to have the property appraised, and will close subject to your approval of the appraisal.

Now hire an appraiser, and tell him you want an estimate of fair market value. In the event the appraisal comes in at $90,000, or thereabouts, you will close on the contract with confidence. In the event the appraisal comes in far below the $90,000 figure, say $75,000, then you will pass. You have invested a nominal amount of money, and either way it works out it was worth it.

The same technique will work with personal property of hard to determine value. Suppose someone approaches you with a work of art, supposedly of high value, which he will wholesale for quick cash. Sign an agreement subject to having the painting appraised. In the event the seller refuses, then you may have learned why he is willing to sell so cheaply.

In neither of the cases above would I let the seller hold my deposit. A deposit on a contract with any contingencies, should be held by a third party until those contingencies have been satisfied. I prefer to have my attorney hold the deposit. In the event there is ever a dispute, I will be assured of a fair settlement.

Using Time To Your Advantage

Deadlines, time schedules which must be met, set the framework for any negotiation. In a situation where neither party is in a hurry to consummate the deal, the deal generally dies from boredom.

Conversely, when one party has a deadline to meet, the negotiation will generally result in a deal *immediately prior to that deadline*. In our class negotiating sessions, they nearly always strike a deal within thirty seconds of the time limit.

Knowing what deadlines are important to the other party is obviously an advantage. Determining what those deadlines are and how critical they are takes practice and some empathy for their position. One of the important items to determine in your telephone conversation with the owner is whether there is any time pressure to sell.

First, you have to ask some well directed questions to see if they have a deadline. If they tell me they are buying a new house, I always ask when they are moving. The answers range from "the truck just pulled up out front" to "whenever we sell".

Answers between those extremes state "before school opens", "before Christmas", "before the baby is born", and "by the time the new house is finished". Once you have that answer, you have to dig a little deeper to see if they are giving you the real answer. Sellers sometimes invent an answer that they think a buyer would like to hear.

To stay objective I try to categorize deadlines into one of the following three groups:

Type A: The party involved will suffer substantial financial loss *or* his reputation would suffer irreparably.

Type B: The party may have a financial loss, but relative to it's overall situation, it will be nominal. (A $100,000 loss to General Motors is nominal). Any damage to reputation can be mended and will be quickly forgotten.

Type C: The party may be inconvenienced, but is willing to put up with it rather than take less for his position.

In the event you are looking for a house and want to negotiate with someone with a deadline, find someone leaving a house unsold while they move to another house. I try not to negotiate with someone unless they have definite moving plans, or the house is already empty. In other words I look for Type A's and avoid wasting time talking to those who are not anxious.

If they are moving when the new house is finished, or maybe when the sellers of their "new" house vacate, I ask about where it is, and how the construction is going. I want to get a feeling for how important it will be to them to move in right away when their new house is available.

I know how eager we were to move into our new house. We moved in before the builder was completely finished. I want to find someone that eager before I try to buy their house. Although the date that their house is finished is not a Type A deadline, it would certainly give them peace of mind to be rid of their old house before they took possession of the new one.

A car dealer will be anxious to sell at year end, but consider the anxiety of the homeowner, who has been transferred out of state and is moving next week. They have but one product to sell and a deadline which they must meet or suffer a relatively large financial loss.

If Sears does not sell a refrigerator, they will be in business the next day, trying again. Their loss is the profit they did not make and the cost of inventory for the unsold item.

When a family of modest means fails to sell their home, and moves to another house, the results can be devastating to the family finances and mental health. Most families do not have the cash flow necessary to make the payments on the old house, and then rent or buy another one. In addition, both houses must be maintained. In the summer the grass will grow and in the winter, the pipes may freeze. As the time to move grows closer, these sellers become Type A's, and hopefully people with whom you can make a deal.

Desperate Deadlines

Sellers of real estate, and other larger items, sometimes are selling for financial reasons. They may be having difficulty making house or car payments. They may have a large lump sum payment, often called a balloon, due soon, without any means of paying that payment.

Sellers with financial problems are often reluctant to talk to strangers about them. Your line of questioning must be more subtle to gather this type of information. You may ask if their present loan is assumable. In the event the sellers are in or near foreclosure, the lender may want to be paid in full.

In buying real estate, I encounter a number of owners who are in danger of losing their property in foreclosure. By the time I see them, foreclosure is only a day or two away.

These people are often still negotiating for a price significantly higher than the loan balance, even though they will lose everything in the event they do not sell their position within hours. They are really Type A's , but are acting like Type C's. Most people who lose their properties in foreclosure have had offers which they have refused hoping for more. The offer they finally accept generally comes the day before or the day of the sale. Of course, if they do nothing they get to accept the results of the sale as the final offer.

A significant number of properties are sold every day in this country through the foreclosure process. Although many of these properties have debts greater than the value, and are abandoned for that debt, thousands have equity which could have been sold prior to the sale.

This points out a paradox in negotiating with people (as opposed to Vulcans or computers who are completely logical). Faced with a deadline which brings with it great financial loss and embarrassment, people seem to ignore the deadline.

Some people become almost comatose under unusual pressure. Those who are not used to negotiating for large sums of money find it easier to make no decision at all, falsely assuming that this is the safest path.

CHAPTER SEVEN

FINANCING, BIDDING AND TRADE-INS

Before you make any purchase, inquire as to what type of financing might be available on the purchase and what kind of warranties will protect your purchase. An article being sold on a cash only, no guarantee basis, should be able to be purchased at a substantial discount over one which will be serviced by the seller and financed either by the seller or by other financing institutions.

The longer the term that a seller or bank will finance a product, probably the longer life that product has. Likewise, the longer a warranty a product would have, the better your chances that the property is well built or the item well constructed.

Don't confuse service contracts with warranties. A service contract is purchased by the buyer in addition to the purchase price. The service contract guarantees the seller will work on whatever he sold you for the life of the contract.

Bidding Pays - Sometimes

A friend recently decided to buy a new luxury car. When he approached a local dealer, he found they were hesitant to give him any discount on the model he wanted. As he was not in a hurry to buy, he wrote twelve dealers around the state for specifics regarding the model he wanted to purchase and asked for bids. Seven of the dealers responded and he saved nearly 20% which amounted to several thousand dollars on this purchase for the time and effort expended in writing these dealers.

The bidding process described above can save you thousands of dollars on major purchases, and using your telephone and the yellow pages can save you hundreds on smaller purchases. Don't be afraid to make some long distance calls when the cost of what you're buying will justify the expenditure of $20 or $30 long distance bills to save hundreds.

Of course, this technique can be extended to the extreme. To save 20% is good, but if that 20% relates to a one dollar savings and takes three hours of your time, you might examine what your time is worth. On the other hand, the recreational value of shopping for an item sometimes justifies spending the time. Have you ever heard of someone shopping all day and not buying anything at all?

How about someone going to an auction and not buying anything at all? Here is the flip side of bidding, and one that can cost you money.

An auction is a good example of an exciting sale environment, where people often pay more than they intended for an item. They are caught in the frenzy of the sale, and forget their spending limits, if indeed they ever had any. In the event you ever bid at an auction, know what you want to pay for an item, and write it down. Then promise yourself that under no circumstances will you bid higher.

At a real estate auction, the auctioneer and his assistants are trying to get the crowd into an excited state so that the bidding will go higher and higher. Many such sales bring more than fair market value. The auctioneer gets two or more eager buyers bidding against each other, and does his job well by getting the highest price he can for the seller.

Trading Up And Trading In

Look for sellers who are trading up into new items. Some are so excited about their next purchase that they wholesale the existing item in order to get the new one. These excited sellers have little regard for the economics of the situation as their focus is on their purchase and not their sale.

I have a good friend who buys car after car from an acquaintance who "trades up" to a new model every other year. My friend always buys a two year old car, but at a fraction of what a new model would cost. The seller is always happy because he is getting a shiny brand new car. Because he continues to finance his purchases, the only thing he notices is his monthly payments increase slightly each year.

People who want a new appliance, car, house, boat, plane - all sorts of things - often have to determinedly sell the present possession to get the new one. They are sometimes in a position to make a cash buyer a great deal, but the buyer has to ask for one.

The microwave oven we have in our office was purchased from a retail outlet which had taken it in on trade. It had not been cleaned or reconditioned, and was of uncertain value. When I put the manager of the store on the spot for a price, he thought fifty dollars would be fair. After discussing the difficulty of unloading an old, discontinued brand, we agreed on forty dollars, if he would throw in a cookbook. That was five years ago and that old oven works as good as the day we bought it.

Now the other side of the coin: when you trade in an item.

Trading in your used item for a new one has its disadvantages. Although it solves your problem of owning two microwave ovens, or one-too-many cars at the same time, the dealer must build in a profit margin in case he can't sell your trade in for what it is worth.

When you approach a car dealer with the proposition that you want to buy one of his newer models, and trade old Bessie in, he will attempt to impress you with his fairness by asking you what you want for old Bessie. There is a good chance that after some animated negotiating with the sales manager, the salesman will convince his boss to give you what you want for Bessie, in the event you buy today. Some are so excited about getting a high price for their old car that they miss the fact that they are paying more for the new car than they would if they just paid cash.

As a cash buyer, you will always have an advantage. In the event you plan on trading in a car, house or other used item, first negotiate with the seller as though you are a cash buyer. After you have reached an agreement on price and terms, then introduce the fact that you will have to sell your old one first. In the event the seller wants to make a deal he will offer to take yours in trade. You already know what your best cash price is on the item you want to buy, so you can easily figure what the dealer is giving you for your old "unit".

I have used this technique in reverse when trying to sell an expensive house I have purchased. I run an ad that reads like this.

> Spacious Custom Built 3 Bedroom 2 Bath Lakefront
>
> Anxious Owner wants smaller home, will Accept Trade-in. Appraised at $98,500. 366-9024.

I am looking for some one with a smaller home, who wants a high price for the house they have now as a trade in. They want a newer or larger house, but they just aren't going to take a low price for their present home. As I always buy substantially below the market price, I can afford to pay someone with a $65,000 house $68,000 in the event they buy mine at close to appraised price.

The Fine Points Of Financing

This section combines financing guidelines with case studies which illustrate those guidelines. Asking the seller to participate in the financing of the sale can increase your profits. On the other hand, a seller will loan you a much higher percentage of value than a bank would on the same purchase. Therefore the unknowledgeable buyer can, and often does borrow more money against a purchase than he can afford to pay back.

The problem with money easily borrowed, is that it is always harder to repay. The following points should be studied before borrowing:

1. Never borrow money without a source of repayment. An investment should only be financed up to the point where the income it generates will service the debt.

2. Never borrow money to pay interest on existing debt. If you cannot pay your interest obligation, sell an asset and pay off the debt. If there are no remaining assets, you must renegotiate a payment schedule you can afford with your lenders. The only alternative is bankruptcy which is unrewarding for all involved.

3. Avoid borrowing on depreciating assets, unless they produce enough income to repay the debt during their expected lifetime. Non-productive depreciating assets (toys, like motorhomes, boats, cars, etc.) often lose value faster than their loans pay down, causing the owner to sell at a cash loss. My personal policy is never to buy a toy unless I can afford to pay cash for it. Then in the event I had to wholesale it, I would at least put some cash in my pocket.

I realize that this goes against the American Way of "buy now, pay later" (a phrase first uttered by a crafty banker). But, I have noticed that most who buy things now that they can't afford pay a high percentage of their income to the bankers in interest. Although much of this interest may be deductible on your income tax return, you must first earn enough to pay the interest and taxes before you get to keep any for yourself.

4. Interest is an expense which should be minimized in the event you wish to maximize profits. Those who argue that deductible interest is tax shelter have not thought through the consequences of paying interest. It is a deductible expense, as is a plumbing bill on an investment property. Who would ask for a bigger plumbing bill so that they would have a bigger deduction?

People who pay lots of interest may pay little in taxes, but they will also have little profits left over, after interest and tax payments. Who would have more spendable income ? Someone who earned $75,000 and paid $40,000 in interest, or someone who earned $75,000 and paid no interest at all? Using any tax brackets you want, the person with no interest expense will come out ahead.

Dealing With Overfinanced Properties

Some houses have loans larger than the value of the property. These houses have financing in place which eliminates them from consideration, unless the sellers would pay the buyers cash to take over the loan. Take the following house for example.

Fair Market Value	$75,000
Existing Loan	$70,575 payable
	$834 PITI, 12.5%

If the sellers would give me the $4,000 equity in this house I would refuse the gift. Certainly the house would rent for far less than the payments, and if I tried to sell, I would probably have to give it to someone else. I would suggest to the sellers that in the event they paid me $5,000 in cash at closing, I would take title and gamble that I could sell to someone else at the loan balance before my $5,000 ran out. That would be about six months at those payments. In sixteen years, I have had two owners pay me a lump sum to take over their loans.

Four times a year I conduct a seminar where the participants locate, negotiate for and in many instances purchase a house in the class. These are houses for sale by owners, and the object is to buy the house below the market and on good terms.

In the Atlanta seminar this year, the students in the class located a seller with this situation. He owed $70,000 on a house worth about the same amount. His loan was at an interest rate higher than new buyers would have to pay, so he was having trouble finding a buyer.

The group who contacted the sellers offered the following:

> A 36 month lease at the rate of $575 per month, with an option to purchase the property for $73,000 anytime during the 36 months. The buyers would take care of the maintenance.

The sellers were agreeable because they had firm moving plans in less than three weeks and did not want to leave an empty house behind with payments of $834, plus maintenance. In effect the sellers were saying that they would pay the buyers $259 per month or $9324 over the term of the 36 months to take the house off of their hands. The sellers saved their credit, and converted their personal residence that they couldn't sell, to an investment property, with all of it's tax benefits. Their alternative was an empty house with payments that they could not afford.

Keeping Your Seller Honest

When buying a house with little equity with a lease-option, a foreclosure on the first mortgage is a potential problem. This would wipe out your position and be a major inconvenience to the tenant. Your option should give you the right to make the payments on an underlying loan in default with full credit toward the purchase price.

One way to check and see if the loan payments are current is to call the lender who has the first mortgage on a monthly basis to see if they received the seller's payment. By giving the original borrower's name and loan account number, they will tell you if the payment has been received.

Sometimes one part of the deal is critical to you. Suppose you want to buy a house, and have only three thousand dollars for a down payment.

You can afford relatively high monthly payments, but cannot qualify (or don't want to qualify) for a bank loan. You need to find a seller who will sell you a house for three thousand or less down, and finance the balance for you.

First you have to find a seller who is willing and able to sell with only three thousand dollars down. Then you should make an offer asking for a better down payment than you want, plus some other terms you don't need. By asking for eight percent interest along with a two thousand dollar down payment, the seller may well be attracted to the interest rate.

You may be willing to pay ten or even eleven percent interest in the event that the seller will take the two thousand dollar down payment. In fact you would gladly pay ten percent with a three thousand dollar down payment, so you have two points on which you can give a little. This is a simplification of an offer. We have listed before many additional points which you would negotiate in a typical house purchase.

Remember to try to get the seller to focus on a point or points not as critical to you. This way you can make a generous concession, and still have it your way.

Sellers not only have to want to make you a good deal, they have to be able to make you that deal. Some sellers of real estate will literally give you their property, in the event you would take them off of the loans they have stacked up against the property.

Making Your Profit When You Buy

Your purchase price is the one factor which most influences your profit, on an item you buy for investment or resale. Car dealers, shoe stores, and real estate investors have little control over the price they can sell their product for. The buyers in the market will shop for the best price, so you cannot depend on selling for more than the lowest price competitor.

When you make a good buy in the marketplace, you can afford to sell, or rent, for less than your competition. This is the principal on which discount stores with a high volume of sales operate.

When investing in houses, we can afford to rent our houses slightly below the market, because we buy better. This translates into longer term tenants, less vacancy, less management headaches, and higher profits. Our competitors who pay more must charge higher rents, and have the problems associated with those rents, i.e., more turnover.

Negotiating Discounts For Buying In Quantity

In the event you can use, or resell more than one of whatever you are buying, ask for a larger discount. It's good business for the buyer and seller. A friend of mine was recently in a hardware store which was getting out the lawnmore business. They had three top of the line riding mowers left on the floor which were obviously not selling fast. My friend made a good deal on one, and then, being an entrepreneur, asked what kind of deal he could make in the event he bought all three.

The store owner figured for a while and came back with a figure which was about 20% less than the price for one. My friend asked to borrow his phone, and started calling everyone he knew (me included) to sell them a mower at a real bargain price. He sold one immediately, bought the other two himself, and later sold another at a profit.

Asking For Terms That Effectively Lower The Price

If neither cash, nor buying in quantity are getting reactions from the seller, ask what kind of terms are available. Some retailers like Sears charge you eighteen percent (or more) interest when you charge an item and don't pay for it in a month's time. However, for that month they have made you an interest free loan.

As an alternative to their revolving charge plans, many large stores offer what is called a "lay-away" plan. This is a sale where you do not take possession of the merchandise until you have paid for it in full. The good news is that they do not charge you any interest on the money, because they still have the goods.

This plan can work to your advantage when the item you want goes on sale at a time before you need it. The $895 refrigerator goes on sale for $695, but you are short on cash, and don't really want it today. Six months from now would be fine. Buy it on the lay away plan. Put up a one hundred dollar deposit and lock in the sale price. You will lose interest on your $100, but are saving interest on the $595 that you still owe them. In addition they are storing the item at their expense and risk until you take delivery.

Buying Houses On The "Lay Away" Plan

The same strategy can work when buying real estate. In the event a seller of a particular property is not anxious to give up possession, but wants to be sure that the property is sold, try to buy it on the same type of terms.

Take a seller who wants to build a new house, but cannot build until he sells the one he has. In addition he has the problem of where to live when he is building the new house. Offer to pay him a small down payment; three thousand dollars on a seventy thousand dollar house would be reasonable.

You will agree to make him additional payments which will apply in full to the purchase price, and he will remain in possession, until he finds a lot and builds the house of his dreams. This building project would most probably take at least a year. During that year you have tied up the property with a nominal down payment, and the seller has been responsible for the all of the expenses associated with the house. He would be required to maintain the house in the same condition as the day you entered the contract, with any repairs needed, to be deducted from the sale price and down payment at closing.

You tie up a seventy thousand dollar property (worth much more hopefully) with three thousand dollars today, and a couple hundred dollars a month which will be applied to the price. The longer it takes for the seller to build and move, the more the house should appreciate, and the more you will make.

Financing Case Studies

Following are the details of some interesting purchases I have made over the years. In each case, the key to a good buy, was that I identified the sellers problem, and then offered to solve it in a manner that was acceptable to the seller.

Solving A Foreclosure Problem

Last year a couple came to my office to see If I would buy their house. They were behind in their loan payments, and facing foreclosure. They had thirty-five thousand dollars in appraised equity, the difference between the loan's balance and the value of the property. They offered to sell me their equity for ten thousand dollars cash, but the sale would have to be completed within two days to save the house.

They had procrastinated until the last minute and now were willing to sell twenty five thousand dollars below the market. Had I accepted their price, I would have probably made a nice profit. However, as they had come down on their price $25,000 on their own, I tested them with an offer which gave me a better price, but had some benefits for them.

I offered them one thousand, five hundred dollars for the equity they wanted ten thousand dollars for, and agreed that they could stay in the house in return for paying rent. They saw the benefit of remaining in the house rather than moving, and we negotiated a rent a little under the real market rent and they accepted.

Had I paid the ten thousand they wanted I could have rented the house to another party for one hundred a month more. However, I would first have to fix up the house, and spend the time to find that new tenant. By asking, I had received. Common sense told me that had I been in these people's shoes, I would be eager to accept any deal which gave me some relief from the immediate problem. So by offering to solve their problem of where to live and by saving them the embarrassment of being foreclosed, I realized an additional profit.

Had I taken unfair advantage of these people? They had purchased the house years earlier for half what they now owed on the house. They had borrowed additional money to buy more playthings, and had not bothered to pay back the money they had borrowed and spent.

If they had not sold the house to me, someone would have purchased it at the foreclosure sale two days later, and they would have to move without receiving anything. They had the choice of trying to sell to someone else for more in the two days they had allowed themselves to sell their property, or to take a sure thing. I think they made the right choice.

On several occasions I have had to sell things in a hurry to raise money for one deal or another. The less time you allow yourself to sell, the less you will realize for your property, whether it is a car, a diamond ring, or a house. When I sold fast, I sold cheap.

Poor people are always in a hurry to buy and a hurry to sell. That is one contributing factor as to why they are poor. Rich people think in terms of longer time spans. They plan ahead, and buy and sell slowly.

Handling Bad Loans

Recently a seller approached me with a house he had paid $74,000 for a year earlier. He now owed a total of $75,000 on the house at high interest rates and with a negative amortization loan which increased in amount with each payment. He offered to give me the house in the event I would agree to make the payments on the house.

It would take nothing down, but he owed more than the house was worth. I offered to buy the house giving the seller $500 for moving expenses, in the event the lender would settle for less than the amount due on the loan.

The lender agreed to take $61,000 for the $75,000 due them and we closed.

This situation was both very common and quite unique. As often happens, the owner/seller had obligated himself to high payments on a terrible loan. Almost half of his take-home pay a year earlier had been from overtime work, and he did not anticipate that all such work would be eliminated. It was, and he just had to get out of the house.

The unique part of the story is that the lender was willing to accept a substantial discount on a loan that was not in default. Perhaps they didn't want a foreclosure in an area where this would be their only repossessed house; perhaps they saw trouble with these loans coming and just wanted out. For whatever reason, they accepted my offer and I bought the house.

I tell this story to reinforce the ideas that you have to ask for a good deal, and sometimes you may get one, even when you think there is no chance your offer will be accepted. I was delighted, and a little amazed, that my offer was accepted. Make offers you are happy with, and prepared to be thrilled once in a while.

Getting Paid To Buy

Another time a broker approached me for a seller who was "desperate" in his words, to sell. It seems that this seller had borrowed some money from his employer, and secured it by some rental property he had inherited. Now he had spent the money, but could not make the payments on the loan, because there was no income from the property. He was letting a friend live there and did not want to ask him to pay rent.

This loan was now past due and the seller was most worried that he might lose his job, if he did not start making payments. The broker asked me to offer anything.

I offered to take title to the property and agree to pay the loan payments when due, in the event that the seller would agree to pay me four thousand dollars at closing. The broker had never seen an offer that required the seller to pay the buyer money plus give up the property. I had to admit it was a little unusual, but it was an offer, and he was obligated to present it to his principal.

The seller considered the offer and then counteroffered saying that he would pay me two thousand dollars, but I would have to pay the real estate commission. I suggested to the broker that instead of taking a commission, we buy the property together, and take one thousand dollars each. He agreed.

That broker has gone on to make a lot of money because he realized that sellers will do the darndest things (apologies to Art Linkletter), if you will just ask them.

CHAPTER EIGHT

TEN - TEN - TEN: HOUSE BUYING AT A PROFIT

If you are interested in buying a house, especially a house for investment, now is the time to apply some of the ideas in the case studies above and start to make your offers. I have some guidelines called TEN-TEN-TEN designed to help you remember the key elements of a good deal when negotiating.

You want to buy the property below the market price, i.e., wholesale. This takes negotiation, skill, practice, and a seller that has a reason to sell to you below the market price. You can make 47 creative offers to a seller, and that person will turn down every one if he is in a position to wait for the highest retail price.

The seller must need to sell, or simply want to sell, and also be in a position to offer you a good deal. A person who recently purchased at a retail price cannot afford to give you a great deal, no matter how much they want to sell.

At Least Ten Percent Below Market Value

I consider "wholesale" buying at a price at least 10% below the market. That means if you are going to buy an $80,000 house the most you can pay is $72,000. Can you look at an $80,000 house and say, "That house is worth exactly $80,000?" Probably not; it's hard to cut it that close. About the best you can do on estimating the market price of a house is 5% plus or minus. On an $80,000 house you could estimate a range of $77,000 - $83,000, and that's close enough.

The first "10" reminds you that you need to buy at least 10% below the market. Keep in mind, that if you are going to offer to buy a house 10% below the market you are not going to buy every house for sale. Most houses are sold at around their present market value; that is how "market value" is determined. Plan on being patient.

You will also be practicing your negotiation skills. To buy a house at a price 10% below the market price, you have to be able to talk to sellers about why they are selling and how they arrived at the selling price. When you negotiate you discuss the seller's motivations and needs and decide if you can make sense of buying his house. Persuasion has its place, but this is not a high-pressure situation. Skill gets the job done; the sledgehammer approach alienates people.

It is most efficient to obtain some skill by education; there is no need to re-invent the wheel when there are worthwhile books (for instance this one) and seminars to take. But even after you learn from others you need to recognize that it will take some practice to hone your skills. Don't be discouraged if you feel awkward or even scared during your first attempts to talk with sellers. You will improve over time once you overcome the initial reluctance to talk to people.

Whenever your offer is refused, consider it as part of your education. If the seller counteroffers, then you know that you have at least established a dialogue with him and he is considering your thoughts. If your offer is immediately and gleefully accepted by the seller - you may feel that you offered too much. With a little more negotiation could you have purchased the property for less?

A Maximum Interest Rate Of Ten Percent

Now on to the second "10" which is critical. This states that you will pay a maximum of 10% interest. If there are two mortgages or trust deeds you will not pay more than a 10% average between them.

Who is going to loan you money at 10%? The seller! And, unless bank rates come down, sellers are the only people that will ever lend you money at 10%. By the way, if bank rates come down so that a commercial lender will loan money at 10%, then it is no longer a good deal, and you need to revise this to a lower percentage.

It is important to negotiatc over every ⅛th point of interest! You may be surprised how many sellers will give in on the interest if you give them their price. If their price is acceptable to you, or close to what you are willing to pay, don't try to negotiate that point; spend your efforts on lowering the percentage on the money you are borrowing from them. Depending on the price - and how close it is to 10% below the market, you can even go up a couple thousand dollars and get that 10% interest.

I argue long and hard over interest. I know that the cause of negative cash flow is high interest rates. *Interest is not a tax shelter, it is an expense! A costly expense, that should be driven as low as possible in every purchase.*

Maximum Down Payment Of Ten Percent

The final "10" is for the maximum of 10% down payment. There are two principal reasons for this rule. As discussed above, the less you put into the deal the less you can lose. Sometimes deals look much different after you close, and you don't want your entire net worth tied up in one deal.

Other deals may present themselves, and you would want some cash to offer on them. Perhaps you made an error in your estimate of how much work is needed for maintenance or repair on the house. Don't plunk all your money down at closing, for you may need it next week.

Of course, if you have cash to invest it is valuable to use it if you can drive down the price. Be sure to read the sections on using cash to your advantage.

The Ten-Ten-Ten System In Action

Now let's pull together what we have covered so far and show you how you can get started buying houses using TEN - TEN - TEN.

Review the section on reading ads, finding willing sellers, and making telephone calls. How long does it take to make each call? A good prospect with a willing and chatty owner could take up to twenty minutes. If no one is home it won't take any time at all. Budget three hours for yourself; typically about twenty ads could be called in this time.

After you call a number of ads, and talk to several owners, select the best two prospects and go see the houses and talk to the owners. Find out more about the house, neighborhood, price, and terms. Talk to the owner(s) and determine their reasons for selling and what terms they will make available to you.

If there is any possibility that this house could benefit you, make an offer. Be sure to make an offer that you will feel happy with if it is accepted. I know the feeling well of arriving at a house listed above market price and knowing immediately that I could only feel comfortable if I bought it for far less than the asking price. This seller has mislead you about the value, and tricked you into coming out to see his house, hoping that you are dumb enough to pay too much.

When faced with a seller like this one, make a low offer. He has wasted some of your time, so you may as well make his day by offering far less than he expects.

With his approach he probably has had few if any offers, and just may be interested in pursuing the deal with you. *You must make an offer, or you have wasted your time completely.*

Good Deals Come Only To Persistent Buyers

I suggest that you set aside some time every week, or at least on a regular basis, to make some calls and see some houses. If you do this irregularly it will be difficult to gain negotiating skills, and to have a feel for the market. Make a number of phone calls and go out to see the best prospects. When you visit a couple of houses, make an offer on at least one of these houses. If you work at this program it will take about one work day to do a good job.

Don't feel that you need to buy a house the first week you try this program. There aren't that many good deals. You will need time to learn the market, practice negotiations and become comfortable speaking with owners. *Your goal during the first year should be to buy one house.* One house, ONE GOOD DEAL. You can't get much simpler than that. Buy one house; buy it for a good price on good terms. Use the 10 - 10 - 10 program.

You have one year to read local ads, get to know the market, talk to owners, look at prospective buys and make offers. If you work every week, in one year you will have read uncountable ads. Talked to about one thousand owners, and made at least fifty offers. In fifty offers do you think you will be able to find a good deal? One that you can buy at a price 10% below the market; with 10% or less down; with an interest rate of 10% or less? I know you can. Thousands have done it and are doing it every day!

If this is a house you are buying for investment, it is most practical to rent it to someone else, so that they will pay rent to you - and you can make the mortgage payments. So after your first purchase you are now a landlord. You may soon learn a great deal about tenants and management. But with just onc housc you can learn how to manage a little at a time. One house should not be a big management problem. With one house you may go through a bad tenant in the beginning, but then you'll start learning about management. You can get your management problems under control if you just have one house and one tenant to concern you.

Information on my three day class is listed in the back of this book. In that class I cover in detail how to buy and manage a portfolio of single family houses. You will probably want to attend that seminar one day in the event you become serious about buying and investing in houses.

Making It Work On The Street Where You Live

In the area where I live, the house I want to buy for investment, in the right neighborhood costs about $80,000. You learn your market and plug the real numbers from your town into this example.

I look for a house that I think is really worth $80,000. If I'm not sure of the market I always guess low. And keeping with the first "10" rule, I need to offer at least 10% below the market; that's $80,000 - $8000 which equals $72,000. Let's round that off to $70,000. What's $2,000 among friends? If you offer $70,000 you can always up the offer to $72,000, but you can't pull back to $70,000 if you offer too much the first time.

Start your offer a little lower, and once in a while you may get lucky. Or you can negotiate to a higher price and reduce one of the other factors. For instance, down payment. Under 10 - 10 - 10 you would pay a maximum of $7,000 down. But if you offer a lower purchase price, and then raise it you may have even a lower down payment. In this example we are going to assume a down payment of $5,000.

And again, depending on how much money you have available, don't offer the entire $7,000 down payment on the first round. If you start at $2,000 then you have some room to negotiate. Once in a while you will be pleasantly surprised.

Obviously, if you are short of funds, don't offer more than you can actually pay. You may have a plan where you put 5% or less down. You will have to work harder, and pass up some deals that would otherwise work, but you can still be a successful investor.

Here's where we are in the example: an $80,000 house, that you want to purchase for $70,000, and the owners have agreed to a $5,000 down payment. Now you owe $65,000. The maximum combined interest you can pay, and have the numbers work out, is 10%. To complete this part of the offer, you need to know or figure out how much the house will draw in rent.

After all, since you are such an astute investor, I assume that you will want the house to break even on cash flow. That is, that the rent that comes in will cover the mortgage payments, property taxes, insurance premiums, and maintenance.

How much does an $80,000 house rent for? In this area about $650 per month. Plug in the realistic numbers for your area. Right off the top of that amount you need to allow for property taxes, insurance, maintenance and vacancies. You must allow funds for these items before you figure how to make the loan payments.

You look at the taxes for this house, and talk to your insurance company about liability and casualty annual rates. Plan on some vacant days, particularly during the first year. The amount of maintenance will depend on the condition of the house; the fix-up business is expensive in time and money. You can't expect to make many repairs out of the monthly rental amount.

Based on the experience I have had managing properties I allow about $100 a month for taxes, insurance, vacancy and maintenance. That leaves $550. per month, out of the rental amount, to make loan payments, and 12 × $550 = $6,600. If I'm going to owe $65,000 total at 10% interest, do I have enough to make the monthly payments? Just barely.

Of course at this rate I'll only be paying off the loan at the rate of $100. per year. It would be about a 65 year loan at that rate, and probably not acceptable to the seller.

Variable Payment Loans Which Solve Problems

Here is an idea to work with this. I suggest that I will pay $550, per month, for the first five years of the loan. Then pay $600. a month for an additional five years, and then bump the monthly amount to $700. I can calculate that this loan will pay off in a little over twenty-two years. This schedule of payments will allow me to have positive cash flow throughout my ownership.

Another suggestion, especially if there is an existing first mortgage and the seller is going to take back a second mortgage, is to have no payments made on the second mortgage for a period of time. After a couple years, with the right house and careful management, you should be collecting more in rent and therefore have more to spend for mortgage payments.

Whenever you plan a variable amount loan, or a loan where payments start after a period of time, be sure to leave the interest rate alone. It should never go up.

It is most inefficient to go to all the trouble necessary to make an outstanding buy, and then sell the house in a short time. I suggest to my seminar students that they keep an investment house at least until it doubles in value.

Buy a good house that will not give you maintenance or management headaches. Finance it with the thought that you have to be able to afford it for several years. Then hold it until it is worth $160,000. In some boom years in certain areas, houses have doubled in value in two years. Typically it will probably take about six to ten years for a house to double, and some houses will never double.

In the event you live in an area without a long term future of growth, your only appreciation will have to come from inflation. Growing areas get the benefit of the compounded effect of real growth in value due to an increase in demand, coupled with inflation.

How to Make Ten - Ten - Ten Work For You

Would you be willing to work one-half day a week for several years if your efforts would produce an income of $6,000 a month for the rest of your life? This is no scam where you send money into some company and never see it again.

If you follow my buying suggestions above, and really work to buy at least one house each year under the program guidelines, then you can reap the rewards.

Program Goals
After You Buy The First House

After the first year using the 10-10-10 system of buying, you have one house. You buy it right, you rent it to the best tenant possible and you get the management under control. Then you go back to the ads, call people, make offers and buy another house. In your second year, buy another house.

If you worked systematically during the first year, you surely are becoming a better negotiator and know the local real estate market very well. Therefore, you should be able to manage your first house while you scout for the second house you will buy.

And, every consecutive year, buy one more house.

Cashing In
When the First House Doubles In Value

Let's look down the road, conservatively about ten years, and say that the first house you purchased has now doubled in value. You have continued to purchase and now have a portfolio of ten houses. Now it's time to reap some of the rewards of your labor.

Sell the first house. You'll be a master negotiator by now and be able to sell for the full market value. But you cannot keep all the money:

you have to pay off the loan. The loan would have paid down some, but depending on the terms perhaps not much. If the house had a market value of $80,000 when you bought it, the selling price now will be around $160,000 and the loan balance would be about $64,000.

Now with $96,000 you have to pay some taxes. The amount depends on your tax bracket, and of course on the tax rates in force when you sell. Under the current rules, if you are in the 30% tax bracket, for instance, you would pay about $12,000 in taxes.

A word about tax planning. If you plan to hold this house until it doubles in value, you will know about this up-coming sale for a number of years. By continuing to buy houses you will have some tax shelter due to the depreciation. You have the opportunity on each of the houses to do some planning and pay less in taxes.

Even without any tax planning you have $84,000; do you keep all that? No, there's one more item to be paid out of the proceeds. You just sold your first house. And if you keep selling one house a year you will run out of houses. So, every time you sell, you need to buy a replacement investment house.

This first replacement house will probably have a value of $160,000. Now that you've negotiated for years, you should buy it for about $145,000. You will need to allow $14,000 for a down payment from the proceeds on the house you sold.

Now there is $70,000 remaining, and this is yours to spend. This is what you've been working for during the holding period. You can generate this money by buying a few good houses, at good prices, on the right terms and holding them.

If you put the $70,000 in a money market account, you would earn 10%. How much could you withdraw each month for a year, so that at the year's end the account balance would be zero? You can spend all the money this year because next year you are going to sell another house and generate more money.

If you take out about $6,000 a month, which would equal $72,000 for the year, that would be the right amount. You would earn some interest on the money, so the account would be just about out of money when you sell the second house.

What About Inflation?

Is this income stream hedged against inflation? What would happen to the value of the first house if we had 20% inflation? The house would appreciate even more quickly. If a house typically doubles in value in ten years, that is an increase of about 7%. Houses appreciate both independently of inflation, and also at a faster rate than inflation.

The less inflation we have, the lower the interest rates. The lower the interest rates, the more jobs that are created. More jobs mean more people want to buy houses. And the more people that buy houses, the more house prices go up.

I Don't Want To Wait Ten Years; Can I Just Do It In One Year?

If you went out and bought ten houses this year and sold them all next year, would the same program work? Absolutely not.

You probably can't make ten good deals this year. And you couldn't sell them next year and count on generating $70,000. Think of the amount of work to buy ten houses instead of concentrating on finding a great deal on one house.

You have to let them grow up. Let the houses appreciate while you improve your investment and management skills.

CHAPTER NINE

GETTING TO THE OFFER

The more you know about the seller and his product, the more likely you are to make a good buy. The following steps should be taken before making an offer.

Establishing A Relationship With The Seller

Most everyone prefers to do business with a person or place with a reputation for integrity, and with a pleasant atmosphere or personality. I often go out of my way to eat at a certain restaurant, which charges premium prices for its food, because the help is friendly, and thc food is inevitably good.

Have you ever driven an extra mile and paid a premium for an item because you know that the merchant will stand behind the merchandise. Quality merchants have long cchoed "you get what you pay for", and in many cases they are right.

When sellers have a choice of who to sell to, they may discriminate based on your appearance, attitude, and use for the property. A person selling the family home, with continuing ties to the neighborhood, will be curious about you and your potential use for the house.

In the event you were going to convert it to a rooming house for young musicians, they may refuse to sell to you, even though they are eager to sell. They are more concerned about alienating their friends and neighbors, than selling the house. In the event you dress slovenly or act rudely, and then ask the sellers to grant concessions or finance part of the purchase price, again the odds are against their cooperation.

I have borrowed one hundred percent of the purchase price of a house on several occasions from sellers who knew me only a short period of time. However, in that period of time I acted competently, and gave them several examples of other transactions in which I had borrowed and repaid money, which I then invited them to verify. These actions were to convince them that in the event they decided to loan me the money, that they could depend on my payments.

Some buyers of real estate mail out blind offers, asking the sellers to finance part of the purchase price in the form of a note. They are asking people to loan them money, even though they have never met. This happens, but rarely. How much money would you loan to someone about whom you know little or nothing and with no information on whether they'll ever pay you back?

Whether you are borrowing money from a bank or private individual, the more trustworthy you appear, the more likely you are to get the loan.

Conversely, the less trustworthy you appear, the higher the price you will pay for that money you borrow when you find a source willing to lend to you. Nearly anybody can borrow money from a loanshark. The loanshark, however, may charge 12% a week, where a good credit customer of a bank may pay only 12% a year. It is worth a little effort to get the lower rate, not to mention the difference in collection techniques.

The larger the deal, the more important trust is. And, it may be to your benefit to get to know your seller also. You may buy pencils from someone on a street corner for a nickle a piece, and not worry about the quality or whether he really owns them.

If he was selling watches for twenty dollars a piece, there would still be some buyers, even with the dubious ownership. If he was selling a new Mercedes for $5000, even though it was an incredible bargain, there would probably not be many serious inquiries until the authorities arrived. Five thousand dollars is too much to risk on a deal with probable complications, which would cost you much time and money.

Complications arise in real estate transactions also. It is often a benefit for you to get to know the seller, and understandable that the seller will want to look over the buyer.

Does The Seller Want To Sell?

In any market, it is the sellers which make the deals, not the product. It may seem obvious, but you need to find someone who really wants to sell. When you find somebody who is anxious to sell a house, sometimes they are anxious to sell their car, their boat or their furniture, because they are raising money for some purpose. They will make you a good deal for anything they have for sale because they have decided that today is the day.

Most buyers of real estate approach the problem backwards and try to find the perfect piece of real estate, whether that is an apartment building, a warehouse, or a house. Once they find the property they have been searching for, then they try to buy it. Consider the chances that their perfect property is owned by someone whose day it is to make someone a good deal. The chances are much better of spinning the wheel of fortune in some casino.

I've already introduced the idea of looking for good deals on the telephone, and will write more on it shortly. The objective in asking the questions is to find information about the property, and also about the seller. As I mentioned before, it helps to be systematic in your search.

To help me be more objective, I've developed a numerical system to rate each seller. Using a scale of one to ten, I give each seller a value based on the below scale:

1. Does not really want to sell, but the property can be purchased. Often says "everything is for sale at a price" but won't mention his.
2. Is advertising to sell, but won't answer any questions. Does not remember what he paid or anything about the loans. Could be a professional investor or agent selling their own property.
3. A dreamer who wants to buy something else, and has priced his property based on the price of his dream. One seller wanted $11,000 for his equity to buy a new van. The fair market equity was probably half

that amount. I commented to him that it was fortunate that he did not want a Jaguar.

4. Sellers want to move and will start looking for a new house as soon as they sell this one. They just started advertising and if it does not sell soon, they plan to list it with a Realtor.

5. Sellers have found a new home and made a deposit which they will lose, in the event that they don't sell within a short time. Not only is the deposit important, they have told their friends and family about the new house and will sacrifice to get it. They cannot afford to own both houses.

6. Sellers have a pressing physical problem. They are commuting long distances, or perhaps their in-laws have moved in to share the seller's two bedroom, one bath house. They will not die if they don't sell, but life is less appealing.

7. Sellers are moving whether or not they sell, cannot afford two payments, and are nervous about trying to sell or manage a house from across country.

8. Sellers have a financial obligation they cannot meet. It may be the monthly payments, or perhaps a balloon payment due soon. They admit to having a problem, but are still hopeful. They are willing to take a small discount, but not

enough. This house will probably end up in foreclosure.

9. Sellers recognize their problem and are willing to give a buyer the lion's share of the profit to solve it for them. They would discount an equity of $20,000 to $3,000 to salvage what they could.

10. Sellers up against the proverbial wall and admit it. They will buy their way out (pay you to take over their loan), or turn over a good equity for your efforts to make their payments (no promises or guarantees on your part).

Try to match up the sellers in your phone conversations with the above list. I would probably not take the time to go see someone at their house unless they rated a nine or a ten on the above scale. I would ask sellers with a rating of five and above to come see me, and in the event they did, would make an offer, subject to my inspection of the house. In the event they declined my invitation to come to my place to hear my offer, I would put them in a tickler file and call them back in a month to see "if they still have it".

Those sellers who rate less than a five, I like to encourage with statements like, "don't give it away", and "that sounds awful cheap to me". It is a mistake to try to "convert" a low rating seller to a higher rating. Do not try to educate a seller, just search until you find a nine or a ten.

When you sell, hopefully you will have the luxury of acting like a one or a two. Keep in mind that most real estate transactions are at fair market price, and in a typical market, the seller does get all cash.

Only a small percentage of all sellers will be nines or tens. If you drove around town and stopped and talked to all the sellers with signs in their yards, you would probably burn out a set of tires and lose your enthusiasm long before you found a ten. An intelligent system of making phone calls, recording the facts gathered, and then rating the seller's motivation, is a necessity to a successful house investment program.

Sellers With Profit

In addition to finding a seller who wants to sell, it is helpful to find a seller with a profit. In the retail setting the profit margin is the difference in price between the wholesale and retail prices. Retail sellers do have a profit, or they won't be in business very long. Private sellers may or may not have a profit. If they do not, then they probably can't afford to give you a good deal, no matter how anxious they are to sell.

Sellers who have large profits in a property are easier to deal with, than those taking a loss on the sale. In the event your goal is to buy properties at least ten thousand dollars below the market, then you should look for properties with at least ten thousand in equity (the difference between the loan balance and the market price), and hopefully more than that in profit to the seller.

A seller with an eighty thousand dollar house and a seventy five thousand dollar loan would find it difficult to sell to you for ten thousand dollars below the market. A seller with a free and clear house, that they just paid eighty thousand dollars for would likewise probably not sell for a loss.

The combination to look for then is a house which the owners bought below the market themselves, or have owned long enough to realize a substantial profit. Sellers with profits will not fight over the last dollar.

Last summer I sold a house in Massachusetts I had owned for five years as an investment. I had paid just under forty thousand dollars for the house and was blessed with a good tenant and manager who had produced a little net cash flow each year.

A broker produced a contract to buy the house for eighty-nine thousand dollars early last summer, and I accepted it. I had an appraiser value the house a little higher than that, but had a nice profit, and our policy is that you can't take a loss making a profit.

I have learned since that date that I could have commanded a higher price in the event that I had been tougher. After more than fifteen years of making a living investing in real estate, I still sold a little below market. Why? Because I had enough of a profit; another thousand dollars was not critical.

Look for people selling products with large profit margins and you will make better deals. People who put much of their own labor into a product tend to put less value on their labor than they should. Some craftsmen and artists with hundreds of hours of labor, but only a few dollars worth of raw materials in a finished product, will discount their work substantially, especially when there is no broker involved. Fixer-uppers, who take a rundown house and recondition it, will often sell at a good price and on good terms. They again have more labor than materials invested in the deal.

Getting Comfortable

When you first meet the seller, study the way they talk, and react. If they seem comfortable standing, sitting, or laying on the ground, join them if you can. If they lean close to you to talk, or if they keep their distance, try to complement their behavior.

Be yourself as much as possible. In the event you pretend to be someone or something you are not, you will probably send out signals of nervousness which will tend to put the other party on their guard. Private investigators Rockford and Travis Mcgee seem successful when pretending, and so do the con- men of the world. But most of us cannot act convincingly enough to fool ourselves, much less another party.

Be Interested, Act Interested - Keep Negotiations Going

After establishing a relationship with the seller, or the buyer, in the event that you are the seller, then you should instill in the other party the idea that you are eager and willing to buy. Now you should not be eager unless you can negotiate an attractive deal, but you want the other party to get excited about you so that they will continue to negotiate and make concessions.

You want them to know that you are going to buy something even if it is not their particular product. Unless they take you seriously, they will not take the time to tell you what you need to know before making an offer.

When talking to a salesman in a store you get the message across by letting on that you have checked out the competition, and the choice is between his product and his competitors.

The other product seems just as nice, but sells for a little less. If you could just buy his for the same price as the competitors, maybe you would buy it right now. Any redblooded salesman will give you his pitch, and if you stand fast there might be an impromptu sale for your benefit.

When I purchased my last set of tires, I approached the owner of the tire store with a newspaper in my hand showing the competitor's ad. After explaining why his tires were better, he matched their prices. I already thought that his tires were better, plus he offered free road service in the event of a flat. I wanted to buy his tires, and I got that point across by being there. I also wanted a "fair" deal, and by asking for one and keeping the negotiations rolling, that's what I received.

Similarly when the purchase is a house, when I first speak with the seller I always carry the classified section of the paper with all of the house-for-sale-by-owner circled in red. To start things off I ask the seller to find his ad for me. If you have ever tried to find your own ad in the paper you know how frustrating that is. I try to help things along by saying, "there are sure a lot of people trying to sell their houses now, aren't there?". It seems to get them in the right frame of mind.

The Importance Of Patient Listening

Practice listening to people. *A good listener looks the other party directly in the eyes, and listens with his mouth shut.* This may seem trivial and obvious, but try it sometime. You will find it difficult to listen to someone with whom you disagree without losing eye contact or breaking in with your opinion. Try it on your spouse, or, better yet, a teenager.

It is important to practice listening as a valuable negotiating technique. It's easy to listen and nod in agreement to someone with whom you see "eye to eye". Consider the wisdom of that phrase. Someone you see "eye to eye" with is someone with whom you agree. It is important, yet difficult to look someone in the eyes when you are not in agreement, and that's why you need to practice.

People who are negotiating usually have several points on which they differ. Be patient in your listening. It is polite, but even more, when you listen you may learn valuable information that will turn the tables in your favor. The saying that "if you give a man enough rope, he will hang himself", can be applied to the party who talks enough to let the opposition discover the most negotiable points of his position. The person who develops a talent of asking probing questions, and then pays attention to the answers, has a major advantage.

It may be harder than you think to develop a quiet and patient questioning technique, especially if you are naturally chatty as I am. My friend Jimmy Napier, is an excellent negotiator. Jimmy is from a town named Chipley in northern Florida, which is really lower Alabama.

Jimmy is a very patient listener, and very reserved when it comes to talking during negotiations. Jimmy speaks with a Southern drawl, and pauses not only between statements, but occasionally between words. When he talks, he occasionally talks so slowly that you just jump in and help him. When you are negotiating with Jimmy, that is a dangerous thing to do.

Jimmy's slow speech is not because Jimmy's mind is slow. His mind is like a well oiled steel trap. Its works so fast you never see it.

One night several years ago Jimmy and I were attending a party on a riverboat near New Orleans. Jimmy at the time owned a property that I was interesting in buying. After we had both relaxed a little in the cordial atmosphere, I asked Jimmy if he would take $10,000 for his equity in the property.

Jimmy just stared at me as though he hadn't heard me. I repeated myself, and this time he nodded a little that he had heard me, but didn't say anything.

Now Jimmy and I were friends, and I thought that perhaps I had offended him by offering him only $10,000 for an equity which I thought was worth more, but which we both knew Jimmy had bought for less. Finally, the silence became too much for me and then I said, "Well how about $11,000?"

Jimmy's minute of silence paid him one thousand dollars. I have negotiated with Jimmy many times since that night, and I have learned to wait for Jimmy's response, even when it takes a while. You will run into some folks as smart as Jimmy in this world, and I hope you recognize them as being smart enough to sit and think. *A quiet, thinking negotiator has an insurmountable advantage over an impulsive, quick talking, impatient negotiator.*

In the event you like to think on your feet and make fast deals, be aware of this disadvantage, and consciously slow things down when faced with a slow talking opponent.

Patient Telephone Techniques

When I teach the techniques of telephone questioning in my real estate seminar, I stress the importance of asking short questions. The ultimate short question is the one word question, or sometimes a one word statement. "Why" is probably the best question. When you think it is time to make a statement rather than ask a question, the words "oh" and "really" are excellent. When combined with patience, the art of remaining silent at the appropriate times, is powerful.

The following dialogue between the seller of a house and a potential buyer illustrates the power of these techniques. The buyer is obviously in charge.

Buyer: I am calling on your house ad, are you the owner?

Seller: Yes.

Buyer: Silence

Seller: The house is on a real nice lot, and has a great back yard.

Buyer: Oh. (Too much silence and the seller may think you have hung up)

Seller: Yes, the bedrooms are quite large, and the kitchen faces out on the family room. I am sure you would like it if you saw it.

Buyer: Why?

Seller: Because of the good neighborhood, and because the house is in excellent condition. We bought it new five years ago and have put a lot of extras in since we bought it.

Buyer: Really.

Seller: Yes, we have wallpapered both of the bathrooms and installed ceiling fans in two bedrooms and the family room.

Buyer: Why?

Seller: Well when we moved in we thought we would live here forever, and now we are going to move.

Buyer: Why?

Seller: Well my wife has been promoted, but it means a move to Atlanta.

Buyer: When.

Seller: She has to be up there by the end of the month, so we hope to sell and find a place up there before then.

Buyer: Really.

Seller: Yeah, if we don't sell the house, we will probably rent it. We don't want to leave an empty house behind.

Buyer: Why?

Seller: We had to move once before and it took over a year to sell our old house, and making two payments was no fun.

Buyer: Really.

Seller: Yeah, we finally sold it. We don't want to do that again, so if we can't sell, we are going to rent it.

Buyer: Silence

Seller: We have had several people who want to rent it for $600 a month so that will be no problem.

Buyer: Really.

Seller: Yeah, why don't you come out and see the house, I am sure you will like it from talking with you.

Buyer: When?

Seller: Well any evening after five thirty would be fine. We are always home at night, or I could meet you here at lunchtime if that would be better.

Buyer: What about the price?

Seller: The price is $89,500.

Buyer: Silence

Seller: We have had several Realtors look at the house and they agree that its worth that much.

Buyer: Oh.

Seller: Yes, the house down the street just sold for $85,000 and that house was tiny compared to this one.

Buyer: Really.

Seller: Yes, we paid over $75,000 for the house five years ago and we have put a lot into it since then.

Buyer: Silence.

Seller: The house is a good buy at $89,500, but if you like the house we could talk about it.

Buyer: Oh.

Seller: We had one offer from a guy who was trying to steal the house. We're not going to give it away.

Buyer: Oh.

Seller: Yeah, he only offered $79,000. Why, we have a lot more than that in the house right now and we aren't going to take a loss. We're not desperate.

You can see what a conversation can be like when the buyer is patient and thinks before he asks a question.

Contrast that with the following conversation when the buyer talks more and listens less.

Buyer: I saw your ad in the paper. Are you the owner?

Seller: Yes.

Buyer: Can you tell me a little about the house, about how big it is and how much you want for it?

Seller: It's on a large lot, and has three bedrooms, all good sized rooms and a kitchen that looks out onto the family room.

Buyer: How much do you want for the house?

Seller: $89,500.

Buyer: Is that your best price?

Seller: Well, come out and see the house and we can talk about it.

Buyer: The only time that is good for me is after work. How about tomorrow after work?

Seller: That would be fine.

Notice the difference in the questioning styles. The second buyer might not have seemed too chatty to you, but compare the results of the conversations. Although both buyers received the basic information about the house, the quiet and patient buyer knows much more about his seller than the impatient and chatty buyer.

The longer the question you ask, the shorter the answer will be. When you ask a long question you generally give the other party the opportunity to answer with a yes or no, without elaborating.

CHAPTER TEN

MAKING THE OFFER

The moment of truth in any transaction is when the buyer makes the first offer. If it is accepted, the buyer has traded his cash (or whatever he is using to buy with) for the object of his offer. Occasionally buyers have what is called "buyer's remorse". That is the desire to reverse the deal, and get their money back.

The way to avoid a case of "buyer's remorse" is to make a good enough offer, so that you will be delighted in the event the seller accepts. The following rules will help you structure the offer so that you will be happy with the results, in the event of an acceptance.

Never Mention The First Price

At this stage you have done your homework, and know about what the property you are buying is worth. In most cases it is hard to establish an exact value, so a range of values will do.

The RCA twenty-one inch color portable you are buying may range in price from $299 up to $399. Your goal is to get it at or below the low end of that range, with an extended warranty. A house you are trying to buy may be worth between $70,000 and $80,000. Again you are shooting for the low end of that price range with good terms from the seller.

If the seller starts off at the high end of the price range, you must compensate on the low side of what you want to pay in order to have a chance of compromising somewhere near your target. With the television, if the store owner starts off at $399, you may ask what goes with it at that price. In the event he thinks you are interested at the high price he may offer a stand, or perhaps another small appliance in the store as an incentive to get you to pay the high price.

With a house seller, after they state a price, whether it be high or low, ask them about the terms of the sale. The terms on a house purchase can be as important as the price. The details of financing are discussed in a later chapter.

In the event the seller refuses to give you his price and says "make me an offer", he is probably just trying to see how much he can get. This point is illustrated at the upper end of the price scale by the negotiations which reportedly took place between Bill Zeckendorf and Howard Hughes. See, *The Autobiography of William Zeckendorf*, c. 1970, published by Holt, Rinehart and Winston.

Hughes had sent word to Zeckendorf through an intermediary that he was interested in selling his real estate and stock holdings and would meet to discuss a sale. Zeckendorf, along with Laurence Rockefeller flew to Los Angeles to negotiate a purchase.

Hughes refused to establish a price so Zeckendorf offered him three hundred and fifty million dollars, and backed up his offer with a nineteen million five hundred thousand dollar cashiers check. Hughes refused the offer stating it was not enough. When asked what was enough Hughes would not state a figure.

After some discussion, Zeckendorf asked if they were close, and Hughes refused to react. Zeckendorf then offered four hundred and fifty million and Hughes refused. Zeckendorf made one more offer of five hundred million, which Hughes again refused.

The deal was never consummated, probably because the Hughes was not that serious about selling. He probably had an amount he would have sold for, but it was so high, that the buyers were not willing at that price.

Let The Other Party Start The Negotiations Process

Most of you are aware of this concept. The owner usually states the selling price and hopes you will hand over the money and complete the deal at the full price. You are looking for a better deal, and the temptation is to jump in with your first offer immediately after the other party sets his first "limit".

Restrain yourself, and see if you can get the negotiations started without actually naming a price. If you give a number, that is absolutely the lowest price you will ever get. If you are quiet you may be pleasantly surprised.

Ask if the stated price is the best he can do. Ask if there have been any problems with this model. Discuss any visible flaws. Ask what the price is today, so he'll have no more expenses with this item. Ask if there is a discount for paying cash. If you are interested in free delivery, accessories or a warranty, ask if he will add them in to make the deal.

It is likely you will get a lower price, and the amount of this reduction gives you an idea of the seller's flexibility. Be polite, smile and be patient; give the seller a chance to talk. If the seller refuses to budge on the price, that tells you something also.

I remember a buying expedition in Mexico when I was much younger. I had wandered into one of the many shops, and negotiated what I thought was a great deal on a chess set. It must have been obvious to the merchant that I thought I had made one of the better deals since Columbus. After he had my cash safely in his hand he asked if I would like another set at the same price.

At a later time, but still early in my career I was negotiating with a bank over a car loan which was in default. The car had been wrecked, and was uninsured at the time. To make a long story short, the owners had disappeared and the bank had attached a lien on a property I was purchasing. In order to clear the legal title I was trying to negotiate a cash settlement with the bank.

The bank's lien was approximately $5,000, and they stated that as the amount they wanted. I knew that unless the bank settled with me that the property would probably go into foreclosure and their lien would be wiped out.

I discussed this with the officer in charge of the matter, before making my first offer of $2,500 to settle the lien. He quickly accepted my offer, which ruined my day.

Had I been more patient and asked for their best settlement price that day, he probably would have stated a lower number than $5,000, which would have enabled me to eventually negotiate to a lower price than $2500.

After several negotiations such as the ones above I have tried harder to let the other party lower their limits as I hold relatively stable. By making some concessions you show you are cooperating in the negotiations. By letting the other party make larger concessions, you are profiting.

In the seminar I teach we have a negotiating session between two class members. The object of the session is for one person to buy from the other person an item of indeterminable value, such as an autographed drawing by my three year old son.

The buyer is given an amount of cash known to him, but not to the seller. The seller has to buy the picture from me for five dollars, and then is free to sell it for as much as he or she can, and pocket the profit. The buyer is told that he must buy the picture at some price or give back the money. In the event he buys the picture, then any leftover cash is his to keep.

In a recent class I gave the buyer $31.00 in cash. The seller knew that she had only seven minutes to conclude a deal or she'd be stuck with the picture. After some preliminary pleasantries the buyer and seller tried to get each other to commit to a price. The seller finally admitted that she would take not one penny less than $100 for the picture.

The buyer offered one dollar. Almost immediately the seller made her second offer of five dollars. Yes, you read that right, five dollars. Now I'm not sure why the seller came down so far so fast, but the buyer's next offer was $1.50 and they negotiated right up to the time limit and finally settled at $4.00.

Had the seller come down in price a little more slowly, no doubt she would have ended up with more money. As it was she lost a dollar on the deal, since originally she bought the picture for $5.00, but hopefully learned a lesson which will probably save her thousands on her next real estate purchase.

Deciding What To Offer

Now is the moment; it's time to make your offer. What do you say?

Following the rule, "let the other party mention the first price", sets one price limit in the negotiations. If the seller says he wants $77,000 for his house, then $77,000 is the most you will have to pay. Your first offer should be low enough so that you have room to increase it without exceeding the limits you set for the purchase.

The next rule is to ask for more of a concession than you really need.

After the seller establishes the most he expects from a deal it is your turn to make an offer. Your first offer should be optimistic, and for less than you ultimately expect to pay. In the event the sellers are eager to sell and you have laid the groundwork so that they believe you to be a serious buyer, they will not end the negotiations because you make an offer below their expectations.

Before you make your first offer, you should establish the top dollar you are willing to pay for an item. You establish that dollar figure, by considering several factors:

What is the item really worth? Twenty-two cent postage stamps are worth twenty-two cents. If you could buy them for twenty cents, that would be a bargain. Unfortunately, other than government denominated stamps and coins, few things have their value printed on its face.

What is a new "Ajax 24" model riding lawn mower worth? Three different dealers in town have about the same price on the mower. They must pay less for the mower than they sell it for or they would not still be in business. The value of that mower may vary from dealer to dealer, as they may have paid differing prices when they bought, and their overhead expenses allocated to that mower may differ.

By spending enough time and writing enough letters, you could probably find out what the dealers paid for those mowers. That factor alone will not tell you the lowest price you can offer and buy one.

It is more efficient (and more fun) to learn by simply making them an offer that you are happy with and see how they respond. If the asking price is $699, and after some shopping you decide it is a fair deal at that price, but would be a good deal at $599, and a great deal at $499, start at the great deal level. Remember to make your offer to the owner, not an employee.

A good guide to what a more expensive piece of capital equipment is worth on a wholesale level, is to find out how much your bank will loan against that particular item. Banks have "loan values" on automobiles, boats, computers, etc. and should not loan any more than what they could realize in a forced sale. Generally a purchase at the "loan value" is a good buy.

With jewelry, collectables, antiques, and numismatics, there is often a large spread between the retail price, and the price a dealer will pay you on a cash sale. The cash value of these items should not be confused with the "appraised" value which often reflects the retail price.

This wholesale cash value would be the price you would pay for a "great deal". It would be the dealer's cost, assuming he bought at wholesale.

Another question to ask yourself is "why are you buying?" If you are buying to make a profit, then establish a minimum acceptable profit for the time and money you will invest in the deal. When buying a house in the $60,000 range, you should have at least a $5,000 cash profit going in. That is to say you should be able to sell the house the day you close and put $5,000 in your pocket after paying all of the expenses.

If you are buying an item to use in your business or home, then your concern is to get the best available price, without spending an extraordinary amount of time.

Always Make At Least One Offer

After going through the preliminary steps of researching, and finding an item which meets all of your criteria, you have wasted your time unless you make an offer. *Disregard for a moment what the seller says he wants, or has to have, and tell him what you are willing to do right this moment.*

A car dealer may state emphatically that $9,755 is as low as he could possibly sell that particular car. In the event the car meets your criteria, and your research shows that it has been sold for less, make your offer. You will find that when you tell the dealer that all you will pay is $8,400, he will either refuse (probably with great indignity) or try to talk you up to a higher price.

When buying houses, you often are given a convincing sales pitch over the phone, which leads you to meeting the owner at the house. The seller claims that his house is priced well below the market, is in excellent condition, and he is desperate to sell. When you arrive at the property, you double check the address, assuming you're at the wrong place.

The house is not in the pristine condition described by the owner, and upon closer inspection appears to be priced above, not below the market. This seller has told you a story to get you out to the house in hopes he could sell it to you.

How would you react to this seller? Most would be aggravated, because the seller has intentionally misstated the facts. You probably would spend only a little time in the house, and then leave with a mumbling " don't call me, I'll call you"

If this seller has told his version of the truth to you, he is doing the same to everyone. Most buyers who see the house will respond with your initial "let me out of here" reaction. But you've spent some of your time, and you shouldn't let it be for nothing.

This turkey has aggravated you; why leave without returning the favor? If he is asking $79,500 for the house, offer him $55,000.

The worse that will happen is he will order you out of his house, and you were leaving anyway. Every once in a while, they may counteroffer with a reasonable price. Remember, this seller probably does not get many offers. At the right price you will start to like the house, if not the seller.

Do You Understand The Deal? Can You Explain It?

Hold your breath one more second before you give your offer. Do you understand what you are offering? Do you understand it so well that you can explain it to an interested, but possibly unenthusiastic party? Sometimes I've been so caught up in the negotiations phase that when I conceive an incredibly brilliant plan I may not realize that it is cute but makes no sense at all.

We have a rule at our house that I have to be able to explain any purchase to my wife.

For example, a friend approached me with an offer to buy part interest in a bank. I became enthused because of his enthusiasm and because of the glamour of owning part-interest in a bank. Later, when I tried to explain to Valerie what a great deal owning part of a bank can be, she asked me a simple question which stopped me in my tracks: Why?

Would we make any profit? Would there be any monthly cash flow or tax benefits? Would we be able to sell easily and get our money back if we needed it? Couldn't we use the same amount of money to buy something else that would make us a bigger profit? What experience have you had with banks anyhow?

Although those questions are tough to answer, they are the questions you should ask about any investment. In the event you can't answer them intelligently (to the satisfaction of your spouse) you should either continue to research the investment or stay away from it.

Any time you are buying an investment, it should be clear to you how you will make a profit. In the event that is not clear enough for you to explain to your spouse and/or your CPA, you should avoid that investment. Many people buy investments because they are afraid to admit they know nothing about them.

CHAPTER ELEVEN

GOOD DEALS ARE MADE, NOT BORN

You Have To Ask For A Good Deal

It would be unusual for someone to force a good deal on you. You have to use your skill, accept the possibility of rejection, understand that not everyone in the entire world is going to like you - and ask sellers to make you a good deal.

I've already started you thinking in this way in the section above where I suggested that you engage the seller in discussion and see if he will make the first price concession. Be imaginative and flexible. Ask for a discount, ask for a warranty, ask for....

Most people start by asking for a price reduction. If you ask for a discount every way that you can think and are making no progress, change direction. Ask if the seller would throw in something extra, in the event you paid in cash.

It may be a felt tip pen on the checkout counter of an office supply store. It could be a tie or a belt in a men's store where you have just spent thirty minutes buying and being fitted for a new suit. It may be an extended warranty on a new roof, or new air conditioner. It could be a better room at a hotel where they won't give you a cheaper room. It could be a month's free rent in an apartment. Wherever you are and whatever you are buying, remember the five most important words in a negotiator's memory, "Ask, and you shall receive".

A seller who can reproduce what he is selling you has an incentive to give you a discount for buying more than one copy. Most items are cheaper, when bought by the case, or truckload. A truckload of refrigerators would scare off most buyers. Someone building an apartment complex may need a truckload.

As a landlord in the business of maintaining properties, I ask for and receive at least a ten percent discount at all hardware, paint, and building supply stores. I have a friend who retired from building construction years ago, but still demands, and receives contractor's prices wherever he goes.

In the event you find a merchant who would agree to give you a good break on the price, in the event you purchased more than one of an item, think of friends or associates who may want one. I had a friend call me a few weeks ago to offer me a deal on a copier at about half price. He had found a dealer who would make him a great deal if he bought the last four copiers from him. As he only wanted one, he was trying to find someone else who could use one.

I called to register for a seminar - on negotiation - several years ago. I naturally asked if there was a discount available. After consulting with the instructor and author of the course, the secretary told me the price would be lower if two registered together. I wrote that down, and then asked what the price would be for three. It was a little lower, so I asked what the price would be if I registered five together. The price came down again.

I then called five friends and told them that I could get them into the class at a discount, if they wanted to attend. We all attended and received the discount.

Using Cash To Your Advantage

Always ask for a discount when paying cash! Whether you are buying an eighty thousand dollar house, or a forty nine cent greeting card, get in the habit of asking for a discount. Many times you will be turned down, but many times you will receive a discount.

Who would be most likely to give you a discount for offering to pay cash?

1. A merchant with an immediate need for cash to pay a supplier. (Many suppliers give a discount for cash or quick payment)
2. A merchant who has been burned with bad checks.
3. A merchant who pays a percentage of the sale to a credit card company, and who then may have to wait for his money.
4. Anyone with a serious cash flow problem, who has no time for a check to clear.
5. Someone with a simplified bookkeeping system, who doesn't want to be bothered with balancing a bank statement or a profit and loss statement.
6. Most people. For some reason, a pile of "real money" is much more alluring than a check for the same amount.

Developing good habits is a trait successful people have. Asking for a discount for paying cash is a great habit. Even when you get turned down, you are learning to deal with rejection, which is a skill a good negotiator must have.

In the event you are bothered when someone rejects your offer, you will make an offer to try and please them. That habit will cost you a lot of money. In the event you would receive an average discount of two percent on all of your purchases this year, how much would you save? You may as well assume that you will spend everything that you will make; we all seem to. Take your income this year and multiply it by 2%. For instance, $20,000 × 2% = $400.; $50,000 × 2% ^{5} $1,000. What you save may not make you rich, but it will certainly repay you for the price of this book.

By the way, two percent should not be your goal. Expect much higher. Mastercard, Visa, American Express, and all of the rest of the credit cards, charge merchants a percentage of the sale to process the paperwork, and make a profit, of course. The discount may be as low as 2% for a high volume customer such as a large department store, but smaller merchants may be paying two to three times that much.

In addition, if down the road, the customer disputes and refuses to pay his bill, the credit card company will come back and charge the merchant's account. Some of the card companies don't pay the merchant right away, which means, the merchandise is gone, with no money to pay the suppliers. The merchant also has an obligation to authorize the card with the company to see if it is stolen, and if the customer is current on his bill. This takes time, and a slip up will cost the merchant the amount of the sale.

All of these are reasons a credit card merchant would rather have your cash and will give you an incentive to pay in cash. To get this discount you must be dealing with the owner of the store, or someone who will benefit by you not using the credit card. A salesman at a big department store receives no benefit from you paying cash, and therefore will give you no discount.

An owner of a business who realizes that he will lose the amount of the discount from the amount of his sale will gladly talk with you. I was paying my bill at a Chinese restaurant and had my credit card in my hand. The man at the register appeared to be the owner, and asked how the meal was. I complimented him on a fine meal, and then asked if he would give a discount if I paid with cash, instead of by credit card. The bill was $21.80 and he accepted $20.00.

Recently I purchased a set of tires for my car and the bill was $429 (after some lengthy negotiations). When presenting my credit card for payment I could see the disappointment on the owner's face. He had signs posted around that he accepted this card. When I unfolded four one hundred dollar bills and asked if he would rather have the cash, he readily accepted.

Self-employed contractors who paint, plumb, electrify, mow lawns, and perform other labor intensive tasks, have an especially strong affinity for cash. For some the cash is mad money, for a new fishing pole or other gadget. For some it is a way to beat the system.

In the event you are repairing a business property, and need a receipt so that you can deduct the cost of the repair, make sure you get an adequate receipt when you pay cash. Otherwise the savings you realize by paying cash will be more than offset by the extra taxes you will have to pay. A one thousand dollar repair will save a taxpayer in the thirty-five percent bracket three hundred and fifty dollars in taxes. It is hard to negotiate that big of a discount for cash.

The time to ask for this discount is at the conclusion of the job, not when you are negotiating the original price. A two hundred and twenty-nine dollar job can often be paid for with two crisp one hundred dollar bills.

Always ask with a smile, like you share a little secret. In the event the vendor or contractor becomes indignant, give him a quizzical look, implying that you always get a discount for cash, so what's his problem. If he's still refusing, ask him why he won't give a discount for a cash payment today. If he is still holding out, just smile and say "I had to ask", and ask him to mail you a bill.

At this point he may reconsider, or may just mail you a bill for the agreed-on amount. The worst that can happen is that you pay the full amount. You have nothing to lose by asking, but a little time.

An associate of mine purchased a business by going to the owner's house with a stack of one hundred dollar bills that totaled $30,000. Thirty Thousand Dollars was the top price he was willing to pay for this business. He and the owner had been in negotiations for some time, and were within five thousand dollars of agreeing. The owner was visibly moved by the pile of cash.

My associate said that he had given a lot of thought to how much he could pay for the business, and that this was going to be his best offer. The seller, hoping for a little more counteroffered at $33,000. At that point the buyer picked up a bill off of the stack and said, ‘‘now my best offer is $29,900.’’ The seller thinking that he would get at least the $30,000 now really began to sweat. He said that he would accept the $30,000. With that the buyer picked up one more bill, making the offer $29,800. The seller accepted the $29,800. price. Seeing a pile of money that could be yours disappear one bill at a time, can bring tears to your eyes.

The Cash Advantage In Buying Houses

Many people talk about putting little or no cash into a real estate purchase. This idea is a necessity when you begin your buying career, as I did, with literally no money to put into a deal. Self-respecting bankers wouldn’t loan me any, either, so the habits of patience and persistence were required - or I might not own anything now.

Another reason is that putting more cash into a deal doesn’t improve the return on your investment. If you put an extra $5,000 down just because you have it, you have that much more tied up in that piece of real estate. And that property will only go up so much. So you limit your return when you put ‘‘extra’’ cash into the deal.

On the other hand, if you have cash and can use that cash as leverage to drive down the purchase price, then this is an excellent return on your money.

Some sellers need a certain amount of cash, and since this can be a premium item in the market, some will reduce the price to get cash. A seller that has owned a house for a number of years, and at the time of sale has a relatively high profit can afford to drop the price if you offer the cash he wants.

Jimmy Napier's "2% Rule" states that for every dollar cash that you put in the seller must reduce the price by two dollars. If the price we are agreeing to is $80,000, but the seller wants $5,000 in cash, then I'm going to knock the price down to $70,000.

In some parts of the county "cash to mortgage", where the buyer pays the seller at closing the entire sales price above the mortgage balance, is almost a religious tenet. If you deal with sellers who feel this way - and you have cash to spend - you can use their insistence on cash to drive down the price. If they are unyielding, leave them for another, less demanding buyer.

There is, of course, a limit to how much people will reduce the price. And some sellers just need too much cash, and you won't be able to buy a house from them unless you have a great deal of available cash and they are willing to drastically reduce the price.

CHAPTER TWELVE

AFTER THE OFFER: OBJECTIONS AND COUNTEROFFERS

Now you've done it. Gathered your courage to make one of the world's best offers.

If the seller jumps right in and accepts it, you probably offered too much. If they are eager to take this amount, then they probably would have considered less. If the seller is less enthusiastic, then you have entered the period of negotiation.

Be Open - Encourage Counteroffers

The challenge is to appear friendly, so that you do not scare off the seller with your first offer, without looking too friendly. With your first offer you asked for more than you really expected to receive. You must now take on the appearance of someone who really expects to get what he asked for, but is reasonable enough to listen to a plausable alternative.

Consider how young children old ask for an extended bedtime. Wide eyed and expectant, they deliver the question with a look that says "this is very important to me". In a few years they will verbalize the message saying, "I'll just die if I can't stay up and watch that show".

In both cases they are trying to communicate that they really want this extension. You know and they know that you are the final authority, so they want you to stay friendly, and keep the negotiations open. They don't want to provoke you into a absolute position of NO.

Likewise, when you make an offer, even an offer considerably below what the seller expects, you must do it in a way that does not provoke the seller into taking that absolute position of NO.

The more time you have spent with the seller, and the better you know each other, the more likely he is to make a counteroffer, and keep the negotiations open. This is one reason why it is important to establish a relationship with the seller before making the first offer.

A low offer made to a complete stranger will generally be rejected without a counteroffer. Imagine your response to a buyer who knocks on the door of a house you have for sale and offers you eighty percent of your asking price. You would probably tell him to buzz off. He has insulted your intelligence and your financial position with his offer.

But what if that same buyer had invested a few hours getting to know you and your house. And then, after asking many questions, the buyer sat down with you and made the same offer. You might not accept, but you would continue the conversation, and the negotiations.

You encourage counteroffers by appearing friendly, not hostile. In the event you go around making offers punctuated with the words, "Take it or leave it", you will find most people leave it.

One of my favorite people who teaches negotiating techniques is a grand lady named Dee Fountain from Salt Lake City. Dee always says, "Don't tell me what you won't do, tell me what you will do!" Dee says this, as she says almost everything, with a smile.

Dee gives you the accurate impression that she is there not just to make a deal, but to help you if she can. The combination of this attitude with her smiling nature, and persistence, makes Dee an excellent negotiator.

As much as possible, within your own personality, adopt a positive, "we can do it" attitude, and keep the ball rolling.

Negotiate Only With Parties Who Can Make A Binding Decision

Does the person you are negotiating with have the authority to make a decision? When I buy real estate, I refuse to make an offer unless all persons necessary to sign a contract and deed are in the room. In the event the approval of a third party is required I want that person there or available by phone.

When you negotiate with one owner of a property, often a spouse is involved. The party with whom you are negotiating may accept your offer, but the spouse's signature is necessary to bind the deal. Often when the spouses confer they will decide to ask for more, or approach another buyer to see if he may pay more.

This technique, called "shopping the offer", is common in the real estate business, where most agents represent sellers, and have a duty to get the highest possible price for the seller. Of course a commissioned agent gets paid more as the price increases, so there is a two-fold reason for getting a higher price.

A Realtor once called to sell me an apartment building. The seller was anxious and he thought I could get a good buy in the event I closed quickly. I offered $134,000 for a building that was listed and worth about $170,000. The Realtor was a little shocked at my low offer, and I insisted that I be present when he presented it to the seller.

He was sure that she would not accept. I was hopeful because I had researched what she had paid for the building and offered her a small profit. I reasoned that if she was truly anxious she might accept my offer.

When we met with the seller, I made a point of letting her know how long I had lived in town and how well established I was. I offered to have her check out my credit and gave as a reference the president of a well known bank. This conversation before entering negotiations let her feel more comfortable with me.

The broker then presented my offer. She questioned several points including the price, and then said she would let me know in the morning. Although I hated to leave without an acceptance or counteroffer, I felt that she was close to accepting, and decided not to pressure her.

The next morning I called the broker to find out her response. He told me that there had been another offer early that morning for one thousand dollars more than mine and she accepted it.

The broker, upon seeing how close she was to an acceptance, had called a friend of his who had topped my offer. I learned from that experience to make offers which make people accept or reject them without the opportunity to "shop them".

In the event the broker had secured an offer at a substantially higher price, then I would have not had any hard feelings. But, in this case he solicited my offer, then gave another buyer the advantage of my skill by offering the property to him at a slightly higher price. Had he offered me the same deal, I would have gladly accepted and both buyer and seller would have been satisfied. Needless to say, I will never make another offer through that broker.

Ordering The Negotiations To Your Advantage

You should choose one of the items of least importance to you to test the waters. When negotiating a house purchase, the price and the terms of any seller financing are the most important items. In the event of a sale which will give the seller all cash, then the price is the most important item.

Generally the item of most importance to you should be negotiated last. The most important item to you may not be the most important item to the seller. Typically in a house deal, the seller concentrates on price. I have purchased several properties at the seller's price, because they have conceded terms to me which more than offset the high price.

When the seller is going to take part of the purchase price in the form of a note (often secured by a mortgage or deed of trust), then the payments and interest rate on that note may be as important as the price. In the event you anticipate seller financing when purchasing, then negotiate this financing toward the end of the negotiations.

Here is a list of topics to cover in negotiations, ordered as I would prefer them discussed for a typical house purchase, with the seller holding some of the financing.

Closing date

Date of possession (not always the closing date)

Personal property included in the sale

Repairs to be made to property prior to closing

Who will pay for the out-of-pocket closing costs

Buyer and seller liability under the contract

Down payment and terms of any paper to be held by the seller

Price

CHAPTER THIRTEEN

COPING WITH DIFFERENT NEGOTIATING STYLES

Negotiations And Intimidators

There are those who will try to intimidate you by their actions and words. In the event this bothers you, simply leave - unless you really want the deal. Blowing smoke at you, making you stand while they sit, or purposely facing you into the sun or another bright light are old intimidation devices.

These are designed to encourage you to make a quick deal, just so you can escape the presence of your "tormentor". By making you a little uncomfortable, they hope to get your emotions working instead of your brain. These techniques do work. Consider how someone decorates their office who wants to give you the impression that they are more knowledgeable than you.

They have a large imposing desk, and a large chair for them with a lower chair for you, so that you are looking up at them. Plaques and diplomas adorn the walls. These are all there to give them credibility, while you have to build yours.

Bankers and lawyers who have limited authority to negotiate, as they are generally agents for other principals, build these fortresses, to give the illusion of power and knowledge. In the event you have what they need, the tables often turn.

Jimmy Napier, Jack Miller and I were in an attorney's office one day trying to buy a property his doctor-client owned. This attorney had read the book on setting up an office. It had one of the largest desks I had seen, in addition to a fireplace and a hound dog curled up in the corner. We were seated in chairs considerably shorter than his.

We had been chatting for a few moments when his secretary called the attorney to the door for something. Jimmy asked if he could use his phone for a quick call, and went around the desk, sat in the chair, and dialed the phone.

Jimmy continued to sit in that chair, saying that he had been put on hold, for the balance of our meeting. Jimmy in a not too subtle way had shown the attorney that he was not intimidated by his office. Jimmy relaxed in the comfortable chair while the attorney paced the floor.

As the attorney was billing his client by the hour, he was now eager to show some results of this meeting. We were willing buyers and his client was an anxious seller, who had no doubt called the attorney many times about disposing this property. An attorney that bills by the hour can still only charge a good client a reasonable amount for a standard real estate transaction, so the attorney was himself anxious to make a deal, and reclaim possession of his chair.

We purchased his client's property on terms that delighted us. Later that day when I asked Jimmy who he called, he told me "time and temperature."

Bankers have mastered intimidation for a different reason. They don't want people asking too many questions. They build marble commercial palaces and fill them with smartly uniformed employees and rubber tree plants, so you do not ask embarrassing questions.

They like to know everything about you before they trust you with some of "their" money, but will tell you little about what they are doing with "your" money after you deposit it. Many have put up with the aggravation, waiting and paperwork it takes to apply for an institutional loan, only to be turned down just before they needed the money, after being led to believe they had the loan.

A friend of mine was in a bank to close a loan after filling out all the forms and months of waiting. The bank officer had the loan documents ready to go, but kept her waiting while he attended to much more important business, like chatting on the phone. Finally he stopped talking long enough to tell her that the rate on the loan had increased since they first agreed to loan her the money. He asked her to sign away her life on numerous forms, and said he would try to get her a check. She stood up with a smile, said no thanks, and left.

Bankers, because of the marble buildings and printed forms, assume that whatever deal they propose will be unquestionably accepted by the customer. Go to a loan closing with a bottle of white out and paint out all of the parts of a loan document you don't like, and watch the reaction.

They have found safety in standardization, and it takes an act of the board to accept anything less than their printed paperwork.

Sometimes the seller will be represented by an attorney at the closing on a property. This attorney will many times try to "earn" his fee in the eyes of his client by trying to make the deal a little bit better. In the event he, acting as an agent for his buyer, tries to change the terms of the sale, he has in effect reopened negotiations. If he stated that the seller will not close unless the interest rate is increased on the money owed to the seller, the buyer has the option of closing or walking away.

This would be a risky maneuver unless they thought the buyer really wanted the deal. Once, Jack Miller, who I've mentioned previously, was at a closing where he was buying a house. The sellers' attorney tried to renegotiate some of the terms to his clients advantage. Jack smiled, closed his brief case, and walked out. He left the attorney to explain to his clients that the sale was off and that they would have to now find another buyer.

We purchased a house on quite favorable terms last year, where the seller agreed to loan us money at well below-market interest rates. The seller did this because we agreed to close the sale in a week, and pay her off in seven years. After signing a contract that we all understood and agreed to, she sent a copy to her attorney.

When he saw the interest rate, he called me immediately to say that under no circumstances would his client close with these terms. The deal was off unless we would pay more interest.

I responded, as I always do, by saying that we would gladly back out of the deal. In fact after we had signed the contract with his seller, we had found another deal we liked much better, but had to pass, because we could not afford both. Now we could buy the other one.

This was not the response he anticipated, and when he called his client to tell her that he had "saved her", it was her turn to blow her stack. She had called the movers, and was moving within a week. She wanted to be in Indiana by Thanksgiving. He got the message that if he did not put the deal back together, he had better be willing to buy the house himself on the same terms.

It was one polite and friendly attorney that called my office again that afternoon, to see if we were still planning on a closing later that week. We agreed, because it was a very good deal. But I was tempted to let it pass.

Although some sellers have difficult personalities, sellers rarely try to intimidate a buyer as an agent might. When dealing directly with a seller, be yourself, and spend the first few minutes as you would on a first date, trying to establish common ground for a relationship.

Only after you are feeling comfortable, proceed to ask more questions and work into making your offer. The larger the item you are buying, the more time you should spend in this preliminary stage. When checking into a hotel, you may chat with the clerk only a few seconds before asking for a better rate on your room. When buying a house you may spend an hour or more just getting to know the seller.

A seller who likes you is more likely to make you a better deal. Coming on like Attila the Hun may be your last resort after the desk clerk has told you for the third time that they are full and have lost your reservation. Appealing to people's good side and begging for mercy is often more productive, especially if you are asking for price concessions.

Working With Imtimidators

There are several ways to do business, either with or around people who try to intimidate you. One way is Jimmy's approach. Simply turn the tables. Show the intimidator that you are not really impressed with his act.

In the event you are dealing with an aggressive salesman who has led you up the path to the mountain, and now expects you to buy, try saying: "Say, that was really good! Do many people still fall for that approach?"

If you can say it with a straight face I guarantee the salesman will laugh. I find that complimenting a good salesman's technique puts him more at ease. This sometimes lets you make a good deal, even with a pro.

In the event you are not getting the results you want, think about going over the person's head with whom you are dealing. Everyone answers to someone, and most of us answer to someone mortal. An attorney's principal is his "boss", although some seem to occasionally confuse the relationship. A banker, even the chairman of the board, is answerable to his board and the stockholders. A letter to all of the board members, will get his attention.

The higher up the ladder of authority you move, the less important the decision is to the person who must finally make it. Because the decision is less important, it is easier for him to make, and you will have your answer. A decision to sell a house that the bank owns for $5,000 less than the amount the bank has in it, would be a major decision for a new bank officer. In the event he is going to make a decision, it would have to be after careful deliberation, and probable consultation with his superiors. He will not jeopardize his position over that decision.

The president of the bank is used to writing off loans many times that amount, and may see the decision as a good move, and make the decision instantly.

Even the board of directors and stockholders are not the final authority. The banking business is regulated by the government. In the event you receive no satisfaction from the board of directors, appeal to the government agency in charge.

Preparing For Intimidators

Robert Ringer, in his book "Winning Through Intimidation" stresses the importance of being prepared before approaching a situation where someone may try to take advantage of you. Ringer was a real estate broker, who specialized in "big deals". The big commissions associated with a big deal are typically negotiated down to a fraction of the normal percentage, because you are dealing with heavy weight buyers and sellers.

A six thousand dollar commission on the sale of a one hundred thousand dollar house may seem reasonable to all parties involved. A six hundred thousand dollar commission on a ten million dollar sale, will look excessive to everyone but the broker trying to collect it.

Ringer was involved in putting together the big deals and was constantly being negotiated out of part of the commission. At the closings you would have a seller who owned a ten million dollar property, a buyer who could afford to purchase a ten million dollar property, their attorneys, and Mr. Ringer, the broker.

Now that the broker had done the work of bringing the buyer and seller together, they could finish the deal without him and would try to squeeze him out of his commission. Many times the amount of cash the buyer would have would be enough to satisfy the seller, but not enough to pay the commission and the seller. In those cases the buyer and seller would say to the broker, "we can close today if you agree to take a $60,000 commission, otherwise the deal is off."

When in the brokerage business in the early seventies, I found myself in several similar situations. As a commissioned agent, no sale, means no pay. After spending hundreds of hours, and often thousands of dollars advertising a property and entertaining potential buyers, sometimes you really needed a payday. When the broker looks a little lean, and is sweating profusely, the principals know they can make a deal. Faced with a sure sixty thousand dollars, or going home empty handed, most would crack and settle for the smaller figure.

Ringer learned quickly. After experiencing the above described treatment, he decided to use a little intimidation of his own. At the next closing he brought along several well dressed and intelligent looking attorneys. He of course introduced his "staff" to everyone present, and sat back cool and relaxed.

When the time came to "put the squeeze" on the commission, one of his attorney's suggested that unless the commission was paid in its entirety, that they would litigate the matter and tie up the property for an indefinite period of time. After the buyers and sellers consulted with their "staffs" they made a little better offer. Ringer stuck to his guns and collected the entire amount.

This show costs Ringer some attorney's fees, but netted him a much large commission. His book is good reading, and especially informative for commission salespeople.

How To Avoid Being Intimidated

Buyers can take comfort in the fact that there are generally many more sellers than buyers. Occasionally the converse is true for short periods causing a shortage. These shortages are generally remedied in short order by sellers manufacturing whatever there is that is in short supply and high demand.

Because of this sellers are generally more eager to please than buyers, and less likely to be intimidating. In the event a seller makes the mistake of giving you a hard time, just smile, and then leave. Even when you really want to buy what he is selling, let him think that he lost your business for a day or so, and then return. His attitude should show improvement, or give him the old smile again.

Responding to an intimidator by using similar tactics, such as loud speech or screaming, only escalates the confrontation. When I was selling real estate on commission I once presented an offer to a seller for about one half of his asking price. He turned red in the face, and threw a tantrum any two year old would be proud of. Once I was comfortable that he was not going to cause me any bodily harm, I relaxed and enjoyed the show.

He was embarrassing his family, but I knew that he would soon cool down, and when he did we discussed a counteroffer which was ultimately accepted.

Try to recognize intimidators and their tactics early in a negotiating situation, so that they will not scare you into an unwise decision in a moment of passion. When you recognize the technique, take a deep breath and count to ten. Then pay attention to what is being said. Sometimes there will be a clue which will help your cause.

CHAPTER FOURTEEN

CLASSIC NEGOTIATING STYLES

Part of the fun of negotiating is the people you meet. There are some sellers who belong in the theater. It has occurred to me that the more vocally resistant the seller is, the more he wants you to make a higher offer.

The following descriptions are of the types of negotiators I have met most often. Fortunately, some are once in a lifetime experiences. A person who loses self control while negotiating will rarely conclude the negotiations successfully. Some negotiators pretend to lose control to influence the other party. This technique is powerful as you will see below, but it takes an accomplished actor to pull it off.

Visit any courtroom, and you will see actors. Attorneys pleading their clients' cases, are often pleading for lives, or millions of dollars. Both the attorneys and their clients are acting in what may be the performance of their life. Business deals can attract similar talent. Try to enjoy the show without becoming part of the act.

Please disregard the gender associated with the following examples. The names were picked to make the reading easier, and the characteristics of each type occur with equal frequency in either sex.

Characters To Recognize

WARY WILLY: Willy is a quiet fellow, who is adverse to giving out information. He answers questions with questions, like "why do you want to know". After a few minutes with Willy, you get the impression that he knows more than he will ever tell you.

You must avoid asking Willy questions which can be answered with a yes or no, or that is the answer you will hear. Willy will avoid mentioning the first price. To negotiate with Willy, you must research first and then make an offer based on your research.

If Willy was selling a house, research what he paid for it, and what his neighbors have paid, before starting negotiations. Present your offer along with your research, to show that you know what you are talking about, even without his help. Now that Willy knows that you are a serious buyer, and not just another talker, he may enter into serious negotiations.

Willy can be monumental timewasters. Sellers who will not respond to direct questioning over the phone, are rarely motivated enough to make you a good deal. Some motivated sellers are tightlipped about some facts which they consider none of your business.

Indirect questions, like "would you consider renting the house if it does not sell?" can give you valuable information about how much cash the seller needs in order to move. A seller who will rent a house will receive little up front cash. Probably a security deposit, and two months rent, are all they can hope for. With that knowledge you can determine if the house would be a good buy with that much cash invested, and start with that offer.

CHATTY CHARLIE: Charlie is the opposite of Willy. He will talk your ear off, telling you more than you ever wanted to know about his product.

Charlie talks so much, that he runs out of facts, but that does not slow him down. Many real estate salesmen (not the successful ones) are like Charlie. The challenge is to separate the fact from the fiction.

Charlie can be turned into an asset by carefully questioning some of his more outlandish statements. You cannot call him a liar, or he will become offended (for a while anyway). By getting across that you know some of what he states is farfetched, he will be less generous with his rhetoric.

Steer the conversation and let him ramble after questions like, "Why are selling?" Cut short rambling by breaking in and asking another question. This is rude, but people who breathe through their ears as they talk non-stop, are used to it, and will respond to the next question with zest.

CHARMING CATHY: She is a gracious and near perfect hostess. She will compliment you on your good taste, good sense, and shrewd negotiating ability. You will face little apparent resistance in your questioning, but closer examination will reveal that you are learning little about her real situation. She passes on the hard questions with statements like, "I will have to look that up".

Many good, high commissioned salespeople adopt this personality. Think of the salesperson at an exclusive clothing store. Didn't most everything that you liked look "just wonderful" on you. What about a salesperson at a highpriced jewelry store. Have you ever tried on a ring that wasn't "stunning"? They even call over their fellow salespeople to show them how great it looks on you.

Some really lay it on thick. "Doesn't he look just like Tom Selleck in that jacket? No, really I'm not kidding". If you catch yourself looking in the mirror after a comment like that, you are in trouble.

These salesmen, or sellers, get you to like them so you feel like a heel if you don't buy from them. In small ticket sales, this tactic often succeeds. We all like to be liked, and some pay a lot of money for that fleeting moment of perceived friendship.

With more expensive items, like a car or house, the seller or salesman is generally trying to steer you to a high price, or away from some detracting detail, like a bad engine or bad plumbing.

It is fine to respond smilingly to this kind of attention, but do not lose sight of what you are trying to accomplish. You will be shocked as to how less friendly these people can become when they find out that you will not pay their price, or buy what they are selling.

Tenants often "court" landlords with all smiles, until the landlord stops buying their excuses for why the rent is late. Then they transform into snarling, little demons hurling insults, as you explain that you enjoyed their story, but it will not replace paying the rent.

SAD SALLY: Sally will appeal to your generous side. She is being forced to sell, and you can see that from the tears welling up in her eyes. She seems most cooperative, but like Cathy above, often sidesteps important questions. You must understand the facts about what she is selling, not just the story she tells you about why she is selling.

A counselor friend of mine tells me that most people tell us the story they think we want to hear when they sell. Some of these stories have grown in detail and clarity with repetition. The tellers of these tales actually believe that they are true after a while.

Some sad tales are true of course. Once a lady tried to sell me her house after her husband had left her. She had just come home from the hospital with twins, and both babies had problems which required constant nursing attention. Her husband could not handle the situation and disappeared. She was out of money and about to lose the house.

A situation like this will bring out the charitable side of nearly everyone, and this woman deserved some help. However, it would be foolish to buy her house from her for too much money, just because of her misfortune. When faced with a situation like this one, keep charity separate from business. In the event you can buy the house at a good price, do it. Regardless of whether you buy, you can make the person a gift. In this way you can be objective about how much you will pay for something, and be as generous as you wish after the emotions have subsided.

CROOKED CAMILLE: Camille is to be avoided if you can recognize her. She deals with greedy people, who let avarice overrule their common sense. Camille may approach you to buy a genuine Rolex watch for only $125. Now most everyone knows that a Rolex watch on its worst day is worth many times that amount and, would be wary.

It either does not really belong to Camille (a nice way to say she stole it) or it's not really a Rolex. Some people will not pass it by, and will probably offer Camille $95 trying to make a good deal better. She of course will protest, and then accept, as her profit margin is still acceptable.

Occasionally Camille will dabble in real estate. One of her favorite scams is to rent a nice home, with a bad check. The greedy landlord who is charging too much rent will be her target. This landlord is glad to see anybody. It's hard to rent a $600 a month place for $800, so he has had few interested parties.

When Camille falls in love with the place, and wants to move in "this very instant", the landlord beams with anticipation. She takes her checkbook out of her Gucci bag, and writes him a check for two months rent and the security deposit. The out of town check bothers the landlord, but Camille looks so good that he makes a very expensive exception.

It will take a couple of weeks for the check to bounce, and Camille will insist that you redeposit the check, as the bank made a mistake. In most states the landlord will have to evict Camille, in order to get possession of the property. This will take a few more weeks, and you can bet that Camille is not a good housekeeper.

Occasionally after Camille rents a place, she will run an ad in the paper which looks like this:

> Must sell this weekend. $90,000 house reduced to $74,500. Will take $3000 down and finance at 10%. Call for appointment 344-3232.

This is an attractive ad and will produce a lot of phone calls. How can she sell a house that she is renting (or not renting). She has no legal right to sell anything, but will again attract those who are bound to 'steal' something.

We ran across this scam in Southern California. The house was sold to several purchasers, and she gave out a Realtor's card, when she took their deposits on the house. She told the buyers to contact the Realtor in ten days to set up a closing. Again the price was not critical to Camille as she had a low cost in the house.

To avoid buying from Camille, never be in too big of a hurry to complete a deal that is too good to be true. Thoroughly check it out. Any jeweler could authenticate the pedigree of the watch. In the event it was a Rolex, offer a check and see if the seller has a name, and can prove that they are that person. It's hard to cash a check without some identification.

With real estate, a few rules will keep you from giving somebody your money.

1. Always make deposit checks payable to a third party, like an attorney, title company, or bank. By not giving the seller your money, they can't disappear with it if they are crooked.

2. Always have a competent attorney or title company research the title of the property to see who the legal owners are and check how much they owe against the property. Title insurance can be purchased to further protect your investment, and it is a bargain compared to fire insurance.

3. When renting a property, NEVER accept a check for the first months rent or deposit. Bill Nickerson made that point clearly in his excellent book titled *How I Turned $1000 Into $1,000,000 In My Spare Time.* Take cash or the equivalent (Cashier's check, money order, travelers checks). Avoid diamond rings, works of art, and Rolex watches.

TERRIBLE TOM: Tom (the name has been changed to protect the terrible), has a temper which he controls at will. When the tables can be turned to his advantage, with a burst of hostility, he lets it fly. This act would be called a tantrum if Tom was three years old, and ignored by a smart parent.

Several years ago I was involved in the renegotiation of a contract for the sale of a house which had called for periodic payments by the buyers. The buyers had not made the payments promptly, and broken many promises they had made to the sellers.

Tom was one of the sellers, and after everyone was seemingly in agreement, Tom jumped up and shouted "I'm not putting up with any more of this", and stomped out slamming the door. The mood of the people remaining in the room was one of shock and disbelief. The people on Tom's side (which I was) had no idea he was going to react like that, so we were as amazed as everyone else.

I volunteered to go after Tom to talk him into coming back. He was outside the building, but not the least bit upset. I returned with the message that Tom was upset over the price, and if the buyers would agree to pay one thousand dollars more, he would return and sign the papers. They agreed, not wanting to upset Tom anymore. This man was obviously treading a fine line as it was.

Tom is not an irrational man. He has just found a way to use his controlled temper to maneuver other people. Tom's act is so good that you are not sure if he is rational at the time of his performance, so your best reaction, should be not to react at all.

If no one takes Tom seriously, he must cut off the negotiations, or return to continue in a civilized manner. If you give in you will lose, because he will continue to use the same tactic until it is no longer is effective.

Some three year olds learn to maneuver their parents using the same tactics as Tom. When a young child knows that he can get his way by screaming in a public place, that parent will hear a lot of screaming in their lifetime.

SILENT SAM: Sam is slow to respond to your questions, and when he does respond, he talks slowly and deliberately. This is a great style to copy, but very difficult for those of us who are bothered by any lull in the conversation. In my family, you have to compete to talk, as everyone has an opinion on everything.

When negotiating, the party who talks the most, often reveals the most about his position. In addition, talkers (I am one so I can talk about them) are typically so busy about thinking about the next important point that they want to make, that they forget to listen to what the other party is saying.

Sam will take advantage of talkers by letting them run. As I mentioned earlier, my friend, Jimmy Napier, is a Sam, and a very good negotiator. I find myself consciously biting my lip to keep from "helping" Jimmy spit out the words, when we are negotiating with each other.

Now Jimmy can talk as fast (or maybe even faster) than I can when he needs to, but he has trained himself to let the other party do most of the talking when discussing his money. Try to recognize Sam early in negotiations. If you don't, in just a little while, Sam will know a lot about your position, and you will know very little about Sam's.

You will probably have to physically trick yourself into not talking, while Sam gets ready to say something. He may pause thirty seconds between thoughts, and for a while between words.

Practice some of Sam's techniques next time you're talking with someone you do not know (your family or friends will think you have gone off the deep end). Notice how chatty they seem, and how much more you can hear when you are not doing all of the talking.

BIG BAD BOB: Bob is from the "I win, you lose" school. He is not content with just winning, he wants a little more than a good deal. Bob is hard to make a deal with, even when you are desperate. He will not survive in any business where there is real competition, as anyone with a choice will deal elsewhere.

Bob is one of the few sellers who will try to intimidate the buyer, not realizing that the buyer has many choices of where to buy. I see Bob often in the role of a landlord "selling" space to tenants. Typically Bob is dealing in low end housing where the tenants have little choice of where to live at the prices they can afford to pay. He can intimidate, and take advantage with high rents and claimed deposits because he knows that they are unlikely to retaliate.

Bob has a hard time buying, because he always asks for a little more than a good deal. He misses many good deals, because he pushes so hard that the sellers refuse to deal with him. Even house sellers under tremendous financial pressure will not sell to Bob, because they would rather lose the house than have him make a profit from it.

Obnoxious, overbearing, (and other adjectives generally reserved for the other guy's attorney), Bob is a hard person with whom to do business, and is best avoided.

Other Challenges

The above descriptions are of those negotiators who seem to reoccur in my dealings with some frequency. There are many others, like a man who was hard of hearing, and had lost his hearing aid. He had done nothing on purpose (or at least I did not think he had) to give him an advantage. However, having to say everything two or three times in a loud voice, put me at a disadvantage.

Non-Americans who have a hard time understanding our language have the same type of advantage as the hard of hearing. You repeat yourself, in different ways to try to be understood, perhaps wondering if their English is as good as yours. When a considerable amount is involved, have an interpreter who will work on your side, converse with the other party.

Those of differing cultural backgrounds do not necessarily play by the rules we are accustomed to in our country.

Other people will negotiate an agreement, and then insist that you live by your side of the bargain, while they ignore their obligations. Avoid dealing with those whose concept of right and wrong differ from your own, unless you are willing to play by their rules.

CHAPTER FIFTEEN

FINAL POINTS

Closers: Getting To Agreement

The next time you make an offer on a new or used car, notice how the salesman "handles" your offer. He will most probably wince a little when you mention your price, and say that he will do his best to get it accepted. He then will disappear to get the approval of his boss.

That wince was not the involuntary physical reaction you or I might have had to a low offer on something we were selling, but a practiced reaction to your first offer. Roger Dawson, a master negotiator who teaches you how to develop a what he calls a flinch, uses the technique in all of his negotiations and at every level.

In the event you are negotiating with your spouse or children (or parents), a flinch will not be as effective as they will see through your mime. But strangers don't know your normal reactions, and the flinch is a very effective first move to get the price lowered.

The salesman was using the wince instead of a counteroffer or an immediate acceptance. Think of what your reaction would be to a car salesman who accepted your first offer with a smile and a handshake. You would naturally assume that you offered too much and there must be something wrong for the salesman to be so anxious to sell. By going through this little ritual, he is leading you to believe that your offer is well below the actual cost of the car and even if he later accepts your offer, you will feel good because you caused him to "sweat it out".

When he returns he will say how close you are to a deal, and ask for a little more. In the event you said that that was your best offer and turned to leave, he would be by you side congratulating you on your negotiating ability and saying that you have made a fine buy.

We were at that point when purchasing our last car. The salesman had told us that this was the best deal he had ever made on this model, and that he hoped he did not lose his job because of it. Then my wife asked him to throw in a set of floormats which were supposed to cost a little over a hundred dollars. He apologized and said that there was just no way he could do that. The mats were handled by another department, and we would have to see them after we finished our business.

Valerie, eight months pregnant and more than a little weary, said, "Well, let's think about it overnight then." The salesman became a little tense, and asked, "If I throw in the mats do we have a deal?", to which we responded yes, and bought a car.

When the salesman said "If I throw in the mats, do we have a deal?" he was using a closer, or a question that would end the negotiation if answered in the affirmative.

Asking For A "No"

Warren Harding, the best salesman I have ever met, use "negative closes". Warren works on the assumption that people are more likely to say "no" than "yes", so he asks a closing question looking for a "no". Warren would have phrased the salesman's question like this, "In the event I throw in the mats, is there any reason we wouldn't have a deal?" When the answer is no, the deal is made.

When closing a deal involving more money, like a house, usually several "closes" are involved. Not only will the buyers and sellers have to agree on price, they must agree on several conditions of the sale.

A question trying to obtain owner financing could be phrased like this." In the event I pay the price you are asking, is there any reason you would not loan me $12,000 for seven years?"

As a buyer you should try to determine what element of the deal is most critical to the seller. One seller may have to net five thousand dollars in cash at the closing. Another seller may not be as critical about the amount of cash he receives, but insist on his price. Another still may really need to close within a few days.

Once you identify the sellers greatest need, try to fulfill it if you can. Then structure the other terms of the transaction so that you can make a nice profit.

Never Steal In Slow Motion

The credit for that line goes to Jack Miller. Jack has made good buys on more properties than anyone I have ever met. Jack makes really good buys because he has the confidence to make quick decisions, involving relatively large sums of money.

In the event someone does offer you a $90,000 house for $70,000, a series of quick actions are necessary on your part to take advantage of the deal. Moving fast on a major purchase is a little like driving fast. When driving a car twenty miles and hour, you can look around, scratch, and fiddle with the radio. Even if you swerve a little, probably nothing will be damaged.

Compare that to driving ninety miles an hour. Now you are intent on watching the road. No time for the radio or to enjoy the scenery, because a little swerve could be fatal.

When you try to buy and close a real estate transaction in a day, things have to happen quickly. While a mistake will rarely prove fatal, it could be very expensive. This is no transaction for the faint of heart or the inexperienced.

We have closed several transactions in one day. In every case we had to pull in some favors and occasionally pay extra to have work done immediately. While an attorney may normally take a week to search the title and prepare the documents necessary to close a transaction, it can be done in a few hours. All it takes is for him or her to drop everything else, and do your work next. The same is true of appraisals, and inspections of the property.

This may cost more than normal, but I am willing to pay double the usual attorney's fees to close a deal, in the event I am buying far enough below the market. A nine hundred dollar law fee is acceptable when it allows you to close a deal ten thousand under the market.

To summarize, real bargains must be contracted for immediately in order to take them off the market. Generally, someone who will sell at a large discount wants the proceeds yesterday. That translates into a dash to the attorney's or title company's office with the contract. Then you need to arrange for the money to be paid to the seller *after the title has been checked and a title commitment has been issued, and the property given a thorough inspection.*

Choose a law firm or title company which has been in business for a while, and which will probably be around for a few years, in case a title problem appears. When buying in a hurry, I prefer to use the best professionals that money can buy, because the inexperienced may make costly mistakes, and the inept may not get the job done in time.

Always Be Willing To Walk Away From A Deal

It is easy to start wanting to close a deal just because you have so much time and effort already invested. Often hours are spent making phone calls, and researching profit margins and sellers' motivations.

Avoid letting any property, or seller, become a personal challenge that you have to buy or beat. A crafty seller or salesman will try to set up a challenge situation, where you feel as though you are about to win. Statements like "we are so close to a deal", are designed to keep you involved. A couple once tried to sell me their large house. They claimed that they were desperate, as many lukewarm sellers do to get some attention. After several phone calls from them and one face to face meeting, they convinced me to come out and see their house. It was a beautiful home, much nicer than any other houses I then owned as investments.

They proceeded to show me all of the extras they had built into the house, and pointed out the other even nicer houses in the neighborhood. After further discussion, I concluded that they indeed needed to sell this nice house in a hurry, or they were going to lose it to their creditors.

I researched what other houses in the neighborhood had sold for, and tried to develop a plan where I could make some money if I bought the house. Finally my wife, noticing I was spending a lot of time on this deal, commented that if it was that hard to see how to make a profit, the deal must be too close.

As usual, she was right. The deal was much too close to market value to be assured of a profit. I was trying to put the deal together because I had come to like the owners and was sympathizing with their position of losing their beautiful home. In addition, I had spent so much time already, I did not want to "waste" that time invested.

The best time to walk away from a marginal deal, is before you buy it. Whenever you find yourself rationalizing that a deal is good, for other than obvious financial reasons, it's time to step back and rethink your reason for buying.

It is easy to fall in love with what you are hoping to buy. Whether it is a spiffy sweater, a new car, a home for your family or an investment, you will not negotiate as good a deal when you become emotionally involved. When you are falling in love, your eyes mist over and you breathe a little faster. Any seller paying attention can see the signs, and it will cost you.

Investors occasionally fall in love with physically attractive real estate, such as a new commercial or office building they can name after themselves. Generally they pay a premium for that ego trip.

CHAPTER SIXTEEN

PULLING IT ALL TOGETHER

You cannot expect to make a good deal on everything you buy - but it never hurts to ask. When you ask the right person, at the right time, your chances are much better. If you are going to save or make money BUYING RIGHT you must overcome being upset when people say "no".

Some people burn out because all they seem to hear is "no", when they ask for a better price. Often they are asking people who won't or can't negotiate, or they are asking the wrong way. I have heard real estate agents present offers I have made, with the opening line, "I know you would never take this, but here is the buyer's offer". These people rarely get offers accepted, and will never figure out why.

Successful buyers spend more time researching the seller's position and product, than they spend trying to buy. Deal only with those who have a reason to make you a good deal.

Once you are confident that you have found the right seller, be patient and be persistent. Don't give up at the first "no", if your common sense tells you that this seller is going to make someone a good deal.

The most common mistake of beginning buyers, is the failure to make an offer. Once you have invested the time in research, ALWAYS make an offer. Even when you don't buy, you learn something about how people react. The more offers you make, the more confident you will be, and the better (for you) your offers will be.

When you encounter a better negotiator than you are, study his or her techniques, but I don't suggest that you try to outsmart them. In the Old West, many almost-great gunslingers never made the history books because they picked on the wrong person at the wrong time. No matter how good you think you are, there is generally someone much better, who by the way may not look good at all.

By doing your homework, you should establish how much you are willing to pay for whatever it is that you are buying. Don't let a master salesman pull your strings and talk you out of more.

Spend Your Time Doing Something You're Good At - And Like

Many successful people seem to play at their work. They would rather work than take time off. Why? Because they like what they do. Do you enjoy what you do for a living? If you don't, you probably fight going to work, and really need time off to recover.

Think about what kind of work you would do if you could choose your career without limitations. Forget for a minute what jobs pay, or the education requirements involved. If you are having trouble, think about the activities you enjoy now.

When I thought about what I like to do most (in the business world), I decided that I liked to buy things. I love spending money, and feel really good when I get an exceptionally good deal on something. Can you relate to that?

Based on this I found a career in which I could do what I enjoy most, and make a living. Now I buy real estate at good prices, and then hold or sell depending on the type of property and my needs for income. This has allowed me and my family to enjoy a lifestyle unavailable to those who have to work for a living in a structured work environment.

I work when I want to, and reserve the right to make as much or little money as I want on an annual basis. I work until we have plenty, and then spend the rest of the time enjoying life. *Success has been defined as not just getting what you want in life, but enjoying what you get.*

If this way of making a living appeals to you, I would like to teach you more about it. Four times a year I teach a class on the right way to buy and manage real estate investments. The class titled MAKING IT BIG ON LITTLE DEALS is geared specifically to the small investor who wants to buy and manage his own property.

In this class the students actually negotiate for, and in most cases purchase a house, using the techniques taught in class. The experience of negotiating a good deal on a house, reinforced by the teaching in the classroom is a learning experience the students never forget.

For a schedule of classes, mail one of the cards in the back of this book, or if they are missing, write to me at 1938 Ringling Blvd., Sarasota, FL 33577. If you are in a hurry, phone for a schedule (813) 366-9024.

I promise, that in the event you trust me with three days of your life, I will help you and your family enjoy a better lifestyle.

ABOUT THE AUTHOR

John Schaub is a native Floridian, who has made his living buying bargain investments for over sixteen years. In 1975 John began teaching others his techniques for BUYING RIGHT and investing in real estate. He is often a featured speaker at national financial conventions, and teaches four popular three-day seminars each year. In the seminars the students apply the classwork in the real world, by negotiating, and, in many cases, purchasing a property in the city where the class is being taught.

His seminar has started thousands on their way to financial independence. In 1983 John's seminar ideas were put on tape and made available in a home study course.

John's course was the original single family house investment seminar. It has continuously been rated as the best course in the country for investors in houses by past students, other instructors and members of the financial press.

For further information and a schedule of upcoming classes write to:

John Schaub
1938 Ringling Blvd.
Sarasota, FL 33577
or call:
(813) 366-9024

Index

phonics lessons

Letters, Words, and How They Work

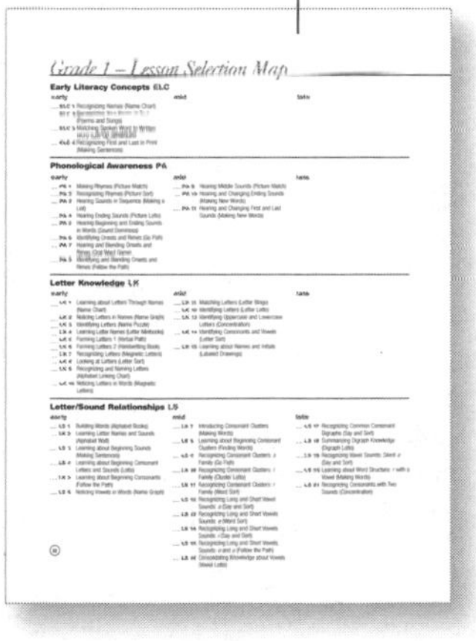

Gay Su Pinnell & Irene C. Fountas — phonics lessons (grade 1)

Gay Su Pinnell & Irene C. Fountas — phonics lessons, grade 1 — TEACHING RESOURCES
- Assessment Guide
- Materials & Routines
- Games
- Templates
- Picture Cards
- Letter/Word Cards
- Bibliographies

Lesson Selection Map
(page 32)

Month-by-Month Planning Guide
(page 36)

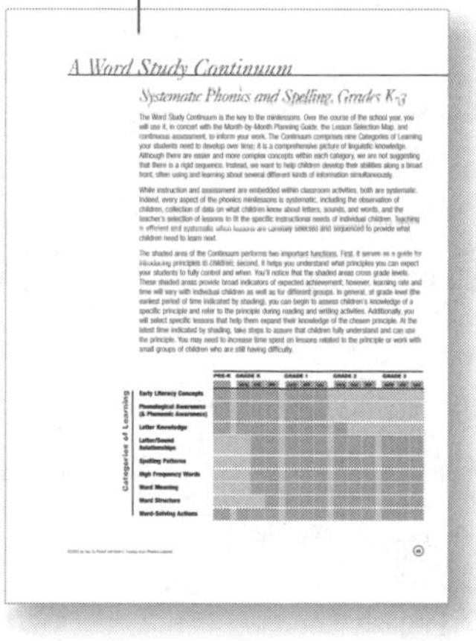

Word Study Continuum
(page 45)

Assessment Guide
(first tab in the *Teaching Resources* binder)

Your Essential Teaching Tools

FirstHand
An imprint of Heinemann
361 Hanover Street
Portsmouth, NH 03801–3912
www.firsthand.heinemann.com

Offices and agents throughout the world

Library of Congress Cataloging-in-Publication Data

Pinnell, Gay Su.
Phonics lessons : letters, words, and how they work / by Gay Su Pinnell and Irene C. Fountas.
p. cm.
Includes bibliographical references.
Contents: [1] Grade K — [2] Grade 1 — [3] Grade 2.
ISBN 0-325-00561-3
1. Reading — Phonetic method. 2. English language — Phonetics. I. Fountas, Irene C. II. Title.

LB1573.3 .P54 2003 2002190837
372.46'5--dc21

Printed in the United States of America on acid-free paper

11 12 13 ML 7 8 9 10

Phonics Lessons

Letters, Words, and How They Work

Contents

ELC Early Literacy Concepts

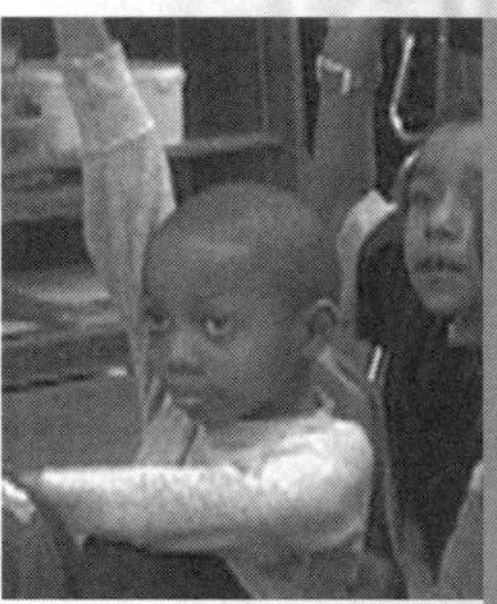

PA Phonological Awareness (including Phonemic Awareness)

LK Letter Knowledge

LS Letter/Sound Relationships

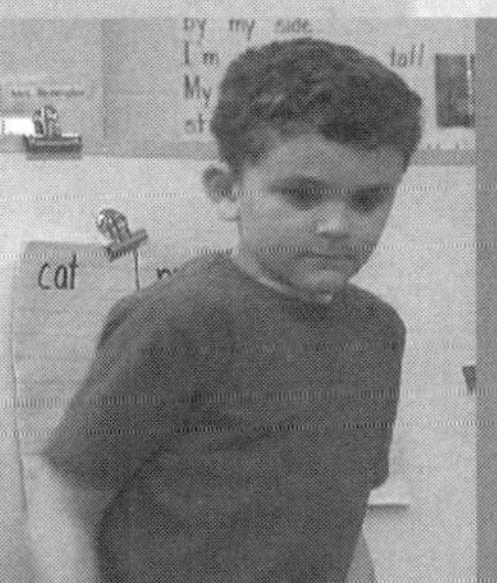

SP Spelling Patterns

HF High Frequency Words

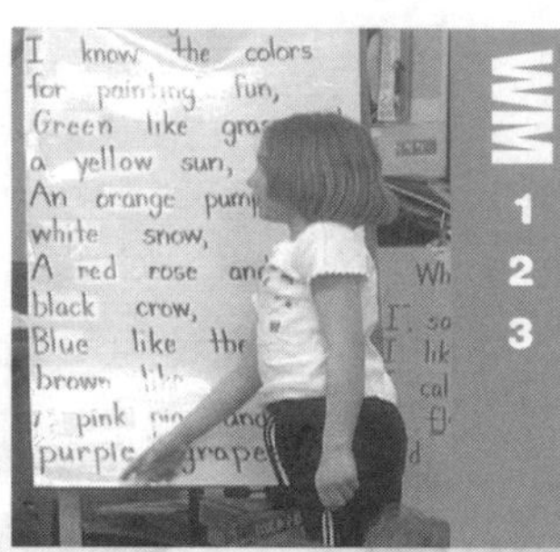

WM Word Meaning

WS Word Structure

WSA Word-Solving Actions

Phonics: Why and How

Welcome to *Phonics Lessons: Letters, Words, and How They Work, Grade One,* a collection of one hundred minilessons. These brief minilessons (so-called to emphasize their targeted focus in both content and delivery) enable you to help children attend to, learn about, and efficiently use information about letters, sounds, and words. While the lessons are most appropriate for first graders, they also work for second graders who have not yet developed control of related principles. The lessons take into account what children already know and help them acquire the knowledge and concepts they need to learn next. You may connect the lessons to word solving in reading and writing across the language and literacy curriculum or use them as prototypes for other phonics minilessons that you design yourself. Most important, each lesson is organized around a language principle—an essential understanding about language and how it works—thus enabling you to plan and teach efficiently and systematically.

Why Teach Phonics?

The true purpose and promise of phonics instruction is to expand and refine children's reading and writing powers. In the complex processes of reading and writing, letters, sounds, and words are the keys to help children grasp and use language as a tool. Most children acquire this tool and learn how to use it at school under the guidance of a skilled teacher who provides a wide range of learning opportunities. While this volume focuses on children's learning about letters, sounds, and words, *phonics is not a complete reading program, nor is it even the most important component of a reading program.* The lessons here enhance but do not take the place of experiences with texts. Phonics instruction as described here takes only about ten or fifteen minutes of explicit teaching each day, with students spending an additional ten to twenty minutes a day applying and sharing what they have learned.

What's the Best Way to Teach Phonics?

Children learn phonics best as part of a wide range of engaging literacy experiences accompanied by rigorous teaching. As teachers work alongside readers and writers, they demonstrate effective behavior, draw attention to important information, and prompt children to use their knowledge. The great majority of time in the classroom is devoted to reading and writing continuous text. Children learn to solve words "on the run" while reading for meaning and writing to communicate. The curriculum is content rich and includes a range of instructional approaches, from demonstration and explicit teaching to support for children's independent work.

In the arguments about what constitutes effective instruction, two issues often arise:

- Should instruction be explicit or *implicit,* that is, embedded in the processes of reading and writing?
- Should we teach children directly or allow them to discover or generalize essential concepts for themselves?

These two areas of tension make designing instructional programs in literacy quite a challenge.

Children learn much more than we teach them; they often astound us with the creativity of their insights. One goal of our teaching is to help children become active examiners and analyzers of print. We want them always to be searching for connections and patterns, to form categories of knowledge, and to have a store of examples to which they can refer.

In the tug-of-war between direct teaching and discovery, going to extremes can be dangerous. Leaving everything to discovery will almost surely mean that many children will not attend to or acquire the understanding they need. Yet assuming that children learn only through direct teaching may lead us to neglect the power of the learning brain, that is, the excitement that makes learning real.

We believe that well-planned and organized direct teaching of language principles is critical but that our lessons must also contain an element of inquiry. In these minilessons, the principle is stated in simple language appropriate for use in the classroom, but the children are also encouraged to categorize words, notice features of letters and words, and search for examples. In any lesson, you decide whether to state the principle first and then generate examples that will make it clear, always leaving room for children to notice more about letters, sounds, and words, or to show some clear examples first and invite children to make connections and generalizations. The combination of discovery and direct teaching makes learning efficient; teaching prompts discovery.

Direct Teaching		**Discovery**	
——————▶		——————▶	
Principle	**Examples**	**Examples**	**Principle**

The Word Study Continuum

The Word Study Continuum is the key to the phonics minilessons. You will use it, in concert with the Month-by-Month Planning Guide, the Lesson Selection Map, and continuous informed assessment, to guide your work over the course of a school year. The Continuum comprises nine Categories of Learning. Each category showcases multiple principles your students will develop over time. It is a comprehensive picture of linguistic knowledge. While there are easier and more complex concepts within each category, we are not suggesting that there is a rigid sequence. Instead, we want to help children develop their abilities along a broad front, often using and learning about several different kinds of information simultaneously. The Continuum gives us as teachers an extensive and organized understanding of the body of knowledge that forms the foundation for expert word solving.

As we set out to construct this Continuum, we examined a wide range of research on language and literacy learning over several decades, and we asked both teachers and researchers for feedback. At the heart of literacy is a language process in which children use what they know about the language they speak and connect it to print (Clay 1991). As teachers, we are simultaneously helping children expand their oral language capabilities while we work with them on the understandings needed for literacy. The semantic, syntactic, and phonological systems of language all contribute to literacy learning. Readers must understand the relationships between language and the graphic symbols that represent sounds and words (Moats 2000). Decades of research have shown that when they are meaningfully engaged in using print, children develop awareness of these relationships early (Read 1971; Treiman 1985). It is especially important that children develop awareness of the phonological system, learn about letters, and develop understanding of sound-to-letter relationships and of words and how they work (see Adams 1990; Armbruster, Lehr & Osborn 2001; Clay 1991, 1998, 2001; Juel 1988; Juel, Griffith & Gough 1986; Moats 2000; National Institute of Child Health and Human Development 2001; Pressley 1998; Snow, Burns & Griffin 1989). Our task as teachers is to organize our own knowledge and design systematic ways to present the information to children and help them use it for reading and writing. We found surprising agreement on the knowledge needed to become an expert word solver. It represents an inventory of knowledge that, together, will form a strong foundation for becoming literate.

Let's look at the nine Categories of Learning in more detail.

Nine Categories of Learning

Early Literacy Concepts

Most early literacy concepts are developed through early reading and writing experiences. These concepts include distinguishing between print and pictures, understanding the concept of letters and words, and learning that print has directionality (in other words, in English we read from top to bottom, left to right). Basic lessons help children use their own names as resources in learning about letters, sounds, and words. Even if your first graders are very knowledgeable, you may still want to use name charts and some name exercises in the first weeks of school to help students feel welcome.

Phonological Awareness (and Phonemic Awareness)

We recommend extensive work in reading aloud and shared reading to develop phonemic awareness. Songs, rhymes, and poetry provide students with the background and examples to participate fully in your minilessons in this area. In first grade, children are learning to control onsets and rimes; identify initial, final, and medial consonants, and identify, separate, and blend sounds to make words.

Letter Knowledge

Children need many different experiences with letters in order to learn "what to look for" when distinguishing one letter from another. They learn that there are many different letters in the set called the "alphabet," and that each letter is just a little different from the others. First graders are learning to recognize, name, and use the letters of the alphabet in many contexts. They can also write letters legibly with efficient motor movements.

Letter/Sound Relationships

Understanding the relationships between letters and letter clusters and sounds is basic to understanding the way words are structured. First graders can connect letters and letter clusters to sounds, recognize several sounds that may be connected to the same letter, and use several letters that may be connected to the same sound.

Spelling Patterns

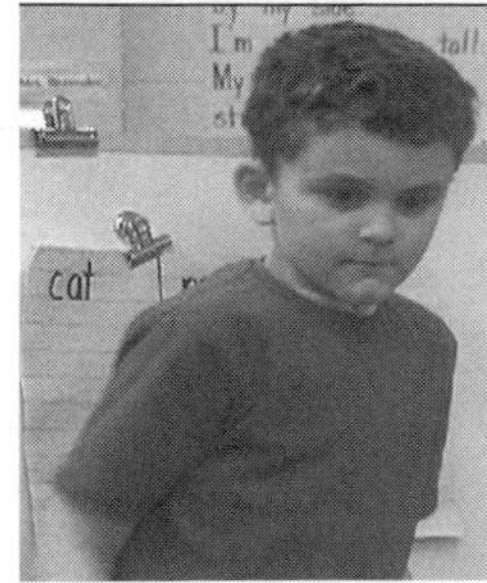

First graders are able to spell some familiar words and word endings (*in* and *s* for example) quickly and automatically. And for those words they write often, they may know conventional spelling. They can also check their spelling for accuracy.

High Frequency Words

High frequency words are also learned in many other components of the language and literacy framework, especially shared/interactive writing and guided reading. Lessons on high frequency words are connected to the word wall. First graders can quickly recognize 100 to 150 high frequency words they know while reading continuous text.

Word Meaning

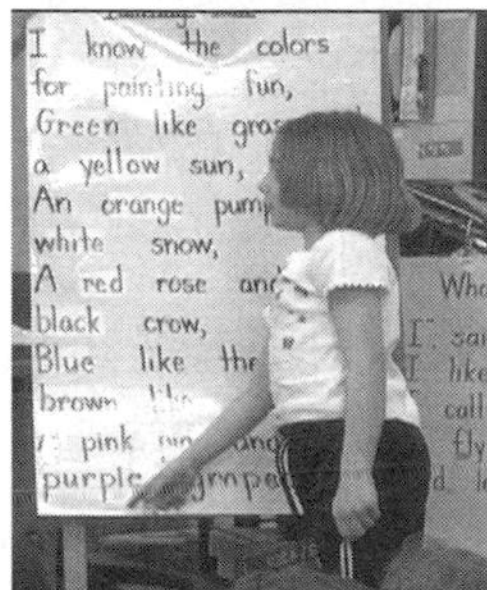

Children need to know the meaning of the words they are learning to read and write. It is important for them constantly to expand their vocabulary as well as develop a more complex understanding of words they already know. This section of the Continuum describes understandings related to the development of vocabulary—labels and concept words, such as colors, numbers, and days of the week.

Word Structure

Beyond simple word patterns, children in first grade begin to understand how words are related to each other and how they can change words by adding parts. First graders may recognize and use syllables, simple contractions, compound words, plurals, affixes, and possessives.

Word-Solving Actions

Word solving refers to the strategic actions that readers take when they use their phonics knowledge while reading or writing continuous text. These strategies are "in-the-head" actions that are invisible, although we can infer them from some overt behavior; for example, children will sometimes make several attempts at words, revealing their hypotheses. Or, children may work left to right on a word (sometimes called "sounding out"); they may also make connections with other words. Good readers tend to use these in-the-head word-solving actions in connection with meaning and knowledge of language so that the reading is smoother, makes sense, and is accurate. They are fitting all systems together. First graders learn to solve words "on the run" while reading with fluency and understanding.

Learning Your Way Around the Minilessons

We have designed these minilessons so that as you use them, you will always consider the particular children you teach. You will decide which lessons to use and whether or not to modify them to meet the needs of your particular students. Certainly, you will note the connections you can make to your own students' discoveries and learning about letters, sounds, and words across the Language and Literacy Framework. Although we present the lessons in a standard format, each one is inherently different because of the conversations you will have with the children you teach. Your students will offer their own examples and make their own connections, and you will enrich their learning as you acknowledge and extend their thinking.

We have included a generous sampling of lessons in each of the nine Categories of Learning. Our goal is to provide clear prototypes from which you can create your own lessons (see *Teaching Resources,* Blank Lesson Template) using the Word Study Continuum that will develop the understanding your students need to experience over time. Within each category, the lessons are numbered for ease of reference, *but we are not implying an unalterable sequence.* Nevertheless, if you are new to teaching or have not taught phonics before, you may want to follow this sequence, because within each learning category we have clustered principles from easier to harder. But easy and hard are relative terms; they refer to students' previous experience, and only you as a teacher know the children's learning background. As you implement these lessons, you will not only learn more about children's development of word-solving strategies but you will also gain invaluable insight into our English linguistic system. Ultimately, feel confident in building your own sequence of explicit lessons that moves your students systematically toward a flexible and powerful range of strategies.

Each lesson title reflects the content of the lesson. The subtitle indicates the type of activity children will do in the Apply section.

GENERATIVE LESSONS provide a recurring structure you can use with similar items within a knowledge set, for example, to teach beginning consonants. As children acquire knowledge, they build systems for similar learning that accelerate the learning.

All materials needed for TEACH, APPLY, and SHARE sections of the lesson are listed. Specific materials (pictures, word cards, activity templates, etc.) are provided as reproducibles in the accompanying binder, *Teaching Resources.* If children are rotating through a center, you need only enough materials for one small group to work with at a time. If they are working individually, as partners, or in simultaneous small groups, you will need additional materials.

Generative Lesson

early
mid
late

3

Learning about Beginning Sounds

Making Sentences

What do your students already know, and what do they need to learn next? Your insights about your own students will guide your choice of lessons and help you plan instruction that targets your students' learning needs.

Consider Your Children

Use this lesson to help the children become more conscious of the sounds at the beginning of words. It will be helpful to children who have grasped the alphabetic principle but who are just beginning to hear sounds in words and to connect them to letters.

Working with English Language Learners

English language learners will enjoy reading sentences that incorporate their names. These sentences will make them feel recognized. As much as possible, pronounce the names accurately in the children's own languages. To be more confident that children understand the sentences, work from their own ideas and concepts. You may want to have children draw pictures or use actions to help them understand the action words in the sentences.

You Need

- Pocket chart.
- Sentence strips that use children's names and names of characters in books to demonstrate that words can sound the same at the beginning and sometimes start with the same letter.

From *Teaching Resources:*

- Four-Box Sheets.

Understand the Principle

It is essential that children learn to hear sounds in words, eventually identifying the sequence of sounds, so that they can connect them to letters. By comparing words, children can more easily notice the sounds in them.

Explain the Principle

"You can hear the sound at the beginning of a word."

"Words can start with the same sound and the same letter."

LS 3
LETTER/SOUND RELATIONSHIPS

CONTINUUM: LETTER/SOUND RELATIONSHIPS — RECOGNIZING SIMILAR BEGINNING CONSONANT SOUNDS AND THE LETTERS THAT REPRESENT THEM

205

Typically, it takes several years for young children to learn English as a second language and to learn to read, write, and think consistently in their new language. As you adjust the lesson for English language learners, your instruction becomes clearer and more explicit in ways that help all your students. (See Guidelines: Working with English Language Learners.)

We help you understand the language principle underlying each minilesson so you can teach with clarity and a well-defined purpose.

Each lesson highlights a key principle from the Word Study Continuum.

Concise, clear language "rings inside students' heads." Avoid jargon and technical labels; use a common language that enables you to reach your readers and writers simply and easily. Sometimes you will show children examples and invite them to think of the principle; other times, you will state the principle, give a few examples, and invite the children to add examples. You determine which approach will be more effective.

Modify the steps for implementing the lesson to fit your own group of children. Much will depend on your children's experience and how well you have taught routines.

We take you through the lesson step by step, suggesting effective language you might use. Sometimes, the lesson is oral only, without written examples. Make frequent use of the pocket chart to hold pictures, letters, and words (or use chart paper on an easel). Occasionally, you may write the principle on the chart before the lesson and generate examples with children during the lesson.

plan

teach

Brown Bear bumps
Peter Piper picked peppers
Nancy naps
Diego drives
Rachel runs
Cindy sleeps
Jimmy jumps
Lisa laughs
Caroline cries
Sarah sleeps

Mary
Mother
Brown
Bear

In each Teach section, we provide a sample chart that you and your children might create. Some depict the chart in process; some depict the final result.

Explain the Principle

"You can hear the sound at the beginning of a word."

"Words can start with the same sound and the same letter."

1. Tell the children they are going to learn more about the first sounds they hear in words.
2. Suggested language: "You have been thinking about the sounds in words. If you say two words, you can tell that they begin with the same sound. *Mary* and *Mother* have the same sound at the beginning."
3. Have the children say the two words and then write them on the whiteboard so they can see the letter at the beginning. Repeat the process with *Brown Bear.*
4. Suggested language: "Can anyone think of another word that has the same sound at the beginning? [Children respond.]" Write their response on a card strip and put it in the pocket chart.
5. Suggested language: "Now we are going to use your names and then think of a word that starts the same and tells something you can do."
6. Demonstrate with your name or the name of someone in the class: *Mary mows, Sam sees.* Try to get an action word for about ten students in the class, writing each on a card strip.

206

We repeat the principle in language suitable for children that you may refer to during your teaching.

Children work independently (individually, with partners, in small groups) to apply and practice what they've learned in the lesson.

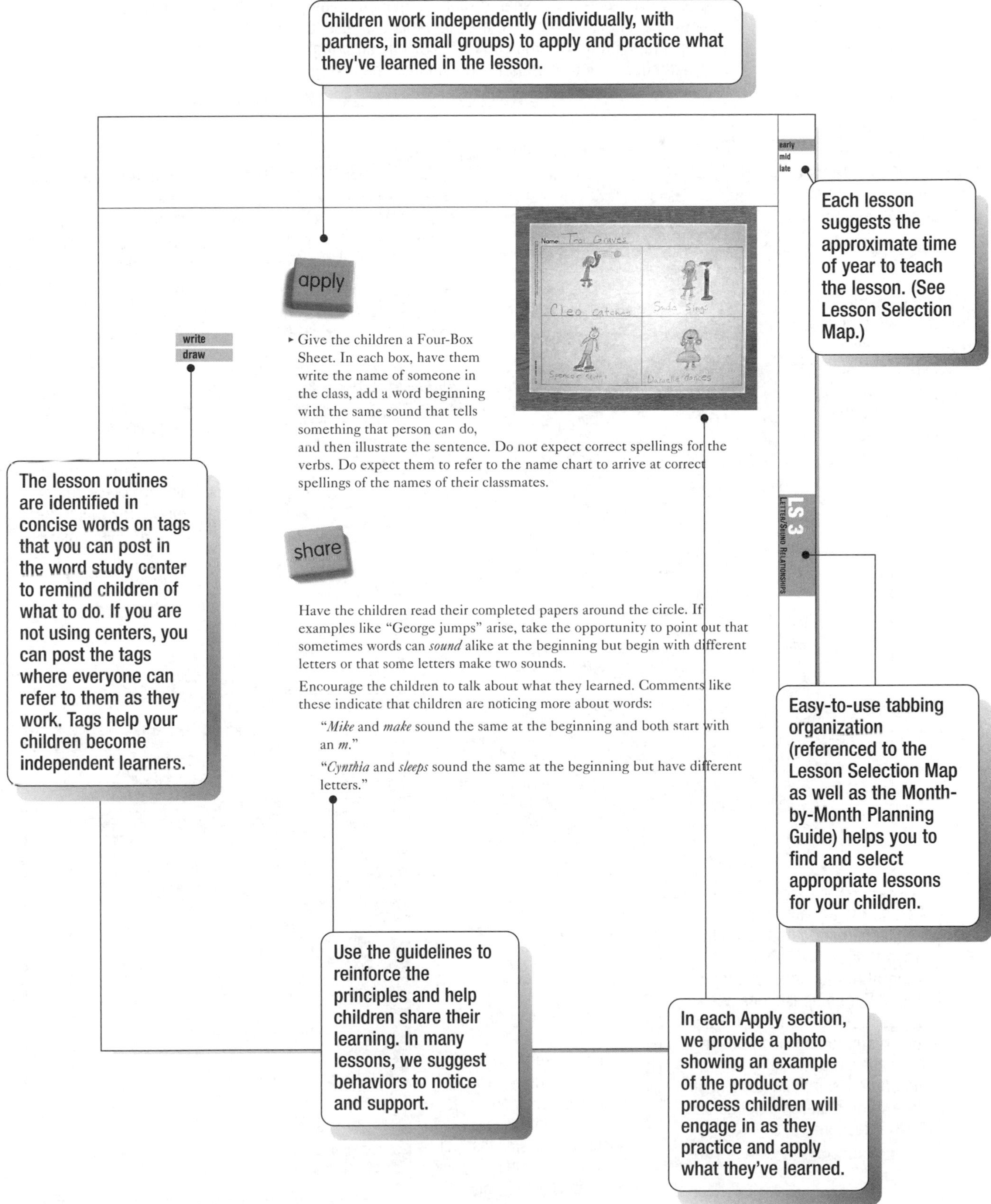

Each lesson suggests the approximate time of year to teach the lesson. (See Lesson Selection Map.)

▸ Give the children a Four-Box Sheet. In each box, have them write the name of someone in the class, add a word beginning with the same sound that tells something that person can do, and then illustrate the sentence. Do not expect correct spellings for the verbs. Do expect them to refer to the name chart to arrive at correct spellings of the names of their classmates.

The lesson routines are identified in concise words on tags that you can post in the word study center to remind children of what to do. If you are not using centers, you can post the tags where everyone can refer to them as they work. Tags help your children become independent learners.

Have the children read their completed papers around the circle. If examples like "George jumps" arise, take the opportunity to point out that sometimes words can *sound* alike at the beginning but begin with different letters or that some letters make two sounds.

Encourage the children to talk about what they learned. Comments like these indicate that children are noticing more about words:

"*Mike* and *make* sound the same at the beginning and both start with an *m*."

"*Cynthia* and *sleeps* sound the same at the beginning but have different letters."

Easy-to-use tabbing organization (referenced to the Lesson Selection Map as well as the Month-by-Month Planning Guide) helps you to find and select appropriate lessons for your children.

Use the guidelines to reinforce the principles and help children share their learning. In many lessons, we suggest behaviors to notice and support.

In each Apply section, we provide a photo showing an example of the product or process children will engage in as they practice and apply what they've learned.

Connect learning across the Language and Literacy Framework through interactive read-aloud, shared reading, guided reading, interactive writing, and independent writing. Your observations across learning contexts will help you think of specific connections you can bring to your children's attention; add your own notes to enhance the lesson.

We provide a variety of useful bibliographies in Teaching Resources.

For each lesson, we provide two suggested read-aloud titles chosen specifically to support the principle and work of each lesson.

Link

Interactive Read-Aloud: Read aloud books that emphasize alliteration. Ask the children to say words that start alike and listen for the sound at the beginning. See *Teaching Resources,* Alliteration Bibliography, for more examples.

- ***Spring Fever*** by Eve Merriam
- ***Busy Buzzing Bumblebees*** by Alvin Schwartz

Shared Reading: Read poems and rhymes that use alliteration such as "Betty Botter" or "The Big Black Bug" or "Swim, Swan, Swim" (see *Sing a Song of Poetry*). Have the children locate words that sound alike at the beginning and have the same first letters.

Guided Reading: Help the children notice the first letters of words and connect them to words they know. For example, a child who is reading the word *make* can "get his mouth ready" by beginning to say the *m* sound because he knows several other words that start like it.

Interactive Writing: When the children are trying to write words, help them connect the beginning sound to other words they know: "Does it sound like *me* at the beginning?" "Could it be *m* as in *me*?"

Independent Writing: In conferences, prompt the children to say the word and think about the beginning sound.

assess

- Notice the children's use of beginning sounds as they attempt to read or write unfamiliar words.
- Select four or five words, say each word, and ask the children to tell another word that starts the same.

Expand the Learning

Repeat the same process with adjectives: *Smart Sam, Jumping John.*

Make a collection of words that start with a particular letter. Children can look for words in the interactive writing they have completed and in poems used for shared reading.

Play a name game by substituting another letter for the first letter of everyone's name: *Mary, Fary; Sam, Wam.*

Connect to Home

Have children take home their sentence drawings; on the reverse side they can write and illustrate sentences about family members *(Dad drives, Jesse jumps).*

If children need more experience, you can repeat the lesson format using these suggestions for variations, different examples, or more challenging activities.

These are not homework assignments; rather, they are ways you can help family members and caregivers make connections between home and school.

Assess the impact of the minilesson and application in ways that are informal and integral to the work children are doing. For some lessons, we suggest using the more formal and systematic procedures in the Assessment Guide (in *Teaching Resources*) to help you determine children's needs for further lessons.

Available separately: *Sing a Song of Poetry* provides reproducibles of hundreds of your favorite rhymes, songs, and poems that will help children use and enjoy oral and written language.

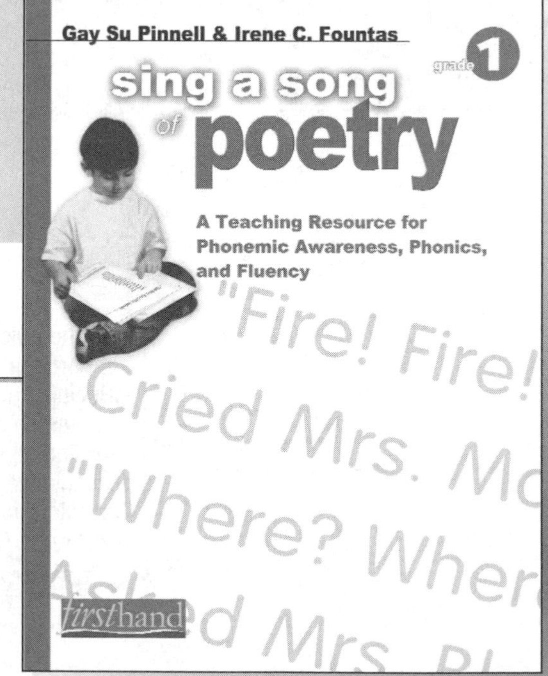

Gay Su Pinnell & Irene C. Fountas
grade 1
sing a song of poetry
A Teaching Resource for Phonemic Awareness, Phonics, and Fluency
firsthand

Teaching Resources is your comprehensive professional resource for everything from diagnostic assessment to an Alphabet Linking Chart.

The Assessment Guide includes more formal, performance-based Assessment Tasks across the nine Categories of Learning.

We've provided a variety of bibliographies listing hundreds of books categorized for ease of use. They include Language Play, Rhymes, Poetry, Songs, and Read-Alouds.

You will find descriptions of and directions for the materials and daily routines most important for your classroom. These are comprehensive lists of the hands-on materials and activities that undergird effective teaching.

Additionally, look for picture, word, and alphabet cards, templates, and reproducibles to make an array of your own cards and ready-to-use booklets. We include game materials and directions for Lotto, Concentration, and Follow the Path. We also provide numerous reproducibles for student activities.

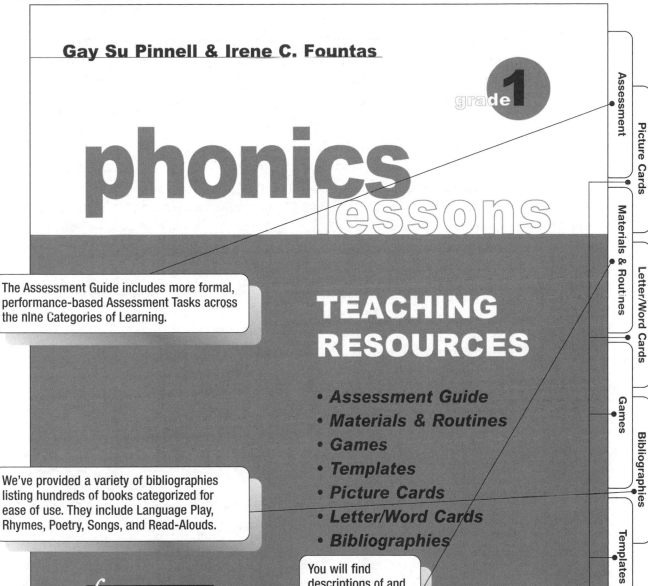

Get to Know Your First Grader

Essential Literacy Concepts Every First Grader Should Know

The most effective teaching is responsive teaching—sensitive instruction that addresses the needs of children. Every lesson in *Phonics Minilessons* begins with a consideration of your children. What do they know, and what do they need to know? Your guiding question as you use the phonics minilessons is: "What are the essential literacy concepts my students need to understand to become accomplished readers and writers?"

Entering first graders who have made good progress in a literacy-rich kindergarten will be able to recognize and enjoy rhymes when they hear them read aloud. They will hear and realize that words have syllables and they also attend to the first parts of words (letters or letter clusters that form the "onset") and ending parts ("rimes," with vowels). They will know the names of the letters of the alphabet and most of the sounds related to consonants and easy-to-hear vowels. They will have become aware of the sounds in words and be able to identify single sounds and to make connections among words by the way they sound.

They will also have experience writing words and can demonstrate the movements necessary to form letters. A number of the easy high frequency words they write will have conventional spellings; they will also attempt the spelling of other words by using their letter/sound knowledge and known words as analogies for writing others.

Beginning first graders who have heard stories read aloud will recognize syntactic (grammatical) structures that are particular to written language; for example, "Oh," said Mary. "Please come in." Moreover, many understand basic principles about how print works. They can read simple texts with one or two lines of print. They use meaning and language, as all readers do, and also check on their reading using what they know about high frequency words they recognize and the letter/sound knowledge they have.

Finally, if they come from a rich kindergarten experience, children will have high expectations of print. They will see writing as something they can and want to do; they will see stories as a source of enjoyment, whether hearing them read or reading simple ones for themselves. As they engage in literacy experiences, they continually learn more. They add to the richness of their experience, the concepts they know, and the ways they are able to use print.

Not every learner will have the rich background described above. In spite of good teaching and a richly supplied classroom, some children may not have zeroed in on key aspects of literacy or found it confusing because of limited background experiences. Or their kindergarten year may have been interrupted. There are dozens of reasons why children may be more or less advanced in their literacy learning. We cannot force all children into the same mold. We need to meet them where they are in their literacy learning and build on their strengths.

In the lessons in this book, we provide very basic information to children but encourage them to use their knowledge across all activities in the Language and Literacy Framework. Some will go well beyond the specifics of any given lesson by expanding their discoveries in writing, reading, and word study. At the same time, it is helpful to have in mind some basic concepts that are important for first graders to learn during a year of instruction. There will always be individual variation, but these goals help us construct an efficient curriculum that will serve as a foundation for good teaching.

We'll explore six different important areas of word learning (outlined in the figure on the following page), each of which is essential for becoming a skilled user of written language. More extensive discussions of first-grade learners may be found in McCarrier, Pinnell & Fountas (2000), Pinnell & Fountas (1998, Chapter 9), and Fountas & Pinnell (1996, Chapter 2). The expectations inherent in these descriptions are consistent with recommended literacy standards for kindergarten through third grade (New Standards Primary Literacy Committee, National Center on Education and the Economy and the University of Pittsburgh, 1999).

Phonemic Awareness

Our oral language is communicated through sounds that we put together to form the words, phrases, and sentences that have special meaning for other speakers. Children learn oral language easily and interactively within their homes and communities, but a closer look is needed as they draw on their oral language knowledge in becoming literate.

Words Children need to be able to hear the individual words in the sentences that they speak. We are reminded of the five-year old who said, "Why can't I hear the spaces when I talk?" That young child was just becoming aware of written language and its characteristics. In fact, there are no spaces in oral language; there may be pauses, but they certainly do not come after each word or our speech would sound robotic. Exposure to written language will help them sort out and become more aware of individual words.

Syllables One of the first steps in noticing the sounds in words is to be able to hear the parts, or *syllables.* Emergent readers often think a two-syllable word like *into* is really two words and try to point to two letter clusters as they read very simple early stories. If you draw it to their attention, children can hear the "breaks" in the word and clap them.

Rhymes Children become aware of the sounds in words through hearing and enjoying rhymes. They learn to recognize pairs of rhyming words and to produce them. As they say words slowly—for example, as they attempt to write words—they become aware of easy-to-hear consonants in both initial and final positions in words.

Names In becoming aware of sounds, children make powerful connections with their own names. They learn to segment and combine words by the beginning consonant, or *onset,* and what follows the vowel, or *rime.* Children are literally learning to "take words apart" and "put words together" orally.

Individual Sounds—Phonemes To take on written language, children must realize that words are made up of separate sounds, or *phonemes.* Called *phonemic awareness,* this critical knowledge opens the door to the alphabetic principle—that is, that there is a relationship between letters and sounds; however, it refers only to what you hear, not to what you see.

Literacy Concepts Every First Grader Should Know

Phonemic Awareness—first graders are learning to:

- Recognize rhyming words and blend onsets and rimes to form words orally.
- Identify initial, final, and medial consonant sounds in words; separate the sounds in words and blend them to make a word.

Letters and Sounds—first graders are learning to:

- Recognize, name, and use the letters of the alphabet in many contexts.
- Connect letters and letter clusters to sounds, recognize several sounds that may be connected to the same letter, and recognized several letters that may be connected to the same sound.
- Write all letters legibly with efficient motor movements.

Reading Words—first graders are learning to:

- Know the regular ways letters and sounds correspond and use them to recognize or solve regularly spelled one- and two-syllable words.
- Solve words by recognizing letter clusters, onsets and rimes, and other patterns.
- Know the meaning of a wide range of words that they meet in reading texts.
- Recognize about 150 high frequency words quickly and automatically.

Writing Words—first graders are learning to:

- Use their knowledge of letters and sounds to write words legibly.
- Spell some familiar words and word endings (*in* and *s,* for example) quickly and automatically.
- Know conventional spelling for words that they write often.

Processing Strategies in Reading—first graders are learning to:

- Quickly recognize the 150 high frequency words they know while reading continuous text.
- Use knowledge of letters, letter clusters, word patterns, and known words to solve words while reading continuous text.
- Use knowledge of letters, sounds, and words to monitor and correct their reading.
- Check letter/sound and word knowledge against meaning and a sense of language structure so that their reading makes sense, sounds right, and looks right.
- Notice, make sense of, and learn the meaning of new words as they encounter them in reading.
- Notice and use simple punctuation as a guide to phrasing and reading for meaning.

Processing Strategies in Writing—first graders are learning to:

- Produce known words quickly while writing continuous text.
- Produce writing that contains a large proportion of conventionally spelled high frequency words.
- Check their writing for accurate spelling and punctuation.

Phonemic awareness is an important part of the curriculum in kindergarten, in which children learn to enjoy language and play with it. By the end of first grade, we would expect that children would have consolidated their knowledge of the sounds of language. They will know that words are made up of sequences of individual sounds and be able to identify beginning, medial, and ending sounds. They have learned to connect words by the way they sound so that they can form categories of words. For example, Peter can provide this kind of information about words that he hears:

- Tree starts like to and ends like be.
- Tree has a /t/[1] sound at the beginning; next is the same sound as in *run*, and it ends with an /e/ sound.
- Tree rhymes with *see, bee, key.*

Some entering first graders may have just discovered the sounds in words and will need many opportunities and much teaching assistance to become sensitive to phonology, or the sound system of the language. By the end of grade 1, phonemic awareness should be firmly established, as well as the ability to hear and manipulate sounds in flexible and playful ways.

Phoneme Chart

We examine forty-four phonemes. The actual sounds in the language can vary as dialect, articulation, and other factors in speech vary. The following are common sounds for the letters listed.

Consonant Sounds

b /b/ box	**n /n/ nest**	**ch /ch/ chair**
d /d/ dog	**p /p/ pail**	**sh /sh/ ship**
f /f/ fan	**r /r/ rose**	**wh /hw/ what**
g /g/ gate	**s /s/ sun**	**th /th/ think**
h /h/ house	**t /t/ top**	**th /TH/ the**
j /j/ jug	**v /v/ vase**	**ng /ng/ sing**
k /k/ kite	**w /w/ was**	**zh /zh/ measure**
l /l/ leaf	**y /y/ yell**	
m /m/ mop	**z /z/ zoo**	

Vowel Sounds

/ă/ hat	**/ā/ gate**	**/o͞o/ moon**	**/û/ bird**
/ĕ/ bed	**/ē/ feet**	**/o͝o/ book**	**/ə/ *about***
/ĭ/ fish	**/ī/ bike**	**/ou/ house**	**/ä/ car**
/ŏ/ mop	**/ō/ boat**	**/oi/ boy**	**/â/ chair**
/ŭ/ nut	**/ū/ mule**	**/ô/ tall**	

Letters and Sounds

At the same time they are learning about sounds in words, children are developing familiarity with the orthographic system. Through many experiences with the letters of the alphabet, they learn the distinctive features that make one letter different from every other letter, and they learn the names of letters. They learn the movements necessary to write letters. When children can identify a letter by its features, they can then attach a sound to it. First-grade children are learning to recognize, name, and use the letters of the alphabet in many different contexts as well as to attach sounds to letters.

The relationship between letters and sounds in English is a complex one. While many words have regular spellings (for example, *can* and *nap* have three letters and three sounds), most spellings are more complex. Words may have four letters and three sounds *(make)* or five letters and three sounds *(night)*. Children learn how to map the sounds of the language onto the print system. First graders need to learn to connect letter clusters and patterns of letters to sounds in words. Also, as they grow in their understanding, they will realize that many letters can be connected to more than one sound, and some sounds are connected to more than one letter or letter cluster.

[1] A letter enclosed by slash marks indicates the *sound* rather than the name of the letter.

We also expect first graders to develop efficient, legible handwriting so that they can write fluently and others can read their products. Not all first graders will enter your class knowing the alphabet and the relationship between letters and sounds. Indeed, it is not at all unusual for some children not to understand the alphabetic principle (that there is a relationship between letters and sounds). In that case, you will need to give extra attention to the alphabet, connecting letters and sounds in children's names and exploring them in many different ways.[2] With a strong base of letter and sound knowledge, children can gradually expand their awareness of the complexities of English words.

Reading Words

Through a wide range of reading and writing activities, children soon acquire a small core of words or a reading vocabulary that they know by "sight"—that is, they do not need to use letters and sounds to read these words but recognize them as whole entities quickly and automatically. Generally, children leave kindergarten with the knowledge of a few words and can recognize and write their names. As they come into first grade, their names are still an important resource in literacy learning. They provide powerful examples of letter/sound relationships, letter clusters, and word parts.

First graders are learning to use letter/sound correspondence to figure out one- and two-syllable words that are spelled regularly. They are also learning a wider range of letter clusters and patterns in words and can recognize and use word parts, such as onsets and rimes. They are accumulating a larger number of high frequency words that they recognize quickly and automatically, and this resource will grow to about 100 to 150 words by the end of first grade.

Writing Words

First graders are building their store of known words. They write many high frequency words quickly, with efficient handwriting, and they use their knowledge of letter/sound relationships and word parts to make good attempts at spelling new and complex words they can write. By the end of first grade, they made many connections between words and are ready for the more systematic and formal study of words that will come in second grade.

Processing Strategies in Reading

As kindergartners, most children have begun to read very simple texts of one or two lines. This active processing of text enables children to simultaneously put into action all of the information they have been gathering about letters, sounds, and words. They begin, as Clay (2001) has said, to "assemble working systems" for constructing meaning from print. As first graders, they expand these working systems to read longer stretches of texts that have more complex meaning.

The typical pattern of growth in first grade is remarkable. Children begin the year either not reading or reading, with pointing, a few lines of print with very easy words. They read aloud and

[2] If your entire class has very low phonemic awareness and knowledge of letters and sounds, you may want to consult our *Phonics Minilessons: Letters. Words, and How They Work, Kindergarten* (Heinemann, 2002).

use pictures in combination with print. We know that they monitor and correct their reading because this behavior is overt. By the end of grade 1, they can read with fluency texts that have many multisyllable words and many lines of print (see Fountas & Pinnell 1996; Pinnell & Fountas, 1999). They are, for the most part, reading silently and do not need to depend on the pictures to learn about or solve the words in texts, although illustrations do extend meaning and provide enjoyment. They can solve words by seeing how they look, by using letters and sounds, and by making connections between words. They check letter/sound and word knowledge against their sense of meaning and of how language should sound. They read with phrasing, using simple punctuation as a guide. As they read, they notice, make sense of, and learn the meaning of new words, expanding their vocabulary. They are solving words "on the run" while reading for meaning.

Processing Strategies in Writing

As writers, first graders are learning to produce longer pieces of text that contain a large proportion of conventionally spelled words. They quickly recognize known words and write them fluently. Their writing is legible because they have internalized efficient habits of handwriting, and they can check their writing for accurate spelling. They can use simple punctuation such as periods, question marks, and exclamation marks; they often incorporate layout features (such as words in all capitals) to make their writing more interesting. These young writers know and use a range of word-solving strategies while keeping in mind what they want to write.

What to Do If Children Are Learning to Speak English

You are likely to have many children in your class who can speak not only one language but are learning a second or even a third language. If English is an additional language, then it will be important that you understand and value the child's expansion of both home and school language. Usually, it takes several years for young children to learn English as a second language and to become able to read, write, and think consistently in their new language.

You will want to adjust your teaching to make sure that English language learners have access to your teaching about letters, sounds, and words. Often, these adjustments are minor and easy to implement, but they are necessary to promote essential understandings on the part of these learners. In addition, many of these adjustments will help all of the children in your classroom because they help to make instruction more explicit and clear.

Following, we have placed some general suggestions for each of four areas—oral language, reading, writing, and phonics instruction. It is obvious that these four areas overlap and are interconnected. Work in one area will tend to support learning in all other areas as well.

Guidelines: Working with English Language Learners

Oral Language

1. Show children what you mean when you give directions. You may need to act out certain sequences of action and have children do it while you coach them. Have them repeat directions to each other or say them aloud as they engage in the activity. Support them during their first attempts rather than expecting independence immediately.
2. Give English language learners more "wait and think" time. You could say, "Let's think about that for a minute" before calling for an answer. Demonstrate to students how you think about what you are going to say.
3. Paraphrase and summarize for students. Repeat the directions or instructions several different ways, watching for feedback that they understand you. Paraphrase until you can see that they understand.
4. Use pictures and objects that children understand and that connect to their homes and neighborhoods. At the same time, avoid examples that may be completely strange to children and to which they have difficulty bringing meaning.
5. Use short simple sentences in shared reading, interactive writing, and oral conversations. Avoid complex, embedded sentences that children will find hard to follow if they are just learning English. When a complex sentence is used (for example, in read-aloud or shared reading), watch for evidence of confusion on the part of students and paraphrase with simpler sentences when necessary.
6. Bring children's familiar world into the classroom through family photos, holiday souvenirs, and objects from home. Expand children's world by bringing in other objects that will give them new experiences.
7. Demonstrate using language structures while talking about familiar topics. Involve children in games that require repeating these simple language structures, for example: "My name is _____." "_____ has two brothers." "I like to eat _____." "Josiah likes to (verb)."
8. Make instruction highly interactive, with a great deal of oral language surrounding everything children are learning.
9. Expand the activities using children's names. Be sure that you are pronouncing all children's names correctly and clearly as you draw their attention to the particular word that is a child's name. Help children learn the names of other children in the class by using them in sentences and placing them on charts.
10. Engage English language learners in repeating and enjoying songs, rhymes, and repetitive chants. Incorporate body movements to enhance children's enjoyment of songs, rhymes, and chants and help them remember and understand the language better.

Reading

1. Provide an extensive collection of simple alphabet books so that children can encounter the same letters, in the same sequence, with picture examples in different texts.
2. Read aloud often to students; in general, it is wise to increase the amount of time that you read aloud and discuss books with students. Be sure that the material you are reading to students is comprehensible, that is, within their power to understand with your support.
3. Stick to simple and understandable texts when you read aloud to students. Watch for signs of enjoyment and reread favorites. Rereading books to children will help them acquire and make use of language that goes beyond their current understandings.
4. Be sure that children's own cultures are reflected in the material that you read aloud to them and that they read for themselves. They should see illustrations with people like themselves in books. They should see their own culture reflected in food, celebrations, dress, holidays, everyday events, and so on.
5. Understand that shared reading involves children in a great deal of repetition of language, often language that is different from or more complex than they can currently use in speech. This experience gives children a chance to practice language, learn the meaning of the words, and use the sentence structure of English.
6. Use a shared reading text over and over, inserting different names or different words to vary it. Rhythmic and repetitive texts are beneficial to English language learners. This repetition will give children maximum experience with the syntax of English and will help them to develop an implicit understanding of noun-verb agreement, plurals, and other concepts. Once a text is well known in shared reading, it can serve as a resource to children. Revisit shared reading texts for examples of language structure and for specific words and their meaning.
7. As soon as English language learners can join in easily in shared reading, know some high frequency words, and independently read shared reading texts with high accuracy, consider including them in guided reading groups. Guided reading is a very valuable context for working with English language learners because you can scaffold their reading and their language through an introduction that clears up confusion and you can observe them closely to gain information as to the accuracy and ease of their reading. Through observation and discussion, you can find what is confusing to them and respond to their questions.
8. Be sure to use oral language, pictures, concrete objects, and demonstration when you introduce stories to help children untangle any tricky vocabulary or concepts they are reading in texts for themselves in guided and independent reading. They may encounter words that they can "read" but do not understand.
9. Help them in guided reading relate new words to words they already know. During and after reading, check with children to be sure they understand vocabulary and concepts; build into lessons a time when they can bring up any words they did not know.
10. Include word work on a regular basis in the guided reading lessons for English language learners. Make strong connections to what they have been learning in phonics and word study.

Writing

1. Value and encourage children's drawing as it represents thinking and connects their ideas to early writing.
2. Have children repeat several times the sentence they are going to write so that they will be able to remember it. If the sentence is difficult for children to remember, that may be a sign that it is too complex for their present level of language knowledge; consider simplifying the structure or rephrasing the sentence so that it is easier for students.
3. Focus on familiar topics and everyday experiences in interactive writing so that children can generate meaningful sentences and longer texts. Reread the piece of interactive writing many times, encouraging fluency as children gain control over the language.
4. Guide children to produce some repetitive texts that use the same sentence structure and phrases over and over again, so that children can internalize them.
5. Know that once a text has been successfully produced in interactive writing and children can easily read it, this text is a resource for talking about language—locating specific words, noticing beginning and ending sounds, noticing rhymes, and so on.
6. Encourage English language learners to write for themselves. Demonstrate how to think of something to write and repeat it so that you remember it. Demonstrate how to say words slowly, providing more individual help and demonstration if needed.
7. Surround children's independent writing with a great deal of oral language. Talk with them and help them put their ideas into words before they write. Encourage them to tell their stories and share their writing with others and extend their meanings through talk.
8. Provide a great many models of writing for English language learners—interactive writing, shared reading, charts about people in the room or experiences. Encourage them to reread and revisit these models to help them in their writing. In the beginning, they may use phrases or sentences from charts around the room, varying their own sentences slightly. Gradually, they will go beyond these resources, but models will be a helpful support for a time.
9. Learn something about the sound system of the children's first language. That knowledge will give you valuable insights into the way they "invent" or "approximate" their first spellings. For example, notice whether they are using letter/sound associations from the first language or whether they are actually thinking of a word in the first language and attempting to spell it.
10. Accept spellings that reflect the child's own pronunciation of words, even if it varies from standard pronunciation. Notice the strengths in the child's attempts to relate letters and sounds. Show that you value attempts rather than correcting everything the child writes.

Phonics and Word Study

1. Use many hands-on activities so that children have the chance to manipulate magnetic letters and tiles, move pictures around, and work with word and name cards.
2. Be sure that the print for all charts (ABC charts, name charts, shared writing, picture and word charts, etc.) is clear and consistent so that children who are working in another language do not have to deal with varying forms of letters.
3. Make sure your English language learners are not sitting in an area that is peripheral to the instruction (for example, in the back or to the side). It is especially important for these learners to be able to clearly see and hear all instruction.
4. Provide a "rehearsal" by working with your English language learners in a small group before you provide the minilesson to the entire group. Sometimes they may find it more difficult than other children to come up with words as examples; however, only a few minutes (for example, thinking of *s* words) will help these learners come up with responses in whole-group settings. It will not hurt them to think about the concepts twice because that will provide greater support.
5. Use real objects to represent pictures and build concepts in children's minds. For example, bring in a real lemon that children can touch and smell rather than just a picture of a lemon. When it is not possible to use real objects to build concepts, use clear pictures that will have meaning for children. Picture support should be included whenever possible.
6. Be sure to enunciate clearly yourself and accept children's approximations. If they are feeling their own mouths say the sounds (or approximate), they will be able to make the connections. Sounds and letters are abstract concepts and the relationships are arbitrary. It will be especially complex for children whose sound systems do not exactly match that of English. They may have trouble saying the sounds that are related to letters and letter clusters.
7. Accept alternative pronunciations of words with the hard-to-say sounds and present the written form to help learners distinguish between them. Minimal pairs (sounds that are like each other, have similar tongue positions, and are easily confused, such as *s* and *sh, r* and *l, sh* and *ch, f* and *v*) are often quite difficult for English language learners to differentiate. English language learners often have difficulty with inflected endings *(s, ed).*
8. Speak clearly and slowly when working with children on distinguishing phonemes and hearing sounds in words, but do not distort the word so much that it is unrecognizable. Distortion may confuse English language learners in that it may sound like another word that they do not know.
9. Use the pocket chart often so that children have the experience of working with pictures and words in a hands-on way. They can match pictures with words so that the meaning of words becomes clearer.
10. Work with a small group of English language learners to help them in the application activity and make your instruction more explicit. Notice concepts that they find particularly difficult and make note to revisit them during word work.

Inside the Classroom: Organizing to Teach

As the schedules demonstrate, ideally, your explicit phonics lessons are embedded in a rich language and literacy framework that offers an organized combination of experiences, each of which contributes uniquely to children's literacy development. We describe a Language and Literacy Framework for First Grade that features three blocks for learning: Language and Word Study, Reading Workshop, and Writing Workshop

Language and Literacy Framework		
Language and Word Study	**Whole Group**	**Community Meeting/Calendar** **Interactive Read-Aloud** **Language and Word Play** **Modeled/Shared Reading** **Modeled/Shared/Interactive Writing** **Phonics/Word Study Minilesson** ► **Active Exploration/Application** ► **Sharing and Evaluation** ► **Connection to Reading and Writing**
Reading Workshop	**Small Group and Individual Work**	**Guided Reading** **Independent Work in Centers** **Sharing and Evaluation**
Writing Workshop	**Whole Group, Small Group, and Individual Work**	**Minilesson** **Writing and Individual Conferences** **Guided Writing** **Sharing and Evaluation**

Language and Word Study

Language and Word Study includes a variety of activities designed to immerse children in language and help them learn about it. We recommend about thirty to forty-five minutes for the Language and Word Study block.

Interactive Read-Aloud As they hear written language read aloud, children learn about the structure, or syntax, of written language, which is different in many ways from oral language. Being read to aloud is very important for first graders, because the patterns and specialized vocabulary are the foundation not only for learning to read for themselves but for expanding their comprehending strategies as they move into more complex texts. The texts you select should contain language that delights children through rhyme and sound.

Modeled/Shared Reading Modeled reading or reading in unison from an enlarged text helps children experience texts that are more complex than they can read on their own. In addition, they see and participate in a powerful demonstration of reading. Behaving as readers with the support of the group, they develop early reading behaviors, start to recognize high frequency words, and learn to use letters and sounds as critical and important information (see Hundley & Powell 1999).

As children become more competent in reading for themselves, they will still enjoy reading poems, chants, and songs together. Shared reading is an excellent context for demonstrating how children can locate both familiar words and new words by using letter/sound knowledge. Shared reading also offers opportunities to help children attend to and use punctuation as well as to demonstrate word solving.

Modeled, Shared, and Interactive Writing In shared writing, a group of children compose a common text. Guided by the teacher, they are able to develop a meaningful letter, description, story, label, sign, or note. The teacher and children compose the text together; then, with children providing input, the teacher writes the text, which is reread many times. Interactive writing involves "sharing the pen"; children make contributions by coming up to the easel and writing some of the words and letters (for a detailed description, see McCarrier, Pinnell & Fountas 2000).

Modeled, shared, and interactive writing are transitional tools that expose the process of writing in a very explicit way. Children are helped to remember the next word in their message, say it slowly, and think of the letters and sounds. They also use high frequency words they know and make connections between words that start or end alike and have similar parts. Teachers make special use of the name chart as a tool in this process.

Shared/interactive writing is an ideal way to bring content-area study into the language arts. Children can compose and write pieces connected to science, mathematics, or social studies. They can also compose and write simple stories. Instruction in shared/interactive writing shifts in relation to the experience of the children:

1. At first, you will write the words children do not know but call children up to the chart to contribute a letter or word they do know (or "nearly know").
2. Over time, children will contribute more letters and words, although you will still limit the number of times you call individuals up to the chart (time is limited and you want to focus children's attention on only a few aspects of writing).
3. The focus of interactive writing lessons changes gradually to emphasize more and more sophisticated aspects of word structure, for example, moving from beginning and ending consonants to letter clusters to word patterns.
4. As children develop a large core of high frequency words, you write more of the easy words yourself, focusing on words that have more instructional value.
5. Finally, you will rely mostly on modeled or shared writing, using interactive writing only when there is something very interesting for children to learn about words.

By the end of first grade, you will still be using shared writing to help children get language down on paper for many purposes. You can also use interactive writing with small groups of children who need more support in developing their writing strategies—both in composing and in constructing messages.

Phonics and Word Study During Language and Word Study, you will provide a brief, lively minilesson on some principle related to the use of letters, sounds, or words. The minilesson is followed by an application activity in which the children explore the principle. The minilessons in this volume are appropriate for first graders. Select many of the easier concepts from the Continuum for children who are less experienced, and move on to the more challenging concepts if your group, in general, is more advanced.

Reading Workshop

The reading block includes guided reading and independent work. We recommend about sixty to seventy-five minutes for reading workshop.

Guided Reading Guided reading is specific small-group instruction on effective reading strategies (see Fountas & Pinnell 1996, 1998). Groups are homogeneous based on students' development of a reading process at a particular point in time. Using a gradient of texts organized according to level of difficulty, you select a book that is within the learners' control but offers a small amount of challenge. You introduce the book and then each member of the group reads the text softly to himself or herself.

While children are reading, you observe their behavior (including but not limited to their application of phonics principles) and interact with them briefly. These interactions support and reinforce the principles you are teaching in word study. Following the reading, you discuss the meaning of the story and teach processing strategies. Often, at the end of the lesson, you will do some quick work with words using magnetic letters, the chalkboard, or a white dry-erase board. Here again is an opportunity to reinforce principles that have been explored in word study.

Independent Work While you are working with a small group of children in guided reading, the other children are engaged in a variety of independent activities. Many teachers like to use "centers," in which children work with materials in designated areas of the room: sorting word cards at the pocket chart, using manipulatives in the word study center, reading books in the classroom library, listening to books read aloud on tape in the listening center, and so on. (Children have been taught specific routines for working in the centers, one center or activity at a time.) Other teachers prefer to work with the whole class on most activities or for children to work at their desks or tables. Either option is effective, as long as children are engaged in active, interesting, effective reading, writing, and word study. The minilessons in this book can be used with either option.

Sharing and Evaluation At the end of the reading period, you may want to reconvene the whole group so that children can share some of their discoveries using the word study principle you've taught.

Suggestions for Managing and Using Centers for Word Study

- Clearly organize supplies so that only one kind of material is in a single container.
- Label supplies with both words and pictures.
- Using words and pictures, label the place on the shelf where the container is stored.
- Have all supplies that children will need for a given activity organized and available.
- Teach children routines for getting and returning materials.
- Establish and explicitly teach the routines that will be needed for a learning activity.
- Post simple directions in the center using both words and pictures.
- Limit the number of routines children are expected to follow—a few essential activities can be varied to explore different principles (for example, sorting).
- Stick to a consistent schedule.
- Introduce only one new application activity each day—typically, children will engage in one activity related to a principle over a period of three to five days.
- Place needed resources (charts, word wall) on the wall near the center so that they will be available.
- "Walk through" the activity so that you can accurately estimate the time it will take.
- Allocate an appropriate amount of time for selected activities and teach children the routines so that they can perform them at a good rate.
- Teach children to speak softly while working independently and model this behavior by speaking softly yourself.
- Have regular meetings with children to self-evaluate the productivity of work in the word study center.

Examples of Productive Literacy Activities

- Reading independently from "browsing boxes" filled with little books that are very easy for children because they have been read in shared or guided reading.
- Enjoying books on tape.
- Exploring, letters, sounds, and words in connection with a minilesson.
- Exploring writing and drawing.
- Exploring books and enjoying illustrations in the classroom library.
- Building familiar poems in a pocket chart.

Writing Workshop

The writing workshop involves a minilesson on some aspect of writing, time for children to work on their own writing with teacher support, and sharing. We recommend about sixty minutes for writing workshop.

Writing Minilesson A writing minilesson is designed to demonstrate principles related to the conventions and craft of writing. The first minilessons may be procedural— showing children how to use paper and other writing materials, for example. With inexperienced first graders, early minilessons will focus on simple topics such as where to start writing on a page, how to say words slowly, how to use spaces, how to make illustrations match your story, how to tell stories, and how to think about something to write. With children who have had a great deal of experience in reading and writing, you can move on to more sophisticated topics.

Writing and Conferring Children write independently while you interact with individuals and sometimes with small groups (guided writing), helping them clarify and expand their messages. Individual conferences are a good time to remind children of what they have learned in word study minilessons. You will also gather very valuable information that will help you select and design effective and timely future word study minilessons. Writing is especially important for first graders because they are examining the details of written language and using all of the letter, sound, and word knowledge that they have accumulated.

Sharing and Evaluation Children discuss their writing in a brief sharing period at the end of the period. Besides talking about the meaning and voice of the stories children write, you can reinforce what they've been learning in your word study minilessons.

Phonics Minilessons That Really Work

Materials Make a Difference

When you teach a minilesson, it is very important to do so in a clearly defined space in which all children can see and hear easily. They should be able to sit comfortably on the floor without touching other children. You will want an easel, a small white dry-erase board, markers, magnetic letters, and a vertical magnetic board. You will also need a pocket chart on which you can post letters or words on cards large enough for the whole group to see. The name chart and Alphabet Linking Chart are useful tools to have nearby, close enough for you to point to. Children should be able to see the word wall from where they sit.

Basic Principles: Designing/Implementing Effective Minilessons

Designing Effective Minilessons

- Focus on one principle that is appropriate and useful for your students at a particular point in time.
- State the principle in simple, clear terms.
- Think of a few good examples in advance so that you have them ready to show the students.
- Have in mind why you selected the minilesson, which probably will help you connect it to children's work in other components of the language/literacy framework; make connections explicit.
- Have in mind how you can connect your minilesson principle to the children's names (on the name chart).
- Design an application activity that students can do independently (after being taught routines), and that will be productive in their learning.
- Design multilevel activities that permit advanced students to go beyond the given activity and make more discoveries and allow children who are less experienced to complete the minilessons.

Implementing Effective Minilessons

- Have all materials organized and quickly available.
- Be sure that all children can see and hear as you demonstrate the principle or write examples on a chart.
- Make a clear statement of the principle as you begin the lesson, or clearly state the principle at the end as children come to their own conclusions from examples.
- Use a conversational rather than a lecture style. Promote interaction so children can be active, engaged learners.
- Invite interaction so that children bring their own knowledge to bear on the application of the principle.
- Invite children to connect the principle and examples to their names; use names as examples when possible.
- Share examples and add examples from children (if children are unable to provide some examples, then either the principle is not clearly stated or it is too difficult).
- Keep minilessons brief; a few examples are enough.
- Make connections to previous word study minilessons or understandings and discoveries made in any other component of the Language and Literacy Framework.
- Check for understanding by asking children to locate and talk about examples.
- Summarize the minilesson by returning to the principle and stating it again.
- Place an example on the word wall for the children's response when teaching minilessons on words.
- Demonstrate the application activity explicitly so that you know children can perform it independently.
- Provide all necessary materials for the application activity in one place—for example, the word study center or a clearly defined and organized materials center.
- Convene children for a brief sharing period so that they can comment on what they have learned and you can reinforce the principle again.

We recommend using black or dark-colored markers on white or cream-colored chart paper. You may want to use colored transparent highlighter tape to emphasize certain words or letters, but, in general, it is better not to clutter up the examples with color-coding, which is usually a distraction for children. Also, it may confuse them; we want them to look at the distinctive features of letters—not the color! If you have set up centers in your classroom, be sure that all the necessary materials are readily available in the word study center where students will use the application. If students work at their own tables, arrange materials in a central area or on each table. If the activity is new or difficult, place a model in clear view so that children can check their results. For additional information about the materials, read the Material Description List in *Teaching Resources*.

Classroom Routines for Effective Teaching

Routines refers both to the basic routines of how to live and learn in the classroom (where to store materials or how to participate in a class meeting, for example) and to a series of instructional routines such as making words, sorting pictures, and creating name puzzles that children will use again and again as they learn a range of concepts. Teach the routines carefully when you first begin using word study minilessons. First demonstrate the activity precisely, and then have everyone do it at once. If you run into a logistical problem (not having enough magnetic letters, for example), ask children to take turns with a partner or in a small group and check each other. When you know that children can perform the routine on their own, then they can work individually, as partners, or in groups. (You will need to demonstrate the activity again in relation to the particular principle you are exploring in the minilesson.) For a comprehensive overview of routines, see the descriptions and directions in *Teaching Resources;* additionally, you will find many references to routines in the Month-by-Month Planning Guide.

Consider Your Language and Delivery

Minilessons should be conversational. You will want to state the principle clearly at the beginning of the lesson (or at the end, if you think it is appropriate for students to derive it through inquiry and example). Your tone should be that of *I'm going to show you something interesting about how words work* or *What do you notice about these words?* Invite children to make connections to their names and anything else they know. Invite them to contribute further examples and recognize and praise their thinking even if the examples don't quite fit. Always try to understand their thinking and build on a partially correct response. Help them clarify their suggestions as necessary.

Remember that a minilesson is *brief.* Don't let it go on too long. Depending on the particular principle, you'll need only a few examples to make an understanding clear. Your goal is for students to integrate some of these examples into their own thinking so they can connect them to new learning when they are working on their own.

At the end of the minilesson, summarize the understanding you are trying to instill and take another moment to restate the principle. If appropriate, place an example on the word wall. Then explain and demonstrate the application activity.

Options for Application Activities

1. Present the minilesson to the entire class and then involve all children simultaneously in the application activity. They can work individually or with partners as you circulate around the room. Immediately follow the activity with sharing.
2. Present the minilesson to the entire class, but involve children in application activities in small groups that you supervise. Have the rest of the children involved in independent reading/writing activities. Follow the activity with sharing as soon as all groups have completed it.
3. Present the minilesson to the entire class and explain the application activity. Have children complete it first (simultaneously for the whole group) and then move to another independent activity. Work with small groups in guided reading or writing while children work independently.
4. Present the minilesson to the entire class and explain the application activity. On the same day, have children rotate to a word study center to complete the activity. Have a brief sharing at the end of the period.
5. Present the minilesson to the entire class and explain the application activity. Over several days, have children rotate to a word study center to complete the activity. Have a brief sharing at the end of each day. Ask the children who participated to talk about what they learned.

So What Did We Learn? Sharing and Evaluation

After independent work, convene a brief sharing period in which children can discuss the principle and share their examples. This community meeting is a good way to ask children to evaluate themselves. You can ask how many completed the activity and ask them to evaluate their work. Recognizing their independent work gives it value and emphasis. If you have made a chart, refer to it again and restate the principle. You may want to add some of their examples. Recognize children's thinking as they share their ideas. Make further connections with reading and writing in other components of the Language and Literacy Framework.

Your Essential Tools for Teaching

Phonics Lessons and *Teaching Resources* comprise multiple tools that work together to support your teaching. The tools are:

- The Lesson Selection Map
- The Assessment Guide (in *Teaching Resources*)
- The Month-by-Month Planning Guide
- The Word Study Continuum: Systematic Phonics and Spelling

The Lesson Selection Map

The Lesson Selection Map catalogs all Grade 1 lessons by Continuum category and suggested time of year (early, middle, or late). In creating this Map, we considered how children's experience is likely to build throughout the year as a result not only of the direct teaching of principles related to letters, sounds, and words but also of their daily experiences hearing written language read aloud and participating in shared, independent, and guided reading and interactive and independent writing.

Again, this Map is not a rigid sequence; it is a continuum of easier to harder principles. It will help you think in broad strokes about the program you are designing for the children in your classroom, which must always be considered in light of your observations and assessments of what your students know and can do at any given point. If children are very knowledgeable and experienced, you may decide that some lessons can be abbreviated or omitted. If children are very inexperienced in a given area, lessons may need to be repeated using different examples.

A whole year of lessons may seem overwhelming; however, keep in mind that:

- Any one lesson takes ten minutes or less.
- Some lessons can be skipped or shortened.
- Some lessons will go very quickly because children have acquired most of the requisite knowledge already through reading and writing in the classroom.

Even if you do not use all the lessons, reflecting on the Map will help you be aware of the entire body of knowledge that is important for first graders to acquire as a foundation for literacy learning.

The Map contains two kinds of information:

- Using the rows, you can take one category of the Continuum and follow children's development of a principle from easier to harder throughout the year. For example, lessons on phonological awareness begin with songs, rhymes, and chants. You'll help your students become more sensitive to the sounds of language by having them match rhyming pictures and listen for the parts in words. Later in the year you will give closer attention to individual sounds in words and help your students develop insights into the structure of words by identifying and manipulating these sounds. Each category of the Continuum offers room for growth throughout the year.
- You can look down the columns to get a sense of the understanding children are building across the entire continuum. Working across categories, you ensure that children not only develop phonological awareness but also learn to look at print—distinguish letters and learn their names—as well as think about word meanings and become familiar with some high frequency words that will help accelerate their learning.

Look at the Map both ways. Your students might be more advanced in one area than another. It is obvious that planning a program is not always neat and tidy; however, the concept of easier to harder, in combination with assessment, should allow you to design an efficient program that:

- Makes the most of what children know by allowing them to work at the edge of their knowledge.
- Ensures clear, explicit teaching and meaningful practice to deepen conceptual knowledge.
- Ensures that principles do not have to be taught again and again.
- Does not blindly demand that you spend time on exercises teaching what children already know.

Here are some easy directions for using the Map as a practical tool in lesson planning:

- Reproduce a copy of the Map to keep in the front of your lesson-planning book. (Another copy of the Map is included in *Teaching Resources.*)
- When you have used a lesson, highlight it on the Map or place a check on the line next to it.
- Write additional lessons that you design and implement in the empty spaces in each section.
- Make notes about adaptations that are helpful to your children because of their native language, background, or culture.
- If you determine that children do not need a particular lesson because they have learned the principle in some other context, cross out the line or highlight it in another color.

Used in this way, the Map becomes a record as well as a planning tool, because you will know at a glance what you have taught (or determined not to be necessary) and what you need to consider teaching next.

Grade 1 – Lesson Selection Map

Early Literacy Concepts ELC

early

___ **ELC 1** Recognizing Names (Name Chart)
___ **ELC 2** Recognizing Your Name in Text (Poems and Songs)
___ **ELC 3** Matching Spoken Word to Written Word (Cut-Up Sentences)
___ **ELC 4** Recognizing *First* and *Last* in Print (Making Sentences)

mid

late

Phonological Awareness PA

early

___ **PA 1** Making Rhymes (Picture Match)
___ **PA 2** Recognizing Rhymes (Picture Sort)
___ **PA 3** Hearing Sounds in Sequence (Making a List)
___ **PA 4** Hearing Ending Sounds (Picture Lotto)
___ **PA 5** Hearing Beginning and Ending Sounds in Words (Sound Dominoes)
___ **PA 6** Identifying Onsets and Rimes (Go Fish)
___ **PA 7** Hearing and Blending Onsets and Rimes (Oral Word Game)
___ **PA 8** Identifying and Blending Onsets and Rimes (Follow the Path)

mid

___ **PA 9** Hearing Middle Sounds (Picture Match)
___ **PA 10** Hearing and Changing Ending Sounds (Making New Words)
___ **PA 11** Hearing and Changing First and Last Sounds (Making New Words)

late

Letter Knowledge LK

early

___ **LK 1** Learning about Letters Through Names (Name Chart)
___ **LK 2** Noticing Letters in Names (Name Graph)
___ **LK 3** Identifying Letters (Name Puzzle)
___ **LK 4** Learning Letter Names (Letter Minibooks)
___ **LK 5** Forming Letters 1 (Verbal Path)
___ **LK 6** Forming Letters 2 (Handwriting Book)
___ **LK 7** Recognizing Letters (Magnetic Letters)
___ **LK 8** Looking at Letters (Letter Sort)
___ **LK 9** Recognizing and Naming Letters (Alphabet Linking Chart)
___ **LK 10** Noticing Letters in Words (Magnetic Letters)

mid

___ **LK 11** Matching Letters (Letter Lotto)
___ **LK 12** Identifying Letters (Letter Lotto)
___ **LK 13** Identifying Uppercase and Lowercase Letters (Concentration)
___ **LK 14** Identifying Consonants and Vowels (Letter Sort)
___ **LK 15** Learning about Names and Initials (Labeled Drawings)

late

Letter/Sound Relationships LS

early

___ **LS 1** Building Words (Alphabet Books)
___ **LS 2** Learning Letter Names and Sounds (Alphabet Wall)
___ **LS 3** Learning about Beginning Sounds (Making Sentences)
___ **LS 4** Learning about Beginning Consonant Letters and Sounds (Lotto)
___ **LS 5** Learning about Beginning Consonants (Follow the Path)
___ **LS 6** Noticing Vowels in Words (Name Graph)

mid

___ **LS 7** Introducing Consonant Clusters (Making Words)
___ **LS 8** Learning about Beginning Consonant Clusters (Finding Words)
___ **LS 9** Recognizing Consonant Clusters: *s* Family (Go Fish)
___ **LS 10** Recognizing Consonant Clusters: *l* Family (Cluster Lotto)
___ **LS 11** Recognizing Consonant Clusters: *r* Family (Word Sort)
___ **LS 12** Recognizing Long and Short Vowel Sounds: *a* (Say and Sort)
___ **LS 13** Recognizing Long and Short Vowel Sounds: *e* (Word Sort)
___ **LS 14** Recognizing Long and Short Vowel Sounds: *i* (Say and Sort)
___ **LS 15** Recognizing Long and Short Vowel Sounds: *o* and *u* (Follow the Path)
___ **LS 16** Consolidating Knowledge about Vowels (Vowel Lotto)

late

___ **LS 17** Recognizing Common Consonant Digraphs (Say and Sort)
___ **LS 18** Summarizing Digraph Knowledge (Digraph Lotto)
___ **LS 19** Recognizing Vowel Sounds: Silent *e* (Say and Sort)
___ **LS 20** Learning about Word Structure: *r* with a Vowel (Making Words)
___ **LS 21** Recognizing Consonants with Two Sounds (Concentration)

Spelling Patterns SP

early

__ **SP 1** Learning Common Short Vowel Word Patterns: *a (i, o, u)* (Making Words)
__ **SP 2** Learning Common Short Vowel Word Patterns: *e (a, i, o, u)* (Making Words)
__ **SP 3** Learning Phonograms: *-at, -an* (Closed Word Sort)

mid

__ **SP 4** Summarizing Easy (Two-Letter) Patterns (Word Sort)
__ **SP 5** Learning Phonograms: *-ate, -ake, -ike* (Word Sort)
__ **SP 6** Learning Phonograms: *-an* (Open Sort)
__ **SP 7** Learning Phonograms: *-an, -ake, -at, -ay, -and* (Open Sort)

late

__ **SP 8** Consolidating Knowledge about Phonograms (Open Sort)
__ **SP 9** Noticing Features of Words (Word Wall Mystery Sort)
__ **SP 10** Learning about Vowels and Silent *e* (Building Words)

High Frequency Words HF

early

__ **HF 1** Learning High Frequency Words 1 (Making and Writing Words)
__ **HF 2** Learning High Frequency Words 2 (Making and Writing Words)
__ **HF 3** Learning High Frequency Words 3 (Building Words with Magnetic Letters)
__ **HF 4** Learning High Frequency Words 4 (Locating Words in Text)
__ **HF 5** Learning High Frequency Words 5 (Making and Writing Words)

mid

__ **HF 6** Learning High Frequency Words 6 (Lotto)
__ **HF 7** Learning High Frequency Words 7 (Follow the Path)
__ **HF 8** Learning High Frequency Words 8 (Concentration)

late

Word Meaning WM

early

__ **WM 1** Learning Days of the Week (Making Books)

mid

__ **WM 2** Recognizing Synonyms (Synonym Match)
__ **WM 3** Recognizing Words That Go Together (Word Sort)

late

Word Structure WS

early

__ **WS 1** Exploring Syllables (Name Graph)
__ **WS 2** Making Plurals: Adding *s* (Word Match)

mid

__ **WS 3** Making Plurals: Adding *es* (Word Match)
__ **WS 4** Learning about Contractions: *I'm* (Poems and Songs)
__ **WS 5** Adding *s* and *ing* (Building Words)

late

__ **WS 6** Adding *ed* (Word Sort)
__ **WS 7** Learning about Contractions with *is* and *will* (Contraction Concentration)
__ **WS 8** Learning about Contractions with *are* and *not* (Contraction Concentration)
__ **WS 9** Summarizing Contractions (Follow the Path)
__ **WS 10** Identifying Syllables in Words (Word Sort)

Word-Solving Actions WSA

early

__ **WSA 1** Saying Words Slowly to Predict Letter Sequence (Words in Sentences)
__ **WSA 2** Changing the First Letter of a Word (Magnetic Letters)
__ **WSA 3** Changing and Adding Beginning Sounds (Sound Substitution Game)
__ **WSA 4** Recognizing Words Quickly (Magnetic Letters)

mid

__ **WSA 5** Using What You Know about Words (Making New Words)
__ **WSA 6** Changing the Last Letter of a Word (Making Words)
__ **WSA 7** Changing the Last Letters of Words (Making New Words)
__ **WSA 8** Noticing Word Parts (Magnetic Letters)
__ **WSA 9** Changing Ending Parts of Words (Building Words)
__ **WSA 10** Changing the Middle of Words (Magnetic Letters)
__ **WSA 11** Adding and Removing Letters to Make Words (Making Words)
__ **WSA 12** Changing First and Last Word Parts (Making New Words)

late

__ **WSA 13** Putting Words Together (Building Words)
__ **WSA 14** Learning How to Learn Words 1 (Choose, Write, Build, Mix, Fix, Mix)
__ **WSA 15** Learning How to Learn Words 2 (Look, Say, Cover, Write, Check)
__ **WSA 16** Learning How to Learn Words 3 (Buddy Check)
__ **WSA 17** Learning How to Learn Words 4 (Making Connections)
__ **WSA 18** Learning How to Learn Words 5 (Test Your Knowledge)

The Assessment Guide

There is a time to use systematic, planned tasks that are designed to gather information about particular aspects of children's growing word knowledge. Performance-based assessment may involve observation, but it also represents more formal structured experiences in which the tasks are standardized. Standardization of the procedure creates a reliable assessment situation that is more objective than daily ongoing observation. The goal is to get a picture of what each student can do independently. Usually, you do not actively teach during a performance-based assessment, but you may make teaching points after the neutral observation.

The Assessment Guide includes more formal, performance-based Assessment Tasks across the nine Categories of Learning. You can use these tasks in multiple ways: as diagnostic tools to determine what your students know and need to know; as monitoring tools to help you keep track of your teaching and your students' learning; and as documentation of the teaching and learning you and your students have accomplished. You and your colleagues may even decide to place some of the summary sheets in your children's permanent cumulative folders as a way to create a schoolwide record of the phonics and word study program.

As noted, the opportunities for informal assessment are embedded in each lesson in the Assess feature. Look for more formal assessment opportunities across the nine Categories of Learning in the Assessment Guide inside *Teaching Resources.*

The Month-by-Month Planning Guide

The Month by Month Planning Guide outlines and describes a year of instructional contexts and ways to organize that instruction—whole-group, independent, and small-group work. It also lists the instructional routines (which include everything from where to store supplies to how to play Alphabet Lotto) you will need to teach so that children will be able to complete the application activities. Although you'll teach only a few new routines each month, children's knowledge accumulates. Once a routine (sorting, for example) has been learned, children can use it again and again in different ways. Finally, our yearly plan suggests specific lessons by month, from easier to harder, and lists specific competencies that you can determine through observation and assessment. These simple assessments of what children can do will help you identify children who are having more difficulty and may need repetition or additional word study work in a small group.

This yearly plan is a ladder of support as you work with children over time. Don't worry if your group does not progress in precisely the same way this plan implies. They may learn more rapidly in one area than another, but referring to the plan will help you reflect on areas where you need to invest more instruction.

If you are new to teaching (or new to teaching in this area), you may want to follow this month-by-month plan closely. You will learn from the experience and over the year will begin to see how you can adapt the plan for greater effectiveness with your own students and also how you can teach more efficiently.

Here's a more detailed look at how the year is broken up and the progression of activities.

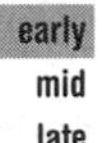
mid
late

Early Grade 1

First grade is an important year for students. In nine short months, they are expected to transition from reading very simple one-line texts and writing a few words to reading complex texts with many pages and few pictures and writing longer pieces with many conventionally spelled words. The change in first graders is fascinating and impressive. Equally important, they are learning the social skills, independence, and collaboration that will guide them toward a successful school experience. The first six weeks of grade 1 are important in establishing order and creating a community of learners. You want children to share with and support each other and to treat you, materials, and each other with respect. Your work with them on classroom routines is very important and worth the time spent. You will want to have a very predictable schedule and a highly organized classroom. Teach children gradually and explicitly how to move about the room, use materials, and follow directions.

early
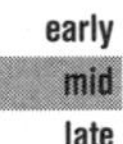
late

Middle Grade 1

By December most children will have settled into the routines of first grade and can perform them automatically; that is, they have learned how to live, work, and learn in the classroom. They can sustain independent work for sufficiently long periods of time and be responsible for themselves and for materials. You will still need to be explicit and clear in your demonstrations and to reteach routines if things are falling apart for some children. A good suggestion for October, November, and December is to enjoy holidays but keep the excitement contained. There are many other worthwhile topics of interest for first graders to discuss.

early
mid
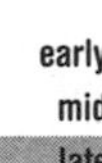

Late Grade 1

In the last three months of first grade, children are able to work much more systematically with word study. They will gradually increase the amount of text they can process in reading, and many will move from reading short books to beginning chapter books and from oral to silent reading much of the time. They begin to plan their writing more carefully and to revise it when needed. This is probably a time when you will want to establish systematic word study, the Buddy Study system. You will teach the routines for the five-day study system. Once the system is established, you can add these activities to your word study program. Any of the lessons listed for late grade 1 are appropriate for use with the system. As children begin to work more systematically on spelling, you will use fewer lessons each week; however, the children will be working with good examples and learning the principles, which ultimately will lead to more generalized learning.

Month-by-Month Planning Guide—September

During the first month of school, you will be continually assessing your students' knowledge of letters, sounds, and words so that you can make good decisions about lessons to teach and how to teach them. At the same time, you will be teaching them some valuable routines that will help them work together and learn in your classroom. Build a repertoire of stories, songs, rhymes, and chants that they enjoy and that will heighten their awareness of language sounds and written symbols and provide examples on which you can draw. Work mainly with the group as a whole and move quickly between activities. Each day:

- Several times a day, read aloud stories that have repetition, rhyme, and enjoyable language. Select books that are easy for children to follow and that will engage them through humor, interesting characters, and easy-to-remember language. Read favorite selections several times and invite children to join in.
- Use enlarged texts for shared reading. Teach children how to follow along as you read aloud and point to the words. To begin, choose simple one- and two-line poems and other messages.
- Work with names to help children use them as tools. Prepare a name chart.
- Begin simple interactive writing. You might begin with simple sentences that use children's names, for example, "Carole has a red dress."

Establish the routine of a focused phonics lesson followed by an application activity and then sharing. Follow the application activity with a sharing period. A good arrangement is to teach children to sit in a circle or square on the floor so that everyone can see and hear what is being shared. Sharing discoveries should be quick; not every child can share something every day. It is very important to establish sharing as a routine, however, because this time:

- Builds accountability for the application activity in that children want to report their discoveries.
- Sharpens their thinking *during* application because they are mentally preparing to share.
- Sets up a routine that encourages discoveries beyond the precise lesson you have taught.
- Gives you valuable information about what children have learned from the lesson and application activity.

For the first month of school, select lessons that help children attend to sounds and letters and at the same time build community among the members of your class. There is no more powerful word for a child than his/her name. Even though many first graders already know their names, lessons using names will be quick and help them use their knowledge as a resource. If they do not know how to read/write their names, then it is very important to focus on names intensively during the first week of school. Also select lessons to help develop phonological awareness, for example, focusing on hearing rhymes and on exploring letters and learning to look at print.

Organization of Instruction: *Whole class; some independent work as teacher circulates.*

Learning Contexts

Introduce reading aloud, shared reading, interactive writing, independent writing, and drawing. Show children the classroom and the materials. Build a repertoire of songs, chants, familiar stories, poems, and rhymes. Build a sense of community by teaching the children to care for the room and use routines in an orderly way. Be sure the children know one another's names and your name. Conduct assessments to determine how much you need to work on early literacy concepts, phonological awareness, and letter identification by shape and name. Establish the routine of a regular lesson followed by an application activity and sharing. Establish responsibility for taking materials home. Set up the word wall with children's names and add other words to it as children become familiar with them.

New Routines to Teach

- Sitting, moving, listening to instructions; getting a turn to speak; singing and chanting as a group;, listening to a story; and participating in shared reading and interactive writing.
- Using materials and putting them away.
- Identifying class activities (for example, "circle time") and introducing the basic daily schedule.
- Using the name puzzle and the name chart (locating, matching, etc.).
- Using the pocket chart: (1) placing picture cards in it and taking them out; (2) putting in sentence strips and taking them out; (3) highlighting words or letters with transparent tape.
- Matching picture cards.
- Sorting picture cards.
- Building words with magnetic letters.
- Clapping syllables.
- Saying words slowly to identify sounds.
- Using the word wall.

Suggested Lessons

ELC 1 Recognizing Names (Name Chart)
ELC 2 Recognizing Your Name in Text (Poems and Songs)
ELC 3 Matching Spoken Word to Written Word (Cut-Up Sentences)
ELC 4 Recognizing *First* and *Last* in Print (Making Sentences)
PA 1 Making Rhymes (Picture Match)
PA 2 Recognizing Rhymes (Picture Sort)
PA 3 Hearing Sounds in Sequence (Making a List)
LK1 Learning about Letters Through Names (Name Chart)
LK 2 Noticing Letters in Names (Name Graph)
LK 3 Identifying Letters (Name Puzzle)
LS 1 Building Words (Alphabet Books)
LS 2 Learning Letter Names and Sounds (Alphabet Wall)
WS 1 Exploring Syllables (Name Graph)
WSA 1 Saying Words Slowly to Predict Letter Sequence (Words in Sentences)
WSA 2 Changing the First Letter of a Word (Magnetic Letters)

Assessment — Children Can:

- Perform basic classroom routines that you have taught.
- Read their names and locate them in text.
- Build and write their names.
- Say the names of the letters in their names.
- Notice and talk about the similarities and differences among letters.
- Copy words accurately.
- Match pictures of items that start the same.
- Join in on poems, songs, rhymes, and chants.
- Clap words to represent syllable breaks.
- Recognize rhymes and match words that rhyme.
- Say words slowly and identify some of the sounds.

October

By October, children should understand the schedule and have internalized the basic classroom routines. If they still have difficulty with transitions or using materials, you'll want to reteach routines and emphasize them with consistency because now you will want to be introducing some more complex routines that will allow them to work independently. Continue to build children's knowledge of familiar stories, chants, songs, and rhymes so that they have a repertoire of examples. Complete initial assessments so that you have good understanding of what students know about letters, sounds, and words.

Continue reading aloud, shared reading, interactive writing, independent writing and drawing, and play activities. Work mainly with whole-group activities, but have some time every day when children work independently as you circulate and guide them. Introduce centers slowly, one at a time, using your judgment and observation as to when children are ready to learn another independent activity. When children can work independently for twenty to thirty minutes, call together a guided reading group, beginning with one group and adding groups as it becomes possible. In guided reading, you can help them take on new texts that have not been read to them. These first guided reading groups will be quite short, actually about ten to fifteen minutes, so you will still have time to assist individuals as needed while they are working independently on word study application activities and in other centers.

Set aside time for writing and continue to monitor and encourage children to compose messages and spell words for themselves. Help them hold the pencil correctly and emphasize directional movements in writing. Help them use their knowledge of sounds and letters.

Continue teaching and reinforcing basic classroom routines including those related to any centers you have opened. Add several new routines, including using the word wall: (1) knowing the purpose of the word wall; (2) placing words on the word wall; (3) reading the word wall; and (4) locating words on the word wall. Be sure that you spend enough time on basic application activities listed below in New Routines to Teach.

Teach the Trip and Line-Up games as an ongoing quick way for children to practice on the bodies of knowledge children have developed so far. For example, to line up, each child says a word that starts with /p/ or a word with *-at.* These games represent a new routine to teach in February; once they are learned, you can fill some transition times with opportunities to learn in an enjoyable way.

Organization of Instruction: *Whole class; some independent work as teacher circulates; some small-group guided reading.*

Learning Contexts

Continue reading aloud, shared reading, interactive writing, independent writing, and drawing, in connection with a phonics lesson followed by an application activity and sharing. Most of the time you will be working with the class as a whole: all the children engage in the application activity simultaneously. You will be teaching routines that the children will eventually perform independently. As the children become more proficient, try working with one small group in guided reading while other children do the word study activity and some independent reading and writing. Continue to build the repertoire of songs and rhymes children know and increase their knowledge of high frequency words through shared reading and interactive writing. An important routine to establish in interactive writing is saying words slowly.

New Routines to Teach

- Reinforcing basic classroom routines so that they become automatic.
- Using the word wall.
- Putting together cut-up sentences (demonstration).
- Saying words and clapping syllables.
- Saying words slowly.
- Matching word by word (demonstration).
- Playing Lotto.
- Playing Sound Dominoes.
- Playing Go Fish.
- Playing Follow the Path.
- Using letter minibooks.
- Making letters using the Verbal Path.
- Using the handwriting book.
- Sorting letters.
- Building and writing words.
- Using word cards (at school or at home).

Suggested Lessons

PA 4 Hearing Ending Sounds (Picture Lotto)
PA 5 Hearing Beginning and Ending Sounds in Words (Sound Dominoes)
PA 6 Identifying Onsets and Rimes (Go Fish)
PA 7 Hearing and Blending Onsets and Rimes (Oral Word Game)
PA 8 Identifying and Blending Onsets and Rimes (Follow the Path)
LK 4 Learning Letter Names (Letter Minibooks)
LK 5 Forming Letters 1 (Verbal Path)
LK 6 Forming Letters 2 (Handwriting Book)
LK 7 Recognizing Letters (Magnetic Letters)
LK 8 Looking at Letters (Letter Sort)
LK 9 Recognizing and Naming Letters (Alphabet Linking Chart)
LK 10 Noticing Letters in Words (Magnetic Letters)
LS 3 Learning about Beginning Sounds (Making Sentences)
HF 1 Learning High Frequency Words 1 (Making and Writing Words)
WM 1 Learning Days of the Week (Making Books)
WS 2 Making Plurals: Adding *s* (Word Match)
WSA 3 Changing and Adding Beginning Sounds (Sound Substitution Game)

Assessment—Children Can:

- Perform new routines you have taught.
- Identify the number of syllables in a word.
- Hear words in a sentence.
- Hear and identify beginning sounds in words.
- Hear and identify ending sounds in words.
- Identify onsets and rimes.
- Blend onsets and rimes.
- Say words slowly and identify several sounds in sequence.
- Read the Alphabet Linking Chart accurately.
- Read the days of the week and months of the year.
- Form letters correctly that you have demonstrated using a Verbal Path.
- Recognize and name the letters of the alphabet.
- Change the first letter of a word to make a new word.

Month-by-Month Planning Guide—November

By November, children will be working independently for about 45 minutes to an hour, and you can work with a full range of guided reading groups. You will still be doing a great deal of whole-group instruction and continuing to build the children's repertoire of stories, songs, and poems. Shared reading and interactive writing continue to be important learning contexts because they allow children to behave like readers and writers in a highly supported way. Intensive work in reading aloud, shared reading, and shared writing exposes children in an authentic way to all of the concepts that they will be using more explicitly in word study throughout the year. Continue to support children in writing; the number of words they can write quickly and automatically will be expanding, and you will also see evidence of their increased knowledge of letters and sounds.

Work closely, sometimes using small groups, with children who do not have full control of basic classroom routines. If most children have trouble with a particular routine, you may need to redesign it to make it easier. You could also take a look at the way you have organized materials or posted directions.

Phonics lessons by now will have assumed a routine structure in that children will know to listen and participate during the lesson, engage independently in the application activity, and share what they have learned. Model and encourage children to go beyond the lesson in actively learning about words; observe their behaviors for insight into their thinking.

New routines to teach include games such as Concentration and Letter Bingo. Children will be applying sorting, Lotto, and locating to different principles and will continue to expand their knowledge of high frequency words. Select lessons that help them become flexible in hearing and connecting words by beginning, middle, and ending sounds. Lessons also help them systematically learn and say common phonograms or word patterns, and continue to expand their knowledge of high frequency words. By now, children should not need phonological awareness instruction, but be aware of children who may need some extra help on hearing sounds in words.

Organization of Instruction: *Whole class; independent work at centers or at desks or tables; small-group guided reading.*

Learning Contexts	New Routines to Teach	Suggested Lessons	Assessment—Children Can:
Continue working with all elements of the Language and Literacy Framework, increasing time spent on independent reading, writing, and word study. Expand the number of activities children do independently, including reading, writing, listening, and word study. Work with children on the routines until they can perform them independently. Convene two, three, or four guided reading groups daily. Establish responsibility for taking home materials and using them as directed (work with caregivers).	▸ Working further with handwriting books. ▸ Working independently in centers (or at desks or tables) on word study activities. ▸ Building words. ▸ Using a Making Words Sheet to record words. ▸ Matching words by looking at letters. ▸ Locating words with masking cards.	**LS 4** Learning about Beginning Consonant Letters and Sounds (Lotto) **LS 5** Learning about Beginning Consonants (Follow the Path) **LS 6** Noticing Vowels in Words (Name Graph) **SP 1** Learning Common Short Vowel Word Patterns: *a (i, o, u)* (Making Words) **SP 2** Learning Common Short Vowel Word Patterns: *e (a, i, o, u)* (Making Words) **SP 3** Learning Phonograms: *-at, -an* (Closed Word Sort) **HF 2** Learning High Frequency Words 2 (Making and Writing Words) **HF 3** Learning High Frequency Words 3 (Building Words with Magnetic Letters) **HF 4** Learning High Frequency Words 4 (Locating Words in Text) **HF 5** Learning High Frequency Words 5 (Making and Writing Words) **WSA 4** Recognizing Words Quickly (Magnetic Letters)	▸ Perform new routines you have taught. ▸ Hear and match words with the same middle sound. ▸ Substitute a beginning sound to make a new word. ▸ Identify the vowels and name them. ▸ Build words with *ap, an, ell, est, at, an, in, it, op, ot, ut, og.* ▸ Read the days of the week and months of the year. ▸ Read high frequency words that you have taught and they have made and written. ▸ Identify the first and last parts of a word. ▸ Use known words or word parts to solve a new word.

December

The sequence of phonics lesson, application activity, and sharing will be automatic for you and the children. Moreover, you will have established a large number of resources to which children can refer as they work independently in writing or word study—word wall, word study charts, rhymes, and songs. Establish the Alphabet Linking Chart as an important resource and teach children how to refer to it as they write.

Continue working with guided reading groups; many children will be acquiring and using more sophisticated word-solving skills as they encounter more multisyllable words. Help them use sound-to-letter relationships and word patterns. You will also have established the full structure of the writing workshop—minilesson, independent work with conferring, and sharing. Remember that saying words slowly and representing sounds with letters and letter clusters have maximal benefit in helping children learn letter/sound relationships.

As you make more connections across the language and literacy framework, you will find that children are becoming alert to making their own connections. They will notice known words, letters, and parts of words within instructional contexts such as read-aloud, shared reading, and interactive writing, and they will also be actively using letter/sound knowledge to write more complete words independently.

Increase the time children spend in oral rereading of the texts that you have used in shared reading and also put some books in browsing boxes that are new to them but will be easy. You'll notice that many of the children are pointing, reading accurately, and monitoring their reading using some knowledge of letters and sounds.

You will be working with several guided reading groups (probably three to five). An optional part of guided reading is one or two minutes of "word work" at the end of the lesson. You will be working with principles for solving words; examples do not come from the guided reading lesson but instead are connected to the principles children in the group need to know. Using magnetic letters, help children build words and manipulate letters in words. Take this opportunity to tailor your word study program to the particular children in the group; you can do some intensive work on a principle that they are finding difficult or help them practice an action to automatic use. Word work is only one or two minutes but is highly effective.

By now, children will have mastered most of the routines they need for word study application activities, and only a quick demonstration will be required to help them vary the routine for new content. Lessons help children become more flexible in using ending sounds in words and working with word parts. They will learn more about consonants, consonant clusters, and vowels and also continue to learn more high frequency words.

Organization of Instruction: *Whole class; independent work, some without teacher circulating; two or three small groups.*

Learning Contexts

Continue using all elements of the Language and Literacy Framework, including the phonics lesson and application activity. Increase children's experience in reading and rereading texts. Use the name chart, Alphabet Linking Chart, and word wall as tools. Increase time the children spend on independent activities. Be sure children are writing independently every day and frequently participate in guided reading groups that include word work as appropriate.

New Routines to Teach

- Sorting in many ways (letters, pictures, names, other words).
- Reading independently—going through the whole book, pointing, etc.
- Writing independently—making letters using specific directions in order and then checking the letters.
- Playing Lotto by matching pictures.

Suggested Lessons:

PA 9 Hearing Middle Sounds (Picture Match)
PA 10 Hearing and Changing Ending Sounds (Making New Words)
PA 11 Hearing and Changing First and Last Sounds (Making New Words)
LK 11 Matching Letters (Letter Lotto)
LK 12 Identifying Letters (Letter Lotto)
LK 13 Identifying Uppercase and Lowercase Letters (Concentration)
LK 14 Identifying Consonants and Vowels (Letter Sort)
LS 7 Introducing Consonant Clusters (Making Words)
LS 8 Learning about Beginning Consonant Clusters (Finding Words)

Assessment—Children Can:

- Perform new routines that you have taught.
- Change the beginning or ending sound of a word to make a new word.
- Identify the consonants and vowels.
- Recognize and identify some beginning consonant clusters.
- Read and write high frequency words you have taught.

Month-by-Month Planning Guide—January

In January, continue connecting word study across the language and literacy framework. Add words to the Word Wall as a regular part of your word study lesson; the examples you place on the Word Wall will remind children of the principle they have learned. Model referring to the Word Wall during writing lessons and guided reading lessons. Show children how to use the wall as a constant reference for their independent work.

In lessons, they will be consolidating their knowledge of letters, sounds, and word patterns and can do more in a short period of time during application activities, which will involve a variety of sorting and matching words and using words in games for various purposes. Lessons help children to expand and systematize their knowledge of consonant clusters and to begin learning phonogram patterns. Work toward children's learning of the fifty high frequency words for first grade.

Organization of Instruction: *Whole class; independent work, some without teacher circulating; one or two small groups.*

Learning Contexts	New Routines to Teach	Suggested Lessons	Assessment—Children Can:
Continue using all elements of the Language and Literacy Framework; add guided reading groups as appropriate. Involve children in guided reading as appropriate. Establish "browsing boxes" and the new routines associated with them. As children learn more high frequency words and as you use phonograms in the minilessons, add examples to the word wall. Increase the time children spend on reading and rereading simple texts and on writing.	▸ Playing Concentration. ▸ Matching pictures of words with the same middle sound. ▸ Sorting letters. ▸ Locating words in print. ▸ Building words using phonograms. ▸ Substituting the first letter to make a new word.	**LK 15** Learning about Names and Initials (Labeled Drawings) **LS 9** Recognizing Consonant Clusters: *s* Family (Go Fish) **LS 10** Recognizing Consonant Clusters: *l* Family (Cluster Lotto) **LS 11** Recognizing Consonant Clusters: *r* Family (Word Sort) **SP 4** Summarizing Easy (Two-Letter) Spelling Patterns (Word Sort) **SP 5** Learning Phonograms: *-ate, -ake, -ike* (Word Sort) **HF 6** Learning High Frequency Words 6 (Lotto) **WM 2** Recognizing Synonyms (Synonym Match) **WSA 5** Using What You Know about Words (Making New Words) **WSA 6** Changing the Last Letter of a Word (Making Words) **WSA 7** Changing the Last Letters of Words (Making New Words) **WSA 8** Noticing Word Parts (Magnetic Letters)	▸ Perform new routines that you have taught. ▸ Recognize and use consonant clusters in the *s, l,* and *r* families. ▸ Make words with the phonograms *-ate, -ake, -ike.* ▸ Read and write high frequency words you have taught. ▸ Match synonyms you have taught. ▸ Change beginning and ending letters to make new words. ▸ Change onsets and rimes to make new words.

February

The word wall will become an increasingly important tool as children add words to it and use it as a resource in writing and word study. Also, work to fully establish the use of the Alphabet Linking Chart as a tool for making connections. Increase the amount of reading and writing children do independently and add reading groups as appropriate. Children will have learned to hold and use a pencil or marker for drawing and writing and, with your support, increase their control over the manual task. You may want to assess children's knowledge of high frequency words toward the end of the month. Select lessons that systematically establish children's knowledge of vowel sounds in words and begin to explore simple aspects of word structure such as plurals and contractions. Show children how they can use their knowledge of high frequency words to read words quickly and of word patterns to solve new words quickly. Help them develop fluency in adding and removing letters to make new words.

Organization of Instruction: *Whole class; independent work, teacher circulating to reinforce new routines; one or two small groups.*

Learning Contexts

Continue to add words to the word wall and use it as a tool. Help children notice word parts in their names as you work with phonograms. Use Line-Up games to practice concepts that the children know (such as first and last sounds of words). Increase the time children spend on reading and rereading texts as well as on writing.

New Routines to Teach

- Playing Line-Up games using various kinds of knowledge
- Playing Trip games.
- Using a Verbal Path (saying directions while writing a letter).
- Naming letters in words (spelling).
- Pointing to words while reading.

Suggested Lessons

LS 12 Recognizing Long and Short Vowel Sounds: *a* (Say and Sort)
LS 13 Recognizing Long and Short Vowel Sounds: *e* (Word Sort)
LS 14 Recognizing Long and Short Vowel Sounds: *i* (Say and Sort)
LS 15 Recognizing Long and Short Vowel Sounds: *o* and *u* (Follow the Path)
LS 16 Consolidating Knowledge about Vowels (Vowel Lotto)
SP 6 Learning Phonograms: *-an* (Open Sort)
SP 7 Learning Phonograms: *-an, -ake, -at, -ay, -and* (Open Sort)
HF 7 Learning High Frequency Words 7 (Follow the Path)
HF 8 Learning High Frequency Words 8 (Concentration)
WM 3 Recognizing Words That Go Together (Word Sort)
WS 3 Making Plurals: Adding *es* (Word Match)
WS 4 Learning about Contractions: *I'm* (Poems and Songs)
WS 5 Adding *s* and *ing* (Building Words)
WSA 9 Changing Ending Parts of Words (Building Words)
WSA 10 Changing the Middle of Words (Magnetic Letters)
WSA 11 Adding and Removing Letters to Make Words (Making Words)
WSA 12 Changing First and Last Word Parts (Making New Words)

Assessment—Children Can:

- Perform new routines that you have taught.
- Identify the long vowel sounds.
- Identify the short vowel sounds.
- Sort words according to phonogram pattern.
- Make plurals by adding *s*.
- Make plurals by adding *es*.
- Recognize contractions when they see them in text.
- Quickly recognize and locate high frequency words that are embedded in text.

onth Planning Guide—March

early mid late

easingly proficient in their independent work, ...nd writing for longer periods of time. Through ...uided reading, you can expand their ability to ...s and engage in word solving. Consistently use the ...ption at the end of guided reading lessons for children ...ving more difficulty with concepts. In lessons, bring c... knowledge of vowels and of consonant digraphs into summ...ary form and have them use their knowledge in application activities. Explore simple compound words.

Teach children how to create and maintain a Words to Learn sheet that will be kept in the writing workshop folder. You can add words to the list from the assessment of high frequency words as well as from children's own writing. Get ready for the Buddy Study system by teaching children how to choose exemplar words from the phonics/spelling lesson and write them on an index card for you to check. Begin with only a few words, three or four. Establish the board with a library card pocket with each child's name on it; teach children to keep their word cards in it.

Organization of Instruction: *Whole class; independent work, teacher circulating to reinforce new routines; individual conferences; concurrent small groups.*

Learning Contexts

Continue using all elements of the Language and Literacy Framework and making connections between word work, reading, and writing. Continue the lesson, application, and sharing structure, but work toward adding a more formal study system for words. When children demonstrate a high level of independence in word study, begin to have children choose several words to write and build with magnetic letters. Add a "Words to Learn" list to children's writing workshop folders.

New Routines to Teach

- Using Choose, Write, Build, Mix, Fix, Mix.
- Creating and maintaining a Words to Learn list.
- Playing Lotto with vowels.
- Making new words by changing middle clusters.
- Putting compound words together and taking them apart.
- Sorting words according to consonant digraphs.
- Using a card to record words.

Suggested Lessons

LS 17	Recognizing Common Consonant Digraphs (Say and Sort)
SP 8	Consolidating Knowledge about Phonograms (Open Sort)
WSA 13	Putting Words Together (Building Words)
WSA 14	Learning How to Learn Words 1 (Choose, Write, Build, Mix, Fix, Mix)

Assessment—Children Can:

- Perform new routines you have taught.
- Match words with the same long and short vowel sounds.
- Recognize and categorize consonant digraphs—*sh, ch, wh, th.*
- Read and write high frequency words you have taught.
- Change vowel clusters in the middle of words to make new words.
- Identify the component words of compound words.

April

As you add components to the framework, do not neglect reading aloud to children. Extensive experiences in hearing stories and nonfiction texts will build a valuable foundation of concepts and vocabulary for reading complex texts at the end of first grade and into second grade. Continue to use the word wall and Alphabet Linking Chart as tools. You will want to take some words off the word wall to make room for examples from your phonics/spelling lessons; build this action in as a regular routine.

Work through the five days of the Buddy Study system several times with your students. They may already know how to choose, write, and build words. Teach the next four days: Look, Say, Cover, Write, Check; Buddy Check; Make Connections; and Buddy Test. After the lesson, remind them of this sequence of actions by quickly demonstrating them and having all children in the class do it at the same time. Over the next four days, teach each routine by demonstration and then have children do it. During sharing time, have children self-evaluate their efforts. Repeat this process over the next two or three weeks, being very specific about the expectations for checking words and writing carefully. As children learn the routines, they can work quicker. If necessary, use a timer set to a reasonable work period. What you want is for children to internalize the amount of time needed for the routine; they should work carefully but steadily.

Organization of Instruction: *Whole class; independent work, teacher circulating to reinforce new routines; individual conferences; concurrent small groups.*

Learning Contexts	New Routines to Teach	Suggested Lessons	Assessment—Children Can:
Engage children in writing and reading for longer stretches of time, and continue working with guided reading groups. You will have introduced the first day of the Buddy Study system by having children choose, write, and build words. Provide a daily lesson to reinforce day one and then teach the other routines of the system over four days. Have children engage in the routines simultaneously so that you can circulate and guide them. Go over these routines each week of the month.	▸ Using Buddy Check. ▸ Using Buddy Test. ▸ Finding words on the word wall—noticing patterns. ▸ Using Look, Say, Cover, Write, Check. ▸ Playing Lotto with digraphs. ▸ Making Connections Sheet. ▸ Sorting words according to meaning. ▸ Using a card to check words.	**LS 18** Summarizing Digraph Knowledge (Digraph Lotto) **SP 9** Noticing Features of Words (Word Wall Mystery Sort) **WSA 15** Learning How to Learn Words 2 (Look, Say, Cover, Write, Check) **WSA 16** Learning How to Learn Words 3 (Buddy Check) **WSA 17** Learning How to Learn Words 4 (Making Connections) **WSA 18** Learning How to Learn Words 5 (Test Your Knowledge)	▸ Perform new routines you have taught. ▸ Navigate the Buddy Study system thoroughly and comfortably.

Month-by-Month Planning Guide—May/June

In most places, May and the first part of June mark the end of a year of learning. All children should leave first grade with a large and rich store of knowledge of stories, poems, rhymes, letters, sounds, and words that they have learned. They will see themselves as readers and writers and be ready for the much more challenging work they will meet in second grade. In May, continue to use lessons exploring word structure, for example, using endings and contractions. Use the steps of the Buddy Study system.

Organization of Instruction: *Whole class; independent work, teacher circulating to reinforce new routines; individual conferences; concurrent small groups.*

Learning Contexts

Continue all elements of the framework and implementing the Buddy Study system weekly as an addition to the lesson, application, and sharing structure. Perform final assessments for the year and look at children's progress in learning about letters, sounds, and words. If possible, send home reading and writing materials for children to use over the summer. Send home children's writing workshop folders.

New Routines to Teach

- Building words by adding endings.
- Playing Concentration—consonants.
- Playing Concentration—contractions.
- Playing Follow the Path—contractions.
- Making lists of words (from building).
- Sorting words with silent *e*.

Suggested Lessons

LS 19 Recognizing Vowel Sounds: Silent *e* (Say and Sort)
LS 20 Learning about Word Structure: *r* with a Vowel (Making Words)
LS 21 Recognizing Consonants with Two Sounds (Concentration)
SP 10 Learning about Vowels and Silent *e* (Building Words)
WS 6 Adding *ed* (Word Sort)
WS 7 Learning about Contractions with *is* and *will* (Contraction Concentration)
WS 8 Learning about Contractions with *are* and *not* (Contraction Concentration)
WS 9 Summarizing Contractions (Follow the Path)
WS 10 Identifying Syllables in Words (Word Sort)

Assessment—Children Can:

- Perform new routines you have taught.
- Identify silent *e* and demonstrate the way silent *e* influences vowel sounds.
- Identify the two sounds that some consonants make.
- Demonstrate understanding of simple contractions involving *is, will, are,* and *not* by moving from component words to contraction and from contraction to component words.

The Word Study Continuum

Systematic Phonics and Spelling, Grades K–3

The Word Study Continuum is the key to the minilessons. Over the course of the school year, you will use it, in concert with the Month-by-Month Planning Guide, the Lesson Selection Map, and continuous assessment, to inform your work. The Continuum comprises nine Categories of Learning your students need to develop over time; it is a comprehensive picture of linguistic knowledge. Although there are easier and more complex concepts within each category, we are not suggesting that there is a rigid sequence. Instead, we want to help children develop their abilities along a broad front, often using and learning about several different kinds of information simultaneously.

While instruction and assessment are embedded within classroom activities, both are systematic. Indeed, every aspect of the phonics minilessons is systematic, including the observation of children; collection of data on what children know about letters, sounds, and words; and the teacher's selection of lessons to fit the specific instructional needs of individual children. Teaching Is efficient and systematic when lessons are carefully selected and sequenced to provide what children need to learn next.

The shaded area of the Continuum performs two important functions. First, it serves as a guide for introducing principles to children; second, it helps you understand what principles you can expect your students to fully control and when. You'll notice that the shaded areas cross grade levels. These shaded areas provide broad indicators of expected achievement; however, learning rate and time will vary with individual children as well as for different groups. In general, at grade level (the earliest period of time indicated by shading), you can begin to assess children's knowledge of a specific principle and refer to the principle during reading and writing activities. Additionally, you will select specific lessons that help them expand their knowledge of the chosen principle. At the latest time indicated by shading, take steps to ensure that children fully understand and can use the principle. You may need to increase time spent on lessons related to the principle or work with small groups of children who are still having difficulty.

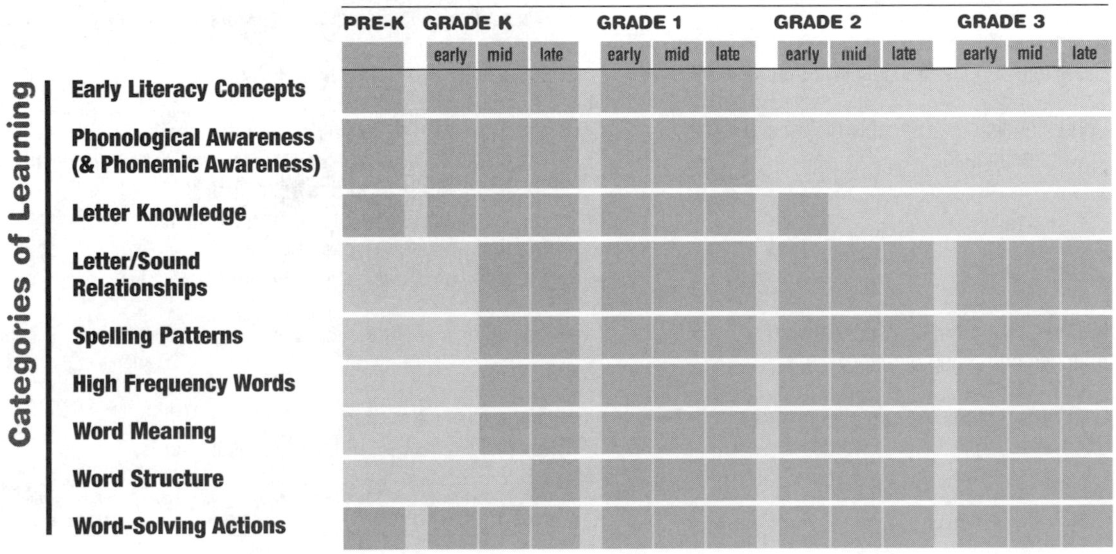

Categories of Learning	PRE-K	GRADE K			GRADE 1			GRADE 2			GRADE 3		
		early	mid	late	early	mid	late	early	mid	late	early	mid	late
Early Literacy Concepts													
Phonological Awareness (& Phonemic Awareness)													
Letter Knowledge													
Letter/Sound Relationships													
Spelling Patterns													
High Frequency Words													
Word Meaning													
Word Structure													
Word-Solving Actions													

Early Literacy Concepts

Learning about literacy begins long before children enter school. Many children hear stories read aloud and try out writing for themselves; through such experiences, they learn some basic concepts about written language. Nearly all children begin to notice print in the environment and develop ideas about the purposes of print. The child's name, for example, is a very important word. Kindergartners and first graders are still acquiring some of these basic concepts, and they need to generalize and systematize their knowledge. In the classroom, they learn a great deal through experiences such as shared and modeled reading and shared and interactive writing. Explicit teaching can help children learn much more about these early concepts, understand their importance, and develop ways of using them in reading and writing.

Early Literacy Concepts

PRE-K | GRADE K (early, mid, late) | GRADE 1 (early, mid, late) | GRADE 2 (early, mid, late) | GRADE 3 (early, mid, late)

Principle	Explanation of Principle
Distinguishing between print and pictures	"We read the print to find out what the words say."
Understanding the purpose of print in reading	"We look at the print to read the words in stories and other messages."
Understanding the purpose of print in writing	"We write letters and words so readers will understand what we mean."
Recognizing one's name	"Your name has letters in it." "Your name starts with a letter that is always the same." "Your name starts with a capital letter. The other letters are lowercase." "Your name is always written the same way." "You can find your name by looking for the first letter."
Using letters in one's own name to represent it or "write" a message	"You can write the letters in your name." "You can use the letters in your name along with other letters to write messages."
Understanding the concept of "letter"	"A letter has a name and a shape."
Understanding the concept of "word"	"A word is a group of sounds that mean something." "A word in writing is a group of letters with space on either side."
Using left-to-right directionality of print	"We read and write from left to right."
Understanding the concepts of *first* and *last* in written language	"The first word in a sentence is on the left." "The last word in a sentence is before the period or question mark." "The first letter in a word is on the left." "The last letter in a word is before the space." "The first part of a page is at the top." "The last part of a page is at the bottom."
Understanding that one spoken word matches one group of letters	"We say one word for each word we see in writing."
Using one's name to learn about words and make connections to words	"Your name is a word." "You can connect your name with other words."

Early Literacy Concepts, continued

PRINCIPLE	EXPLANATION OF PRINCIPLE
	PRE-K · GRADE K (early, mid, late) · GRADE 1 (early, mid, late) · GRADE 2 (early, mid, late) · GRADE 3 (early, mid, late)
Locating the first and last letters of words in continuous text	"You can find a word by noticing how it looks." "You can find a word by looking for the first letter." "You can check a word by looking at the first and last letters."
Understanding the concept of a sentence	"A sentence is a group of words that makes sense."
	PRE-K · GRADE K (early, mid, late) · GRADE 1 (early, mid, late) · GRADE 2 (early, mid, late) · GRADE 3 (early, mid, late)

Phonological Awareness

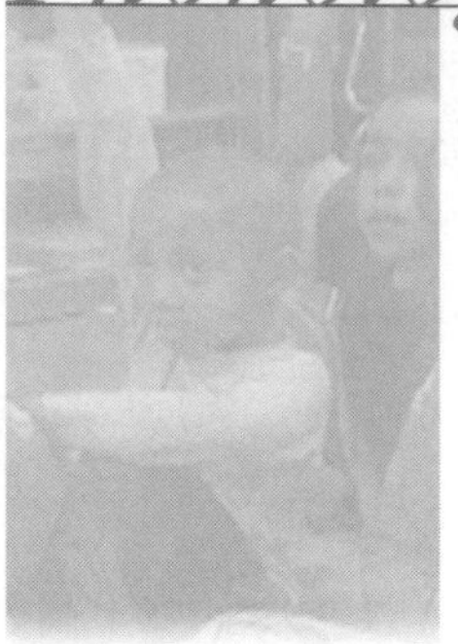

Phonological awareness is a broad term that refers to both explicit and implicit knowledge of the sounds in language. It includes the ability to hear and identify words (word awareness), rhymes (rhyme awareness), syllables (syllable awareness), onsets and rimes (onset and rime awareness), and individual sounds (sound awareness).

Phonemic awareness is one kind of phonological awareness. Phonemic awareness refers to the ability to identify, isolate, and manipulate the individual sounds *(phonemes)* in words. Principles categorized as phonemic awareness are labeled Phonemes [PA] in this Continuum.

Phonological awareness (and phonemic awareness) is taught orally or in connection with letters, when it is called *phonics.* Phonics instruction refers to teaching children to connect letters and sounds in words. While very early experiences focus on hearing and saying sounds in the absence of letters, most of the time you will want to teach children to hear sounds in connection with letters. Many of the lessons related to this section begin with oral activity but move toward connecting the sounds to letters. You will not want to teach all of the PA principles in this Continuum. It is more effective to teach children only two or three ways to manipulate phonemes in words so that they learn how words work.

Principles related to letter/sound relationships, or phonics, are included in the letter/sound relationships category of this Continuum.

Phonological Awareness (including phonemic awareness)

	Principle	Explanation of Principle
Words	Hearing and recognizing word boundaries	"You say words when you talk." "You can hear words in a sentence if you stop after each one. [*I - have - a - dog.*]"
Words	Segmenting sentences into words	"You can say each word in a sentence. [*I - like - to - go - shopping.*]"
Rhyming Words	Hearing and saying rhyming words	"Some words have end parts that sound alike. They *rhyme* [*new, blue*]." "You can hear the rhymes in poems and songs." "You can say words and hear how they rhyme."
Rhyming Words	Hearing and connecting rhyming words	"You can hear and connect words that rhyme [*fly, high, buy, sky*]."
Rhyming Words	Hearing and generating rhyming words	"You can make rhymes by thinking of words that end the same. [*I can fly in the ___.*]"

(Grade bands: PRE-K; GRADE K early, mid, late; GRADE 1 early, mid, late; GRADE 2 early, mid, late; GRADE 3 early, mid, late)

Phonological Awareness, continued

PRE-K | GRADE K (early, mid, late) | GRADE 1 (early, mid, late) | GRADE 2 (early, mid, late) | GRADE 3 (early, mid, late)

	Principle	Explanation of Principle
Syllables	Hearing and saying syllables	"You can hear and say the syllables in a word [*to-ma-to, tomato*]." "Some words have one syllable [*cat*]." "Some words have two syllables [*can-dy, candy*]." "Some words have three or more syllables [*um-brel-la, umbrella*]."
	Blending syllables	"You can blend syllables together [*pen-cil, pencil*]."
Onsets and Rimes	Hearing and segmenting onsets and rimes	"You can hear and say the first and last parts of a word [*c-ar, car; pl-ay, play*]."
	Blending onsets with rimes	"You can blend word parts together [*d-og, dog*]."
Phonemes [PA]	Hearing and saying individual phonemes (sounds) in words	"You can say a word slowly." "You can hear the sounds in a word [*m-a-k, make*]."
	Segmenting words into phonemes	"You can say each sound in a word [*b-a-t*]."
	Hearing and saying two or three phonemes in a word	"You can say a word slowly to hear all the sounds [*r-u-n*]."
	Hearing and saying beginning phonemes in words	"You can hear the first sound in a word [*s-u-n*]." "You can say a word to hear the first sound."
	Hearing and saying ending phonemes in words	"You can hear the last sound in a word [*r-u-n*]." "You can say a word to hear the last sound."
	Hearing similar beginning phonemes in words	"Some words sound the same at the beginning [*run, race*]." "You can connect words that sound the same at the beginning [*mother, mom, make*]."
	Hearing similar ending phonemes in words	"Some words sound the same at the end [*win, fun*]." "You can connect words that sound the same at the end [*get, sit, Matt*]."
	Blending two or three phonemes in words	"You can blend sounds together to say a word [*d-o-g = dog*]."
	Adding phonemes to the beginning of words	"You can add sounds to a word [*it + s = sit*]." "You can add sounds to the beginning of a word [*rate + c = crate*]."
	Manipulating phonemes at the beginning of words	"You can change the first sound in a word to make a new word [*not, hot*]."
	Manipulating phonemes at the ending of words	"You can change the last sound in a word to make a new word [*his, him*]."
	Hearing and saying middle phonemes in words	"You can hear and say the sound in the middle of a word [*s-u-n*]."
	Hearing similar middle phonemes in words	"Some words sound the same in the middle [*cat, ran*]." "You can match words that sound the same in the middle [*stop, hot, John*]."
	Hearing four or more phonemes in a word	"You can say a word slowly to hear all the sounds [*s-p-e-n-d*]."

PRE-K | GRADE K (early, mid, late) | GRADE 1 (early, mid, late) | GRADE 2 (early, mid, late) | GRADE 3 (early, mid, late)

Phonological Awareness, continued

Principle	Explanation of Principle
Phonemes [PA]	
Hearing and identifying phonemes in a word in sequence	"You can say a word slowly to hear all the sounds, from first to last [/r/ *(first)*, /ʌ/ *(next)*, /n/ *(last)* = *run*]." "You can write the letter or letters for each sound."
Blending three or four phonemes in words	"You can blend sounds together to say a word [*n-e-s-t* = *nest*]."
Deleting phonemes in words	"You can say words without some of the sounds [*can* – *c* = *an*; *sand* – *s* = *and*]." "You can say a word without the first sound [*ch* – *air* = *air*]." "You can say a word without the last sound [*ant* – *t* = *an*]."
Adding phonemes to the end of words	"You can add sounds to the end of a word [*an* + *d* = *and*; *and* + *y* = *Andy*]."
Manipulating phonemes in the middle of words	"You can change the sounds in the middle of a word to make a new word [*hit*, *hot*]."

PRE-K | GRADE K: early, mid, late | GRADE 1: early, mid, late | GRADE 2: early, mid, late | GRADE 3: early, mid, late

Letter Knowledge

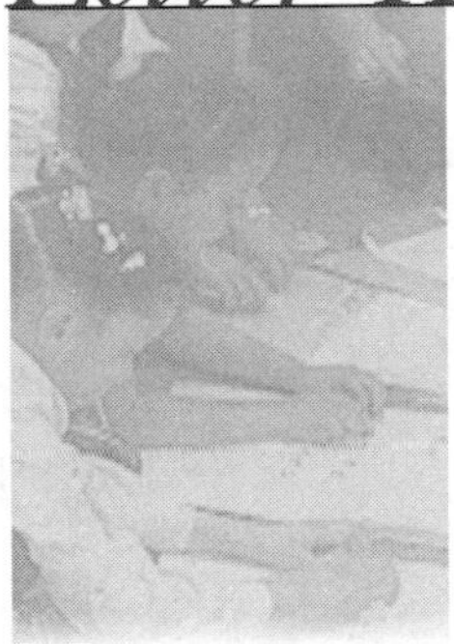

Letter knowledge refers to what children need to learn about the graphic characters that correspond with the sounds of language. A finite set of twenty-six letters, two forms of each, is related to all of the sounds of the English language (approximately forty-four phonemes). The sounds in the language change as dialect, articulation, and other speech factors vary. Children will also encounter alternative forms of some letters—for example, g, g; a, a; y, y—and will eventually learn to recognize letters in cursive writing. Children need to learn the names and purposes of letters, as well as the particular features of each. When children can identify letters by noticing the very small differences that make them unique, they can then associate letters and letter clusters with phonemes and parts of words. Knowing the letter names is useful information that helps children talk about letters and understand what others say about them. As writers, children need to be able to use efficient directional movements when making letters.

LK Letter Knowledge

Letter Knowledge

Identifying Letters

Principle	Explanation of Principle
Understanding the concept of a letter	"The alphabet has twenty-six letters." "A letter has a name and a shape."
Distinguishing letter forms	"Letters are different from each other." "You can notice the parts of letters." "Some letters have long sticks. Some letters have short sticks." "Some letters have curves, circles, tunnels, tails, crosses, dots, slants."
Producing letter names	"You can look at the shape of a letter and say its name."
Categorizing letters by features	"You can find parts of letters that look the same." "You can find the letters that have long sticks [short sticks, curves, circles, tunnels, tails, crosses, dots, slants]."
Understanding alphabetical order	"The letters in the alphabet are in a special order."
Recognizing uppercase and lowercase letters	"A letter has two forms. One form is uppercase (or capital) and the other is lowercase (or small) [*B, b*]." "Your name starts with an uppercase letter." "The other letters in your name are lowercase letters." "Some lowercase forms look like the uppercase forms [*W, w*] and some look different [*R, r*]."
Recognizing consonants and vowels	"Some letters are consonants [*b, c, d, f, g, h, j, k, l, m, n, p, q, r, s, t, v, w, x, y, z*]." "Some letters are vowels [*a, e, i, o, u,* and sometimes *y* and *w*]." "Every word has a vowel."
Understanding special uses of letters	"Your initials are the first letters of your first name and your last name." "You use capital letters to write your initials."

Grade bands: PRE-K | GRADE K (early, mid, late) | GRADE 1 (early, mid, late) | GRADE 2 (early, mid, late) | GRADE 3 (early, mid, late)

Letter Knowledge, continued

	Principle	Explanation of Principle
		PRE-K · GRADE K (early, mid, late) · GRADE 1 (early, mid, late) · GRADE 2 (early, mid, late) · GRADE 3 (early, mid, late)
Recognizing Letters in Words and Sentences	Understanding that words are made up of letters	"Words have letters in them." "Your name has letters in it." "You can say the first letter of your name."
	Making connections between words by recognizing letters	"You can find words that have the same letters in them."
	Recognizing the sequence of letters in words	"Letters in a word are always in the same order." "The first letter is on the left." "You can find the first letter in a word."
	Recognizing letters in words	"You can find letters in words." "You can say the names of letters in words."
	Recognizing letters in continuous text	"You can find letters in sentences and stories."
	Making connections between words by recognizing letter placement	"You can find words that begin with the same letter." "You can find words that end with the same letter." "You can find words that have the same letter in the middle."
Forming Letters	Using efficient and consistent motions to form letters	"You can make the shape of a letter." "You can say words that help you learn how to make a letter." "You can check to see if your letter looks right."
		PRE-K · GRADE K (early, mid, late) · GRADE 1 (early, mid, late) · GRADE 2 (early, mid, late) · GRADE 3 (early, mid, late)

Letter/Sound Relationships

The sounds of oral language are related in both simple and complex ways to the twenty-six letters of the alphabet. Learning the connections between letters and sounds is basic to understanding written language. Children first learn simple relationships that are regular in that one phoneme is connected to one grapheme, or letter. But sounds are also connected to letter clusters, which are groups of letters that appear often together (for example, *cr, str, st, bl, fr*), in which you hear each of the associated sounds of the letters; and consonant digraphs *(sh, ch)*, in which you hear only one sound. Vowels may also appear in combinations *(ea, oa)* in which you usually hear the first vowel *(ai)* or you hear a completely different sound *(ou)*. Children learn to look for and recognize these letter combinations as units, which makes their word solving more efficient. It is important to remember that children will be able to hear and connect the easy-to-identify consonants and vowels early and progress to the harder-to-hear and more difficult letter/sound relationships—for example, letter clusters with two and three letters and those that have more than one sound. You will want to connect initial letter sounds to the Alphabet Linking Chart (see *Teaching Resources*). It is not necessary to teach every letter as a separate lesson. When using the children's names to teach about words, substitute *name* for *word* when explaining the principle.

Letter/Sound Relationships

Consonants

Principle	Explanation of Principle
Recognizing that letters represent consonant sounds	"You can match letters and sounds in words. For example: *b* is the letter that stands for the first sound in *bear.*"
Recognizing and using beginning consonant sounds and the letters that represent them: *s, m, t, b, f, r, n, p, d, h, c, g, j, l, k, v, w, z, qu, y, x*	"You can hear the sound at the beginning of a word." "You can match letters and sounds at the beginning of a word." "When you see a letter at the beginning of a word, you can make its sound." "When you know the sound, you can find the letter." "You can find a word by saying it and thinking about the first sound."
Recognizing similar beginning consonant sounds and the letters that represent them	"Words can start with the same sound and letter [<u>b</u>ox, <u>b</u>ig]."
Recognizing and using ending consonant sounds and the letters that represent them: *b, m, t, d g, n, p, f, l, r, s, z, x, ss, ll, tt, ck*	"You can hear the sounds at the end of a word." "You can match letters and sounds at the end of a word." "When you see a letter at the end of a word, you can make its sound." "When you know the sound, you can find the letter." "You can find a word by saying it and thinking about the ending sound."
Recognizing similar ending consonant sounds and the letters that represent them	"Words can end with the same sound and letter [*duc<u>k</u>, boo<u>k</u>*]."
Recognizing and using middle consonant sounds sometimes represented by double letters: *bb, dd, ll, mm, nn, pp, rr, tt, zz*	"You can hear consonant sounds in the middle of a word." "You can match letters and sounds in the middle of a word." "When you see letters in the middle of a word, you can make their sound." "When you know the sound in the middle of a word, you can find the letter." "Sometimes two consonant letters stand for the consonant sound in the middle of a word." "You can find words by saying the word and thinking about the sound in the middle."

Grade scale: PRE-K | GRADE K (early, mid, late) | GRADE 1 (early, mid, late) | GRADE 2 (early, mid, late) | GRADE 3 (early, mid, late)

	Principle	Explanation of Principle
Consonants	Recognizing and using consonant sounds represented by consonant digraphs: *sh, ch, th, ph* (at the beginning or end of a word), and *wh*	**“Some clusters of consonants stand for one sound that is different from either of the letters. They are called consonant digraphs.”** **“You can hear the sound of a consonant digraph at the beginning or end of a word.”** **“You can match a consonant digraph at the beginning or end of a word with its sound.”** **“You can find words by saying the word and thinking about the sound of the consonant digraph.”**
	Recognizing and using letters that represent two or more consonant sounds at the beginning of a word: *c, g, th, ch*	**“Some consonants make two or more different sounds [*car, city; get, gym; think, they; chair, chorus, chateau*].”**
	Recognizing and using consonant clusters that blend two or three consonant sounds (onsets): *bl, cl, fl, pl, pr, br, dr, gr, tr, cr, fr, gl, sl, sn, sp, st, sw, sc, sk, sm, scr, squ, str, thr, spr, spl, shr, sch, tw*	**“Some consonants go together in clusters.”** **“A group of two or three consonants is a consonant cluster.”** **“You can hear each sound in a consonant cluster.”** **“You can hear and connect consonant clusters at the beginning of words.”** **“You can hear and connect consonant clusters at the end of words.”** **“You can find a word by saying the word and thinking about the first (or ending) sounds.”** **“Knowing a consonant cluster helps you read and write words.”**
	Recognizing and using consonant letters that represent no sound: *lamb, light*	**“Some words have consonant letters that are silent.”**
	Recognizing and using letters that represent consonant clusters at the end of a word: *ct, ft, ld, lp, lt, mp, nd, nk, nt, pt, rd, rk, sk, sp, st*	**“You can hear each sound in a consonant cluster at the end of a word.”** **“You can hear and connect consonant clusters at the end of words.”** **“You can find a word by saying it and thinking about the ending sounds.”** **“Knowing an ending consonant cluster helps you read and write words.”**
	Recognizing and using letters that represent consonant digraph sounds at the end of a word (making one sound): *sh, th, ch, ck, tch, dge, ng, ph, gh*	**“You can hear the sound in a consonant digraph at the end of a word.”** **“You can connect a consonant digraph at the end of a word with its sound.”** **“You can find a word by saying it and thinking about the last sound (consonant digraph).”**
	Recognizing and using letters that represent less frequent consonant digraph sounds at the beginning of a word (making one sound): *gh, gn, kn, ph, wr*	**“You can hear the sound of a consonant digraph at the beginning of a word.”** **“You can connect a consonant digraph at the beginning of a word with its sound.”** **“You can find a word by saying it and thinking about the first sound (consonant digraph).”**
Vowels	Understanding letters that represent consonant sounds or vowel sounds	**“Some letters are consonants and some letters are vowels.”** **“Every word has a vowel.”** **“*A, e i, o,* and *u* are vowels (and sometimes *y* and *w*).”**
	Hearing and identifying short vowel sounds in words and the letters that represent them	**“In some words, *a* sounds like the *a* in *apple* and *can*.”** **“In some words, *e* sounds like the *e* in *egg* and *net*.”** **“In some words, *i* sounds like the *i* in *igloo* and *sit*.”** **“In some words, *o* sounds like the *o* in *octopus* and *hot*.”** **“In some words, *u* sounds like the *u* in *umbrella* and *cup*.”**
	Recognizing and using short vowel sounds at the beginning of words: *at, apple*	**“Some words have one vowel at the beginning [*apple, at, Andrew*].”** **“The sound of the vowel is *short*.”**

PRE-K | GRADE K (early, mid, late) | GRADE 1 (early, mid, late) | GRADE 2 (early, mid, late) | GRADE 3 (early, mid, late)

Letter/Sound Relationships, continued

Vowels

Principle	Explanation of Principle
Recognizing and using short vowel sounds in the middle of words (CVC): *hat, bed*	"Some words have one vowel between two consonants [*hat, bed*] and the sound of the vowel is *short*."
Hearing and identifying long vowel sounds in words and the letters that represent them	"In some words, *a* sounds like the *a* in *name* and *came*." "In some words, e sounds like the *e* in *eat* and *seat*." "In some words, *i* sounds like the *i* in *ice* and *kite*." "In some words, *o* sounds like the *o* in *go* and *boat*." "In some words, *u* sounds like the *u* in *use* and *cute*."
Recognizing and using long vowel sounds in words	"You can hear and say the vowel in words like *make, pail, day*." "You can hear and say the vowel in words like *eat, meat, see*." "You can hear and say the vowel in words like *I, ice, ride*." "You can hear and say the vowel in words like *go, grow, boat*." "You can hear and say the vowel in words like *use, cute, huge*."
Recognizing and using vowels in words with silent *e* (CVC*e*): *make, take, home* A: *make, ate, take, came, same, base* [Exceptions: *are, dance*] E: *Pete, breeze* [Exception: *edge*] I: *bite, bike, five, ice, slime, shine* [Exceptions: *mince fringe*] O: *rode, hole, joke* [Exceptions: *come, some, goose*] U: *use, cube, cute, fume* [Exceptions: *judge, nurse*]	"Some words end in an *e* that is silent and the vowel usually has the long sound (sounds like its name)."
Contrasting long and short vowel sounds in words	"A vowel can have a sound like its name (*a* as in *make*), and this is called a long vowel sound." "A vowel can have a sound that is different from its name (*a* as in *apple*), and this is called a short vowel sound."
Recognizing and using *y* as a vowel sound: *happy, family, my, sky*	"*Y* is a letter that sometimes makes a vowel sound." "*Y* sounds like *e* on the end of words like *happy, funny, family*." "*Y* sounds like *i* in words like *my, sky, by*."
Recognizing and using other vowel sounds: *oo* as in *moon, look; oi* as in *oil; oy* as in *boy; ou* as in *house; ow* as in *cow; aw* as in *paw*	"Some letters go together and make other vowel sounds [*moon, oil, boy, oil, house, cow, paw*]."
Recognizing and using letter combinations that represent long vowel sounds: *ai, ay, ee, ea, oa, ow, ie, ei*	"Some vowels go together in words and make one sound." "When there are two vowels [*ai, ay, ee, ea, oa, ow*], they usually make the sound of the name of the first vowel [*rain, day, meat, seat, snow*]."
Recognizing and using vowel sounds in open syllables: (CV): *ho-tel*	"Some syllables have a consonant followed by a vowel." "The sound of the vowel is long [*ho-tel, Pe-ter, lo-cal*]."
Recognizing and using vowel sounds in closed syllables: (CVC): *lem-on*	"Some syllables have a vowel that is surrounded by two consonants." "The sound of the vowel is short [*lem-on; cab-in*]."
Recognizing and using vowel sounds with *r*: *car, first, hurt, her, corn*	"When vowels are with *r* in words, you blend the vowel sound with *r* [*car, her, fir, corn, hurt*]."

PRE-K | GRADE K (early, mid, late) | GRADE 1 (early, mid, late) | GRADE 2 (early, mid, late) | GRADE 3 (early, mid, late)

Spelling Patterns

Phonograms are spelling patterns that represent the sounds of *rimes* (last parts of words). They are sometimes called *word families.* You will not need to teach children the technical word *phonogram,* although you may want to use *pattern* or *word part.* A phonogram is the same as a rime, or ending of a word or syllable. We have included a large list of phonograms that will be useful to primary-age children in reading or writing, but you will not need to teach every phonogram separately. Once children understand that there are patterns and learn how to look for patterns, they will quickly discover more for themselves.

Another way to look at phonograms is to examine the way simple words and syllables are put together. Here we include the consonant-vowel-consonant (CVC) pattern in which the vowel often has a short, or terse, sound; the consonant-vowel-consonant-silent *e* (CVC*e*) pattern in which the vowel usually has a long, or lax, sound; and the consonant-vowel-vowel-consonant (CVVC) pattern in which the vowel combination may have either one or two sounds.

Knowing spelling patterns helps children notice and use larger parts of words, thus making word solving faster and more efficient. Patterns are also helpful to children in writing words because they will quickly write down the patterns rather than laboriously work with individual sounds and letters. Finally, knowing to look for patterns and remembering them help children make the connections between words that make word solving easier. The thirty-nine most common phonograms are marked with an asterisk.

Spelling Patterns

PRINCIPLE	EXPLANATION OF PRINCIPLE PRE-K · GRADE K (early, mid, late) · GRADE 1 (early, mid, late) · GRADE 2 (early, mid, late) · GRADE 3 (early, mid, late)
Recognizing that words have letter patterns that are connected to sounds (phonograms are spelling patterns)	**" Some words have parts [patterns] that are the same. "** **" You can find patterns [parts] that are the same in many words. "**
Recognizing and using the consonant-vowel-consonant (CVC) pattern	**" Some words have a consonant, a vowel, and then another consonant. The vowel sounds like the *a* in *apple* [*i* in *igloo, o* in *octopus, e* in *egg, u* in *umbrella*]. "**
Recognizing and using simple phonograms with a VC pattern (easiest): *-ad, -ag, -am, -an*, -at*, -ed, -en, -et, -ig, -in*, -it*, -og, -op*, -ot*, -ut*	**" You can look at the pattern [part] you know to help you read a word. "** **" You can use the pattern [part] you know to help you write a word. "** **" You can make new words by putting a letter or letter cluster before the word part or pattern. "**
Recognizing and using more difficult phonograms with a VC pattern: *-ab, -ap*, - ar, -aw*, -ay*, -eg, -em, -ib, -ip*, -ix, -ob, -od, -ow (blow), -ow (cow), -ug*, -um, -un*	**" You can look at the pattern [part] you know to help you read a word. "** **" You can use the pattern [part] you know to help you write a word. "** **" You can make new words by putting a letter or letter cluster before the word part or pattern. "**
Recognizing and using phonograms with a vowel-consonant-silent *e* (VC*e*) pattern: *-ace, -ade, -age, -ake*, -ale*, -ame*, -ane, -ape, -ate*, -ice*, -ide*, ike, -ile, -ime, -ine*, -ite, -ive, -obe, -oke*, -ope, -ore**	**" Some words have a vowel, a consonant, and a silent *e*. The vowel sound is usually the name of the vowel [*a* in *make, e in Pete, i* in *ride, o* in *rode, u* in *cute*]. "**
	PRE-K · GRADE K (early, mid, late) · GRADE 1 (early, mid, late) · GRADE 2 (early, mid, late) · GRADE 3 (early, mid, late)

* Indicates most common phonograms.

Spelling Patterns, continued

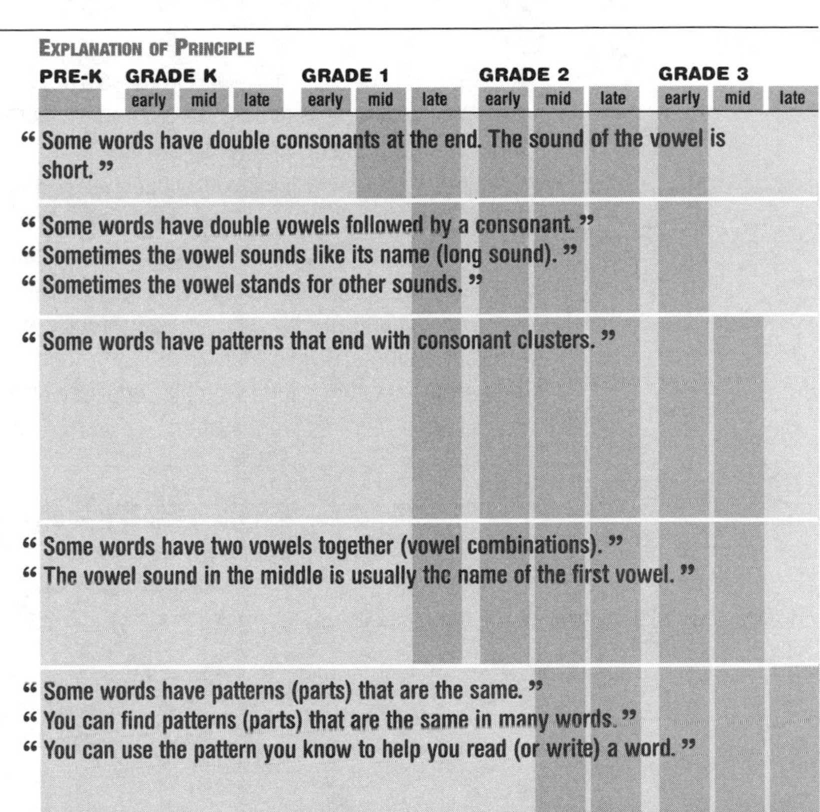

Principle	Explanation of Principle
Recognizing and using phonograms that end with double letters (VCC): *-all, -ell*, -ill*, oll, -uff*	"Some words have double consonants at the end. The sound of the vowel is short."
Recognizing and using phonograms with double vowels (VVC): *-eek, -eel, -eem, -een, -eep, -eer, -eet, -ood, -ook, -ool, -oom, -oon*	"Some words have double vowels followed by a consonant." "Sometimes the vowel sounds like its name (long sound)." "Sometimes the vowel stands for other sounds."
Recognizing and using phonograms with ending consonant clusters (VCC): *-ack*, -act, -alk; -amp, -and, -ank*, -ant, -ard, -ark, -arm, -art, -ash*, -ask, -ath, -aw*, -eck, -elp, -elt, -end, -ent, -esh, -est*, -ick*, -ift, -igh, -ing*, -ink*, -ish, -ock*, -old, -ong, -uck*, -ump*, -ung, -unk*, -ush*	"Some words have patterns that end with consonant clusters."
Recognizing and using phonograms with vowel combinations (VVC): *-aid, -ail*, -ain*, air, -ait, -aw, -ay*, -ea, -ead, -eak, -eam, -ean, -eap, -ear, -eat*, -oad, -oak*	"Some words have two vowels together (vowel combinations)." "The vowel sound in the middle is usually thc name of the first vowel."
Recognizing and using more difficult phonograms (VVCC, VVC*e*, VCC*e*, VCCC, VVCCC): *-aint, -aise, -ance, -anch, -arge, -aste, -atch, -each, -ealth, -east, -eath, -eave, -edge, -eech, -eeze, -eight, -ench, -ight*, -itch, -ooth, -ouch, -ound, -udge, -unch*	"Some words have patterns (parts) that are the same." "You can find patterns (parts) that are the same in many words." "You can use the pattern you know to help you read (or write) a word."

SP
Spelling Patterns

High Frequency Words

A core of known high frequency words is a valuable resource as children build their reading and writing processes. Young children notice words that appear frequently in the simple texts they read; eventually, their recognition of these words becomes automatic. In this way, their reading becomes more efficient, enabling them to decode words using phonics as well as attend to comprehension. These words are powerful examples that help them grasp that a word is always written the same way. They can use known high frequency words to check on the accuracy of their reading and as resources for solving other words (for example, *this* starts like *the*). In general, children learn the simpler words earlier and in the process develop efficient systems for learning words. They continuously add to the core of high frequency words they know. Lessons on high frequency words help them look more carefully at words and develop more efficient systems for word recognition.

High Frequency Words

PRINCIPLE	EXPLANATION OF PRINCIPLE
	PRE-K · GRADE K (early, mid, late) · GRADE 1 (early, mid, late) · GRADE 2 (early, mid, late) · GRADE 3 (early, mid, late)
Recognizing and using high frequency words with one or two letters	**"You see some words many times when you read: *I, is, in, at, my, we, to, me, am, an.*"** **"Some have only one letter: *I* and *a.*"** **"Some have two letters: *am, an, as, at, be, by, do, go, he, in, is, it, me, my, of, on, or, so, to, up, us, we.*"** **"Words you see a lot are important because they help you read and write."**
Locating and reading high frequency words in continuous text	**"When you know a word, you can read it every time you see it."** **"You can find a word by knowing how it looks."**
Recognizing and using high frequency words with three or four letters	**"You see some words many times when you read."** **"Some have three or four letters: *the, and, but, she, like, come, this.*"** **"Words you see a lot are important because they help you read and write."**
Recognizing and using high frequency words with five or more letters	**"You see some words many times when you read."** **"Some have five or more letters: *would, could, where, there, which.*"** **"Words you see a lot are important because they help you read and write."**
	PRE-K · GRADE K (early, mid, late) · GRADE 1 (early, mid, late) · GRADE 2 (early, mid, late) · GRADE 3 (early, mid, late)

Word Meaning

Children need to know the meaning of the words they are learning to read and write. It is important for them constantly to expand their vocabulary as well as develop a more complex understanding of words they already know. Word meaning is related to the development of vocabulary—labels, concept words, synonyms, antonyms, and homonyms. Concept words such as numbers and days of the week are often used in the texts they read, and they will want to use these words in their own writing. When children learn concept words (color words are another example), they can form categories that help in retrieving them when needed. In our complex language, meaning and spelling are intricately connected.

Often you must know the meaning of the word you want to spell or read before you can spell it accurately. In addition to lists of common concept words that children are often expected to know how to read and spell, we include synonyms, antonyms, and homonyms, which may be homographs (same spelling, different meaning and sometimes different pronunciation) or homophones (same sound, different spelling). Knowing synonyms and antonyms will help children build more powerful systems for connecting and categorizing words; it will also help them comprehend texts better and write in a more interesting way. Being able to distinguish between homographs and homophones assists in comprehension and helps spellers to avoid mistakes.

Word Meaning

PRE-K | GRADE K (early, mid, late) | GRADE 1 (early, mid, late) | GRADE 2 (early, mid, late) | GRADE 3 (early, mid, late)

Principle	Explanation of Principle
Recognizing and learning concept words: color names, number words, days of the week, months of the year	"A color (number, day, month) has a name." "Days of the week have names and are always in the same order." "Months of the year have names and are always in the same order." "You can read and write the names of colors (numbers, days, months)." "You can find the names of colors (numbers, days, months)."
Recognizing and using words that are related	"Some words go together because of what they mean: *mother–father; sister–brother;* clothing; animals; food."
Recognizing and using synonyms (words that mean about the same)	"Some words mean about the same and are called synonyms: *begin/start, close/shut, fix/mend, earth/world, happy/glad, high/tall, jump/leap, keep/save, large/big.*"
Recognizing and using antonyms (words that mean the opposite)	"Some words mean about the opposite and are called antonyms: *hot/cold, all/none, break/fix, little/big, long/short, sad/glad, stop/start.*"
Recognizing and using homophones (same sound, different spelling and meaning). (It is not necessary to teach children the technical term *homophone.*)	"Some words sound the same but look different and have different meanings: *to/too/two; there/their/they're; hare/hair; blue/blew.*"
Recognizing and using homographs (same spelling, different meaning and may have different pronunciation—heteronym). (It is not necessary to teach children the technical term *homograph or heteronym.*)	"Some words look the same, have a different meaning, and may sound different: *bat/bat, well/well; read/read; wind/wind.*"
Recognizing and using words with multiple meanings (a form of homograph)	"Some words are spelled the same but have more than one meaning: *beat, run, play.*"

PRE-K | GRADE K (early, mid, late) | GRADE 1 (early, mid, late) | GRADE 2 (early, mid, late) | GRADE 3 (early, mid, late)

Word Structure

Looking at the structure of words will help children learn how words are related to each other and how they can be changed by adding letters, letter clusters, and larger word parts. Being able to recognize syllables, for example, helps children break down words into smaller units that are easier to analyze. In phonological awareness lessons, children learn to recognize word breaks and to identify the number of syllables in a word. They can build on this useful information in reading and writing.

Words often have affixes, parts added before or after a word to change its meaning. An affix can be a prefix or a suffix. The word to which affixes are added can be a *base* word or a *root* word. A base word is a complete word; a root word is a part with Greek or Latin origins (such as *phon* in *telephone*). It will not be necessary for young children to make this distinction when they are beginning to learn about simple affixes, but working with suffixes and prefixes will help children read and understand words that use them as well as use affixes accurately in writing.

Endings or word parts that are added to base words signal meaning. For example, they may signal relationships *(prettier, prettiest)* or time *(running, planted)*. Principles related to word structure include understanding the meaning and structure of compound words, contractions, plurals, and possessives as well as knowing how to make and use them accurately. We have also included the simple abbreviations that children often see in the books they read and want to use in their writing.

Word Structure

PRE-K | GRADE K (early, mid, late) | GRADE 1 (early, mid, late) | GRADE 2 (early, mid, late) | GRADE 3 (early, mid, late)

Syllables

Principle	Explanation of Principle
Understanding the concept of syllable	**"You can hear the syllables in words."** **"You can look at the syllables to read a word."**
Recognizing and using one or two syllables in words	**"You can look at the syllables in a word to read it [*horse, a-way, farm-er, morn-ing*]."**
Understanding how vowels appear in syllables	**"Every syllable of a word has a vowel."**
Recognizing and using three or more syllables in words	**"You can look at the syllables in a word to read it [*bi-cy-cle, to-geth-er, ev-er-y, won-der-ful, li-brar-y, com-put-er, au-to-mo-bile, a-quar-i-um, un-der-wat-er*]."**
Recognizing and using syllables in words with double consonants	**"Divide the syllables between the consonants when a word has two consonants in the middle [*run-ning, bet-ter*]."**
Recognizing and using syllables ending in a vowel (open syllable)	**"When a syllable ends with a vowel, the vowel sound is usually long [*ho-tel*]."**
Recognizing and using syllables ending in a vowel and at least one consonant (closed syllable)	**"When a syllable ends with a vowel and at least one consonant, the vowel sound is usually short [*lem-on*]."**
Recognizing and using syllables with a vowel and silent *e*	**"When a vowel and silent *e* are in a word, the pattern makes one syllable with a long vowel sound [*hope-ful*]."**

early mid late early mid late early mid late early mid late
PRE-K GRADE K GRADE 1 GRADE 2 GRADE 3

Word Structure, continued

	Principle	Explanation of Principle
Syllables	Recognizing and using syllables with vowel combinations	"When vowel combinations are in words, they usually go together in the same syllable [poi-son, cray-on, ex-plain]."
	Recognizing and using syllables with a vowel and *r*	"When a vowel is followed by *r*, the *r* and the vowel form a syllable [*corn-er, cir-cus*]."
	Recognizing and using syllables made of a consonant and *le*	"When *le* is at the end of a word and preceded by a consonant, the consonant and *le* form a syllable [*ta-ble*]."
Compound Words	Recognizing and understanding simple compound words: *into, itself, myself, cannot, inside, maybe, nobody, outside, sunshine, today, together, upset, yourself, without, sometimes, something*	"Some words are made up of two words put together and are called compound words." "You can read compound words by looking at the two words in them."
	Recognizing and understanding more complex compound words: *airplane, airport, another, anyone, anybody, anything, everyone, homesick, indoor, jellyfish, skyscraper, toothbrush, underground, whenever*	"Some words are made up of two words put together and are called compound words." "You can read compound words by looking at the two words in them."
Contractions	Understanding the concept of contractions	"A contraction is one word made from two words [*can + not = can't*]. A letter or letters are left out and an apostrophe is put in." "A contraction is a short form of the two words."
	Recognizing and understanding contractions with am: *I'm*	"To make a contraction, put two words together and leave out a letter or letters. Write an apostrophe where letter(s) are left out. Here is a contraction made with *I + am: I'm*."
	Recognizing and understanding contractions with is: *here's, he's, it's, she's, that's, there's, what's, where's, who's*	"To make a contraction, put two words together and leave out a letter or letters. Write an apostrophe where the letter(s) are left out." "Many contractions are made with is: *here + is = here's*."
	Recognizing and understanding contractions using will: *I'll, it'll, he'll, she'll, that'll, they'll, we'll, you'll*	"To make a contraction, put two words together and leave out a letter or letters. Write an apostrophe where the letter(s) are left out." "Many contractions are made with will: *I + will = I'll*."
	Recognizing and understanding contractions with not: *aren't, can't, couldn't, didn't, doesn't, don't, hadn't, hasn't, haven't, isn't, mustn't, needn't, shouldn't, wouldn't*	"To make a contraction, put two words together and leave out a letter or letters. Write an apostrophe where the letter(s) are left out." "Many contractions are made with not: *can + not = can't*."
	Recognizing and understanding contractions with are: *they're, we're, you're*	"To make a contraction, put two words together and leave out a letter or letters. Write an apostrophe where the letter(s) are left out." "Many contractions are made with are: *they + are = they're*."
	Recognizing and understanding contractions with have: *could've, I've, might've, should've, they've, we've, would've, you've*	"To make a contraction, put two words together and leave out a letter or letters. Write an apostrophe where the letter(s) are left out." "Many contractions are made with have: *should + have = should've*."

PRE-K | GRADE K (early, mid, late) | GRADE 1 (early, mid, late) | GRADE 2 (early, mid, late) | GRADE 3 (early, mid, late)

Word Structure, continued

Principle	Explanation of Principle
Contractions	
Recognizing and understanding contractions with is or has: *he's, it's, she's, that's, there's, what's, where's, who's*	"To make a contraction, put two words together and leave out a letter or letters. Write an apostrophe where the letter(s) are left out." "Many contractions are made with is and/or has: *he + is = he's* [*He's going to the zoo*]; *he + has = he's* [*He's finished his work*]."
Recognizing and understanding contractions with would or had: *I'd, it'd, she'd, there'd, they'd, we'd, you'd*	"To make a contraction, put two words together and leave out a letter or letters. Write an apostrophe where the letter(s) are left out." "Many contractions are made with would or had: *she + would = she'd; they + would = they'd.*"
Recognizing and understanding contractions with us: *let's*	"To make a contraction, put two words together and leave out a letter or letters. Write an apostrophe where the letter(s) are left out." "Many contractions are made with us: *let + us = let's* [*Let's go*]."
Plurals	
Understanding the concept of plural	"Plural means more than one."
Recognizing and using plurals that add *s: dogs, cats, apples, cans, desks, faces, trees, monkeys*	"Add *s* to some words to show you mean more than one [make them plural]." "You can hear the *s* at the end."
Recognizing and using plurals that add *es* when words end with *x, ch, sh, s, ss, tch, zz: buzzes, branches, buses, boxes, dishes, kisses, patches, peaches, quizzes*	"Add *es* to words that end with *x, ch, sh, s, ss, tch,* or *zz* to make them plural." "The *s* at the end sounds like /z/."
Recognizing and using plurals that change the spelling of the word: *child/children, foot/feet, goose/geese, man/men, mouse/mice, ox/oxen, woman/women*	"Change the spelling of some words to make them plural."
Recognizing and using plurals that add *s* to words that end in a vowel and *y: boys, days, keys, plays, valleys*	"Add *s* to words that end in a vowel and *y* to make them plural."
Recognizing and using plurals that add *ies* to words that end in a consonant and *y: babies, candies, cities, countries, families, flies, ladies, ponies, skies, stories*	"Change the *y* to *i* and add *es* to words that end in a consonant and *y* to make them plural."
Recognizing and using plurals that change *f* to *v* and add *es* for words that end with *f, fe,* or *lf: wolves, hooves, lives, scarves, selves, shelves, wives*	"Change *f* to *v* and add *es* to words that end with *f, fe,* or *lf* to make them plural."
Recognizing and using plurals for words that end in a consonant and *o* by adding *es: heroes, potatoes, volcanoes, zeroes*	"Add *es* to words that end in a consonant and *o* to make them plural."
Recognizing and using plurals for words that end in a vowel and *o* by adding *s: kangaroos, radios, rodeos*	"Add *s* to words that end in a vowel and *o* to make them plural."
Recognizing and using plurals that are the same word for singular and plural: *deer, lamb, moose, sheep*	"Some words are spelled the same in both the singular and plural forms."

PRE-K | GRADE K (early, mid, late) | GRADE 1 (early, mid, late) | GRADE 2 (early, mid, late) | GRADE 3 (early, mid, late)

Word Structure, continued

PRINCIPLE	EXPLANATION OF PRINCIPLE
Verb Endings — Recognizing and using endings that add *s* to a verb to make it agree with the subject: *skate/skates; run/runs*	**“Add *s* to the end of a word to make it sound right in a sentence.” “She can *run.*” “She *runs.*” “She can *skate.*” “She *skates.*”**
Recognizing and using endings that add *ing* to a verb to denote the present participle: *play/playing; send/sending*	**“Add *ing* to a base word to show you are doing something now.” “I can *read.*” “I am *reading.*” “She can *jump.*” “She is *jumping.*”**
Recognizing and using endings that add *ed* to a verb to make it past tense: *walk/walked; play/played; want/wanted*	**“Add *ed* to the end of a word to show that you did something in the past.” “I can *play* a game today.” “I *played* a game yesterday.” “I *want* to play.” “I *wanted* to play.”**
Recognizing and using endings that add a *d* to a verb ending in silent *e* to make it past tense: *like/liked*	**“Add *d* to words ending in silent *e* to make the *ed* ending and show it was in the past.” “I *like* vanilla ice cream.” “I *liked* vanilla ice cream, but I don't anymore.”**
Recognizing and using endings that add *ing* to words that end in a single vowel and consonant to denote the present participle: *run/running; bat/batting; sit/sitting*	**“Double the consonant and add *ing* to words ending in a single vowel and consonant.” “I can *run.*” “I am *running.*”**
Recognizing and using endings that add *ing* to words ending in silent *e* to denote the present participle: *come/coming; write/writing; bite/biting*	**“Drop the *e* and add *ing* to most words that end with silent *e.*” “Will she *come?*” “She is *coming.*” “I can *write.*” “I am *writing.*”**
Recognizing and using endings that add *ing* to words that end in *y* to denote the present participle: *carry/carrying; marry/marrying*	**“Add *ing* to words that end in *y.*” “I can *carry* the flag.” “I am *carrying* the flag.”**
Recognizing that *ed* added to a word to make it past tense can sound several different ways	**“When you add *ed* to a word, sometimes it sounds like */d/*: *grabbed, played, yelled.*” “When you add *ed* to a word, sometimes it sounds like */ed/* (short *e* plus the /d/ sound): *added, landed, melted.*” “When you add *ed* to a word, sometimes it sounds like */t/*: *dressed, liked, talked, laughed, walked.*” “Sometimes you change the *y* to *i* and add *ed* and the ending sounds like /d/: *cried, fried, carried.*”**

PRE-K | GRADE K (early, mid, late) | GRADE 1 (early, mid, late) | GRADE 2 (early, mid, late) | GRADE 3 (early, mid, late)

Word Structure, continued

Principle	Explanation of Principle
Verb Endings	
Recognizing and using endings that add *es* to a verb: *cry/cries; try/tries; carry/carries*	"You can add endings to a word to make it sound right in a sentence." "Change the *y* to *i* and add *es* to words that end in a consonant and *y*." "I can *carry* the flag." "She *carries* the flag."
Recognizing and using endings that add *es* or *ed* to verbs ending in a consonant and *y* to form present or past tense: *cry/cries/cried; try/tries/tried*	"You can add word parts to the end of a word to show you did something in the present or in the past." "Change the *y* to *i* and add *es* or *ed* to words that end in a consonant and *y*." "I can *try* to run fast." "He *tries* to run fast." "We *tried* to run fast in the race yesterday."
Recognizing and using endings that add *ed* to verbs ending in a single short vowel and consonant or a vowel and double consonant to make it past tense: *grab/grabbed; grill/grilled; yell/yelled*	"You add word parts to the endings of words to show you did something in the past." "Double the consonant before adding *ed* to words ending in a short vowel and one consonant. Add *ed* if the word ends with a vowel and a double consonant." "She can *yell* loud." "She *yelled*, 'Run!'" "Mom can *grill* the hot dogs." "Mom *grilled* the hot dogs." "*Grab* the end of the rope." "She *grabbed* the end of the rope."
Recognizing and using endings that add *er* to a verb to make it a noun: *read/reader; play/player; jump/jumper*	"Add *er* to a word to talk about a person who can do something." "John can *read*." "John is a *reader*."
Recognizing and using endings that add *er* to a verb that ends with a short vowel and a consonant: *dig/digger; run/runner*	"Double the consonant and add *er* to words ending in a short vowel and one consonant." "Sarah can *run*." "Sarah is a *runner*."
Recognizing and using endings that add *r* to a verb that ends in silent *e: bake/baker; hike/hiker*	"Add *r* to words that end in silent *e* to make the *er* ending." "I like to hike." "I am a *hiker*."
Recognizing and using endings that add *er* to a verb that ends in *y: carry/carrier*	"Change the *y* to *i* and add *er* to words that end in *y*." "He can *carry* the mail." "He is a mail *carrier*."

Grade-level bands: PRE-K; GRADE K (early, mid, late); GRADE 1 (early, mid, late); GRADE 2 (early, mid, late); GRADE 3 (early, mid, late)

Word Structure, continued

Principle	Explanation of Principle
Adjectives—Comparatives and Superlatives	
Recognizing and using endings that show comparison *(er, est): cold/colder; hard/harder; dark/darker; fast/faster; tall/taller; rich/richest; thin/thinner/thinnest*	" Add *er* or *est* to show how one thing compares with another. " " John can run *fast,* but Monica can run *faster.* " " Carrie is the *fastest* runner in the class. "
Recognizing and using endings that show comparison for words ending in *e: pale/paler/palest; ripe/riper/ripest; cute/cuter/cutest*	" Add *r* or *st* to words that end in silent *e* to make the *er* or *est* ending. " " Jolisa has a *cute* puppy. " " Matthew has a *cuter* puppy. " " Jaqual has the *cutest* puppy. "
Recognizing and using endings that show comparison for words ending in a short vowel and a consonant	" Double the consonant and add *er* or *est* to words that end in a short vowel and one consonant. " " The red box is big. " " The blue box is bigger. " " The green box is biggest. "
Recognizing and using endings that show comparison for words ending in *y: scary/scarier/scariest; funny/funnier/funniest*	" Change *y* to *i* and add *er* or *est* to words that end in *y.* " " Ciera told a *funny* story. " " Kyle's story was *funnier* than Ciera's. " " Amanda told the *funniest* story of all. "
Prefixes	
Recognizing and using common prefixes (*re* meaning *again*): *make/remake; tie/retie*	" Add a word part or prefix to the beginning of a word to change its meaning. " " Add *re* to mean *do again.* " " I *made* the bed and took a nap. I had to *remake* the bed. "
Recognizing and using common prefixes (*un* meaning *not* or *the opposite of*): *do/undo; tie/untie; known/unknown; believable/unbelievable*	" Add a word part or prefix to the beginning of a word to change its meaning. " " Add *un* to the beginning of a word to mean *not* or *the opposite of.* " " I don't *believe* it. That is *unbelievable.* " " I *tied* my shoes and then they came *untied.* "
Recognizing and using more complex prefixes (*im, in, il, dis* [meaning *not*]): *possible/impossible; valid/invalid; like/dislike*	" Add a word part or prefix to the beginning of a word to change its meaning. " " Add *im, in, il,* or *dis* to the beginning of words to mean *not.* " " That is not *possible.* It is *impossible.* " " We cannot *cure* the disease. It is *incurable.* " " It is not *legal.* It is *illegal.* " " I do not *like* broccoli. I *dislike* broccoli. "
Possessives	
Recognizing and using possessives that add an apostrophe and an *s* to a singular noun: *dog/dog's; woman/woman's, girl/girl's, boy/boy's*	" A person, animal, place, or thing can own something. To show ownership, you add *'s* to a word. " " The collar belongs to the *dog.* It is the *dog's* collar. " " The ball belongs to the *girl.* It is the *girl's* ball. " " The *book* has a cover. It is the *book's* cover. "
Recognizing and using possessives for words that end in *s: dogs' dishes, pigs' houses, Marcus' papers, Charles' lunch box*	" If a word already ends in s, just add an apostrophe to show ownership. " " Those balls belong to the *boys.* They are the *boys'* balls. " " Here is *Marcus'* lunch box. It belongs to *Marcus.* " " The *girls* are getting the jump ropes. The ropes belong to the *girls.* They are the *girls'* jump ropes. "
Abbreviations	
Recognizing and using common abbreviations: Mrs., Ms., Mr., Dr., St., Ave., Rd., months of the year, days of the week	" Some words are made shorter by using some of the letters and a period. " " They are called abbreviations. "

PRE-K | GRADE K (early, mid, late) | GRADE 1 (early, mid, late) | GRADE 2 (early, mid, late) | GRADE 3 (early, mid, late)

WS Word Structure

Word-Solving Actions

Word-solving actions are the strategic moves readers and writers make when they use their knowledge of the language system to solve words. These strategies are "in-the-head" actions that are invisible, although we can infer them from some overt behavior. The principles listed in this section represent children's ability to *use* the principles in all previous sections of the Continuum.

All lessons related to the Continuum provide opportunities for children to apply principles in active ways; for example, through sorting, building, locating, reading, or writing. Lessons related to word-solving actions demonstrate to children how they can problem-solve by working on words in isolation or while reading or writing continuous text. The more children can integrate these strategies into their reading and writing systems, the more flexible they will become in solving words. The reader/writer may use knowledge of letter/sound relationships, for example, either to solve an unfamiliar word or to check that the reading is accurate. Rapid, automatic word solving is a basic component of fluency and important for comprehension because it frees children's attention to focus on the meaning and language of the text.

Word-Solving Actions

Principle	Explanation of Principle PRE-K · GRADE K (early, mid, late) · GRADE 1 (early, mid, late) · GRADE 2 (early, mid, late) · GRADE 3 (early, mid, late)
Recognizing and locating words (names)	"You can find your name by looking for the letters in it."
Making connections between names and other words	"You can find the letters that are in your name in other words." "You can connect your name with other names [<u>M</u>ark, <u>M</u>aria]." "You can connect your name with other words [<u>Ma</u>rk, <u>ma</u>ke]."
Using the letters in names to read and write words: *Chuck, chair*	"You can connect your name with the words you want to spell or read."
Using known words to monitor reading and spelling	"You can use words you know to check on your reading."
Using first and last names to read and write words	"You can think of the first and last names you know to help you read and spell words [*Angela, Andy*]."
Recognizing and spelling known words quickly	"You can read (or write) a word quickly when you know how it looks [*the*]." "When you know how to read some words quickly, it helps you read fast." "When you know how to write some words quickly, it helps you write fast."
Using letter/sound knowledge to monitor reading and spelling accuracy	"You can use what you know about letters and sounds to check on your reading (and writing)."
Using parts of known words that are like other words: *my/sky; tree/try; she/shut*	"You can use parts of words you know to read or write new words."
Using what you know about a word to solve an unknown word: *her, mother*	"You can use what you know about words to read new words."

PRE-K · GRADE K (early, mid, late) · GRADE 1 (early, mid, late) · GRADE 2 (early, mid, late) · GRADE 3 (early, mid, late)

Word-Solving Actions, continued

Taking Words Apart to Solve Them

Principle	Explanation of Principle (PRE-K · GRADE K · GRADE 1 · GRADE 2 · GRADE 3; early · mid · late)
Saying words slowly to hear sounds in sequence	"You can say words slowly to hear the sounds." "You can hear the sounds at the beginning, middle, or end of a word." "You can write the letters for the sounds you can hear." "You can say words slowly to hear the sounds from left to right."
Changing beginning letters to make new words: *sit/hit; day/play*	"You can change the first letter or letters of a word to make a new word."
Listening for sounds to write letters in words	"You can say words slowly to hear the sounds." "Hearing and saying the sounds help you write words."
Changing ending letters to make new words: *car/can/cat*	"You can change the last letter or letters of a word to make a new word."
Changing middle letters to make new words: *hit/hot; sheet/shirt*	"You can change the middle letter or letters of a word to make a new word."
Using letter/sound analysis from left to right to read a word	"You can read words by looking at the letters and thinking about the sounds from left to right."
Learning to notice the letter sequence to spell a word accurately	"You can make a word several times to learn the sequence of letters."
Studying features of words to remember the spelling	"You can look at a word, say it, cover it, write it, and check it to help you learn to spell it correctly."
Noticing and correcting spelling errors	"You can write a word, look at it, and try again to make it 'look right.'" "You can notice and think about the parts of words that are tricky for you." "You can write words to see if you know them."
Noticing and using word parts (onsets and rimes) to read a word: *br-ing*	"You can use word parts to solve a word." "You can look at the first and last parts of a word to read it."
Changing the onset or rime to make a new word: *bring/thing; bring/brown*	"You can change the first part or the last part to make a new word."
Adding letters to the beginning or end of a word to make a new word: *in/win; bat/bats; the/then*	"You can add letters to the beginning of a word to make a new word." "You can add letters to the end of a word to make a new word."
Adding letter clusters to the beginning or end of a word to make a new word: *an/plan; cat/catch*	"You can add letter clusters to the beginning or end of a word to make a new word."
Removing letters or letter clusters from the beginning of words: *sit/it; stand/and; his/is*	"You can take away letters from the beginning of a word to make a new word."
Removing letters from the end of a word to make a new word: *and/an; Andy/and; kite/kit*	"You can take away letters from the end of a word to make a new word."

WSA Word Solving Actions

Word-Solving Actions, continued

PRE-K | GRADE K (early, mid, late) | GRADE 1 (early, mid, late) | GRADE 2 (early, mid, late) | GRADE 3 (early, mid, late)

Principle	Explanation of Principle
Taking Words Apart to Solve Them	
Recognizing and using word parts (onsets, rimes) to read a word: *br-ing, cl-ap*	"You can notice and use word parts to read (or write) a new word." "You can look at the first part and last part to read a word."
Taking apart compound words or joining words to make compound words: *into, sidewalk, sideways*	"You can read compound words by finding the two smaller words." "You can write compound words by joining two smaller words."
Removing letter clusters from the end of a word to make a new word: *catch/cat*	"You can take away letter clusters from the end of a word to make a new word."
Removing the ending from a base word to make a new word: *sit/sits/sitting; big/bigger/biggest*	"You can take off the ending to help you read a word."
Breaking down a longer word into syllables in order to decode manageable units: *for-got-ten*	"You can divide a word into syllables to read it."
Making Connections Between and among Words to Solve Them	
Connecting words that mean the same or almost the same: *wet/damp*	"You think about the words that mean almost the same."
Connecting words that start the same: *tree/tray*	"You can connect the beginning of a word with a word you know."
Connecting words that end the same: *candy/happy*	"You can connect the ending of the word with a word you know."
Connecting words that have the same pattern: *light/night; running/sitting*	"You can connect words that have the same letter patterns."
Connecting words that sound the same but look different and have different meanings: *blew/blue*	"You can read words by noticing that they sound the same but look different and have different meanings."
Connecting words that rhyme: *fair/chair*	"You can think about words that rhyme."
Connecting words that look the same but sometimes sound different and have different meanings: *read/read*	"You can read words by remembering that some words look the same but sometimes sound different and have different meanings."
Connecting and comparing word patterns that look the same but sound different: *dear/bear*	"You can read words by remembering that some words have parts or patterns that look the same but sound different."
Connecting and comparing word patterns that sound the same but look different: *said/bed*	"You can read words by remembering that some words have parts or patterns that sound the same but look different."

PRE-K | GRADE K (early, mid, late) | GRADE 1 (early, mid, late) | GRADE 2 (early, mid, late) | GRADE 3 (early, mid, late)

Early Literacy Concepts

Learning about literacy begins long before children enter school. Many children hear stories read aloud and try out writing for themselves; through such experiences, they learn some basic concepts about written language. Nearly all children begin to notice print in the environment and develop ideas about the purposes of print. The child's name, for example, is a very important word. Kindergartners and first graders are still acquiring some of these basic concepts, and they need to generalize and systematize their knowledge. In the classroom, they learn a great deal through experiences such as shared and modeled reading and shared and interactive writing. Explicit teaching can help children learn much more about these early concepts, understand their importance, and develop ways of using them in reading and writing.

Connect to Assessment

See related ELC Assessment Tasks in the Assessment Guide in *Teaching Resources:*

- Name Writing
- Name Locating 1
- Name Locating 2
- Word Location
- Word-by Word Matching
- Letter and Punctuation Locating
- First and Last

Develop Your Professional Understanding

See *Word Matters: Teaching Phonics and Spelling in the Reading/Writing Classroom* by G.S. Pinnell and I.C. Fountas. 1998. Portsmouth, New Hampshire: Heinemann.

Related pages: 5, 8–10, 47–48, 67–69, 76–77, 88–89, 123, 141–142, 252, 254.

1 Recognizing Names

Name Chart

Consider Your Children

This is a good "first day of school" activity that will help you learn just how much your first graders already know about letters and words. Even though many of your children may already know how to read and write their names, you may still want to use the name chart to build community. Early on, the name chart helps the children learn about uppercase and lowercase letters, initial letters and sounds, and putting letters together to form words. Once the children control these early concepts, you can use the name chart to make a variety of connections: "The word *make* has a silent *e* just like Jake's name." "Carly's name starts with the word *car*."

Working with English Language Learners

Recognizing their own names in print and hearing them said aloud will provide English language learners with a point of entry to speaking, reading, and writing English. It's important that you learn how to pronounce their names accurately in their languages, and say those names often. Help the children find their names as a way of orienting them to print. Give English language learners many opportunities to locate their and their classmates' names quickly on the name chart, which will be an important resource for them in writing.

You Need

- Pocket chart.
- Magnetic letters.

From *Teaching Resources:*

- Name cards (Pocket Chart Card Template) with each child's name. Make each initial letter a different color to emphasize the first position: the *A* in *Alisa* could be red, the rest of the name black; the *B* in *Bobby* could be blue, the rest of the letters black; the *C* in *Courtney* and *Chris* could be green; etc.
- Name Tracing Cards (Pocket Chart Card Template); see description in the Overview section of Materials & Routines in *Teaching Resources.*
- Alphabet Linking Chart.

Understand the Principle

The single most important word to a child is his name. Beginning with their own names, children need to realize that words are made up of distinct letters and that words are always spelled with the same letters in the same order.

Once children learn these principles with names, they can apply them to other words.

Explain the Principle

"Your name starts with a letter that is always the same."

"Your name starts with a capital letter. The other letters are lowercase."

"You can find your name by looking for the first letter."

plan

Explain the Principle

"Your name starts with a letter that is always the same."

"Your name starts with a capital letter. The other letters are lowercase."

"You can find your name by looking for the first letter."

① Tell the children that they are going to learn to use what they know about their names.

② With the children, prepare a preliminary chart containing their first names, categorized by first letter. Place each name card in a pocket chart as you review the names. (Alternatively, if the children already know their first names well, you may want to place first and last names on the chart.)

③ Hold up each name card, point to the child's name, and say it, emphasizing the first sound. Suggested language: "This is Alisa's name. Alisa starts with an *A*. Say Alisa. [Children respond.] Say A for Alisa. [Children respond.] Alisa, put your name on the chart." Repeat with each child.

④ When the chart is completed, have the children take turns finding uppercase and lowercase letters and naming them. (If this is difficult, see Lessons LK 12 and LK 13.) Suggested language: "When you write your name, the first letter is an uppercase letter and the rest of the letters are lowercase." Model writing one or two names. Make connections to the Alphabet Linking Chart. Then read the chart again with the children.

⑤ After completing the preliminary chart using the name cards, copy them onto a permanent name chart. Print should be large enough for all the children to see. Keep it in clear view in the meeting area so you can refer to it during reading, writing, and word study activities.

trace
draw
mix
fix
mix (3x)
write

- Prepare a name tracing card for each child so that he can glue it onto a piece of paper, trace each letter, and then draw a picture of himself. These pictures can be stapled into a class book of names or placed in alphabetical order on a bulletin board.
- Have the children, using the name cards as models, use magnetic letters to make their names three times, mixing up the letters each time.
- Then have children write their names on a piece of paper or blank large name card. If the children have difficulty writing their names, have them write as much as they can.

Have the children show their pictures and read their names. They can exchange names with a partner and show them and read them.

Go quickly through the names again. Review the concept of uppercase and lowercase letters.

Link

Interactive Read-Aloud: Read aloud the name chart again quickly each morning for a week. Read alphabet books (see *Teaching Resources,* Alphabet Books Bibliography) that focus on children's names, such as

- ***So Many Bunnies*** by Rick Walton
- ***A My Name Is Alice*** by Jane Bayer

Shared Reading: After reading and enjoying a poem or chant, such as "Good Morning Mrs. Hen" or "Five Little Speckled Frogs" (see *Sing a Song of Poetry*), use the children's names to play a word game: "I'm thinking of a word in our poem that starts with an uppercase *R* like Rebecca." Have the children use a masking card, flag, or highlighter tape to locate the word.

Guided Reading: When the children come to a new word, show them how they can use what they know about names to figure out new words: "That starts like Jason. *Jason, just.*"

Interactive Writing: Look for opportunities to use the name chart to help write words in texts you are creating with the children: "*Will* starts like William; William, can you come up and make your *W*?"

Independent Writing: Prompt the children to use the name chart as a reference to help them write words: "That starts like Nicole and Nicky."

assess

- Observe whether the children can find their names and the names of others by thinking about the sounds and letters.
- Notice whether the children use their names as resources for interactive writing and independent writing.
- Have the children write their names on paper. These will be quick indicators of children's control in forming the letters of their names.

Expand the Learning

If the children know a lot of letters, simply use the name chart as a reference and make connections to it during phonics lessons.

If the children know very few letters and have had very little experience with print, continue using the name chart to have them work with their names:

Read the chart together. Then have individual children locate their names by first thinking about the first letter.

Play a game: "I'm thinking of a boy whose name starts with *A*. He has a red shirt." Let children guess by going up and pointing to the name and reading it.

After the children know the names and first letters, locate names by the last letters or the next letters: "I'm thinking of a girl whose name starts with *C*. The next letter is *a*."

Connect with Home

Give the children a sheet of class names. (Use Word Card Template in *Teaching Resources.*) The children can read the list to family members.

Then, using magnetic letters or letter cards (see *Teaching Resources*), the children can make their names and the names of three classmates several times.

Recognizing Your Name in Text

Poems and Songs

Consider Your Children

To recognize their names within a text, children must know some visual signposts to search for. Use this lesson after students have worked, even briefly, with the name puzzle. Be sure they can find their names on the name chart, represent their names in writing using at least one or two letters, and/or build their names with magnetic letters and check them against a model. Children need many experiences in quickly locating their names in a variety of texts. You will find several good examples in *Sing a Song of Poetry*, such as "Good Morning to You," "Happy Birthday," "Who Stole the Cookies from the Cookie Jar?" and "Are You Sleeping?" In addition, consider using your own innovations on texts: "Jimmy wore his black shoes" (based on *Mary Wore Her Red Dress*), for example, or "Kecia, Kecia, what do you see? I see Maria looking at me" (based on Bill Martin's *Brown Bear, Brown Bear, What Do You See?*).

Working with English Language Learners

Be sure that you go over the poems in a shared way so the English language learners can join in easily and use their own names within them. Be sure you can pronounce the children's names correctly. Using their names sets up a welcoming and friendly atmosphere. Showing that you value all children's names helps create a sense of community. Provide more repetitions for children who find it difficult to remember the poems.

You Need

- Name songs or chants on charts or sentence strips for pocket chart.
- Pocket chart.
- Name chart (see Lesson ELC 1).
- Photocopies of name songs or chants. Use Blank Book Page Template.

From *Teaching Resources:*

- Names on cards with Velcro® if needed (Pocket Chart Card Template).
- Cards with initial letters of some names (Pocket Chart Card Template).

Understand the Principle

Starting with their names, children learn that words may be recognized by noticing the visual features of letters. They may be able to recognize their names in isolation, but they also need to be able to search through a line of print and locate a word. Names are an ideal way to begin locating words and noticing the distinctive features of letters.

Explain the Principle

"Your name is always written the same way."

"Your name has letters in it."

plan

Explain the Principle

"Your name is always written the same way."

"Your name has letters in it."

① Let the children know that they are going to learn more about how to read names.

② Put a "name song" on a chart, with blank spaces for names to be substituted.

③ First read the chant or sing the song to the tune of "This Old Man," placing name cards in the blank spaces (use Velcro® on the back of the name cards, or put the song on a pocket chart). If you use the example in the illustration, elongate "friends" to span two notes of the tune (alternatively, you could add "And" to the beginning of the third and sixth lines). You may involve the children in several ways.

④ One way is to use shared reading to read the entire text, including the name substitution. Using this option, you are supporting the reading of the names.

⑤ A second option: Select a name and ask children to look at it carefully but not say it. Place it in the appropriate spot; then read up to the name, pointing word for word. Drop out and let children guess the name. Afterward, ask children to talk about how to "read" the name.

⑥ A third option is to place the first letter of a name in the blank space and ask what name or names would work there. This will draw attention to the first letter of the word. If children already notice the first letter, place or write more than the first letter and have them predict the name(s).

⑦ Then invite the children to read or sing the text with you. Repeat this several times, each time inserting different name cards.

8 Gather the children in a circle to teach them an oral game based on Bill Martin's *Brown Bear, Brown Bear, What Do You See?* Give each child a name card of one of their classmates and ask them to look at it but place it face down. Start with everyone sitting, legs crossed, in a circle. You begin the chant by asking one child (Kevin, for example), "Kevin, Kevin, who do you see?" Kevin responds by looking at the name card he has and calling out the name. If Kevin's name card says Mary, then the chant begins again with the whole class asking, "Mary, Mary, who do you see?" Continue until all children have been called on.

apply

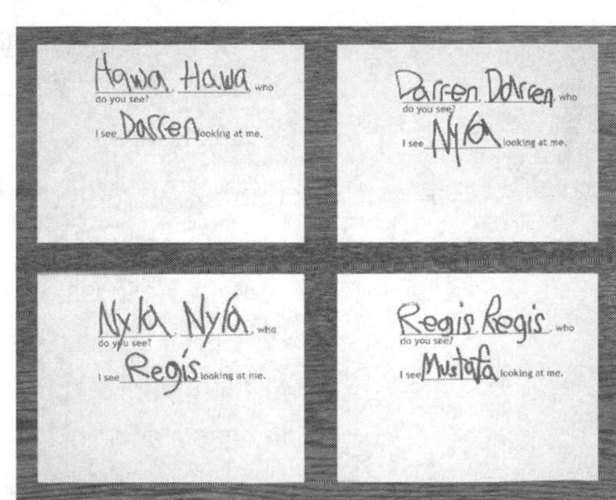

write
draw
read

- Give each child four copies (stapled together) of the patterned text you just taught them: ______, _____, who do you see? I see ________, looking at me" (see *Teaching Resources*, Blank Book Page Template). Have the children write the names of classmates in the blanks, using the name chart as a reference, on the page. Be sure each child links the previous verse to the next one by using the name that ends a verse to begin the next verse. They illustrate each page with a picture that matches the text and then read the book to a partner.

Ask the children what they have noticed about names. Comments like the following will let you in on their thinking:

"It starts with a capital letter."

"Some of our names start the same."

"You look at the letters to know it's your name."

Link

Interactive Read-Aloud: Read aloud books that feature a similar pattern, such as

- ***I Went Walking*** by Sue Williams
- ***Polar Bear, Polar Bear, What Do You Hear?*** by Bill Martin, Jr.

Shared Reading: You may want to make a big book of name songs and poems, such as "A Birthday Song" or "Going to the Fair" (see *Sing a Song of Poetry*), so that children can read them. After using them in enlarged-print form, consider photocopying the song, poem, or chant so children can have individual copies to read at home.

Guided Reading: During word work, have the children, using the name chart as a reference, make several names using magnetic letters. When children come to an unfamiliar word in a text, prompt them to use the beginning sounds in names as a link.

Interactive Writing: Use the name songs and poems as resources for words in interactive writing. Look for opportunities to create text using children's names.

Independent Writing: Encourage the children to put their names on their writing papers. You can also give them photocopies of songs they know well (see *Sing a Song of Poetry*) and have them put their name in the blanks and draw pictures.

assess

- Notice the children's progress in recognizing their own names and others' names.
- Notice evidence of the children's growing ability to make connections between names and between names and other words (beginning sounds, ending sounds, patterns such as double letters).
- Notice children's progress in writing their names accurately and with fluency.
- Ask every child to write his or her name on a piece of paper. The attempts will provide useful data for analyzing young children's control of name writing.

Expand the Learning

Using many of the same poems, songs, or chants, insert the names of favorite storybook characters (for example, Chrysanthemum, Peter Rabbit, or Lily) and place them in the pocket chart for shared reading.

Connect with Home

Have the children take home the book they made and read it with family members.

3 Matching Spoken Word to Written Word

Cut-Up Sentences

Consider Your Children

You may want to use *Concepts About Print* (Clay 2000) or ELC Assessment Task—Word-by-Word Matching to determine whether children understand directionality and word-by-word matching. (Alternatively, ask each child to point to the words of a simple text while you read.) If these behaviors are well established, this lesson will not be necessary. Using a piece of interactive writing or poems from shared reading, work intensively with children who still need more experience to be sure this early understanding becomes automatic.

Working with English Language Learners

Many children have difficulty with the sentence structure of English because their own language has different syntactic rules. Allow English language learners to approximate sentences without correcting them; they will gradually become familiar with English syntax if they have many opportunities to hear language read aloud and to participate in lessons where it is easy for them to use English syntax. Give English language learners more opportunities to practice saying sentences.

You Need

- Chart paper.
- Pocket chart.

From *Teaching Resources:*

- Blank word cards (Pocket Chart Card Template).
- Cut-up Sentence Strips (see description in the Overview section of Materials & Routines in *Teaching Resources*).

Understand the Principle

Children need to understand that sentences are made up of words and that written words are defined by white space. These concepts are a foundation for learning to match word by word in reading and for learning to identify and solve individual words while reading and writing.

Explain the Principle

“We say one word for each word we see in writing.”

plan

Explain the Principle

“We say one word for each word we see in writing.”

① Mention that today children are going to learn more about how to write words in sentences.

② Before the lesson, display several sentences written on a chart or placed in the pocket chart. Compose sentences about children in the class, such as *Marty likes to play football.*

③ Read the sentences to the children, pointing under each word, and have them read with you after they have heard it. With one sentence, have the children notice how many times you point: “When I read *Maxine likes to draw pictures,* I pointed five times.”

④ Ask what the children notice about the way the words are written.

⑤ Create more sentences with the children using a pocket chart. Suggested language: “Today we are going to write some more about the children in our class. We’ll write about some of you each day. We are going to write the words for each sentence on these cards.”

⑥ Pick a child’s name and generate a statement about her: “Sujarta loves to ride her bike.” Guide them to create a simple text, but be sure that the language is the children’s own and that they can repeat it. If children are more advanced, let the sentence go to a second line.

⑦ After the sentence about the first child (for example, Sujarta) is decided, tell children that *Sujarta* is the first word in the sentence and write it on the first card. Suggested language: “The first word in our sentence is *Sujarta.* Let’s say the sentence. [Children respond.] *Sujarta loves to ride her bike.*”

⑧ Move on to the second word. Suggested language: “What is the second word?” [Children respond.] Write the word on a card and place it right after *Sujarta* (or invite a student to do it). Point out that you are leaving space between the words and invite the children to read it together as you point.

9. Continue until the sentence is written on cards. It is not so important that children know the words *second, third, fourth,* etc.; you may simply ask for the "next" word, reading up to the blank card. You will want them to know the word *last.*

10. Place a period after the last word. Read it all together and ask children to check to see whether they have left spaces between words.

11. Repeat the process with more children's names, rereading each time you add a word. Help children see that each word stands alone and that some sentences are shorter or longer than the others. Point out how the period means to stop. Clap multisyllable words and show how they are still one word with space on either side. Finally, read the whole story at once.

mix
cut
glue
draw

- Make sentence strips (on tag board if possible, which is easier for children to manipulate) of one or two sentences from the chart you created for this lesson. Write each word of the sentence (out of order) in a box. Have the children cut out the word boxes and glue them on a paper to create the sentence and illustrate it. If the children need a model, they can refer to the lesson chart to check their work.
- Alternatively, have the children draw someone in their families and tell one thing about the person, approximating the spelling of words. They can write each word of their message on a small card and glue the cards underneath the drawing to form a sentence.

Have children share the sentence they have put together or written.

Link

Interactive Read-Aloud: Read aloud books that have large bold print so children can see the spaces between words, such as

- ***Bear in a Square*** by Stella Blackstone
- ***Little White Dog*** by Laura Godwin

Shared Reading: Invite one child to use a long, slim pointer to point while classmates read the text. Be sure the child is lifting the pointer and placing it crisply under each word; guide the hand if needed. Use short poems such as "The Boy in the Barn" or "Little Robin Redbreast" (see *Sing a Song of Poetry*).

Guided Reading: Prompt the children to point crisply under words, using the same finger each time. Ask them, "Did it match?" or "Did you have enough words?" Your goal is to help them monitor their reading by pointing and matching the words.

Interactive Writing: Explicitly point out spaces; reread messages word by word, pointing crisply at each word. Be sure the children leave a good space before starting a new word by showing them where to start.

Independent Writing: Ask the children to check their writing to be sure they are leaving spaces. Remind them that when they leave good space, their readers will be able to understand their stories.

assess

- Observe the children's writing products to determine whether they are using spaces.
- Notice whether the children say one word for each word they see in writing.
- Observe the children in independent reading to determine whether they are noticing individual words and pointing word by word.
- Check which children still have some difficulty with word-by-word matching, directionality, and use of space. Work with them in a small group until this early understanding is established.
- If a child is having extreme difficulty leaving space between words in writing, you may consider (with the child's permission) making cuts between the words and gluing them on a separate paper with exaggerated white space. Then invite the child to reread the sentence and help him see that it is now easier to read. Remind the child to do the same when he continues to write.

Expand the Learning

Create more sentences about children in the class and make a class book, with a page (including a drawing or photo) for each child.

If needed, give the children more cut-up sentences from a familiar text (for example, an interactive writing text you created) to glue, illustrate, and reread.

Connect with Home

After a sentence has been produced about every child and that child has illustrated it, create an 8½" x 11" class book. Send home a photocopy of the whole book for children to read with family members.

4 Recognizing First and Last in Print

Making Sentences

Consider Your Children

Use *Concepts About Print* (Clay 2000) or "ELC First and Last" in *Teaching Resources* to determine the extent to which children know the concept of *first* and *last* in relation to print. This assessment will let you know where to focus the lesson. Choose a text appropriate for the children's present knowledge. When referring to uppercase and lowercase letters, use language common in your school (capital and small letters, for example). Focus on first/last letter or first/last word before combining the concepts. For children who are very inexperienced, work with only one concept in a lesson, building others in further lessons.

Working with English Language Learners

English language learners often seem as if they do not know the answers to questions when in reality they do not understand the vocabulary you are using in your instruction. For example, they may know the concept of *first word* but not understand the term in English. Be sure you demonstrate by pointing and make your directions very explicit. If you know comparable words in the children's first languages, use them. This lesson involves composing and writing sentences. Be appreciative of children's approximations and realize that they may not yet have full control of English language syntax.

You Need

- Sentences on a chart.
- Photocopied sheets with words from lessons placed in mixed-up order.
- Highlighter tape.
- Highlighter markers.

Understand the Principle

First and *last* have particular meanings when applied to print. You will be using these words as you talk with children about the letters in words, the words in a sentence, and the sentences or parts of a text, so it is important that they understand what you mean. The first letter of a word is the first graphic symbol on the left; the last letter is the symbol farthest to the right.

A sentence is a grammatical construct that children may know implicitly but that is too complex to explain at this time. However, they can learn to produce sentences, to place capital letters at the beginning, and to put a period at the end. They can also label the first and last words of a sentence.

Explain the Principle

"The first word in a sentence is on the left."

"The last word in a sentence is before the period or question mark."

"The first letter in a word is on the left."

"The last letter in a word is before the space."

"The first part of a page is at the top."

"The last part of a page is at the bottom."

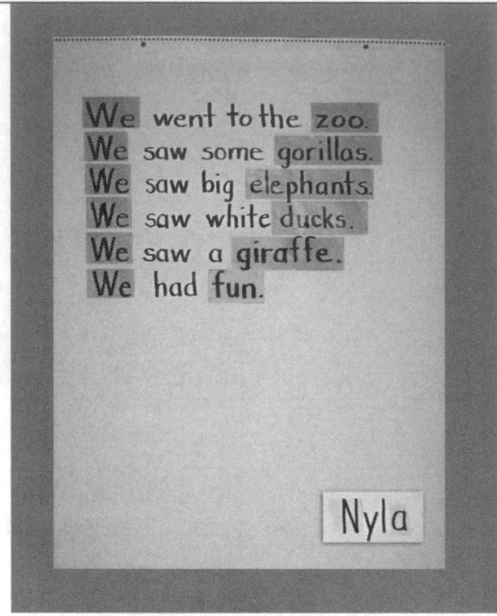

Explain the Principle

"The first word in a sentence is on the left."

"The last word in a sentence is before the period or question mark."

"The first letter in a word is on the left."

"The last letter in a word is before the space."

"The first part of a page is at the top."

"The last part of a page is at the bottom."

① Tell your children they are going to learn about *first* and *last.*

② Begin with a name or single word, holding the cards up individually rather than arranging them in a line. You do not want children to think of them as a sentence.

③ Suggested language: "This is Nyla's name. What is the *first* letter of Nyla's name? [Children respond.] That's right, it's an *N.* The first letter is the one on the left. It is at the beginning of the word. It's a capital letter because all of our names begin with a capital letter."

④ "What is the *last* letter of Nyla's name? [Children respond.] That's right, it's an *a.* The last letter is at the end of the word." Move your finger or a pointer left to right. Remember that children may not understand the terms *left* and *right.* It will be necessary to point to the letters as you say them.

⑤ "I'm going to make the first letter of Nyla's name yellow. [Demonstrate.] I'm going to make the last letter of Nyla's name orange." Use highlighter tape, plastic, or highlighter marker, or underline the letters. (Circling the letters can obscure the features of the letter.)

⑥ Repeat the process with a single word within a sentence, pointing out the first letter comes after a space and the last letter comes just before a space.

⑦ Select a familiar text and begin with one sentence. Suggested language: "The *first word* of the sentence is *We.* It has a capital letter and it is the first word on the left. Let's read it. [Children respond.] The *last word* in the sentence is *zoo.* We put a period at the end of the sentence. [Demonstrate.]"

⑧ Have the children practice finding the first and last words in this sentence and in several others in the story. Use highlighter tape to identify the first and last words in sentences.

⑨ Suggested language: "We have been talking about *first* and *last.* What is the first letter in this word? [Indicate a word—children respond.] What is the last letter? [Children respond.] When we are talking about a sentence, we know that the first word is the one on the left with a capital letter, and the last word is right before the period. If we are talking about the first part of the story, it is at the top. The last part is at the bottom."

⑩ Remember that later you may have to explain that sometimes the first word of a sentence is in the middle of the line and comes after the period. When the children begin to read texts with this layout, teach another minilesson or point it out explicitly during guided reading.

⑪ Conclude the lesson by having the children quickly point out examples of *first* and *last.*

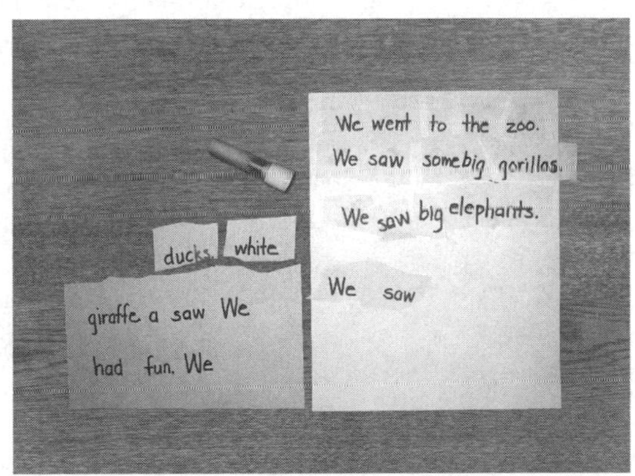

cut
glue
read
tell

- Choose a familiar text. (Don't use poems because the lines may not be sentences.) Write the words in random order on a sentence strip. Children cut up the words to re-create the sentences, using the chart as a reference, and glue the words on paper.
- They take turns reading a sentence to a partner and telling the first and last words of that sentence.

Using a familiar text on a chart, play a game: "The first letter of the word I am thinking of is *m*. The last letter is *n*." The children search the text for the answer. After your demonstration, the children can pose the questions and call on someone to answer.

Link

Interactive Read-Aloud: Read aloud books that have large print (see *Teaching Resources,* Large Print Books Bibliography) so the children can notice the letters and words, such as

- ***The Cat Barked?*** by Lydia Monks
- ***Feathers for Lunch*** by Lois Ehlert

Shared Reading: Have the children locate known words by predicting the first letter in poems such as "This Little Hand" or "I Know a Little Puppy" (see *Sing a Song of Poetry*). Have them say the word, tell what letter it would begin with, and then find it with a masking card or flag. Have children point out the first and last words of a sentence.

Guided Reading: After reading and discussing a text, have the children turn to a particular page and ask them to locate the first/last word in a particular sentence or the first/last letter in a particular word.

Interactive Writing: When showing the children how to write a word or when a child comes to the easel to write, use the terms *first* and *last* to talk about words. Point out the last word of the sentence and ask the children what punctuation to use.

Independent Writing: When you confer with children, use the terms *first* and *last.* Encourage the children to say their sentences out loud to evaluate whether they make sense. Encourage the children to use capital letters at the beginning of sentences and punctuation at the end.

assess

- Notice whether the children are looking or pointing in the right place when you use the terms *first* and *last.*
- Have the children highlight the first/last word in a sentence you give them. Have them do the same with the first/last letter in two or three words. Work in a small group with children who still have difficulty with the concept.
- Notice the children's use of the words *first* and *last* in talking about their writing.

Expand the Learning

If you concentrated only on the concept of *first* for this lesson, do another lesson on the concept of *last,* or on both *first* and *last.*

If you concentrated only on letters in words, move on to talk about words in sentences.

Connect with Home

Give the children copies of the text you used in the lesson. Ask them to highlight the first and last words in the sentences. Tell them to take the text home, read the sentences to their family members, and explain why the words are highlighted.

Phonological Awareness

Phonological awareness is a broad term that refers to both explicit and implicit knowledge of the sounds in language. It includes the ability to identify and make rhymes, hear syllables in words, hear the parts of words (onsets and rimes), and hear individual sounds in words.

Phonemic awareness is one kind of phonological awareness. Phonemic awareness refers to the ability to identify, isolate, and manipulate the individual sounds *(phonemes)* in words. Concepts categorized as phonemic awareness are labeled PA in this Continuum.

Phonological awareness (and phonemic awareness) is taught orally or in connection with letters, when it is called *phonics.* Phonics instruction refers to teaching children to connect letters and sounds in words. While very early experiences focus on hearing and saying sounds in the absence of letters, most of the time you will want to teach children to hear sounds in connection with letters. Many of the lessons related to this section begin with oral activity but move toward connecting the sounds to letters. You will not want to teach all of the PA principles in this Continuum. It is more effective to teach children only two or three ways to manipulate phonemes in words so that they learn how words work.

Principles related to letter/sound relationships, or phonics, are included in the letter/sound relationships category of this Continuum.

Connect to Assessment

See related PA Assessment Tasks in the Assessment Guide in *Teaching Resources:*

- Hearing Word Boundaries
- Hearing and Identifying Syllables
- Hearing and Identifying Rhymes
- Hearing and Identifying Beginning Consonant Sounds
- Hearing and Identifying Ending Consonant Sounds
- Hearing and Identifying Beginning Vowel Sounds (Short)
- Hearing and Identifying Short Vowel Sounds
- Hearing and Identifying Long Vowel Sounds
- Hearing and Identifying Sounds in Words
- Blending Word Parts
- Segmenting Word Parts
- Blending Sounds to Make Words
- Segmenting Sounds in Words
- Adding Sounds to Words
- Taking Sounds Away

Develop Your Professional Understanding

See *Word Matters: Teaching Phonics and Spelling in the Reading/Writing Classroom* by G.S. Pinnell and I.C. Fountas. 1998. Portsmouth, New Hampshire: Heinemann.

Related pages: 5, 63–64, 76–77, 82, 90–91, 95, 98–99, 137.

1 Making Rhymes

Picture Match

Consider Your Children

Use this lesson after the children have listened to and joined in as you read poems and rhyming stories. They should also have participated in some shared reading of rhymes so that they have an internal sense of rhyming words. This lesson will bring rhymes to their direct attention and help them realize what is meant by the word *rhyme.* Be sure that the children know the names of the objects in the pictures.

Working with English Language Learners

Be sure that your English language learners have had a great many experiences with rhymes and songs in shared reading and that they know and can repeat some rhymes that are meaningful and enjoyable to them. These rhymes will be resources for thinking of other rhymes. Children who are unfamiliar with English phonology will need many experiences to be able to hear rhymes and understand the concept. Be sure that English language learners can say and understand the meaning of the picture cards that you use for matching. (They may need to say the labels many times.) Discard those that are too far from their experience or that you cannot explain. Start with a limited set of pairs and gradually increase the set as children build understanding of the concept of rhyme.

You Need

- Pocket chart.
- Magnetic letters.

From *Teaching Resources:*

- Picture Cards, Rhymes: *bell–shell, box–fox, ring–king, car–jar, hat–cat, dog–frog, nail–pail, fire–tire, house–mouse, ball–wall.*
- Word cards (Word Card Template) for the picture labels.
- Four-Box Sheet.
- Pocket Chart Card Template.

Understand the Principle

Children naturally enjoy rhymes. Attention to rhymes increases their awareness of the sounds of language and forms a foundation for hearing the individual sounds in words, which is essential for successful early reading and writing.

Children must be able to hear the sounds in words before they can attach letters to them; awareness of rhyme is a beginning step.

Explain the Principle

“Some words have end parts that sound alike. They *rhyme.*”

“You can hear and connect words that rhyme.”

plan

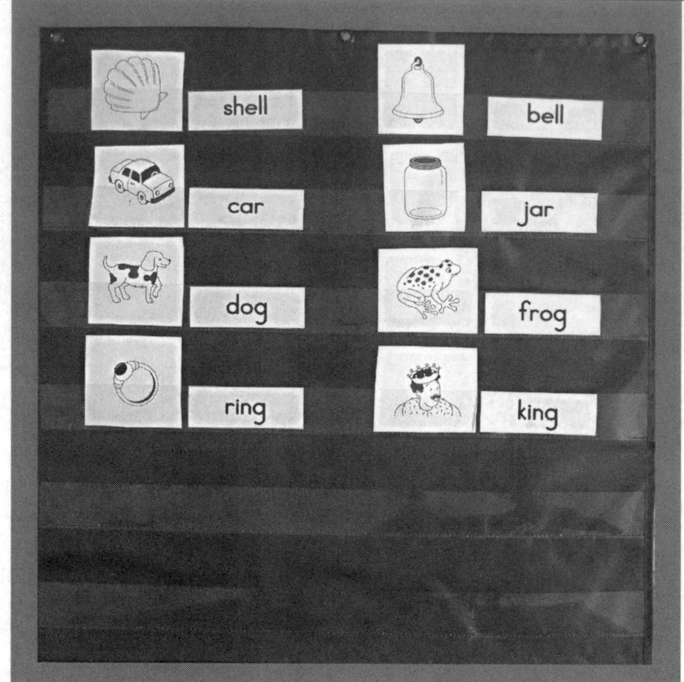

Explain the Principle

"Some words have end parts that sound alike. They *rhyme.*"

"You can hear and connect words that rhyme."

① Let children know they are going to learn something about words.

② Show the picture of a shell and ask the children to say the word. Then show the picture of a bell and have them say it. Suggested language: "*Shell, bell.* What do you notice?" Children will likely say that they end the same, or rhyme.

③ Place another four or five pairs of pictures in the pocket chart.

④ Place any picture to the left side (*ring,* for example) and ask the children to find one that rhymes (*king,* for example). Have a child place the picture next to its rhyme. Suggested language: "Some words have parts that sound alike. They rhyme. You can hear and connect words that rhyme."

⑤ "Now I'm going to put the words beside the pictures. What do you notice?" Guide the children to notice the parts that are alike.

⑥ "Today you are going to connect four pairs of words that rhyme. Line up your picture cards. Take one picture and match it to one that rhymes until you make four pairs. Then put the words for what the pictures are under or next to them by taking magnetic letters and making each word below the picture. Finally, write the words on the Four-Box Sheet. You will need to make four pairs of rhyming words."

early
mid
late

PA 1 Phonological Awareness

take
match
make
write

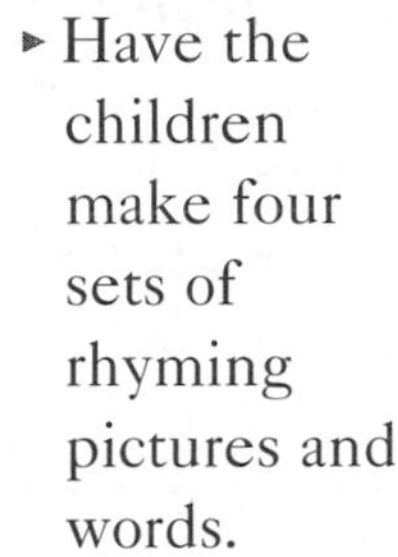

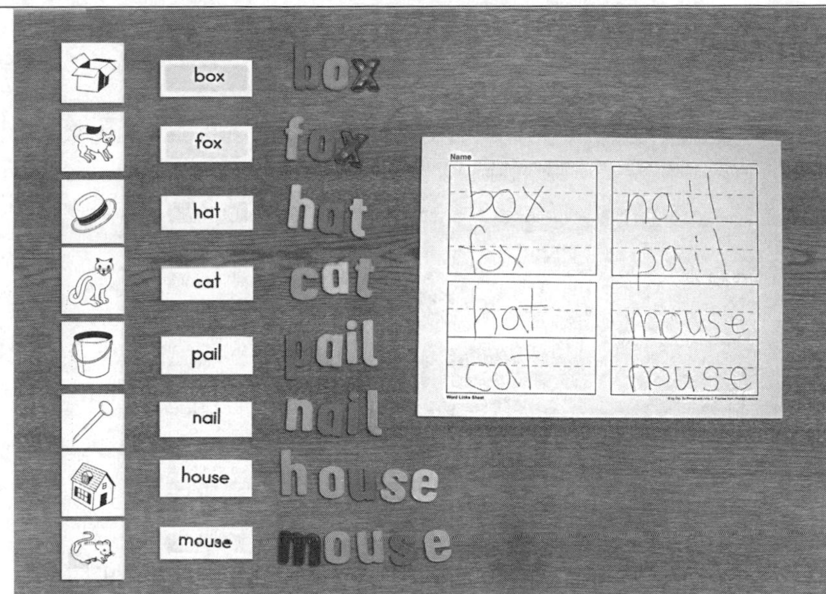

- Have the children make four sets of rhyming pictures and words.
- If the children are able to attempt writing the words, have them write their four word pairs on the Four-Box Sheet.

Have the children read their rhyming pairs of pictures to a partner.

Link

Interactive Read-Aloud: Read aloud many wonderful rhyming books (see *Teaching Resources,* Rhymes Books Bibliography), such as

- ***Tracy's Mess*** by Elise Petersen
- ***Quacky Quack-Quack!*** by Ian Whybrow

Shared Reading: After enjoying poems and songs, such as "The Clever Hen," "Jack in the Box," or "Ball-bouncing Rhymes" (see *Sing a Song of Poetry*), have children use a masking card or highlighter tape to find pairs of rhyming words.

Guided Reading: During word work, have children make two or three words with magnetic letters and make a rhyming word to go with each.

Interactive Writing: As children write, point out words that rhyme. Have them listen for the sounds in the words and get a good look at the letter patterns.

Independent Writing: To help a child write a new word, tell her another word she knows that rhymes (and has the same ending part). The word she knows will help her think about the new word—*out, shout,* for example.

assess

- Select four or five sets of pictures and ask a child to say and make rhyming pairs.

Expand the Learning

Repeat the lesson with a greater variety of rhyming pictures (see *Teaching Resources,* Picture Cards, Rhymes).

Have the children play Rhyming Lotto (see *Teaching Resources,* Directions for Bingo and Lotto). Glue one part of a pair in the square on the game card. The second picture of the pair is part of the deck of cards from which the children draw. They take a card, say the name, and cover a box on their card if they have a picture that rhymes.

Connect with Home

Send home a sheet of rhyming pictures (see *Teaching Resources,* Picture Cards, Rhymes) and Lotto game cards (see *Teaching Resources,* Games, Lotto Game Card) so that children can play Rhyming Lotto with family members.

2 Recognizing Rhymes

Picture Sort

Consider Your Children

Use this activity after the children have experienced much shared reading of poems, chants, and songs. Through engagement with shared texts they will become more sensitive to the sound patterns of language. If rhyming is a very new concept for the children, begin with only two or three pairs of words. This activity is designed for hearing only, but you may move on to the next step, which is putting words under the pictures to look at letter similarities.

Working with English Language Learners

For games like this one, you will be using the same picture cards over and over. English language learners will be developing a repertoire of labels that they know and can say and use in different ways. Be sure they understand the procedures of the game; you may want to work with a small group, playing the game for a short time with each child in turn. When you read books aloud, stop and call attention to rhymes that the children know so that they begin to understand that they will meet the same words and labels in other contexts.

You Need

- Highlighter tape.
- Pocket chart.

From *Teaching Resources:*

- Rhyming pictures (selected pairs) (Picture Cards, Onsets and Rimes).
- Two-Way Sort Extension.
- Two-Way Sort Cards or Sheets.
- Masking Card.

Understand the Principle

Hearing and identifying words that rhyme, or sound alike at the end, helps the children realize that a word is made up of a sequence of sounds. Listening for these units of sound, they become sensitive to individual sounds and clusters of sound.

Recognizing rhymes enables the children to match clusters of symbols on a page. Knowing about rhymes helps them identify word parts in word solving.

Explain the Principle

“Some words have end parts that sound alike. They *rhyme.*”

Explain the Principle

"**Some words have end parts that sound alike. They *rhyme.***"

① Explain to the children they'll be thinking and learning about words that rhyme.

② Begin with easy rhyming words. Have the children say the labels of the pictures you have lined up on the left of the pocket chart.

③ Suggested language: "Some words sound alike at the end. Listen to these two words: *bee, tree.* [Point to the pictures as you say the words.] Now say those words with me. [Children respond.] They sound alike, don't they? When they sound alike at the end, they rhyme."

④ Guide the children to talk about how the words sound alike at the end. Then demonstrate matching the other three pairs of words, having the children say them with you.

⑤ Line up the pictures of the *bee, cat, car, fish,* and *fan* in a column on the left of the pocket chart. Then have one child demonstrate finding pictures that have labels that rhyme and saying both words to check them. Ask the class to judge whether the words rhyme.

⑥ Do this demonstration several times if needed. Then show the children how to match pictures on a Two-Way Sort Card, each time saying the words aloud.

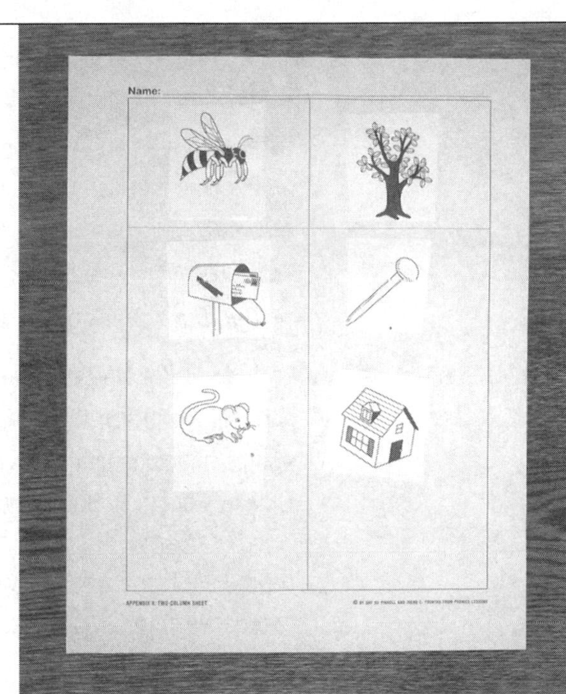

say
match

- Have the children place a key picture at the top left of the Two-Way Sort Card and a rhyming picture at the top right. Ask them to select pictures and find pictures that rhyme until they have created ten rhyming pairs.
- Use the Two-Way Sort Extension to continue the two columns as needed.

Read a poem together and use a masking card or highlighter tape to find pairs of words that rhyme.

Link

Interactive Read-Aloud: Read aloud books and poems that use rhyme (see *Teaching Resources,* Rhymes Books Bibliography) in an enjoyable way, such as

- ***One Duck Stuck*** by Phyllis Root
- ***Pigs in the Mud*** by Lynn Plourde

Shared Reading: Read a variety of rhymes, poems and songs together, such as "A Wise Old Owl" or "Willy Boy, Willy Boy" (see *Sing a Song of Poetry*). After the children know them, have them identify easy rhyming words. An alternative is to cover the second rhyme in a pair on a first reading of a text and invite the children to predict the rhyme. Then uncover the word to confirm predictions.

Guided Reading: During word work, make a few words with magnetic letters or write them on a whiteboard. Invite the children to give a word that rhymes and make it or write it below.

Interactive Writing: When a piece of interactive writing has rhyming words, point them out to the children. When a text is completed, say a word and have the children find a word on the chart that rhymes.

Independent Writing: Point out pairs of words that rhyme in a child's writing.

assess

- Notice the children's ability to recognize rhymes and put rhyming pairs together.
- Notice spontaneous recognition of rhymes in shared reading.
- Say four or five words and ask the children to give a rhyming word for each one.

Expand the Learning

Repeat the picture sort using different pictures. As an added challenge, include some words that do not rhyme with any others in the set.

After children have read simple poems (see *Sing a Song of Poetry*) many times in shared reading, have them glue the poems in a personal poetry book and illustrate them. On some poems, they can identify and highlight rhyming words.

Connect with Home

Have the children take home photocopies of the rhyming pictures to cut apart and match.

Encourage family members to play rhyming games: "I'm thinking of a word that rhymes with *store.*" (Answer: *floor* or *door.*)

3 Hearing Sounds in Sequence

Making a List

Consider Your Children

Most of the work on this principle is accomplished during interactive writing as you help the children spell the words they want to write. This lesson is most successful if the children have participated in a great deal of interactive writing, during which saying words slowly has been modeled and elicited. Also, the children should know most letters and be able to hear some of the dominant consonants in words, as well as some easy-to-hear vowel sounds. A few lessons formatted like this one make the knowledge the children have gained through daily interactive writing explicit. A lesson like this one is appropriate when the children are producing a number of the sounds in words.

Working with English Language Learners

Saying words slowly will make the phonology of English words more available to English language learners and will help them considerably in their writing. Be sure that you enunciate clearly and provide many demonstrations. Accept the children's approximations as they pronounce words. Some sounds may be very difficult for them, and they will eventually need to remember the graphic sign even if they cannot say all parts of the word. They will probably make their own internal connections with idiosyncratic pronunciations of words.

You Need

- Chart paper.

From *Teaching Resources:*

- Picture cards whose labels include vowel sounds (Picture Cards, Short Vowel Sounds and Long Vowel Sounds).
- List Sheet.

Understand the Principle

Children need to understand that words are made up of sequences of sounds. They need to learn how to isolate and identify a large number of these sounds and understand the alphabetic principle—that there is a relationship between letters and sounds in words.

Hearing sounds in sequence makes it possible for children to think analytically about words and lays a foundation for writing more of the letters in words and digging deeper into print to decode words.

This lesson goes beyond phonological awareness to demonstrate the connections to print, but the major strategy children will use is saying words slowly and identifying sequences of sounds.

Explain the Principle

“ You can say a word slowly to hear all the sounds, from first to last. ”

plan

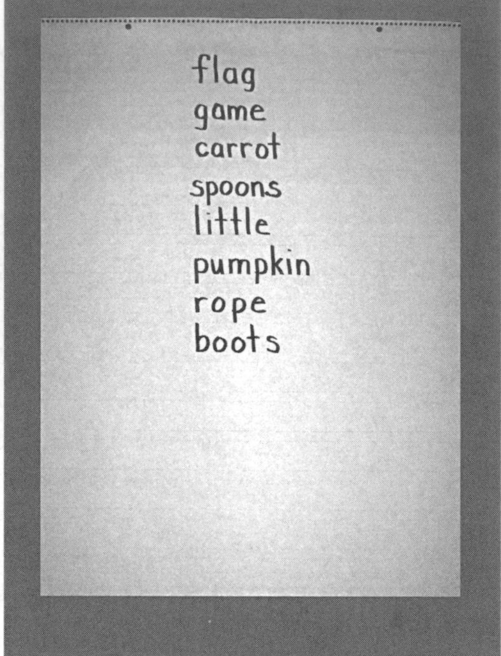

flag
game
carrot
spoons
little
pumpkin
rope
boots

Explain the Principle

“You can say a word slowly to hear all the sounds, from first to last.”

① Mention that today children will be learning to write the sounds they hear in words.

② From the interactive writing you have done, select about ten words the children have found challenging, words they had to say slowly and listen carefully to for the sounds. Alternatively, collect some words from the children’s own writing. Examples might be *little, flag, spoons, carrot, pumpkin, boots, game.* Do not expect the children to generate all sounds in these words. The goal is for them to listen and generate some consonant and vowel sounds; you will be filling in the rest of the word.

③ Suggested language: “If you say a word slowly, you can hear some of the sounds in it. You are getting really good at doing that. Today we are going to work with some words from your writing over the last few weeks, and we are going to think hard about the sounds.”

④ “Let’s start with the word *flag.* Say it slowly. What can you hear?” Children respond by saying it slowly and offering their analyses.

⑤ Accept their responses and comment on them. For example, if a child says *g* or makes the /g/ sound, you can say, “Yes, that is at the end of the word. Keep that in mind and let’s say it again and think about the beginning of the word.” Alternatively, you can write the *g* on the chart and ask for other sounds, which you place in the correct position. If children offer vowels other than *a*, recognize that the letter is a vowel and show the conventional spelling.

⑥ Work until the children have generated what they can, including the vowel sound, and then fill in the missing letters yourself. Demonstrate running your finger under the word and saying it slowly. Show the children how checking like this helps you know if you have connected all of the sounds you can.

7. Repeat using *game*. Here you might want to comment that there is an *e* on the end of the word that is silent. There is no sound connected with it, but you put it on the word to make it look right.

8. Do the same thing using four or five of the other words you have selected. Notice how many of the sounds the children can produce. Children may analyze a sound correctly but suggest the wrong letter—*k* for *carrot*, for example. Recognize their thinking and say it could start that way, but in print, the letter is *c*.

9. Suggested language: "You can hear lots of the sounds in words. Today you are going to write some words. Choose at least five pictures and write the word for each of them. Say each word slowly and write as many of the letters as you can."

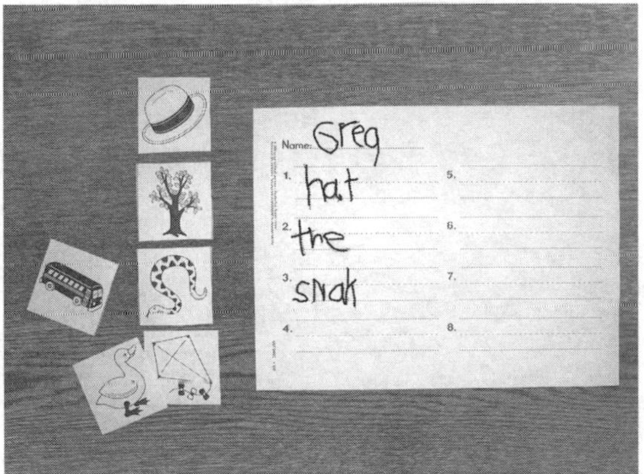

say
write
read

- Have the children choose a minimum of five pictures. For each, ask them to say the label slowly, writing the letter for each sound they hear on the list sheet. Then have each child read her list to a partner.

Have the children read the words on their list sheet to a different partner. Comment on how many of the sounds they heard and wrote a letter for. Do not insist on conventional spelling. Collect the sheets to give you information for planning future lessons.

Link

Interactive Read-Aloud: Read aloud books that contain familiar words, supported by pictures, that emphasize sounds. Say some words slowly so that students can hear all the sounds. Examples are:

- ***Boats*** by Byron Barton
- ***To Market, To Market*** by Anne Miranda

Shared Reading: In a text that the children have read several times, such as "Way Down South" or "Two Little Dogs" (see *Sing a Song of Poetry*), cover a few key words with a stick-on note. When you approach the covered word, have children say it and predict what the first letter and some subsequent letters will be. Then remove the stick-on note so they can check their prediction.

Guided Reading: When a child comes to a word he or she doesn't know, instead of telling what it is, ask, "Could it be [word]?" Ask the child to say it slowly and check the letters.

Interactive Writing: Ask the children to say a word slowly and think about the letters. They can suggest many of the letters, after which you will fill in the rest for standard spelling.

Independent Writing: When the children are attempting to spell new words, encourage them to say the word slowly and represent as many letters as they can. (If the children already *know* a word, they should simply write it quickly rather than saying it slowly to identify sounds. This technique is tedious when it's not necessary.)

assess

- Examine the list sheets for information about which children are able to represent letters in words accurately in their writing.
- Observe whether the children are using letter/sound cues to check their reading and to solve new words in their reading.
- Give a "spelling test" using words in this exercise. Don't grade the test, but use it as an assessment. Notice which children are representing all easy-to-identify sounds. Notice which sounds are hard to identify.

Expand the Learning

After a few weeks, repeat the lesson with more words the children have been attempting to spell. This lesson can be very quick.

Have the children say words they are trying to write several times to identify more of the sounds in each word.

Ask the children to generate a sequence of sounds as you write the corresponding letters.

Connect with Home

Have the children take home the words they wrote with a brief note asking family members to notice the sounds children have represented.

Encourage caregivers to have their children say words slowly and think about the sounds in the word whenever they write. Explain that the children's approximations will lead to standard spelling because they will be learning more every time they write.

4 Hearing Ending Sounds

Picture Lotto

Consider Your Children

Use this lesson after the children have had some experience matching pictures whose labels have the same beginning sound. We have not included lessons on beginning sounds in this Grade 1 book, but there are many in the Kindergarten book. If your children need work on beginning sounds, you can adapt this lesson for that purpose. Matching words with ending sounds is an oral exercise, not a visual one; for example, *soap* and *rope* end with the same sound but not the same letter. Later you may add the written label to each picture so children can begin to connect their knowledge of sounds to letters.

Working with English Language Learners

You may need to work with a small group of English language learners to clearly articulate the words and say and hear the last sound. Be sure the children are saying the words themselves rather than just listening as you say them. You will be using picture cards for this Lotto game. Be sure they know and can say the names of the labels they will be using and that they understand the words *first* and *last* in English. Go over the labels and have them say the words several times. Also, act out the directions when you are demonstrating how to play Lotto. The first time English language learners play the game, either observe and coach them or play with them so that you are sure they understand the basic directions.

You Need

- Pocket chart.

From *Teaching Resources:*

- Picture cards (Picture Cards, Ending Consonant Sounds).
- Lotto Game Cards.
- Directions for Bingo and Lotto Games.

Understand the Principle

Being able to hear the sequence of sounds in words (what *first* and *last* mean) and identify words with the same ending sound helps children connect letters with the sounds they represent.

Once children can identify ending sounds and connect letters with them, they can use this information to distinguish words and solve them while reading and writing.

Explain the Principle

“ Some words sound the same at the end. ”

“ You can connect words that sound the same at the end. ”

Explain the Principle

“Some words sound the same at the end.”

“You can connect words that sound the same at the end.”

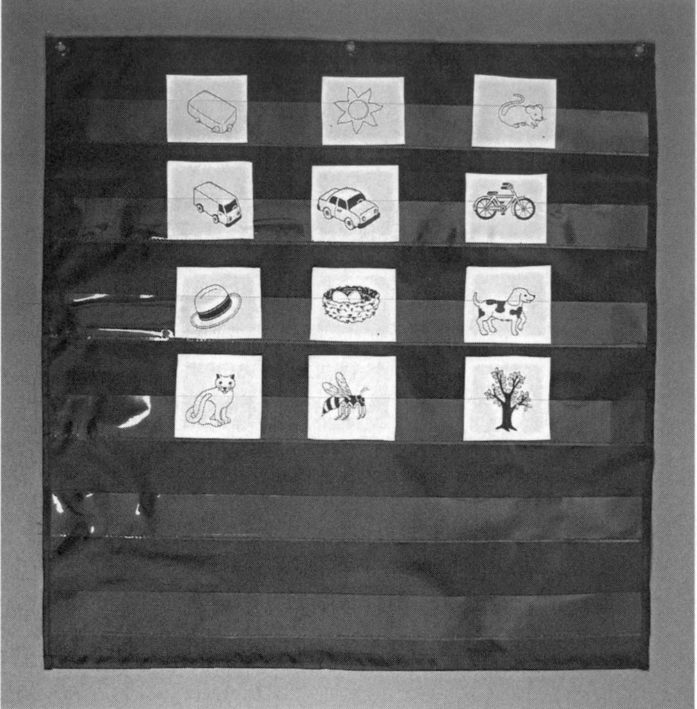

① Let children know they are going to learn how to match pictures whose names sound the same at the end, like *snake* and *bike* (accentuate the final sound).

② Place twelve picture cards in a pocket chart in a rectangular pattern (a facsimile of a Lotto card). Have a stack of other picture cards available: *cup, snake, fan, train, bus, truck, bag, kite, vest, jar.*

③ Suggested language: “Today we are going to learn to play a game called Picture Lotto. In this game you get to match pictures whose names sound alike at the end. Let’s try it with the pictures I have in the pocket chart. Let’s say the names of these pictures and listen for the last sound of the word.” Have the children say the names. Some of them may identify the last sound by letter or say it in an isolated way.

④ “I’m going to draw a picture card from this stack and see if I can match it to the pictures on my card.”

⑤ Hold up the first picture card. Suggested language: “I can see that this is a cup. Now I’m going to see if there is a picture on my card that sounds like *cup* at the end. Can anyone see something that ends like *cup*?” Children respond with *soap*.

⑥ Model checking *cup* and *soap* by saying both words. Have the children say both words as well to check whether they sound alike at the end. Place the picture of the cup over the picture of the soap.

⑦ Draw additional cards one at a time, saying both words to check a potential match. (Cards that do not match anything on the pocket chart are placed face down at the bottom of the pile.)

⑧ Suggested language: "I've covered all the spaces on my square. That's what you do to win the Picture Lotto game. Remember to say both words to check your matches."

⑨ Ask the children to discuss what you have to do to fill your Lotto card. Then ask three children to demonstrate the game in a circle on the floor. Show them how to take turns drawing cards and matching them to the pictures on their game cards. The first to fill the game card wins.

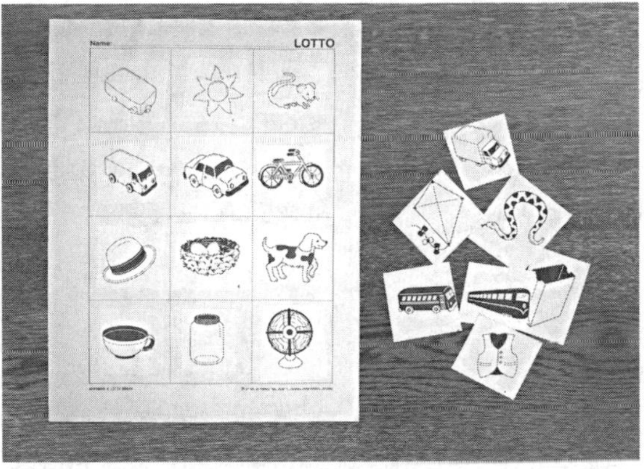

take
say
match

- Have the children play Picture Lotto. If you have enough picture cards and game cards (they can be photocopied), several games can be played at once.

Ask the children to talk about some of the matching words they found while they were playing Picture Lotto. Comments like "If it's a rat, it ends like cat, but if it's a mouse it ends like bus" mean children are becoming more flexible in their phoneme awareness.

Link

Interactive Read-Aloud: Read aloud books that draw attention to the ending sound in words, and emphasize the ending sounds. Examples are:

- ***Grandma's Cat*** by Helen Ketteman
- ***Window Music*** by Anastasia Suen

Shared Reading: Draw the children's attention to words that sound alike at the end: "Can someone find a word in our poem (or story) that ends like *do*?" Use rhyming poems such as "My Apple" or "Little Sally Watters" (see *Sing a Song of Poetry*).

Guided Reading: During word work, show the children a word and ask them to think of another word that sounds the same at the end. Write or make the second word. Repeat with three or four pairs of words.

Interactive Writing: When thinking how to write a word, have the children say it slowly and connect it to a name or other word that ends the same.

Independent Writing: Encourage the children to say words slowly when they are writing and to connect them to names or other words that end the same.

assess

- Notice whether the children are able to connect ending sounds of words during interactive and independent writing.
- Place picture cards in the pocket chart. Hold up additional picture cards, asking individual children to say the name of the picture card and match it with one in the pocket chart that has the same ending sound. Evaluate which consonant sounds the children are hearing and connecting.

Expand the Learning

Have children play the game numerous times with different game cards and sets of pictures.

Connect with Home

Encourage family members to use time spent shopping or riding in the car to play games with their children based on the way words sound. Explain that they say a word and ask their child to think of another word that ends with the same sound (*grass, bus,* for example).

5 Hearing Beginning and Ending Sounds in Words

Sound Dominoes

Consider Your Children

Use this lesson when the children understand the concept of *first* and *last* in written language and also know that words are made up of sounds that you can hear. They should be able to say words slowly and match words that have the same beginning and/or ending sound. In this lesson, they will be hearing both beginning and ending sounds and interchanging them flexibly.

Working with English Language Learners

Be sure that English language learners can identify the objects in pictures and say the words, emphasizing both beginning and ending sounds. Go over the pictures used in the Sound Dominoes game several times so that identifying the names will be easy. Act out the game and demonstrate it explicitly from beginning to end. The first time English language learners play Sound Dominoes, play the game with them to be sure that they understand the directions.

You Need

From *Teaching Resources*:

- Selected picture cards (Picture Cards, Beginning Consonant Sounds and Ending Consonant Sounds).
- Directions for Sound Dominoes.

Understand the Principle

The ability to hear and identify sounds at the beginning and end of words is essential if children are going to connect the sounds in words with letters and letter clusters.

Knowing how to say words and think of corresponding letters will help children monitor their reading for accuracy and solve words in reading and spelling.

Explain the Principle

" You can hear the first sound in a word. "

" You can hear the last sound in a word. "

plan

Explain the Principle

“ You can hear the first sound in a word. ”

“ You can hear the last sound in a word. ”

① Tell your children they are going to learn how to play Sound Dominoes.

② Take the picture of the house and tape it to the board.

③ Say the word the picture represents and ask the children what they hear at the end. Suggested language: “*House.* What sound do you hear at the end? [Children respond.] Yes, /s/. Now I'm going to tape up another picture.”

④ Tape the picture of the sun so that it is beside the picture of the house. “What sound does this word begin with? [Children respond.] What sound do you hear at the end? [Children respond.]”

⑤ Select a picture that starts with *n* (*nest,* for example) and tape it beside the picture of the sun.

⑥ Explain to the children that they will have turns taking one picture from the pile to see if it starts like the previous picture ends.

⑦ If it does, they connect it. If it does not, they can keep it to use later.

⑧ The goal is to continue to connect picture cards until they are all used.

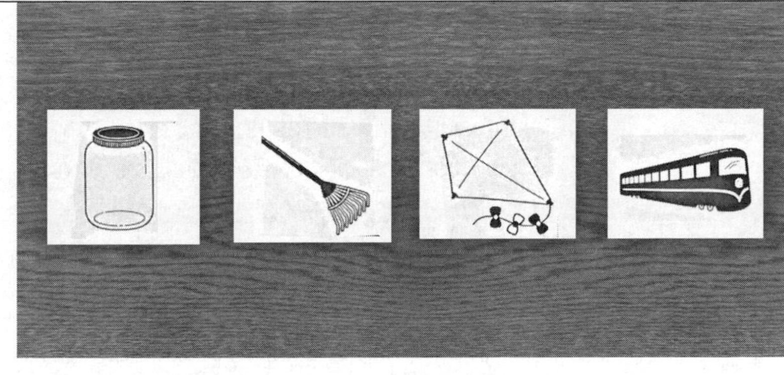

say
connect
say

► Have the children (individually or with a partner) play Sound Dominoes using the set of pictures and connecting them on the tabletop. When they are done connecting a row of pictures, have children say the words.

Have the children sit in a circle. Ask each child to say a word. The next child gives a word that starts like the previous word ends. Continue until all children have had a turn.

Link

Interactive Read-Aloud: Read aloud alphabet books and books with alliteration (see *Teaching Resources,* Alphabet Books and Alliteration Bibliography), such as

- ***Tomorrow's Alphabet*** by George Shannon
- ***Alphabet Under Construction*** by Denise Fleming

Shared Reading: After enjoying a poem such as "Five Fat Peas" or "Dingle Dangle Scarecrow" (see *Sing a Song of Poetry*), chant, or song, have the children use a masking card or highlighter tape to mark words that start or end like a word you name.

Guided Reading: When the children come to an unknown word, invite them to say the word they think would come next. Ask, "What letter would you expect to see first?" Then have them check the first letter of the word.

Interactive Writing: Before writing a new word, get the children to say the word slowly. Ask what they hear first. You might want to ask for middle letters or write them yourself. Then ask for the last sound.

Independent Writing: Prompt the children to say words and listen for the first/last sound.

assess

- Observe how easily and quickly the children match beginning and ending sounds.
- Place a row of Beginning Consonant Sounds and Ending Consonant Sounds picture cards on the table and ask the children to find matches first for beginning and then for ending sounds.
- Prepare a page with two columns and one word at the top—*kite,* for example. Have the children cut out and glue pictures that start like *kite* in the first column and pictures that end like *kite* in the second column.

Expand the Learning

Have the children play the game again with a different selection of pictures.

Add short-vowel consonant-vowel-consonant pictures (Picture Cards, Consonant-Vowel-Consonant).

Connect with Home

Send home a packet of photocopied pictures and directions so that children can play Sound Dominoes with family members.

6 Identifying Onsets and Rimes

Go Fish

Consider Your Children

Use this activity after the children have learned to hear and clap syllables in words and have participated in shared reading of rhymes and songs. Be sure the children know the meaning of *first* and *last* in connection with the sequence of sounds and letters. The technical terms *onset* and *rime* are not necessary to understand the concept. This lesson sets up a routine for word play that can be used at any time during the school day. Whenever you have a minute or two of down time, you can make a game of one or two quick examples.

Working with English Language Learners

The phonology of English may be difficult for children who are just beginning to speak it; however, they are fast learners who are very flexible in taking on new sounds. Repeat the names of the objects in the pictures and have the children say them; discard those that are not within the children's experience. Use real objects or act out meanings. Give English language learners many opportunities to say the names of the items in pictures before expecting them to play the game. The first time, play Go Fish yourself with a small group to show them the routines.

You Need

From *Teaching Resources:*

- Picture cards (two matching sets) (Picture Cards, Onsets and Rimes).
- Go Fish cards (Deck Card Template).
- Directions for Go Fish.

Understand the Principle

Syllables are easy word components for children to recognize because they can hear them. Syllables can be further broken down into the *onset,* which consists of whatever is before the vowel, and the *rime,* which is the vowel and whatever comes after it (in that syllable). A syllable can be a single word *(tell)* or a word can have several syllables *(telephone),* but except for single-sound words like *a* and *oh,* every syllable has an onset and a rime. Hearing, identifying, and blending onsets and rimes will alert children to the sounds of words and are natural precursors to analyzing these sounds.

Explain the Principle

“You can blend word parts together.”

“You can hear and say the first and last parts of a word.”

plan

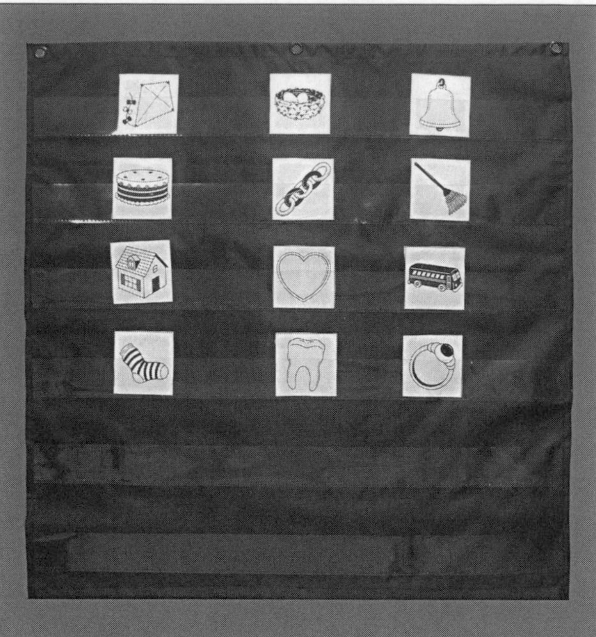

Explain the Principle

"You can blend word parts together."

"You can hear and say the first and last parts of a word."

1. Tell children that today they are going to play a listening game.

2. Suggested language: "I'm going to say the first part of a word and then I'll say the last part: *c–ar*. I can put those parts together to make a word, *c–ar, car*. See how I say it as two parts, *c–ar*, and then I say them smoothly as one word, *car*?"

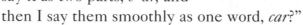

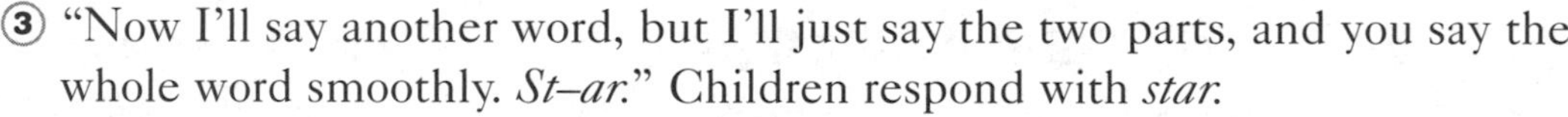

3. "Now I'll say another word, but I'll just say the two parts, and you say the whole word smoothly. *St–ar*." Children respond with *star*.

4. Repeat using several more words, each time saying the two parts and then having the children say the whole word: *f–ar, far; t–ar, tar; b–ar, bar*. Give them feedback on their response. You may need to say the parts more than once.

5. Take a collection of pictures (examples are *heart, house, swing, ring, chain, cheese, cake, dress, bus, glass, sock, nest, bell, rake, tooth;* include a variety so that the children will generalize across patterns) and place them on an easel or in the pocket chart. Suggested language: "I'm going to say the first part and last part of a word. It will be one of the pictures. Tell me which one it is."

6. Let the children say the first and last part of a word for others to guess and say the whole word smoothly. This requires both identifying the parts and blending them together.

7. Demonstrate how to play Go Fish using picture cards.

ask
match

► Have the children play Go Fish using a deck of cards that includes several sets of matching pictures. Each child is given five cards to start. Taking turns, they ask one of the other players for a card that matches one of the cards they are holding, saying the word in parts: "Do you have *f–ish*?" If the other child has a picture of a fish, he responds by blending the parts together and saying *fish*. He gives the card to the first player. The first player now has a match and puts it down on the table. If the second player does not have a match, he says, "Go Fish," and the first player takes a picture card from the deck. The first player with no cards wins the game.

Have each child select a word from the game and say the word and its parts.

Link

Interactive Read-Aloud: Read aloud rhyming books, emphasizing the parts of words. Call attention to the way words end. Examples are:

- ***Cows Can't Fly*** by David Milgrim
- ***My Crayons Talk*** by Patrica Hubbard

Shared Reading: Use poems such as "Fishy-fishy" or "Fire! Fire! Cried Mrs. McGuire" (see *Sing a Song of Poetry*). Say the parts in a word and have the children locate the whole word with a masking card or highlighter tape. Alternate by pointing to a word and having the children say its parts.

Guided Reading: During word work, say the parts of a few words and have the children blend them together. Then give them a few words and have them say the parts.

Interactive Writing: Have the children say a word and think about the first and last parts as they write it. If the children understand vowels, point out that the last part contains the vowel.

Independent Writing: Encourage the children to say the words they want to write and think about the letters they need for the first part and the last part.

assess

- Observe whether the children can identify and blend the parts of syllables and words. A quick check with pictures of two or three words will tell you whether they understand how to identify the parts and blend them.

Expand the Learning

Repeat this minilesson if the children are not using the concept in their own writing and reading. Explicitly show them how to think about a word they want to write, say it, and identify the first part and last part.

If the children find this task very easy, try words with consonant blends at the beginning: *string, train,* or *cheese,* for example.

Connect with Home

At a meeting or in a newsletter, teach family members to play a word game with their children in which the adult says the first and last parts of the word and the child blends them together. Be sure family members choose one-syllable words that start with a single consonant or cluster of consonants (for example, *big, stripe*). You may wish to send home a list of words that they can use for the game (see *Teaching Resources,* Word Cards, Syllables). Emphasize that the activity should be quick and fun and that the idea is to make children curious about words and get them to enjoy manipulating sounds.

7 Hearing and Blending Onsets and Rimes

Oral Word Game

Consider Your Children

This activity introduces the children to segmenting and blending and helps them become more flexible with words. Use this lesson after they have had experience clapping words into syllables and have participated in shared reading of rhymes and songs. Be sure the children know the meaning of *first* and *last* in connection with the sequence of sounds and letters. The technical words *onset* and *rime* are not necessary to understand the concept. This lesson sets up a routine for word play that can be used at any time during the school day. Whenever you have a minute or two of down time, you can make a game of one or two quick examples.

Working with English Language Learners

Blending onsets and rimes requires a somewhat abstract concept of words, awareness of word parts, and precise pronunciation, which may be quite difficult for English language learners. Accept approximations and praise the children for attempts to blend words. Provide many demonstrations of blending word parts. Use words that are known and meaningful to the children.

You Need

From *Teaching Resources:*

- Picture Cards, Onsets and Rimes.

Understand the Principle

The structure of syllables helps children begin to analyze them and to hear sounds. Each syllable has an *onset,* which consists of whatever is before the vowel, and a *rime,* which is the vowel and whatever comes after it (in that syllable). A syllable can be a single word *(to),* or a word can have several syllables *(tornado),* but every syllable has a rime and most syllables have an onset. If children can hear the first and last parts of syllables and words and blend them together, they have taken the first step toward word analysis by letter and sound.

Explain the Principle

“You can hear and say the first and last part of a word.”

“You can blend word parts together.”

plan

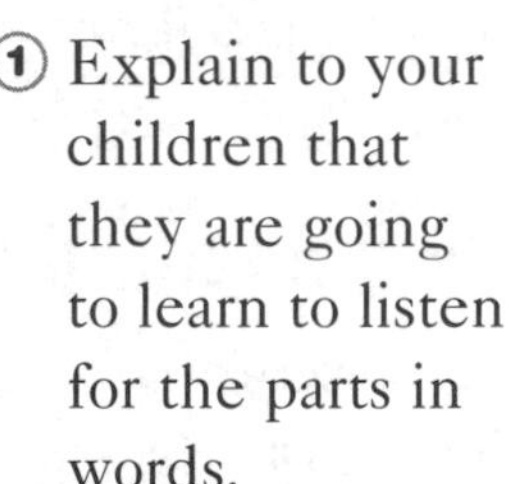

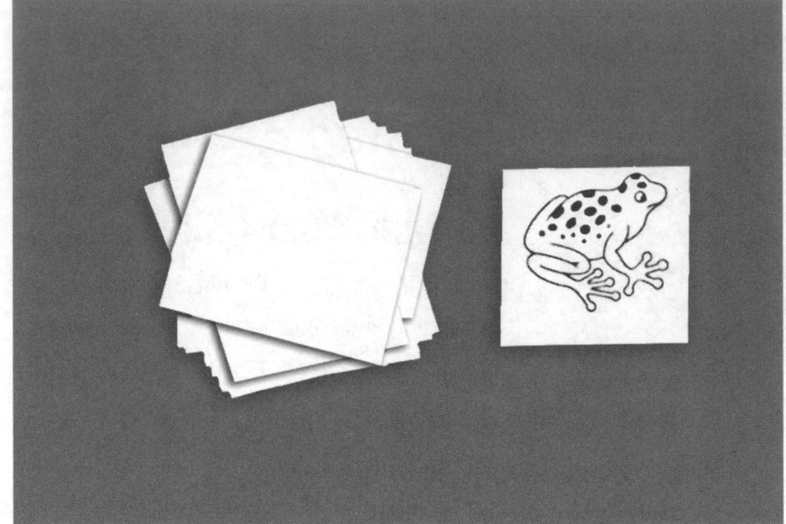

Explain the Principle

“You can hear and say the first and last part of a word.”

“You can blend word parts together.”

① Explain to your children that they are going to learn to listen for the parts in words.

② Suggested language: “When you say a word, you can hear the first part. Say *top*. [Children respond.] Now I’ll say the first part by itself and then I’ll say the last part: *t–op*, *top*. You say that. [Children respond.]”

③ “Let’s try another one. Say *st–op*. [Children respond.] When I say those two parts smoothly, the word is *stop: st–op*, *stop*. I’ll say the parts of some words, and you say the whole word smoothly. Try *m–op*. [Children respond.]”

④ Have the children try *c–op, cop; fl–op, flop; pl–op, plop*. Then do the same with *f–ish, fish; d–ish, dish; r–ake, rake; c–ake, cake; c–ar, car; st–ar, star; b–ar, bar*. Vary the words so that children can generalize across patterns.

⑤ Now take a collection of pictures and have the children take turns identifying the parts of the words the pictures represent by giving the onset and the rime.

⑥ Demonstrate how to play the partner word game explained below.

take
say parts
say word

▸ Have the children play the following word game with a partner. One child takes a picture from a pile of fifteen to twenty cards and pronounces the first part and the last part of the word the picture represents. The partner blends the parts together and says the word smoothly. They proceed through all the cards in the pile. Then they mix up the cards and reverse roles.

Give each child one picture. In turn, have children say the word the picture represents, say the parts, and say the word.

Link

Interactive Read-Aloud: Read aloud books that emphasize rhyme and the pleasure of hearing language, such as

- ***Timothy Tunny Swallowed a Bunny*** by Bill Grossman
- ***These Hands*** by Hope Lynne Price

Shared Reading: Using a familiar text such as "Five Little Leaves" or "Hanky Panky" (see *Sing a Song of Poetry*), say the parts of a word and have the children find the word in the text and mark it using a masking card, flag, or highlighter tape.

Guided Reading: During word work, make a few easy words with magnetic letters and have the children tell the first and last parts. You can have them move the letters apart and put them together.

Interactive Writing: Have the children say a word and think about the first and last parts as they write it. If the children understand vowels, point out that the last part contains the vowel.

Independent Writing: Encourage the children to say the words they want to write and think about the letters they need for the first part and the last part.

assess

- Give the children two or three words and observe whether they can identify the first and last parts.

Expand the Learning

Repeat the lesson with a variety of other picture cards.

Connect with Home

At a meeting or in a newsletter, teach family members to play a word game with their children in which the first and last parts of a word are segmented. Give them a sheet of onset/rime pictures (see *Teaching Resources,* Picture Cards, Onsets and Rimes) to use. Emphasize that the activity should be quick and fun and that the idea is to make children curious about words and get them to enjoy manipulating sounds.

8 Identifying and Blending Onsets and Rimes

Follow the Path

Consider Your Children

Present this lesson after the children have had experience clapping words into syllables and have participated in shared reading of rhymes and songs. Use one-syllable words for this lesson. Be sure the children know what *first* and *last* mean. (They don't need to know the technical words *onset* and *rime* to understand the concept.) This lesson sets up a routine for word play that can be used any time during the school day. For example, while the class is waiting for another activity to begin, you can make a game of one or two quick problems.

Working with English Language Learners

English language learners will need a great deal of practice saying and blending onsets and rimes before they can use this information independently to play Follow the Path. Be sure they can identify and say the labels of the pictures used in the game. Demonstrate Follow the Path from beginning to end, and work with them in a small group until you know they understand the rules. Plenty of practice will help them become much more fluent with identifying and blending onsets and rimes, but practice periods should be no longer than two or three minutes.

You Need

- Follow the Path Game Board.

From *Teaching Resources:*

- Picture Cards, Onsets and Rimes.
- Directions for Follow the Path.

Understand the Principle

As children become more aware of the sounds in words, they learn to identify syllables. Each syllable has an *onset,* the sound before the vowel, and a *rime,* the vowel and whatever comes after it (in that syllable). A syllable can be a single word *(cat),* or a word can have several syllables *(caterpillar),* but most syllables have onsets and all have rimes.

Teaching children to hear, identify, and blend onsets and rimes gives them a foundation for thinking analytically about words. It is a natural way for them to break up words before learning about individual phonemes.

Explain the Principle

“You can hear and say the first and last part of a word.”

“You can blend word parts together.”

plan

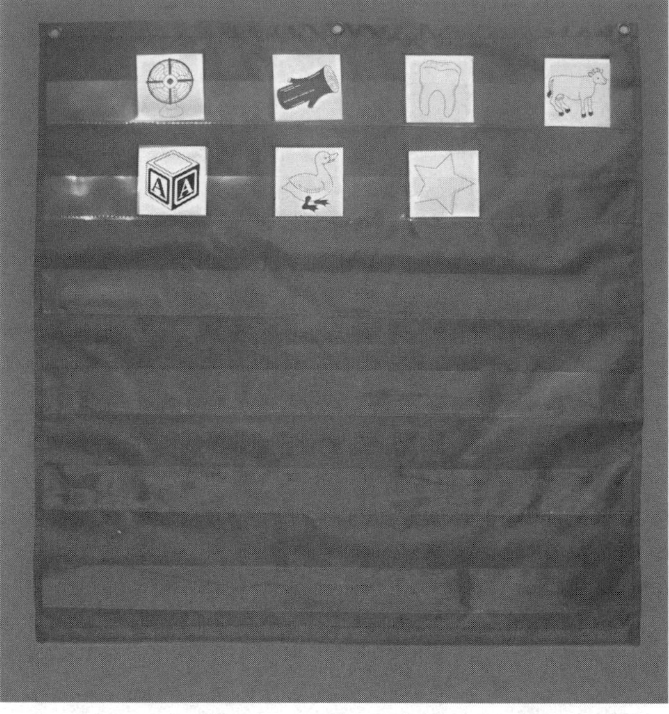

Explain the Principle

"You can hear and say the first and last part of a word."

"You can blend word parts together."

① Tell children that they are going to learn more about the parts of words by playing a game.

② Suggested language: "When you say a word, you can hear the parts. Say *tack*. [Children respond.] Now I'll say the first part by itself and then I'll say the last part: *t–ack*, *tack*. You say that. [Children respond.]"

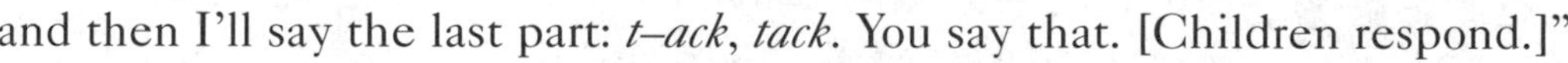

③ "Let's try another one. Say *b–ack*, *back*. [Children respond.] Try *black*, *bl–ack*. [Children respond.]"

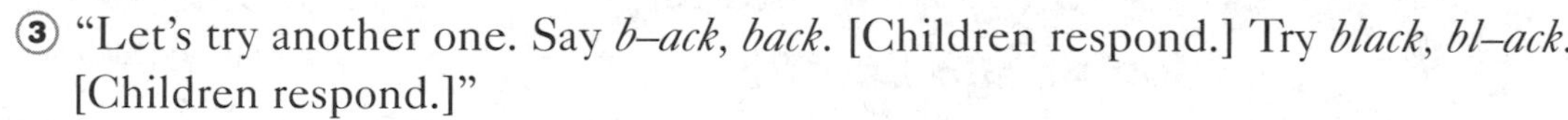

④ Have the children try *shack*, *pack*, *stack*, *crack; top*, *stop*, *shop*, *plop*, *mop; sip*, *nip*, *slip*, *snip*, *grip*, *flip; fan*, *man; stand*, *band*, *sand.*

⑤ Hold up a series of pictures and have the children take turns quickly saying the onset and the rime in the label for each.

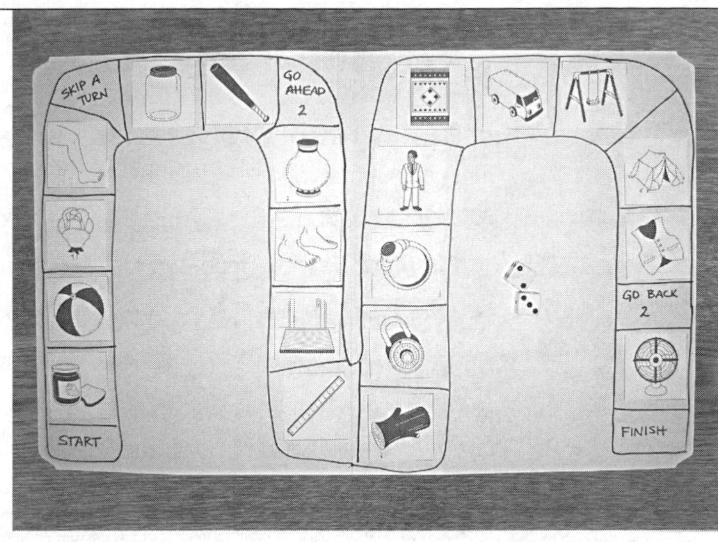

move
say word
say parts
say word

- Have the children play Follow the Path. Place pictures on the spaces (perhaps leaving a few "free spaces"). The children throw a die to determine the number of spaces to move forward. When they land on a space, they say the word that represents the picture, then say the first and last parts of the word separately, and finally say the word again *(string, str–ing, string)*.

Have the children share some examples from the game and demonstrate identifying first and last parts.

Link

Interactive Read-Aloud: Read aloud books that contain one-syllable words that rhyme, such as

- ***Big Black Bear*** by Wong Herbert Yee
- ***Here Comes Henny*** by Charlotte Pomerantz

Shared Reading: Put a stick-on note over the last part (rime) of a few words in a poem, chant, or song such as "I Don't Suppose" or "I Have Two Eyes" (see *Sing a Song of Poetry*). Read the verse, using the first part (onset) of these words to predict the last part. Uncover each word to confirm the prediction.

Guided Reading: When a child stops at a word he doesn't know, cover the last part of the word with your finger and say, "Say the first part." When you remove your finger, the child should be able to complete the word that fits in the sentence and check to be sure the word he says "looks right."

Interactive Writing: Have the children say a word and think about the first and last parts as they write it. If the children understand vowels, point out that the last part contains the vowel.

Independent Writing: Encourage the children to say the words they want to write and think about the letters they need for the first part and the last part.

assess

- Notice whether the children can identify the first and last parts of words. A quick check of two or three examples will tell you whether they have grasped the concept.

Expand the Learning

Begin with a blank Follow the Path Game Board (again with a "free space"). The children throw a die and draw a picture card, then say the word and the parts. If they can do it, they move the number of spaces indicated on the die.

Repeat the lesson using onset/rime and short-vowel picture cards (see *Teaching Resources*).

Connect with Home

At a meeting or in a newsletter, teach family members to play a game with their children in which they say the first and last parts of one-syllable words, perhaps in categories such as colors, clothing, food, or kitchen utensils (for example, *bl–ack, h–at, gr–apes, sp–oon*). Emphasize that the activity should be quick and fun and that the idea is to make the children curious about words and get them to enjoy manipulating sounds.

9 Hearing Middle Sounds

Picture Match

Consider Your Children

This lesson works best after the children have worked with their names and have participated in interactive writing. They should also be able to hear consonants at the beginning and end of words. In this lesson, the children will learn an important routine for matching middle (vowel) sounds. One of the issues in matching pictures is that the children may not have the same label for the picture in mind. In picture sorting, this doesn't matter: their own labels will work. The point is for them to say the words and think about the sounds. Over time, they will accumulate labels for all of the picture cards in *Teaching Resources* and be able to use those labels to think about sounds, letters, and words in different ways.

Working with English Language Learners

Matching pictures and saying the words and listening to the medial sounds will help English language learners acquire the phonology of the new language. Saying these words slowly, slightly emphasizing the medial sound, will make them more available than when they are heard within the rapid pattern of normal speech. Be sure that English language learners know, understand, and can say the picture labels before they are expected to match them by the medial sound. Play the matching game with a small group so that they understand the task. Provide several demonstrations.

You Need

- Pocket chart.

From *Teaching Resources:*

- Picture Cards, Long Vowel Sounds and Short Vowel Sounds.
- Two-Way Sort Card or Sheet.

Understand the Principle

Children need to say and hear medial sounds in words to develop a beginning understanding of the structure of words. The vowel sounds within words are difficult to hear. Some very brief practice attending to them in the absence of letters may help children listen more carefully to all parts of words, forming a foundation for comparing words and connecting sounds with letters and letter clusters.

Adding the print later helps children begin to relate the sounds of the language to the symbols on the page.

Explain the Principle

“You can hear and say the sound in the middle of a word.”

“Some words sound the same in the middle.”

“You can match words that sound the same in the middle.”

Explain the Principle

"You can hear and say the sound in the middle of a word."

"Some words sound the same in the middle."

"You can match words that sound the same in the middle."

1. Tell children they are going to learn how to listen for the middle sound in words.

2. In a pocket chart, place a picture card with the label that has the sound of *a* as in *cat*. Have other pictures ready, some that have the /a/ sound in the middle (choose words that have regular spelling patterns: *tub*, *cube*, for example).

3. Have the children say the word *cat* slowly and think about the sound in the middle of the word.

4. Suggested language: "You have been thinking hard about the beginning sounds of words and the ending sounds. Today we are going to think about some of the sounds in the middle of words. This is a word you know. Say *cat*. [Children respond.] What do you hear at the beginning? [Children respond.] What do you hear at the end of *cat*? [Children respond.] Now say the word *cat* and think about the sound in the middle."

5. After the children generate the /a/ sound, you may want to write the word *cat* to confirm their understanding, but just work with pictures for the comparisons at first.

6. "*Cat* has an /a/ in the middle. I've got some pictures here. [Hold up the picture of the van.] Let's say the name of the thing in this picture and see if it sounds like *cat* in the middle. *Cat*, *van*—they sound the same in the middle. Say them with me." The children say the words, *slightly* exaggerating the middle sound but keeping the words smooth rather than segmenting them.

7. Demonstrate with one or two more picture cards. Be careful not to use pictures whose labels start or end like *cat* for this first demonstration. Some sample pictures might be *pan*, *van*, *fan*, *bug*, *soap*, *tub*, *bean*, *tree*, *mop*. These labels provide some good contrasts, so that the children can just listen for the /a/ sound.

8 Help the children establish the routine of saying the two words and placing the picture card either under the picture of the cat in the first column or putting it in the second column because it doesn't match.

9 "We are going to play a game to decide which pictures are of things that sound like *cat* in the middle and which are not. First say *cat* and then say the name of the picture, like this. [Demonstrate.] By saying both words, you can tell whether the sound is the same in the middle."

10 If the words have the same middle sound, put the picture under the cat. If they do not, put the picture on the right under the question mark. Work your way through the stack of pictures, inviting children to join in.

say
put
read

- Have the children use the pictures to complete a two-way sort. They take out and mix up all the pictures. Then they match each picture to the picture of a cat by saying both words slowly and deciding whether it belongs under cat. If it doesn't belong, they place it in the right column. Then have them say the labels of the pictures under cat to a partner.

Select a familiar poem or chant (see *Sing a Song of Poetry*). Invite two or three children to find a word that sounds like *cat* in the middle.

Link

Interactive Read-Aloud: Read aloud books that repeat the same middle sounds many times throughout the text, such as

- ***Time for Bed*** by Mem Fox
- ***Better Not Get Wet, Jesse Bear*** by Nancy Carlstrom

Shared Reading: Bring the children's attention to words in the text that have the same sound in the middle—*cat/hat,* for example. Use poems such as "I Never Had a Dog That Could Talk" *(pig/jig, June/moon, had/that)* or "I Went Downtown" *(sour/flower, sharp/harp)* (see *Sing a Song of Poetry*).

Guided Reading: When solving an unfamiliar word, ask the children to check beyond the first letter for the vowel to be sure they are right.

Interactive Writing: Have the children say a word slowly and think how to write it beyond the first letter.

Independent Writing: Encourage the children to say the words they want to write and think how to write the vowel in the middle. Do not expect conventional spelling of vowels, but encourage the children to make an attempt at representing each sound with a letter.

assess

- Notice whether the children can identify the picture cards with /a/ in the middle.
- Observe whether the children can come up with good attempts at writing vowels during interactive and independent writing.

Expand the Learning

Repeat the lesson with other vowels as medial sounds (see *Teaching Resources,* Picture Cards, Short Vowel Sounds and Long Vowel Sounds).

Sort words with two different vowel sounds in the middle—words with /a/ as in *cat* and words with /o/ as in *mop,* for example.

Introduce a three-way sort (see *Teaching Resources,* Three-Way Sort Sheet Template) using three different medial sounds.

Connect with Home

Reproduce and cut apart a collection of small pictures. Give the children a piece of paper with a key picture (a cat, for example) at the top above a large circle. Have the children select pictures whose labels have the same middle sound (see *Teaching Resources,* Picture Cards, Consonant-Vowel-Consonant) as the key picture and glue them in the circle. Show them how to say the name of the key picture along with each picture in the circle when they take the paper home.

Hearing and Changing Ending Sounds

10

Making New Words

Consider Your Children

Use this activity after the children have had a great deal of experience saying and hearing sounds in words, matching ending sounds of words, and associating letters and sounds. Start with very easy phonograms. It will be much harder for the children to think of ending-sound examples than beginning-sound examples, because often the vowel sound changes when you change the last sound. Be sure the children know the meaning of *first* and *last* in relation to the sequence of sounds in words. Use this routine for word play at various times during the school day.

Working with English Language Learners

English language learners should be asked to change the sounds of words that they know and understand. Use the very easiest examples to begin with and recognize the children's attempts at pronunciation. As the children learn to manipulate sounds using simple, familiar examples, the phonology of English will become more apparent.

You Need

- Magnetic letters.

From *Teaching Resources:*

- Picture Cards, Ending Consonant Sounds.

Understand the Principle

As the children become more aware of the sounds in words, they learn to isolate and identify them and to recognize their position. This helps them connect sounds and letters, which in turn helps them begin to decode words and monitor their reading of continuous text.

Removing one sound and replacing it with another helps learners understand how to use knowledge of one word to write or read another.

Explain the Principle

" You can say a word to hear the last sound. "

" You can change the last sound in a word to make a new word. "

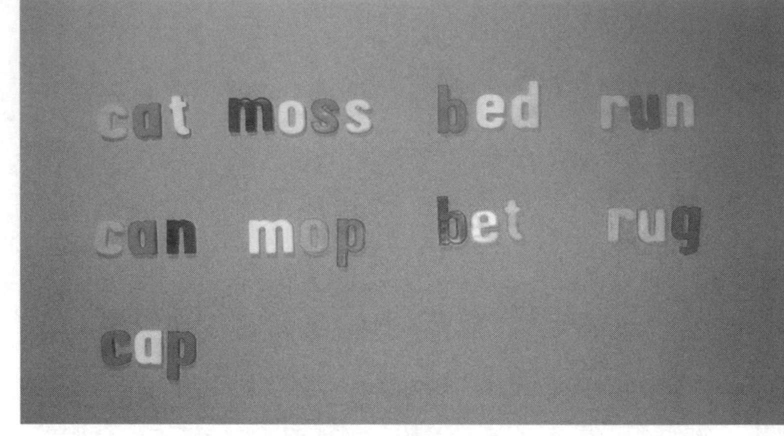

Explain the Principle

"You can say a word to hear the last sound."

"You can change the last sound in a word to make a new word."

① Mention to children that they'll be playing a word game.

② Suggested language: "We're going to play a word game today. When you say a word, you can hear the last sound, can't you? Say *cat*. [Children respond.] What's the last sound? [Children respond.] Say the last sound by itself. [Demonstrate if needed; children respond.] Now I'm going to say the word *cat* and I'm going to change the last sound to an /n/. Say the sound of *n*. [Demonstrate; children respond.] Listen while I change the last sound of *cat. Cat, can*. What did I change? [Children respond.]"

③ "Now change the last sound to /p/, *cap*. [Children respond.]"

④ "Let's try another one. The last sound of *moss* is. . . . [Children respond.] Now change the last sound to /p/, *mop. Moss, mop*."

⑤ Continue with two or three more examples. Use the same language each time so that the children know exactly what it means to change the last sound: "Say *bed*. Change the last sound to /t/. Say *run*. Change the last sound to /g/."

⑥ Continue with five or six more examples chosen from the following:

pat–pad	*lip–lid*	*can–cat*
hug–hum	*map–mad*	*hit–hip*
bit–big	*him–his*	*cut–cup*
fit–fill	*run–rub*	*sit–sip*
hat–ham	*sun–sub*	*cot–cob*
pin–pit	*tip–tin*	*win–will*

⑦ Ask the children to offer examples. Tell them that sometimes when you change the last sound, you don't get a real word.

take
say
change and say
make

► Have the children use selected picture cards to play this game with a partner. They say a word. Their partner changes the ending sound, says the new word, makes it with magnetic letters, and reads it. They reverse roles until each partner has made five words.

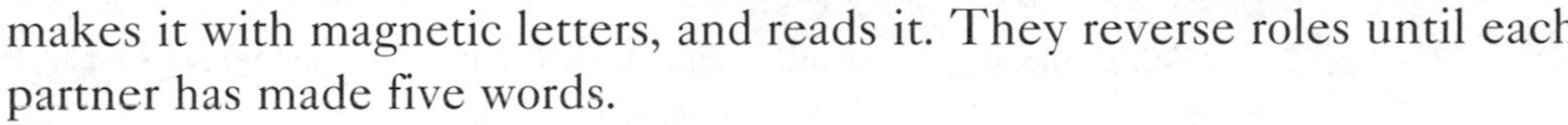

Have the children share their own examples and demonstrate changing last sounds.

Link

Interactive Read-Aloud: Read aloud books that play with words, such as

- ***Bear Day*** by Cynthia Rylant
- ***Little Black Truck*** by Libba Moore Gray

Shared Reading: Use poems and nursery rhymes such as "I Know Something" or "I Went Downtown" (see *Sing a Song of Poetry*) that include words that end alike.

Guided Reading: During word work, make a word with magnetic letters. Change the last letter to make a new word. Have the children use magnetic letters to do the same with a few words.

Interactive Writing: If an appropriate example arises, use the whiteboard to demonstrate making new words by changing the last sound. In this case, the children will be changing the last sound and seeing the letter change at the same time.

Independent Writing: Encourage the children to get to words they want to write by using known words and changing one of the sounds.

assess

- Notice whether the children can create a word by changing the ending sound of another word. A quick check of just two or three examples will tell you whether they understand the concept.
- Notice whether the children provide appropriate examples during the game.

Expand the Learning

Repeat the lesson using different examples (see *Teaching Resources,* Picture Cards, Consonant-Vowel-Consonant and Onsets and Rimes).

Make a game of some quick examples at the start or end of an instructional period or while lining up.

For a funny variation, take some of the names of the children in your class and change the last sound.

Connect with Home

At a meeting or in a newsletter, teach family members to play a word game with their children in which they call out the one-syllable names of items around the house or yard and then change the last sound—for example, *yard/yarn, rug/run, pan/pad.* Emphasize that the activity should be quick and fun and that the idea is to make the children curious about words and get them to enjoy manipulating sounds.

Hearing and Changing First and Last Sounds

Making New Words

Consider Your Children

Use this activity after the children can easily manipulate sounds in words by changing the last sound. This game increases the challenge by asking them to change either the first *or* last sound, thus creating greater flexibility. The children are thinking about the sounds rather than the spellings of these words, so the words used need not have the same internal spellings. (Use this as an oral activity at first, but add print quickly.)

Working with English Language Learners

Manipulating the sounds in words will help your English language learners realize how words work in English. You may want to use the Alphabet Linking Chart (see *Teaching Resources,* Materials & Routines) because it contains the key words that they will use for connecting sounds and letters. Be sure that the children know and can say the key words on the chart. Select words from the chart to provide the first examples of how to change first and last letters to make new words. Then use very simple examples that the children understand and can pronounce in a way that is close to conventional English.

You Need

- List of word pairs.
- Magnetic letters.

From *Teaching Resources:*

- Selected Picture Cards, Consonant-Vowel-Consonant, with labels that allow children to change the first or last letter to make a new word.
- Lined Four-Box Sheet.

Understand the Principle

As children become more aware of the sounds in words, they learn to isolate and identify them and to recognize their position. This helps them connect sounds and letters, which in turn helps children begin to decode words and monitor their reading of continuous text.

Manipulating sounds helps learners understand how to use knowledge of one word to write or read another.

Explain the Principle

“You can hear the first and last sounds in a word.”

“You can change the first or last sound in a word to make a new word.”

plan

Explain the Principle

"You can hear the first and last sounds in a word."

"You can change the first or last sound in a word to make a new word."

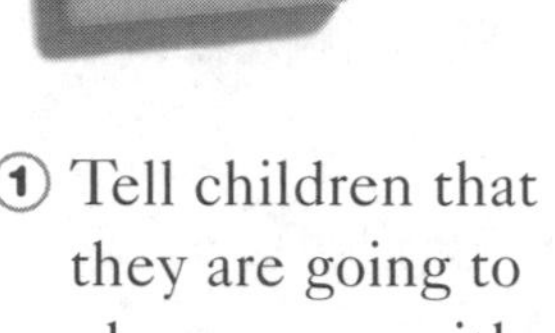

1. Tell children that they are going to play a game with sounds and words.
2. Suggested language: "You know how to change the first sound in a word to make a new one, don't you? Can someone think of an example? [Children respond.] You also know how to change the last sound in a word to make a new one, right? [Children respond with examples.] Today you need to listen very carefully. I might ask you to change the first sound *or* the last sound."

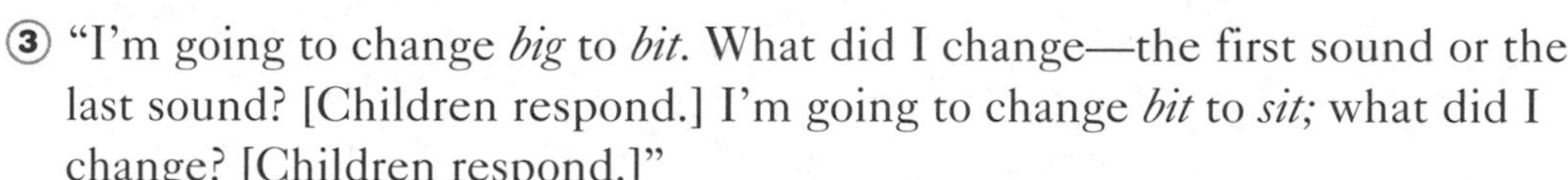

3. "I'm going to change *big* to *bit*. What did I change—the first sound or the last sound? [Children respond.] I'm going to change *bit* to *sit;* what did I change? [Children respond.]"
4. "Now let's play a game. Say *fan*. [Children respond.] Change the first sound to /m/. [Children respond.] Say *man*. [Children respond.] Change the last sound to /t/. [Children respond.] Say *mat*. You can change the first sound and the last sound."
5. Go through examples that keep children thinking about first and last sounds—for example, *hat, mat, map, cap; nail, pail, paid, maid; fog, log, lot, pot; red, bed, bet, set.*
6. Next introduce print and demonstrate the process. Say a word. Make it with magnetic letters. Say a new word and change the letters.
7. Finally, take the Lined Four-Box Sheet and show how to write the word pair in each box.

take
say
make
write
change
write

▸ Have the children, using selected picture cards, create pairs of words and record them on a Lined Four-Box Sheet. Have them select a card, say the word, make it with magnetic letters, write it on the first line, change the first or last letter to make a new word, and write the new word on the second line of the box.

Have the children share their own examples that demonstrate changing beginning and ending sounds in words.

Link

Interactive Read-Aloud: Read aloud books that encourage play with words, such as

- ***The Alphabet Keeper*** by Mary Murphy
- ***Flappy Waggy Wiggly*** by Amanda Leslie

Shared Reading: After reading and enjoying a text such as "Sing Sing" or "A Snail" (see *Sing a Song of Poetry*), select two or three words to make with magnetic letters. Invite a child to change the first or last letter to make a new word and read it to the class.

Guided Reading: During word work, make a few words with magnetic letters or on the whiteboard. Change the first or last letter each time to make a new word. Have the children do the same with three or four words at their tables.

Interactive Writing: If an appropriate example arises, use the whiteboard to demonstrate making new words by changing the first or last sound. In this case, the children will be changing the sound and seeing the letter change at the same time.

Independent Writing: Encourage the children to write unfamiliar words by changing one of the sounds in a familiar word.

assess

- Notice whether the children can create new words by changing beginning and ending sounds. A quick check of just two or three examples will tell you whether they understand the concept.

Expand the Learning

If needed, repeat the lesson with other words.

Introduce a minute or two of word play between instructional periods or while lining up. Say a word and ask the children to change the first or last letter to make another word.

Connect with Home

At a meeting or in a newsletter, teach family members to play word games with their children in which they change first and last sounds: *mat/hat/ham; mop/hop/hot.* Emphasize that the activity should be quick and fun and that the idea is to make the children curious about words and get them to enjoy manipulating sounds.

Letter Knowledge

Letter knowledge refers to what children need to learn about the graphic characters that correspond with the sounds of language. A finite set of 26 letters, two forms of each, is related to all of the sounds of the English language (approximately 44 phonemes). The sounds in the language change as dialect, articulation, and other speech factors vary. Children will also encounter alternative forms of some letters—for example, g, g; a, a; y, y—and will eventually learn to recognize letters in cursive writing. Children need to learn the names and purposes of letters, as well as the particular features of each. When children can identify letters by noticing the very small differences that make them unique, they can then associate letters and letter clusters with phonemes and parts of words. Knowing the letter names is useful information that helps children talk about letters and understand what others say about them. As writers, children need to be able to use efficient directional movements when making letters.

Connect to Assessment

See related LK Assessment Tasks in the Assessment Guide in *Teaching Resources:*

- Alphabet Test
- Letter Writing
- Matching Uppercase and Lowercase Letters
- ABC Order Sorting
- ABC Order Writing

Develop Your Professional Understanding

See *Word Matters: Teaching Phonics and Spelling in the Reading/Writing Classroom* by G.S. Pinnell and I.C. Fountas. 1998. Portsmouth, New Hampshire: Heinemann.

Related pages: 7–8, 46–47, 47–48, 69–72, 87–88, 90–93, 123, 138–139, 141–142, 143–147, 252–254.

1 Learning about Letters Through Names

Name Chart

Consider Your Children

The class name chart is important for the children who have limited knowledge of letters and sounds and who know very few words. Use this lesson early in the year to bring the group together as a community and teach the children to use their names as a resource. You can begin with first names, but for an advanced group, you may want to include both first and last names (or add last names after a few days). Following this lesson, make a permanent class name chart on large newsprint or tag board to display next to your easel so that it will be there for you and the children to make continual links in reading and writing.

Working with English Language Learners

Seeing their names on the chart will help English language learners feel welcome in the classroom and is also the best way to make them aware of the concept of letters, words, and sounds. This chart will be an important resource as they learn about letters; the connections they make to their names will help them generalize knowledge. Be aware that the pronunciations of names will vary and that the English sound-to-letter relationships won't always apply. You will of course teach regular sound-to-letter relationships in other lessons, but tell the children that names are often different from other words. Help everyone in the class say everyone's name correctly in the appropriate language.

You Need

- Pocket chart.

From *Teaching Resources:*

- Name cards, two for each child (Pocket Chart Card Template).

Understand the Principle

Beginning with their own names, children need to realize that words are made up of distinct letters and that words are always spelled with the same letters in the same order. This principle sets the scene for noticing spelling patterns in words.

Explain the Principle

" You can find letters in names [words]. "

" You can say the letters in names [words]. "

plan

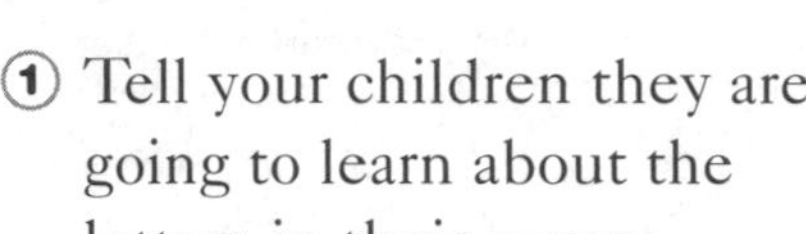

Explain the Principle

" You can find letters in names [words]. "

" You can say the letters in names [words]. "

1. Tell your children they are going to learn about the letters in their names.
2. Prepare cards for the pocket chart with the children's first names on them. Print should be large enough for all the children to see. In alphabetical order, hold up each child's name, say it, and ask class members to repeat it. Then, have each child put her name on the chart as you point to the appropriate pocket.
3. Suggested language: "This is Ariel's name. Ariel starts with an *A*. Say Ariel. [Children respond.] Say A for Ariel. [Children respond.] Ariel, put your name on the chart."
4. Read the chart with the children.

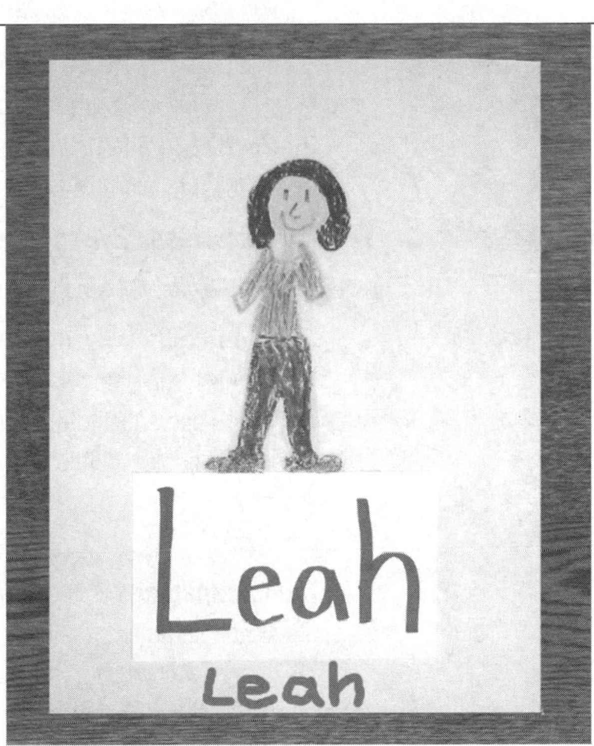

glue
write
draw

- Have another name card for each child that she can glue onto a large sheet of drawing paper, write her name underneath, and then draw a self-portrait. These pictures can be stapled into a class book of names or placed in alphabetical order on a bulletin board.

Have children show their pictures and read their names. They can exchange names with a partner and show them and read them.

Read the name chart one more time. Ask children what they have noticed about their names. Invite comments like these, which indicate children are noticing features of words and making connections between words:

> "Tanya and Troy have the same letter at the beginning."
>
> "Chelsey has a *y* like Troy."
>
> "Brittany and Vanessa have double letters."
>
> "The first letters used most often are *a*, *c*, and *j*."

Link

Interactive Read-Aloud: Read aloud books that focus on children's names, such as

- ***From Anne to Zach*** by Mary Jane Martin
- ***Away from Home*** by Anita Lobel

Shared Reading: Read the name chart again quickly each morning for a week. Use poems in which you can substitute names, such as "Jack Be Nimble," "Little Peter Rabbit," or "Mary Wore Her Red Dress" (see *Sing a Song of Poetry*).

Guided Reading: As the children are reading a text and come to a difficult word, help them make connections with the letters and sounds represented on the name chart. For example, if a child comes to the word *have,* you can say, "That starts like Harry."

Interactive Writing: Refer to the name chart to show the children how to make letters ("a *p* like the *p* in *Peter*").

Independent Writing: Have the children write their names on their drawings and other writing. Remind them they can use the letters in their names while writing.

assess

- Ask every child to write his name without looking at a model; look at the products to see how many letters the children are producing.
- Notice whether the children use their names as resources for interactive writing and independent writing.

Expand the Learning

Play a game: "I'm thinking of a girl whose name starts with *J* and who has a *t* in her name." Let children predict by going up and pointing to the name and reading it.

After the children know the names and first letters, locate names by the last letter or the next letter: "I'm thinking of a girl whose name starts with *S.* The next letter is *u.*"

Connect with Home

Have children take their name cards home and find something that starts with the same letter to glue on the cards.

Have them write their names and the names of family members.

2 Noticing Letters in Names

Name Graph

Consider Your Children

This lesson works best when most of the children can read their own names and some of the names of other children. They should be noticing the details of words and making connections between names and other words.

Working with English Language Learners

The English language learners in your classroom may have richly diverse names. Make every effort to say the children's names as they pronounce them. You may need to explain to the children that sometimes the sounds in names are different from sounds in the English words they are reading. Have all the children work to pronounce all the names of their classmates correctly.

You Need

- Pocket chart.

From *Teaching Resources:*

- Name cards (Pocket Chart Card Template and Word Card Template).

Understand the Principle

By studying their own names, children become more aware of the features of words. They learn that it is important to notice beginning letters and think about their labels and sounds.

By making connections between names, they begin to generalize knowledge of first letters. They also learn other aspects of word structure, such as number of letters and ending letters.

Explain the Principle

“You can find names [words] that begin with the same letter.”

“You can find names [words] that end with the same letter.”

plan

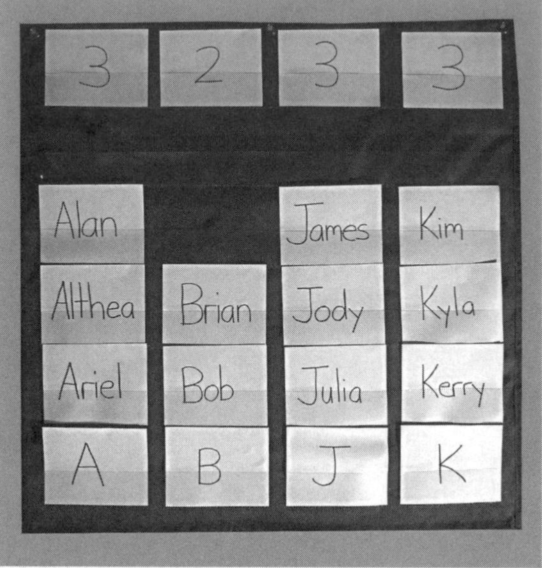

Explain the Principle

“You can find names [words] that begin with the same letter.”

“You can find names [words] that end with the same letter.”

① Let children know that today they are going to think about the letters in their names.

② In the pocket chart, have each appropriate first letter at the bottom of a column. Have name cards for each child. (Name cards should be of equal size and contain equal-size letters so that the graph will be attractive visually and the children can see relationships.) You will be placing name cards above each letter, making a graph.

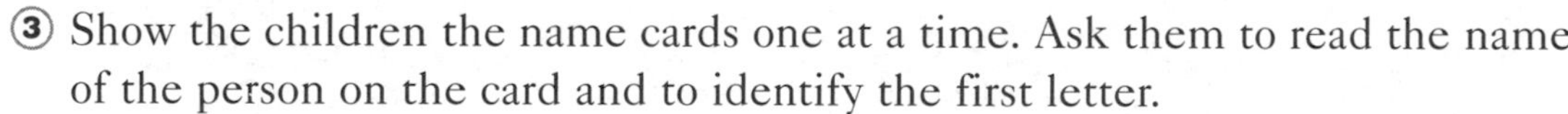

③ Show the children the name cards one at a time. Ask them to read the name of the person on the card and to identify the first letter.

④ Suggested language: “Today we are going to see how many of us have the same first letter in our names. Whose name is this? [Hold up the card for Ana.] What is the first letter? [Children respond.] That’s right, an *A*. I’m going to put it right above the *A* on our pocket chart. Whose name is this?” And so on.

⑤ Continue showing the names and asking the children to categorize them on the pocket chart.

⑥ Then count the number of children in each letter category. Place the number above the column for each letter.

⑦ Ask the children to locate names with certain features: (a) names that start with a vowel; (b) names that start with a consonant cluster; (c) names that have four letters; (d) names that have double letters in them.

⑧ Quickly sort the names by number of letters and ask the children to identify how you sorted them. Suggested language: “Find a name with four letters. Who is it? Find a name with eight letters. Who is it?”

⑨ Tell the children they will be working with name cards. Their task is to sort them by the first letter and then to sort them one other way. Ask the children to think of more ways to sort names. They may come up with:

- By the ending letter.
- Names that have double letters and names that just have single letters.
- Names of girls and boys.

sort
read

- Have the children sort name cards according to the first letter and read them to a partner.
- Alternatively, they can work in pairs, with one person reading each name and the other person putting it into the right column.
- Then each child should sort the names in one other way and the partner should guess the way of sorting.

Invite children to discuss what they have noticed about their names and the names of their classmates. Generate comments like:

> "No people have just one or two letters in their names."
>
> "Hanmeiwei has the longest name."
>
> "Patrick has a *k* at the end."
>
> "More people's names begin with an *M* than any other letter."
>
> "Five people have double letters in their names."
>
> "Ana has the word *an* in it."

Link

Interactive Read-Aloud: Read aloud books that contain alliteration (see *Teaching Resources,* Alliteration Books Bibliography), such as

- ***Some Smug Slug*** by Pamela Edwards
- ***Watch William Walk*** by Ann Jonas

Point out that the words sound alike because they start with the same letter.

Shared Reading: Following the reading of a poem or chant, such as "Slip On Your Raincoat" or "Three Elephants" (see *Sing a Song of Poetry*), have the children find words that begin like their names. For example, have Jonda find a word that begins like her name *(jump, just).*

Guided Reading: In stories the children are reading, help them notice names and the letters in them. During word work, have the children make a few words with magnetic letters. Point out the first letters in each.

Interactive Writing: Make connections to letters in names (or parts of names) as children connect to the words they want to write in shared/interactive writing. Use word endings such as the *al* in Randal.

Independent Writing: Encourage the children to use the name chart as a resource for writing words.

assess

- Notice the children's ability to quickly remember the first letters of their names and the names of others.
- Notice the children's use of their names and the names of classmates as resources for writing words.
- Observe the children's ability to make connections to names during interactive writing.

Expand the Learning

Make another name chart with last names added. Have the children sort the last names in the same ways.

Connect with Home

Send home a blank Word Card Template (see *Teaching Resources*) on tag board. Have family members write the names of friends and family in each box. After cutting the cards, children and family members can sort them according to first or last letters.

3 Identifying Letters

Name Puzzle

Consider Your Children

Although this lesson will not be necessary for most first graders, it will help those who have limited knowledge of letter names and are just beginning to recognize the distinctive features of letters. You may want to use it with a small group of children who need more work. For some, begin with just their first names; others who are further along may work with both first and last names. Have all the children in the group work together seated in a circle on the floor so you can direct and observe. Repeat this lesson as necessary until each child has full control of the letters in her or his first and last name and can make them without a model. Then send the name puzzle home.

Working with English Language Learners

Use the terms *name, word,* and *letter* as you work with the children. Guide English language learners to use these words themselves so they will develop familiarity with and fluency in talking about written language. Demonstrate the pronunciation of names and be sure that you are saying them as accurately as possible in the children's own language. Say the letters of each child's name and have the child repeat the letter name. Work with the letter puzzle each day until English language learners can put their names together easily and say the letter names.

You Need

- Large envelopes with children's first names on them (and room to add the last names).
- File folders in four different colors (to simplify distribution).
- Cut-up names inside the envelopes (using the same color stock as the folder helps keep the pieces from getting mixed up).
- Box or tub to keep name puzzles in as long as they are in use.

From *Teaching Resources:*

- Directions for Name Puzzle.

Understand the Principle

By putting together their names, children learn how to look at letters and notice distinguishing features and orientation. They learn that words are made up of letters and that the order of letters is always the same.

These concepts are important in recognizing words by sight using letter patterns and also in beginning to recognize spelling patterns.

Explain the Principle

"You can find letters in words."

"You can say the names of letters in words."

Explain the Principle

"You can find letters in words."

"You can say the names of letters in words."

① Tell your children they are going to learn how to put together their name puzzles.

② Suggested language: "Today, I'm going to give each of you your own name puzzle and show you how to put it together. First, take out the letters. Spread them out in front of you. Then match each of the letters with the letters in your name. Be sure they are exactly the same." Demonstrate placing each letter under the right letter, emphasizing that it has to look the same (including orientation). You may want to demonstrate on a vertical surface so that all the children can see clearly.

③ Demonstrate how to check letter by letter: *E–E, m–m, i–i, l–l, y–y*. Say the letters as you demonstrate checking. Remember that some children may not be able to say all the letters in their names at first.

④ Prompt the children to notice different characteristics of their names. For example, you might ask them to point to and name the vowels. You might also ask them to notice names that start the same, end the same, or have the same number of letters. Be sure to allow for the children's own discovery about letters and patterns in their names and the names of their classmates.

match
point
say
mix

- Have the children sit in a large circle on the floor. Give each child a colored file folder with their name puzzles in envelopes inside the folder. Helping one child (perhaps seating her in the middle of the circle), guide her through the steps of taking out the letters, placing them under the letters in her name, and checking letter by letter.
- Show the children how to mix up the letters and do it again.
- Have children mix up the letters and make their names three times.
- With their name puzzles flat in front of them, have children sit in a circle and talk about what they have noticed about their names. Look for comments like these:

  "My name starts like Ronni's—with an *R*."

  "I have an *r* in the middle of my name."

  "There are three children in our class that have an *R* at the beginning of their names."

  "I have a double letter in my name."

  "Some names are short and some names are long."

Have the children take turns reading their names and pointing under and saying each letter. When they come to a letter they don't recognize, tell them.

Have the children who know their first names easily also read the letters of their last names.

Show the children how to put their name puzzles away in a box or tub. Collect the puzzles by calling out each color.

Link

Interactive Read-Aloud: Read aloud books that have characters' names in the title, such as

- ***Alice and Aldo*** by Alison Lester
- ***Mary Wore Her Red Dress and Henry Wore His Green Sneakers*** by Merle Peeke

Shared Reading: Read poems such as "Polly Put the Kettle On" and "Mary Wore a Red Dress" (see *Sing a Song of Poetry*). Have the children use a masking card or highlighter tape to locate names. Then have them say each letter in the names they mark.

Guided Reading: During word work, have the children use magnetic letters to make and mix their names three times.

Interactive Writing: Write stories with the children's names in them: "Stuart likes to play ball. Madeleine likes to eat pizza." "Billy likes his new shoes."

Independent Writing: Encourage the children to use their names as resources when writing words. Encourage the children to write their names on their papers.

assess

- Observe each child's ability to put together his name, letter by letter, from left to right.
- Notice the children's attention to correct orientation of letters.
- Notice the children's ability to accurately spell their names.

Expand the Learning

When the children can put together their names and check them with the model, have them put them together left to right. Then have them put together the names without the model and check.

When the children can put together their first names easily, add their surnames to the puzzle.

When the children can put together their first names easily, have them put together a partner's name or a family member's name and check it.

Connect with Home

First graders who need this activity will quickly learn how to put together their names. When they know the routine for putting together the name puzzle, let them take it home to show their family members.

4 Learning Letter Names

Letter Minibooks

Consider Your Children

This lesson establishes the routine for working with letter minibooks. Children do not have to know any letters of the alphabet before beginning the letter books, but they should have worked with the name chart (ELC 1 or LK 1), name puzzle (LK 3), and Alphabet Linking Chart (LK 5) and have a beginning understanding of how to use these tools. Also, they should have had some practice writing their names. We suggest this sequence: *(b, m, r, s) (t, g, n, p) (c, h, f, d) (l, k, j, w) (y, z, v, q, x)*. If the children know quite a few letters, you can introduce two letter books in this first lesson and follow quickly with the rest. If the children have excellent letter knowledge or used personal letter books in kindergarten, you may not want to use this lesson in first grade.

Working with English Language Learners

Letter minibooks are an important tool for your English language learners to use at home: they contain pictures of objects with labels and will help them acquire a repertoire of nouns that they know. Have them use the minibooks at school until you are sure they know how to use them, store them, and care for them. For each minibook, go through the pictures carefully; have the children say the labels and then read the book several times. Have them locate the first letter of each word and say the letter, then read the word.

You Need

- Small storage boxes with children's names on them. (A small tissue box with the top cut completely open works well. Cereal boxes cut in half are also good.) Each child will need to store twenty-six books.
- Small pictures to glue in the books.
- Writing materials and crayons.
- Assembled *Rr* books for children using the Letter Book Template.

From *Teaching Resources:*

- Letter Book Template.
- Alphabet Linking Chart (Materials & Routines).

Understand the Principle

Many first graders know the names of the letters of the alphabet but may not have the quick, automatic letter recognition that helps them notice aspects of print, connect letters to sounds, and check on their reading.

Connecting letter names to their shapes gives children useful labels for identifying these important tools. It helps them understand teachers and parents as they point out and talk about letters.

Explain the Principle

“A letter has a name and a shape.”

“You can look at the shape of a letter and say its name.”

plan

Explain the Principle

“A letter has a name and a shape.”

“You can look at the shape of a letter and say its name.”

① Show children a box with a set of letter books and tell them that they will have their own boxes and books. Suggested language: “Today you are going to get a letter book.” Show the *Rr* book. “This book is about the letter. . . .” Children respond.

② “That’s right. It has *r* on the front. This is the uppercase *R* and this is the lowercase *r*.” Point to the letters. “This is a picture of a ring, which begins with *r*.” Point to the picture of the ring. “On this line, I am going to write my name.” Demonstrate.

③ Then show the first page of the book. “On this page, it says *r* at the top and here is a picture of a rose. Here is the word *rose,* which has an *r* at the beginning.” Trace the *r* at the top of the page, say the label of the picture, *rose,* trace the letter *r* in the word *rose* (children may not fully understand what the *beginning* of a word is, so point to the letter), and read the word.

④ Suggested language: “On this page, I read the letter, *r,* at the top, and trace it. Then I say the name of the picture, *rose,* trace the *r* in the word, and then read it.” Demonstrate pointing to the letter, tracing the letter, saying the picture label, tracing the first letter of the word, and reading the word on this page and page 3.

⑤ Suggested language: “On the last page, I see the *r* at the top and I get to choose [or draw] a picture there to go with *r*.” Have small precut pictures ready for children to use, or they can draw something. Demonstrate tracing the *r* and gluing in a picture. Tell the children to write the word on the line below. Turn back to the front of the book.

⑥ Suggested language: "You are going to get your own *Rr* book, and now I'm going to show you how to read your book." Go through the book reading the letter, saying the name of the picture, and reading the label.

⑦ "On the front cover, you say the letter name and the name of the picture and write your name on the blank line. On page 2, trace the letter at the top, say the name of the picture, trace the first letter of the word, and say the word. Do the same on page 3. On page 4, trace the letter at the top, choose your own picture, and write the name of the picture. Then read the whole book again from the beginning."

⑧ Read the Alphabet Linking Chart, A, a, apple, B, b, bear, etc., with the children.

say letter
say picture
write name

trace letter
say picture
trace letter
read word

trace letter
glue picture
write word
read word

- Give each child an *Rr* book and have everyone work simultaneously at tables while you circulate and help children.
- After they have learned this routine, they can perform it on their own with other letters.

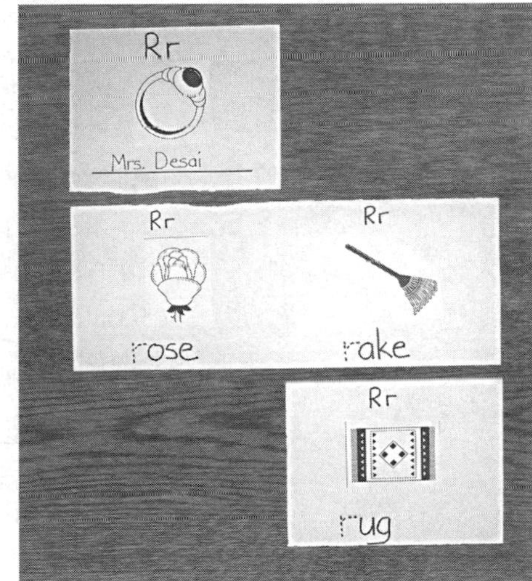

Have the children show a partner the picture they glued in and tell the label.

Have the children read their books to a partner, taking turns pointing and reading.

Link

Interactive Read-Aloud: Read aloud alphabet books (see *Teaching Resources,* Alphabet Books Bibliography, for additional examples), such as

- ***Animal Parade*** by Jakki Wood
- ***The Awful Aardvarks Go to School*** by Reeve Lindbergh

Shared Reading: After reading and enjoying a poem, song, or chant, such as "Little White Rabbit" or "Moon, Moon" (see *Sing a Song of Poetry*), name letters and have the children find them in the text using a masking card or highlighter tape.

Guided Reading: Use a letter book to help individual children who have difficulty with the initial letter and sound in a word. For example, a child who is trying to read the word *run* might be prompted, "Look, that word starts like *ring*" as you point to the word and picture of *ring* in the minibook. Have the children who need more letter/sound work read several of their letter minibooks quickly at the end of a group lesson.

Interactive Writing: Use letter minibooks to help the children connect the sound with the letter needed in a piece of writing. You can also make connections with the Alphabet Linking Chart (see *Teaching Resources,* Materials & Routines) and the name chart (ELC 1 or LK 1).

Independent Writing: Pull out a particular letter minibook to help a child associate sounds with the letters.

assess

- Observe whether the children can locate letters by name on the Alphabet Linking Chart and in texts.
- Observe whether the children can produce the name of the letter.
- Give a quick test of letter names using letter cards or a letter chart (or use the letter minibooks); don't present the letters in alphabetical order.

Expand the Learning

Repeat this lesson with different letter books. Go over routines until children understand and can perform the steps independently. After that, you can work quickly on a letter, saying its name and connecting it with any print in the room.

Have children read their letter minibooks independently or to partners.

Have a small group read their books to partners.

Connect with Home

In a meeting, show family members the letter minibooks and the storage boxes. After children have practiced the routines for eleven or twelve books, send the boxes home; children can then take each book home after making them. Encourage family members to keep the box in a special place and to make sure the books are always stored there. Have children read each book to a family member.

Encourage caregivers to get a set of lowercase magnetic letters for the refrigerator to make names and other easy words they know. (See *Teaching Resources,* Materials & Routines, Ways to Use Magnetic Letters at Home.)

5 Forming Letters 1

Verbal Path

Consider Your Students

The procedures in this lesson may be used many times for different letters, both lowercase and uppercase. Since children encounter mostly lowercase letters in the texts they read, begin with them. Work on letters that most children know or "nearly know." Use the children's names as a resource. Once the children have grasped the principle, the lessons will be quite short because they will have developed a system for learning the verbal path for forming a letter and the physical movements to make a letter. When attending to and gaining control of the movements, children need to use large movements. Lined paper may therefore be distracting. The children must have good control of efficient movements before being asked to attend to size, lines, etc. Many writers develop neat handwriting without using lines.

Working with English Language Learners

Be sure English language learners hear and say the verbal directions enough times to know what they mean. As they do more handwriting and think about and say the motions, they will take on new letters faster. At a meeting for caregivers, demonstrate efficient ways to help the children so that family members know the reason the children are using the verbal path and what it means.

You Need

- MagnaDoodle®.
- Dry-erase marker or chalk.
- Whiteboard or chalkboard.
- Sand/salt in a box.
- Sandpaper letters or newsprint and crayons.

From *Teaching Resources,* Materials & Routines:

- Verbal Path for the Formation of Letters.
- Letter Formation Charts.
- Letters Made in Similar Ways.

Understand the Principle

Learning efficient movements for making letters helps children feel how the letter is formed. It helps fix the features of the letter in the child's mind and visual memory so that it can be identified. An additional benefit is the growing legibility of their writing.

Explain the Principle

"You can make the shape of a letter."

"You can say words that help you learn how to make a letter."

"You can check to see if your letter looks right."

plan

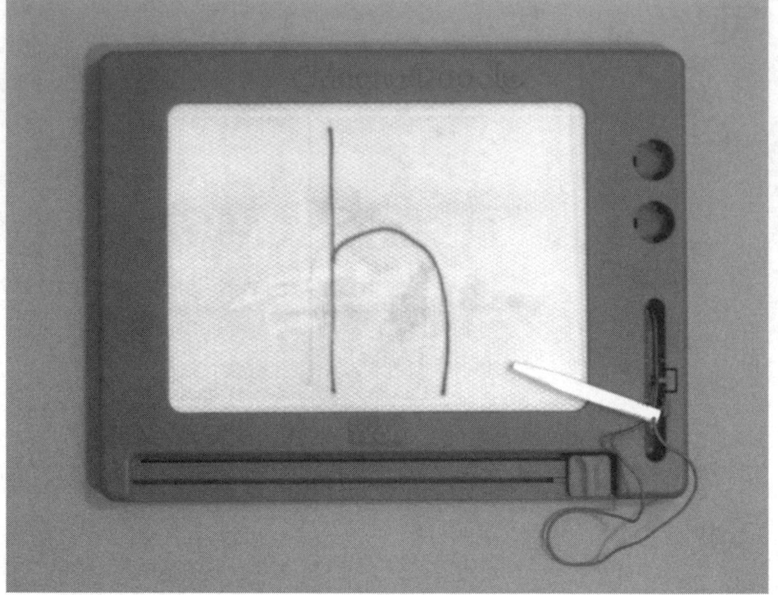

Explain the Principle

"You can make the shape of a letter."

"You can say words that help you learn how to make a letter."

"You can check to see if your letter looks right."

① Tell your children you're going to show them how to make really good letters.

② Say the name of a letter and then demonstrate how it is formed using the simple, clear language in Verbal Path for the Formation of Letters: "I'm going to make *h*. To make a lowercase *h*, you pull down, up, curve, and down." Make the letter slowly as you describe the movement.

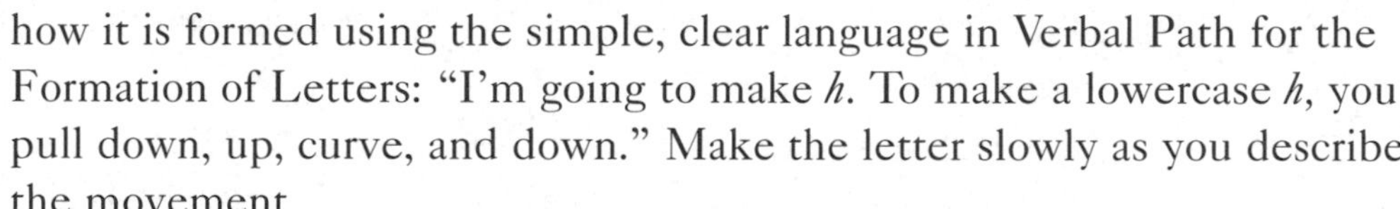

③ Make the letter again and invite the children to say the verbal path with you as you write.

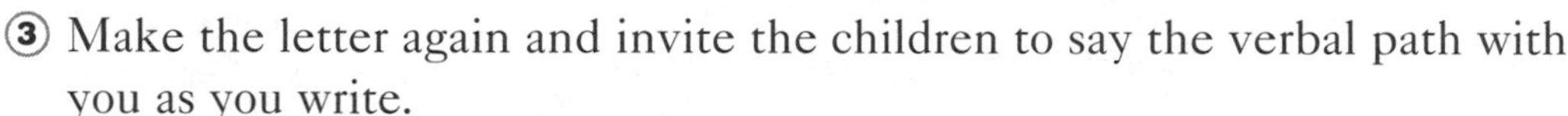

④ Invite the children to say the verbal path and make the letter in the air a few times and then on the carpet in front of them. (Asking children to make the letter on the back of the child in front of them is not helpful and disrupts the group.)

⑤ Work with a group of letters that start in the same place—*h*, *l*, and *b*, for example. (See *Teaching Resources*, Letters Made in Similar Ways for groups of letters starting in the same place.)

⑥ On a large piece of newsprint, teach the children how to make "rainbow letters." Write the letter in pencil yourself and place dots and arrows on it with a black marker. Each child writes and says the motions for the letter, tracing over your model in ink or crayon of a different color. Demonstrate with four or five colors. If you have time, have every child trace over the letter. When finished, you will have a large, multicolored letter one child can take home—perhaps someone with that letter in her name.

⑦ Demonstrate two or three ways you want children to make letters:

Write the letters in a flat box containing salt or sand.

Trace sandpaper letters.

Write the letters with dry-erase markers on laminated letter cards with dots and arrows.

make
say
write

- Have the children make today's letters using several different media, talking about thc motion as they do so. (Make a large version of the Letter Formation Chart to put up as a reference.)

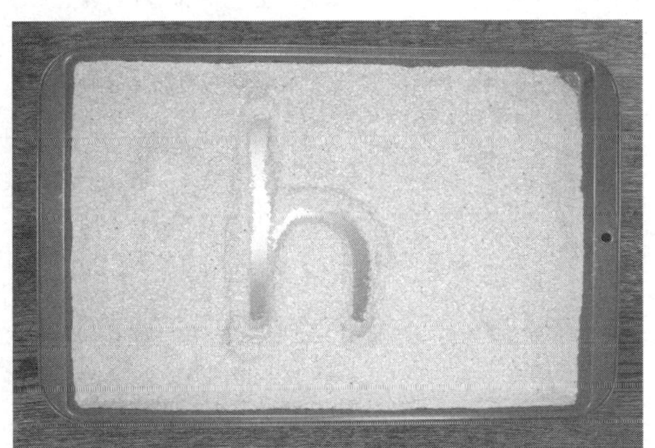

- Have the children make two of each letter on a paper to be turned in.

Have several children say the motions for today's letters.

Hold up the cards and ask what children noticed about today's letters. (You may need to model this process at first.) Comments like these will help you understand what the children are noticing about the distinctive features of letters:

"They are all tall letters."

"You pull down to make them all."

"The *b* is different because it has a circle."

"The *l* is different because it just has the stick."

"The *h* is different because it has a tunnel."

Link

Interactive Read-Aloud: Read aloud alphabet books that emphasize sounds as well as names, such as

- ***ABC Discovery*** by Izhar Cohen
- ***Goblins in Green*** by Nicholas Heller

Shared Reading: When reading a very familiar poem, such as "Where, Oh, Where Has My Little Dog Gone" or "What Do You See" (see *Sing a Song of Poetry*), or a piece of interactive writing, play a game by describing a letter while making it in the air and then asking the children to find an example.

Guided Reading: During word work, have the children find a particular letter and make the form in the air.

Interactive Writing: Use language to describe the motions when you model writing a letter they find difficult. When a child is writing a letter at the easel, use language to describe motions.

Independent Writing: Encourage the children to use efficient motions when writing and to say the motions if that helps them.

assess

- Observe the children to see if their handwriting is getting more efficient.
- Evaluate the children's written products to determine whether their handwriting is becoming more legible.
- Ask all your children to write a series of letters that you dictate. Identify the letters to which you need to continue to pay detailed attention.

Expand the Learning

Repeat the lesson with other lowercase letters: *a, c, e, g, o, f; i, j; p, r, m, n; d, q, k; u, v, w, y; x, z.* It may not be necessary to go over every letter in this kind of detail.

Repeat the lesson with uppercase letters that children are making in an inefficient way or find to be difficult.

Have children practice forming the letters using individual laminated letter tracing cards (see *Teaching Resources,* Materials & Routines, for directions).

Connect with Home

At a meeting, explain to family members why you are describing the motions for forming letters.

Give caregivers a copy of the uppercase and lowercase alphabet with the dots and arrows (Letter Formation Charts, see *Teaching Resources,* Materials & Routines) so that they can use them at home.

Caution family members not to expect perfect handwriting right away and say that you do not correct your students' handwriting when they are concentrating on what they want to say and represent with letters. Mention that you teach handwriting in special lessons.

6 Forming Letters 2

Handwriting Book

Consider Your Children

It is important to work intensively on handwriting early in Grade 1 so that the children learn efficient movements for writing letters. Use this lesson near the beginning of the year to establish the procedures for using a handwriting book. The routine, which takes only a few minutes and is easy to manage, is best used after the children are accustomed to using writing materials (paper, markers, pencils), can follow simple directions, can work independently for five or more minutes, and are using mostly conventional letters in their approximated writing. This lesson will be especially important if the children have had very little opportunity for handwriting or if they have formed the habit of holding pencils awkwardly and making letters inefficiently.

Working with English Language Learners

Demonstrate the task so that the children say the words and simultaneously make efficient motions for writing letters. Focus on only one or two letters at the beginning. If you are storing handwriting books in colored boxes, be sure English language learners know the English color words needed. Demonstrate and practice having the children take out the books, get writing material, write a page of letters, and put them away in the right place. These routines will be used over and over, so the time spent learning them is well worth it.

You Need

- A handwriting book for each child (a lined paper-covered composition book cut in half horizontally).
- Enlarged handwriting book for demonstration.
- Baskets or boxes for storing handwriting books.
- Newsprint and crayons.
- Class name chart (see Lesson ELC 1).

Understand the Principle

Learning efficient movements for making letters helps children remember the features of the letters. Saying words to fit the motions will help students remind themselves of the best way to make a letter. Frequent practice until the movements are established will help children become more efficient and fluent writers. Handwriting lessons take only a few minutes a day and are a way to help children practice regularly.

Explain the Principle

“You can make the shape of a letter.”

“You can check to see if your letter looks right.”

“You can say words that help you learn how to make a letter.”

plan

Explain the Principle

"You can make the shape of a letter."

"You can check to see if your letter looks right."

"You can say words that help you learn how to make a letter."

1. Tell children that today they are going to learn how to practice their handwriting.
2. Hold up a handwriting book. Suggested language: "Today we are going to start working with our handwriting books. This is my handwriting book, which I will use to show you what to write. On the front, it says 'My Handwriting Book,' and here is my name. [Demonstrate.]"
3. "Each of you will have your own book, and you will keep it in one of these boxes. [Point out the boxes of handwriting books.] The color of your box matches the dot on your book. Each time when you finish your book, you will need to put it back in the right box, and the dot will help you remember."
4. "I'm going to be showing you how to write letters on each page of this book. Every time you use your handwriting book, you will be writing a page of letters or words. This book is going to help you do your best writing."
5. "Today, we're going to practice forming *b* by making a 'rainbow' letter. Watch while I make a big *b* with a pencil. Pull down, up, and around." Make the *b*—on newsprint—about twenty-four inches tall. Have children practice making the *b* in the air and remind them of the routine. Then have them take colored crayons or markers and trace over the *b* (each time a little further out) while describing the motions. The colors will form a rainbow-like letter. (At the end of the day, let one child take the "rainbow" *b* home.)
6. If this routine is easy for the children, you can introduce two or three letters each time you do a handwriting lesson.

⑦ Show the children what you want them to do in their handwriting books. Explain that they will see a letter at the beginning of the line and they will make the letter carefully several times to fill the row.

trace
say
write
check

- Have the children add to the "rainbow letters" by choosing a color and tracing over each large letter while saying the verbal directions.
- Have the children take their own handwriting books and practice writing a line of the letters you modeled, creating a page of letters like the one you started.

Have the children demonstrate saying the motions to make letters.

Have the children show a partner the best letter they made in each line.

Have several children demonstrate finding their handwriting books in the colored boxes and putting them away.

Link

Interactive Read-Aloud: Read aloud alphabet books (and emphasize noticing letters), such as

- ***Old Black Fly*** by Jim Aylesworth
- ***Alphabet Soup: A Feast of Letters*** by Scott Gustafson

Shared Reading: Have the children locate letters they worked with in the lesson in poems such as "The Vowel Song" or "A Snail" (see *Sing a Song of Poetry*) or other texts using masking cards or flags (see *Teaching Resources,* Materials & Routines).

Guided Reading: During word work, have the children find the particular letter they learned. Model the formation on the whiteboard.

Interactive Writing: Describe the motions (see *Teaching Resources,* Verbal Path for the Formation of Letters) when you are modeling a letter on the whiteboard or when a child is writing a letter at the easel. Have the children "check" the letter and its formation after it is written. Have children locate a "really good" *b* (or any letter) after a piece is written.

Independent Writing: Encourage the children to say the motions while writing letters that are hard for them. Point out really good examples of letters that they write so that they can begin to self-assess.

assess

- Evaluate the children's writing to determine other handwriting lessons they need.
- Observe the children while they are writing to determine whether they are using efficient movements to write letters.

Expand the Learning

Repeat the lesson for the next day or two if the children are not getting and putting away handwriting books properly. It is very important for this routine to become automatic.

When the children are working in writing workshop, their attention should be focused mostly on what they want to write—the message—so you will not want to overemphasize letter formation. You can encourage them to use the verbal directions when needed and to do their best work. Accept approximations as children gradually gain control.

Repeat the lesson with the other lowercase letters. See the suggested teaching order in Letters Made in Similar Ways (see *Teaching Resources,* Materials & Routines).

Repeat the lesson with uppercase letters.

Connect with Home

Give family members a copy of the uppercase and lowercase alphabet with the dots and arrows indicating the required motions (see *Teaching Resources,* Materials & Routines, Letter Formation Charts) so that they can use them at home.

Encourage caregivers to have their children who are just learning how to make letters form the letters using finger paint, watercolors and a brush, a brush in water on the sidewalk, or their finger or a stick in a sandbox.

At a meeting, show caregivers the handwriting books and tell them that children will be bringing them home when they are filled up.

7 Recognizing Letters

Magnetic Letters

Consider Your Children

This lesson establishes the routine for sorting letters. It will be helpful to the children who have not noticed the details or shapes of letters and do not know many letter names. Work with three or four letters at a time, selecting letters that are dissimilar in shape. We suggest this sequence: *(b, m, r, s, i), (t, g, n, p, o), (c, h, f, d, a), (l, k, j, w, u) (y, z, v, q, x, e).* If your children have very little experience with letters, work with only two or three different letters with more examples of each.

Working with English Language Learners

Provide clear demonstrations so that English language learners understand what you mean by sorting items into categories. Talk about the features of letters and point them out. Have the children touch the letters while you are demonstrating the principle. Previous experience with picture cards will help them understand the routine. Children who have had very little experience with the letters that represent English (those whose own language has a different alphabet) will need many experiences sorting magnetic letters. Start with a few letters that are dissimilar and gradually expand the set.

You Need

- MagnaDoodle®.
- Magnetic letters on a vertical surface.
- Basket of magnetic letters.
- Name chart (see Lesson ELC 1).

From *Teaching Resources:*

- Alphabet Linking Chart.

Understand the Principle

Many first graders will know the alphabet, but others will need some explicit work focusing their attention on the important features of the letters. Recognizing and naming letters quickly and easily is an important skill for beginning readers and writers; it is the basis for connecting letters and sounds. Although the name of a letter does not necessarily connect with its sound, the label is necessary in order to talk about letters. The alphabet is also an important organizing tool.

Explain the Principle

"A letter has a name and a shape."

"Letters are different from each other."

"You can notice the parts of letters."

plan

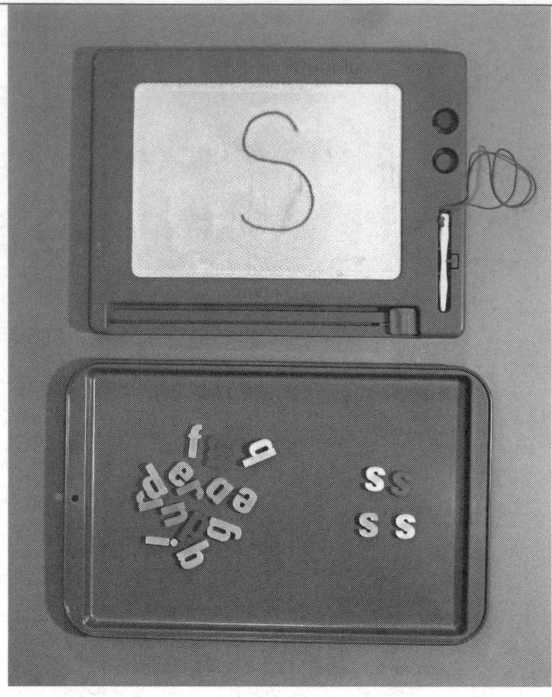

Explain the Principle

“A letter has a name and a shape.”

“Letters are different from each other.”

“You can notice the parts of letters.”

1. Explain to your children that they'll be learning how to notice letter parts. Be sure that all the children can see the MagnaDoodle® and the magnetic surface clearly. Begin with some *s*s, *t*s, and *m*s on the magnetic surface, plus several other letters. (For very inexperienced children, limit the number of other letters.)
2. Suggested language: “I'm going to make a letter.”
3. Make the letter on the MagnaDoodle®, being sure that the line is thick and black.
4. “This is an *s*. Say *s*. [Children respond.] Say *s* softly. [Children respond.] Say *s* louder. [Children respond.] To make *s*, pull back, in, around, and back. This is an *s*. It is a lowercase *s*. Who can find an *s* on the Alphabet Linking Chart? Who can find an *s* on the name chart? Now, I'm going to find an *s* among the magnetic letters.”
5. Demonstrate finding an *s* among the letters on the magnetic surface. Place the *s* clearly away from the others. Then ask several children to come up and find other *s*s and group them with the first one. Provide help as needed so that the process moves quickly.
6. Say the name of the letter each time you place it in the group. Also show the children how to “check” the group by pointing to each *s*, looking closely, and saying its name.
7. Repeat the process with the letter *m* and then with the letter *t*. Then tell the children that they will be finding *s*s, *m*s, and *t*s.

look
match

- Give the children a basket of mixed magnetic letters. Have children spread their collection of magnetic letters out on the table or a magnetic cookie sheet and group all the *s*s, *m*s, and *t*s together.
- Have them choose three other key letters and repeat the process.

Have the children discuss what they noticed about *s*, *m*, and *t*. Demonstrate and encourage comments like these, which give the children practice saying letter names and indicate they are looking closely at the letters as they sort them:

"*s* is curvy."

"*s* sounds like a snake and looks like a snake."

"I have an *m* in my name."

"*t* is like a cross."

"*m* has two humps."

Link

Interactive Read-Aloud: Read aloud alphabet books (and emphasize the shape of the letters as you read) such as

- ***The Hullabaloo ABC*** by Beverly Cleary
- ***Miss Spider's ABC*** by David Kirk

Shared Reading: Name letters and have the children locate them in poems such as "Slowly Slowly" or "The Moon Shines Bright" (see *Sing a Song of Poetry*) or other texts with a masking card or highlighter tape.

Guided Reading: After reading and discussing a text, engage the children in some quick letter sorting on the magnetic board.

Interactive Writing: Use names of letters to help the children locate the letter needed in a piece of writing. Make connections with the Alphabet Linking Chart (see *Teaching Resources,* Materials & Routines) and with the name chart (Lesson ELC 1).

Independent Writing: Point out letters by name when conferring with the children.

assess

- Observe whether the children find letters quickly and match and check them.
- Notice whether the children can produce the name of a letter quickly.
- Give a quick test using cards or a chart of letters that are not in alphabetical order. Ask the children to quickly say the names of the letters.

Expand the Learning

Repeat this lesson with different letters. (In Consider Your Children, we have suggested a sequence for lowercase letters, which are more useful to children.)

Repeat the lesson and mix in uppercase letters.

After children understand the routines for finding and grouping specific letters, increase the challenge by having a larger group of distracting letters. Prompt the children to work quickly and to check their groupings.

If your assessment indicates that the children have learned most of the letters, it will not be necessary to give every letter this attention.

Connect with Home

Encourage family members to sort letters in different ways (see *Teaching Resources,* Materials & Routines, 25 Ways to Use Magnetic Letters at Home). If children do not have magnetic letters at home, send home multiple copies of letter cards for them to use.

8 Looking at Letters

Letter Sort

Consider Your Children

This lesson teaches children how to sort letters, which is a useful routine during the first part of the year. It is especially helpful to children who have limited knowledge of letters and are just beginning to learn to look at print. You may want to use it with a small group of children who are less experienced than the group as a whole. Limit the number of letters and categories for children who have extreme difficulty. Include the entire alphabet, uppercase and lowercase, for children who already know most of the letters.

Working with English Language Learners

In this lesson, you identify key letters and ask the children to find letters that have similar features. Use the specific terms that describe letter features and ask the children to repeat these terms. It is particularly important for English language learners to internalize this information. Encourage them to explore letters and find relationships. Observe or work with three students at a time so that you can find out what they are attending to and can encourage them when they make connections. Repeat this lesson as many times as necessary until English language learners can perform the sorting task easily. Be sure that the form of the letters you use is consistent. You may need to work with a small group and go slowly, looking at no more than two features at a time.

You Need

- Magnetic letters.

Understand the Principle

Children must learn how to look at print. That means they need to learn how to notice the distinctive features of a letter—what makes it different from every other letter. These differences are very small, but a child must learn to see these distinctive features before a sound can be attached to a given letter.

Explain the Principle

“ Letters are different from each other. ”

“ You can notice the parts of letters. ”

plan

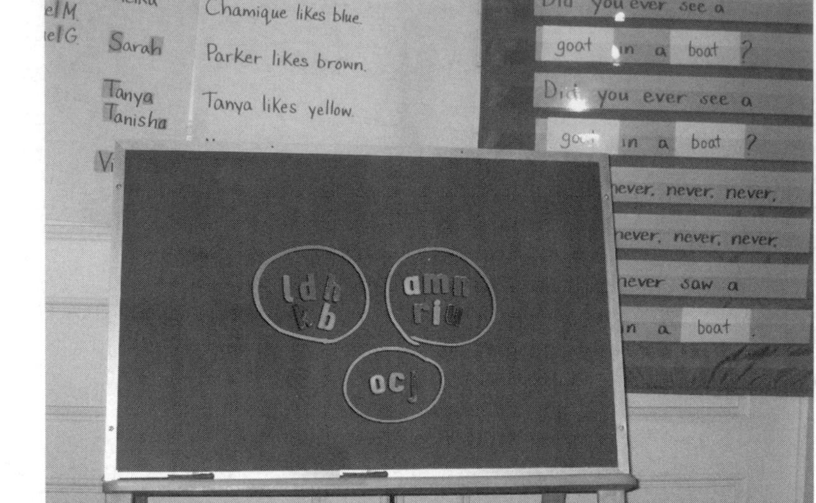

Explain the Principle

“ Letters are different from each other. ”

“ You can notice the parts of letters. ”

① Let children know that today they’re going to learn how to look carefully at letters.

② Using a magnetic easel or cookie sheet placed on an easel, show the children an array of fifteen or so lowercase letters.

③ Suggested language: “Every letter looks different from every other letter. These are lowercase letters. One of the ways that letters are different is that some of them have tall sticks and some of them have short sticks. Some have no sticks.”

④ “Here is a letter with a tall stick [show *h*]. Here is a letter with a short stick [show *n*]. What is different?” Children respond and talk about the letters.

⑤ Introduce more letters: *d, a, m, l, k, r, b, i, u, j, y, p, n.* Ask the children in which category each letter belongs—long stick, short stick, or no stick.

⑥ Draw a circle around the categories—tall stick, short stick, no stick.

⑦ Ask, “Can anyone think of another way to put letters together?” Some children may suggest ideas like “letters that have circles and letters that don’t have circles.” Demonstrate one or two other simple ways to sort letters.

⑧ Then demonstrate how to do a three-way sort. Place three letters that have a distinctive feature (long stick, short stick, no stick) at the top of the magnetic board. Using the rest of the letters, take one letter at a time and place it under the letter with a similar feature.

choose
place
check

- Have the children sort the letters *l, d, h, a, m, n, k, b, r, i, u, j, y, p, g* into three categories: long sticks, short sticks, and no sticks. Partners can check each other's work.
- Ask partners to find one more way to sort letters and prepare to share it with the group.

Invite the children to discuss what they have noticed about the letters they have sorted. Invite comments like these:

"Some letters are tall and some are short."

"Some letters have dots and some do not have dots."

"Some letters have curves and some have straight lines."

"Some letters have tunnels."

"Some letters have zigzags or points and others have curved lines."

Link

Interactive Read-Aloud: Read aloud alphabet books that draw attention to the distinctive features of letters, such as

- ***Chicka Chicka Boom Boom*** by Bill Martin, Jr.
- ***Alphabatics*** by Suse MacDonald

Shared Reading: Read poems or sing songs such as "Merrily We Roll Along" or "I've Got a Dog as Thin as a Rail" (see *Sing a Song of Poetry*). Ask the children to locate letters that have long and short sticks within words and to name the letters.

Guided Reading: During word work, have the children sort letters several ways (see *Teaching Resources*, Ways to Sort Letters).

Interactive Writing: When the children are making a letter, mention that the letter has a long or short stick or no stick.

Independent Writing: During writing conferences, guide children to notice and talk about features of letters.

assess

- Notice the children's ability to sort letters into categories.
- Examine the children's writing to note letter formation.

Expand the Learning

Sort letters with circles and letters with tunnels: *a, d, b, u, n, m, o, q, h, g.*

Sort letters with tails and letters with no tails: *a, b, c, d, e, f, g, h, i, j, k, l, m, n, o, p, q, r, s, t, u, v, w, x, y, z.*

Sort letters with crosses and letters without crosses: *t, f, h, d, v, a.*

Sort letters with dots and letters without dots: *i, j, f, t, g, x.*

Sort letters with straight sticks and letters with curves: *c, x, o, k, s, t, w, x, y, z, l.*

Sort letters with straight sticks, letters with curves, and letters with *both* straight sticks and curves: *a, b, c, d, e, f, g, h, i, j, k, l, m, n, o, p, q, r, s, t, u, v, w, x, y, z.*

Connect with Home

Send home a set of letters on individual cards and ask children to sort them by long and short sticks and/or other categories. You may want to send home a list of Ways to Sort Letters (see *Teaching Resources*).

9 Recognizing and Naming Letters

Alphabet Linking Chart

Consider Your Children

This lesson establishes different routines for "reading" the Alphabet Linking Chart and for using it as a tool. (The chart differs slightly from the one used in kindergarten in that there are two sounds for *c* and *g*.) It is especially helpful to children who have not noticed the details or shapes of letters and who do not know many letter names. It helps all the children learn how to use the chart as a tool in their own writing.

Working with English Language Learners

The Alphabet Linking Chart is a very helpful tool for English language learners. Many repetitions of "reading" this chart will help these children internalize the names of the letters of the alphabet and connect them with the graphic figures. Varying the task will help English language learners recognize the letters by name automatically, knowledge that will help them understand and respond to classroom instruction.

You Need

- MagnaDoodle®.
- Name chart (see Lesson ELC 1).

From *Teaching Resources:*

- Alphabet Linking Chart (enlarged) and pointer.
- An Alphabet Linking Chart for every child.

Understand the Principle

Rapid, automatic letter recognition is helpful to children as they learn letter/sound relationships and begin to use print to check their reading and solve words using letters and sounds. Knowing the letter names and connecting them to the shapes helps children understand the language of the classroom. Knowing how to use the Alphabet Linking Chart helps children with their writing and reading.

Explain the Principle

" A letter has a name and a shape. "

" You can look at the shape of a letter and say its name. "

plan

Explain the Principle

" A letter has a name and a shape. "

" You can look at the shape of a letter and say its name. "

① Let children know that they'll be learning more about letters.

② Suggested language: "Today we are going to learn some ways to read the Alphabet Linking Chart. This chart is important because it helps you remember the names of the letters, how they sound, and how they look. One of the things you can do when you are working in class is to read the Alphabet Linking Chart, and that will help you remember the letter names, sounds, and shapes."

③ Demonstrate reading the chart with a thin pointer. Be sure that the pointer (or your arm) does not obscure the children's view of the letters, because it is very important that they be able to see them clearly. Read the chart, letter by letter, saying *A–a, B–b, C–c, D–d,* etc. Suggested language: "That's one way to read the chart. Let's do it together." Repeat with the children.

④ Suggested language: "Now let's read it another way. This time I am going to skip every other letter." Demonstrate: *A–a, C–c, E–e, G–g,* etc. Have the children join you. This task will be much more difficult for them, so you may need to proceed more slowly. They will have to look at the letters rather than just remembering their ABCs.

⑤ Suggested language: "Now I'm going to show you another way. This time I am going to read the letter and say the name of the picture." Read *A–a–apple, B–b–bear,* etc. Have the children join you.

⑥ Suggested language: "Let's try one more way. This time I am going to read just the words under the pictures." Read *apple, bear, cat, celery, dog, egg,* etc. Have the children join you.

⑦ "We'll be learning lots of ways to read this chart. Today, each of you will be getting a small copy of this Alphabet Linking Chart. Take your pointing finger and read the chart two different ways to your partner. Then bring your chart to sharing time."

read
read
color

▸ Have the children read the chart two ways to a partner. Then have them color the pictures with markers, crayons, or colored pencils.

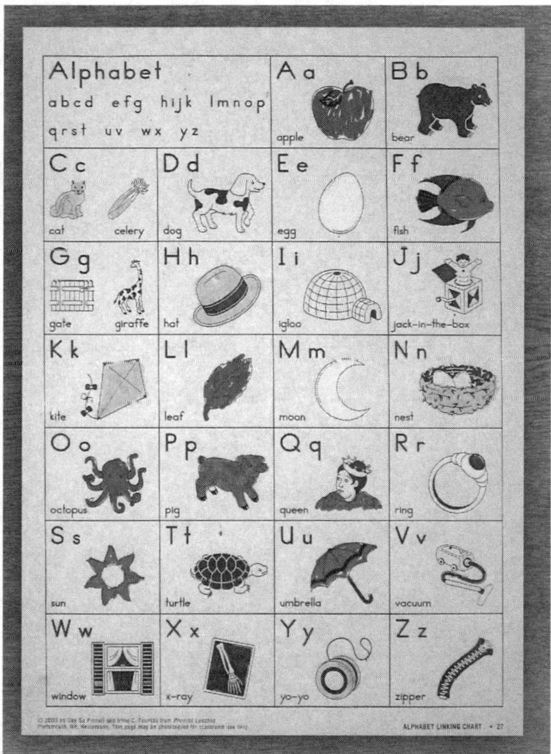

Have the children demonstrate reading the chart, skipping every other letter, with a new partner.

Link

Interactive Read-Aloud: Read aloud alphabet books, such as

- ***Q Is for Duck*** by Mary Elting
- ***The Absolutely Awful Alphabet*** by Mordicai Gerstein

Shared Reading: Read the Alphabet Linking Chart a different way for several days until the children know the chart very well. Have the children use a masking card or highlighter tape to locate particular letters in poems or other texts such as "I Don't Suppose" or "Five Little Sparrows" (see *Sing a Song of Poetry*).

Guided Reading: Have individual children read the Alphabet Linking Chart with you. During word work, show the children a magnetic letter and have them find the letter on the chart.

Interactive Writing: Use the names of letters to help the children locate the letter needed in a piece of writing. Make connections with the Alphabet Linking Chart and with the name chart (ELC 1 and LK 1).

Independent Writing: Point out letters by name when conferring with the children.

assess

- Observe whether the children can find letters quickly on the Alphabet Linking Chart.
- Notice if they can say the names of letters quickly.
- Observe whether the children can use the Alphabet Linking Chart as a resource during interactive or independent writing.
- Point randomly to letters on the chart and ask the children to read the letters and say the names of the pictures.

Expand the Learning

Teach the children additional ways to read the chart, increasing the level of challenge. Here are some possibilities: (1) read every other box, starting with *b;* (2) start in the middle of the chart and read back and forth to the same place; (3) alternate halves of the group reading letters, saying the names of pictures, or reading words; (4) read only the consonants; (5) read only the vowels; (6) read down the columns; (7) read the chart backward; (8) have one partner or one half of the group read the letters on the chart, the other partner or half of the group read the word below the picture.

Connect with Home

Give the children a small version of the Alphabet Linking Chart to read at home.

10 Noticing Letters in Words

Magnetic Letters

Consider Your Children

In this lesson, you show children how to build words and check them, a routine that will be useful as a foundation for writing as well as reading. The lesson is based on children's knowledge of the alphabet and their understanding of the alphabetic principle. Determine children's knowledge of letters by using the alphabet inventory in the Assessments Guide (see *Teaching Resources*). Also notice what words children are learning. When the children know only a few high frequency words, use them for the word-building activities. Start with a small number of words. Gradually increase the number of words they can build.

Working with English Language Learners

It is important that English language learners learn the names of the letters so they can understand classroom instruction. They may need several demonstrations of letters and names, and at the beginning you may want to work with a small set of letters (for example, find all the *b*s in a set of four different letters). Begin with letters that are very different from each other and have the children say the name of the letter each time they find it.

You Need

- Chart.
- Magnetic letters.
- Magnetic surface.

From *Teaching Resources:*

- Making Words Sheet.
- Word Cards, High Frequency Words.

Understand the Principle

Grasping the alphabetic principle is a fundamental understanding for beginning readers and writers. Children must simultaneously recognize letters by their distinctive visual features and connect those letters to the sounds that they hear in words. They also need to recognize letters that are embedded in words.

Building words that they have seen before in shared reading and interactive writing will help children make those connections as they work with words they know. Once a word has been experienced in many ways, it is phonologically more available to children.

Explain the Principle

" You can find letters in words. "

plan

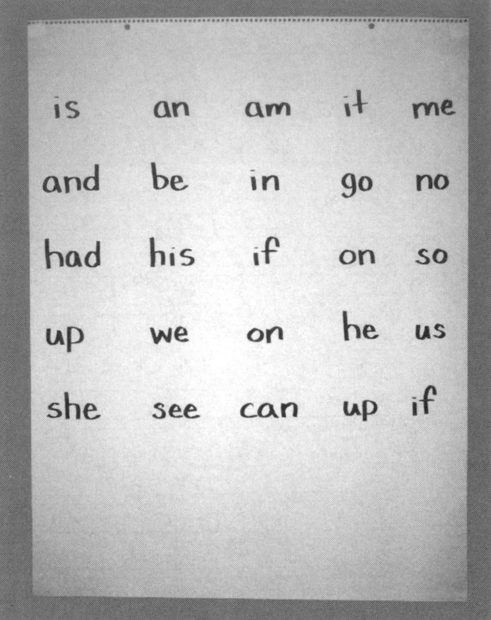

is an am it me
and be in go no
had his if on so
up we on he us
she see can up if

Explain the Principle

“You can find letters in words.”

① Tell your children you are going to help them learn more about the letters in words.

② Have some high frequency words on a chart on the easel or on the chalkboard. Start with words the children have seen and located before in shared reading and interactive writing. These may be “word wall” words or other familiar words. Use fewer words if the children are less experienced. (The words selected here have “regular” letter/sound relationships.)

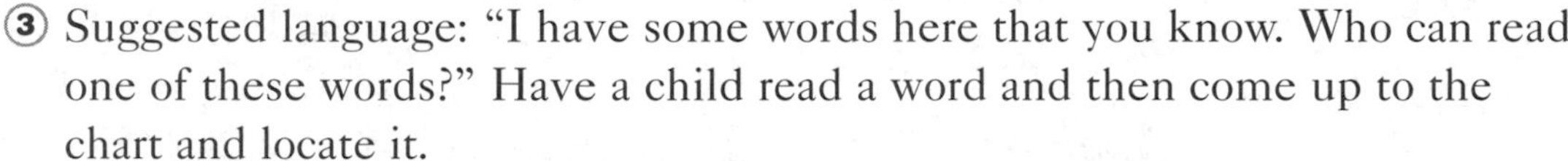

③ Suggested language: “I have some words here that you know. Who can read one of these words?” Have a child read a word and then come up to the chart and locate it.

④ Suggested language: “I'm going to make this word with magnetic letters.”

⑤ Using a cookie sheet or other magnetic surface, demonstrate making the word and checking it letter by letter, saying the names of the letters *(a–a, n–n, d–d)*.

⑥ Suggested language: “You can check your word another way, too. Move your finger under the word and say it slowly. You can hear the sounds.”

⑦ Demonstrate running your finger under the word. Suggested language: “You can hear the *a*, the *n*, and the *d* at the end—*a–n–d*.”

⑧ Ask the children to demonstrate moving a finger under the word and then identifying the sounds and letters.

⑨ Continue the demonstration with other words.

take
make and mix (3x)
check and say
write

- Give the children a set of high frequency word cards and a Making Words Sheet. Include the words used in the lesson.
- Have the children place a word card in the left column, make the word and mix it three times with magnetic letters, checking it letter by letter each time, check it by saying it slowly while moving a finger under it to check the sounds, and then write the word in the last column.

Ask the children to talk about what they learned from building words. Have visible the chart of words with which they worked. Comments like these will give you information about what children are learning about words:

> "I know *is* because I read it."
>
> "*Is* and *in* start the same."
>
> "*Me* and *he* rhyme."
>
> "To make *and*, you add a *d* to *an*."

Link

Interactive Read-Aloud: Read aloud ABC books to reinforce and extend letter learning, such as

- ***Accidental Zucchini*** by Max Grover
- ***A Is for Amos*** by Deborah Chandra

Shared Reading: After reading and enjoying a poem such as "1, 2, 3" or "Aunt Maria" (see *Sing a Song of Poetry*), have the children locate known words in the text using a masking card or highlighter tape. Ask them to check the words by moving a finger under them and saying them slowly to check the sounds.

Guided Reading: After reading and discussing a text, have the children find a particular word on a page you specify ("Find *can* on page 3"). Ask them to check the word by saying it slowly and sliding a finger under it as they say it.

Interactive Writing: Write yourself words that the children already know, but ask them to check the spelling by saying words slowly and matching the letters with the sounds.

Independent Writing: Encourage the children to say words slowly and represent all the sounds they can hear. Also encourage them to check the word they wrote by moving a finger under it and thinking about the sounds. The goal is not accuracy but learning to think about letters and sounds and their order in words.

assess

- Observe the children's growing ability to recognize the letters of the alphabet and a few high frequency words.
- Notice whether the children are able to check the sounds and letters in the words they read and write.

Expand the Learning

Extend the lesson by repeating it with more words. For a very inexperienced group of children, you will want to start with a few words and gradually increase the set.

Show the children how, in their own writing, they can check the word by saying it slowly and thinking about the letters and sounds.

Connect with Home

Help family members understand how to help children to build words with magnetic letters or letter cards (see *Teaching Resources,* 25 Ways to Use Magnetic Letters at Home). Explain that it is important for children to check the letters and sounds by sliding a finger under the letters in the word as they read it.

You may want to send home word lists that reflect the particular words children need to practice.

11 Matching Letters

Letter Lotto

Consider Your Children

This lesson establishes the routine of playing Bingo, which can be used for many purposes. The activity is appropriate for children who have little letter knowledge, who know upper- but not lowercase letters, who do not recognize letters quickly and automatically, or who can say the alphabet but do not readily recognize letters when they are embedded in words. Use this lesson after the children have worked with the name chart and can read most of the names of the children in the class.

Working with English Language Learners

This lesson will be especially helpful to English language learners who have little letter knowledge. Play the game with a small group (or the whole class) several times so that they can easily follow the procedures. Using their names will provide a great deal of practice saying the names of the letters and noticing distinctive features of letters. Some English language learners may not be able to say all the names of the letters, but matching them by form will build their knowledge of the features.

You Need

- Two enlarged Lotto game boards.
- Selected stick-on letters from children's names.

From *Teaching Resources:*

- Directions for Lotto.
- Lotto Game Cards.
- Letter cards (multiple sets).

Understand the Principle

Being able to recognize letters quickly and automatically is basic to the ability to decode and recognize words rapidly. Children need thorough, flexible knowledge of letters' visual features so they can distinguish them when they are embedded in print.

Explain the Principle

"Letters are different from each other."

"You can notice the parts of letters."

plan

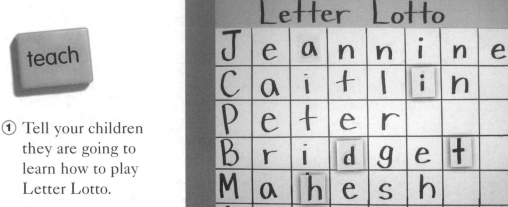

Explain the Principle

" Letters are different from each other. "

" You can notice the parts of letters. "

1. Tell your children they are going to learn how to play Letter Lotto.

2. Suggested language: "You have been learning to read the names of the children in our class. Today we are going to play a game with our names. It's called Letter Lotto."

3. Have the children read the names on the enlarged Lotto charts. Then select one child to be your partner to show everyone how to play the game.

4. Suggested language: "Here are some letter cards [or you may use stick-on notes]. I'm going to take one and look at it and say the name of the letter. Then I am going to see if I have a letter that matches it. If it's uppercase, I'll look for an uppercase letter. If it's lowercase, I'll look for a lowercase letter."

5. Demonstrate taking a letter and finding a match by comparing it with the letters on your game board. Let's say you draw an *h*. Suggested language: "The letter I've drawn is *h*. Mahesh has an *h*." Place the card [or stick-on note] with the *h* over one of the *h*s in Mahesh's name. "I keep on taking cards as long as I can find a letter to match." Demonstrate taking cards and matching letters until there is no match. Put the nonmatching letter in another pile, face down.

6. Then instruct your partner to take a turn. Moving quickly, continue taking turns until one player covers all of the letters on the card and says, "Lotto."

7. Show children the letter cards and Lotto game boards they will use to play Letter Lotto with their classmates.

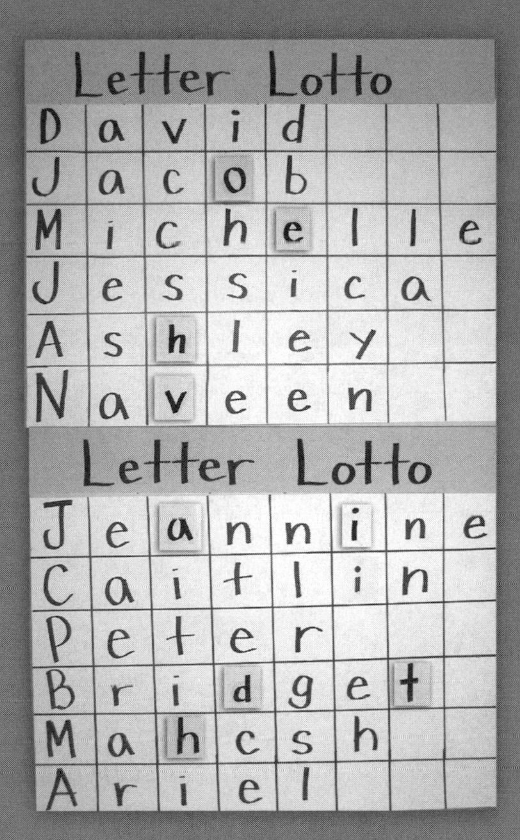

apply

take
say
match

- Have the children play Letter Lotto in groups of two, three, or four.

Invite the children to discuss what they learned from playing Letter Lotto. Look for comments like these:

> "Sometimes you have more than one letter that matches."
>
> "The capital letters are only at the beginning of names."
>
> "You have more lowercase than uppercase letters to match."
>
> "Remembering where the letters are helps you find a match."

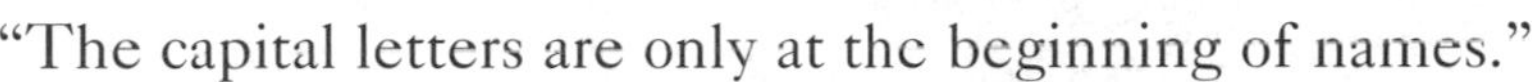

Link

Interactive Read-Aloud: Read aloud alphabet books to reinforce and extend letter knowledge, such as

- ***Pignic*** by Anne Miranda
- ***Animalia*** by Graeme Base

Shared Reading: Name letters and have the children locate them quickly in poems such as "Three Jolly Gentlemen" or "Nut Tree" (see *Sing a Song of Poetry*) or other texts you are reading together. Have them say whether letters are at the beginning of words or the end of words.

Guided Reading: During word work, have the children quickly match letter pairs in uppercase or lowercase form.

Interactive Writing: Use names of letters to help the children locate the letter needed in a piece of writing. Make connections with the Alphabet Linking Chart (see *Teaching Resources*) and with the name chart (see Lessons ELC 1 and LK 1).

Independent Writing: Point out letters by name when conferring with the children about their writing. Show them how to use the Alphabet Linking Chart as a resource.

assess

- Have the children quickly find letters in names, on the Alphabet Linking Chart, and in a simple page of print (about three lines). Identify children who need more work on letters in a small group.

Expand the Learning

Change the words on the game cards to color words, number words, days of the week, high frequency words, or last names.

Play a game like Simon Says: "Everyone who has an *a* stand up." "Everyone who has a *y* sit down."

Connect with Home

Give the children photocopies of the Letter Lotto Game Cards along with two or three copies of the alphabet squares. Children can take them home, cut up the letters, and play Letter Lotto with family members using names of friends or family members on the cards.

12 Identifying Letters

Letter Lotto

Consider Your Children

Use this lesson after the children have learned many letters and have matched pictures according to beginning sounds. You can focus on lowercase letters, uppercase letters, or matching upper- and lowercase letters, depending on how much your children know about letters.

Working with English Language Learners

This lesson uses the terms *uppercase* and *lowercase* to describe letters. It will take many experiences working with letters to help your English language learners sort out the two categories as well as the way uppercase and lowercase letters are matched. Provide as many demonstrations as necessary to help them look closely to notice the differences and similarities between uppercase and lowercase letters. Be sure they understand the sorting process; you may want to work with them in a small group.

This lesson will give English language learners a chance for more practice identifying and matching letters quickly. It is important for children to "overlearn" these important letter shapes and to associate them with names so that they can focus their attention on letters during your instruction.

You Need

- Magnetic letters (uppercase or lowercase).
- Two baskets.

From *Teaching Resources:*

- Directions for Lotto.
- Lotto Game Cards.
- Letter Cards (lowercase or uppercase) (if you use them instead of magnetic letters).

Understand the Principle

Children need to distinguish the features that make one letter different from other letters and an uppercase letter different from its lowercase form. Learning the shapes and their labels helps them talk about letters and connect letters and sounds.

Explain the Principle

"A letter has two forms."

"One form is uppercase (or capital) and the other is lowercase (or small)."

"Some lowercase forms look like the uppercase forms and some look different."

plan

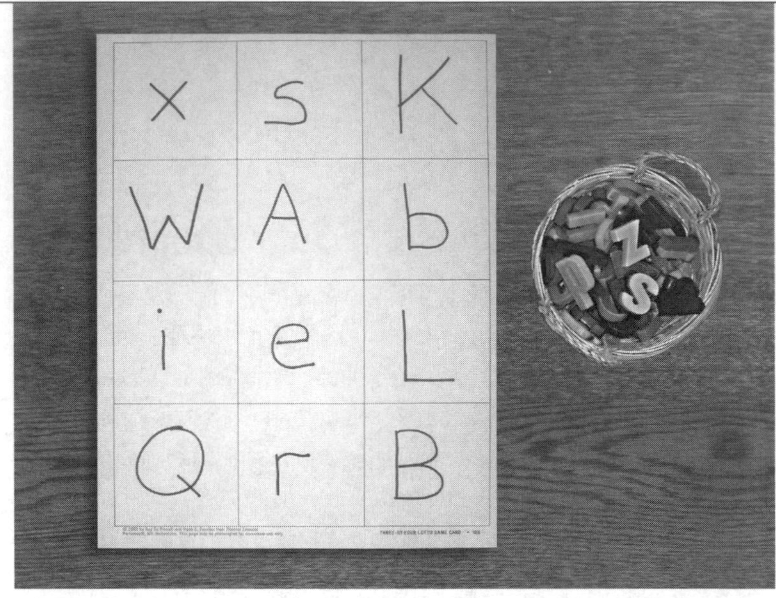

Explain the Principle

"A letter has two forms."

"One form is uppercase (or capital) and the other is lowercase (or small)."

"Some lowercase forms look like the uppercase forms and some look different."

① Explain to children that they are going to learn how to play Letter Lotto so they can learn more letters.

② Remind them that a letter has a name and shape. (Show a few examples.)

③ Tell them a letter can be uppercase or lowercase. (Show examples.)

④ Explain that some letters look just the same in the uppercase and lowercase form. (Show examples.)

⑤ Show the children the three-by-four Letter Lotto Game Card. Suggested language: "Today you are going to play Letter Lotto. In each box is a letter. You put your hand in the basket and take out one magnetic letter. Say the letter name and whether it is uppercase or lowercase (lowercase *b*, for example) and then look for the matching letter on your card. In this case, if you have a lowercase *b* on your Lotto game card, place the letter in the box. If you do not, place it in the second basket. Then the next person takes a turn. The first person who fills all the boxes on the Lotto card wins the game."

⑥ When all the letters in the first basket are used, put the discarded letters in the first basket to be used again.

say
look
match

▸ Have the children play Letter Lotto. Observe the children to be sure they understand the routine of the game and are taking turns. Remind the children to say the letter name out loud.

Ask the children to share what they noticed about letters. Listen for comments like these:

> "Every letter has two shapes."
>
> "You can tell the little *b* by the tall stick and circle."

Link

Interactive Read-Aloud: Point out interesting type treatment of letters and words to children in the layout of the text you are reading. Two books with good examples are:

- ***Blueberry Shoe*** by Ann Dixon; the capital letter at the beginning of the page is enlarged.
- ***Louella Mae, She's Run Away!*** by Karen Alacór; the last word of each sentence is in a larger font.

Shared Reading: After reading and enjoying a text such as "My Bike" or "Mouse in a Hole" (see *Sing a Song of Poetry*), have the children say and locate both uppercase and lowercase letters with a masking card, flag, or highlighter tape.

Guided Reading: After reading a text, have the children locate two or three words by saying the word and searching for the first letter.

Interactive Writing: Have the children use the Alphabet Linking Chart (see *Teaching Resources*) as a reference to write lowercase letters in words.

Independent Writing: Encourage the children to use lowercase letters in their independent writing (except for the first letter of names and the first letter of the first word in a sentence).

assess

- Place uppercase letters on a table and have a child match them with their lowercase forms. Notice which letters the child is confusing.
- Give the children a sheet with selected lowercase letters in one column and have them write the capital letter for each (or vice versa). Or have children draw lines to match a sheet of uppercase and lowercase letters.

Expand the Learning

Have the children play Letter Lotto with all uppercase letters or all lowercase letters.

Use both lowercase and uppercase letters and have children match lowercase letters with uppercase letters or vice versa.

Connect with Home

Give the children Lotto Game Cards and letter cards (see *Teaching Resources*) to take home so they can play Letter Lotto with family members.

13 Identifying Uppercase and Lowercase Letters

Concentration

Consider Your Children

Most children need many ways in which to learn about letters. Use this lesson after your children have worked with the name chart and name puzzles and know that there are uppercase and lowercase letters. They need to work with their names and notice that the names begin with an uppercase letter and the rest of the letters are lowercase. Some children may need more work with name puzzles and also with using their names in interactive writing before they fully control the concepts in this lesson. Others may have good alphabet knowledge and will be able to play Concentration quickly.

Working with English Language Learners

Be sure that children have had a great deal of experience working with their names and with magnetic letters. They should know most of the letter names although not all. Teach and demonstrate the rules of Concentration and observe children playing it so that you are sure they understand the tasks. This activity requires remembering the letters and their forms, so be sure that children can identify individual letters.

You Need

- Uppercase and lowercase magnetic letters.

From *Teaching Resources:*

- Directions for Concentration.
- Concentration cards (use the Deck Card Template).

Understand the Principle

Knowing the uppercase and lowercase alphabet helps children learn that every letter looks different from every other letter and that every letter has a name, critical information in order to be able to relate letters and sounds and begin to decode words.

Some uppercase and lowercase letter forms are similar in shape. Others look quite different to children. Lowercase letters are generally more difficult to learn. Connecting the lowercase letters with their uppercase form will help children learn to recognize and name the lowercase letters.

Explain the Principle

“A letter has two forms.”

“One form is uppercase (or capital), and the other is lowercase (or small).”

plan

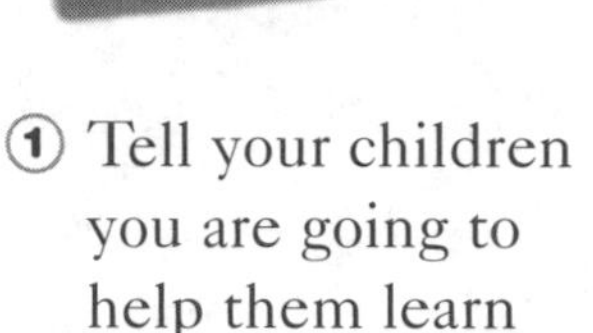

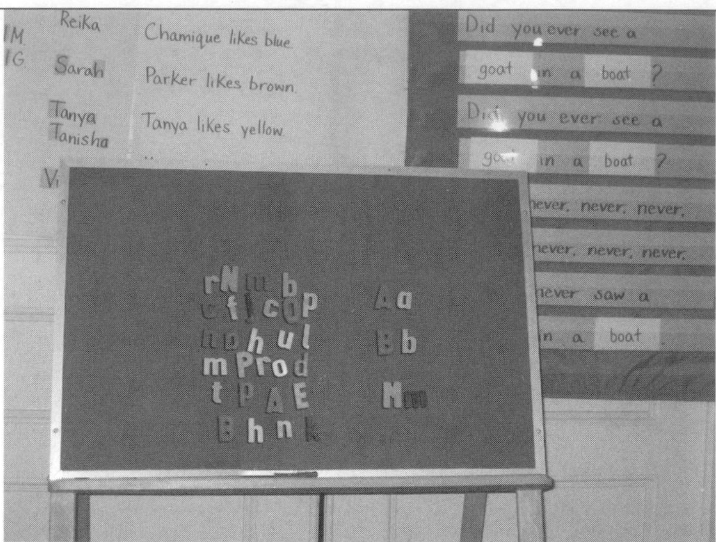

Explain the Principle

" A letter has two forms. "

" One form is uppercase (or capital), and the other is lowercase (or small). "

① Tell your children you are going to help them learn more about letters.

② Place a selection of uppercase and lowercase letters (about twenty-five) on a magnetic board or easel.

③ Suggested language: "You know that all of these are letters in the alphabet. Let's look at the alphabet chart. Can someone find the uppercase *A*?" One child demonstrates. "Now can you point to the lowercase *a*?" Point out two more uppercase and lowercase pairs. "Now look at our name chart. Barry's name starts with an uppercase *B*. Can someone find a lowercase *b* on the name chart?" Point out several more uppercase and lowercase pairs in the children's names.

④ Suggested language: "Now look at these letters on the easel. I'm looking for an uppercase *A*." Have the children find it with their eyes. Then point to the uppercase *A*. "Were you right? I'm going to put the uppercase *A* over here [place it to the right], and now I'm looking for the lowercase *a*." Let the children search for the lowercase *a*. Then place it beside the uppercase *A* on the right.

⑤ Repeat the process with several other letters, showing the children how to look for and group the uppercase and lowercase pairs. Say the name of the letter each time.

⑥ Suggested language: "Today you are going to play the Concentration card game with uppercase and lowercase letters. All of the game cards are face down on the table. You turn over a card and say the name of the letter and whether it is uppercase or lowercase. Then you turn over another card and say the name of the letter and whether it is uppercase or lowercase. If the cards are the uppercase and lowercase forms of the same letter, you get to keep them." Play a demonstration game with two children.

apply

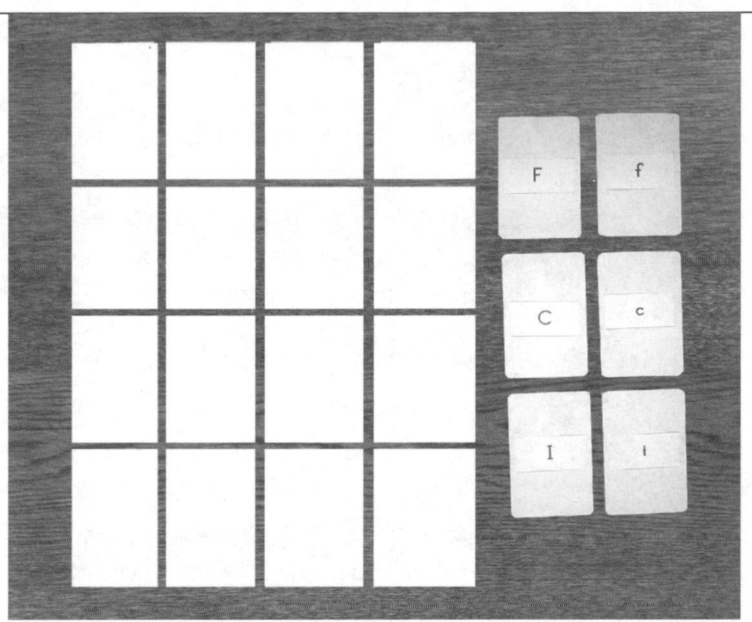

turn
say
turn
say
match

- Have the children play Concentration, matching uppercase and lowercase letters. Each time they turn over a card, they say the name of the letter and tell whether it is uppercase or lowercase. The player with the most pairs at the end wins the game.

share

Have the Alphabet Linking Chart (showing both uppercase and lowercase letters) handy. Have the children share what they noticed about how uppercase and lowercase letters are alike or different by pointing to and talking about specific examples. Model and elicit comments like these, which indicate that the children are noticing features of letters:

"Uppercase *K* and lowercase *k* look alike."

"Uppercase *O* and lowercase *o* are just alike except one is bigger."

"Some lowercase letters are tall."

"All uppercase letters are tall."

"Uppercase *H* and lowercase *h* don't look alike."

Link

Interactive Read-Aloud: Read aloud alphabet books, taking time to point out uppercase and lowercase letters (see *Teaching Resources,* Alphabet Books Bibliography for more titles). Two examples are:

- ***26 Letters and 99 Cents*** by Tana Hoban
- ***A Book of Letters*** by Ken Wilson-Max

Shared Reading: After reading and enjoying a poem or chant such as "Monday Morning" or "Out" (see *Sing a Song of Poetry*), have the children take turns showing an uppercase letter and having a classmate locate a lowercase match in the text.

Guided Reading: Draw the children's attention to a word at the beginning of a sentence and to the same word within a sentence. Point out that the word is the same, but one starts with an uppercase or capital letter and the other starts with a lowercase letter.

Interactive Writing: Show the children how to use uppercase letters appropriately (first letter of sentence, name, etc.). Model using lowercase letters to write the text.

Independent Writing: Encourage the children to use lowercase letters in writing and to use capital letters at the beginning of names and lowercase letters for the rest of the name.

assess

- Notice whether the children can match uppercase and lowercase letters encountered in random order.
- Notice the children's ability to recognize high frequency words whether they start with uppercase or lowercase letters.
- Notice the children's use of lowercase letters in their writing.
- Give children uppercase and lowercase letters (or only lowercase letters) in two columns. Have them draw lines to match the letters. Notice which children need more work on letters.

Expand the Learning

Invite the children to tell a word that begins with each letter they turn over as they play Concentration.

Have the children say the letter name and case and then say what letter comes next in the alphabet.

Connect with Home

Give the children a set of uppercase and lowercase letter cards (see *Teaching Resources*) to take home so they can play Concentration with family members.

14 Identifying Consonants and Vowels

Letter Sort

Consider Your Children

Use this lesson after the children know most of the letters of the alphabet and can recognize and name them quickly in words. They should also know the terms *first, middle,* and *last* as applied to letters in words, know some simple high frequency words, and know some words with regular spelling.

Working with English Language Learners

It may take many repetitions for English language learners to be able to say the words *consonant* and *vowel*. There may also be confusion because they have heard letter forms called *letters* and the names of the letters; this is now a third label. You may want to use simple sentences that you have the children repeat after you: "These letters are called consonants." "These letters are called vowels."

You Need

- Magnetic letters.
- Highlighter markers.
- Copies of name chart (use the Word Card Template in *Teaching Resources*).

Understand the Principle

The words *consonant* and *vowel* are useful labels that will allow children to talk about the principles related to how words work. If they can learn these two broad categories early, these words will be in their vocabularies when they later explore more complex principles.

It may be helpful to show that *y* is a vowel in words that have no other vowel such as *my, by, sky.* Later, children will also learn that *w* sometimes functions as a vowel, but it is not necessary to mention it at this time.

Explain the Principle

"Some letters are consonants."

"Some letters are vowels."

"Every word has a vowel."

plan

Explain the Principle

"Some letters are consonants."

"Some letters are vowels."

"Every word has a vowel."

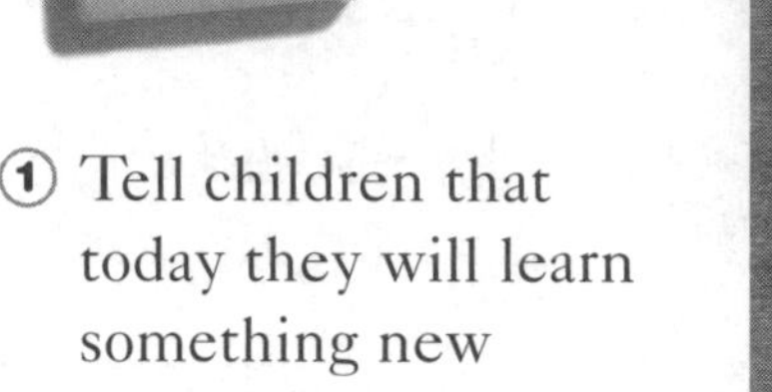

① Tell children that today they will learn something new about letters.

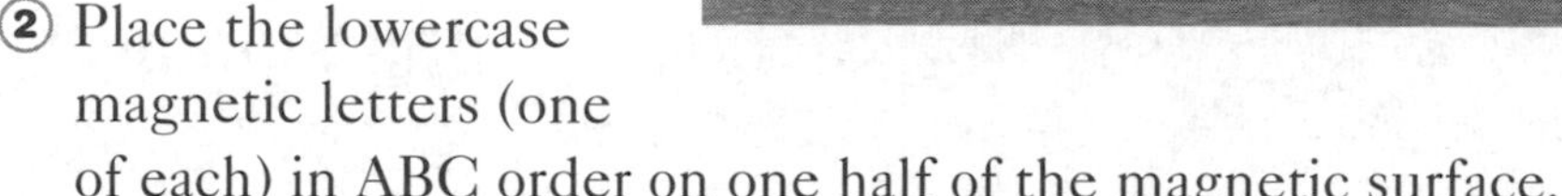

② Place the lowercase magnetic letters (one of each) in ABC order on one half of the magnetic surface.

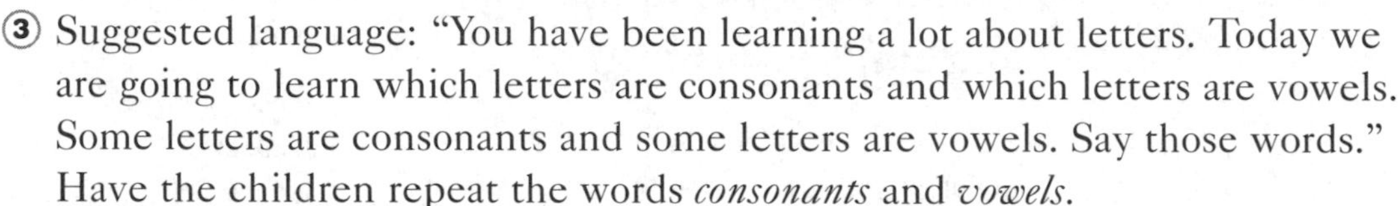

③ Suggested language: "You have been learning a lot about letters. Today we are going to learn which letters are consonants and which letters are vowels. Some letters are consonants and some letters are vowels. Say those words." Have the children repeat the words *consonants* and *vowels*.

④ Make *sit* in magnetic letters and have the children read it. Suggested language: "Look at this word that you know. What is it? [Children respond.] In this word, the first letter, *s*, is a consonant; the middle letter, *i*, is a vowel; and the last letter, *t*, is another consonant."

⑤ Place additional magnetic letters of the vowels on the bottom of the surface. "These are the letters that are vowels. They are *a*, *e*, *i*, *o*, and *u*, and sometimes *y*. We're going to hunt for the vowels as we say the alphabet. The first one we'll look for is *a*. Who can find it?" Have a child find the *a* on the left side of the display and move it to the right side.

⑥ Suggested language: "We found *a*. Now we are going to look for *e*. You clap when we come to the *e*." Continue reading the alphabet as you point. When you come to *e*, move it to the right side. Repeat the process, each time telling the children what to look for.

⑦ Place one set of vowels back in the alphabet, but leave the other set of vowels as a model. Go through the process again more quickly, having the children clap when you come to a vowel, and put the vowels on the other side. This time, don't tell them what vowel to look for.

⑧ Turn to the name chart and have the children determine whose name begins with a consonant and whose begins with a vowel.

sort
highlight
read

- Place one complete set of lowercase magnetic letters (letters cards are an alternative) in a margarine tub, milk carton, or other container. On a flat or vertical surface divided into two areas, have the children place consonants on the left and vowels on the right. Include more than one of each letter to make the task more complex.
- When they have finished sorting, have the children take a copy of the class name chart and highlight all the vowels, then read the name chart to a partner.

Ask the children to share anything they notice about vowels in words. They may say things like:

> "Every word has a vowel. "
>
> "*Y* is a vowel sometimes."
>
> "Some words have two vowels."
>
> "Vowels can go at the beginning, middle, or end."

Link

Interactive Read-Aloud: Read aloud alphabet books and have the children clap when you come to a vowel. Two good books are:

- ***Alligators All Around*** by Maurice Sendak
- ***Alphabears*** by Kathleen Hague

Shared Reading: Read the alphabet chart, first just the consonants and then just the vowels. Ask the children to point out the vowels and/or consonants in a word that they locate in a familiar text.

Guided Reading: During word work, have the children make three or four words with magnetic letters and tell which letters are consonants and which are vowels.

Interactive Writing: When a word is being written, have the children check to see whether it has a vowel and name it. Tell what position the vowel is in—first, middle, last.

Independent Writing: Encourage the children to check words they have written to be sure that they have vowels.

assess

- Notice whether the children are able to identify vowels quickly.
- Have the children locate the vowels in three or four words.

Expand the Learning

Play Follow the Path (see the directions in *Teaching Resources,* Materials & Routines) emphasizing consonants and vowels. Have the children throw the die, land on a letter, say the letter name, and say whether it is a consonant or a vowel.

Connect with Home

Have the children take home letter cards (see *Teaching Resources*) to sort into consonants and vowels. They can make a few words and check to make sure each word has a vowel.

15 Learning about Names and Initials

Labeled Drawings

Consider Your Children

This lesson is appropriate for children who don't yet know all the letters. Use it after the children have worked with the name chart (ELC 1 and LK 1) and name puzzles and know some of the uppercase letters. If your children already know most of the uppercase and lowercase letters and can read and write their names, this lesson will probably not be needed. You can quickly show these children what the word *initials* means as a way of helping them distinguish the uses of capital and lowercase letters.

Working with English Language Learners

English language learners will enjoy working with their names in a different way. This lesson illustrates uses of uppercase letters and will also introduce the idea that a single letter or set of letters can stand for an entire word. Explain the word *initials,* use it several times, and have children say it.

You Need

- Pocket chart or chart with Velcro®.
- Name and initial cards with Velcro® (use the Pocket Chart Card Template in *Teaching Resources*).

Understand the Principle

Children need to learn that there are special conventions in written language: names can be represented by initials. Focusing on their initials and those of their friends also helps children expand their ability to quickly recognize and name letters and understand the different uses of uppercase and lowercase letters.

Explain the Principle

“You use capital letters to write your initials.”

“Your initials are the first letters of your first name and your last name.”

plan

Our Names	Our Initials
Ariel Adams	A.A.
Chelsea Brown	C.B.
Chris Beton	C.B.
Andrea Carter	A.C.
Julita Cruz	J.C.
Kali Darby	K.D.
David DiBercio	D.D.
Bridget Gleason	B.G.
Vrinda Kumar	V.K.
Dalila Lehmkuhl	D.L.
Carlos Martin	C.M.
Cadeo Nguyen	C.N.
Aisling O'Hara	A.O.
Tony Oliviera	T.O.
Michelle Stanton	M.S.

Explain the Principle

“You use capital letters to write your initials.”

“Your initials are the first letters of your first name and your last name.”

① Explain to children that they are going to learn about writing their initials.

② Show the children the name chart with their first and last names. Suggested language: “You can read and write your names. Today you are going to be doing something special with your names—writing your initials. Does anyone know what initials are?”

③ Some children will know their initials, but they may not be able to describe exactly what initials are. Suggested language: “Initials are a short form of your name. Instead of writing your whole name, you just write the first letter of your first name and the first letter of your last name. Watch while I write Ariel’s initials.” Use a whiteboard to demonstrate.

④ “Ariel’s first name starts with . . . ? [Children respond.] An *A*. So I’m going to write an *A* here.” Write a capital letter large enough for all children to see. “Her last name is *Adams*, which begins with . . . ? [Children respond.] Another *A*. So I’m going to write an *A* here.” Show the children the initials. “These are Ariel’s initials—*A. A.* What do you notice?”

⑤ Model and encourage comments like these:

> “They are the same letters as at the beginning of her name.”
>
> “They are both *A*s.”
>
> “They are capital letters.”
>
> “They have periods after them.”

⑥ Do one or two more sets of initials so that the children get the idea. Then, invite each child to come up and find her initials, which are on cards (use

Velcro® or a pocket chart), and match them to the name. Tell the children to look for the letter at the beginning of their first names and then for the letter at the beginning of their last names.

7. Each time, ask the children in the class to think of what the individual is looking for. The activity will become easier and faster as more initials are eliminated.

8. Then invite the children to write their initials in the next column.

9. Keep the chart in the classroom for a few weeks.

draw
label

- Have the children draw pictures of themselves and a friend on a blank piece of paper. Then have them label their pictures with the names and initials of each person shown.

Play a mystery game: "I'm thinking of someone whose initials are P. C. Who is it?" Encourage children to find the name quickly. Or: "I'm thinking of two people who have the same initials."

Link

Interactive Read-Aloud: Ask children to quickly think of initials for the characters in children's books: Curious George = C.G.; Brown Bear = B.B. They will increase their ability to identify the first letters of names quickly. Also read aloud books that include names and initials, such as

- ***Bill and Pete*** by Tomie de Paola
- ***Mike Mulligan and His Steam Shovel*** by Virginia Lee Burton

Shared Reading: Read the name and initials chart. Read poems that incorporate the children's names, such as "Tommy Snooks" or "Old Dan Tucker" (see *Sing a Song of Poetry*), but use initials instead of names.

Guided Reading: Notice any initials that appear in the stories the children read, such as D.W. in Marc Brown's series featuring Arthur.

Interactive Writing: Try using someone's initials instead of the name and having the children guess who the person is. Have the children "sign" the piece of writing with their initials.

Independent Writing: Let the children put their initials instead of their names on their papers. Later, hold up some of the papers and ask the class who wrote them.

assess

- Check their papers to be sure that the children understand the concept of initials. Check to see whether they are using uppercase letters with periods.

Expand the Learning

Give the children a piece of drawing paper with two circles. Have them write the initials of the girls in one and the boys in the other. This will require thinking about and searching for (or writing from memory) each person's initials. They can use the class name chart on the wall (without the model of initials).

Connect with Home

Have the children write the initials of their family members and friends and bring them back to school to share.

Letter/Sound Relationships

The sounds of oral language are related in both simple and complex ways to the twenty-six letters of the alphabet. Learning the connections between letters and sounds is basic to understanding written language. Children first learn simple relationships that are regular in that one phoneme is connected to one grapheme, or letter. But sounds are also connected to letter clusters, which are groups of letters that appear often together (for example, *cr, str, ch, st, bl, fr*), in which you hear each of the associated sounds of the letters; and to consonant digraphs *(sh, ch),* in which you hear only one sound. Vowels may also appear in combinations *(ea, oa),* in which you usually hear the first vowel *(ai)* or you hear a completely different sound *(ou).* Children learn to look for and recognize these letter combinations as units, which makes their word solving more efficient. It is important to remember that children will be able to hear and connect the easy-to-identify consonants and vowels early and progress to the harder-to-hear and more difficult letter/sound relationships—for example, letter clusters with two and three letters and those that have more than one sound. You will want to connect initial letter sounds to the Alphabet Linking Chart (see *Teaching Resources*). It is not necessary to teach every letter as a separate lesson. When using the children's names to teach about words, substitute *name* for *word* when explaining the principle.

Connect to Assessment

See related LS Assessment Tasks in the Assessment Guide in *Teaching Resources:*

- Identifying and Representing Sounds in Words
- Matching Beginning Consonant Letters and Sounds
- Matching Ending Consonant Letters and Sounds
- Matching Consonant Clusters and Sounds
- Matching Beginning Consonant Digraphs and Sounds
- Matching Ending Consonant Digraphs and Sounds
- Matching Short (Tense) Vowel Letters and Sounds
- Matching Long (Lax) Vowel Letters and Sounds
- Writing Words

Develop Your Professional Understanding

See *Word Matters: Teaching Phonics and Spelling in the Reading/Writing Classroom* by G.S. Pinnell and I.C. Fountas. 1998. Portsmouth, New Hampshire: Heinemann.

Related pages: 46–48, 71–73, 90–93, 123, 141.

1 Building Words

Alphabet Books

Consider Your Children

Check the children's knowledge of letters and their ability to generate beginning consonants for simple pictures (such as the ones on the Alphabet Linking Chart, *Teaching Resources*). This lesson will benefit children who have little letter knowledge and/or who have made very few letter/sound connections.

Working with English Language Learners

This lesson will enable English language learners to identify and explore words in many different contexts. Building words from alphabet books will help them notice the visual features of words and make connections among them, especially by first letter and sound. Encourage them to say the words aloud and check them letter by letter with the words in the book.

You Need

- A large, simple alphabet book that has a picture and letter and one corresponding word on each page.
- Magnetic letters and a magnetic surface.

From *Teaching Resources:*

- List Sheets.
- A variety of alphabet books chosen from the Alphabet Books Bibliography.
- Alphabet Linking Chart.

Understand the Principle

Knowing the alphabetic principle, as well as how to use letter/sound relationships in word solving, is basic to the ability to read proficiently. Children need to understand that there is an important connection between the sounds in words and the letters and their placement in words.

Explain the Principle

" You can match letters and sounds in words. "

" You can match letters and sounds at the beginning of a word. "

plan

teach

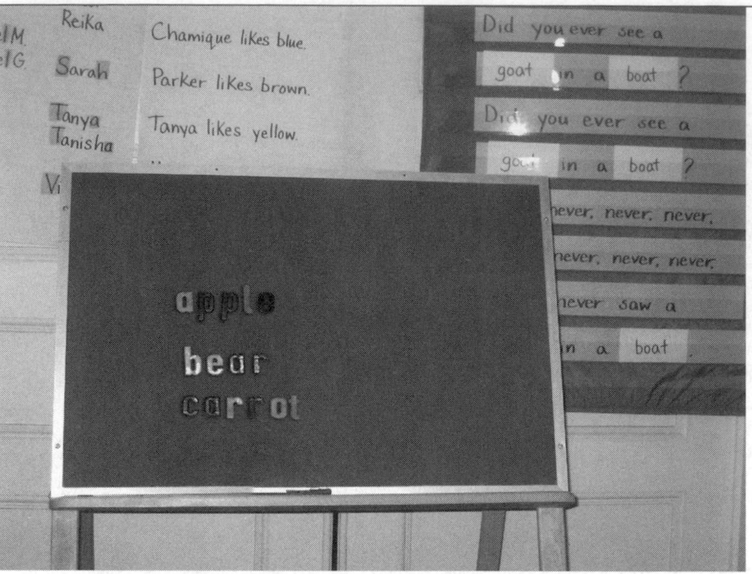

Explain the Principle

“ You can match letters and sounds in words. ”

“ You can match letters and sounds at the beginning of a word. ”

① Tell the children they are going to learn about letters and their sounds.

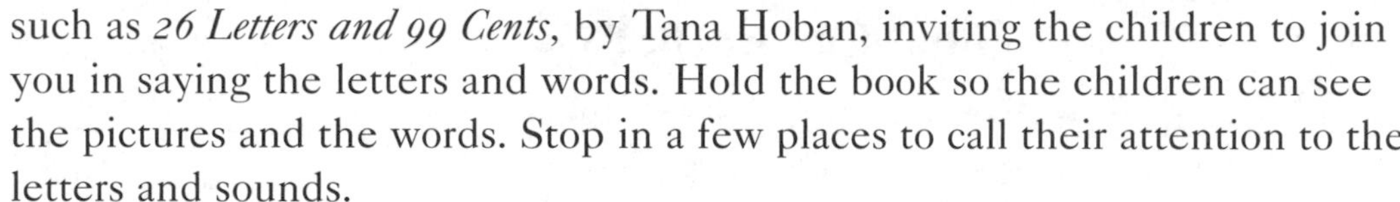

② Read a simple enlarged-print alphabet book such as *26 Letters and 99 Cents*, by Tana Hoban, inviting the children to join you in saying the letters and words. Hold the book so the children can see the pictures and the words. Stop in a few places to call their attention to the letters and sounds.

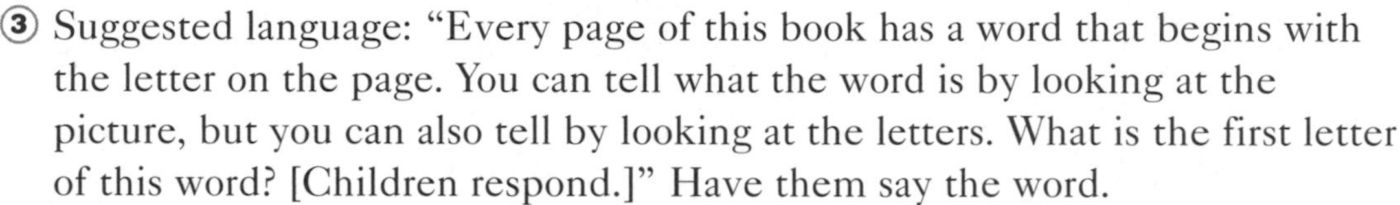

③ Suggested language: “Every page of this book has a word that begins with the letter on the page. You can tell what the word is by looking at the picture, but you can also tell by looking at the letters. What is the first letter of this word? [Children respond.]” Have them say the word.

④ Suggested language: “Say the word. [Children respond.] You can hear the *a* at the beginning of the word.” You may want to exaggerate or elongate the *a* slightly so that the children can attend to the sound but don’t distort the word too much.

⑤ “You can hear the sound at the beginning and you can see the letter. We’re going to make and write some of the words in this alphabet book.”

⑥ Demonstrate making the word *apple* and show how to check letter by letter to be sure that the word you built is accurate *(a–a, p–p, p–p, l–l, e–e).* Suggested language: “After you check the letter, say it and move your finger under it.”

⑦ Have the children say the word. “You can hear the sound at the beginning and see the letter. You can hear other sounds, too. What else can you hear in *apple*?” Invite the children to talk about the other sounds and point out the letters representing them. Emphasize that the letters have to be in the same sequence every time you build or write the word.

8. Show the children how to write the word in the next column and check it.
9. Repeat the demonstration with several other words in the book.
10. Explain to the children that they will be building words from an alphabet book and then writing them. (If children are very inexperienced, it may be enough for them simply to build and check the words.)

make
check
say
write

- Give the children simple alphabet books, along with a list sheet and some magnetic letters. Have them turn to each page in the book. Have the children make and build at least ten different words with magnetic letters, checking each word letter by letter and then saying it slowly to check it.
- They write each word on the list sheet. If you don't have enough alphabet books, children can use the Alphabet Linking Chart as a resource for words.

Ask the children to talk about what they learned from building words. Comments like these will give you information about what children are learning about words:

"The first letter of *zebra* is *z*."

"*Pumpkin* starts with *p*."

"You can hear the first sound of the word."

Link

Interactive Read-Aloud: Read aloud alphabet books, such as

- ***The Letters Are Lost*** by Lisa Campbell Ernst
- ***ABC Like Me*** by Nancy Carlson

Shared Reading: Use poems such as "Bears Eat Honey" or "Bat, Bat" (see *Sing a Song of Poetry*). Have the children locate specific words in the text by saying the word and thinking about what letter they would expect to see at the beginning.

Guided Reading: Prompt the children to notice the first letters of words they are reading in texts. Show them how to "get your mouth ready for it" by looking at the word and making the sound of the first letter. Rereading by making the sound of the first letter will help children solve the word. Also, prompt them to check whether the word "looks right" (noticing the first letter of the word).

Interactive Writing: Have the children slowly say a word they want to write and think about what the first letter would be. Write the word and have them check their prediction.

Independent Writing: Encourage the children to say words slowly and represent all the sounds they can hear. Also encourage them to check a word they've written by moving their finger under the word and thinking about the sounds. The goal is not accuracy but learning to think about letters and sounds.

assess

- Notice the children's ability to connect letters and sounds and to use the first sound/letter of a word to write the word and to check their reading.
- Notice whether the children are able to write most of the sounds in words they attempt in independent writing.

Expand the Learning

Increase the challenge of the application by having the children look at the word in the book, cover it, and then make it without a visible model. They then uncover the word and check it.

Have the children engage in the same process using other alphabet books.

Have the children make a word from the alphabet book and then make other words they know (or they can find in alphabet books or on the word wall) that begin with the same letter.

Connect with Home

Send home several letter minibooks (see *Teaching Resources*) each day. Have children use magnetic letters or letter cards (see *Teaching Resources*) to make the words and check them.

2 Learning Letter Names and Sounds

Alphabet Wall

Consider Your Children

This lesson helps the children become aware of and learn to use an overall framework—the alphabet—to categorize letters, sounds, and words. The alphabet wall is a reference and resource in the classroom that children can use as they read and write and study words. It helps the children solidify their knowledge of letters, letter/sound relationships, and first letters and sounds in words. It will help children with limited letter and sound awareness expand their knowledge. You can use the board to work with small groups of children who need more experience. Your alphabet wall may eventually turn into a word wall. For children who have limited knowledge of the letters and sounds, preplace one key picture in the box beside the letter. For a less experienced group, work with the whole group, doing as many squares a day as is practical. (One letter per day is far too slow a pace; try for at least three or four.)

Working with English Language Learners

Creating an alphabet wall will help children widen their English speaking vocabulary and learn words that are related to one another. Introduce the objects in the bags to children so that they know the English names for objects before they begin the activity. Alternatively, work with a small group so that when they encounter the objects, you can give them the name and have them repeat it.

You Need

- Bulletin board divided by letters of the alphabet. Be sure letters are clearly printed in a dark color on a white or cream background. Leave space to insert pictures, glue on small objects, and print a few words.
- Bags (one for each letter) containing small objects (e.g., a button, a penny, a crayon, a stamp, a buckle, a pencil, a piece of candy, an eraser, a balloon, a paper plate, a napkin) or pictures (see *Teaching Resources,* Beginning Consonant Sounds Picture Cards) that can be glued onto paper and placed into the letter squares.

Understand the Principle

Words and pictures can be categorized by the beginning sound. Children say the word and hear and identify the first sound; at the same time, they look at and identify the letter and connect it to the sound.

Once children can perform these operations, they will be able to use beginning letter/sound relationships in reading and writing.

Explain the Principle

“You can match letters and sounds in words.”

“You can hear the sound at the beginning of a word.”

“You can match letters and sounds at the beginning of a word.”

plan

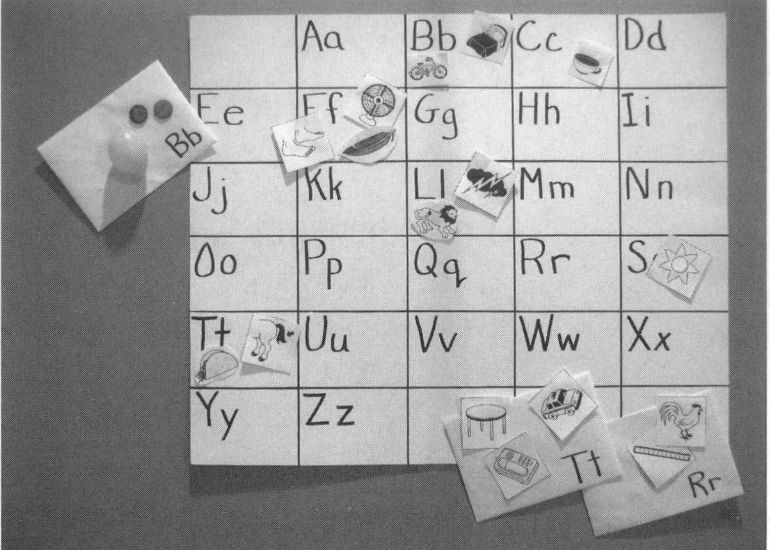

Explain the Principle

“ You can match letters and sounds in words. ”

“ You can hear the sound at the beginning of a word. ”

“ You can match letters and sounds at the beginning of a word. ”

① Explain to the children that they are going to learn more about letters and sounds.

② Show the children the bulletin board with letters only. Suggested language: “You know some of the alphabet letters and their sounds. Today we are going to make a big alphabet wall that will help us learn more about letters and their sounds.”

③ Have a collection of pictures (or small objects) beginning with each sound in the alphabet in separate bags or envelopes. Take one bag of pictures/objects. Select a letter whose form, name, and related sound most children know.

④ Suggested language: “This is a *boat.* Say *boat.* [Children respond.] I’m going to put the picture of the boat under the *Bb.* [Glue on quickly.] This is a *ball.* Where would I put the *ball*? [Children respond.] So under the *Bb,* we have *boat* and *ball.* Say those words. [Children respond.] They sound alike at the beginning, don’t they? And they both start with *b.*”

⑤ Continue modeling the process with two or three other letters, drawing pictures or objects from the bags. Let the group decide where they go on the alphabet chart.

⑥ Tell the children they are going to be given a piece of white paper that will fit in the squares on the alphabet bulletin board. Show them how to take each picture or object out of the bag, say its name, and glue it on the paper. Finally, they should say the names of all the pictures or objects on their paper and place them in the appropriate squares on the alphabet bulletin board.

take
say
draw or glue
read

▸ Have the children work independently, each child with a different letter bag. They take the objects or pictures out of the bag, say the name of each, and draw it or glue it on a paper. After drawing or gluing all the pictures or objects, they say all the names to a partner.

Invite individuals to place their squares on the alphabet wall and say the name of each picture or object until you have completed the entire alphabet. (This may take several days.)

Link

Interactive Read-Aloud: Read aloud alphabet books such as the ones below to reinforce and expand the children's knowledge of the alphabet.

- ***Toby's Alphabet Walk*** by Cyndy Szekeres
- ***The Wacky Wedding*** by Pamela Edwards

Shared Reading: Read or sing the children's new alphabet wall to the tune of "A, You're Adorable," using one word from each box. (If you don't know the tune, make up your own.) Repeat the song over several days using different words from the letter squares.

Guided Reading: During word work, play a quick game: make a word with magnetic letters and ask the children to tell a word that starts with the same letter. Repeat with five or six more words.

Interactive Writing: As the children attempt to write new words, link the words they want to write with the alphabet wall.

Independent Writing: Encourage the children to use the alphabet wall as a resource. They can use the letters as models when they are unsure how to make a letter. They can also refer to the chart when saying words slowly and thinking of the first letter and also when writing high frequency words.

assess

- Notice whether the children can read the alphabet wall.
- Say words and have the children quickly point to the letter representing the first sound.

Expand the Learning

When the alphabet wall has served its purpose, cut it apart and make it into a big alphabet book that children can continue to read in a shared way or in pairs.

Glue the squares onto larger pieces of brown paper so that children can search for and add pictures.

Connect with Home

Give children individualized small blank stapled books (see *Teaching Resources,* Blank Book Page Template) with six or seven letters that are especially important for them to learn more about. Have family members help children collect and glue in or draw pictures representing words that have a first sound corresponding to the letter. Family members' names can also be entered into these books.

3 Learning about Beginning Sounds

Making Sentences

Consider Your Children

Use this lesson to help the children become more conscious of the sounds at the beginning of words. It will be helpful to children who have grasped the alphabetic principle but who are just beginning to hear sounds in words and to connect them to letters.

Working with English Language Learners

English language learners will enjoy reading sentences that incorporate their names. These sentences will make them feel recognized. As much as possible, pronounce the names accurately in the children's own languages. To be more confident that children understand the sentences, work from their own ideas and concepts. You may want to have children draw pictures or use actions to help them understand the action words in the sentences.

You Need

- Pocket chart.
- Sentence strips that use children's names and names of characters in books to demonstrate that words can sound the same at the beginning and sometimes start with the same letter.

From *Teaching Resources:*

- Four-Box Sheets.

Understand the Principle

It is essential that children learn to hear sounds in words, eventually identifying the sequence of sounds, so that they can connect them to letters. By comparing words, children can more easily notice the sounds in them.

Explain the Principle

"You can hear the sound at the beginning of a word."

"Words can start with the same sound and letter."

Explain the Principle

“You can hear the sound at the beginning of a word.”

“Words can start with the same sound and the same letter.”

① Tell the children they are going to learn more about the first sounds they hear in words.

② Suggested language: “You have been thinking about the sounds in words. If you say two words, you can tell that they begin with the same sound. *Mary* and *Mother* have the same sound at the beginning.”

Brown Bear bumps
Peter Piper picked peppers
Nancy naps
Diego drives
Rachel runs
Cindy sleeps
Jimmy jumps
Lisa laughs
Caroline cries
Sarah sleeps
Mary
Mother
Brown
Bear

③ Have the children say the two words and then write them on the whiteboard so they can see the letter at the beginning. Repeat the process with *Brown Bear.*

④ Suggested language: “Can anyone think of another word that has the same sound at the beginning? [Children respond.]” Write their response on a card strip and put it in the pocket chart.

⑤ Suggested language: “Now we are going to use your names and then think of a word that starts the same and tells something you can do.”

⑥ Demonstrate with your name or the name of someone in the class: *Mary mows, Sam sees.* Try to get an action word for about ten students in the class, writing each on a card strip.

write
draw

▸ Give the children a Four-Box Sheet. In each box, have them write the name of someone in the class, add a word beginning with the same sound that tells something that person can do, and then illustrate the sentence. Do not expect correct spellings for the verbs. Do expect them to refer to the name chart to arrive at correct spellings of the names of their classmates.

Have the children read their completed papers around the circle. If examples like "George jumps" arise, take the opportunity to point out that sometimes words can *sound* alike at the beginning but begin with different letters or that some letters make two sounds.

Encourage the children to talk about what they learned. Comments like these indicate that children are noticing more about words:

> "*Mike* and *make* sound the same at the beginning and both start with an *m*."
>
> "*Cynthia* and *sleeps* sound the same at the beginning but have different letters."

Link

Interactive Read-Aloud: Read aloud books that emphasize alliteration. Ask the children to say words that start alike and listen for the sound at the beginning. See *Teaching Resources*, Alliteration Bibliography, for more examples.

- ***Spring Fever*** by Eve Merriam
- ***Busy Buzzing Bumblebees*** by Alvin Schwartz

Shared Reading: Read poems and rhymes that use alliteration such as "Betty Botter" or "The Big Black Bug" or "Swim, Swan, Swim" (see *Sing a Song of Poetry*). Have the children locate words that sound alike at the beginning and have the same first letters.

Guided Reading: Help the children notice the first letters of words and connect them to words they know. For example, a child who is reading the word *make* can "get his mouth ready" by beginning to say the *m* sound because he knows several other words that start like it.

Interactive Writing: When the children are trying to write words, help them connect the beginning sound to other words they know: "Does it sound like *me* at the beginning?" "Could it be *m* as in *me*?"

Independent Writing: In conferences, prompt the children to say the word and think about the beginning sound.

assess

- Notice the children's use of beginning sounds as they attempt to read or write unfamiliar words.
- Select four or five words, say each word, and ask the children to tell another word that starts the same.

Expand the Learning

Repeat the same process with adjectives: *Smart Sam, Jumping John.*

Make a collection of words that start with a particular letter. Children can look for words in the interactive writing they have completed and in poems used for shared reading.

Play a name game by substituting another letter for the first letter of everyone's name: *Mary, Fary; Sam, Wam.*

Connect to Home

Have children take home their sentence drawings; on the reverse side they can write and illustrate sentences about family members *(Dad drives, Jesse jumps).*

4 Learning about Beginning Consonant Letters and Sounds

Lotto

Consider Your Children

Use this lesson after the children can name most letters of the alphabet and have demonstrated that they can hear sounds in words, match pictures by sound, and understand the concept of matching letters and sounds. In this lesson they work with the range of initial consonant sounds.

Working with English Language Learners

Go over the picture cards with children so that you are sure they know the English words for each item. Have them repeat the words, slightly emphasizing the beginning sounds. You may want to have them practice matching letters with the pictures on cards before actually playing the game. Work with them in a small group the first time they play Lotto.

You Need

- Pocket chart.

From *Teaching Resources:*

- Picture Cards, Beginning Consonant Sounds.
- Consonant Letter Cards. (Use cards with uppercase letters, both uppercase and lowercase letters, or lowercase letters.)
- Lotto Game Cards.
- Directions for Lotto.

Understand the Principle

Children do not need to learn all the letters of the alphabet before reading stories, but knowing letters and their relationship to sounds in words is valuable information as they read their first storybooks. It is important for children to learn to identify beginning sounds and connect letters to them so that they can use this information to solve words and check on their reading.

Explain the Principle

“You can match letters and sounds in words.”

“When you see a letter at the beginning of a word, you can make its sound.”

“When you know the sound, you can find the letter.”

plan

Explain the Principle

"You can match letters and sounds in words."

"When you see a letter at the beginning of a word, you can make its sound."

"When you know the sound, you can find the letter."

① Tell the children they are going to learn about the sounds they hear at the beginning of words.

② Show the children a picture and ask them to find another picture that starts with the same sound. For example, show *duck* and ask them to tell another word that starts like *duck—doll,* for example. Ask the children: "What letter would you expect to see first in *duck* and *doll*?" Children respond.

③ Repeat the process with three or four other examples, helping the children understand that you can hear the sound at the beginning of a word, and when you know the sound, you can find the letter that goes with it.

④ Place twelve picture cards in a three-by-four pattern in a pocket chart (include the ones you've already used as examples).

⑤ Suggested language: "Today we are going to learn to play a game called Lotto. In this game you get to match letters with the first sounds of words. Let's try it with the squares of pictures I have in the pocket chart." Go over the pictures, naming each.

⑥ Invite a child to be your partner. Show children the pile of consonant letter cards.

⑦ Suggested language: "On these cards, I have some letters. I'll mix them all up and then take one. I'm going to see if it is the first letter of one of the pictures on my square."

⑧ Take a card. "I have a *p*. Do I have a picture of something on my card that starts with *p*? [Children respond.] Yes, I have a pig. I'm going to put a piece of paper on top of the pig and draw again." Continue drawing until there is no match.

9 Then let your partner take a card. The other children can help him find the match and cover it with a piece of paper.

10 Continue taking cards and covering squares until one person "wins" by covering all the squares. If you run out of letters, mix them up and start retaking cards from the pile.

11 Tell the children they will be playing Lotto with consonant letters and pictures.

12 Ask the children to discuss what you have to do to fill your Lotto card. Then demonstrate the game with three children in a circle on the floor. Show them how to take turns drawing cards and matching them to the letters on their squares. The first to fill the card wins.

take
match
say

- Have the children play the Beginning Consonant Lotto game in groups of three or four. If you have enough letter cards and game cards, several games can be going on at once.

Ask the children to share some of the first letters and words they matched while playing Lotto. Ask them to talk about what helped them. They may say: "I said the word and thought about the first sound."

Make it clear that sometimes a picture can be called two different things (for example, *horse* and *pony*). You can make a first sound match using either name.

Link

Interactive Read-Aloud: Read aloud stories with alliteration (see *Teaching Resources,* Alliteration Books Bibliography, for more examples) that draw attention to beginning consonant sounds, such as

- ***Miss Mary Mack*** by Mary Ann Hoberman
- ***Four Famished Foxes and Fosdyke*** by Pamela Edwards

Shared Reading: When rereading familiar texts such as "Jack Sprat" or "Johnny Appleseed" (see *Sing a Song of Poetry*), mask the first letter of a word. Ask the children to read up to the word and predict the first letter by thinking about the sound.

Guided Reading: When the children come to an unfamiliar word, prompt them to say the first sound and think what would make sense.

Interactive Writing: When preparing to write a word, have the children say it slowly and think about what the first letter is likely to be.

Independent Writing: Encourage the children to say words slowly when they are writing and to write the first letter.

assess

- Observe whether the children are able to generate beginning letters of words when they are writing.
- Notice whether the children can say the first sound of a word while reading.
- Notice whether the children can use the first letter/sound of a word to monitor and check on their reading.
- Place picture cards in the pocket chart and ask the children to match letters.

Expand the Learning

Have the children play the game several times with different pictures.

Have them play the game with letters written on the game cards and a pile of pictures to draw from.

Connect with Home

Give children a Lotto Game Card with letters on it and a pile of Beginning Consonant Sounds picture cards (see *Teaching Resources*) in a sealable bag. Have them take the bag home and play this reverse version of the game with family members.

5 Learning about Beginning Consonants

Follow the Path

Consider Your Children

This lesson will be beneficial for children who need to make more letter/sound connections or who need to become more automatic and flexible in recognizing and using first letters and sounds. Conduct a quick assessment of the children's ability to use first letters by having them connect pictures and letters that represent the first sounds. If the children are having difficulty relating the letter to its sound, use all letter cards. If they are having difficulty relating the sound to the letter, use all picture cards. If your goal is the children's flexibility with both, use a mixture of letter and picture cards.

Working with English Language Learners

Help English language learners pronounce words clearly, both by listening for the beginning sound and by feeling how their lips and tongue are working. Also be sure that they know the names for the objects in the pictures they are using for Follow the Path. Accept approximations for the words that are difficult for them to say. You may want to review the routines for the game with a small group.

You Need

- Follow the Path Game Board (with blank spaces).

From *Teaching Resources:*

- Picture Cards, Beginning Consonant Sounds.
- Letter Cards.
- Directions for Follow the Path.

Understand the Principle

Making connections between the first sound and first letter of a word is an important beginning action in word solving. As they read continuous text, children can learn to say the first sound of the word (prompted by recognizing the letter and connecting it to the sound) as a way of solving the word. This is a first step in noticing and using other letter/sound connections. Children can also use knowledge of the first letter and sound to monitor their reading.

Explain the Principle

" You can hear the sound at the beginning of a word. "

" You can match letters and sounds at the beginning of words. "

plan

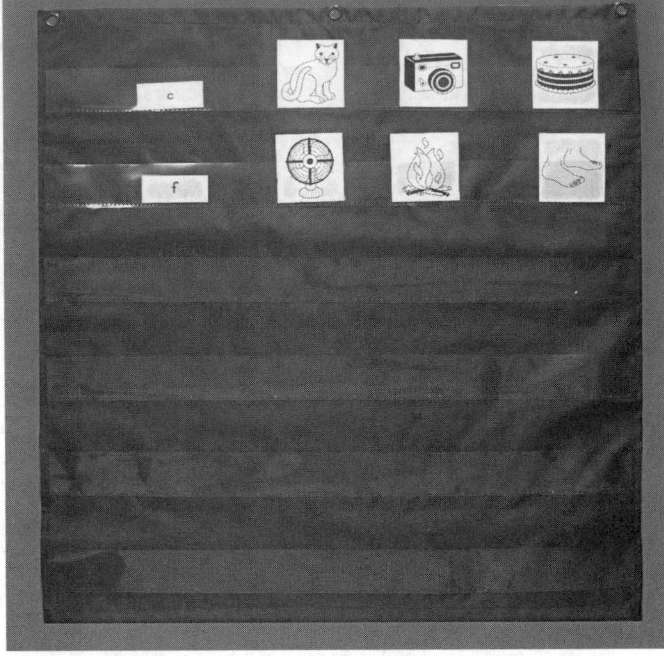

Explain the Principle

"You can hear the sound at the beginning of a word."

"You can match letters and sounds at the beginning of words."

① Explain to the children that they are going to learn more about letters and sounds.

② Suggested language: "You are learning to use the first sounds and letters of words to help you read and write. What is this letter?" Hold up a letter and ask the children to name the letter and then to think of words that start with that letter. You might also work the opposite way: "What is this picture?" Hold up a picture and ask the children to name the picture and tell the first letter of the word.

③ The goal of this lesson is to help the children become more automatic and flexible in recognizing and using first letters and sounds. Continue with several examples, selecting mostly pictures and letters that represent the letters and sounds the children are still learning.

④ Suggested language: "You are going to be playing a game today with letters and pictures. It is called Follow the Path."

⑤ Show the children how to play Follow the Path by taking a card from the pile. If they take a picture card, they say the word it represents and then say the name of the first letter. If they take a letter card, they say the name of the letter and say a word that starts with that letter. (If the children are very inexperienced, you may want to use only picture cards or only letter cards at the beginning; however, moving back and forth between pictures and letters will help the children become more flexible in using their knowledge.)

⑥ Invite a child to be your partner and demonstrate playing the game.

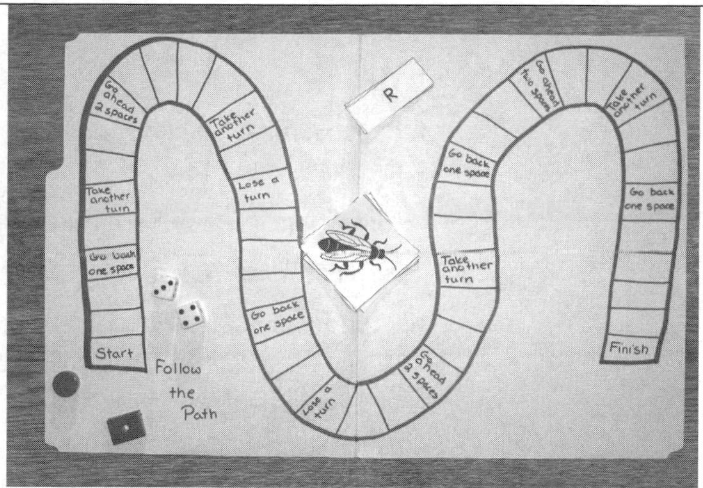

apply

throw
take
say
move

- Have the children play Follow the Path using a game board and a die. You may want to write "take another turn" on a few spaces to add some spice. Each child has a marker on the board. They throw a die. Then they take a picture card and say the word and first letter (or a letter card and say the letter and a word). If they give the correct response, they move the number of spaces on the die. Otherwise they remain where they are on the board. Then the next child takes a turn.

Ask the children to discuss how they were able to identify the first letters and sounds for the Follow the Path game. Watch for comments like these:

> "I looked for the first letter and thought about the sound."
>
> "I said the word and thought about the letter."
>
> "I thought of other words I knew that started the same."
>
> "I knew it from the word wall."

Point out that noticing the first letter will help them read the word.

Link

Interactive Read-Aloud: Read aloud books with alliteration, such as

- ***Six Sandy Sheep*** by Judith Enderle
- ***Watch William Walk*** by Ann Jonas

Shared Reading: On a familiar text such as "The Boy in the Barn" or "The Elephant Who Jumped a Fence" (see *Sing a Song of Poetry*), cover up some words that offer the children a chance to use their knowledge of beginning consonant sounds. Have them read up to the word and predict what the next word will be and what letter they will expect to see. Say, "What will you expect to see at the beginning if the word is ________?" Uncover the word to have them check their prediction.

Guided Reading: Show the children how to read up to a word and "get your mouth ready for it" by saying the first sound. Next have them locate words in text by first saying the word and the letter they expect to see at the beginning.

Interactive Writing: Have the children say a new word they want to write and think about the beginning sound. They can predict the letter; then, write the letter and have them check the prediction.

Independent Writing: Encourage the children to record the first sound/letter of words they want to write even if they do not know how to spell the entire word.

assess

- Notice the children's ability to connect consonants and letters at the beginning of words.
- Notice the extent to which the children are representing first letters in the words they write and how they are using first letters in reading.

Expand the Learning

Continue to play Follow the Path with an expanding set of letters and sounds.

Expand the cards to include consonant clusters and words that begin with vowels (see *Teaching Resources*).

Have the children play the game with ending sounds.

Connect with Home

At a meeting or in a newsletter, teach family members to play Follow the Path with their children and explain that the game will help children learn words to get them started in reading and writing.

Send home small copies of the Follow the Path Game Board. Children can use their letter cards to play it.

6 Noticing Vowels in Words

Word Graph

Consider Your Children

Before using this lesson, be sure that the children have worked with their names using the name puzzle and name chart. Check to see whether they can locate their names and at least partially write them. Also, the children should have some familiarity with the categories *consonant* and *vowel* when it comes to letters. This lesson will help inexperienced children learn what vowels are because of the personal connections with their names, but some children may need more demonstrations. Have children locate vowels in their own and others' names to give them more practice if necessary.

Working with English Language Learners

This lesson will help the children become more conscious of the visual details in words and draw attention to the role of vowels in words. It is useful for English language learners to learn to identify the vowels as a defined set of letters so that they will give them more attention in reading and spelling. Beginning with their names sets the scene for further work with vowel letter/sound relationships.

You Need

- Poster-size graph.
- Name chart.

From *Teaching Resources:*

- High Frequency Word Cards.
- Three-Way Sort Sheets.

Understand the Principle

Knowing the names of the vowels and being aware that all words have at least one vowel helps children develop a beginning understanding of the role of vowels in spelling patterns. This understanding, along with the important understanding that connections between vowels and sounds are influenced by where they appear in words, is necessary to learn how vowels function.

Explain the Principle

“Some letters are consonants and some letters are vowels.”

“Every word has a vowel.”

“*A, e, i, o,* and *u* (and sometimes *y* and *w*) are vowels.”

plan

Explain the Principle

“Some letters are consonants and some letters are vowels.”

“Every word has a vowel.”

“*A, e, i, o,* and *u* (and sometimes *y* and *w*) are vowels.”

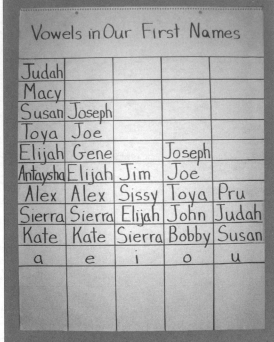

Vowels in Our First Names

Judah				
Macy				
Susan	Joseph			
Toya	Joe			
Elijah	Gene		Joseph	
Antaysha	Elijah	Jim	Joe	
Alex	Alex	Sissy	Toya	Pru
Sierra	Sierra	Elijah	John	Judah
Kate	Kate	Sierra	Bobby	Susan
a	e	i	o	u

① Let the children know they are going to learn about vowels.

② Start with a premade graph with the vowels on the bottom and a grid above each of the five letters. You will be writing the children’s names in the spaces above each vowel.

③ Begin by looking at an ABC chart. Highlight the five vowels and talk about how they are special because every word has at least one vowel and often more than one.

④ Suggested language: “Today we are going to see what vowels are in each of our first names.”

⑤ Show the premade poster-size graph with the vowels on the bottom and a grid above each of the five letters. Start with your own name or a name of one of the children.

⑥ Suggested language: “My first name is Kate. Look at my name on the name chart. What vowels do I have in my name? [Children respond.] I have an *a* and an *e*. In my neatest handwriting, I am going to write my name in a space above the vowels *a* and *e*.”

⑦ Continue to model this action. For example, have Sierra come up and write her name three times, above *i*, *e*, and *a*. Have Susan come up and write her name above *u* and *a*.

⑧ Once the children understand the task, leave the graph out and have the children come up and sign their names during independent work time or the following morning as they enter the classroom.

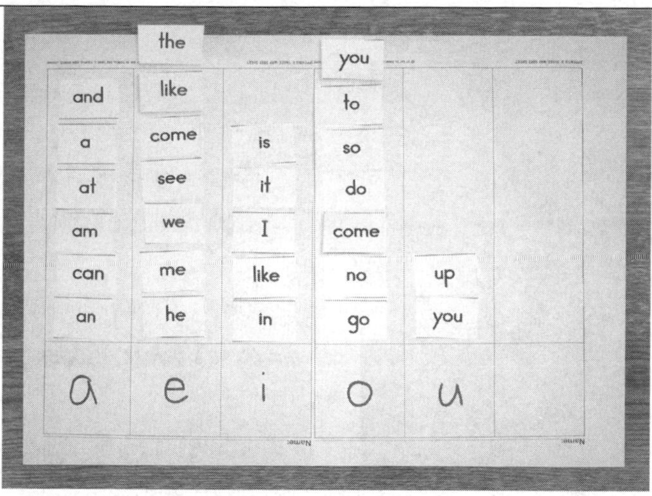

read
write

▸ Give each child a sheet of high frequency words and two Three-Way Sort Sheets taped together (from behind) to create a wide chart. (Before making the copies, designate the bottom row of boxes as the key boxes and write one vowel in each box. One column will not be used.) Explain to the children that they will build the graph from the bottom (as in the graph of their names), writing each high frequency word in the column above the vowels contained in the word. Then, in pairs, children take turns reading every other column to their partner.

Have the children discuss what they have noticed about their names. Generate sentences like:

"Seven people have an *a* in their names."

"Only three people have a *u* in their names."

"Sierra and Elijah both have *a*, *i*, and *e*."

Link

Interactive Read-Aloud: Read aloud books such as the ones below, emphasizing a few vowel letters and sounds when you come to them.

- ***Once I Was . . .*** by Niki Clarke Leopold
- ***Ms. MacDonald Has a Class*** by Jan Ormerod

Shared Reading: On a familiar text such as "Six Little Ducks" or "Listen to the Tree Beat" (see *Sing a Song of Poetry*), have the children locate words and identify the vowels in them. Highlight or point out words in the poem that illustrate the organizing principles. For example: "Find a word with the vowel *a*. Find a word with two vowels. Find a word that begins with a vowel."

Guided Reading: During word work, have the children build three or four words with a common vowel pattern (such as -*at*) and have them identify the vowel.

Interactive Writing: Using a "shared pen," write a title for the graphs created in this lesson.

Independent Writing: Have the children find words around the room that have a particular vowel. They can create a graph as they did in the application.

assess

- Check to see how many of the children can identify the vowels in the Alphabet Linking Chart and can identify vowels in four or five words.

Expand the Learning

Repeat the activity with other sets of words—the remaining high frequency words, color words, days of the week, number words, months of the year, short vowel words, beginning consonant words.

Connect with Home

Give the children another copy of the *a, e, i, o, u* and *y* combined Three-Way Sort Sheets used in the application, as well as a Word Card Template (see *Teaching Resources*) on which to write names. Have them take these materials home and make a graph of the names of people in their families or extended families and friends.

7 Introducing Consonant Clusters

Making Words

Consider Your Children

This lesson will be effective when the children know most of the consonants and their related sounds. In this lesson, they learn how to blend together more than one consonant sound. Consonant clusters are also referred to as *consonant blends* or just *blends.* For a very first lesson on consonant clusters, you may want to work with only one cluster as described in this lesson. If your children are able, work with two or three clusters in this first lesson. If you are focused on one consonant cluster, it will be important that you have a very short lesson. This should be a short simple introduction to the concept of a consonant cluster.

Working with English Language Learners

Before using this lesson, check to be sure that English language learners can easily identify individual consonant letter/sound relationships. Use words that you know they understand and can pronounce. The *tr* cluster may sound like *ch* to English language learners, so it will be important to say it slowly. Have children say it for themselves and look at the letter cluster. Also, be sure that children understand the meaning of the words you are using as examples.

You Need

- Magnetic letters and vertical surface.

From *Teaching Resources:*

- Picture Cards, Beginning Consonant Clusters.
- Four-Box Sheets.

Understand the Principle

Consonants frequently occur together in words. Understanding that you can hear the sound connected to each of the letters, although they are blended smoothly when you say the word, helps children recognize these particular word patterns. Eventually, they will become accustomed to recognizing the frequently occurring consonant clusters as a unit, making decoding more efficient.

Explain the Principle

“Some consonants go together in clusters.”

“A group of two or three consonants is a consonant cluster.”

“You can hear each sound in a consonant cluster.”

plan

Explain the Principle

“ Some consonants go together in clusters. ”

“ A group of two or three consonants is a consonant cluster. ”

“ You can hear each sound in a consonant cluster. ”

① Explain to children that they are going to learn something new about consonants.

② Suggested language: “You have been learning a lot about consonants and the sounds that go with them. There are some consonants that go together in many words, and they are called consonant clusters.”

③ Show a picture of a tree and have the children say the word with you.

④ Make *tree* with magnetic letters and ask the children to read it.

⑤ Explain that *tree* starts with *t* and the next letter is *r*. (You can ask the children to name the letters.)

⑥ Suggested language: “*T* and *r* go together in many words. *Tr* is called a *consonant cluster*. Say *tree*.” Children respond.

⑦ Work with the children to help them understand and hear both the *t* and *r* in *tree*. It will be tricky because *tr* is very close to the sound of *ch*.

⑧ Show pictures and make several more examples of words that begin with the consonant cluster *tr*, for example, *truck, train, triangle*.

⑨ It will also be effective to simply say words clearly, write them on the board or make them with magnetic letters, and have children think about the first two or three letters that make the consonant cluster (for example, *try*, *tray*, *trick*, *treat*, *trash*, *trail*, *trip*).

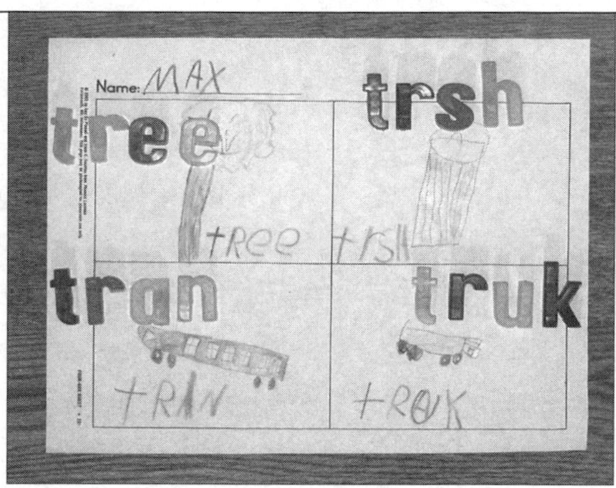

make
illustrate
write

- Give each child a Four-Box Sheet. In each box, using magnetic letters, they make a word that begins with the consonant cluster *tr*. Then they illustrate the word and write the word below the illustration. Encourage the children to write at least one letter for each sound they hear. It will be important for you to notice whether the children can write the consonant clusters correctly, but you should not expect them to be able to spell the rest of every word conventionally.

In groups of four, have each child in turn read all four words.

Begin a reference chart for letter clusters at the beginning of words (see LS 11, Recognizing Consonant Clusters: *r* Family). In the first column, place three or four *tr* words.

Link

Interactive Read-Aloud: Read aloud books that emphasize repetition of letter clusters, such as

- ***Get to Work, Trucks*** by Don Carter
- ***I Stink*** by Kate McMullan

Shared Reading: Point out letter clusters in texts that the children are reading, such as "Auntie, Will Your Dog Bite?" or "Choo-Choo Train" (see *Sing a Song of Poetry*). Ask the children to locate words with *tr* using a masking card or highlighter tape.

Guided Reading: Have the children locate words that begin with letter clusters. After reading, have the children go back to look at examples of words that begin with letter clusters. You can include any letter cluster that occurs, rather than sticking to *tr* words. This action will help the children notice letter patterns in words. Have children who need more experience build *tr* words during word work.

Interactive Writing: When the children want to write a word that has a letter cluster at the beginning, point out that the two sounds are a letter cluster. Highlight letter clusters on pieces of interactive writing children have produced.

Independent Writing: Encourage the children to hear and represent sounds of letter clusters in their writing.

assess

- Notice whether the children, in their writing, are representing the sounds of both letters in a letter cluster.
- Have the children connect pictures and letter clusters.

Expand the Learning

Repeat the lesson with other letter clusters: *br, gr, fr, cr, dr,* and *pr.* You will not need to have a separate lesson on every type of letter cluster. Once the children understand the concept by exploring three or four types of letter clusters, they will quickly learn the rest and can then sort and work with many different types of letter clusters.

If the children find letter clusters easy to understand, go on to help them understand clusters with three letters: *scr, str, spr.*

Connect with Home

Give children letter cards to cut up and make words with letter clusters at home.

Generative Lesson

8 Learning about Beginning Consonant Clusters

Finding Words

Consider Your Children

Use this lesson when the children can easily hear sounds in words, know most consonant sounds, have worked with common phonograms, and understand the substitution principle (that you can change a word by changing the beginning sound/letter). The children should also have a core of known words that they can use as examples.

Working with English Language Learners

Be sure that the examples you use on the chart are within English language learners' speaking vocabularies and that the poem you select is one that they can understand and learn with your help. Read it in an enjoyable way many times until children know it and can say it with little support. Point to the words as you have them read it; if they know the poem well, you may want to support individual children as they point to the words. Talk about the meaning of the words in the poem (for example, *sneezy* and *freezy*), so that you are sure students know the individual words and what they mean. Invite the children to share their own experiences and connect them to the poem. Once the poem is well known, the words will be more familiar and you can have children locate words, match letters, and so on.

You Need

- Copies of "Four Seasons."
- Highlighters.

Understand the Principle

Consonant clusters are some of the most frequently occurring word patterns. It is important for children to begin to notice consonants that frequently occur together and to understand that you can hear the sound connected to each of the letters, although they are blended smoothly when you say the word.

Explain the Principle

"Some consonants go together in clusters."

"A group of two or three consonants is a consonant cluster."

"You can hear each sound in a consonant cluster."

plan

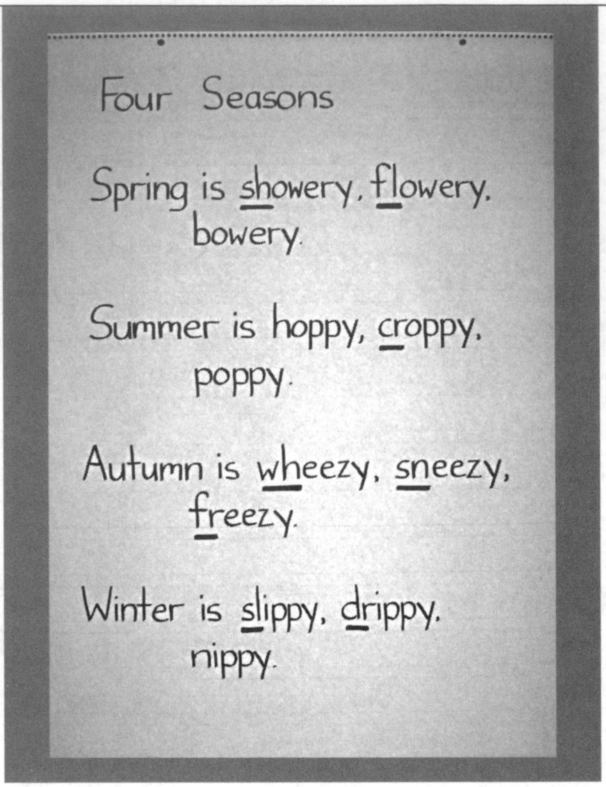

Four Seasons

Spring is showery, flowery,
bowery.

Summer is hoppy, croppy,
poppy.

Autumn is wheezy, sneezy,
freezy.

Winter is slippy, drippy,
nippy.

teach

Explain the Principle

“Some consonants go together in clusters.”

“A group of two or three consonants is a consonant cluster.”

“You can hear each sound in a consonant cluster.”

① Tell the children they are going to learn about consonant letters that go together.

② Display the poem “Four Seasons” on the easel and read it several times (see *Sing a Song of Poetry*).

③ Suggested language: “This word is *flowery*. The first sound in *flowery* is. . . . [Children respond.] The first sound in *bowery* is *b*. Now, listen to the word *croppy*. [Say *croppy* slowly and have the children say the word.] What do you hear?”

④ Children will respond that they hear *c* and *r*. Highlight the *cr* in *croppy* on the easel and ask the children to check the word to see if they were right. Do the same with *sneezy*. Go over one or two more examples of words in the poem with single consonants and consonant clusters.

⑤ Say several more words that have either one or two consonants at the beginning. Ask students to tell you the column in which to write them. You will need to explain that *sh* and *wh* are clusters of two consonants but we hear only one sound.

⑥ Ask the students to identify consonants that you often see together at the beginning of a word: *sl*, *dr*, *wh*, etc. Underline these pairs in red on the chart. Don’t try to make an exhaustive list, but make students aware that there are common letter patterns.

⑦ Suggested language: “We often see two consonants together at the beginning of a word. When two consonants are together at the beginning of a word, you can usually hear the sounds of both. Sometimes the two letters make one sound, as in *wheezy* or *showery*." This statement repeats the principle, but it is not necessary to write it on the chart.

The Itsy Bitsy Spider
The itsy bitsy spider
went up the water spout.
Down came the rain and
washed the spider out.
Out came the sun and
dried up all the rain.
And the itsy bitsy spider
went up the spout again.

highlight
read
glue
illustrate

- Have a copy of the poem "Four Seasons" for each child. Have them highlight or underline all the consonant clusters at the beginning of words in the poem and then read the poem to a partner. They can glue the poem in a poetry or word study notebook and illustrate it.
- You might also give them copies of two or three other poems. (*Sing a Song of Poetry* contains many examples, such as "The Itsy Bitsy Spider.")

Have the children share the words they found in the poem and tell the consonant clusters they found.

Ask them to discuss what they found out about consonant clusters. Comments like these indicate that the children are exploring words and applying the principle:

"You see *f* and *l* together a lot."

"I found *c* and *r* together at the beginning of a word."

"I found three consonants together at the beginning of *spring*."

Link

Interactive Read-Aloud: Read aloud books such as those below, stopping at one or two words with consonant clusters. Ask the children to point out the consonant cluster and listen for the individual consonant sounds.

- ***In the Swim*** by Douglas Florian
- ***Without Wings, Mother, How*** by Norma Farber

Shared Reading: After reading poems such as "The Old Woman" or "Soda Bread" (see *Sing a Song of Poetry*) together, have the children use a masking card or highlighter tape to show a few words with consonant clusters. On the first reading of a poem, you might cover a few words with beginning consonant clusters with stick-on notes. Stop before each word so that students can predict the beginning letters.

Guided Reading: During word work, make words with consonant clusters on an easel or whiteboard. If appropriate in the introduction or while teaching processing strategies, point out one or two words in the text that begin with consonant clusters.

Interactive Writing: Encourage children who need more help understanding the concept to come up to the easel and write the consonant cluster letters.

Independent Writing: Call attention to words with consonant clusters that children have spelled correctly.

assess

- Ask children to write 5–10 words with consonant clusters that you dictate to them.

Expand the Learning

Find words with consonant clusters in the poems you have been using for shared reading.

Have the children sort word cards with consonant clusters and those that have single consonants.

Have the children sort word cards by where the consonant cluster appears in the word (beginning, middle, end).

Connect with Home

Teach family members to play a consonant cluster word game with their children on a walk or in the supermarket. The adult says a word with a consonant cluster and the child tells the letters.

9 Recognizing Consonant Clusters: s Family

Go Fish

Consider Your Children

It will be important to work with many different beginning consonant sounds before moving to work with a variety of consonant clusters. Use this lesson with children who have a good grasp of consonants and corresponding sounds and can identify them in words. They may have already noticed that some letters often appear together at the beginning of a word.

Working with English Language Learners

For this lesson, the children will need to identify the objects in pictures and associate them with letters representing first letters. It will help your English language learners if you select pictures that they have worked with and for which they know the English labels. Be sure that they understand the procedures for the Go Fish game. Play it yourself with a student as a demonstration, explaining the game as you go. Then, have all students play it so you can observe. Work with a small group of students if they are having difficulty.

You Need

- Magnetic letters. (You may substitute word cards made using the Pocket Chart Card Template in *Teaching Resources*).
- Deck of Go Fish Cards (use the Beginning Consonant Clusters Word Card and Deck Card Template in *Teaching Resources*). Suggested words: *scale, scar, scout, scarf, snack, snail, snake, sneaker, sneeze, snap, skin, skip, sky, skirt, skid, skim, smack, smell, smile, smoke, smooth, smart, stem, star, stick, still, stop, stand, space, spell, spend, speed, spill, sport, swell, sweet, swim, sweat, string, strong, street, stream.*

From *Teaching Resources*:

- Directions for Go Fish.

Understand the Principle

Efficient readers and writers understand that there are patterns of letters that often appear together. They quickly learn to attach sounds not just to individual letters but to the larger unit or "cluster" of letters. This makes decoding more efficient and writing more fluid.

There are several families of consonant clusters: the *s* family, *r* family, and *l* family, among others. Some clusters have three letters, such as *spr* and *str.*

Explain the Principle

"Some consonants go together in clusters."

"You can hear each sound in a consonant cluster."

plan

Explain the Principle

"Some consonants go together in clusters."

"You can hear each sound in a consonant cluster."

1. Explain to children that you are going to teach them how to notice letters in words.
2. Suggested language: "You know how to listen for the first sound in words. What sound do you hear first in *soup*? [Children respond.] Take a look at these."
3. Put the words below on the board with magnetic letters or on cards in a pocket chart:

   scar *smile* *skip* *snack*

   spot *stick* *swim*
4. Point to and read the words. "What two sounds and letters do you hear first?" Have children tell the two sounds and two letters.
5. "So all of the words begin with two consonants together, and you can hear each sound. The two consonant letters together are called consonant clusters."
6. Explain how to play Go Fish. Children start with five cards each as their hand and try to create pairs of words that start with the same letter—for example, *slice, slim.* After laying down any matches in their hands, players ask another player for a word that begins with a particular cluster: "Do you have a word that begins like *spell*?" If the other player has such a word, he surrenders it, and the pair of cards is put down on the table. If the other player does not, he says "Go fish" and the original player takes a card from the deck. The first child to get rid of all her cards wins the game.

ask
match

▸ Have children play Go Fish in groups of two, three, or four.

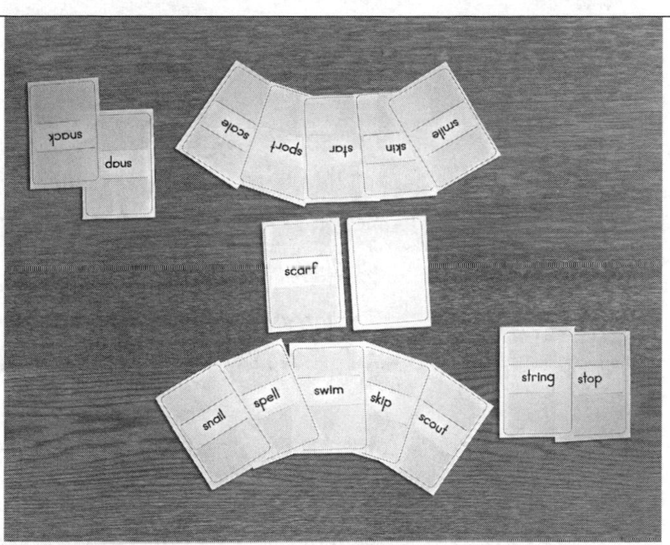

Ask the children to tell one word from the game that begins with a consonant cluster. Create a list of words on a chart.

Link

Interactive Read-Aloud: Read aloud books that have many words with consonant clusters, such as

- ***When It Starts to Snow*** by Phillis Gershator
- ***Cherry Pies and Lullabies*** by Lynn Reiser

Shared Reading: Use songs and poems with consonant clusters, such as "Six Little Snowmen," "A Snail," and "Itsy Bitsy Spider" (see *Sing a Song of Poetry*). Have the children use a masking card or highlighter tape to locate words that begin with consonant clusters.

Guided Reading: After the lesson, have the children locate two or three clusters in the text.

Interactive Writing: As the children contribute a word that begins with a consonant cluster, have them say it slowly and listen for the two or three sounds.

Independent Writing: Remind the children to write the two or three sounds they hear at the beginning of words with clusters.

assess

- Observe the children as they play the game and make note of children who need your help in small group work to understand and identify letter clusters.
- After the children have worked with several different letter clusters, prepare a pencil-and-paper test that requires them to identify pictures, say the words they represent, draw lines between the pictures and the words, and underline the letter cluster.

Expand the Learning

Have the children play the game with different words. See Beginning Consonant Cluster word cards in *Teaching Resources,* which include many words containing consonant clusters.

Connect with Home

Send home a deck of consonant cluster cards so children can play Go Fish with family members.

10 Recognizing Consonant Clusters: 1 Family

Cluster Lotto

Consider Your Children

Use this lesson with children who know the letters of the alphabet well and understand that letters and sounds are connected. They should be able to connect most consonants with sounds. They may have started to notice letter clusters in shared reading or interactive writing. In this lesson, you can focus on one cluster family or on several. It is important that children see the clusters as a word part and understand they can hear each sound.

Working with English Language Learners

Be sure that children say and understand the names for each picture on the Lotto cards. Have them say the words themselves rather than just listening to your pronunciation. Demonstrate saying the names of the letters and matching letter clusters with the picture cards. If children do not already know Lotto, demonstrate the game; you may want to work with a small group to be sure they can say and hear the letter clusters at the beginning of the word.

You Need

- Pocket chart.
- Chips or cards to cover game card squares.
- Magnetic letters (if not using pocket chart).
- Word Cards (use the Word Card Template in *Teaching Resources*). Suggested words: *black, clap, flag, glad, blank, class, flame, glass, blue, clay, flat, blister, clean, fly, glue, flip, globe, flea, cloud, place, closet, flew, plan, plate, slick, play, slide, slice, plum, slip, plus, slow.*

From *Teaching Resources:*

- Pocket Chart Card Template.
- Lotto Game Card.
- Directions for Lotto.

Understand the Principle

Efficient readers and writers recognize that consonants are often found together, and they learn to use these larger units in connection with the sounds. There are several groups of consonant clusters with two sounds—including the *l* cluster, the *r* cluster, and the *s* cluster, as well as clusters with three letters or sounds. When children learn to recognize and use clusters, they can read words more efficiently.

Explain the Principle

“Some consonants go together in clusters.”

“You can hear each sound in a consonant cluster.”

plan

Explain the Principle

“Some consonants go together in clusters.”

“You can hear each sound in a consonant cluster.”

① Explain to the children that today they are going to think about some word parts.

② Put the words below, in random order, on the board with magnetic letters or on cards in the pocket chart:

glass	*fly*	*black*
glad	*flip*	*blue*
clap	*slip*	*plum*
class	*slice*	*plan*

③ Point to and read the words and ask the children what they notice about them. They will notice that each word begins with two consonants and the second consonant is *l*.

④ Explain that each word begins with a consonant cluster and you can hear each sound in the cluster. (These words are in the *l* family cluster.)

⑤ Have a child sort the words so that the words that start the same are together.

⑥ Explain to the children that today they are going to play Consonant Cluster Lotto. They will each have a game card with words that begin with consonant clusters. They also have a deck of cards to draw from. They take a card and read the word. If they have a word that starts with the same cluster, they can cover the word on the game card with a chip or square of paper. If they do not, they do not cover a word on the game card. They place the card face down next to the deck. The first person to cover all the squares on the game card wins the game.

take
say
match

▸ Have the children play Consonant Cluster Lotto in groups of three or four. If time allows, they can play the game more than once for practice, swapping game cards with another child.

Invite the children to give one word that begins with a consonant cluster and say the cluster.

Link

Interactive Read-Aloud: Read aloud books that feature many words that begin with consonant clusters, such as

- ***Up the Ladder Down the Slide*** by Betsy Everitt
- ***Sleep, Little One, Sleep*** by Marion Dane Bauer

Shared Reading: After reading and enjoying a poem, such as "Slowly, Slowly," "A Cloud," or "A Horse and a Flea and Three Blind Mice" (see *Sing a Song of Poetry*), have the children use a masking card, flag, or highlighter tape to locate words that begin with consonant clusters.

Guided Reading: During word work, make some words with clusters. Change the cluster to make new words.

Interactive Writing: As the children try to write a new word containing a consonant cluster, have them say it slowly and listen for the two consonant sounds at the beginning.

Independent Writing: As the children write, remind them to say words and write the first two sounds they hear.

assess

- Observe the children's use of consonant clusters at the beginning of words to decode words in reading or in their spelling.

Expand the Learning

Have children play the game several times with different game cards.

Vary the Lotto game by having the children take picture cards instead of word cards. They match the name of the picture with a word on the game card.

Connect with Home

Give the children a set of Lotto Game Cards and word cards in a plastic bag so they can play the game with family members.

Recognizing Consonant Clusters: r Family

Word Sort

Consider Your Children

This lesson will be effective when the children know most of the consonants and their related sounds. They should understand the concept of a consonant cluster and have worked with several of the *r* clusters alone, as in Lesson LS 7. In this lesson, the children focus on the *r* family of clusters in order to be able to recognize these word parts quickly when reading.

Working with English Language Learners

This lesson gives children a chance to apply and generalize their knowledge of letter clusters that include the letter *r*. Provide many demonstrations of pronunciation and help students say words for themselves, accepting approximations. Include words that children understand. By this time, students should be accustomed to sorting; this lesson will help them focus on the first letter of the cluster and become familiar with words they can connect to each *r* cluster. You may want to use the Picture Cards, Beginning Consonant Clusters (see *Teaching Resources*) to support word meaning with children who have a more limited vocabulary.

You Need

- Magnetic letters and a magnetic vertical surface.

From *Teaching Resources:*

- Word Cards (Beginning Consonant Clusters).
- Three-Way Sort Cards.
- Three-Way Sort Sheets (optional).

Understand the Principle

Consonant clusters appear frequently in words. Recognizing these patterns quickly and automatically makes decoding more efficient. Understanding that you can hear the sound connected to each of the letters, although they are blended smoothly when you say the word, helps children understand these particular word patterns. When children are able to recognize and use clusters, their word solving is more efficient.

Explain the Principle

“Some consonants go together in clusters.”

“You can hear each sound in a consonant cluster.”

plan

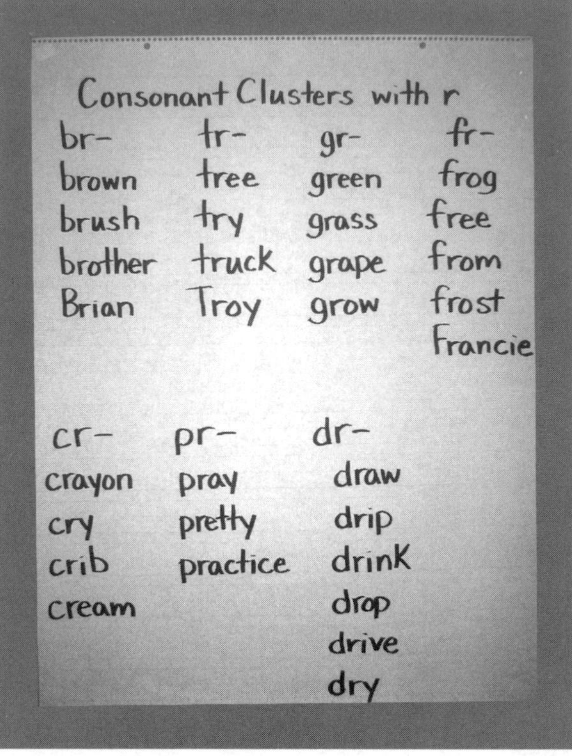

Consonant Clusters with r
br- tr- gr- fr-
brown tree green frog
brush try grass free
brother truck grape from
Brian Troy grow frost
Francie
cr- pr- dr-
crayon pray draw
cry pretty drip
crib practice drink
cream drop
drive
dry

Explain the Principle

" Some consonants go together in clusters. "

" You can hear each sound in a consonant cluster. "

1. Let the children know that today you're going to help them notice more about the letters in words.
2. Starting with a blank chart, write seven words or make them with magnetic letters *(brown, tree, green, frog, crayon, pray, draw)* at the top of seven columns. Ask the children what they notice about the words. They will notice that all words begin with two consonants and the second one is *r*.
3. Explain to the children that there are several consonant clusters that have *r* as a second letter and that together you are going to make a chart with words for each pattern. Invite the children to give two or three additional examples to create a reference chart as above. If children are less experienced, you may want to complete the chart over two or three days.
4. Write the title "Consonant Clusters with *r*" at the head of the columns. Suggested language: "You know a lot of words that have consonant clusters with *r*. You can use this chart to help you remember them, and we can add more words as you find them."
5. Suggested language: "Today you are going to sort words that start with the same pattern."
6. Demonstrate the three-way sort with word cards.

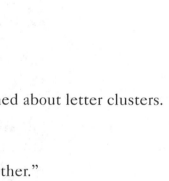

say
sort
read
write

- Have the children use a Three-Way Sort Card (with *fr*, *pr*, and *cr* at the top) and word cards to sort words according to consonant clusters.
- Tell the children to take word cards and place them under the correct column. Then they should read each column to a partner.
- Finally, have them write the words in three columns on a sheet of paper (or in a Word Study Notebook or on a Three-Way Sort Sheet) with the key word at the top of each column.

Have the children talk about what they have learned about letter clusters. Encourage comments like these:

"A lot of consonant clusters have *r* in them."

"A consonant cluster is two letters that go together."

"My name has a consonant cluster in it."

Link

Interactive Read-Aloud: Read aloud books that emphasize repetition of consonant clusters, such as

- ***Here Comes Henny*** by Charlotte Pomerantz
- ***Warthogs in the Kitchen*** by Pamela Edwards

Shared Reading: Point out consonant clusters in texts that the children are reading such as "The Squirrel" or "Three Elephants" (see *Sing a Song of Poetry*). Ask the children to use a masking card, flag, or highlighter tape to locate words with consonant clusters containing *r*. They will start to notice that there are *r* clusters in the middle of words but not at the end of words.

Guided Reading: Have the children locate words that begin with consonant clusters. After reading a text, have the children go back to look at one or two examples of words that begin with consonant clusters. Have the children who need more experience build words with *r* consonant clusters during word work.

Interactive Writing: When the children want to write a word that has a consonant cluster, remind them that they can hear both sounds in clusters. Highlight consonant clusters on pieces of interactive writing the children have produced.

Independent Writing: Encourage the children to hear and represent sounds of consonant clusters in their writing.

assess

- Notice whether the children, in their writing, are representing the sounds of both letters in a consonant cluster.
- Have the children connect five pictures with the corresponding consonant clusters.

Expand the Learning

Repeat the lesson with *l* family clusters *(bl, fl, cl, pl, gl, sl)* and *s* family clusters *(sl, sn, sp, st, sw, sc, sk, sm)*.

If the children find consonant clusters easy to understand, go on to help them understand clusters with three letters: *scr, str, spr, spl*.

Have the children play Lotto with a family of consonant clusters or with all varieties. The cards to be drawn from the deck have pictures. The individual Lotto Game Cards have consonant clusters on them such as *br, st, pl*. The children draw cards with pictures and match the consonant clusters on their cards.

Connect with Home

Give the children a Three-Way Sort Sheet (see *Teaching Resources*) and a sheet of words containing consonant clusters and have them do a three-way sort with family members.

12 Recognizing Long and Short Vowel Sounds: a

Say and Sort

Consider Your Children

This lesson is appropriate when the children know the term *vowel* and the five letters usually associated with it. The goal is to help them listen for and identify short and long vowels in words. After working with the long and short sounds of *a,* continue with the long and short sounds of the other vowels. This lesson is followed by other lessons that require contrasting the long and short vowel sounds in words. You will want to provide many lessons related to the sounds of vowels in words prior to working with these contrasts. Vowels are most easily learned in a variety of phonogram patterns. You will find many lessons on simple short and long vowel patterns (phonograms) in the section on spelling patterns and will want to use many of them prior to this consolidation.

Working with English Language Learners

Use the word *vowel* with English language learners and be sure that they can identify at least the five primary vowels. Use examples for the chart that they understand and can pronounce with your help. Provide many repetitions; have children say the words slowly and work for independence. Slightly exaggerate the vowel sounds of the words without distorting them too much.

You Need

From *Teaching Resources:*

- Word Cards (Long Vowel Sounds and Short Vowel Sounds) containing *a* vowel sounds.
- Two-Way Sort Sheets.

Understand the Principle

One of the most difficult letter/sound concepts for children to understand is the role of vowels in words. Vowel sounds are affected by the consonant sounds around them. Vowels may be "short" (tense) or "long" (lax), depending on their position in words. Children need a great deal of experience with vowels in order to notice the common and regular patterns in words as well as the exceptions.

Explain the Principle

" A vowel can have a sound like its name (*a* as in *make*), and this is called a long vowel sound. "

" A vowel can have a sound that is different from its name (*a* as in *apple*), and this is called a short vowel sound. "

plan

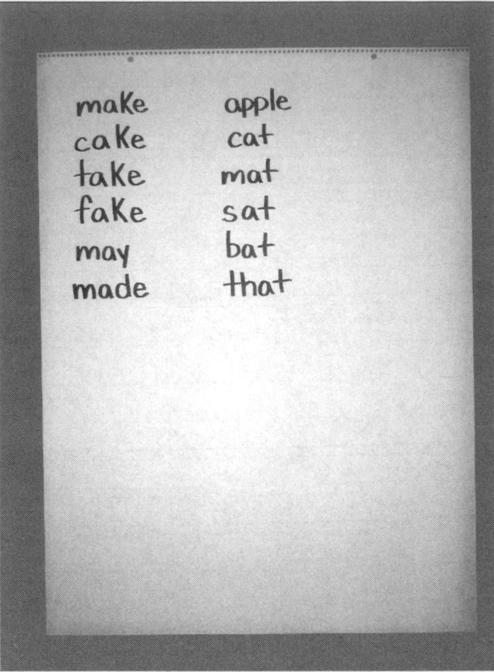

make
cake
take
fake
may
made
apple
cat
mat
sat
bat
that

Explain the Principle

"A vowel can have a sound like its name (*a* as in *make*), and this is called a long vowel sound."

"A vowel can have a sound that is different from its name (*a* as in *apple*), and this is called a short vowel sound."

1. Explain to the children that today they are going to learn about the vowel *a*.
2. Brainstorm with the class words with the vowel *a*. If the children give examples that are neither long nor short *a* (such as *call, was, watch*), write them outside the columns or on another chart and explain that although they have *a* in them, the sound that the *a* represents is different.
3. Record their suggestions by the sound of the *a* (see the example chart above).
4. Once the children begin to notice how you are categorizing their suggestions, ask them to tell you under which column to record the new words. Then explain that the words in the first column have an *a* that sounds like the *a* in *make* and the words in the second column have an *a* that sounds like the one in *apple*.
5. Suggested language: "You know a lot of words that have the letter *a* in them. You know many words that have an *a* that sounds like the *a* in *make*. Let's read them." Have children read down the list of these words as well as the other columns.
6. Suggested language: "Today you are going to write words that have *a* like *make* or *a* like *apple*. First, you read the word and then put your card in one of two piles."
7. Demonstrate sorting the cards into two piles. (If you are using the pocket chart, place them in two columns.)
8. Explain to the children that after they sort their words, they will list the words in each pile in two columns on the Two-Way Sort Sheet. The words that have the same *a* vowel sound as *make* will be written on the left, and the words that have the same *a* vowel sound as *apple* will go on the right.

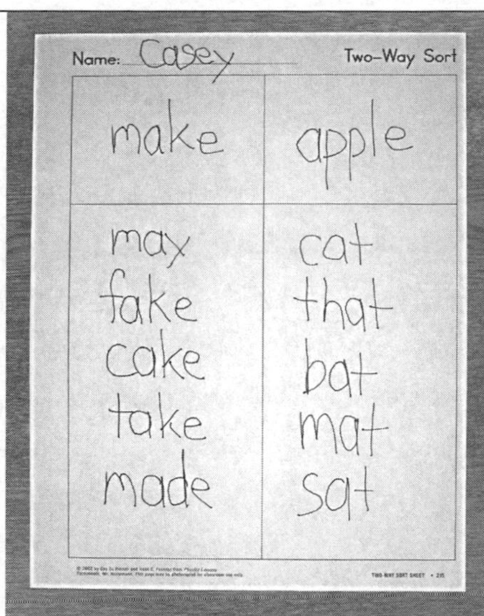
Name: Casey Two–Way Sort

make	apple
may fake cake take made	cat that bat mat sat

say
sort
write
read

- Give each child a set of word cards containing long *a* sounds and short *a* sounds. Also give them a Two-Way Sort Sheet. Have each child say a word, place it in the correct pile, and then write it in the correct column on the Two-Way Sort Sheet. Finally, have them read their list to a partner.

Have partners read their lists to each other one contrasting pair at a time. (The first partner reads a long *a* word followed by a short *a* word; then the second partner reads a line of contrasting words.)

Link

Interactive Read-Aloud: Point out one or two words that have long and short vowel sounds while reading aloud books, such as

- ***My Friend Bear*** by Jez Alborough
- ***Have You Seen My Cat?*** by Eric Carle

Shared Reading: After reading and enjoying a poem, such as "Away Down East, Away Down West," or "Bat, Bat" (see *Sing a Song of Poetry*), have the children use two different color highlighters or highlighter tape to find two or three words that have the *a* sound in *make* or the *a* sound in *apple*.

Guided Reading: During word work, have the children make two or three simple short *a* words. Do the same with words with the long *a* vowel sound.

Interactive Writing: When writing new words, prompt the children with language such as, "It's like the *a* in *make,*" or "It's like the *a* in *cat.*"

Independent Writing: Prompt the children to think about the sound of *a* in words they are writing. Have them tell whether it sounds like the *a* in *apple* or the *a* in *make.*

assess

- Check whether the children can categorize words with the long *a* or short *a* vowel sound.
- Give the children a paper with pictures and letters in columns to match. Identify the children who need more work in a small group.

Expand the Learning

Repeat the lesson with other words until the children have a good understanding of the contrasting sounds.

Connect with Home

Give the children a sheet of pictures representing five words containing the long *a* vowel sound and five words containing the short *a* vowel sound. (Limit the words to those with the single vowel *a* unless you have worked with the other vowels.) Have children cut out the pictures and sort them into two columns and write the words the pictures represent on a folded sheet of paper.

13 Recognizing Long and Short Vowel Sounds: e

Word Sort

Consider Your Children

This lesson is appropriate when the children know the term *vowel* and the five letters usually associated with it. Also, they should be able to hear and identify a range of sounds in words, including beginning and ending consonants and consonant clusters, so that they are better able to attend to the complexities of vowel sounds and their relationship to letters. Begin with very easy examples. Working with phonograms containing *e* will be helpful.

Working with English Language Learners

By the time you use this lesson, English language learners will understand the concept that letters can be connected to more than one sound. They will have become more flexible in their letter knowledge. Encourage them to search for many connections between sounds and letters. Understanding that *e* can be connected to two different sounds or can be silent in words will help them understand how words work. Provide many repetitions and use words that they already have in their speaking vocabulary.

You Need

- Chart paper and marker.

From *Teaching Resources:*

- Three-Way Sort Sheets.
- Word Cards (Long Vowel Sounds and Short Vowel Sounds) containing *e* vowel sounds.

Understand the Principle

Once children understand that vowel sounds are affected by the consonants around them and that two or more sounds are connected to the letters *a, e, i, o,* and *u,* they will increase their ability to connect and solve words. As they work with vowels within phonograms, many experiences will be required to help them understand regular letter/sound relationships as well as exceptions.

Explain the Principle

“In some words, the *e* sounds like the *e* in *eat* and *seat.*”

“In some words, the *e* sounds like the *e* in *egg* and *net.*”

“Some words end in an *e* that is silent and the vowel usually has the long sound.”

teach

Explain the Principle

“In some words, the *e* sounds like the *e* in *eat* and *seat.*”

“In some words, the *e* sounds like the *e* in *egg* and *net.*”

“Some words end in an *e* that is silent and the vowel usually has the long sound.”

① Tell children that today they'll be learning about vowels in words.

② Have a chart (leaving room for headings to be added) with four or five examples of words that have *e* that sounds like the *e* in *see* (long vowel sound), words that have *e* as in *egg* (short vowel sound), and words with silent *e*.

Sounds of the vowel e

Sounds like e in see	Sounds like e in egg	Silent e
seat	net	cake
meet	wet	Kite
me	best	like
tree	messy	hope
green	bed	cute
read		
eat		
he		

③ Read each column and ask the children to listen for the sound of *e* and tell what they notice about it.

④ Suggested language: “I'm going to read you some words. Every word I read has the letter *e* in it. Listen for the sound it makes.”

⑤ Point to and read each word in a column and ask the children what they notice. They will notice that the *e* in the first column sounds like its name. They may also notice that sometimes it is an *e* by itself and other times there are two vowel letters together making the *e* sound.

⑥ After guiding the children to generalize this principle, write “sounds like *e* in *see*” at the top of the column and tell the children the vowel sound is a long *e*.

⑦ Repeat the process with the short *e* words in column two and the silent *e* words in the third column—each time guiding the children to generalize the important principle.

⑧ To summarize, explain to the children that the vowel sound of *e* can be long (as in *see*), short (as in *egg*), or silent (as in *cake*).

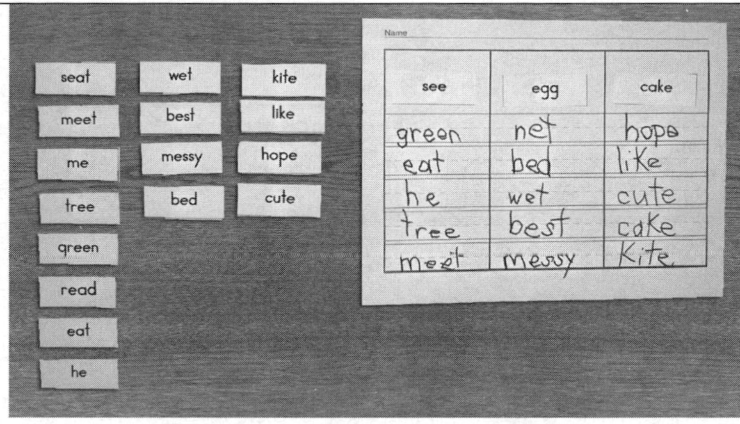

say
sort
write
read

- Have the children use a Three-Way Sort Sheet and a set of word cards containing long and short *e*s. Be sure to select words with silent *e* from the long vowel group, such as *kite* and *game*. Have the children write the key word "*see*" at the top of the first column and the key word "*egg*" at the top of the second column. In the third column have them write the word "*cake*." Remind the children to underline all the *e*s in the key words.
- Have the children sort the cards into three piles. Pile 1 sounds like the *e* in *see* and has *ee* or *ea*. Pile 2 sounds like the *e* in *egg*. Pile 3 has silent *e*.
- Then, have the children record the results of their sorting on the Three-Way Sort Sheet.
- Finally, have them read their lists of words to a partner.

Invite the children to suggest one or two other words to add to each column on the chart.

Link

Interactive Read-Aloud: Select words that have *e* sounds and help children notice how they look after reading aloud books, such as

- ***Animal Music*** by Harriet Ziefert
- ***Pet Show*** by Ezra Jack Keats

Shared Reading: After reading and enjoying a text, such as "Five Little Sparrows" or "Mary's Canary" (see *Sing a Song of Poetry*), have the children use a masking card or highlighter tape to locate words with long *e* and short *e* sounds.

Guided Reading: After reading and discussing a text, have the children turn to a specific page and find a word that has a clear long or short *e* sound. Repeat the process with two or three more words.

Interactive Writing: While writing, have the children notice words with *e* as in *see* and *e* as in *egg.*

Independent Writing: Prompt the children to think about the sound of *e* in words they are writing. Help them link new words to the key words *see* and *egg.*

assess

- Notice whether the children are able to read words with short *e* and long *e* sounds. Be sure to observe whether they are checking the sounds in the word with the sense of the sentence they are reading.
- Check whether the children can categorize words with *e* vowels. Give children a paper with pictures and letters in columns that they are to match. Identify children who need more work in a small group.

Expand the Learning

Repeat the lesson using other words with the three sound patterns from this lesson (or other *a, i, o,* or *u* patterns) to give children more practice.

If the children have a strong understanding of the principles in this lesson, you may want to create a Follow the Path game (see *Teaching Resources,* Materials & Routines) for further practice. On each space of the path, write a word that has a long *e*, short *e*, or silent *e*. Have the children read the word and tell whether the *e* is long, short, or silent.

Connect with Home

Give children photocopied lists of the words you used in the lesson, along with a Three-Way Sort Sheet. They can cut the words apart and sort them at home. You can add more vowel word cards to their collections later.

14 Recognizing Long and Short Vowel Sounds: i

Say and Sort

Consider Your Children

This lesson is appropriate when your children know the term *vowel* and the five letters that are usually associated with it. The goal is to help them focus on the vowel *i* and help them understand two sounds that the vowel *i* makes. Prior to this lesson, you will want to work with many simple short and long vowel patterns (phonograms) from lessons within the "Spelling Patterns" section.

Working with English Language Learners

This lesson will help English language learners listen closely to vowel sounds in words and differentiate between long and short sounds of *i*. Demonstrate word pronunciation and work with children until they can say the words themselves. Accept approximations; they may have to make their own connections to the letters based on how they can pronounce the words. Be sure the examples you use are in children's speaking vocabulary.

You Need

- Pocket chart.

From *Teaching Resources:*

- Pocket Chart Card Template.
- Word Cards (Long Vowel Sounds and Short Vowel Sounds) containing *i* vowel sounds.
- Two-Way Sort Sheets (lined).

Understand the Principle

More experience in connecting and sorting words containing contrasting vowel sounds will help children understand that vowel sounds are related to their position in words. Building experience with identifying vowel sounds will contribute to decoding and spelling abilities.

Explain the Principle

"In some words, the *i* sounds like the *i* in *ice* and *kite.*"

"In some words, the *i* sounds like the *i* in *igloo* and *sit.*"

plan

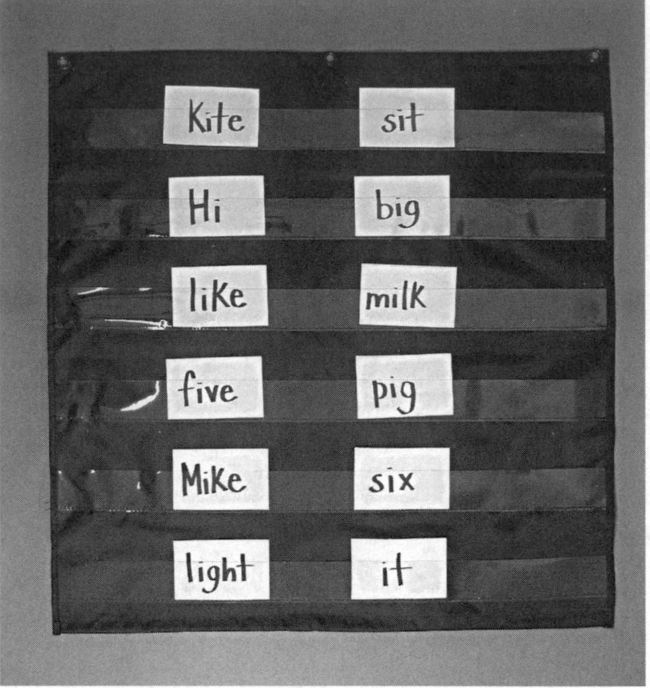

Explain the Principle

“ *In some words, the i sounds like the i in ice and kite.* ”

“ *In some words, the i sounds like the i in igloo and sit.* ”

① Explain to children that today you are going to teach them more about the sounds vowels make in words.

② Using pocket chart cards and a pocket chart, place the word *kite* and the word *sit* at the top of two columns.

③ Show one word at a time from a pile of words that have the long or short *i* vowel sound. Ask the children to read the word and tell you whether the vowel sound goes with *kite* or *sit*. Place it under the correct key word until you have four or five words in each column.

④ If the children suggest words that have the sound of long *i* but do not have an *i* (*fly* or *my*, for example), recognize their good thinking and explain to them that the sound is *i* but it is represented by a different letter. You can place it outside the chart or include it in the column with the associated sound.

⑤ Guide the children to generalize that the *i* sound can be long as in *kite* or short as in *sit*. Suggested language: “You know a lot of words that have *i* in them. You can see that some words have an *i* that sounds like its name. It is called a long *i* when it sounds like its name. Some words have an *i* like in *sit*. That sound is a short vowel sound. Today you are going to practice reading words that have a long vowel sound or a short vowel sound.”

⑥ Demonstrate reading, sorting, and writing words containing the vowel *i* in two columns on a Two-Way Sort Sheet.

sort
write
read

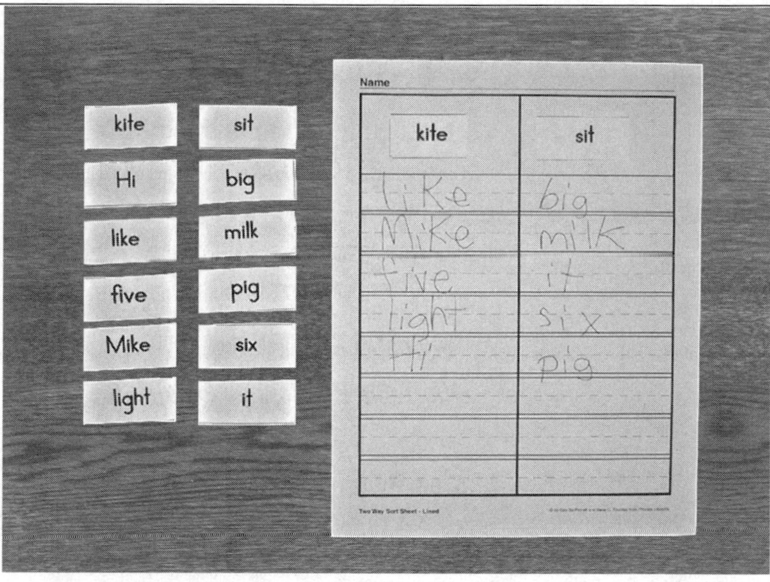

▸ Give the children a Two-Way Sort Sheet and a list of words containing long and short vowel *i* sounds. Have the children say and sort the words into piles of long and short vowel sounds. Then ask them to write the words in two columns on the Two-Way Sort Sheet under the key words *kite* and *sit*. Finally, have them read their lists to a partner.

Show the children four or five additional words. Invite them to place the words in the appropriate column in the pocket chart.

Link

Interactive Read-Aloud: In books you are reading aloud, select two or three words, such as the names of characters or the name of a place, and have the children tell whether the words go with *kite* or *sit*. Examples are:

- ***Moonlight Kite*** by Helen Buckley
- ***The Table Where Rich People Sit*** by Byrd Baylor

Shared Reading: In familiar texts, such as "Roosters Crow" or "There Was an Old Man of Peru" (see *Sing a Song of Poetry*), have the children use a masking card or highlighter tape to find two or three words with the long or short *i* vowel sound.

Guided Reading: During word work, make two or three words with the short *i* vowel sound and have the children read them. Do the same with two or three words with the long *i* vowel sound.

Interactive Writing: Reinforce the vowel sound of *i* by telling the children that a word they are going to write sounds like the *i* in *kite* or the *i* in *sit*.

Independent Writing: Prompt the children to think about the sound of *i* in words they are writing.

assess

- Notice the children's ability to read words with the short or long *i* sound.
- Observe the children's ability to write words with short *i* or long *i*. If they are saying the words slowly and listening for the sounds, they should be able to write most of the words successfully.
- Dictate four or five words with the long or short *i* sound in them to determine the children's understanding of the letter/sound relationship.

Expand the Learning

Repeat the lesson with a greater variety of words with long and short *i*.

Have the children play Follow the Path (see *Teaching Resources,* Games) with pictures representing words containing the long or short *i* sound in each space. When they land on a space, have them read the word and tell whether it has a long or short vowel sound.

Connect with Home

Give the children a sheet of easy-to-read long and short *i* vowel words. Have them cut out the words and sort them into two piles and glue them on a sheet of paper.

Add more vowel word cards to the children's home word collections.

15 Recognizing Long and Short Vowel Sounds: o and u

Follow the Path

Consider Your Children

This lesson is appropriate when your children know the term *vowel* and the five letters usually associated with it. The idea is to help the children notice and learn ways of thinking about how vowels function in words and how they sound different in different words. If this lesson follows many others on vowels and vowel patterns from this section and the spelling patterns section, children should be able to assimilate the concepts quickly.

Working with English Language Learners

Be sure that English language learners know how to play Follow the Path and that they can read and know the meaning of the words you are using in the lesson and in the game. Ask the children to offer their own examples and notice the connections they are making.

You Need

- Follow the Path Game Board.

From *Teaching Resources:*

- Pocket Chart Word Card Template.
- Word Cards (Long Vowel Sounds and Short Vowel Sounds) containing *o* and *u* vowel sounds.
- Directions for Follow the Path.
- List Sheets.

Understand the Principle

As the children learn more about vowel sounds, they will increase their ability to notice the details of words as they read and spell them. They will also be able to give more attention to less regular letter/sound relationships.

Explain the Principle

" A vowel can have a sound like its name (*o* as in *go, u* as in *use*), and this is called a long vowel sound. "

" A vowel can have a sound that is different from its name (*o* as in *hot, u* as in *umbrella*), and this is called a short vowel sound. "

plan

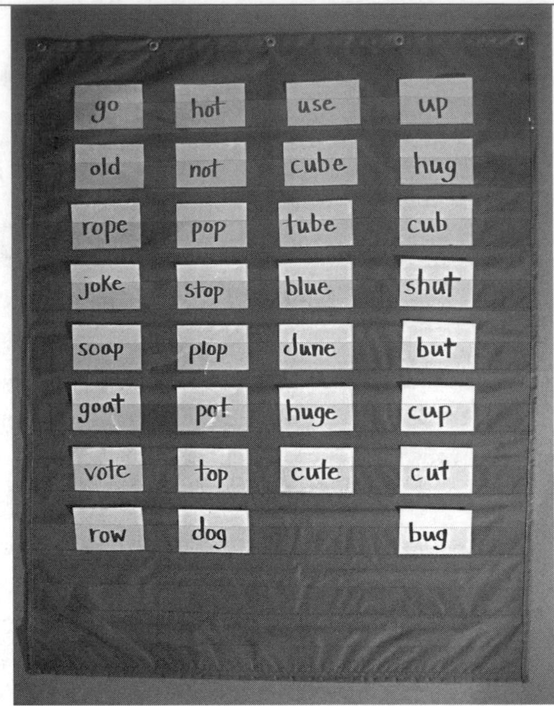

Explain the Principle

"A vowel can have a sound like its name (*o* as in *go, u* as in *use*), and this is called a long vowel sound."

"A vowel can have a sound that is different from its name (*o* as in *hot, u* as in *umbrella*), and this is called a short vowel sound."

1. Explain to the children they are going to learn how to listen for and notice vowel letters and sounds in words.
2. Start out with three or four words in each column in the pocket chart and have the children read them with you. After reading the words in each column, focus the children's attention on the first column, adding a few more examples.
3. Suggested language: "All of these words have the vowel *o* and it sounds like its name. It is called a long vowel sound. [Read the words in the next column.] All of these words also have an *o* in them. The *o* sounds like *o* in *hot.* The vowel sound is different from its name. It is called a short vowel sound."
4. Continue with the columns for long and short *u*.
5. Have the children read down the list of words in each category. Suggested language: "In these words, the *u* has the sound that you hear in *use.* Let's read all of these words and listen for the sound of *u* in the middle. What do you notice about these words?"
6. The children may say (or you may point out) that the words all end in *e*.
7. Repeat the process with the words with *u* as in *cup* and ask the children what they notice about the words. The point here is not to have the children repeat a rule but to begin to see words in categories.
8. Explain to the children that they are going to play Follow the Path. They will each have a marker and they will share a board with a partner. They take turns, throwing a die, moving the correct number of spaces, reading the words, and telling whether they hear a long or short vowel sound.

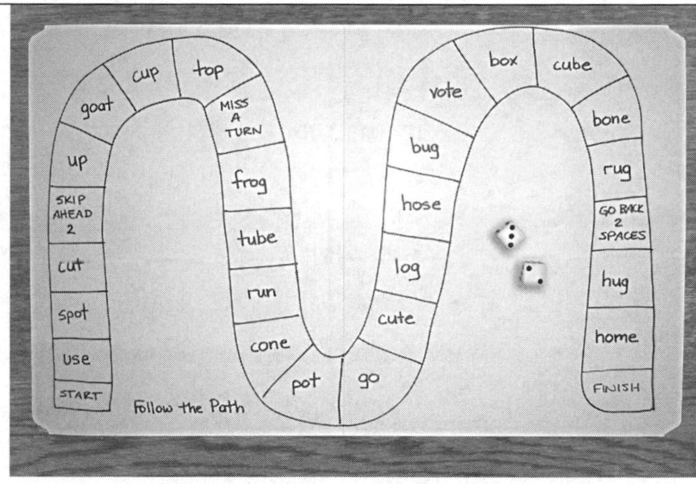

throw
move
read
tell

▸ Have the children play Follow the Path. On each space there is a word containing a long *o* or *u* or a short *o* or *u* vowel sound. Children take turns throwing the die, moving the marker, reading the word, and telling whether the word includes a long or short vowel sound.

Invite four or five children to give additional words that have an *o* or *u* vowel sound that sounds like its name. Continue adding words to the lists throughout the week.

Link

Interactive Read-Aloud: Point out long or short vowel sounds in the names of two or three characters or places when reading aloud books, such as

- ***Bear Day*** by Cynthia Rylant
- ***Sleepy Bears*** by Mem Fox

Shared Reading: Before reading a text, such as "Alice Where Are You Going?" or "There's Music in a Hammer" (see *Sing a Song of Poetry)*, cover four or five words containing long *o* or *u* vowel sounds with stick-on notes. In the first reading of the text, stop at the covered words and invite the children to predict the word in the text. Have them tell whether the word has a short or long vowel sound.

Guided Reading: After reading and discussing the text, have the children turn to two or three words on specific pages and ask them to tell whether the vowel sound is long or short.

Interactive Writing: Before writing a word together, have the children say it slowly with you and tell whether the vowel sound they hear is long or short.

Independent Writing: Prompt the children to listen for the vowel sound as they write words. You may want to point out that when a vowel sounds like the name of the letter, it is called a "long" vowel.

assess

- Select four or five words that have long or short *o* or *u* vowel sounds. Dictate these words or ask the children to read them.
- Observe the children when they write words containing *o* or *u* to determine the patterns they control.

Expand the Learning

Play Follow the Path (see *Teaching Resources,* Materials & Routines) with words containing the full range of long and short vowel sounds *(a, e, i, o, u).* Write a vowel on each side of a die or block. The children roll the die and see a letter name. They move their marker to the next word on the path that has that vowel. They read the words and tell whether the vowel sound is long or short.

Connect with Home

Give the children a photocopy of a Follow the Path Game Board and a pile of cards with *a, e, i, o, u* written on them so they can play the game at home with family members. They use the cards to move forward on the board.

16 Consolidating Knowledge about Vowels

Vowel Lotto

Consider Your Children

This lesson is appropriate when your children know and have worked with the five vowels. The children will have looked at the vowels one at a time and done some graphing or sorting. The idea is to help the children notice and learn ways of thinking about how vowels function in words and how they sound different in different words. Be sure the examples you use are words the children know and can read.

Working with English Language Learners

When English language learners have worked with all of the vowels, they will begin to bring their knowledge together and summarize it. This body of information will help them understand how words work. By the time you use this lesson, the children will have had the opportunity to make many connections with the vowels in words even if their pronunciation is slightly different from your own. Provide many opportunities for the children to say the words and categorize them. Work with a small group of children who are still having difficulty with vowel categorization.

You Need

- Chart paper and marker.

From *Teaching Resources:*

- Lotto Game Card.
- Directions for Lotto.
- Word Cards (Short Vowel Sounds and Long Vowel Sounds).

Understand the Principle

Children need a great deal of experience with vowels in order to notice the common and regular patterns in words as well as the exceptions. Consolidating and systematizing their knowledge of regular letter/sound relationships for vowels will give them powerful categories that will serve as resources in reading and writing.

Explain the Principle

“A vowel can have a sound like its name (*a* as in *make*), and this is called a long vowel sound.”

“A vowel can have a sound that is different from its name (*a* as in *apple*), and this is called a short vowel sound.”

plan

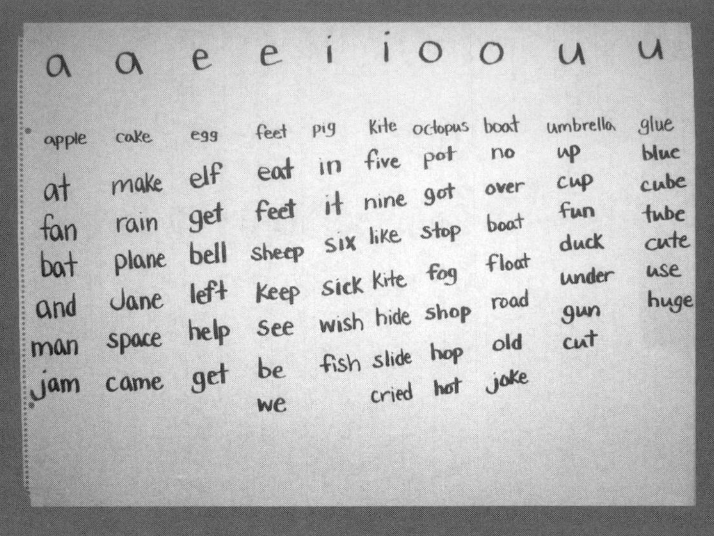

Explain the Principle

“ A vowel can have a sound like its name (*a* as in *make*), and this is called a long vowel sound. ”

“ A vowel can have a sound that is different from its name (*a* as in *apple*), and this is called a short vowel sound. ”

① Tell the children you are going to help them think about all the vowel sounds they know in words. Review the five vowels with the children. Use previously made vowel charts or begin a new summary chart (like the one pictured) that will replace them.

② Suggested language: “You know a lot about vowels now. Two sounds for each vowel are on this chart. Let’s think of examples for *a* as in *apple*.” Continue adding examples until you have at least three or four words for each vowel sound on the chart.

③ Suggested language: “Today you are going to play Vowel Lotto.” Demonstrate playing Lotto with a game card. In each space on the game card is a word with a long or short vowel sound. The deck of cards contains two each of the key word cards used in this lesson’s chart *(apple, cake, egg, feet, pig, kite, octopus, boat, umbrella, glue).*

④ Children take turns taking a word card, reading the word, saying the name of the vowel and whether it is long or short. Then they look on their game cards for a word that has the same vowel sound. If they have one, they cover it with a marker and the next child takes a turn. The first child to cover all the spaces wins the game.

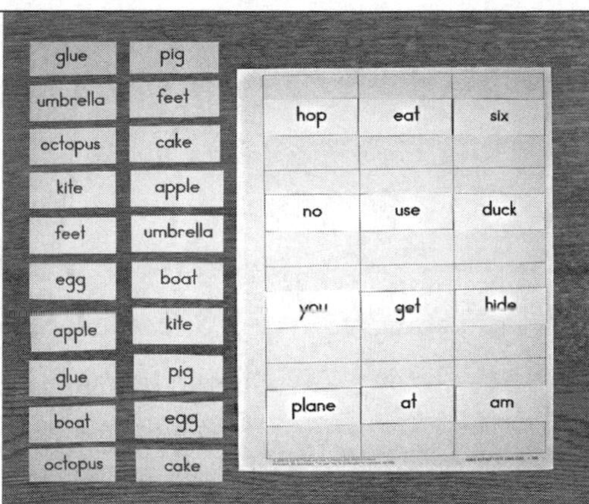

take
read
match
cover

- Have the children play Vowel Lotto with a partner or in groups of three or four. They will have the opportunity to practice all the vowel sounds and can use the reference chart if necessary.

Invite the children to give one or two words you can add to each category on the chart.

Link

Interactive Read-Aloud: Read aloud books that emphasize vowel sounds, such as

- ***Tracy's Mess*** by Elise Petersen
- ***I Swapped My Dog*** by Harriet Ziefert

Shared Reading: In familiar texts, look for words with specific vowel sounds and ask the children to locate them with a masking card or highlighter tape. Be sure to link the words to the key words they know. For example: "Can you find a word that has an *a* sound like *apple* or an *a* sound like *cake?*"

Guided Reading: Help the children notice the vowels and vowel combinations in words that they are trying to solve. During word work, have children who need more experience make words with regular vowel patterns.

Interactive Writing: While writing, have the children notice words with vowels. Use the summary chart as a resource for spelling or add examples to it.

Independent Writing: Prompt the children to say words slowly and to think about how to represent the sounds of the vowels.

assess

- Check whether the children can categorize words with regular vowel patterns.
- Notice whether the children are including at least one vowel in every word they try to spell, even if the spelling is not quite accurate.
- Notice whether the children's spelling of words with regular vowel patterns is becoming more conventional.

Expand the Learning

Extend the children's understanding of vowels by exploring different vowel combinations in words that have a long or short sound—the *ay* in *day,* the *aight* in *straight,* or the *ai* in *pail,* for example.

Connect with Home

Send home Lotto Game Cards and a sheet of Long and Short Vowel word cards (see *Teaching Resources*) so that children can play Vowel Lotto with family members.

Increase the children's collections of long and short vowel words so that they can sort the full range of words at home.

17 Recognizing Common Consonant Digraphs

Say and Sort

Consider Your Children

This lesson will be effective when your children know most of the consonants and their related sounds. The way you use this lesson will depend on your assessment of children's current knowledge. Be sure they know what you mean by the *beginning* and *end* of a word; demonstrate with letters. If the children have very little familiarity with these consonant clusters, start with one and gradually deal with the others in later lessons. You may also want to concentrate only on beginning sounds and look at ending sounds later. On the other hand, if the children have considerable experience with digraphs, one lesson that summarizes this information may be sufficient. It is not essential to use the technical term *digraph* for the children to understand the principle that a group or cluster of consonants can make one sound. If you do decide to use the term, have the children repeat it and be sure that they understand what you mean.

Working with English Language Learners

Some sounds may be difficult for English language learners to say because they vary so much from their own language. Accept approximations and provide many opportunities for them to say the words and to make their own connections to letters based on what they hear. Use words that are meaningful to them, and be sure they know how to listen for both the beginning and ending sounds of words.

You Need

- Magnetic letters and a magnetic vertical surface.

From *Teaching Resources:*

- Word Cards (Consonant Digraphs). Suggested words: beginning *sh* words—*shack, shame, shape, shake, shark, sharp, ship, shop, shell, shelf, shoe, shadow, shut, she, shock, shine, shoot, shawl, shout, show, shade, share, sheep, shirt, short, shed;* ending *sh* words—*brush, cash, fish, dish, wish, trash, push, mash, bush, dash, flash, hush, rash, wash, crash, crush.*
- Two-Way Sort Sheets.

Understand the Principle

Consonants frequently occur together in words. Some consonant digraphs make one sound that is different from either of the letters in the digraph. Quick, automatic recognition of these letter patterns and the associated single sound makes decoding more efficient.

Explain the Principle

“Some clusters of consonants stand for one sound that is different from either of the letters. They are called consonant digraphs.”

“You can hear the sound of a consonant digraph at the beginning or end of a word.”

plan

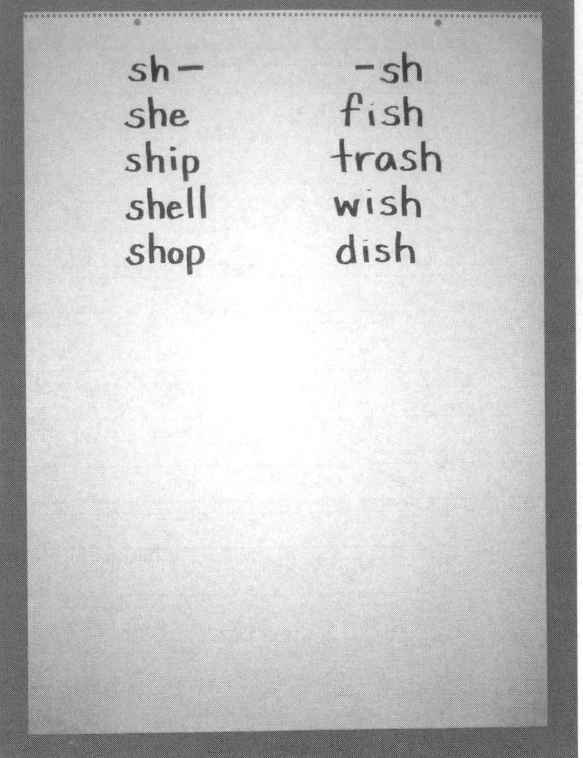

sh–
she
ship
shell
shop
–sh
fish
trash
wish
dish

Explain the Principle

"Some clusters of consonants stand for one sound that is different from either of the letters. They are called consonant digraphs."

"You can hear the sound of a consonant digraph at the beginning or end of a word."

① Tell the children they are going to learn more about consonants and their sounds.

② Suggested language: "You have been learning about consonant clusters." Prompt the children to discuss consonant clusters and to give some examples. (See Lesson LS 16.)

③ "There are some consonants that come together and make only one sound. You know this word." Make *she* with magnetic letters. The children read the word.

④ Suggested language: "*She* starts with a consonant cluster, *sh*. The two letters go together to make one sound." The *sh* is called a consonant digraph. Make the sound of *sh*. Using magnetic letters, make several other examples of words that begin with *sh*. Have the children read them and think about the sound at the beginning and the two letters that represent it.

⑤ Repeat the process with words that have *sh* at the end.

⑥ As a summary, create a chart of three or four words that start or end with *sh*. If needed, you may want to review the list one more time, underlining or highlighting the *sh* in each word.

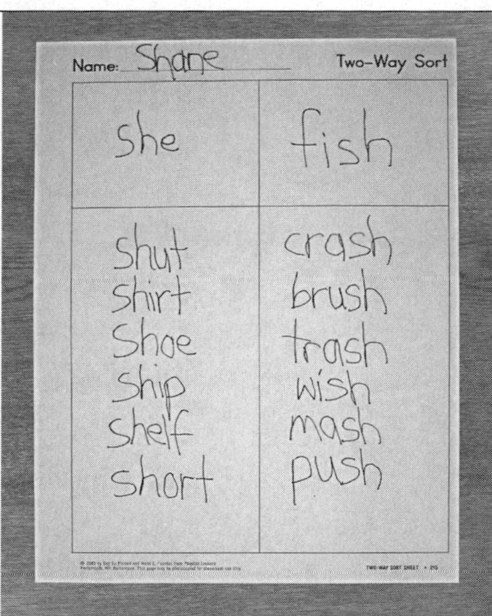

sort
write
read

- Give the children an asortment of *sh* words, some words beginning with *sh* and others ending with *sh*.
- Have the children sort the words into two piles, beginning and ending. Then, have them write *she* and *fish* as key words on a Two-Way Sort Sheet. Next, have them consult their sorted piles and pick six words to write in each column. Finally, have them read their lists to a partner.

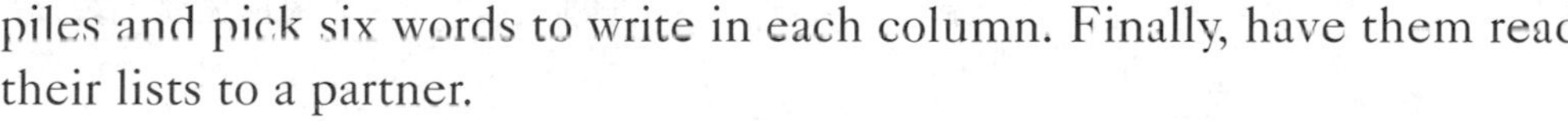

Have the children read their lists to a different partner. You may want to add more *sh* words to the chart.

Help the children notice whether any of the names on the name chart have *sh* in any position (Shayla and Keisha, for example; children may also notice words that have the sound but are spelled differently—like Tricia or Latitia). Have the children place highlighter tape on the *sh* cluster.

Link

Interactive Read-Aloud: Read aloud books that emphasize repetition of digraph sounds, such as

- ***Sheep on a Ship*** by Nancy Shaw (and other entries in this series)
- ***What Do You See When You Shut Your Eyes?*** by Cynthia Zarin

Shared Reading: Point out *sh* words in the texts children are reading. After reading and enjoying a poem such as "Can You Wash Your Father's Shirt?" or "Slip on Your Raincoat," have them apply highlighter tape to or underline the *sh* at the beginning, middle, or end of words.

Guided Reading: After reading, have children go back to look at examples of words that begin with *sh*. This action will help the children notice the letter pattern in words. Have children who need more experience build simple *sh* words (*she, shop,* for example) during word work.

Interactive Writing: When the children want to write a word that has *sh* at the beginning, make connections to the words on the chart. Highlight *sh* letter clusters on pieces of interactive writing children have produced.

Independent Writing: Encourage the children to hear and represent the *sh* sound as they write.

assess

- Notice whether the children, in their writing, are representing the *sh* sound with the correct letters.
- Notice whether the children, in their reading, are able to begin *sh* words with the appropriate sound.
- Dictate four or five words that have *sh* in them.

Expand the Learning

Teach the lesson using picture cards representing words that have *sh* in them (see *Teaching Resources,* Picture Cards, Beginning Consonant Clusters and Digraphs).

To make the task more challenging, mix in some other words (*stop, frog, snow,* for example).

Repeat the lesson with other consonant digraphs: *th, ch, wh.*

Connect with Home

Give the children a sheet of different *sh* words (see *Teaching Resources,* Word Card Template) to sort with family members. You can gradually add words containing other digraphs.

18 Summarizing Digraph Knowledge

Digraph Lotto

Consider Your Children

This lesson summarizes your children's learning about consonant digraphs. It will be most effective if it follows lessons on the beginning and ending sounds *sh, ch, wh,* and *th* (no words end in *wh*) (Lesson LS 17). If you have created an *sh* chart in Lesson 17, you can begin with that chart and add more categories to the chart in this lesson. You can decide whether it is approriate to use the technical term *digraph* with your children. The digraph *th* can make two different sounds, the sound in *the* and the sound in *think.* Be prepared for children to notice the two sounds of *th.* You may want to teach this summary lesson with words that begin with consonant digraphs and teach a different lesson with words that end with consonant digraphs.

Working with English Language Learners

By the time you use this lesson, children will know the concept of digraphs and be able to identify them in words. Be sure that English language learners know and can say the names of the pictures in the Lotto game. Have them identify the digraph by saying the names of the letters, the beginning sound, and the word. Play the game with them in a small group to be sure they are saying the names of the pictures, saying the names of letters, and playing the game as designed.

You Need

- Summary chart.
- Markers.

From *Teaching Resources:*

- Lotto Game Cards.
- Directions for Lotto.

Understand the Principle

Noticing and using consonant letters that go together to make one sound will increase children's efficiency in solving words as they are reading and writing. The more they can see these letter patterns as larger units, the less attention decoding will require.

Explain the Principle

“Some clusters of consonants stand for one sound that is different from either of the letters. They are called consonant digraphs.”

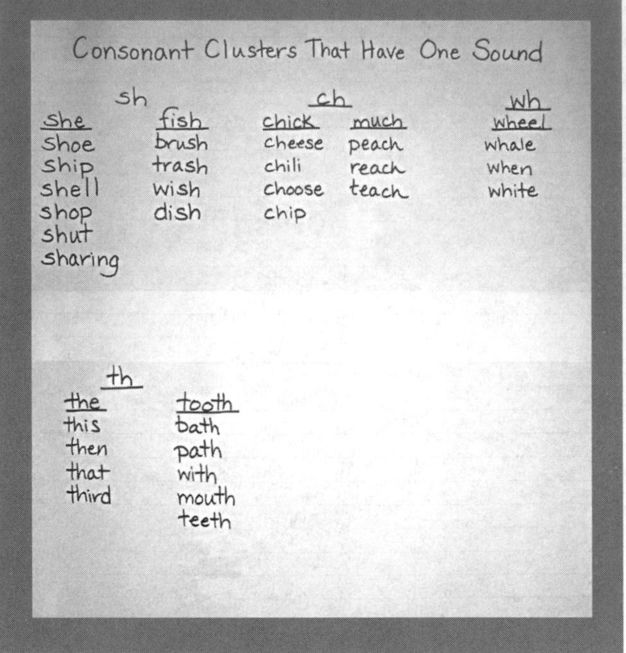

Consonant Clusters That Have One Sound
sh
she
shoe
ship
shell
shop
shut
sharing
fish
brush
trash
wish
dish
ch
chick
cheese
chili
choose
chip
much
peach
reach
teach
wh
wheel
whale
when
white
th
the
this
then
that
third
tooth
bath
path
with
mouth
teeth

Explain the Principle

“ Some clusters of consonants stand for one sound that is different from either of the letters. They are called consonant digraphs. ”

① Let the children know they are going to learn more about consonant clusters that have one sound.

② Suggested language: “You have been learning about consonant clusters like *sh* that have one sound.” Have the children read the examples for *sh* at the beginning of the word. “You also know that *sh* can be at the end of a word.” Have the children read the examples for *sh* at the end of a word.

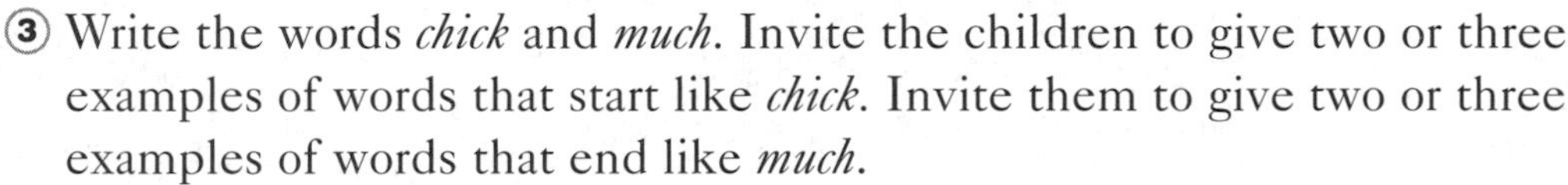

③ Write the words *chick* and *much*. Invite the children to give two or three examples of words that start like *chick*. Invite them to give two or three examples of words that end like *much*.

④ Write the words *the* and *tooth* at the top of two adjoining columns. Invite the children to give two or three words that start with *th* and two or three words that end with *th* or have *th* in the middle as you write them on the chart.

⑤ Finally, write the word *wheel* on the top of a column and invite the children to give examples of words that begin with *wh*.

⑥ As a review, invite the children to read each column of words. Ask them to talk about what they noticed about the words. Look for comments like these:

“There are two letters, but they make only one sound.”

“The sound is different from the sound of the letter by itself.”

“The letters can be at the beginning or the end of the word.”

“There aren’t any words that end with *wh*.”

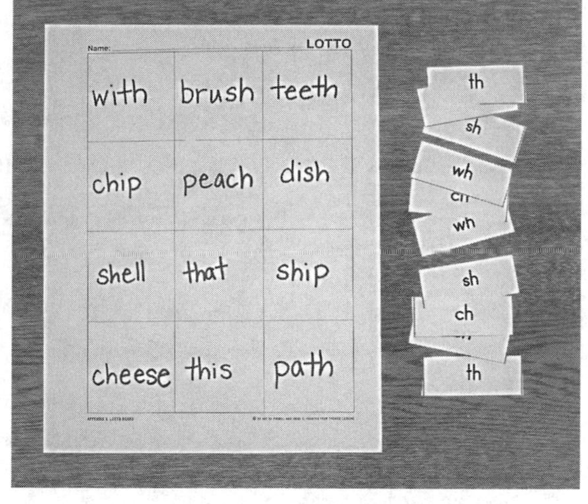

take
match
say
cover

- Have the children play Digraph Lotto with a partner or in groups of three or four. On the Lotto Game Card, write words that start or end with *ch*, *sh*, *th*, or *wh*. Give the children a pile of cards that have the four consonant digraphs written on them (several of each).
- Have the children take turns taking a card from the pile and looking on their game cards for a word that starts or ends with the digraph. If they find one, they read the word and cover it with a marker. The first player to cover all the words on the card wins the game.

Select four or five children to read each column of the chart together while one child points to each word.

Remind the children to use the chart as a reference when they are thinking about how to write a word.

Link

Interactive Read-Aloud: Read aloud books that emphasize repetition of digraph sounds, such as

- ***The Tenth Good Thing About Barney*** by Judith Viorst
- ***When Mama Comes Home Tonight*** by Eileen Spinelli

After reading and enjoying the story, find one or two examples of words that begin or end with these sounds and have children say them. Add examples to the summary chart.

Shared Reading: Point out words with consonant digraphs in poems children are reading such as "Clever Hen" or "Dingle Dangle Scarecrow" (see *Sing a Song of Poetry* for many more examples). Have the children highlight (with tape or pen) or underline digraphs at the beginning, in the middle, or at the end of words.

Guided Reading: After reading and discussing a text, have the children locate words that begin with any of the digraphs. During word work, write a few words that begin or end with consonant digraphs on a whiteboard for the children to read quickly.

Interactive Writing: When the children want to write a word that has a consonant cluster that makes one sound, make connections to the words on the summary chart. Highlight letter clusters on pieces of interactive writing the children have produced.

Independent Writing: Encourage the children to refer to the summary chart until they can write words with consonant digraphs independently.

assess

- Notice whether the children, in their writing, are representing consonant digraphs with the correct letters.
- Observe whether the children, in their reading, are able to begin consonant digraphs with the appropriate sounds.
- Have the children write a word that begins with each consonant digraph.

Expand the Learning

Have the children play Lotto with game cards that have a different variety of words with consonant digraphs (see *Teaching Resources,* Word Cards, Beginning and Ending Consonant Digraph Sounds).

Show the children how to add *-er* to words that end in consonant digraphs (*teacher,* for example).

Help the children notice that the *ch* sound is represented by *tch* in words such as *match* and *catch.*

Connect with Home

Give the children a list of five or ten words that have consonant digraphs. Have them make the words with magnetic letters or letter cards (see *Teaching Resources*) and read them to a family member.

19 Recognizing Vowel Sounds: Silent e

Say and Sort

Consider Your Children

This lesson is appropriate when your children recognize the sounds of vowels and are familiar with some of the letter patterns in the spelling pattern lessons. They should be able to read and write a number of words with silent *e* and be ready to look at them in categories.

Working with English Language Learners

Sorting these words will help English language learners attend closely to the vowel sounds in words. This task will be easier if you help them think about the name of the letter and connect it with the long vowel sound they are hearing. Encountering many examples of words with silent *e* will help them internalize the principle; be sure that the examples you use are in their speaking vocabulary. Work with a small group of children who are having difficulty with some of the words.

You Need

- Pocket chart.

From *Teaching Resources:*

- List Sheets.
- Pocket Chart Card Template.
- Word Cards (Long Vowel Sounds) that contain silent *e*.

Understand the Principle

Our alphabetic system is complex, and there are often more letters than sounds within a word. A helpful generalization for children to know is that when a word ends in *e*, sometimes you do not hear a sound for that *e*. It is a common phonogram pattern with the vowels *a, i, o,* and *u.* (There are a few *e* words, such as *Pete.*) The long *u* sound is tricky because it can sound like /oo/ in *blue* or the /u/ in *cute.* The difference is slight but noticeable, with the *u* in *cute* sounding more like the name of the letter. The *u* in *blue* is not precisely the long sound of *u* but is closer to that category than to the short sound.

Explain the Principle

"Some words end in an *e* that is silent, and the vowel usually has the long sound (sounds like its name)."

plan

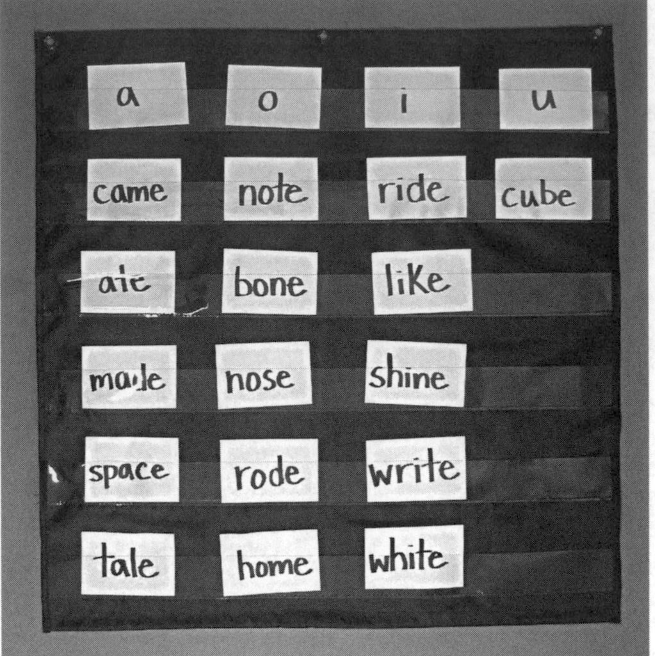

Explain the Principle

“Some words end in an *e* that is silent, and the vowel usually has the long sound (sounds like its name).”

① Tell the children they are going to learn more about vowels in words.

② Start with one column of four words *(came, ride, note, cube)* in a pocket chart. Have the children read the words with you as you point to them.

③ Suggested language:
“What do you notice about all of these words?”

④ The children will likely tell you that all of the words have an *e* at the end and that it is silent.

⑤ Take the words out of the column and place them across the bottom of the pocket chart, leaving the key words.

⑥ Invite the children to come up to a pile of word cards, take the top one, read it to the class, and place it in the pocket chart under the appropriate key word.

⑦ Include words like *come* and *trouble* in the pile. When they are drawn, show the children that sometimes you see words that end with a silent *e* and the vowel sound is different from how you would expect it to sound.

⑧ Tell the children they will be sorting and writing words with silent *e*.

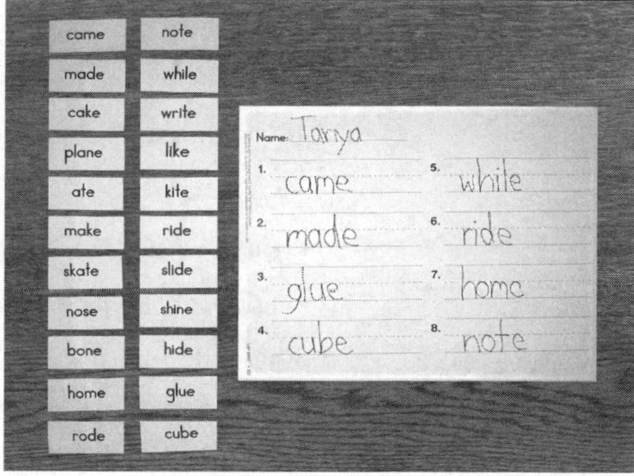

sort
read
write

▸ Have the children work with a set of about twenty words with silent *e*. Ask the children to say and sort the words in piles according to vowels. Once the words are categorized, ask them to read the words in each group to a partner. Then have them write two examples for the vowel sounds on the list sheet.

With the children, add one or two more examples to the chart.

Link

Interactive Read-Aloud: Read aloud books that emphasize long vowel sounds, such as

- ***Hush Little Baby*** by Sylvia Long
- ***Edward the Emu*** by Sheena Knowles

Shared Reading: In familiar texts such as "One, Two, Three, Four, Five" or "I Know Something" (see *Sing a Song of Poetry*), have the children use a masking card or highlighter tape to locate two or three words with silent *e*.

Guided Reading: Help the children notice new examples of words with silent *e*. You may also find words with silent *e* that do not fit this principle. Make a collection of those words to examine later during word work. Have the children make two or three words with silent *e* if more work is needed.

Interactive Writing: While writing, have the children notice words with silent *e*. Suggested language: "This word has an *e* on the end to make it look right. It is a silent *e*."

Independent Writing: Prompt the children to think about how words look and to say the word to consider whether it might have a silent *e*.

assess

- Check whether the children can categorize silent *e* words by noticing the vowel.
- Ask the children to read a randomly ordered list of words with silent *e* that fit this principle.

Expand the Learning

Repeat the lesson with other words that have silent *e*.

Look at other word patterns that have a final *e* and categorize them: *apple, trouble, challenge, choose, moose, sense, fudge, bridge, freeze.*

Connect with Home

Send home word cards with silent *e* for children to sort according to vowels and read to family members. They can glue their sorts on a sheet of paper.

20 Learning about Word Structure: r with a Vowel

Making Words

Consider Your Children

Use this lesson when your children know the common letters and associated sounds and have worked with some phonograms. They will have constructed many words with *r* in interactive writing and may have noticed that the *a* in *part* or *car* sounds different—almost as if it is part of *r*. Children should also know some high frequency words that contain this sound (*car* and *for*, for example).

Working with English Language Learners

English language learners will be able to hear the *r* but may not realize that there is a vowel before it because the sounds blend. It may help them to clap the syllables. Remind the children that every word (and every syllable) has a vowel in it. Use words that are in children's speaking and listening vocabularies.

You Need

- Easel and chart paper.
- Magnetic letters.

From *Teaching Resources:*

- List Sheet.

Understand the Principle

When young children first begin to write, they often use the letter *r* to represent the sounds spelled as *ar, ir, er, ur,* and *or*. From the point of view of a child who knows the letter name *r*, this makes sense. As they grow more proficient, spellers need to know that when a vowel is followed by *r*, it often sounds different from that same vowel in other positions; they need to think about the letter cluster that includes a vowel with the *r*. This cluster may appear in the middle, at the beginning, or at the end of words, and there is always a vowel with the *r*. To decide *which* vowel to use, children will need to think not only about the sound but also about how the word looks.

Explain the Principle

"When vowels are with *r* in words, you blend the vowel sound with the *r*."

plan

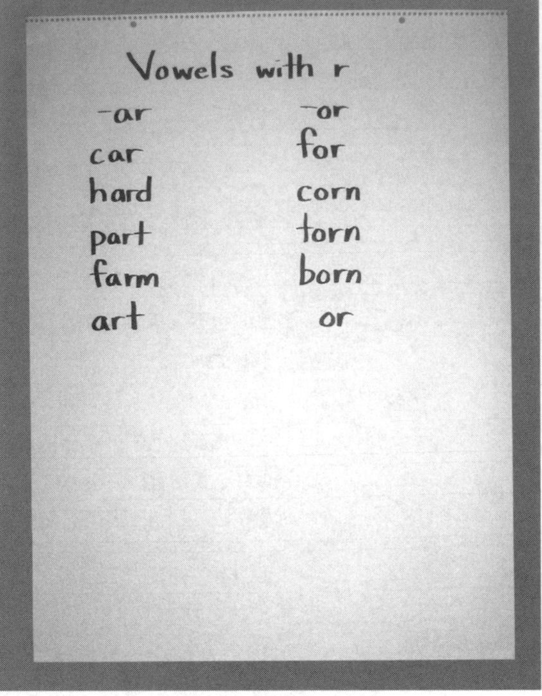

Vowels with r
-ar
car
hard
part
farm
art
-or
for
corn
torn
born
or

Explain the Principle

"When vowels are with *r* in words, you blend the vowel sound with the *r*."

① Explain to the children that they'll be learning about vowels and the letter *r* in words.

② Write *car* on the chart.

③ Suggested language: "Here is a word you know. [Children respond.] Yes, it's *car*. What part of the word says *ar*? [Children respond.]"

④ Write *-ar* at the top of the column and ask the children to generate some other examples of words they know that have *-ar*. You can use the word wall as a resource. If the children offer examples of words that have other vowels, recognize that they are getting the idea. As an option, you can write *-ir* or *-ur* words in a column to the far right. If they give *-or* examples, start another column.

⑤ Explain that it is hard to hear the difference in the vowels when they are right before *r*. Introduce the *-or* column to the children by writing the word *for*. Suggested language: "Here is another word you know that has a vowel with *r*. Say *for*. [Children respond.] Now say *car*. [Children respond.] Can you hear a little bit of difference?"

⑥ Discuss the difference with the children, but caution that you can't always hear the difference when there is a vowel with *r*. Sometimes you have to think about how the word looks or connect it with other words. Place *-or* at the top of the second column and generate more examples that have *-or*.

⑦ Summarize the lesson by stating the principle orally. Suggested language: "Today we have learned that when vowels are next to the letter *r* in words, the vowel sound changes."

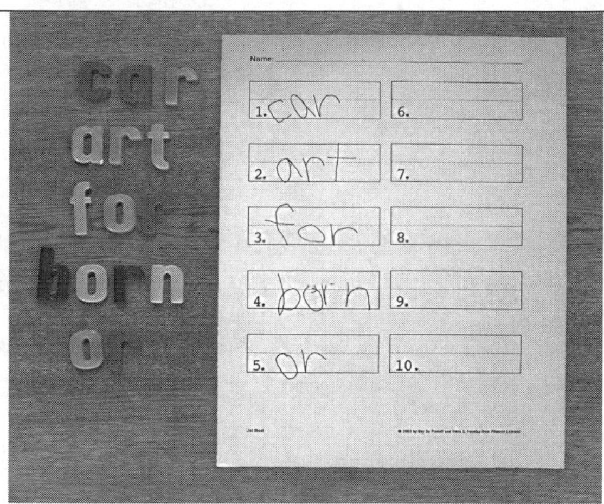

make
write
read

- Have the children use magnetic letters and/or letter cards to make five *-ar* and five *-or* words. Have them list their words on the list sheet and read them to a partner.

Have the children share some of the words they made. Add one or two examples of *-ar* and *-or* words to the word wall (or highlight words that are already there). Ask the children what they noticed about these words. Encourage comments like these:

"*Ar* can be at the beginning of the word or after the first letter or at the end."

"*Or* is a word all by itself but *ar* isn't."

"*Chart* and *part* rhyme."

"You can make *car* into *cart* by adding a *t* at the end—like *go-cart*."

"There's an *ar* in Marcella's name."

Link

Interactive Read-Aloud: Read aloud books such as the following and point out one or two words that use vowels with *r.*

- ***Four Fur Feet*** by Margaret Wise Brown
- ***I Heard the Willow Weep*** by Toni Albert

Shared Reading: Call attention to words with *-ar* and *-or* in poems or songs such as "Old Mother Hubbard" or "The Queen of Hearts" (see *Sing a Song of Poetry*). Cover part of the word with a stick-on note and ask children to predict the letters. Uncover it to confirm the prediction.

Guided Reading: During word work, have the children use magnetic letters to make four or five *-ar* and *-or* words.

Interactive Writing: When writing words with *-ar* and *-or*, call attention to the letter cluster and make connections to the chart and the examples on the word wall.

Independent Writing: Encourage the children to make connections to known words with *-ar* and *-or* when writing longer words.

assess

- Notice whether the children can quickly locate *-ar* and *-or* words in guided reading.
- Examine the children's writing to determine whether they are including a vowel before *r* in appropriate words and whether they are using *-ar* and *-or* with increasing accuracy.
- A week or two later, test whether the children are spelling most *-ar* and *-or* words conventionally. Dictate three or four words with a vowel and *r.*

Expand the Learning

Repeat the lesson with two-syllable words that have a vowel and *r,* such as *corner, farmer.*

Repeat the lesson with words that have *-er, -ir,* and *-ur.*

Connect with Home

Send home a sheet of words with *-ar* and *-or* and have the children work with family members to make five words with magnetic letters or letter cards.

Give the children letter cards to take home and make words with a vowel and *r* with family members.

21 Recognizing Consonants with Two Sounds

Concentration

Consider Your Children

This lesson extends children's knowledge of the sounds represented by consonants. Use this lesson after your children have developed a strong understanding of regular consonant letter/sound relationships and also understand that sometimes two or more sounds are connected to a particular letter. Use this lesson after these variations in letter/sound relationships have come up informally in shared reading and interactive writing.

Working with English Language Learners

Some children may just be beginning to connect letters and sounds, but they quickly need to realize that these relationships are complex. Their own languages may not have as much variation in letter/sound relationships as English does. This lesson will help these children look at the words in a more systematic and formal way so that they can form categories.

You Need

From *Teaching Resources*:

- Concentration Cards (made from Beginning Consonants Word Cards and Deck Card Template).
- Directions for Concentration.

Understand the Principle

To become flexible readers and writers, children need to learn that letters and sounds do not necessarily have a one-to-one relationship. Sounds can be represented by several different letters, and letters can be related to more than one sound. Knowing this principle will help children develop a broader understanding of letter/sound relationships and how they can be used to solve words. For example, they will be less likely to substitute *s* for *c* or *j* for *g* when writing.

Explain the Principle

"Some consonants make two or more different sounds."

plan

Some consonants have two sounds
c
cat city
come circus
can celery
cut cents
g
girl gym
get giant
go giraffe
gate

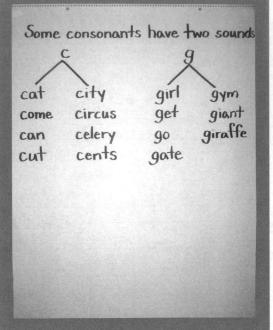

Explain the Principle

“Some consonants make two or more different sounds.”

① Tell children you're going to help them notice something about letters and their sounds.

② Have a chart that is blank at the top but that lists the words that start with *c* on the chart in the illustration.

③ Suggested language: “Listen carefully as I point to and read the words on the chart. [Point to and read the words that begin with *c*.] What do you notice? [Children respond that the first sound is different in the two lists.] That's right. They all start with *c*, but in the first row the *c* sounds like *k* and in the second row it sounds like *s*.”

④ Repeat with the *g* words.

⑤ Elicit responses from the group to arrive at the principle that some consonants have two sounds, providing guidance and suggesting specific language if necessary. Write the principle at the top of the chart to summarize the learning. It will be appropriate for the children to generalize that *c* and *g* have two sounds.

⑥ Invite the children to suggest examples you can add to the list. They may bring up examples that they cannot spell. And they may contribute words that begin with *s* or *j*. If this happens, recognize that these words have the same sound as *one* of the sounds of *c* or *g*, and place them on the chart outside of the columns or write them on a separate chart. (Such examples mean that the children are hearing the sounds and have categorized them; they are searching for subcategories.)

⑦ Explain that they will be playing Concentration with words that begin with *c* and *g*.

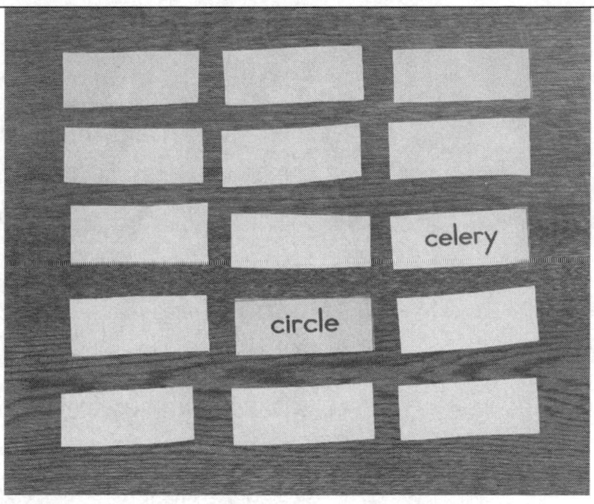

turn
read
match

▸ Have children play Concentration with a partner. On each face down card is a word that begins with *c* or *g* *(cat, can, come, cake, celery, circle, circus, cent; get, go, good, gym, giant, girl).* Use words that children know or can figure out easily as they work together. (You can place a small picture cue on the card if necessary.) Turning over two cards, children read each word. They match word cards that have identical beginning sounds to make a pair. When all the cards have been matched, the game is finished. The player with the most pairs wins.

Ask the children to share some pairs of words that they made while playing the game.

Invite them to suggest additional words to add to the list.

Talk about any patterns they may notice. For example, they may notice that the *ca* always has the same sound, that *ci* sounds like *s*, or that *circus* has both /c/ sounds in it. The principles children come up with may not hold in every case. The important thing is for them to search for patterns.

Link

Interactive Read-Aloud: Draw attention to one or two words that contain /c/ and /g/. Examples of books in which to do this are:

- ***Curious George*** by H. A. Rey
- ***The Giant Jam Sandwich*** by John Vernon Lord

Shared Reading: After reading and enjoying a poem such as "Alice, Where Are You Going?" or "One, Two, How Do You Do?" (see *Sing a Song of Poetry*), have the children use a masking card or highlighter tape to locate words that begin with or contain either sound of *c* or *g*.

Guided Reading: One way to prompt children who are having difficulty reading a word that starts with *c* or *g* is to have them try the other sound. You might say, "It starts like *giant,*" or "It starts like *city,*" or "Try the other sound for that letter."

Interactive Writing: When the children are going to write a new word that starts with *c* or *g,* use prompts that help them consider the two sounds. For example, when children are going to write the word *come,* you might say, "It starts like *Carol.*" Or when the children are going to write the word *city,* say, "It starts like *circle.*"

Independent Writing: When the children are trying to write new words, encourage them to say the word slowly and help them remember that some letters, such as *c* and *g,* have two sounds.

assess

- Notice whether the children are spelling words with *c* and *g* conventionally in their writing.
- Ask the children to write three or four words that start with *c* and *g.*

Expand the Learning

Repeat the lesson with a greater variety of *c* and *g* words.

Teach the lesson focusing on the two sounds of *c* and *g* when they are in other positions within words: *stick, bicycle* (an example of both *c* sounds), *ice, mice, twice, tag, dog, age, page, bridge, large.* Have the children add examples to the list (or make another one) that have the letters and sounds in different positions in the words and underline the *c* or *g* sounds.

Connect with Home

Invite family members and their children to draw a picture that contains as many objects as they can think of whose label has the different sounds of *c* and *g.* An example might be a scene with a *car, garage, gate,* and *cow.* The children can bring the pictures to class and ask other children to identify the *c* and *g* words.

Spelling Patterns

Phonograms are spelling patterns that represent the sounds of *rimes* (last parts of words). They are sometimes called *word families*. You will not need to teach children the technical word *phonogram*, although you may want to use *pattern* or *word part*. A phonogram is the same as a rime, or ending of a word or syllable. We have included a large list of phonograms that will be useful to primary-age children in reading or writing, but you will not need to teach every phonogram separately. Once children understand that there are patterns and learn how to look for patterns, they will quickly discover more for themselves.

Another way to look at phonograms is to examine the way simple words and syllables are put together. Here we include the consonant-vowel-consonant (CVC) pattern in which the vowel often has a short, or terse, sound; the consonant-vowel-consonant-silent *e* (CVC*e*) pattern in which the vowel usually has a long, or lax, sound; and the consonant-vowel-vowel-consonant (CVVC) pattern in which the vowel combination may have either one or two sounds.

Knowing spelling patterns helps children notice and use larger parts of words, thus making word solving faster and more efficient. Patterns are also helpful to children in writing words because they will quickly write down the patterns rather than laboriously work with individual sounds and letters. Finally, knowing to look for patterns and remember them helps children make the connections between words that make word solving easier. The thirty-seven most common phonograms are marked with an asterisk in the Continuum.

Connect to Assessment

See related SP Assessment Tasks in the Assessment Guide in *Teaching Resources:*

- Matching Phonogram Patterns and Words
- Reading Names with Patterns
- Reading Words with Phonogram Patterns
- Reading and Writing Names (Phonograms)
- Hearing and Representing Phonogram Patterns

Develop Your Professional Understanding

See *Word Matters: Teaching Phonics and Spelling in the Reading/Writing Classroom* by G.S. Pinnell and I.C. Fountas. 1998. Portsmouth, New Hampshire: Heinemann.

Related pages: 65, 82, 95, 236.

1 Learning Common Short Vowel Word Patterns: a (i, o, u)

Making Words

Consider Your Children

Use this lesson when your children have had a great deal of experience using letters and sounds to spell words, as well as making connections between words. Interactive writing and shared reading are powerful contexts for noticing the patterns in words. This lesson uses patterns with *a,* but you can expand it to other vowels. The children should understand what words are and be able to hear many consonant sounds in beginning or ending position and connect these sounds to the letters that represent them. They should also have some experience with letter clusters. Remember that it is not productive for children to memorize principles. Rather, you want them to explore examples that will help them internalize the principles.

Working with English Language Learners

Working with regular word patterns will help these children internalize the phonology and letter/sound relationships they will meet in English words. A key idea is to search for patterns; actively working to make connections among words will accelerate their learning of English. Be sure the children understand and can pronounce the words you are using as examples of patterns. You may have to act out words or use some pictures to help them. Praise them for approximations; they will gradually improve.

You Need

- Whiteboard.
- Magnetic letters.

From *Teaching Resources:*

- Two-Way Sort Sheets (lined).

Understand the Principle

Common, regular letter patterns in words are building blocks children can use to generate many more words in writing and develop strategies for taking words apart while reading. While not all words are regular in structure, examining these common patterns helps children learn to *look* for patterns and gradually expand their knowledge of how words "work."

In this lesson they are looking at the phonogram, or *rime* of the word. Within a syllable, the *onset* is the beginning consonant or consonant cluster before the vowel, and the *rime* is the vowel and whatever comes after it—a group of letters commonly found. All words have a rime and most words have an onset. Here we talk about *patterns,* to make the language less technical.

Explain the Principle

"You can look at the pattern you know to help you read a word."

"You can make new words by putting a letter or letter cluster before the word part or pattern."

plan

Some words have patterns that are the same. You can look at the patterns you know to read a word. You can make new words by putting letters or letter clusters before the pattern.

-ap	-an
tap	man
lap	can

Explain the Principle

“ You can look at the pattern you know to help you read a word. ”

“ You can make new words by putting a letter or letter cluster before the word part or pattern. ”

① Let children know they are going to learn how to notice parts, or patterns, in words.

② Suggested language: “You have been noticing the connections between words. Words can be alike at the beginning and they can also be alike at the end—either the last letter or the whole last part of the word. There are some word endings that you see in many different words. Here’s a part you know.” Write *-at* on the whiteboard. “When I put *h* before the word ending, the new word is. . . .” Children respond. “So *-at* is a pattern that you see in many words.”

③ “Let’s look at another pattern.” Write *tap* and *lap* on chart paper. Read *tap* and *lap* and ask the children what they notice. Confirm that *-ap* is a pattern that will be found in many words and get them to give you a few more examples *(nap, map, trap).* “Yes, *-ap* is a pattern. I’ll write it at the top.”

④ Repeat the process with *man* and *can (-an),* having children generate examples. Then have the children read both lists.

⑤ “Now, I’ll write a word that has the pattern of *-ap,* and you see if you can read the word.” Write *sap* or *cap.* Confirm the children’s analysis, and repeat with one or two words that have the pattern of *-an*, for example, *ran, Dan, plan.* The word *plan* introduces extra complexity, so focus the children’s attention on the fact that there is a consonant cluster before the ending. Highlight the *-an.*

⑥ Put an example on the word wall for *-an* and *-ap;* let the children choose the example.

⑦ Summarize the lesson by stating the principles and writing them at the top of the chart. Suggested language: "Today we learned that some words have parts, or patterns, that are the same. We looked at some patterns that have the vowel *a*. You can look at the pattern you know to read a word. You can make new words by putting a letter or letter cluster before the pattern."

⑧ Explain to the children that they will be building words using magnetic letters. Demonstrate the activity.

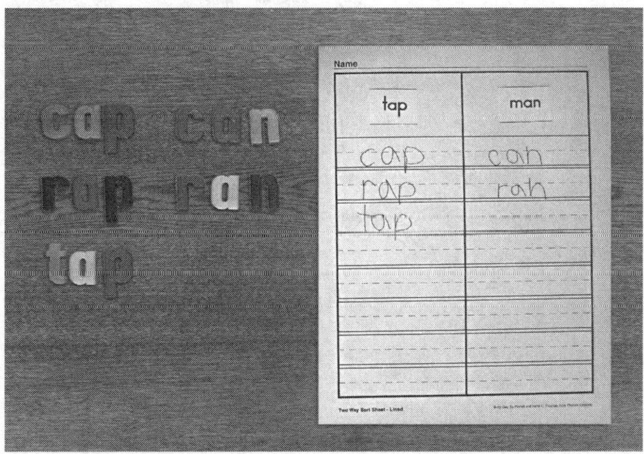

build
mix + build
mix + build
write
read

- Have the children use *tap* and *man* as key words at the top of a Two-Way Sort Sheet. Then have them use magnetic letters to build as many *-ap* and *-an* words as they can. Each time they make a word, have them mix it and remake it two times and then write the word they made on the Two-Way Sort Sheet or in their Word Study Notebook. When they finish, have them read the list to a partner, making sure each is a real word. Even if they come up with a few nonsense words, by reading and writing them they are still applying the principles.

Have some children share the words they made. Add one or two words to the columns on the chart.

Link

Interactive Read-Aloud: Read aloud books that call attention to the ending parts of words (rimes), such as

- ***Each Peach Pear Plum*** by Janet and Allen Ahlberg
- ***Ten Terrible Dinosaurs*** by Paul Stickland

Shared Reading: Read rhymes such as "Mary Ann, Mary Ann," "Thank You," or "Fishy-fishy" (see *Sing a Song of Poetry*) that include words with matching parts in them. Have the children highlight rimes (patterns) with highlighter tape or a colored marker.

Interactive Writing: When writing a word with a regular pattern, show the children on the whiteboard how you can use the pattern to help spell it.

Independent Writing: Remind the children to use the patterns they know when they are writing new words.

assess

- Notice whether the children can use word patterns to spell regular words.
- Give a quick (ungraded) spelling test (four or five words) to see whether the children can use regular word patterns.

Expand the Learning

Repeat the lesson with two or three additional patterns: *-at, -ask, -op, -ot, -ock, -it, -ip, -in, -ing, -ink, -ug, -uck, -ump, -unk, -uck.* Have children use a Two- or Three-Way Sort Sheet (see *Teaching Resources*), depending on their experience.

For variety, have children use letter tiles, onset/rime word cards, or letter cards (see *Teaching Resources*) to make words.

Connect with Home

Have children take home letter cards, Consonant Cluster Cards (Beginning Consonant Digraphs), and regular pattern cards (Rimes) so that they can build and read words. (All these materials are included in *Teaching Resources*.)

Generative Lesson

early
mid
late

Learning Common Short Vowel Word Patterns: e (a, i, o, u)

2

Making Words

Consider Your Children

This lesson brings common word patterns to children's attention. In this lesson you use examples of patterns with *e*, but you can extend the lesson to include other vowels. Use it after your children have learned basic consonant sounds and some vowel sounds and worked with simple phonogram patterns. They should know some high frequency words and have begun to notice connections between words. You will probably want to repeat this lesson several times, adding more phonograms and examples.

Working with English Language Learners

As English language learners become more familiar with the concept of word patterns and begin to connect words and/or place them in categories, they will start to use what they know about spelling patterns to figure out new words that they may know how to say but not how to read or write. Repeat the words many times so they can hear the patterns, and use pictures and actions to help the children understand the meaning of words.

You Need

- Whiteboard.
- Magnetic letters.

From *Teaching Resources:*

- Two-Way Sort Sheets.

Understand the Principle

Recognizing phonograms (regular spelling patterns) that appear in many words will help children understand that they can apply what they know about word structure to figure out new words. They will also begin to understand that searching for and recognizing patterns are valuable to them as readers and writers.

Explain the Principle

“You can look at the pattern you know to help you read a word.”

“You can make new words by putting a letter or letter cluster before the word part or pattern.”

plan

Some words have parts that are the same. You can look at the parts you know to read a word. You can make new words by putting letters or letter clusters before the word part.

-ell	-est
bell	nest
well	best
spell	rest

Explain the Principle

" You can look at the pattern you know to help you read a word. "

" You can make new words by putting a letter or letter cluster before the word part or pattern. "

① Tell the children they'll be learning more about patterns in words.

② Begin with a blank chart. Suggested language: "You have been noticing the connections between words. Sometimes you see the same group of letters at the end of different words. These are called *patterns*. Here is one you know." Write *-ed* on the whiteboard. "You find it in this word." Write *bed* and have children read it. Have children suggest another word with *-ed*. "You can even put two letters in front of the word and make a word—*sled*. What is the same in all these words?" Children respond. "The *-ed* is the same, so it is a pattern."

③ "I'm going to write three words on the chart; you see if you can notice the pattern." Write *bell, well, spell.* The children will notice that *-ell* is the pattern. Write *-ell* at the top of the column. Have the children read the whole list.

④ Suggested language: "Now that you know *-ell* can be a pattern, can you think of another word like that?" The children may suggest (or you may prompt) *tell, sell.*

⑤ Repeat with *nest, best, rest.* The children should quickly see the pattern here and may suggest *test.* Write the pattern label at the top, and have the children read the whole list.

⑥ Using the language "Can you think of a word like that?" will remind the children to connect words in their search for patterns in reading and writing.

⑦ Suggested language: "Noticing the patterns will help you in your reading and writing. Here's a word you might not have read before. What pattern do you notice?" Write *pest* on the whiteboard and invite the children to figure it out. "*Pest* is like *nest*, isn't it? It has the *-est* pattern." Write and have the children quickly figure out *fell, yell, smell, rest, vest, west.*

⑧ You may want to put an *-ell* word and an *-est* word on the word wall.

⑨ Suggested language: "Today you are going to be making words with the *-ell* and *-est* patterns."

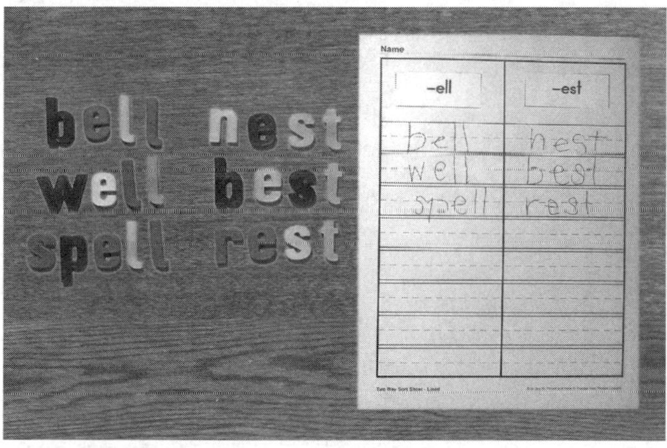

build
mix + build
mix + build
write
read

▸ Using a Two-Way Sort Sheet with two patterns in the key word spots, have the children build *-ell* and *-est* words with magnetic letters three times. Then have them write the words on their Two-Way Sort Sheet or in columns in their Word Study Notebook. When they are finished, they can read their list to a partner. Remind them to be sure they are using real words and to think about what the word means.

Have the children share their words with the group. Add any new examples to the chart.

Ask the children if they built a word and then decided it wasn't a real word. Guide a discussion about how to decide whether a word is "real" or not.

Link

Interactive Read-Aloud: Read aloud rhyming books, such as

- ***A Pig Tale*** by Olivia Newton-John
- ***I Was Walking Down the Road*** by Sarah Barchas

Shared Reading: Using a familiar text such as "Little Sally Waters," "My Favorite Toys," or "I Know Something" (see *Sing a Song of Poetry*), play a game to locate words: "I'm thinking of a word that has the *-est* pattern." Have the children place highlighter tape on common word patterns you have them locate.

Guided Reading: Help the children notice patterns while solving new words. During word work, have children who need more help with the principle use magnetic letters to build *-est* and *-ell* words.

Interactive Writing: Make connections to patterns when the children are writing a word they need in a text. After writing, have them search for word endings that are patterns.

Independent Writing: When conferring with students, help them spell words by using their knowledge of patterns.

Expand the Learning

Repeat the lesson with other patterns: *-in, -ip, -an, -ap, -at, -it, -ot, -ock, -op, -an, -at, -ack, -ick, -ash, -ug, -ill, -ale, -ank, -ing*. Use the Two- or Three-Way Sort Sheet as appropriate.

Connect with Home

Have the children take home letter cards, Consonant Cluster Cards (Beginning Consonant Digraphs), and regular pattern cards (Rimes) so that they can build and read words. (All these materials are included in *Teaching Resources*.)

assess

- Notice whether the children can contribute examples for the chart.
- Look at the children's writing to see whether they are representing patterns in a conventional way.
- Notice whether the children use patterns to solve words while reading.

3 Learning Phonograms: -at, -an

Closed Word Sort

Consider Your Children

In this lesson children learn that patterns in words help them read and write new words. Use it after your children have built words with simple phonograms. Work with two-way sorts first, but move to three-way sorts as children become more proficient. This lesson incorporates a closed sort. In a closed sort, you give the categories and the children find the words that fit; in an open sort, the children sort words and generalize the pattern for themselves. A new element in this lesson is placing words that don't fit in either category. *Teaching Resources,* Common Phonograms List, lists the thirty-nine most common English phonograms. For a complete list of phonograms, see the Word Study Continuum. An extensive list of examples for each phonogram is included in Appendix 15 of *Word Matters: Teaching Phonics and Spelling in the Reading/Writing Classroom.*

Working with English Language Learners

This lesson will give children a chance to act on and systematize their knowledge of word patterns by comparing them with one another. Working with *-at* and *-an* is a very simple way to begin sorting by pattern and allows you to select simple words that English language learners already have in their speaking vocabularies. Be sure to take advantage of any names among the class that fit these regular patterns by including them as examples.

You Need

- Pocket chart.

From *Teaching Resources:*

- Word Cards (*-at* and *-an* words from Short Vowel Sounds mixed with other words for sorting).
- Pocket Chart Card Template.
- Three-Way Sort Cards.

Understand the Principle

There are many useful patterns that children can use. Patterns made up of a consonant-vowel-consonant are among the simplest for developing an early understanding of recognizable word parts. Being able to recognize phonograms quickly helps children decode words, and pattern knowledge will also help them write many new words.

Explain the Principle

“You can look at the pattern you know to help you read a word.”

plan

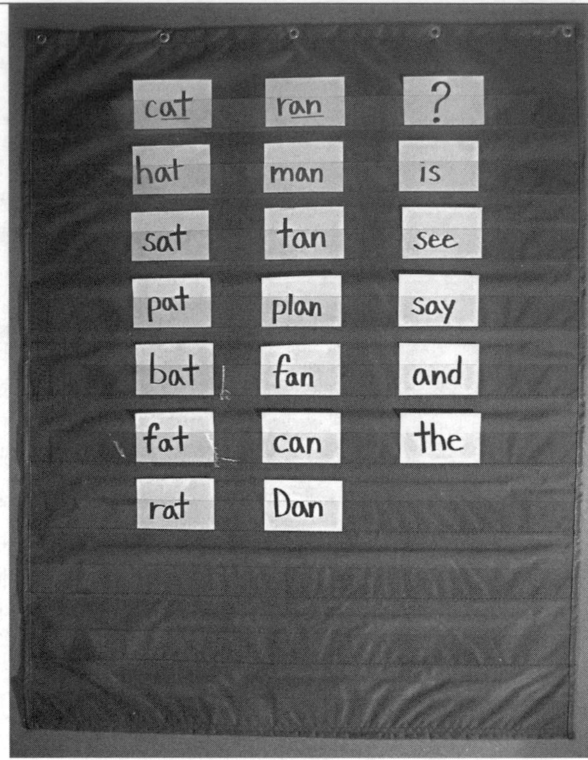

Explain the Principle

"You can look at the pattern you know to help you read a word."

① Explain to the children that today they are going to learn more about the letter patterns in words.

② Suggested language: "We've been looking at the ending parts of words. Let's look at some words that end in *-at* and *-an*." Show five or six word cards with *-at* and *-an*, helping children notice the last part of the word.

③ Suggested language: "Today we are going to sort words by looking at the ending part." Select a word and have children read it. "This word is *mat.* Does it end like *cat* or *ran*?" [Children respond.] That's right, it's like *cat* at the end, so I'll put it under *cat.*"

④ Continue demonstrating how to sort words. Show the children how to place words that do not fit under *-at* or *-an (the, see)* in the column with the question mark.

⑤ Then tell the children they can sort the words themselves. If the children are not accustomed to sorting as an independent activity, have a child demonstrate the process; then mix up the words and have another child do it.

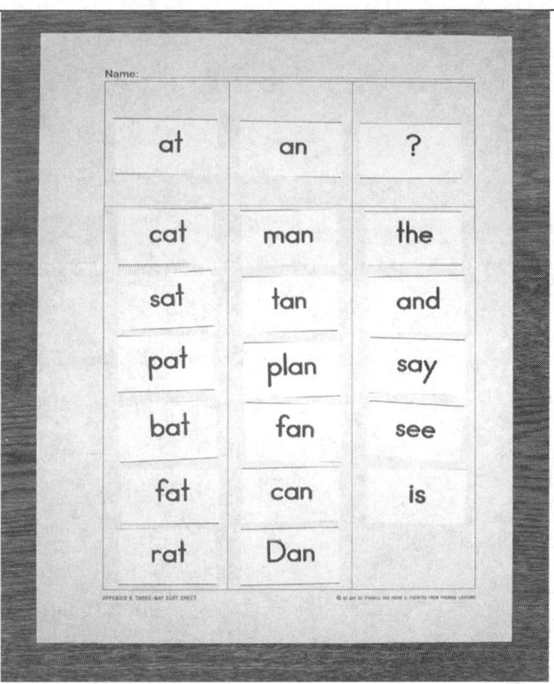

say
sort
read

- Have the children sort words with *-at* and *-an* using Three-Way Sort Cards and a pile of word cards that includes primarily *-at* and *-an* words. Include words without the pattern and have children place them in a column with a question mark in the key word spot. One child takes a turn reading the words and placing them in the correct column (say and sort) while the other observes. Then the partner reads each column. They remove the cards and mix them up, and the second child reads the words and places them in the correct column.

Have the children share what they noticed about the words they sorted. Add a few new words to the chart.

Link

Interactive Read-Aloud: Read aloud books with rhymes that draw attention to ending patterns, such as

- ***Is Your Mama a Llama?*** by Deborah Guarino
- ***Sunflower House*** by Eve Bunting

Shared Reading: After reading and enjoying a poem or song such as "Sam, Sam, the Butcher Man" or "I Had a Little Rooster" (see *Sing a Song of Poetry*), have the children use a masking card or highlighter tape to locate words that have the -*at* or -*an* pattern. See *Sing a Song of Poetry* for many other examples. Expand their collection of words to sort by pattern by adding other phonograms over the next week or so.

Guided Reading: Encourage the children to notice phonograms and other word parts while solving words. During word work, have the children build two or three -*at* or -*an* words with magnetic letters.

Interactive Writing: When the children are attempting to write new -*at* or -*an* words, help them use the pattern in words they already know to help them write the new word.

Independent Writing: Encourage the children to use their knowledge of the -*at* or -*an* pattern as a resource to write other words with the same pattern.

assess

- Check whether individual students can sort -*at* and -*an* words by looking at the endings.
- Look at your running records of reading behavior to determine whether the children are noticing and using -*at* and -*an* patterns to solve words.

Expand the Learning

Repeat the lesson using consonant clusters and digraphs and the -*an* and -*at* pattern (words such as *plan* and *flat*).

Repeat the lesson with other simple phonograms *(-ad, -ag, -am, -ed, -en, -et, -ig, -in, -it, -og, -op, -ot, -ut)*. See *Teaching Resources* for the list of the thirty-nine most common English phonograms.

Connect with Home

Give the children a set of -*at* and -*an* words to take home and sort with family members.

4 Summarizing Easy (Two-Letter) Spelling Patterns

Word Sort

Consider Your Children

This lesson reviews eight easy phonogram patterns. Decide how many patterns you want to summarize at a time. You may not have taught a minilesson on every one of these phonograms, but the children know them because they have explored the concept in many ways and worked with words informally. Over time, build a large summary chart with no more than two or three examples for each phonogram. Children need only one or two examples to generalize the concept and apply it to many other words.

Working with English Language Learners

This lesson helps children systematize and generalize their knowledge of patterns and use patterns to learn to read and write new words. These patterns help English language learners because they can use these consistent letter groupings to take apart new words, pronounce them, and work on their meaning. Make sure the words are repeated many times. Ask the children to add their own examples for the chart; this will give you an idea of their thinking. You can praise them for their attempts even if they are only partially correct.

You Need

- Summary chart.
- Envelopes.

From *Teaching Resources:*

- Word Cards (Short Vowel Sounds).
  Sort 1: *can, pan, man, fan, ran, plan, sat, pat, flat, mat, hat, rat, bat, fat, chat, pin, tin, chin, fin, win, thin, sit, bit, pit, fit, hit, split, spin, spit.*
  Sort 2: *mop, hop, chop, drop, stop, pop, not, pot, hot, spot, lot, rot, jot, but, cut, shut, nut, rut, frog, log, dog, fog*
- Four-Way Sort Sheets.

Understand the Principle

Summarizing their understanding of regular, common spelling patterns helps children become more flexible in using this knowledge to read and write words. The connections children make between words gives them a system for rapidly expanding their reading vocabularies.

Explain the Principle

"You can look at the pattern you know to help you read a word."

plan

-at	-an	-in	-it	-op	-ot	-ut	-og
sat	can	pin	sit	mop	not	but	frog
pat	pan	tin	bit	hop	pot	cut	log
mat	man	chin	pit	chop	hot	shut	dog

Explain the Principle

“ You can look at the pattern you know to help you read a word. ”

① Explain to the children that today they are going to review many patterns they already know.

② Start a summary chart for the number of patterns you want to review: provide the correct number of columns, write the word pattern at the top of each column, and include one easy-to-read example for each pattern listed.

③ Suggested language: “You know a lot of the parts in words. We’re going to review some of the patterns you know.”

④ Go quickly over each column, have the children generate one or two more examples for each pattern, and write them on the chart.

⑤ Have the children take turns choosing a pattern and reading quickly down the words in that column. If children’s names fit any of the patterns, add them to the chart.

⑥ Explain that they are going to do a four-way word sort. Place four key words at the top of a pocket chart. Show the children how to take each word card, read it, and place it under the key word. Tell the children that today they will complete the four-way sort and then write the four columns on a Four-Way Sort Sheet or in four columns in their Word Study Notebook.

apply

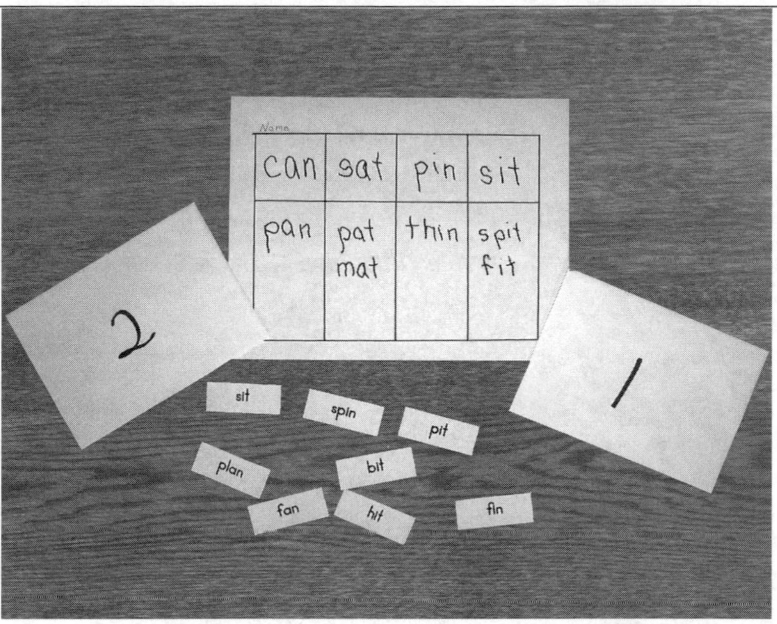

say
sort
write
read

- Have the children take the word cards in envelope 1, say and sort them into four categories, and record the words in four columns on a Four-Way Sort Sheet or in their Word Study Notebooks. After they write the sort, have them read the columns to a partner.
- Repeat the process with the word cards in envelope 2.

Have the children play a game with the summary chart: "What is a word that starts with *m* and ends with *-at*?" Repeat a few times to reinforce the patterns reviewed.

Link

Interactive Read-Aloud: Read aloud books that emphasize vowel sounds and rhymes, such as

- ***Ten Little Bears*** by Kathleen Hague
- ***Mama Zooms*** by Jane Cowen-Fletcher

Shared Reading: Use a variety of poems and songs with simple spelling patterns such as "Hickory, Dickory, Dean" or "I've Got a Dog as Thin as a Rail" (see *Sing a Song of Poetry*). After reading and enjoying the text, say a word with a particular pattern and invite the children to use a masking card or highlighter tape to find a word in the text that has the same pattern.

Guided Reading: Help the children use phonogram patterns to solve words. During word work, have children who need more work with words build phonogram patterns quickly: "Make *sat*. Now make it say *Sam.* Make *at.* Now make it say *pat.* Now make it say *sat.*"

Interactive Writing: When appropriate, have the children use phonogram patterns they know to help them write an unknown word.

Independent Writing: Prompt the children to use phonogram patterns they know to check on the spelling of words.

assess

- Have the children read words from the summary chart in random order.
- Have the children write five pattern words as you say them.

Expand the Learning

Repeat the lesson adding a few more patterns *(-ad, -ag, -am, -ed, -en, -et, -ig)* each time until your summary chart includes about fifteen easy phonogram patterns. (See the Word Study Continuum.)

After the children develop good control of these fifteen phonograms, add phonograms that have a silent *e* and other more difficult phonograms (see the Word Study Continuum).

Connect with Home

Reproduce the summary chart (or sections of it) for each child to take home and read to family members.

5 Learning Phonograms: -ate, -ake, -ike

Word Sort

Consider Your Children

In this lesson, the children learn to notice the consonant-vowel-consonant-silent *e* (CVC*e*) pattern and build words with it. Use the lesson after your children have built words with simpler phonogram patterns. *Teaching Resources* lists the thirty-nine most common English phonograms. For a complete list of phonograms, see the Word Study Continuum. An extensive list of examples for each phonogram is included in Appendix 15 of *Word Matters: Teaching Phonics and Spelling in the Reading/Writing Classroom.*

Working with English Language Learners

Once these children have learned to use simple patterns to sort words, you can rapidly expand those they can identify and connect. Be sure the children can read all the words you are using for the *-ate, -ake, -ike* sort and know the meaning of the words. If they offer other examples, add them to the sort.

You Need

- Pocket chart.

From *Teaching Resources:*

- Word Cards (*-ate, -ake,* and *-ike* words from Long Vowel Sounds mixed with other words for sorting).
- Pocket Chart Card Template.
- Four-Way Sort Cards.
- Four-Way Sort Sheets.

Understand the Principle

Spelling patterns are an excellent resource children can use to generalize and expand their reading and writing vocabularies. Sorting words helps children notice the details and make connections among words.

Explain the Principle

“Some words have parts that are the same.”

“You can find parts that are the same in many words.”

plan

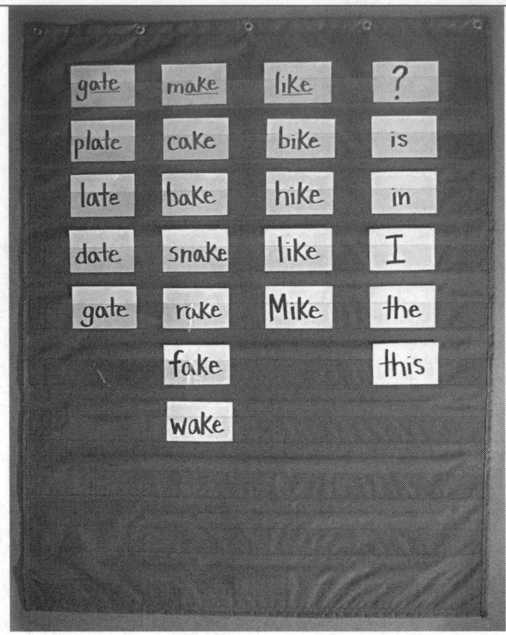

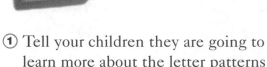

Explain the Principle

"Some words have parts that are the same."

"You can find parts that are the same in many words."

① Tell your children they are going to learn more about the letter patterns in words.

② Suggested language: "We've been looking at the ending parts of words. Let's look at some words that end in *-ate*, *-ake*, and *-ike*." Show five or six word cards with *-ate*, *-ake*, and *-ike*, helping the children notice the last part of the word.

③ "Today we are going to learn more about word patterns by looking at the ending part of words. Read the words on this chart." Have the children read *gate*, *make*, and *like* on the chart or in the pocket chart.

④ Select a word and have the children read it. "This word is *Mike*. Look at the *ending part* of the word. What word on the chart is like *Mike*? You can say the words to help you, and you can look at the words." Demonstrate saying *Mike*, *gate*, *Mike*, *make*, *Mike*, *like*. Also, hold up the *Mike* word card to each word at the top of the column.

⑤ The children may respond that *Mike* and *make* start with the same letter. Suggested language: "They do start with the same letter, *m*. That's good thinking. This time, we are looking at the ending part of the word. Do you see a word that has the same ending part as *Mike*?"

⑥ Demonstrate sorting the words under the examples. Show how to place words that do not fit in the first three columns under the question mark.

⑦ Then tell the children they will be sorting the words themselves. If the children are not accustomed to sorting as an independent activity, have one child demonstrate the process, mix up the words after sorting, and have another child do it.

say
sort
read
write

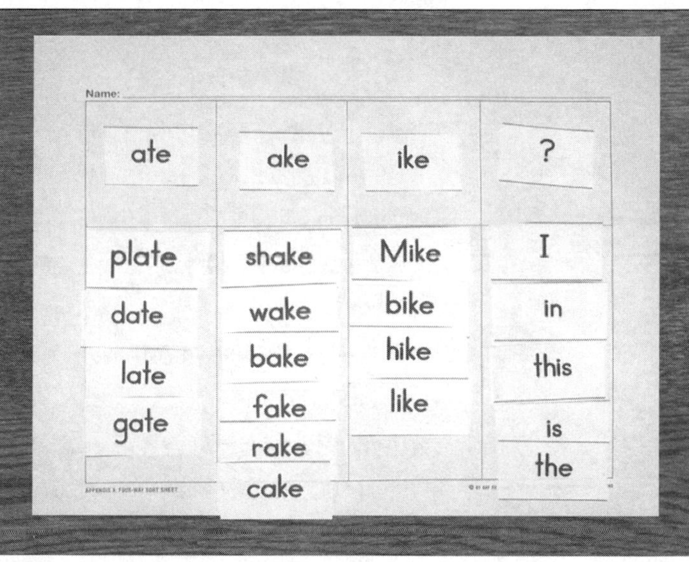

- Have the children sort words ending in *-ate*, *-ake*, and *-ike* using the Four-Way Sort Card or Sheet. When they are done, have them record their complete sort by writing each column of words on a Four-Way Sort Sheet. The Four-Way Sort Extension can be taped or glued to the Four-Way Sort Sheet to accommodate the extra words.

Have the children share what they noticed about the words they sorted. Add a few new words to the chart.

Link

Interactive Read-Aloud: Read aloud books with rhymes that call attention to words that sound alike at the end, such as

- ***The Hungry Thing*** by Jan Slepian and Ann Seidler
- ***There's Nothing to D-o-o-o!*** by Judith Mathews

Shared Reading: After reading and enjoying a text such as "My Bike" or "Apples and Bananas" (see *Sing a Song of Poetry*), have the children locate words with the *-ate, -ake, -ike* patterns using a masking card or highlighter tape. *Sing a Song of Poetry* includes many more texts with words that contain many of these patterns.

Guided Reading: During word work, have the children build two or three words with *-ate, -ake*, and *-ike.*

Interactive Writing: When the children are writing new words with the consonant-vowel-consonant-silent *e* pattern, refer them to an example on the word wall so they can see that many words contain this pattern.

Independent Writing: Encourage the children to use their knowledge of the *-ate, -ake,* and *-ike* phonograms as a resource to write new words.

assess

- Check whether individual children can sort five or six *-ate, -ake,* and *-ike* words by looking at the endings.
- Look at your running records of reading behavior to determine whether the children are noticing and using ending word parts or patterns to solve words.

Expand the Learning

Repeat the lesson with other CVC*e* phonograms *(-ade, -ace, -age, -ale, -ame, -ane, -ape, -ide, -ile, -ime, -ine, -ite, -ive, -obe, -oke, -ore). Teaching Resources* lists the thirty-nine most common English phonograms.

Connect with Home

Give children a set of *-ate, -ake,* and *-ike* words to take home and sort with family members.

6 Learning Phonograms: -an

Open Sort

Consider Your Children

Use this lesson after your children have built words with simple phonograms and have had experience sorting words. This is a simple task to help them learn the process for open sorts. They must be able to read the words. In a closed sort, the children are given the categories and find the words that fit. In an open sort, the children sort words and generalize the pattern for themselves. You will be using very easy examples (words with *-an*) because children are learning a new routine. If this example is not challenging enough for your group, substitute another phonogram pattern.

Working with English Language Learners

Ideally, children will have had experience in sorting and will be ready to notice and form their own categories. Be sure that English language learners can read and understand all the words they are sorting and that the words have patterns with which they are familiar. Have the children talk explicitly about the patterns that they found and the features they are noticing about words.

You Need

- Pocket chart.

From *Teaching Resources:*

- Pocket Chart Card Template.
- Word Cards (Word Card Template):

can	*an*	*a*	*pan*	*man*
I	*the*	*is*	*van*	*are*
of	*no*	*it*	*in*	*to*
pin	*dog*	*me*	*top*	*hit*
win	*day*	*we*	*my*	

- Two-Way Sort Card.

Understand the Principle

Open sorts require that children form their own categories for words, which makes them attend closely to the details and notice connections among words. Determining the underlying principle by which others sort words helps children search for patterns that propel decoding.

Explain the Principle

"You can look at the pattern you know to help you read a word."

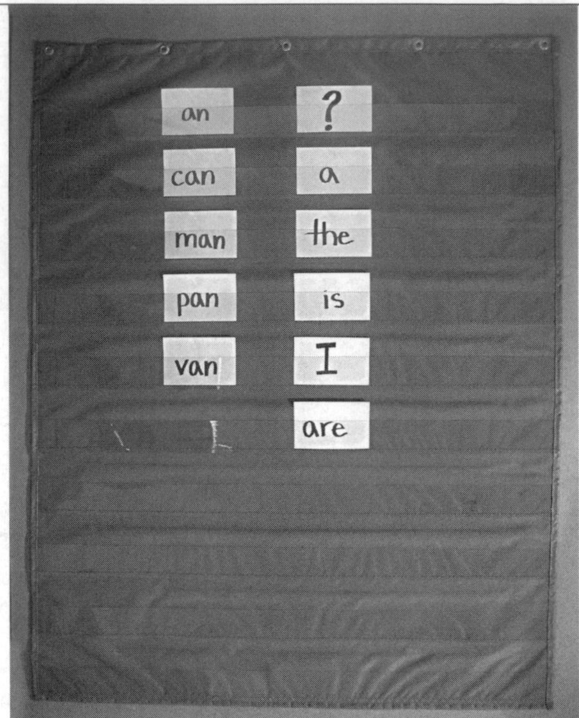

Explain the Principle

"You can look at the pattern you know to help you read a word."

① Tell your children they are going to learn how to notice patterns that are the same in words.

② Show the children how to do an open sort. Suggested language: "We've been looking at the ending parts of words. Today we are going to do some mystery sorts. I'll sort some of these words, and I want you to tell me how I sorted the words—what I was looking at."

③ Demonstrate placing *can*, *an*, *pan*, *man*, *van* in the left column and all other words in the question mark column. Suggested language: "This word is *can*. I'll put it here. This word is *an*. I'll put it here. This word is *pan*. I'll put it with *can*. This word is *the*. I'll put it under the question mark because I don't have anything it goes with." Continue until you have all words sorted into the two categories.

④ Point to the first column. Ask, "Why did I put these words together?" The children will respond that they all end with *-an*. Tell them that you put all the other words under the question mark.

⑤ Suggested language: "When you are making up the way you sort words, you can do it any way you want. You just have to see ways in which the words are alike. Can you see any other ways these words are alike?" Guide the children to think of first letter, last letter, and number of letters. Try out one or two other ways of sorting: words with two letters and those with more than two letters, words that start with consonants and those that don't, and so forth.

⑥ Then tell the children that they can sort the words themselves.

say
sort
tell

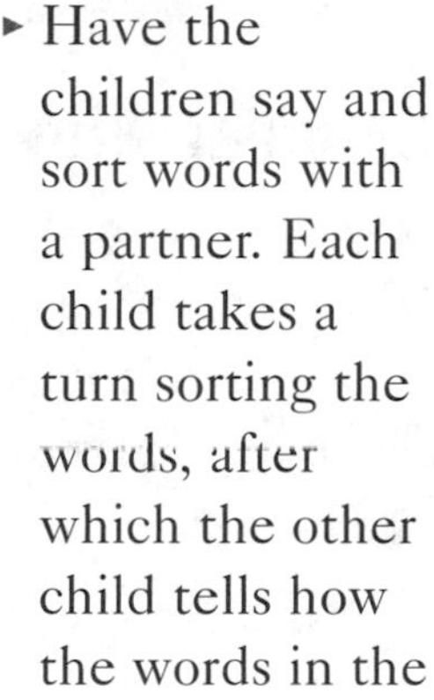

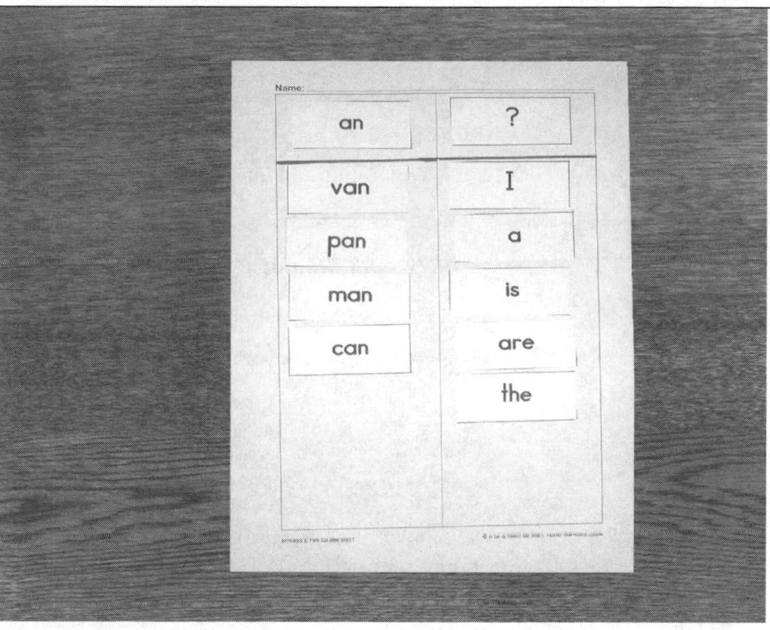

- Have the children say and sort words with a partner. Each child takes a turn sorting the words, after which the other child tells how the words in the first column are alike. Have enough word cards available for children to sort in several ways.
- Pairs can sort the words again another way.

Have the children share the ways they sorted words. You may get some unusual categories, such as "all the words that have an *n*" or "words with tall letters and words that don't have tall letters." These ways of looking at words indicate that children are flexible about noticing word features.

Link

Interactive Read-Aloud: Read aloud books with rhymes that call attention to words that sound alike at the end, such as

- ***Buzz Said the Bee*** by Wendy Lewison
- ***Mouse Mess*** by Linnea Riley

Shared Reading: After reading and enjoying a poem or chant such as "Fishy-fishy" or "Mary Ann, Mary Ann" (see *Sing a Song of Poetry*), have the children use a masking card or highlighter tape to locate specific phonogram patterns: "I'm thinking of a word that starts with *c* and has *an* at the end. Can you find it?"

Guided Reading: If the children have difficulty sorting words, take a minute or two at the end of the lesson to do the sorting activity with them. Use patterns that they need to learn.

Interactive Writing: As the children write new words, help them connect the new words to patterns they know. After writing a text, invite the children to locate words with particular patterns.

Independent Writing: When you confer with the children, prompt them to make connections between words.

assess

- Notice the children's behavior as they sort. Do they work quickly, form the categories easily, and discover the features of words?
- Give the children seven or eight word cards, and have them sort them and tell how the words in a category are alike.

Expand the Learning

Repeat the open sorting lesson with other phonograms (*Teaching Resources* lists the thirty-nine most common English phonograms); choose patterns that you notice the children need to work on.

Connect with Home

Send a sheet of words home with the children and encourage them to sort them in different ways. They can glue them on a sheet and bring them back to school to share.

7 Learning Phonograms: -an, -ake, -at, -ay, -and

Open Sort

Consider Your Children

Use this lesson after your children have built words with simple phonograms and worked with open sorts (see Lesson SP 6). Children are working with phonogram patterns they know, but they will now be asked to work with them in new ways and that will require flexibility. If the lesson is too complicated for your students, reduce the number of categories to two.

Working with English Language Learners

First graders are building a large repertoire of word patterns they know and can sort into categories. Open sorts help English language learners make connections between words. If you are not sure whether they can read the words, work with them in a small group and remove any words that they cannot read and/or do not understand. Add other examples that they suggest.

You Need

- Pocket chart.

From *Teaching Resources:*

- Pocket Chart Card Template.
- Word Cards (Word Card Template):

can	*cat*	*tan*	*pan*	*pay*
fan	*day*	*rat*	*man*	*cake*
rake	*ran*	*say*	*may*	*fake*
than	*bay*	*pat*	*band*	*van*
make	*take*	*sat*	*sand*	*mat*
lake				*bat*

- Four-Way Sort Cards.
- Four-Way Sort Sheets.

Understand the Principle

Open sorts require that children form their own categories for words, which makes them attend closely to the details and make connections among words. Determining the underlying principle by which others sort words helps children search for patterns that aid decoding.

Explain the Principle

“You can look at the pattern you know to help you read a word.”

plan

teach

Explain the Principle

"You can look at the pattern you know to help you read a word."

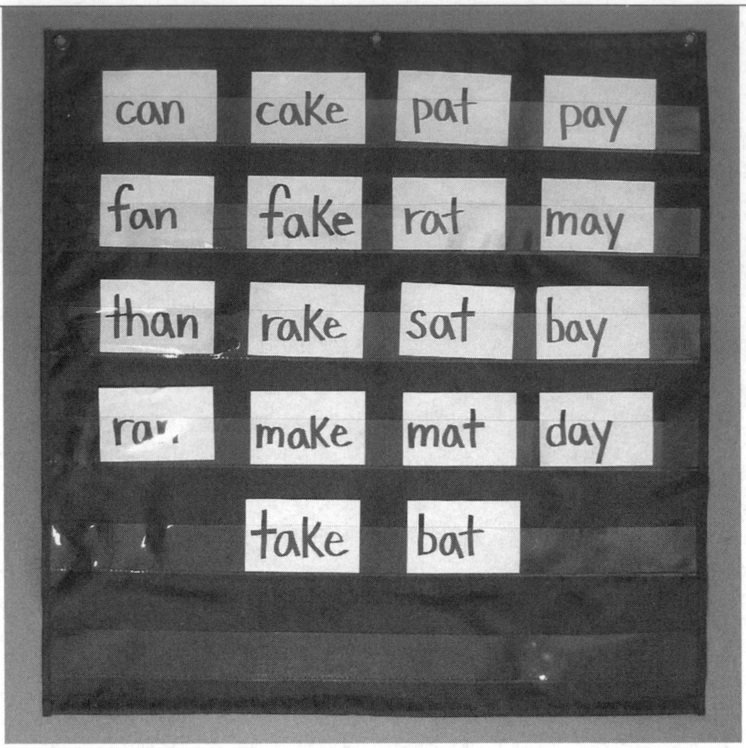

① Explain to children that today they will learn how to notice patterns in words and play a game that will help them learn more about words.

② Suggested language: "We've been looking at the ending parts of words. Today we are going to do some mystery sorts. I'll sort some of these words, and I want you to tell me how I sorted the words—what I was looking at."

③ Model sorting words into four categories. Include only words that fit into one of the categories.

④ Suggested language: "This word is *make*. I'll put it here. This word is *pat*. I'll put it here. This word is *bake*. I'll put it with *make*." Continue until you have sorted all the words.

⑤ Point to the first column. Ask, "Why did I put these words together?" The children will respond that they all end with *-ake*. Repeat for the other columns. This process will prepare the children for working on other open sorts.

⑥ You may want to review by doing one more mystery sort using *-and* words.

⑦ Then tell the children that they will be doing their own word sorts.

apply

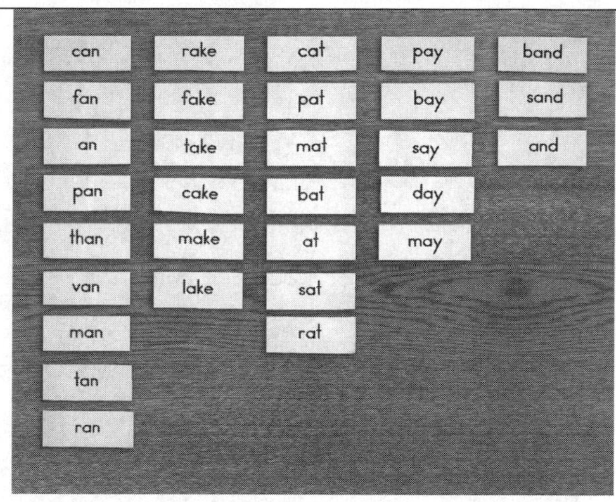

say
sort
read
tell

- Have the children sort the set of word cards on a Four-Way Sort Card. When they finish, have them work with a partner who tells how the words were sorted.
- In this lesson there are five phonograms used. Children can work with their partners and create another sort. They can sort four at a time on the sort card or sort five at a time on the table surface. When they are finished, record some of their sorts.

share

Invite two or three children to say, sort, and read the words. Then have the class tell the category.

Link

Interactive Read-Aloud: Read aloud books with rhymes that call attention to words that sound alike at the end, such as

- ***Bears in Pairs*** by Niki Yektai
- ***Barn Cat*** by Carol Saul

Shared Reading: After reading and enjoying a text such as "A Horse and a Flea and Three Blind Mice" or "The Old Man and the Cow" (see *Sing a Song of Poetry*), select six or seven words and write them on word cards. Read the words and sort them into categories of your choice and invite the class to tell how they were sorted.

Guided Reading: Prompt the children to notice phonogram patterns when trying to solve words as they read. Use language such as "Do you see a part you know?" or "What do you know that might help you?" or "Do you know a word like that?"

Interactive Writing: After a piece is finished, underline familiar phonograms or place highlighter tape on them.

Independent Writing: Encourage the children to use their knowledge of phonograms as a resource in writing words.

assess

- Write five or six words with phonogram patterns the children should know and ask them to read the words quickly.
- Use the same words but have the children write them.

Expand the Learning

Repeat the lesson over time using all thirty-nine most common phonograms (see list in *Teaching Resources*).

Connect with Home

Send home sheets of words containing the patterns you are working with in the lessons. Have children say, sort, read, and tell how they are sorted with family members.

8 Consolidating Knowledge about Phonograms

Open Sort

Consider Your Children

Use this lesson, in which words can be sorted by first letters, number of letters, ending letters, and ending parts, after the children have built many words and have learned how to sort words into different categories. You will want to select words with particular features, such as phonogram patterns. You may also want to include some of the names of children in the class.

Working with English Language Learners

You will want to show English language learners how a set of words can be sorted several ways, each time looking at different features. This will greatly increase their knowledge of how letters and sounds work, as well as draw their attention to larger clusters of letters. You want them to become much more flexible in the way they look at words, and these open sorts will help. Give explicit demonstrations of how to identify and talk about the categories they form for words.

You Need

- Pocket chart.

From *Teaching Resources:*

- Pocket Chart Card Template.
- Word Cards (Word Card Template):

May day my pan pat
fan come rat take cake
rake ran sat man fake
than say bike pay van
make like be see tan
Mike Mary Bill lake bat
to the hike by fat
mat is play bay boy
me blue cat can

- Four-Way Sort Cards (or use table surface).

Understand the Principle

Open sorts require that children form their own categories for words, which makes them attend closely to the details and make connections among words. Determining the underlying principle by which others sort words helps children search for patterns that aid decoding. Varying the way words are sorted helps children become more flexible in noticing features of words.

Explain the Principle

"You can look at the pattern you know to help you read a word."

plan

Explain the Principle

"You can look at the pattern you know to help you read a word."

① Mention to the children that today they are going to learn how to notice more word patterns.

② Suggested language: "We've been looking at the ending parts of words. Today we are going to do some more mystery sorts. These are all words you can read because you know the parts. I'll sort some of these words, and I want you to tell me how I sorted the words—what I was looking at."

③ Have words already sorted like this (number of letters): *by, be, to, is, me, my; May, day, pan, pat, fan, rat, ran, sat, man, say, pay, van, see, tan, bat, the, fat, mat, boy, cat, can, come, take, cake, rake, fake, than, bike, make, like, Mike, Mary, Bill, lake, hike, play, blue.*

④ Ask the children to look at your sort carefully and think about why you put these words together. Point to a category and ask, "What is the same about these words?"

⑤ Then repeat the process with the words sorted like this (initial consonants): *May, my, man, make, Mike, mat, me; pan, pat, pay, play; be, by, bay, boy; come, cake, can,* with the rest of the words in the question mark column. Ask the children to look at your sort carefully and think about why you put these words together. Point to a category and ask, "What is the same about these words?"

⑥ Guide the children to discuss the fact that the words all start with the same letter.

⑦ Then, repeat the process, this time putting together three of the following sets, with the rest of the words in a question mark category: *may, day, say, pay, play, bay; pan, fan, ran, man, than, van, tan, can; pat, rat, sat, bat, fat, cat; cake, rake, fake, make, lake; hike, bike, like.*

⑧ Point to the first column. Ask, "Why did I put these words together?" The children will respond that they all end with *-ay*. Repeat for the other columns. Guide the children to conclude that the words are sorted by the *ending part* of the word.

⑨ Encourage the children to think of new ways to sort the words.

⑩ Show the children how to take turns in pairs, one child saying and sorting and the other guessing the categories.

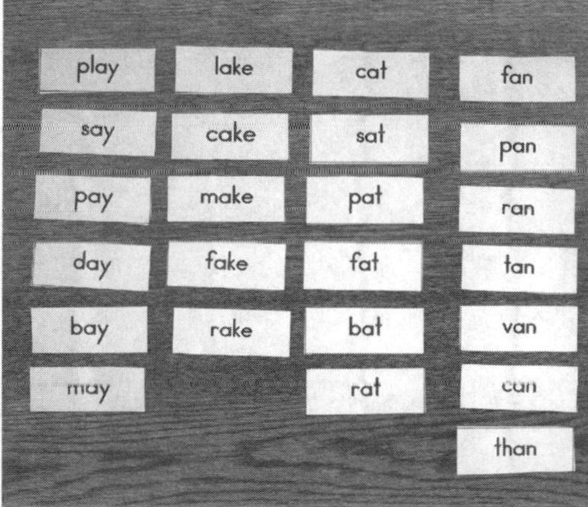

say
sort
read
tell

► Have the children sort a set of words four ways while their partner watches. The partner tells how the words were sorted. When they are finished, they can switch roles and repeat the process.

Have the partners share ways they sorted and give an example in each category.

Link

Interactive Read-Aloud: Read aloud books with rhymes that call attention to words that sound alike at the end, such as

- ***Play Day*** by Bruce McMillan
- ***Five Little Kittens*** by Nancy Jewell

Shared Reading: Continue reading enlarged texts of nursery rhymes and songs such as "Aunt Marie" or "Chitterabob" (see *Sing a Song of Poetry*). Point to two or three words and ask the children how the words are the same.

Guided Reading: Help the children learn how to use what they know about words to figure out new words. Use language such as "That word ends like [word]" or "Do you see a part you know?"

Interactive Writing: Go back to pieces of interactive writing to find examples of words with phonograms or words that start alike.

Independent Writing: Notice and encourage the children to make connections between words to help them write new words. Help the children use the examples on the word wall as a resource.

assess

- Give the children a set of nine or ten word cards and ask them to create two or three categories.

Expand the Learning

Create new word sorts using many words the children know, some words they "almost know," and a few new words. Have the children use the same set of word cards over several days so that they become very familiar with the word set.

Connect with Home

After they have learned to sort words in open categories, encourage the children to keep a large collection of words that they know in a shoebox. They can demonstrate sorting them in different ways for their families.

9 Noticing Features of Words

Word Wall Mystery Sort

Consider Your Children

In selecting words for this lesson (there should be at least twenty), think about all the words your children are likely to know. A good place to start is the word wall—words children have encountered in interactive writing, shared reading, or a word study minilesson and know or "almost know." In this lesson, the children take a closer look at these known words and make connections between them.

Working with English Language Learners

Check English language learners' reading and understanding of the words they are sorting and remove words that are too difficult for them. For this open sort, you will be using a wide variety of words, high frequency words as well as words that illustrate the principles you have been teaching in lessons. There will also be words that illustrate patterns. It will help English language learners to develop flexibility in sorting words in many different ways.

You Need

- Pocket chart.

From *Teaching Resources:*

- Pocket Chart Card Template.
- Word Cards (Pocket Chart Card Template and Word Card Template) of the selected words. Here's a suggested list:

at	*love*	*you*	*my*
go	*see*	*it*	*got*
and	*is*	*we*	*stop*
went	*with*	*to*	*in*
me	*is*	*like*	*was*
the	*he*		

- Two-Way Sort Cards.

Understand the Principle

As children become familiar with letters and words, they begin to notice visual patterns, which is an important step in understanding how words work. It is important for them to notice a variety of features. Sorting and connecting words in different ways will heighten their awareness of letters and patterns and increase the flexibility with which they work with words.

Explain the Principle

" Some words have parts that are the same. "

" You can find patterns that are the same in many words. "

plan

Explain the Principle

"Some words have parts that are the same."

"You can find patterns that are the same in many words."

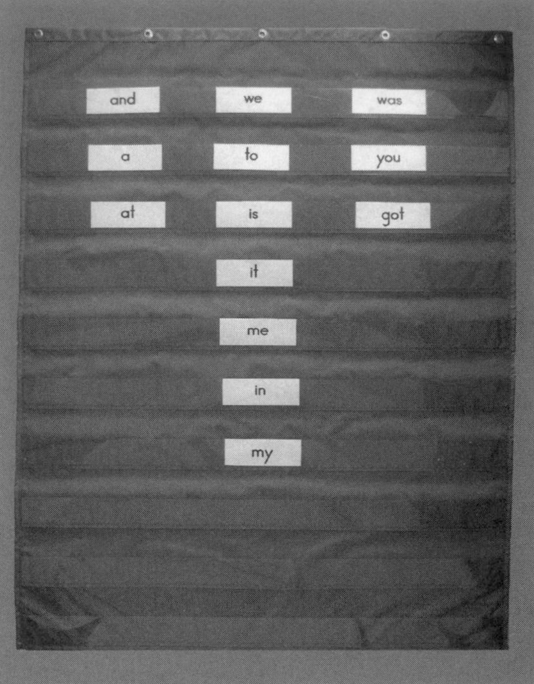

1. Let the children know that today you are going to help them notice patterns in words.
2. Give each child a word card (containing a word from your selected grouping) as a "ticket" to the group meeting. Have each child say the word and place it in the pocket chart. You can have duplicates of some words, if necessary.
3. Then hold up particular word cards one after another, asking the group to read them. Place them on the right side of the pocket chart in a selected pattern—for example, words containing the vowel *i* or words with a consonant-vowel-consonant (CVC) pattern. Then ask, "What do you notice about my words?"
4. The children will discover that every word has an *i* in it (or whatever your criterion was).
5. Repeat the process by selecting words containing another letter or letter pattern. You can select words that have the same first letter, last letter, or middle vowel. Or you can select a group of words that *do not* have a certain letter. Vary the patterns so that the children will become flexible in looking for them.
6. Demonstrate the activity until all the children know what you mean by selecting words that are alike in some way.

say
sort
read
tell

- In pairs, one child sorts the word cards two different ways using a Two-Way Sort Card. The partner tells how the words are sorted. Then the children reverse roles.

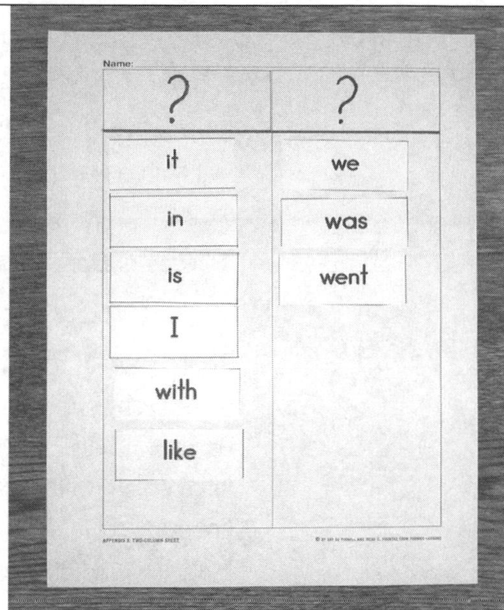

After two or three days, ask the children to share the ways in which they sorted words. Ask one child to do a "mystery sort" for the whole group and have children guess.

Link

Interactive Read-Aloud: Read aloud books that emphasize connections between words, such as

- ***The Alphabet Keeper*** by Mary Murphy
- ***The Alphabet Tree*** by Leo Lionni

Shared Reading: After reading and enjoying a text such as "I Know Something" or "I Went Downtown" (see *Sing a Song of Poetry*), select three or four words that have similar features (for example, three or four words ending in *e*). Invite the children to use highlighter tape or a highlighter pen to mark the words.

Guided Reading: Encourage the children to make connections between the words they know and new words they encounter in texts. Use language such as "What do you know that might help you?" or "Do you see a part that can help?"

Interactive Writing: Make explicit connections between words on the word wall and words that the children are writing. After writing the piece, make connections among words in the text.

Independent Writing: Encourage the children to use words on the word wall as resources for their spelling.

assess

- Notice whether the children are representing word patterns in their writing.
- Notice whether the children are connecting words in shared or guided reading.

Expand the Learning

Sort word wall words into several different groups, varying the patterns. Discuss the fact that a word may fit into more than one group (for example, *the* could be grouped with words that have three letters and with words that end in *e*).

Connect with Home

Send home a group of word wall words on cards for children to read and sort with their families and caregivers.

Learning about Vowels and Silent e

10

Building Words

Consider Your Children

Use this lesson after the children have had a great deal of experience working with simple phonogram patterns and have dealt with meaningful print. They should know some high frequency words and have begun to notice connections between words. The lesson focuses on two related structures, consonant-vowel-consonant (CVC) and consonant-vowel-consonant-silent *e* (CVC*e*). The principle applies to many CVC words, but there are also many exceptions that you will need to explain to children as they come up.

Working with English Language Learners

When working with phonograms, children have been internalizing a CVC pattern. Adding silent *e* exposes them to an additional word structure. Be sure English language learners understand what you mean when you say the words *consonant* and *vowel* and also that they have learned the CVC patterns you use in the lesson. Provide as many demonstrations as necessary of changing from CVC to CVC*e*.

You Need

From *Teaching Resources:*

- Word Cards (from CVC and Short Vowel Sounds): *mad, can, man, van, cap, tap, bat, fat, hat, rat, hid, slid, dim, slim, fin, let, win, shin, spin, twin, rip, tap, grip, bit, kit, rob, hop, mop, slop, not, hum, cub, tub, hug, cut, map, sat, rag, pad, fig, lid, job.*
- Letter Cards for the letter *e.*
- List Sheets.

Understand the Principle

After children have had many opportunities to hear meaningful print read aloud and engaged in shared (and some independent) reading of meaningful text, they are ready to look at the structure of words. Understanding the structure of simple words helps children learn to search for patterns and apply them to reading and spelling words. Rather than thinking of words as thousands of separate entities to be memorized, they make connections between words and form categories that help them in word solving.

Explain the Principle

“ Some words have a consonant, then a vowel, and then another consonant. The vowel sounds like the *a* in *apple* [*e* in *egg*, *i* in *igloo*, *o* in *octopus*, *u* in *umbrella*]. ”

“ Some words have a consonant, a vowel, a consonant, and then a silent *e*. The vowel sounds like the *a* in *make* [*e* in *Pete*, *i* in *ride*, *o* in *rode*, *u* in *cute*]. ”

plan

mad	made	hid	hide	not	note	cub	cube
can	cane	bit	bite	hop	hope	cut	cute
cap	cape	Kit	Kite	rob	robe	hug	huge

Explain the Principle

"**Some words have a consonant, then a vowel, and then another consonant. The vowel sounds like the *a* in *apple* [*i* in *igloo*, *o* in *octopus*, *e* in *egg*, *u* in *umbrella*].**"

"**Some words have a consonant, a vowel, a consonant, and then a silent *e*. The vowel sounds like the *a* in *make* [*e* in *Pete*, *i* in *ride*, *o* in *rode*, *u* in *cute*].**"

① Tell the children they are going to learn how to look at letter patterns in words.

② Write eight key words in pairs at the top of the chart.

③ Suggested language: "You have been noticing how words are connected and have been thinking about consonant and vowel sounds. Today we are going to look at two kinds of words. You know this word, *mad*. This word is like *mad;* it is. . . ." Children respond.

④ Suggested language: "What do you notice about these two words—*mad* and *made*?" Elicit and watch for comments like these:

"*Mad* doesn't have an *e*."

"In *made*, the *a* sounds like the letter."

⑤ The children will likely notice that the vowel *a* in each word has a different sound. Guide them to the principle that the word with a silent *e* at the end has the long *a* sound, which sounds like the vowel's name.

⑥ Suggested language: "When you add an *e*, the vowel says its name." Go through the rest of the examples, discussing and stating the principle for each one.

⑦ Then write *can* under *mad*. Suggested language: "Remember that when you add an *e*, the vowel says its name." Write *cane*. "*Mad* and *made*, *can* and. . . ." Let the children read and discuss the word *cane*, which they may not have encountered previously. They can nevertheless apply the rule.

⑧ Restate the principle and do one or two more examples for each key pair. The idea here is not to learn these individual words but to understand this word pattern.

⑨ The children may bring up words like *let* and *lete*. If they don't, bring up some words yourself and show them how to say them and think whether adding the *e* makes a real word that they know.

⑩ Explain to the children that they will be adding *e* to words. Suggested language: "You are going to take some cards that have three-letter words on them. Try adding an *e* and saying the word. Think, is this a real word? If you think so, write it on your list. Try to get ten words on your list to share with the class. If you are not sure whether your word is a real word, you can write it and we'll talk about it later."

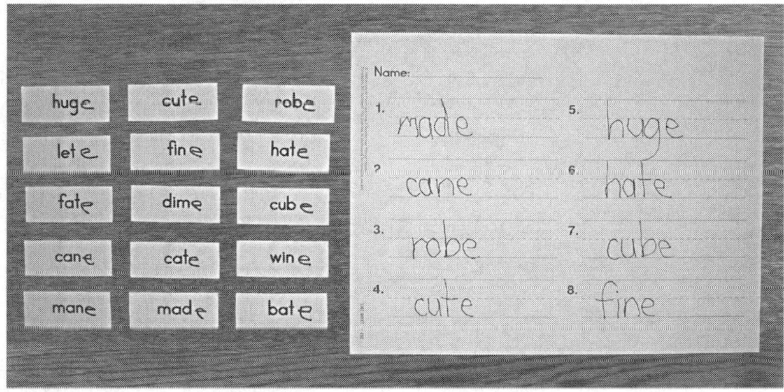

make
write
read

▸ The children take the set of CVC word cards and add an *e* to each. They list ten real words on the list sheet or in their Word Study Notebook and read them to a partner.

Have children share some examples and add them to the chart. When you come across words that are not real (with *hum, hume,* for example, point out that you would say this word with *u* as in *cute,* but it isn't really a word). Children may create real words but not understand them. For *van, vane* or *sat, sate,* explain what the word means). Or they may create a real word, incorrectly spelled. With *pad, pade,* explain that *paid* is the real spelling of the word.

Link

Interactive Read-Aloud: Read aloud books that provide opportunities for children to notice patterns. Examples are:

- ***Mad Isn't Bad*** by Michaelene Mundy
- ***The Flyaway Kite*** by Steve Bjorkman

Shared Reading: Using a familiar text such as "The Lady and the Crocodile" or "Mary Had a Little Lamb" (see *Sing a Song of Poetry*), play a game in which you ask children to use a masking card or highlighter tape to locate words: "Who can find a word with silent *e*? Who can find a word like *mad* with an *e* at the end?"

Guided Reading: Help the children notice CVC and CVC*e* patterns as part of teaching processing strategies. During word work, have the children who need more help with the principle make CVC words with magnetic letters and then add *e* and read the word.

Interactive Writing: When writing a CVC*e* word in a text the children are composing, show them the process. Write the CVC word on a whiteboard. Then have the children slowly say the word they want to write to determine whether the letter "says its name." If it does, ask the children whether they need a silent *e*.

Independent Writing: When conferring with the children, point out CVC and CVC*e* words.

assess

- Notice whether the children can come up with examples for the chart.
- Look at the words the children wrote on their papers to determine whether they understand the principle.
- Dictate four or five words with CVC or CVC*e* patterns.

Expand the Learning

Revisit the principle and add more examples to the chart.

Have the children do the activity with a different set of CVC words.

Have the children find and highlight CVC*e* words in photocopies of poems they have read as a group (*Sing a Song of Poetry* contains many examples).

Connect with Home

Give the children a card with four or five CVC words to take home. Have them use magnetic letters to make the CVC words and then add *e* and say the new word.

High Frequency Words

A core of known high frequency words is a valuable resource as children build their reading and writing processes. Young children notice words that appear frequently in the simple texts they read; eventually, their recognition of these words becomes automatic. In this way, their reading becomes more efficient, enabling them to decode words using phonics as well as attend to comprehension. These words are powerful examples that help them grasp that a word is always written the same way. They can use known high frequency words to check on the accuracy of their reading and as resources for solving other words (for example, *this* starts like *the*). In general, children learn the simpler words earlier and in the process develop efficient systems for learning words. They continuously add to the core of high frequency words they know. Lessons on high frequency words help them look more carefully at words and develop more efficient systems for word recognition.

Connect to Assessment

See related HF Assessment Tasks in the Assessment Guide in *Teaching Resources:*

- Reading High Frequency Words
- Writing High Frequency Words

Develop Your Professional Understanding

See *Word Matters: Teaching Phonics and Spelling in the Reading/Writing Classroom* by G.S. Pinnell and I.C. Fountas. 1998. Portsmouth, New Hampshire: Heinemann.

Related pages: 35–41, 44–46, 71–72, 88–90, 237–238.

Generative Lesson

Learning High Frequency Words 1

Making and Writing Words

Consider Your Children

This lesson is the first in establishing the high frequency words for Grade 1. Think about your children's experience and the likely level of their word knowledge. Choose either the list of twenty-five high frequency words or the list of fifty (which includes the twenty-five) (see *Teaching Resources*). Have the children read and/or write the words. Select words that children have seen before in shared reading and interactive writing but do not fully control. Once children have learned forty or so words (in other words, most of the initial fifty), these activities will not be necessary. You may want to move on to the hundred-word list, which includes the initial fifty.

Working with English Language Learners

Most high frequency words are abstract function words rather than concrete nouns, so be sure the high frequency words you use are decipherable to English language learners with your support. It is especially important to use these words in the context of sentences so that English language learners become familiar with hearing them and know how they are used. Construct sentences for each one that will be meaningful to the children and that they can repeat. For example: "I see John." Then John says, "I see Mike," and the phrase is repeated until everyone in the group has been called on. (Then create more complex sentences; for example, "Johnny can ride. So can I.")

You Need

- Magnetic whiteboard, chalkboard, or chart with Velcro®.
- Magnetic letters.
- Dry-erase markers or chalk.

From *Teaching Resources:*

- High Frequency Word Cards.
- Making Words Sheets (two per child).

Understand the Principle

Knowing some common words does not interfere with children's learning of the alphabetic principle and developing strategies for decoding words; in fact, these known words are an important resource and support system for early readers. Knowing some high frequency words allows beginning readers to read simple, meaningful texts—and thus to practice important early reading behaviors—before they are fully able to use letter/sound information to solve words. High frequency words are also powerful examples; children connect new words to these familiar words by using beginning letters or sounds. Sorting these words helps them become more familiar with the details of print.

Explain the Principle

"You see some words many times when you read."

"Words you see a lot are important because they help you read and write."

plan

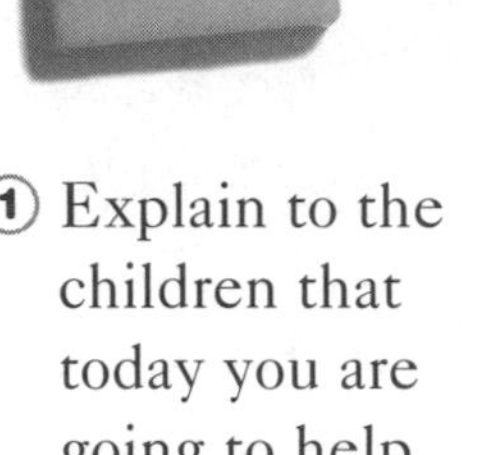

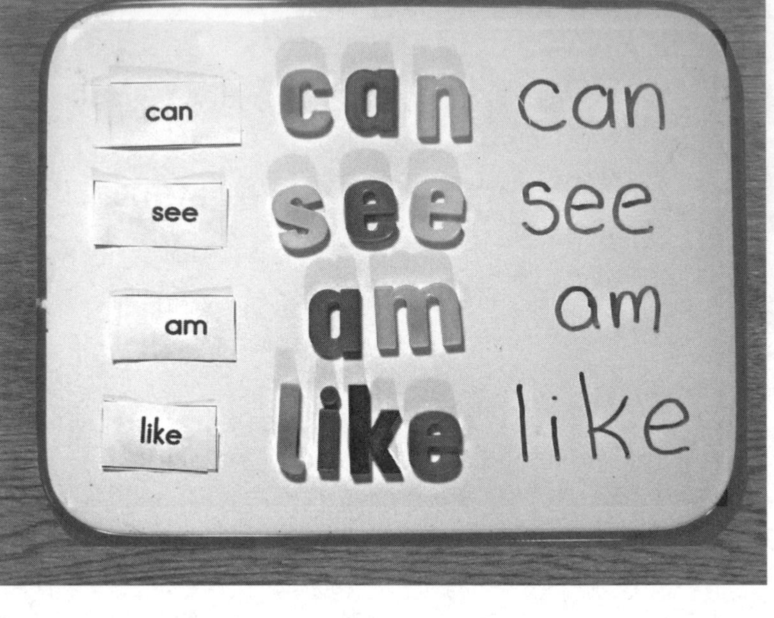

Explain the Principle

"You see some words many times when you read."

"Words you see a lot are important because they help you read and write."

① Explain to the children that today you are going to help them learn some important words.

② Place a high frequency word card (*can*, for example) on the pocket chart (or write the word on a chart or magnetic whiteboard).

③ Build the word with magnetic letters or letter cards.

④ Ask the children what they notice about the word. They may offer comments like:

"*Can* has three letters."

"It has a vowel in the middle."

"It starts like *cat*."

"It has *an* in it."

⑤ Then write the word quickly from beginning to end without stopping. Explain that there are some words you need to know how to read quickly or write quickly.

⑥ Repeat this process with more high frequency words. Ask the children to assist you on some of the steps in making the words.

⑦ Show the children the Making Words Sheet. Explain that they should take a word card, place it in the first column, say it, make and mix the word with magnetic letters (or letter cards) three times in the second column. They place a check in the box each time they make it. Then they write the word in the last column.

take
say
make, mix (3x)
write

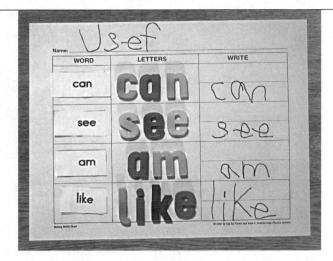

- Give the children a copy of the Making Words Sheet and word cards for the high frequency words used in the lesson.
- Have the children complete the sheet as shown above, working alone or in pairs. (If they work in pairs, one partner can make and write the words and the other partner can check them, or they can alternate the functions on every other word.) If you want the children to work with more words, give them two stapled Making Words Sheets to use.

Have the children read the word sheet to a different partner. You may want to invite two or three children to the board to make or write a word quickly.

Link

Interactive Read-Aloud: Call children's attention to some of the high frequency words when you are reading aloud books with large print (*Teaching Resources,* Large Print Books Bibliography, lists many other titles), such as

- ***Where's Spot?*** by Eric Carle
- ***Nuts to You*** by Lois Ehlert

Shared Reading: After reading poems and stories such as "All By Myself," "Colors," and "Lavender's Blue" (see *Sing a Song of Poetry*), have the children look for high frequency words they know and read them aloud. Have the children use a masking card or highlighter tape to identify particular words.

Guided Reading: After the reading the text and discussing it, give the children two or three high frequency words to locate in the text or write quickly.

Interactive Writing: When the children want to write a high frequency word they have studied, have them think about how the word looks. Then have a child write it quickly on the chart. (When the children know high frequency words and can write them quickly, you'll want to write them yourself rather than take the time for a child to come up to the easel to write them. Remind them that they know how to read and write the word quickly.)

Independent Writing: Encourage the children to write high frequency words quickly rather than copying them from the word wall. Then they can use the word wall to check themselves.

assess

- Notice how quickly the children recognize high frequency words in reading.
- Observe whether the children can write high frequency words quickly and accurately.
- After the children have practiced making and writing a series of high frequency words, check their knowledge periodically and review the words if necessary.

Expand the Learning

Teach children how to use a personal word box or word ring, in or on which they place the words they know and "almost know" and that they can eventually take home (see *Teaching Resources,* Materials & Routines). Give each child word cards for the high frequency words they already know, including the words in this lesson. Have the children take out all the words in their box and place them in three piles: "I know it," "I'm not sure," and "I don't know it." Upper-grade partners, volunteers, or you can check their work. The goal is to get all the words in the "I know it" pile.

Have children select five words from their box or ring to build and write.

Connect with Home

Communicate with family members about the purpose of their child's word box. Be sure children know the words in their boxes, as well as how to take them out, work with them, and put them back, before letting them take the box home.

Learning High Frequency Words 2

Making and Writing Words

Consider Your Children

This lesson is the second in establishing the high frequency words for Grade 1. If you have already presented the previous lesson (Lesson HF 1), the children will be very familiar with the routine and the lesson will move quickly. Select words that children have met before in shared reading and interactive writing but do not fully control. The goal is quick reading and writing of words.

Working with English Language Learners

Building and writing high frequency words will help English language learners attend to the details they will need to remember when reading or writing the words. Knowing some English words in detail will help the children connect their own pronunciation and grasp of the sound system and the letters and letter combinations that they see. Be sure that the children can say the words they are making and writing. By the time you use this lesson, your English language learners will know a small core of high frequency words and also know how to say, make, and write them. Encourage them to look carefully at words and learn more. Be sure you verify their ability to recognize and say words before they take word cards home. Show them how to use these word cards themselves if there are no English speakers in the home.

You Need

- Magnetic pocket chart, whiteboard, or chart with Velcro®.
- Magnetic letters.
- Dry-erase markers.

From *Teaching Resources:*

- High Frequency Word Cards.
- Making Words Sheets (two per child).

Understand the Principle

Children use a core of known high frequency words as anchors to monitor and check on their reading. These known words help them read simple texts while engaging in the behavior of reading (left-to-right directionality and word-by-word matching). High frequency words are also powerful examples; children connect new words to these familiar words by using beginning letters or sounds. Sorting these words helps them become more familiar with the details of print.

Explain the Principle

“You see some words many times when you read.”

“Words you see a lot are important because they help you read and write.”

plan

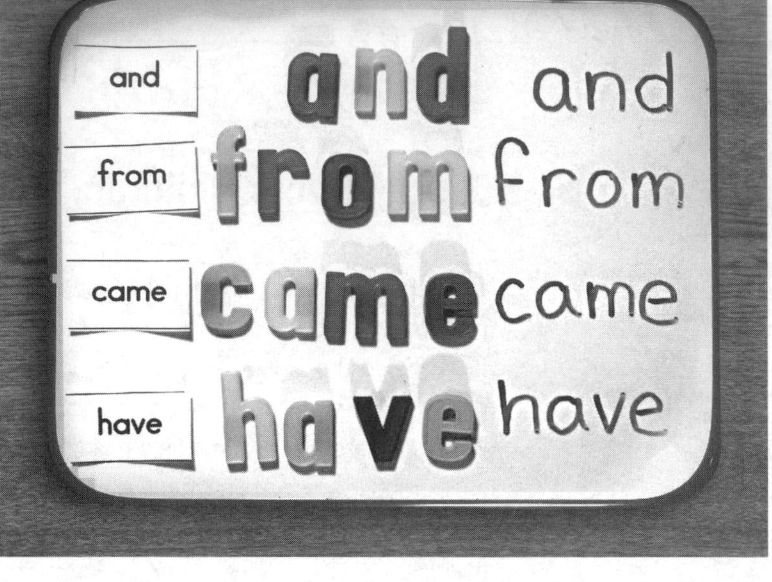

Explain the Principle

"You see some words many times when you read."

"Words you see a lot are important because they help you read and write."

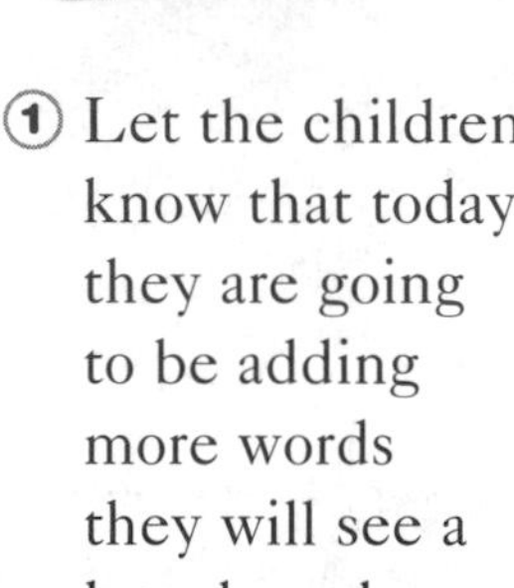

① Let the children know that today they are going to be adding more words they will see a lot when they read and write.

② Place a high frequency word card (*from,* for example) on the pocket chart (or write the word on a chart or magnetic whiteboard).

③ Make the word with magnetic letters or letter cards three times.

④ Ask the children what they notice about the word. They may offer comments like:

> "*From* has four letters."
>
> "It starts with *f.*"

⑤ Then write the word quickly from beginning to end without stopping. Explain that there are some words you need to know how to read or write quickly.

⑥ Repeat this process with more high frequency words. Ask the children to assist you on some of the steps in making the words.

⑦ Show children the Making Words Sheet. Explain that they should take a word card, place it in the first column, say it, make and mix the word three times with magnetic letters (or letter cards), placing a check each time they make the word in the second column. Then they write it in the last column.

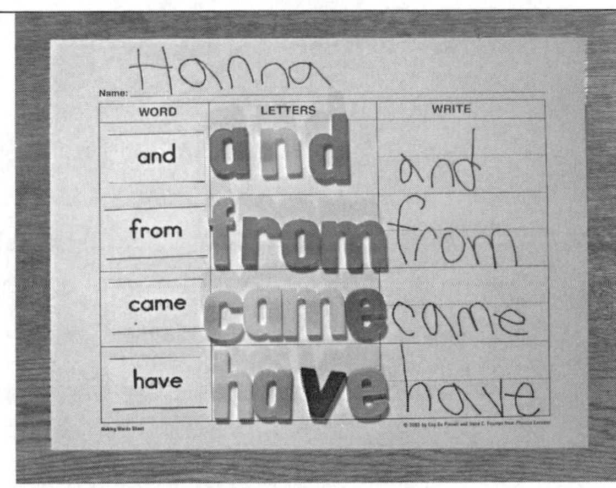

- take
- say
- make, mix (3x)
- say and check
- write

▸ Give the children a copy of the Making Words Sheet and word cards for the high frequency words used in the lesson. Have the children complete the sheet as above, working alone or in pairs. (If they work in pairs, one partner can make and write the words and the other partner can check them, or they can alternate the functions on every other word.) If you want the children to work with more words, give them two stapled Making Words Sheets to use.

Have the children read the word sheet to a different partner. You may want to invite two or three children to the board to make or write a word quickly.

Link

Interactive Read-Aloud: Call children's attention to some of the high frequency words when you are reading aloud books with large print, such as the following (*Teaching Resources,* Large Print Books Bibliography, lists many other titles):

- ***Airport*** by Byron Barton
- ***My Day in the Garden*** by Miela Ford

Shared Reading: After reading a text such as "My Aunt Jane" and "I Have Two Eyes" (see *Sing a Song of Poetry*), have the children find particular high frequency words. Give them two clues: "I'm thinking of a four-letter word that ends with a silent letter" (*come*) or "I'm thinking of a four-letter word that starts with a consonant cluster" (*from*). Have the children mark the words with a highlighter pen or highlighter tape. When you have finished, review all the words you marked by having the children read them with you.

Guided Reading: During word work, have the children make (with magnetic letters) several three- and four-letter high frequency words. Observe how quickly they put them together.

Interactive Writing: Remind the children to write the high frequency words quickly when they contribute to the text. Together you may decide to take some of the high frequency words off the word wall because they know them well.

Independent Writing: When the children finish a piece of writing, teach them how to reread it and check to see whether the words they know how to write are spelled correctly.

assess

- Notice how quickly the children recognize high frequency words in reading.
- Notice whether the children can write high frequency words quickly and accurately.

Expand the Learning

Repeat the lesson with other words the children need to learn. For variety, have the children use foam letters, cardboard letters, plastic link letters, etc. Instead of using word cards, you might want to write words on small ceramic tiles for children to use in the first column of the Making Words Sheet.

Connect with Home

Give children word cards to add to their word boxes. (See *Teaching Resources,* Materials & Routines.)

Give the children a high frequency word grid (see *Teaching Resources,* Materials & Routines) to practice reading the high frequency words down each column with family members. The goal is to develop speed in reading the words.

Learning High Frequency Words 3

Building Words with Magnetic Letters

Consider Your Children

This activity sets up a routine that the children can use in many ways to study word patterns and structure. You can quickly check your children's knowledge of high frequency words by having them read the high frequency word lists in *Teaching Resources.* You can also ask them to write the words. This will provide a good inventory from which to select words for the lesson. Children who can read and write a large number of high frequency words will not need this lesson.

Working with English Language Learners

Working with high frequency words will help English language learners monitor their reading of beginning texts and will make words more available to them phonologically. For this lesson to be effective, children should know the meaning of the words they are making. Saying some of the words in a child's own language is helpful, but direct translations are sometimes not possible. Provide many repetitions and have the children use the words in simple sentences that they understand.

You Need

- Magnetic letters.

From *Teaching Resources:*

- Pocket Chart Card Template.
- High Frequency Word Lists.
- High Frequency Word Cards (optional).

Understand the Principle

As children begin to read and write, it is important for them to establish a core of familiar high frequency words. This core of known words helps beginning readers monitor their reading and check for accuracy. The words are anchors to help them achieve word-by-word matching in early reading. High frequency words are also powerful examples; children connect new words to these familiar words by using beginning letters or sounds.

Explain the Principle

" You see some words many times when you read. "

" Words you see a lot are important because they help you read and write. "

plan

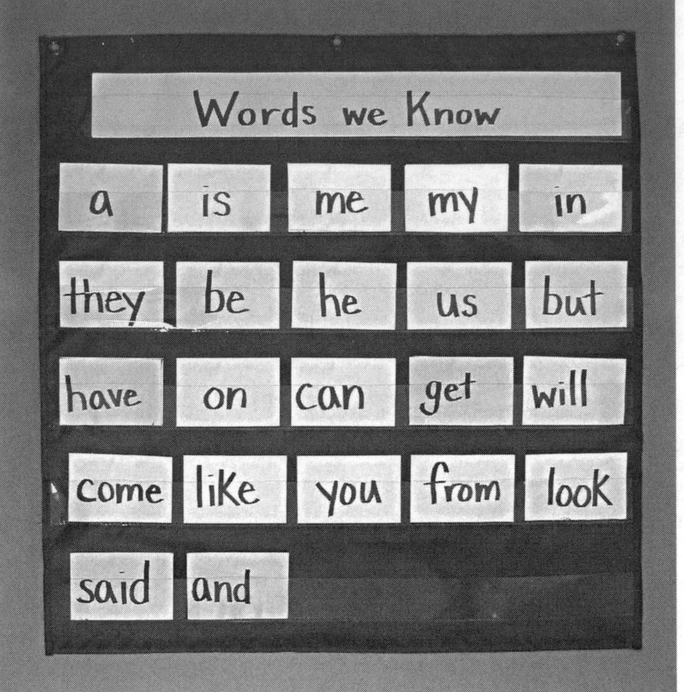

Explain the Principle

“ You see some words many times when you read. ”

“ Words you see a lot are important because they help you read and write. ”

① Tell the children that today they will be working more with the important words they’ve been learning.

② Have some high frequency words printed on cards.

③ Suggested language: “There are some words that we see a lot when we read and use a lot when we write. We need to know how to read them quickly so we don’t have to slow down when we read.”

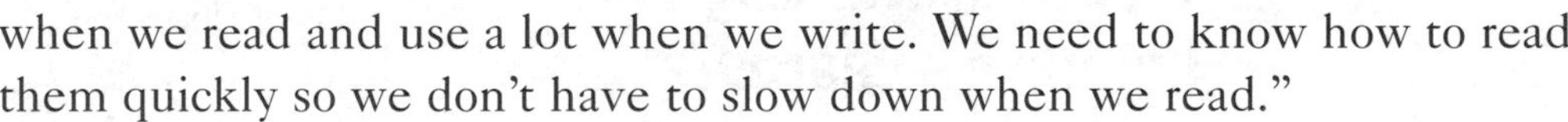

④ Show some simple words that the children know, such as *I*, *a*, *me*. Place the words in the pocket chart or on the chalkboard. Have the children read the words.

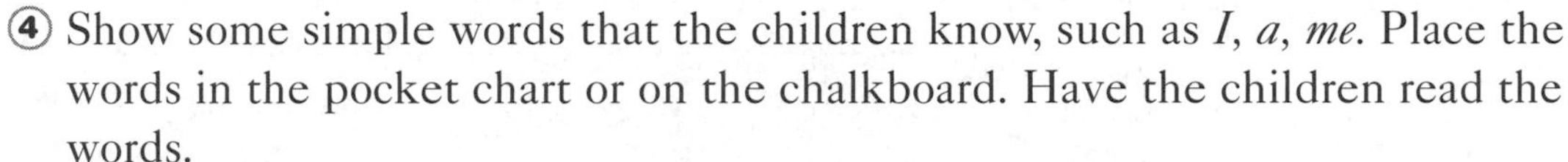

⑤ Add two or three new words, showing them each word.

⑥ Then help them notice the pattern of letters in each word by demonstrating how to make it with magnetic letters. Demonstrate checking the word letter by letter. Suggested language: “When you make a word with letters, check to be sure that every letter is the same from left to right: *m–m*, *y–y*, *my*.” Mix the letters up and have a few children demonstrate making the word quickly and checking it.

⑦ Repeat the process with several words. Each time you add a new word to the board, make it with magnetic letters and check it.

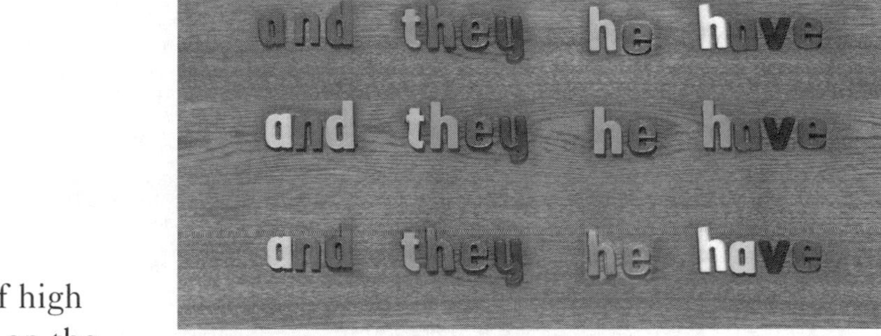

make
read
check
mix

- Place the chart of high frequency words on the wall. Put a colored dot on the words you want the children to make. Have the children use magnetic letters to make each word three times, reading it and checking it each time.
- Alternatively, give the children a pile of word cards. Have them take cards and make the words with magnetic letters.

Have the children talk about what they learned about words. They may simply say and show words they have learned. Encourage comments like these:

> "*Like* starts with an *L* like *Lisa*."
>
> "You have to look at the next letter to tell the difference between *me* and *my*."

Link

Interactive Read-Aloud: Prompt children to notice the high frequency words when you are reading aloud books with large print, such as the following (*Teaching Resources,* Large Print Books Bibliography, lists many other titles):

- ***Bear's Busy Family*** by Stella Blackstone
- ***Chugga-Chugga Choo Choo*** by Kevin Lewis

Shared Reading: Place a stick-on note over one or two high frequency words in a poem such as "My Bike" or "My Big Balloon" (see *Sing a Song of Poetry*). Have the children read up to the words, predicting what word will be next. Have them think about how the word looks: what letters will they see? Then remove the stick-on note so they can check the prediction.

Guided Reading: During word work, have the children make two or three high frequency words with magnetic letters. It's important that they make them quickly.

Interactive Writing: Draw attention to words that the children can write quickly because they know them. Make connections to the word wall and to the poems, chants, and songs that the children have used in shared reading.

Independent Writing: Encourage the children to write the words they know quickly but also to try spelling words they do not know.

assess

- Notice whether the children are making the words correctly and reteach when necessary.
- After the children have learned a series of high frequency words, reassess their knowledge. Some children may not need to work further with high frequency words. Others may need to work with volunteers or in a small group with you to notice features of words.

Expand the Learning

Gradually drop words that children know well and add other high frequency words that they need to know.

Create a high frequency word grid and have children practice it each day. Start with a blank grid (see *Teaching Resources,* Materials & Routines). In each box write a word you have taught until you fill up the sheet. Copy the grid on tag paper and have the children practice reading the words each day until they can read them all. Add a second or third sheet when children are ready for more words.

Connect with Home

Give each child high frequency word cards to take home and sort and practice.

Give them letter cards so they can build words at home.

4 Learning High Frequency Words 4

Locating Words in Text

Consider Your Children

Use this lesson after you have read any easy poem, song, or chant aloud to your children several times and then used it several more times in shared reading in conjunction with an enlarged text. Examples are "Eensy-Weensy Spider," "Rain," and "Jack Be Nimble." Write it on chart paper or, alternatively, on sentence strips to be placed in a pocket chart.

Working with English Language Learners

In this lesson, the children practice finding high frequency words in a text. Be sure the rhyme you select has meaning for your English language learners. After selecting the rhyme, act it out with these students and repeat it enough times for them to be comfortable reading it and matching word by word. This will provide a context for using the words *first* and *last.* Demonstrate the task and have students use the words so that they understand the directions.

You Need

- Chart or pocket chart.
- Highlighter tape or colored plastic strips.
- Highlighter markers (or the children can simply underline).
- Colored stick-on dots.

From *Teaching Resources:*

- High Frequency Word Lists.

Understand the Principle

The concept of *word,* as encountered in print, is important basic knowledge as children begin to read. Children need to learn to discriminate and identify letters that are embedded in words and words that are embedded in text. Being able to locate known words in text helps children monitor their reading. In addition, being able to identify particular high frequency words in text helps them learn how words work.

Explain the Principle

"You see some words many times when you read."

"When you know a word, you can read it every time you see it."

"You can find a word by knowing how it looks."

plan

teach

Eensy-Weensy Spider
The eensy-weensy spider
Climbed up the waterspout.
Down came the rain
And washed the spider out.
Out came the sun
And dried up all the rain,
And the eensy-weensy spider
Climbed up the spout again.

Explain the Principle

"You see some words many times when you read."

"When you know a word, you can read it every time you see it."

"You can find a word by knowing how it looks."

① Tell the children they are going to learn how to read some more words quickly.

② Place an easy poem, chant, or song on a chart or in the pocket chart.

③ Select a few high frequency words that you want the children to locate.

④ Suggested language: "You know the word *and*. This time when we read, stop when you come to the word *and*." Read the poem with the children, stopping at the word *and*. They should be able to recognize *and* easily. You can then look for the word *the*.

⑤ Have the children underline, circle, or place colored highlighter tape over words and letters on the chart. The pocket chart has the advantage of allowing you to place colored plastic over words and letters to highlight them.

⑥ Suggested language: "I'm going to put the colored tape over the word *the*. Now, use your eyes to find another *the*." The children look and one child comes up to point to *the*.

⑦ "Find *the* with a capital letter; find *the* with a lowercase letter."

⑧ Repeat with one or two more words. You can take the highlighter tape (or plastic) off the previous word each time so that children focus on the word they are currently looking for.

⑨ If the children are very familiar with the text and find high frequency words easily, you can vary the task by asking them to:

"Find a word that starts with *a* [any letter]."

"Find a word that ends with *e* [any letter]."

"Find a word with *ed*."

"Find a word with a capital [big, uppercase] letter."

"Find a word that is the first word in a line."

"Find a word that is the last word in a line."

"Find a period [a question mark]."

apply

read
mark
read
draw

- Place a list of high frequency words on the wall for children to see, and place colored dots next to specific ones. Give children a photocopy of the poem you used. Have them read the poem, highlight the high frequency words with a marker or pen, and then read the poem to a partner. Then ask them to illustrate the poem.

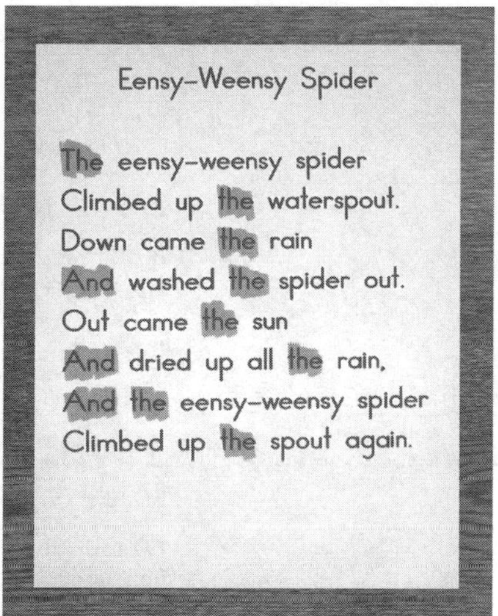
Eensy-Weensy Spider
The eensy-weensy spider
Climbed up the waterspout.
Down came the rain
And washed the spider out.
Out came the sun
And dried up all the rain,
And the eensy-weensy spider
Climbed up the spout again.

share

Have the children suggest words or elements they want others to locate. One child suggests what to look for; have all the children read up to the particular letter, word, word feature, or punctuation and then stop.

Link

Interactive Read-Aloud: Prompt children to notice the high frequency words when you are reading aloud books with large print, such as the following (*Teaching Resources,* Large Print Books Bibliography, lists many other titles):

- ***In the Small, Small Pond*** by Denise Fleming
- ***The Cow That Went OINK*** by Bernard Most

Shared Reading: After reading and enjoying a text such as "My Favorite Toys" or "The Old Gray Cat" (see *Sing a Song of Poetry*), have the children locate one or two high frequency words. While reading, ask them to locate different high frequency words. Locating words should be quick and fun. You would not want to do too much in any single session.

Guided Reading: During word work, write a high frequency word on a whiteboard and have the children read it quickly. Repeat with several more words.

Interactive Writing: Draw attention to words that the children can write quickly because they know them. Make connections to the word wall and to the poems, chants, and songs that the children have used in shared reading.

Independent Writing: Encourage the children to use the texts they know from shared reading as resources for their writing.

assess

- Notice whether the children are able to locate words, word features, or punctuation in the texts that they have read in shared reading.
- Notice whether the children can read, write, and locate high frequency words.

Expand the Learning

Repeat the lesson using other poems, songs, or chants that are familiar to the children (see *Sing a Song of Poetry*) and contain high frequency words (see *Teaching Resources,* High Frequency Word Lists) children need to know.

Connect with Home

Have the children take home a list of high frequency words they can make with magnetic letters or letter cards.

Learning High Frequency Words 5

Making and Writing Words

Consider Your Children

This lesson is the third (see Lessons HF 1 and HF 2) in establishing one hundred high frequency words for Grade 1 (see *Teaching Resources*). In this lesson, your children learn and practice the more complex high frequency words on the list. Most of them contain four or five letters and require the children to pay attention to particular patterns. Select words that the children have seen before in shared and interactive writing but do not fully control. Alter the sample words provided in this lesson based on the words your students know and need to know. If your children already know these sample words, select others.

Working with English Language Learners

As English language learners say, make, and write high frequency words, they will be acquiring a system for learning new words and noticing how letters work together to make words. Be sure that children say the words while making them and read each row after they complete the task—word card, word built in magnetic letters, and word written by the child.

You Need

- Pocket chart, whiteboard, or chart with Velcro®.
- Magnetic letters.
- Dry-erase markers.

From *Teaching Resources:*

- High Frequency Word Cards.
- Making Words Sheets.
- Pocket Chart Word Template.

Understand the Principle

As they begin to read, children acquire a small core of high frequency words that they recognize quickly and automatically. These words are powerful examples; children make connections between them and the words they are learning to solve by other means (such as using letter/sound relationships). These words are also important in the first texts children read and write. They increase children's early confidence in writing. They make simple texts more intelligible; there are fewer words for children to solve using letters and sounds.

Explain the Principle

“You see some words many times when you read.”

“Words you see a lot are important because they help you read and write.”

plan

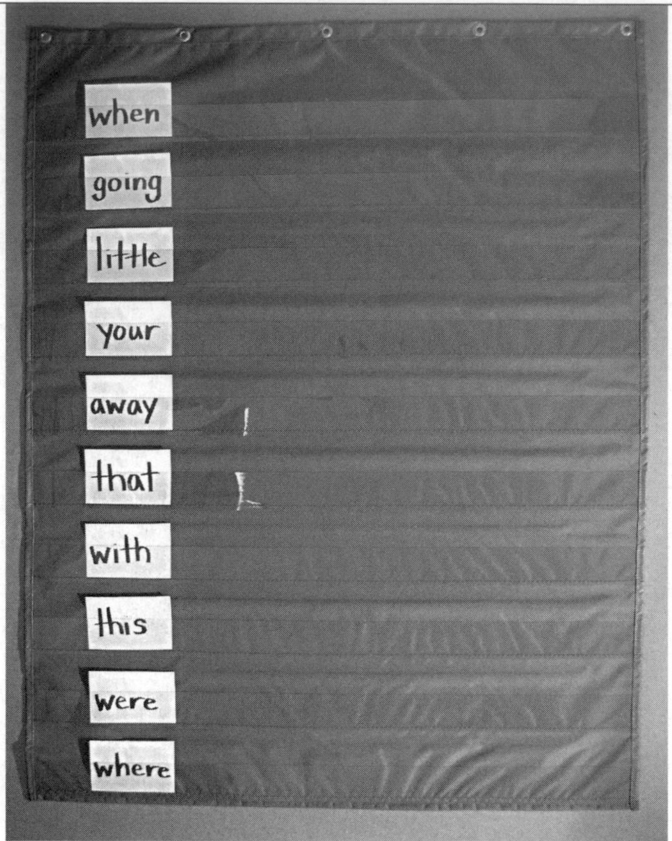

Explain the Principle

"You see some words many times when you read."

"Words you see a lot are important because they help you read and write."

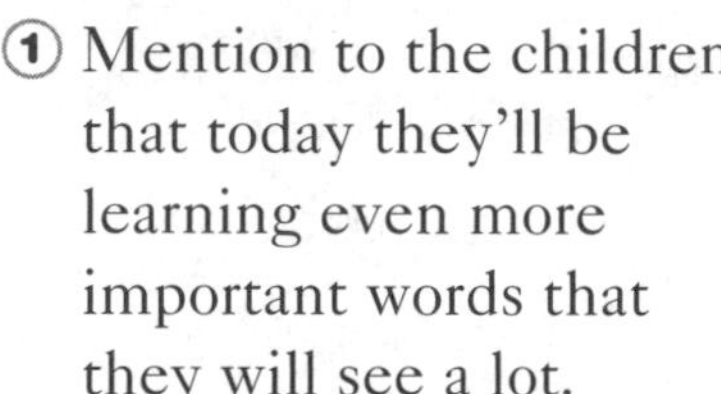

① Mention to the children that today they'll be learning even more important words that they will see a lot.

② Using the pocket chart, place ten words in the left column. Be sure the words are those that most of the children have noticed (or you've brought to their attention) in shared reading and interactive writing.

③ Remind the children of the directions for making and writing words. By now, they should be accustomed to this routine.

④ Show children the Making Words Sheet. Explain that they should take a word card, place it in the first column, say it, and make and mix the word three times with magnetic letters, placing a check in the box each time they make it in the second column. Then they write the word in the last column.

Name: Zoe

WORD	LETTERS	WRITE
that	that	that
with	with	with
your	your	your
were	were	were

say
make, mix, check (3x)
write

- Give the children a copy of the Making Words Sheet and word cards for the high frequency words used in the lesson.
- Have the children complete the sheet as above, working alone or in pairs. (If they work in pairs, one partner can say, make, and write the words and the other partner can check them, or they can alternate the functions on every other word.) If you want the children to work with more words, give them two stapled Making Words Sheets to use.

Create an enlarged high frequency word grid (see *Teaching Resources*, Materials & Routines) using the words from this lesson and any others you have worked with before. Have the children read the word grid across each line with you to reinforce and practice quick word recognition.

An alternative is to place words in a pocket chart or to point to and read words from the word wall.

Play a game with words. Invite the children to think of a way that two of the words on the chart are alike (for example, *the* and *they* start the same way or *that* and *went* end with the same letter or *here* and *there* end the same). This will help them notice more about the patterns in words.

Link

Interactive Read-Aloud: Read aloud large print books so that children can see how words look as you read them. Examples are:

- ***Jasper's Beanstalk*** by Nick Butterworth
- ***The Earth Is Good*** by Michael DeMunn

Shared Reading: Before reading a new poem such as "On Saturday Night" or "Papa's New Glasses" (see *Sing a Song of Poetry*), cover three or four high frequency words with stick-on notes. When you come to the covered word, invite the children to predict what it will be. Uncover the word so they can check the prediction. Ask them to tell you what they notice about the word.

Guided Reading: Following the reading of a text, have the children turn to a page or two and point to particular high frequency words.

Interactive Writing: When you are composing a text to write with your children, think about high frequency words you can include in the sentences.

Independent Writing: Write high frequency words on a sheet taped around the pencil can in the middle of a table so your children can check the words they write. Or place a copy of the 100 High Frequency Words chart in their writing folders so they can use it as a resource.

assess

- Notice how quickly the children recognize high frequency words in reading.
- Observe whether the children can write high frequency words quickly and accurately.
- Have a sheet of the one hundred high frequency words for each child and highlight the ones each knows how to read and write.

Expand the Learning

Repeat the lesson with other words the children need to learn. For variety, have the children use foam letters, cardboard letters, plastic link letters, etc. Instead of word cards, you might want to write words on small ceramic tiles for a child to use in the first column of the Making Words Sheet.

Connect with Home

Send home directions for playing Concentration (see *Teaching Resources*) and several sheets of High Frequency Word Cards. Have children cut out the words and use them to play Concentration.

Generative Lesson

Learning High Frequency Words 6

Lotto

Consider Your Children

Use this lesson after the children know what words are and know enough high frequency words (about fifteen or twenty) to play Lotto. In this game, children will be matching words simply by looking at their visual features, although they will also be saying the words. They can help one another, so every player doesn't have to know every word in isolation to play it. Base the words you select on your assessment of children's knowledge of the list of fifty high frequency words in *Teaching Resources*. Select some words your students know and many that they "almost know."

Working with English Language Learners

Word Lotto will give English language learners the opportunity to encounter words many times and practice reading them. These repetitions will help them establish a core of high frequency words that they can use as examples and that will make their reading of easy texts more meaningful. Assess the children's knowledge of the words they will be using in the game; they should recognize or "almost know" all of them.

You Need

- Pocket chart.
- Colored blank cards to cover words.

From *Teaching Resources:*

- Pocket Chart Card Template.
- Lotto Game Cards.
- Directions for Lotto.
- High Frequency Word Cards.

Understand the Principle

As children begin to read and write, they establish a core of familiar high frequency words. They can use these known words to monitor their reading. The words are anchors to help them with word-by-word matching. High frequency words are also powerful examples because children can connect the beginning letters or sounds of these familiar words with new words.

Explain the Principle

" You see some words many times when you read. "

" When you know a word, you can read it every time you see it. "

plan

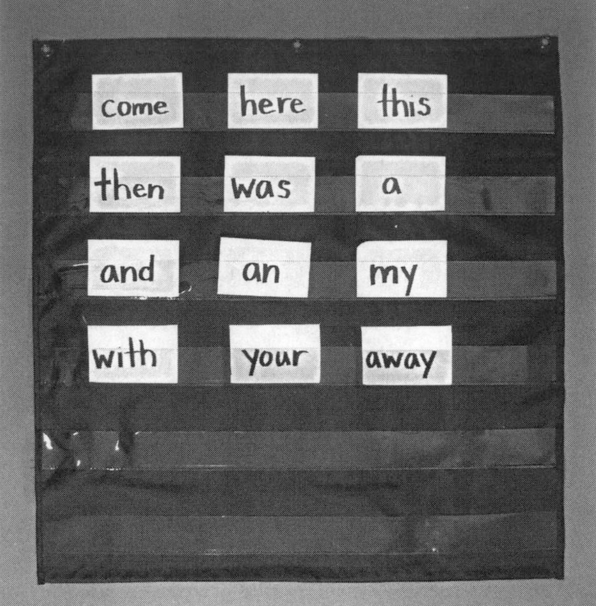

Explain the Principle

"You see some words many times when you read."

"When you know a word, you can read it every time you see it."

1. Explain to the children that they are going to play Lotto with words they need to know.
2. Place twelve high frequency word cards in a rectangular pattern on the pocket chart.
3. Have a stack of face down high frequency word cards that you can take from one at a time.

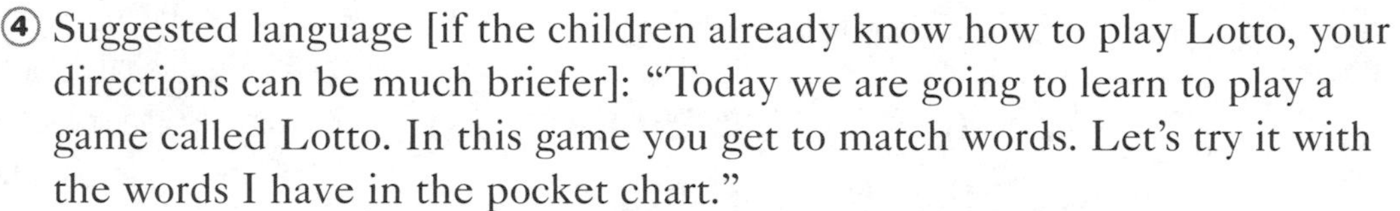

4. Suggested language [if the children already know how to play Lotto, your directions can be much briefer]: "Today we are going to learn to play a game called Lotto. In this game you get to match words. Let's try it with the words I have in the pocket chart."
5. "I'm going to take a word card from this stack and see if I can match it to a word on my game board."
6. Hold up the first word card. Suggested language: "This word is *a*. [Let the children say the word if they can.] Now I'm going to see if there is a word on my game board that looks just like the word *a*. Can anyone see *a* on my card?"
7. Model checking *a* and *a* by pointing to each and saying *a*. Then place a colored blank card over the word, blocking it out.
8. Take cards one at a time, showing how to say and check the words. Some words will not match any on the card, so no words will be covered.
9. When all the words on the chart are covered, say: "I've covered all the spaces on my game board. That's what you do to win the Word Lotto game. Remember to say both words to check your matches."

⑩ Ask children to discuss what they have to do to fill a Lotto card. Then demonstrate the game with three children in a circle on the floor. One child can show and read the word cards aloud. Players who have that word can cover it with a blank card (like Bingo, but all squares must be covered to win). Players can take turns drawing cards, saying the words, and covering the word if they have it.

take
say
match
cover

▸ Have the children play Word Lotto in groups of three or four.

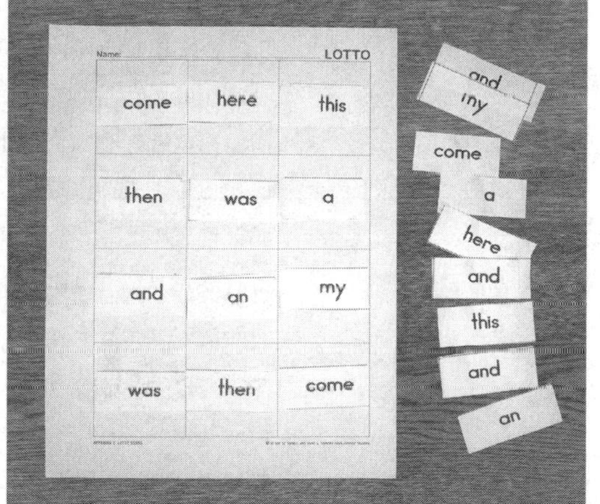

Write some of the words from the lesson on a dry-erase whiteboard and encourage quick recognition.

Hold up a few high frequency word cards one at a time and encourage quick recognition.

Ask the children to show on the word wall some of the words they have learned.

Link

Interactive Read-Aloud: Prompt children to notice the high frequency words when you are reading aloud books with large print, such as the following (*Teaching Resources,* Large Print Books Bibliography, lists many other titles):

- ***Top Cat*** by Lois Elhert
- ***Run Jump Whiz Splash*** by Vera Rosenberry

Shared Reading: When reading poems and stories such as "Polly Put the Kettle On" or "Pumpkin Orange" (see *Sing a Song of Poetry*), draw the children's attention to high frequency words and have them locate them with a masking card or highlighter tape.

Guided Reading: During word work, have the children make a few high frequency words with magnetic letters. You might show a model the first time and then have them make the word a couple more times without the model.

Interactive Writing: Have a child write a high frequency word quickly while others locate it on the word wall.

Independent Writing: Encourage the children to recognize that they know some words in detail. They don't have to construct them by hearing and representing the sounds. They can write them quickly because they know them. In conferences, point out words that children have written quickly because they know them.

assess

- Notice whether the children are able to recognize high frequency words as they read.
- Notice whether the children can write high frequency words quickly.
- Ask the children to write five or ten specific high frequency words. The children should be able to write between seventy-five and one hundred words quickly by the end of the first grade.

Expand the Learning

Repeat the lesson using a greater variety of high frequency words to make the Lotto Game Cards.

Use more difficult high frequency words once the children know the easy ones.

Connect with Home

Give each child a list of high frequency words and a set of letter cards to take home. Have them make the words several times with the letter cards (or with magnetic letters if they have them). Have them read the words to their family members.

Learning High Frequency Words 7

Follow the Path

Consider Your Children

Ongoing assessment of your children's word knowledge will help you select high frequency words for your lessons. After the children know thirty or so high frequency words, they can increase their ability to recognize them quickly and use them flexibly by playing this game. Be careful not to give the impression that *all* words must be "remembered" and recognized on sight. You will be teaching your students many strategies for solving words and will use games like this only for easy high frequency words. You may want to take the list of one hundred high frequency words (see *Teaching Resources*) and highlight all the words each child can read or write.

Working with English Language Learners

Assess English language learners' repertoire of high frequency words to be sure they know the words they will be reading on the Follow the Path game. Provide more practice reading and/or matching words in the pocket chart to help them play the game more easily. You may want to give the children additional chances to play the game until they achieve full control of the set of words.

You Need

- Follow the Path Game Boards.

From *Teaching Resources:*

- Directions for Follow the Path.
- High Frequency Word Cards (optional).

Understand the Principle

Being able to recognize a set of core words quickly and automatically helps beginning readers monitor the accuracy of their reading. These words are anchors for word-by-word matching. High frequency words are also powerful examples because children can connect the beginning letters or sounds of these familiar words with new words. As children learn more words, they develop strategies that will help them learn more quickly.

Explain the Principle

"When you know a word, you can read it every time you see it."

plan

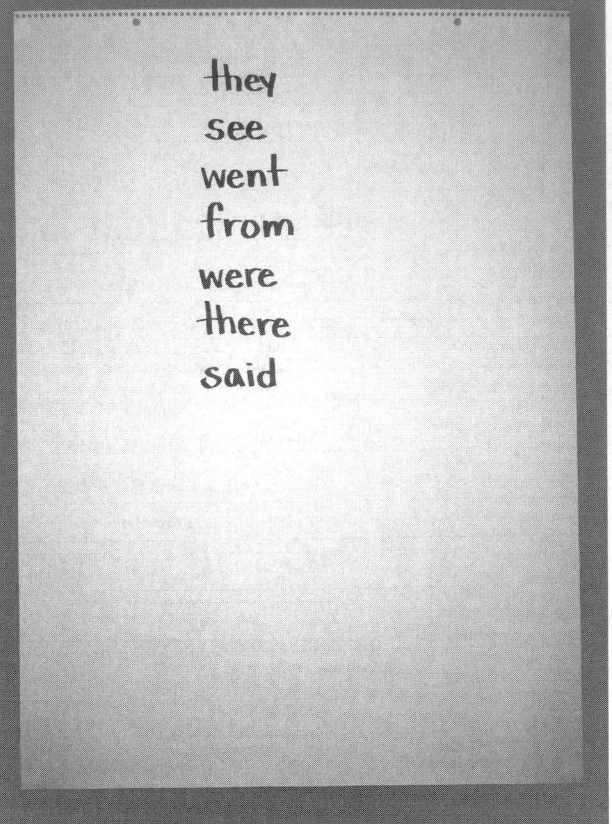

Explain the Principle

"When you know a word, you can read it every time you see it."

① Tell the children you are going to help them think about some important words they've been learning.

② Write some words, one at a time, on a chart. Choose words that most of the children "almost know" or need to practice, along with a few words that are new to most of them.

③ Suggested language: "You are learning a lot of words as you read and write. Sometimes you figure out words by looking at the letters and sounds, but other words you can read very fast because you know them. I'm going to write a list of words on the chart. Take a good look at the words and think about how you will remember the way each word looks."

④ Write the words *they, see, went, from, were, there,* and *said* on the chart.

⑤ The children will likely offer comments such as:

"The word *they* has the word *the* in the first part."

"The word *said* has an *a* and *i* that sounds like *e*."

"The word *went* has four letters and the vowel is *e*."

"The word *see* has two *e*s."

"*Were* and *there* look the same at the end."

⑥ Explain how to play Follow the Path with high frequency words. Suggested language: "Today you are going to play a game with the many words you know or almost know."

⑦ Show the children a Follow the Path Game Board with a high frequency word written on each space (perhaps including free spaces to make the game more interesting). Explain that they are to select a marker and take turns rolling the die and moving the number of spaces indicated. When they land on a space, they must read the word. A player who cannot read the word goes back to the original space. The player who gets to the end of the path first wins the game. (An alternative is to use a game board with a blank path. Children throw a die and move the number of spaces. Then they draw a high frequency word card and read the word. If they read the word correctly, as determined by the other players, they stay in the space. If not, they move back to the original space.)

⑧ Invite a child to be your partner and demonstrate playing the game.

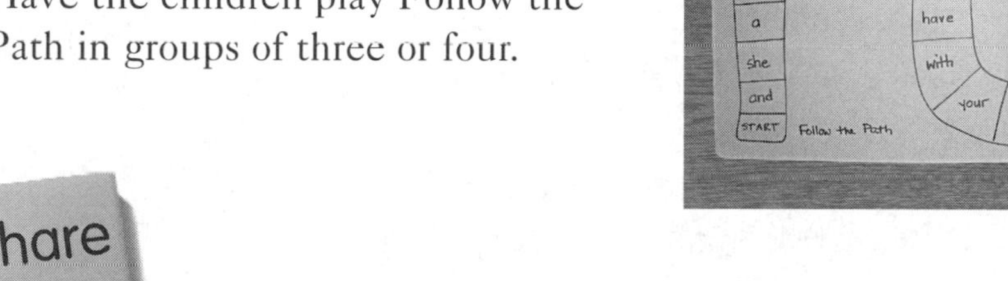

throw
move
read

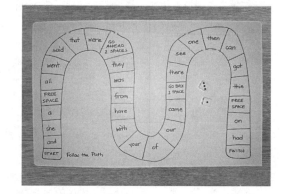

▸ Have the children play Follow the Path in groups of three or four.

Ask the children to discuss how they were able to recognize the words in the game. Look for comments like these:

"I looked at the first letter."

"I looked at the beginning and ending."

"I knew it because it's like [another word]."

"I knew it from the word wall."

Point out that noticing the letters will help them remember words.

Link

Interactive Read-Aloud: Prompt children to notice the high frequency words when you are reading aloud books with large print, such as the following (*Teaching Resources,* Large Print Books Bibliography, lists many other titles):

- ***Hush, Little Alien*** by Daniel Kirk
- ***Hand, Hand, Fingers, Thumb*** by Al Perkins

Shared Reading: Have the children read poems such as "Rooster's Crow" or "Coffee and Tea" (see *Sing a Song of Poetry*), noticing words they know. Have them use a masking card to locate specific words.

Guided Reading: After reading and discussing a text, have the children turn to a particular page and locate a particular high frequency word. Have them find a word several times on the same page.

Interactive Writing: Have the children think about whether they can read a word and write it. (Quickly write the high frequency words they already know well yourself.)

Independent Writing: Encourage the children to quickly write the words they know and help them become conscious of the words they are learning. Encourage them to check their words with the word wall.

assess

- Using the High Frequency Word Lists in *Teaching Resources,* determine which high frequency words the children can read.
- Determine which high frequency words the children can write with conventional spelling.

Expand the Learning

Play Follow the Path with increasingly difficult high frequency words.

Connect with Home

At a meeting or in a newsletter, teach family members to play several kinds of word games (Concentration, Follow the Path, Go Fish, Lotto—see *Teaching Resources* for directions) with their children. Explain that in these games children will learn some words to help them get started in reading and writing. Emphasize that they will also learn phonics skills.

Send home a set of high frequency word cards so that children can practice. Start with easy words you know children can read and gradually include more difficult words.

Generative Lesson

Learning High Frequency Words 8

Concentration

Consider Your Children

Continue to monitor the high frequency words your children know. This lesson will be especially helpful to children who are having difficulty remembering words.

Working with English Language Learners

To cnjoy playing Concentration, English language learners must first have practiced the routines related to the game and be able to recognize the high frequency words used. This exercise will give them a chance to "overlearn" these words so that they can read and write them fluently.

You Need

- Magnetic letters.

From *Teaching Resources:*

- High Frequency Word Cards, two of each word.
- Deck Card Template.
- High Frequency Word Lists.
- Directions for Concentration.

Understand the Principle

Children need to acquire an early reading vocabulary of high frequency words. They use these words to check the accuracy of their reading and maintain momentum. Knowing high frequency words frees children's attention to solve unfamiliar words. High frequency words are examples and resources for solving words while reading and writing.

Explain the Principle

" You see some words many times when you read. "

" Words you see a lot are important because they help you read and write. "

plan

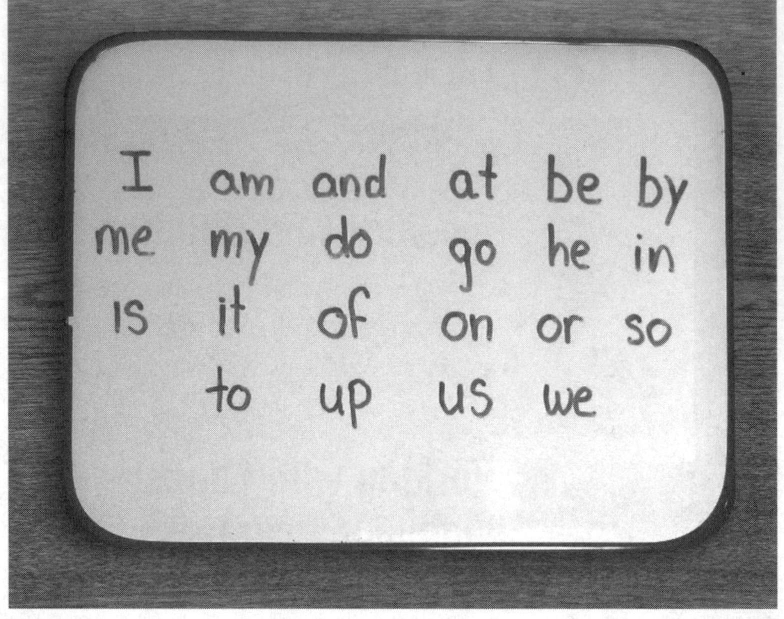

teach

Explain the Principle

"You see some words many times when you read."

"Words you see a lot are important because they help you read and write."

① Tell the children they are going to practice some words that they are going to use many times when they read and write.

② Suggested language: "I'm going to show you some words on the board, and after I go through them, I'm going to ask you to read them quickly."

③ Make ten or more (depending on your children's knowledge of high frequency words) words with magnetic letters and say the word each time.

④ Then write all the words on a whiteboard and have the children read them.

⑤ Explain the game Concentration.

⑥ One at a time, place all the cards face down on the table. Each player, in turn, turns one card over, says the word, turns a second card over, and says the word. If the words are the same, the player keeps the pair. If they are not, the child turns the cards back over, leaving them in the same place. The player with the most pairs at the end wins the game.

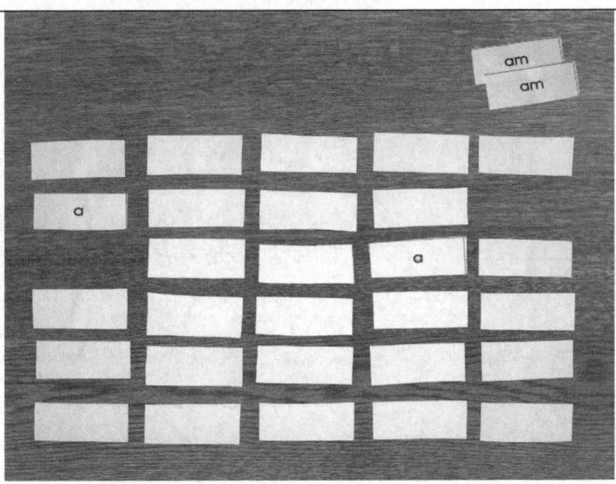

turn
read
match

- Have children play Concentration in groups of two, three, or four.

Invite a few children to go to the easel and make a word from the game with magnetic letters.

Link

Interactive Read-Aloud: Prompt children to notice the high frequency words when you are reading aloud books with large print, such as the following (*Teaching Resources,* Large Print Books Bibliography, lists many other titles):

- ***Barnyard Banter*** by Denise Fleming
- ***What the Sun Sees*** by Nancy Tafuri

Shared Reading: After reading and enjoying poems, chants, and songs, such as "Say and Touch" or "Sing a Song of Sixpence" (see *Sing a Song of Poetry*), have the children highlight particular high frequency words with a masking card or highlighter tape.

Guided Reading: Following the lesson, have the children turn to two or three specific pages and locate some high frequency words.

Interactive Writing: When there are high frequency words to be written, call on the children to write them from beginning to end without stopping.

Independent Writing: Once you have taught particular high frequency words, expect the children to write them correctly, referring to the word wall if necessary.

assess

- Observe the children's ability to recognize high frequency words when reading.
- Dictate four or five high frequency words for the children to write.

Expand the Learning

Repeat the lesson with more high frequency words. The goal is for the children to be able to read and write between seventy-five and one hundred high frequency words by the end of Grade 1.

Connect with Home

Send home a deck of high frequency word cards for children to play Concentration with family members.

Word Meaning

Children need to know the meaning of the words they are learning to read and write. It is important for them to expand their vocabulary constantly as well as develop a more complex understanding of words they already know. Word meaning is related to the development of vocabulary—labels, concept words, synonyms, antonyms, and homonyms. Concept words such as numbers and days of the week are often used in the texts they read, and they will want to use these words in their own writing. When children learn concept words (color words are another example), they can form categories that help in retrieving concept words when needed. In our complex language, meaning and spelling are intricately connected.

Often you must know the meaning of the word you want to spell or read before you can spell it accurately. In addition to lists of common concept words that children are often expected to know how to read and spell, we include synonyms, antonyms, and homonyms, which may be homographs (same spelling, different meaning, and sometimes different pronunciation) or homophones (same sound but different spelling). Knowing synonyms and antonyms will help children build more powerful systems for connecting and categorizing words; it will also help them comprehend texts better and write in a more interesting way. Being able to distinguish between homographs and homophones assists in comprehension and helps spellers to avoid mistakes.

Connect to Assessment

See related WM Assessment Tasks in the Assessment Guide in *Teaching Resources:*

- Reading Concept Words in Isolation
- Reading Concept Words in Sentences
- Identifying Synonyms

Develop Your Professional Understanding

See *Word Matters: Teaching Phonics and Spelling in the Reading/Writing Classroom* by G.S. Pinnell and I.C. Fountas. 1998. Portsmouth, New Hampshire: Heinemann.

Related pages: 78–81, 88–89, 199–205.

1 Learning Days of the Week

Making Books

Consider Your Children

Use this lesson after the children have heard stories that involve days of the week or months of the year and have used these terms in conversations. They should also have had some experience with the calendar (looking at birthdays each month, for example, will prompt them to use the terms). Chances are the children will have heard these terms in their homes and communities but may not understand them as organizational systems. When they have some familiarity with the terms, this lesson will help them systematize their knowledge.

Working with English Language Learners

Be sure that English language learners have had a chance to work with the calendar, perhaps in a small group if other children in the class are already very familiar with it. Give them a chance to read the days of the week and months of the year in order in shared reading. (You can use this lesson to help the children learn any other word categories or sequences they find difficult in English—color words, number words, or holidays, for example).

You Need

- Pocket chart.
- Text of "Sally Go Round" (days of week) on sentence strips.
- Text of "Thirty Days Hath September" (months of year) on sentence strips.

From *Teaching Resources:*

- *On Sunday I Ate . . .* book pages (Blank Book Page Template).

Understand the Principle

The names of the days of the week (and months of the year), as well as the order in which they occur, are concepts that many first graders are expected to know. Often these terms are used as organizing features in the texts they are expected to read. Familiarity with these words will help them understand the structure of these texts.

Explain the Principle

“ Days of the week have names and are always in the same order. ”

plan

Explain the Principle

"Days of the week have names and are always in the same order."

① Tell the children they are going to read the words that tell the days of the week.

② In a pocket chart place the simple text "Sally Go Round." Read the text several times, each time substituting the card with a different day of the week.

③ Finally, place all the days in order and have the children tell what they notice. (For example, they all have *day* at the end; *Sunday* and *Saturday* start the same; *Tuesday* and *Thursday* start the same).

④ Have the children read all the days with you and explain that they have an exact order.

⑤ Explain that they are going to make books about foods they eat each day of the week. Have one completed so you can show an example.

write
write
read
draw

- Using the Blank Book Page Template (see *Teaching Resources*), write at the bottom of the page. Give each child a stapled book with several photocopied pages. Have them write in the name of a day of the week in the first blank—one per page—in order. Next, have them fill in something edible in the second blank, read the sentence, and illustrate each page of the book.

Have the children share books with partners or in groups of three.

Display the books in the classroom for a few days so children can read one another's books.

Link

Interactive Read-Aloud: Read aloud books structured around days of the week or months of the year, such as

- ***The Very Hungry Caterpillar*** by Eric Carle (days)
- ***Dog Days*** by Jack Prelutsky (months)

Shared Reading: Have the children locate days of the week in enlarged texts using highlighter tape or a masking card. See several text examples such as "Monday Morning" or "There Are Seven Days" in *Sing a Song of Poetry.*

Guided Reading: If days of the week appear in texts, have the children locate them before or after reading the text.

Interactive Writing: Create some texts that incorporate the days of the week. For example, you might create a class version of *The Very Hungry Caterpillar* or *Cookie's Week.*

Independent Writing: Encourage the children to refer to a list of days of the week (perhaps on the word wall) when they want to write one of the days.

assess

- Working individually with children, have them locate the days of the week and notice how quickly they are able to do so.
- When the children include the days of the week in their writing, notice how they use the words and the extent to which they can spell them.

Expand the Learning

Repeat the lesson with the months of the year using "Thirty Days Hath September" as the teaching text.

Connect with Home

Encourage family members to refer to the calendar regularly. Explain how they can help children learn the days of the week and months of the year. After the days-of-the-week books have been on display for a while, have children take them home to read to a family member.

2 Recognizing Synonyms

Synonym Match

Consider Your Children

This lesson will be effective if the children have the words you use as examples in their speaking vocabularies. You will also want to be sure that the words are those that your children can read easily, with some support from you. The children should also have had some beginning experience with synonyms in interactive writing as they select words to make their writing more interesting.

Working with English Language Learners

To grasp the concept of synonyms, English language learners will need to know the meaning of both words in a set, at least for most of the examples. Once they understand the idea, finding synonyms and adding them to the chart can be a way of expanding their English vocabularies.

You Need

- Pocket chart.

From *Teaching Resources:*

- Synonym Word Cards.
- Synonym Concentration Cards (Deck Card Template).
- Directions for Concentration.

Understand the Principle

When good readers encounter unfamiliar words in print, they use their decoding skills but also think of alternative words that fit the meaning of the sentence. Knowing that words can mean the same or almost the same thing helps children begin to notice and connect words by meaning. Knowing synonyms helps children make their writing more interesting by varying the words they use.

Explain the Principle

“Some words mean about the same and are called synonyms.”

plan

teach

Explain the Principle

“Some words mean about the same and are called synonyms.”

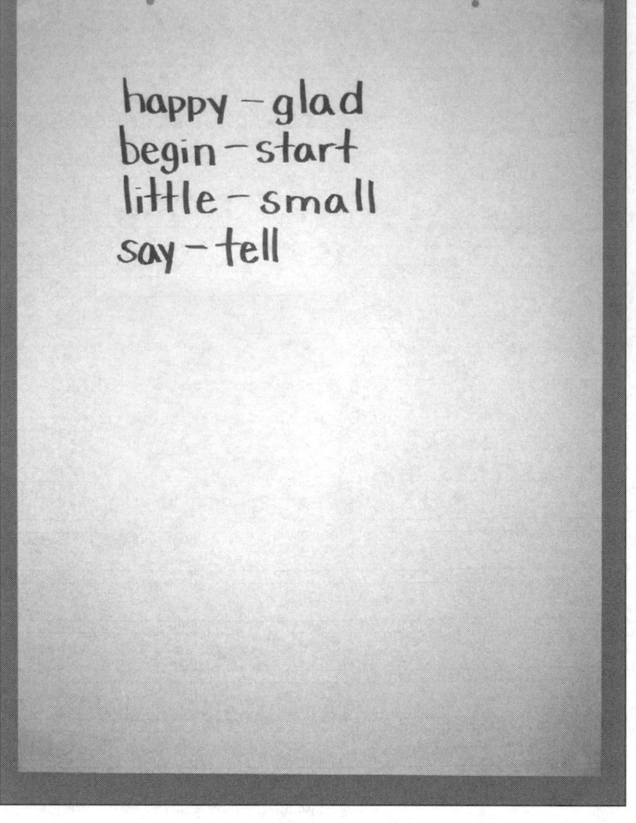

1. Tell the children they are going to learn something new about words.
2. Select four pairs from the synonym word cards (*happy–glad*, *begin–start*, *little–small*, *say–tell*, for example).
3. Point to and say the pairs of words. Suggested language: “What do you notice about the words? [Children respond.] Yes, they mean almost the same thing. We call words that mean almost the same *synonyms*. Say synonyms. Clap with me. Today you are going to make synonym pairs as you play Concentration.”
4. Have the children play Synonym Concentration with a partner or in small groups. They take the set of cards and lay them all flat on the table, face down. They take turns turning one card over, reading it, and then turning over another card and seeing whether it means the same thing. If it does, that player gets the pair of cards. If it doesn't, the cards are turned face down again and the next player takes her or his turn. The player with the most pairs wins.

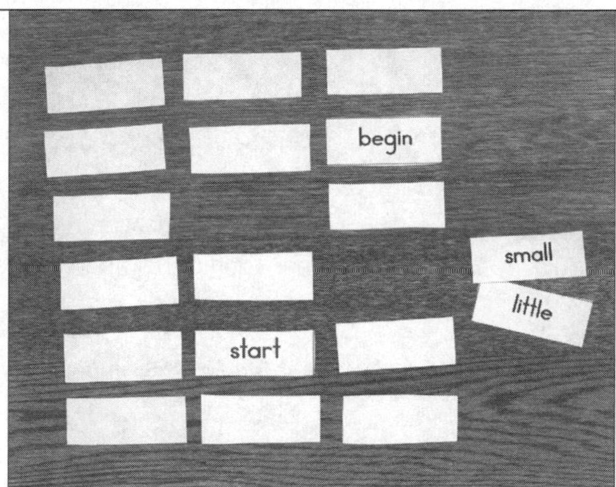

apply

turn
turn
match

- Have the children play Synonym Concentration in groups of two, three, or four, matching pairs of synonyms. The player who makes the largest number of pairs wins the game.

Have the children share a pair of words they matched.

You might want to create a synonym board and invite the children to put pairs of words and illustrations on the board.

Link

Interactive Read-Aloud: Read aloud books that focus on similarities and differences, pointing out synonyms as you come across them. Examples are:

- ***A Huge Hog Is a Big Pig*** by Francis McCall
- ***A Big Fat Enormous Lie*** by Marjorie Sharmat

Shared Reading: Have the children tape a synonym over one or two words in a text such as "A Tiny Seed" or "My Big Balloon" (see *Sing a Song of Poetry*) and read the text with the new words.

Guided Reading: As you discuss a story, use one or two synonyms for words.

Interactive Writing: When the children are composing a text, encourage them to give a synonym for a word in order to make the text more interesting.

Independent Writing: As you confer with the children, help them see places where they can cross out a word and put a more interesting word.

assess

- Observe the children as they play Synonym Concentration to identify those who need more work in a small group or who do not know the labels for the pictures.
- After the children have worked with synonyms for a while, have them make a "synonym book" with words that mean the same on left and right pages. They can write the words and illustrate them. Have them identify the synonyms as they read the book to you.

Expand the Learning

Have children play the game again with different pairs of synonyms.

Repeat the lesson with antonyms.

Connect with Home

Encourage the children to write a pair of synonyms at home to bring in and put on the synonym board.

Give children a deck of synonym cards so they can play Synonym Concentration at home.

3 Recognizing Words That Go Together

Word Sort

Consider Your Children

Use this lesson with your children when they can read a large number of high frequency words and can solve simple words easily. Be sure the words you use for examples are in the children's speaking vocabulary and that they can read them with some support.

Working with English Language Learners

English language learners will know the routine of sorting, but you will need to demonstrate and make clear to them that this time you are asking them to connect words by thinking about what they *mean*. The exercise of putting words into categories will be very helpful to English language learners as they expand their speaking, reading, and writing vocabularies. Begin with simple examples and use pictures if needed.

You Need

- Pocket chart.

From *Teaching Resources:*

- Word Cards (Pocket Chart Card Template) of words in related categories (*clothing, family, fruit,* for example).
- Four-Box Sheets.

Understand the Principle

Good readers and writers form networks of understanding around the words that are in their oral and written vocabularies. They learn to categorize words by their connections, and doing so helps them solve words and check their comprehension while reading.

Explain the Principle

"Some words go together because of what they mean."

plan

teach

Explain the Principle

" Some words go together because of what they mean. "

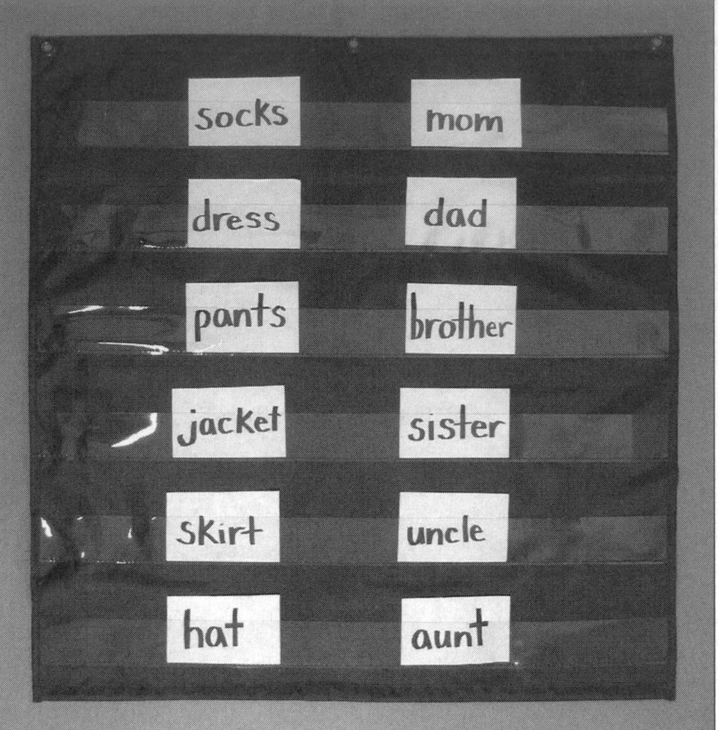

1. Tell the children they are going to think about words that go together.
2. Place some word cards in a pocket chart in random order *(mom, dad, brother, sister, uncle, aunt, socks, dress, pants, jacket, skirt, hat, apple, banana, orange, pear, peach, plum).*
3. Ask the children whether any of the words go together.
4. With their input, create three groups (clothing, family, fruit).
5. Explain that some words go together because of what they mean.
6. Hold up a Four-Box Sheet.
7. Demonstrate how the children will use it, explaining that they are to choose one of three other categories—food, colors, or toys—draw four items that fit in this category (one in each box), and write the name of the item below each drawing. (Note: Children will approximate the spellings. The important point to notice is whether the words fit the category.)

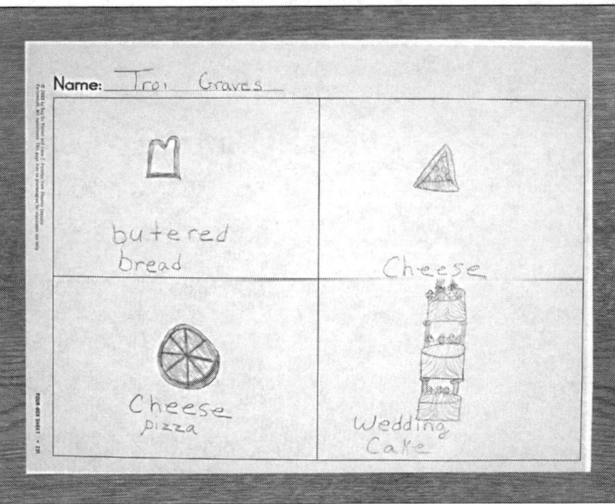

choose
draw
write

▸ Have the children choose a category, draw four pictures on a Four-Box Sheet, and label each item.

Have the children point to each word and read it to a partner.

Link

Interactive Read-Aloud: Read aloud books that are centered around specific categories of activities or things, such as

- ***Who Hops?*** by Katie Davis
- ***Bread Bread Bread*** by Ann Morris

Shared Reading: Select poems in which children can notice categories such as "Apples, Peaches" or "Cap, Mittens, Shoes and Socks" (see *Sing a Song of Poetry*).

Guided Reading: During word work, write three words and ask the children to tell the category.

Interactive Writing: Involve the children in creating texts that involve categories—a family book or a food book, for example.

Independent Writing: Have the children write simple four-page books about family, food, or clothing:

family This is my Mom. This is my Dad. This is my cat. This is my teddy bear.

food I like pizza. I like bananas. I like chocolate. I don't like vegetables.

clothing I have a blue hat. I have a green sweater. I have a yellow raincoat. I have brown shoes.

assess

- Give the children a sheet with about twenty words on it that can be grouped into two or three categories. Have them cut out the words and glue them inside circles, then write the category underneath each circle. Notice how well they understand this concept.

Expand the Learning

Repeat the lesson with other categories.

Connect with Home

Have the children share their Four-Box Sheets with family members.

Ask the children to make a small bag of objects that go together and bring it to school to share.

Ask the children to cut out four magazine pictures that go together.

Word Structure

Looking at the structure of words will help children learn how words are related to each other and how words can be changed by adding letters, letter clusters, and larger parts of words. Being able to recognize syllables, for example, helps children break down words into smaller units that are easier to analyze. In phonological awareness lessons, children learn to recognize the word breaks and to identify the number of syllables in a word. They can build on this useful information in reading and writing.

Words often have affixes, parts added before or after a word to change its meaning. An affix can be a prefix or a suffix. The word to which affixes are added can be a *base* word or a *root* word. A base word is a complete word; a root word is a part with Greek or Latin origins (such as *phon* in *telephone*). It will not be necessary for young children to make this distinction when they are beginning to learn about simple affixes, but working with suffixes and prefixes will help them read and understand words that use them as well as use them accurately in writing.

Endings or word parts that are added to base words signal meaning. For example, they may signal relationships *(prettier, prettiest)* or time *(running, planted).* Principles related to word structure include understanding the meaning and structure of compound words, contractions, plurals, and possessives as well as knowing how to make and use them accurately. We have also included the simple abbreviations that children often see in the books they read and want to use in their writing.

Connect to Assessment

See related WS Assessment Tasks in the Assessment Guide in *Teaching Resources:*

- Syllables in Words
- Recognizing and Using Plurals
- Understanding and Using Contractions
- Compound Words
- Simple Affixes *(s, ed, ing)*

Develop Your Professional Understanding

See *Word Matters: Teaching Phonics and Spelling in the Reading/Writing Classroom* by G.S. Pinnell and I.C. Fountas. 1998. Portsmouth, New Hampshire: Heinemann.

Related pages: 97–98.

1 Exploring Syllables

Name Graph

Consider Your Children

Use this lesson when your children can read their own names and some of the names of their friends. It will help children who are just beginning to be able to clap the syllables of a word to identify the breaks. This strategy is a first step in being able to hear the sounds in words.

Working with English Language Learners

English language learners may already have some awareness of syllables from being encouraged to clap words to help them read and write them. This lesson will help them become more consciously aware of the number of syllables in words and of how awareness of syllable breaks can help them solve words. The repertoire of names in your classroom should provide plenty of variety, but you can also add names of favorite storybook characters (like Clifford) if you have a small class. Help all children in the class pronounce each name as accurately as possible in the appropriate language. This lesson will help English language learners learn their classmates' names, a valuable resource. If they need more practice in clapping syllables, work with them in a small group using other words that are in their speaking vocabulary.

You Need

- Graph (start with a blank graph).
- Name chart (see Lesson ELC 1).

From *Teaching Resources:*

- Name Cards (Word Card Template).
- Name grids filled in with names of class members (Materials & Routines).

Understand the Principle

Syllables are easy for young children to hear, recognize, and use because they represent natural breaks in language. The structure of syllables allows children to break words into component parts so that they are easier to solve. It helps them learn how to take multisyllable words apart.

Explain the Principle

“You can hear the syllables in words.”

“You can look at the syllables to read a word.”

plan

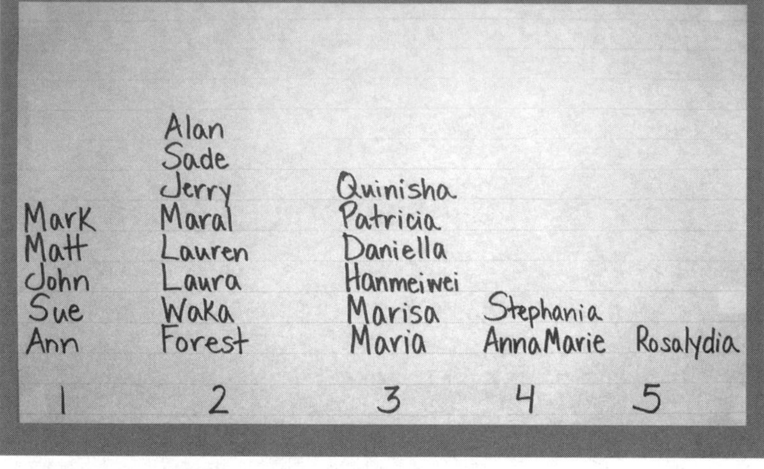

Explain the Principle

"You can hear the syllables in words."

"You can look at the syllables to read a word."

1. Explain to children that they are going to learn how to listen for syllables in their names. Read your class name chart (Lesson ELC 1) together.
2. Display a blank graph with syllable numbers at the bottom.
3. Suggested language: "You have been learning about your names. When you say your name, you can hear the parts and you can clap to help you know how many parts are in your name. I'm going to say someone's name and clap the parts." Demonstrate by saying *Forest*, for example, and clapping each syllable.
4. Suggested language: "How many parts does *Forest* have?" Children respond. "It has two parts. I'm going to write *Forest* over the 2 because it has two parts."
5. Continue saying each child's name, having the children clap and listen for the parts, and writing the name in the appropriate column on the graph.
6. When the graph is finished, quickly read the names in each category and listen for the number of parts. The children should be able to clap syllables by the time they have read all the names together.

early
mid
late

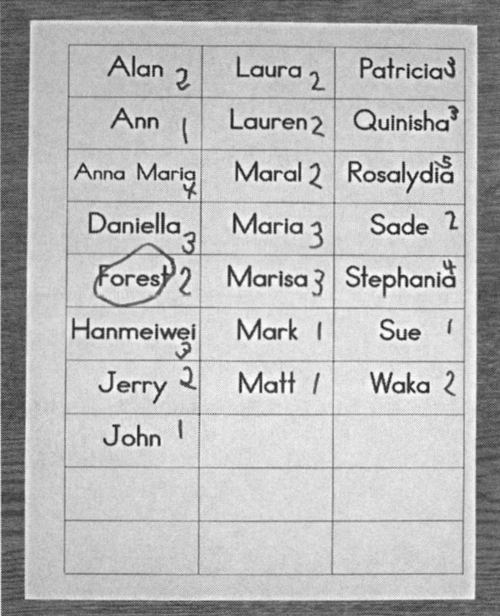

Alan 2	Laura 2	Patricia 3
Ann 1	Lauren 2	Quinisha 3
Anna Maria 4	Maral 2	Rosalydia 5
Daniella 3	Maria 3	Sade 2
Forest 2	Marisa 3	Stephania 4
Hanmeiwei 3	Mark 1	Sue 1
Jerry 2	Matt 1	Waka 2
John 1		

read
clap
tell
write

- Have the children work in pairs. Place a pile of name cards in a basket or tray for partners to use. Each partner selects five names. The first child reads each name, and the partner claps the syllables and tells the number of parts. After the five names have been worked through, the children reverse roles and repeat the process with five more names.
- When the partners finish, each child takes a name grid containing class names. He reads each name and writes the number of parts in the corner of each box. When complete, each child circles his own name on the grid and hands it in.

Have each child say and clap his name and tell the number of parts he hears.

Link

Interactive Read-Aloud: Read aloud books with lots of character names and have the children clap the syllables. Examples are:

- ***Safe, Warm, and Snug*** by Stephen Swinburne
- ***Ms. Bindergarten Celebrates the 100th Day of Kindergarten*** by Joseph Slate

Shared Reading: Have the children locate words with a masking card or highlighter tape in texts such as "My Favorite Toys" or "The Smile Song" (see *Sing a Song of Poetry*) after first clapping them to tell the number of syllables.

Guided Reading: During word work, say five or six words and have the children clap the syllables.

Interactive Writing: When the children are working on an unfamiliar word, have them clap the syllables and work on one at a time.

Independent Writing: Prompt the children to say the syllables of the word to help them write the sounds within it.

assess

- Say four or five words and ask the children to clap the syllables.

Expand the Learning

Repeat the lesson with the children's surnames if they need more experience.

Repeat the lesson with words that the children have used in shared reading and interactive writing.

Play "clap the syllables" while the children are lining up.

Connect with Home

Send home a copy of the graph with blank spaces in each category (or a blank version). Children can place names of their family members and friends in the appropriate spaces.

2 Making Plurals: Adding s

Word Match

Consider Your Children

Use this lesson after your children are familiar with the concept of plural. They should also be skilled in hearing sounds in words. Most children will find it easy to understand the concept of adding *s,* because they will have begun to use the plural form in their own conversations. In this lesson, you will want to help them say the *s* at the end and notice it in the written word.

Working with English Language Learners

You'll want to be sure that English language learners understand the concept of plural as "more than one" as well as the words *singular* and *plural.* If you can, use some words in the children's own languages to help them grasp the idea. You can also use pictures (for example, one dog, two dogs) to illustrate the idea. Work with a small group and ask children to talk about what they are noticing about the words (for example, that in some words the *s* sounds like *z*).

You Need

From *Teaching Resources:*

- Word Cards, Plurals 1.
- Two-Way Sort Cards (optional).
- Two-Way Sort Sheets (two copies).

Understand the Principle

Children need to understand that there are different processes for making nouns plural. They can improve their spelling by saying the word and making a connection between the sound of the ending and the word they are spelling.

Explain the Principle

"Plural means more than one."

"Add *s* to some words to show you mean more than one."

"You can hear the *s* at the end."

plan

Explain the Principle

"Plural means more than one."

"Add *s* to some words to show you mean more than one."

"You can hear the *s* at the end."

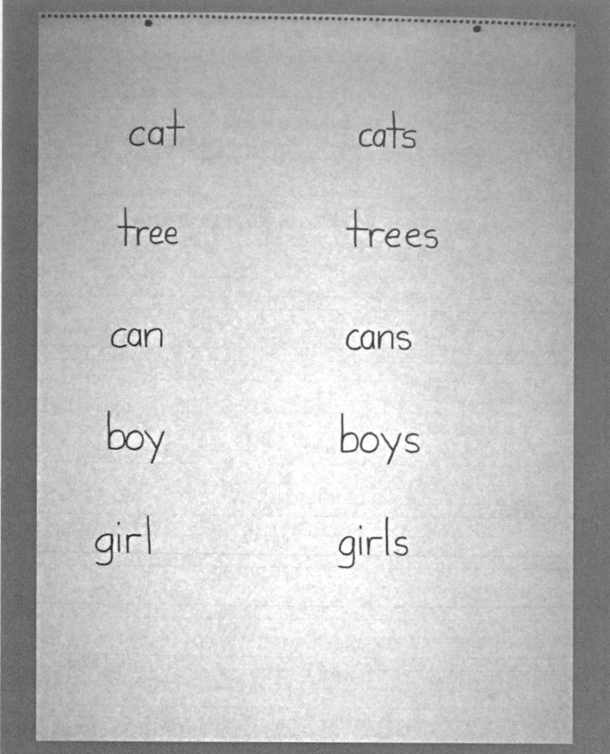

1. Tell children they're going to learn how to add *s* to words when they mean more than one.
2. Begin by having the children orally generate singular and plural forms of simple nouns. Suggested language: "I'll say the word for one thing, and you say the word for more than one." Demonstrate by saying *one cat* and then *two cats*. Follow with words like *tree, can, boy, girl.*
3. After the children can generate plurals by adding *s*, write simple words on the chart and show them how to add *s*. Write the plural form in column 2.
4. Ask the children what they have noticed about the words. You may demonstrate or children may make comments like these, which indicate that children are analyzing words and thinking about the principle:

   "You add *s* if there are two."

   "Some sound like *z* and some sound like *s*."
5. Explain to the children that they will be matching words that mean one and words that mean more than one, or are plural.

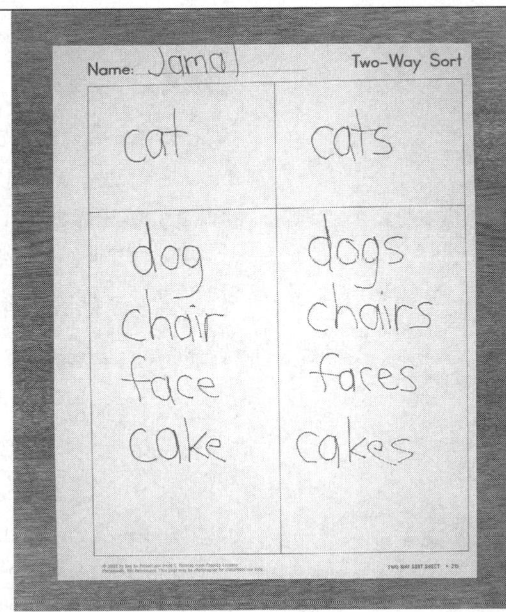

read
match
write

- Have ready thirty cards, fifteen with the singular form and fifteen with the plural form of simple nouns. Children match singular and plural words on the table, or on a Two-Way Sort Card.
- When they have finished, they can write five of their pairs on a second Two-Way Sort Sheet.

Ask the children to share what they noticed about plurals. Place two examples of plurals on the word wall.

Link

Interactive Read-Aloud: Point out an interesting new word that illustrates the principle of this lesson in the books you read aloud. Examples are:

- ***Just One More*** by Michelle Koch
- ***Millions of Snowflakes*** by Mary Siddals

Shared Reading: In the poems you read with the children such as "These Elephants" or Six Little Ducks" (*Sing a Song of Poetry* contains many more selections), find and highlight (with highlighter tape or a masking card) plural nouns that are made by adding *s.*

Guided Reading: During word work, have the children make a few nouns with magnetic letters and add *s* to make them plural.

Interactive Writing: Call attention to the principle. Ask the children who are having difficulty with the principle to come up to the easel and write the plural ending for a simple noun.

Independent Writing: Draw attention to the principle while conferring with the children about their writing.

assess

- Notice whether the children are using conventional *s* plurals in their writing.

Expand the Learning

When the children are very familiar with the plural forms using *s,* remove the singular forms. Then have them sort the plurals by the ending sound (/s/ or /z/). This extension will help children understand that the *s* at the end can have either sound.

Connect with Home

Send home sheets containing the singular and plural forms of another set of simple nouns so that children can cut them apart and match them. (You can use the Word Card Template in *Teaching Resources.*)

3 Making Plurals: Adding es

Word Match

Consider Your Children

Use this lesson after the children are familiar with the concept of plural and have worked with plurals by adding *s.* They should also be skilled in hearing sounds in words and be able to hear the syllable breaks by saying and clapping words.

Working with English Language Learners

Be sure that English language learners have worked enough with simple plurals to understand the concept and are familiar with some good, easy examples. This lesson will expand their knowledge of plurals. Use pictures if necessary to illustrate the words, and work with a small group to be sure that the children can read and talk about the plurals they are making. Invite them to talk about what they notice about words.

You Need

From *Teaching Resources:*

- Word Cards, Plurals 2 and Plurals 1.
- Two-Way Sort Sheets.
- Two-Way Sort Cards (optional).

Understand the Principle

Children need to understand that there are different processes for making nouns plural. They can improve their spelling by saying the word and making a connection between the sound of the ending and the spelling.

Explain the Principle

“Plural means more than one.”

“Add *es* to words that end with *x, ch, sh, s, ss, teh,* or *zz* to make them plural.”

“The *s* at the end sounds like /z/.”

plan

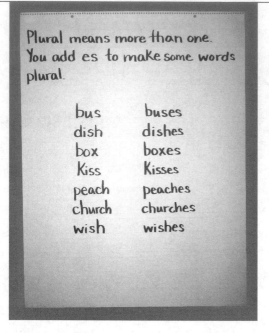

Plural means more than one.
You add es to make some words plural.

bus	buses
dish	dishes
box	boxes
Kiss	Kisses
peach	peaches
church	churches
wish	wishes

Explain the Principle

"Plural means more than one."

"Add *es* to words that end with *x, ch, sh, s, ss, teh,* or *zz* to make them plural."

"The *s* at the end sounds like /z/."

① Tell the children they are going to learn more about words that are plural.

② Begin by reviewing a few of the plurals you made by adding *s* (see Lesson WS 2).

③ Then have the children orally suggest plurals for *bus*. Suggested language: "You know that for most words you add *s* to make it more than one. Today we are going to look at some words that are different. I'll say the word for one thing, and you try to say the word for more than one—one bus." Write *bus* on the chart. Children respond.

④ Suggested language: "That's right—two buses. Now, I am going to write *buses* and you think about what I am adding. Here is another one—*dish*." Write *dish*.

⑤ The children orally produce the plural, *dishes*. Write it on the chart and then ask them to tell you what you are adding to make more than one.

⑥ The children will notice that you have added *es*. Suggested language: "What about the word *box*?" Write *box*. "What do you think I need to add to *box* to make it more than one?" Children may be able to predict *es*.

⑦ Suggested language: "You can hear the *es* at the end of these words. Let's read them." Guide the children to read the words one at a time and listen for the *es* at the end of the words. Some children may observe that it sounds like a *z*.

⑧ Suggested language: "You can hear the parts of these words too. Clap *bus*." Children respond by saying and clapping *bus*. "How many parts does it have?" Children respond by saying one. "Now say and clap *buses*."

9. The children will notice that the plural words have two parts that you can hear.

10. Continue writing singular words on the chart and asking children to say and predict the spelling of the plurals.

11. Ask the children what they have noticed about the words. You may demonstrate, or children may make comments like these, which indicate they are analyzing words and thinking about the principle:

    "You add *es* to some words to make more than one."

    "All of them sound like *z* at the end."

    "All of them have two parts."

12. Explain to the children that they will be adding the *es* words to the singular and plural words they are matching.

read
match
write

- The children will have matched plural forms of nouns that add *s*. Add the *es* singular/plural word cards and mix up the pile. Have the children match singular and plural forms. Then have them choose five singular/plural sets to write on a Two-Way Sort Sheet.

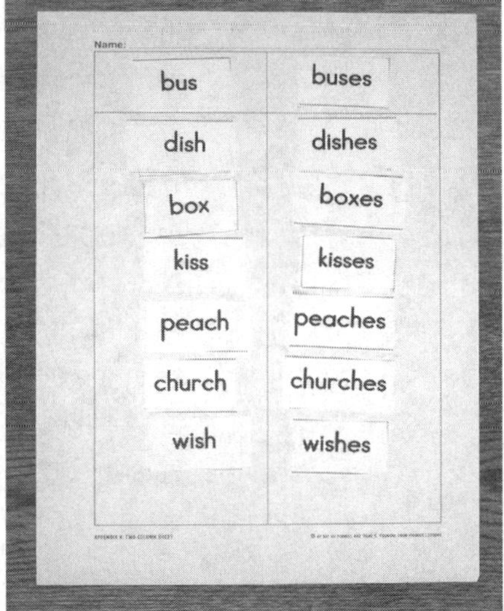

Ask the children to share what they noticed about plurals. Place two examples of plurals with *es* on the word wall.

Link

Interactive Read-Aloud: Read aloud texts with plurals. After reading the text, have the children notice a few plural words to which an *s* or *es* was added to make the plural. Examples are:

- ***One Moose, Twenty Mice*** by Clare Beaton
- ***Toby Counts His Marbles*** by Cyndy Szekeres

Shared Reading: After the children have read familiar poems and songs such as "Papa's Glasses" or "Five Little Sparrows" (see *Sing a Song of Poetry*), have them use a masking card or highlighter tape to locate plural nouns that are made by adding *s* or *es*. (*Sing a Song of Poetry* contains many selections.)

Guided Reading: During word work, make the noun with magnetic letters and then make it again as a plural. Work with several examples on a magnetic board or on the table.

Interactive Writing: Call attention to the principle of adding *es* to a word to make it plural. Ask children who are having difficulty with the principle to come up to the easel and write the plural ending for a simple noun. Have the children say and clap the word to determine the number of syllables. Have them say the word to listen for the *es* sound.

Independent Writing: Draw attention to the principle while conferring with the children as they attempt to write plural words that are formed with *es*.

assess

- Notice whether the children are using conventional plural forms for nouns in their writing.
- Give the children seven or eight singular nouns (with both *s* and *es* words in the group) and have them write the plurals after saying them.

Expand the Learning

When the children are very familiar with *s* and *es* plurals, remove the singular forms. Then have them sort the plurals by the ending sound (/s/ or /z/). This extension will help the children understand that the *s* and *es* at the end can have different sounds.

After the children are familiar with the *es* plurals, give them a list of words that have *sh, ch, x,* and *z* endings. Have children highlight the ending letters that signal the word will have an *es* in its plural form.

Connect with Home

Send home sheets containing the singular and plural forms of another set of simple nouns that you add *es* to make plural. Have children cut them apart and match them.

4 Learning about Contractions: I'm

Poems and Songs

Consider Your Children

Use this lesson after your children have encountered contractions in reading and interactive writing. You may have explained the principle informally as you worked with contractions in context. Probably the children will already know how to read the word *I'm,* but this time you will be using it to explain the principle. If your children are familiar with the idea of contractions in general, you may want to include several more in this lesson.

Working with English Language Learners

For some English language learners, contractions may be a new word structure. If you know parallels in their first language, use them in your explanation. If not, work more with simple sentences to help them understand the way contractions work. For example: *I am a boy. I'm a boy. I am running. I'm running.* Use words and concepts they understand.

You Need

- Magnetic letters.
- Photocopies of "Going to the Fair," "I'm a Little Teapot," or a similar rhyme (*Sing a Song of Poetry* contains many selections).
- Highlighter tape or highlighter pens.

Understand the Principle

Children use contractions in their oral language and often attempt to use them in their writing. They will also encounter contractions in many beginning reading books. Understanding how contractions are formed will help children understand their meanings and promote correct and conventional use of contractions.

Explain the Principle

“A contraction is one word made from two words. A letter or letters are left out and an apostrophe is put in.”

“A contraction is a short form of the two words.”

“To make a contraction, put two words together and leave out a letter or letters. Write an apostrophe where letter(s) are left out. Here is a contraction made with *am: I + am = I'm.*”

plan

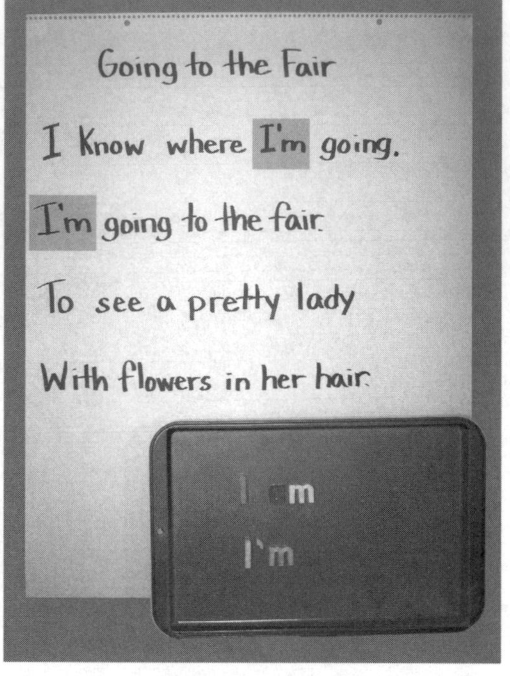

Going to the Fair
I Know where I'm going.
I'm going to the fair.
To see a pretty lady
With flowers in her hair.
I'm

Explain the Principle

" A contraction is one word made from two words. A letter or letters are left out and an apostrophe is put in. "

" A contraction is a short form of the two words. "

" To make a contraction, put two words together and leave out a letter or letters. Write an apostrophe where letter(s) are left out. Here is a contraction made with *am: I + am = I'm.* "

① Tell the children they are going to learn about two words that are sometimes put together.

② Begin by stating the principle. Suggested language: "Some of you have noticed contractions when we read together. A contraction is a word that is made by putting two words together. Let's read these two words." Make *I* and *am* in magnetic letters on a vertical magnetic surface. Be sure all the children can see the letters clearly. Have the children read the words.

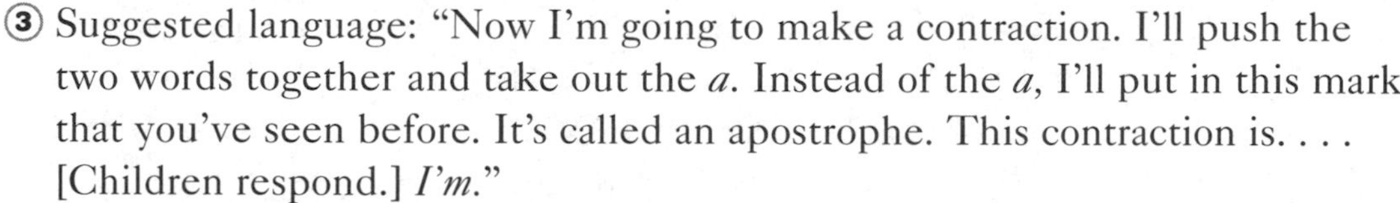

③ Suggested language: "Now I'm going to make a contraction. I'll push the two words together and take out the *a*. Instead of the *a*, I'll put in this mark that you've seen before. It's called an apostrophe. This contraction is. . . . [Children respond.] *I'm*."

④ Using your hands to move the letters, demonstrate going back to *I am* and then making the contraction several times. Describe the action as you do it. Demonstrate and have the children say the word *apostrophe*.

⑤ Suggested language: "Now let's read 'Going to the Fair' together." Read this simple rhyme once or twice. "Do you see a contraction in this poem?"

⑥ Have the children come up to the chart (or pocket chart) and highlight the contraction *I'm*.

⑦ Have the children think about whether they could substitute *I am* in the poem. It might sound a little different, but it would still make sense.

⑧ Tell the children they will be finding the word *I'm* in poems that you have read together.

⑨ Repeat the process with a few other familiar poems and songs.

⑩ Place *I'm* on the word wall.

apply

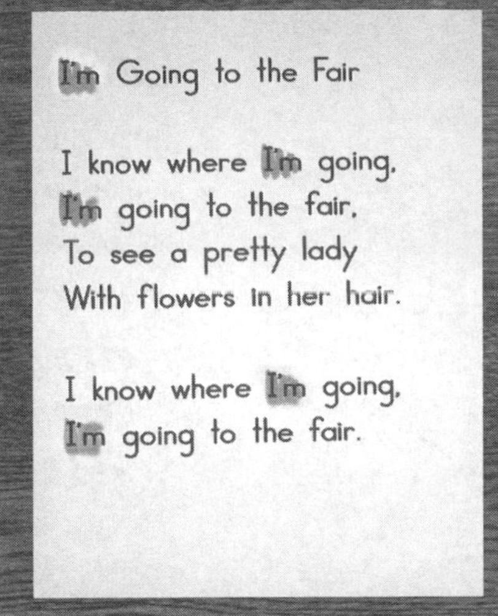
I'm Going to the Fair
I know where I'm going,
I'm going to the fair,
To see a pretty lady
With flowers in her hair.
I know where I'm going,
I'm going to the fair.

highlight
illustrate
glue

- Provide photocopies of poems that you have used in shared reading that have the word *I'm* in them—"Going to the Fair" or "I'm a Little Teapot," for example. Have the children read the poem, highlight *I'm*, and illustrate the poem.
- If the children have personal poetry anthologies, they can glue in the poems and then illustrate them.

share

Have the children read one of the poems again and find the contractions.

Have several children come to the easel and make the contraction by removing *a* and inserting the apostrophe.

Link

Interactive Read-Aloud: Point out the contraction *I'm* when you encounter it in books such as

- ***No Matter What*** by Debi Gliori
- ***The Big Wide-Mouthed Frog*** by Ana Larranaga

Shared Reading: Have the children use a masking card or highlighter tape to locate *I'm* contractions in familiar poems such as "Baby Bumblebee" or "Willy Boy, Willy Boy" (see *Sing a Song of Poetry*) contains many examples.

Guided Reading: During word work, have children who have difficulty understanding the concept make a few simple contractions with magnetic letters.

Interactive Writing: When composing a text, ask the children to decide whether to use *I am* or *I'm.* When the word *I'm* is needed, remind the children that it is a contraction of *I am.*

Independent Writing: Point out contractions when conferring with the children.

assess

- Select two or three contractions and have the children write them.
- Notice whether the children can locate contractions and state the two words that make up the contraction.
- Notice whether they are confusing possessives with contractions.

Expand the Learning

Continue to help children notice contractions during shared reading of new poems and songs. (*Sing a Song of Poetry* contains many examples.)

Once the children understand the concept of contractions, introduce many new ones.

Connect with Home

Send home photocopies of uncopyrighted rhymes that include contractions for children to read with their families.

5 Adding s and ing

Building Words

Consider Your Children

Use this lesson when the children have begun to encounter and notice the endings *s* and *ing* in the simple texts they are reading in shared, independent, and guided reading. They probably are already using their sense of language syntax to check whether their reading sounds right, and they may also have noticed the added letters. This lesson will help them generalize their knowledge and think about language structure in relation to the visual elements.

Working with English Language Learners

Word endings are very challenging to English language learners because often the syntax has not been internalized. They need to encounter words with *ing* and *s* endings many times in reading and writing, be familiar with a number of examples, and implicitly know the correct syntax in simple sentences. If necessary, construct more sentences, using words and concepts the children understand, to give them more practice. Demonstrate saying the words slowly, slightly segmenting the ending to call attention to it. English language learners may find it difficult to determine when sentences do not "sound right," so you may want to work more on that part of the lesson or eliminate it until they grow in experience.

You Need

- Copies of sample sentences.

Understand the Principle

Understanding how language works helps children read more efficiently and write more coherently. Knowing that sometimes you add *s* or *ing* to a word to make it "agree" or "sound right" in a sentence will help children notice and use these endings to decode and spell words.

Explain the Principle

"Add *s* to the end of a word to make it sound right in a sentence."

"Add *ing* to a base word to show you are doing something now."

plan

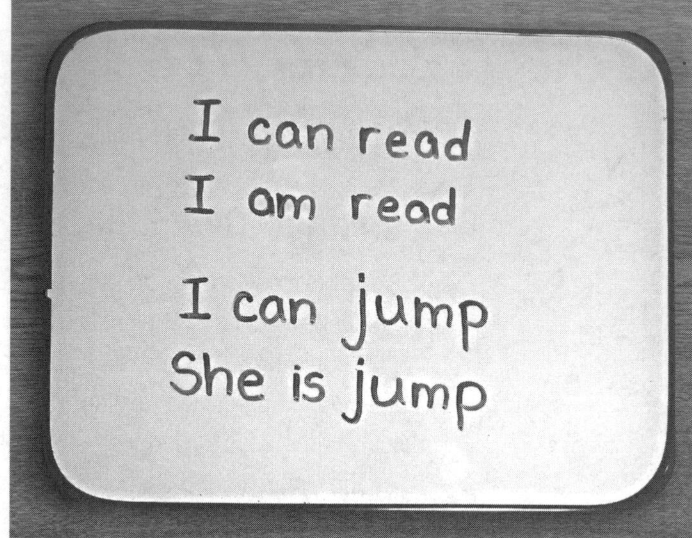

Explain the Principle

“ **Add *s* to the end of a word to make it sound right in a sentence.** ”

“ **Add *ing* to a base word to show you are doing something now.** ”

① Tell children they will be learning more about making words.

② Write the four sentences in the illustration on the chalkboard or whiteboard.

③ Point to and have the children read the first two lines with you.

④ Ask them what they notice. They will tell you the second one doesn't sound right.

⑤ Ask what you should do. When they tell you to add *ing,* write it on the end of the word.

⑥ Repeat with the second pair of sentences.

⑦ Repeat using instances that require the *s* ending:

I skate

She skate

We ride

He ride

⑧ When the children notice that the second sentence in each pair doesn't sound right, add an *s* to *skate* and *ride.*

⑨ Suggested language: "So you can add *s* or *ing* to words to make them sound right in a sentence. You add *ing* to show you are doing something now. You add *s* to show someone else is doing something."

⑩ Some children may have difficulty with this task because their own dialects vary from these conventions or because they have an immature understanding of word structure. Provide many demonstrations and also be sure children have many opportunities to hear and notice these structures in read-aloud and shared reading sessions.

I cook pizza.
She cook s pizza.
He is cooking pizza.

I send my letters.
He send s his letters.
We are sending our letters.

We play games.
She play s games.
They are playing games.

I read a book.
He is reading a book.
We are reading a book.

I sing a song.
She sing s a song.
They are singing a song.

apply

read
cut
glue
add *s* or *ing*
read

- Give the children a sheet containing the five sets of sentences in sentence strips 1 (see *Teaching Resources*, Materials & Routines). Have them read the groups of sentences, cut them into words, and then glue them onto a piece of paper in the correct order, leaving space to add *s* or *ing* in their own handwriting.
- When they finish, have them read the sentences to a partner.

Invite the children to share one sentence each.

Link

Interactive Read-Aloud: Point out *s* and *ing* endings in verbs when you encounter them in books such as:

- ***One Sunday Morning*** by Yumi Heo
- ***Iron Horses*** by Verla Kay

Shared Reading: Choose poems and songs with verbs that have *s* and *ing* endings such as "Five Little Leaves," "Choo-choo Train," or "Five Enormous Dinosaurs" (see *Sing a Song of Poetry*). After enjoying the text, have the children use highlighter tape or a highlighter marker to find these endings.

Guided Reading: During word work, have the children make some verbs, add *s* or *ing,* and read them.

Interactive Writing: Reinforce adding endings to verbs as they come up in stories you write together.

Independent Writing: Point out places writers have used the *s* and *ing* endings on verbs.

assess

- Observe the children as they read and write words with endings. Model what sounds right and looks right as needed.

Expand the Learning

Repeat the lesson with other examples that include verbs with *e* or with a single short vowel before the consonant at the end. Show the children how to take away the *e* *(take–taking)* and double the consonant *(run–running)* before adding *ing.*

Repeat the lesson with sentences that include words to which *d* or *ed* is added (*like–liked* and *play–played,* for example).

Connect with Home

Have children take home their sentences to read to family members.

6 Adding ed

Word Sort

Consider Your Children

Use this lesson after the children have worked with the principle of adding *ed* to base verbs to indicate past tense. They may have noticed that sometimes the *ed* sounds like /t/, and/or they may have mispronounced words such as *lik-ed* when reading them (even though they would not do so when speaking). If your children are not familiar with the *ed* ending, you may want to first work with just one sound and add the rest over a period of several days.

Working with English Language Learners

Inflectional endings are difficult when you are learning another language. Give your English language learners a great deal of experience hearing written language read aloud, participating in shared reading and interactive writing, and reading very simple stories for themselves before you expect them to work with and understand the range of *ed* endings. When they can use words with *ed* endings in sentences and spell them when writing, this lesson will help them recognize *ed* as a word ending rather than just a letter and sound added to a word.

You Need

- Pocket chart.

From *Teaching Resources:*

- Word Cards, -*ed* Endings.
- Three-Way Sort Sheets.

Understand the Principle

Learning how words work includes recognizing and using inflectional endings that add meaning. The inflectional ending *ed* changes the tense of verbs; that is, it indicates that the actions were performed previously. Many stories young children read are written in past tense, so they may have begun to recognize words that have the *ed* ending and many also know some verbs with irregular conjugations (*ran, swam,* for example). They will gain power over words when they learn how the regular past tense works (adding *ed* to the base word).

Explain the Principle

“When you add *ed* to a word, it sometimes sounds like /d/ *(played).*”

“When you add *ed* to a word, it sometimes sounds like /ed/ *(melted).*”

“When you add *ed* to a word, it sometimes sounds like /t/ *(walked).*”

“Sometimes you change the *y* to *i* and add *ed* and the ending sounds like /d/ *(cry–cried).*”

plan

Explain the Principle

"When you add *ed* to a word, it sometimes sounds like /d/ *(played).*"

"When you add *ed* to a word, it sometimes sounds like /ed/ *(melted).*"

"When you add *ed* to a word, it sometimes sounds like /t/ *(walked).*"

"Sometimes you change the *y* to *i* and add *ed* and the ending sounds like /d/ *(cry–cried).*"

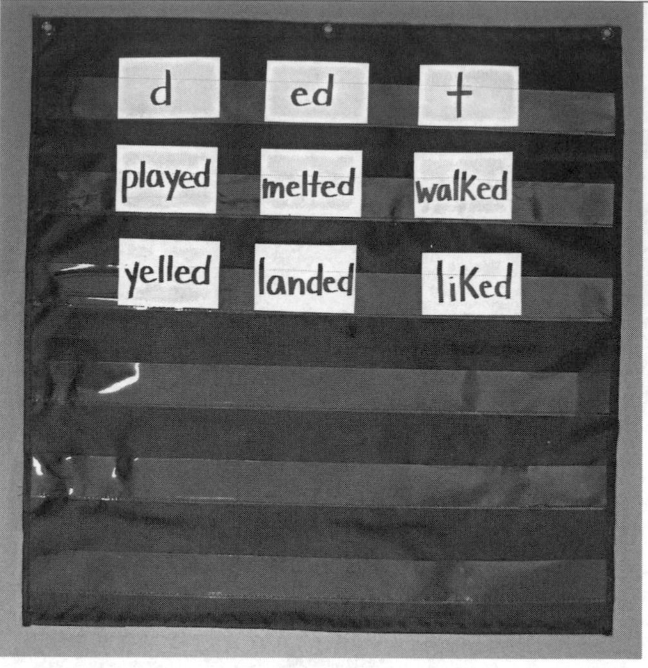

① Tell the children you are going to show them something interesting about words that end in *ed*.

② Place the words *played, melted,* and *walked* in the pocket chart and read each one to the class. Suggested language:

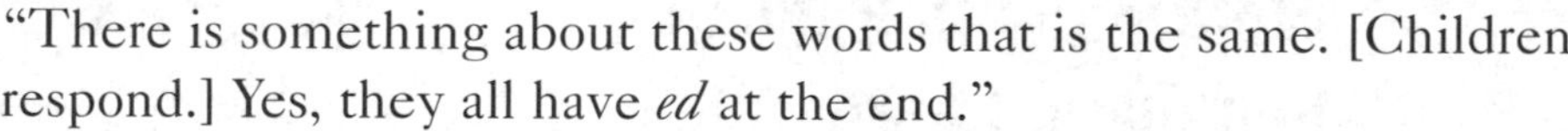
"There is something about these words that is the same. [Children respond.] Yes, they all have *ed* at the end."

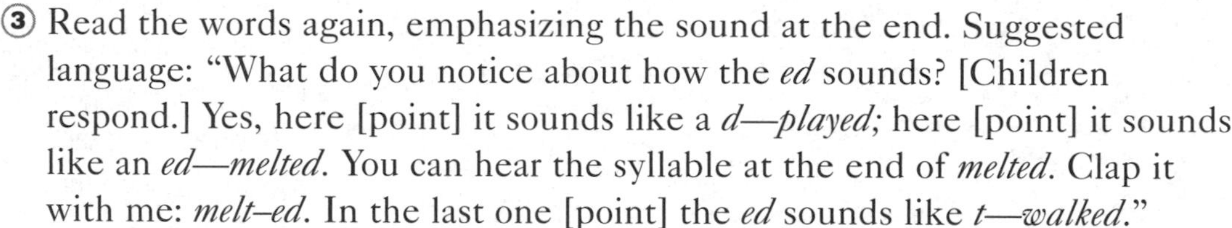
③ Read the words again, emphasizing the sound at the end. Suggested language: "What do you notice about how the *ed* sounds? [Children respond.] Yes, here [point] it sounds like a *d—played;* here [point] it sounds like an *ed—melted.* You can hear the syllable at the end of *melted.* Clap it with me: *melt–ed.* In the last one [point] the *ed* sounds like *t—walked.*"

④ "I'm going to show you some more words, and you tell me where to put them." Show *yelled, landed,* and *liked* and place them on the chart in the appropriate column.

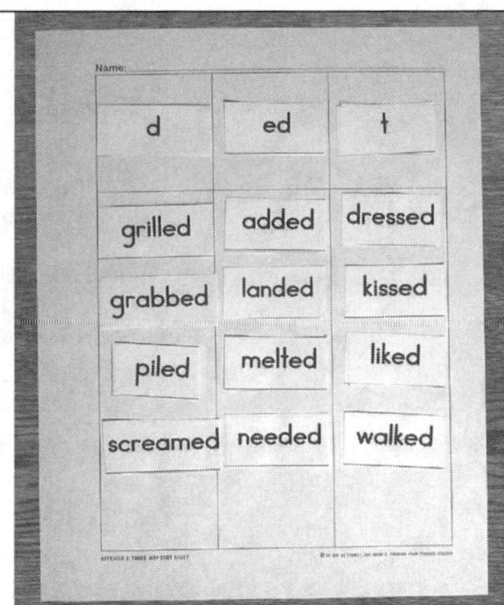

say
sort
write

- Have the children, in pairs, paste *d*, *ed*, and *t* at the top of a Three-Way Sort Sheet.
- Give them the *-ed* endings word cards and ask them to take turns saying each word and placing it in a column until they have placed all the words with the *d* sound, the *ed* sound, and the *t* sound together.

Have the children read one word and tell the category it belongs in.

Link

Interactive Read-Aloud: Point out the category of words ending with *ed* when you encounter them in books, such as

- ***The Cat That Walked By*** by Rudyard Kipling
- ***The Day It Rained Hearts*** by Felicia Bond

Shared Reading: Choose poems and songs with words that have *ed* endings such as "The Elephant Who Jumped a Fence" or "On Top of Spaghetti" (see *Sing a Song of Poetry*). After enjoying the text, have the children use highlighter tape or a highlighter marker to find *ed* endings.

Guided Reading: During word work, have the children make some words, add *ed,* and read them.

Interactive Writing: Reinforce adding *ed* to words as they come up in stories you write together.

Independent Writing: Point out places writers have used *ed* endings.

assess

- Place some sentences on a chart or in the pocket chart and have the children select the present tense or past tense of the verb to put in the empty space. Examples:

  "Sarah said she ______ ice cream. I ______ ice cream, too." *[likes, like]*

  "I like to _____ in puddles. Yesterday I _____ and _____." *[jump, jumped]*

  "We _____ football yesterday. We like to _____ football." *[played, play]*

  "I like to ____ pictures. Yesterday I _______ a pretty picture." *[paint, painted]*

- As an alternative, use the sentences above as a pencil-and-paper test. Have the children write the appropriate words in the blanks.
- Give the children a sheet of paper folded in three columns with these key words: *liked, played, painted.* Give them the following words on a photocopied sheet that they can cut apart: *walked, melted, jumped, yelled, slipped, needed, watched, matched.* Go over the words and pronounce them before the children begin. Have them cut the words apart and glue them under the key words. This will be a record of the extent to which the children realize the three different ways the *ed* ending can be pronounced.

Expand the Learning

Show the children how, with words like *cry* and *carry*, which end in a consonant and *y,* you change the *y* to an *i* before the *ed* is added. Show them it sounds like *d.*

Repeat the lesson with a greater variety of words to which *ed* can be added.

Connect with Home

Have children take the sort sheet home and read it to family members. Send home a new sheet of *ed* words for them to sort.

Learning about Contractions with is and will

Contraction Concentration

Consider Your Children

Use this lesson after your children have encountered contractions in reading and interactive writing and are familiar with the concept but still learning how it works. The children will probably already know how to read many of the words in this lesson, so they can use them to explore the principle.

Working with English Language Learners

It will take many demonstrations for English language learners to understand the concept of contractions and how to make and unmake them. Point out contractions as you encounter them in reading and writing so that they will build familiarity with them. In this lesson the children will be separating simple contractions into the two words that make them up. Work with a small group of English language learners who are having difficulty with the concept. It may help to have them build words with magnetic letters and physically put them together, removing letters.

You Need

- Chart, easel, and markers.

From *Teaching Resources:*

- Directions for Concentration.
- Concentration Cards made from Contraction Word Cards and Deck Card Template. Suggested words: *I'm, I am; she's, she is; he's, he is; that's, that is; here's, here is; I'll, I will; he'll, he will; she'll, she will; they'll, they will.*

Understand the Principle

Knowing how contractions are constructed will help children understand what these words mean when they read them and spell them conventionally when they write them.

Explain the Principle

“To make a contraction, you put two words together and leave out a letter or letters. Write an apostrophe where the letter(s) are left out.”

plan

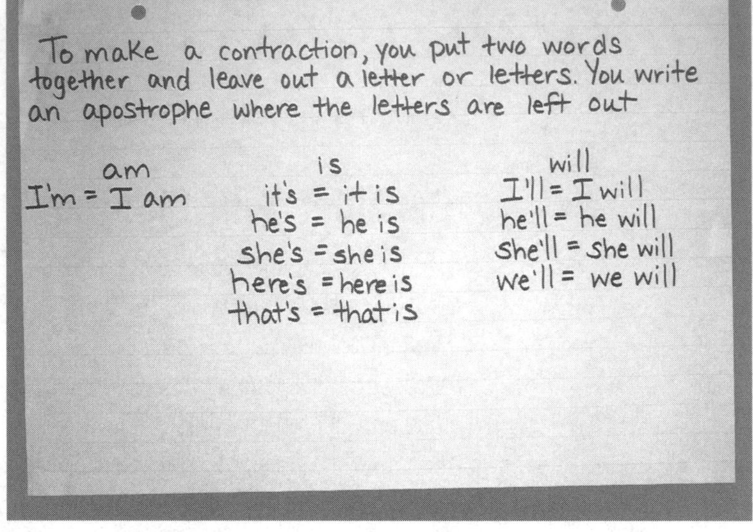

teach

Explain the Principle

“To make a contraction, you put two words together and leave out a letter or letters. Write an apostrophe where the letter(s) are left out.”

① Tell children you're going to teach them about contractions.

② Start with a chart on which you have written the principle. Leave the rest of the chart blank.

③ Begin by stating the principle. Suggested language: “You know that to make a contraction, you put two words together and leave out a letter. You write an apostrophe instead of the letter you leave out.”

④ Write *I'm* on the chart in column 1 and ask the children to read it and tell you the two words that have been put together. Suggested language: “*I* and *am* have been put together. What letter is left out? [Children respond.] And we have put an apostrophe in place of the *a*. [Write an equal sign and *I am* after *I'm*.] This contraction is made with the word *am*, so I'm going to write *am* at the top.”

⑤ Write *it's* in the second column. Suggested language: “This contraction is *it's*. You could say, ‘It's raining.’ What are the two words that are in *it's*? [Children respond.] You're right. You could say, ‘It is raining,’ or ‘It's raining.’ What letter is left out?” Children respond. Write *it is* after an equal sign in the column.

⑥ “I'll write *is* at the top of the second column, because this contraction is made with *is*. Can you think of any more contractions with *is*?”

⑦ Have the children suggest examples, and perhaps add some yourself. Each time, write the contraction and ask the children to tell you the two words that have been put together and the letter or letters that have been left out.

⑧ If a child offers a contraction that does not have *is*, you can put it in an "other" box off to the side, saying, "Yes, that is a contraction. I'm going to write it here so we will remember it later."

⑨ If a child offers a possessive, explain that when you say something belongs to someone, it is not a contraction but you do use an apostrophe. Write it in a "possessives" box to be used later. You are recognizing their good thinking and giving them feedback.

⑩ Go to the third column and repeat the process with words that use *will*, again writing the contraction and asking the children to name the two words and the missing letter.

⑪ Summarize by repeating the principle and saying that they will be adding different kinds of contractions later.

⑫ Have children play Contraction Concentration by matching two-word phrases with the appropriate contraction.

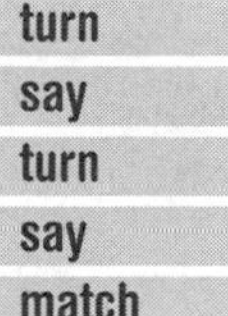

▸ Have the children work with a partner to play Contraction Concentration in groups of two or three.

Have the children share some of the contractions they learned from the game. They can state the contraction and the two words that were put together.

Link

Interactive Read-Aloud: Children will hear and add to their vocabulary a great variety of contractions in books, such as

- ***Moondogs*** by Daniel Kirk
- ***Let's Go Visiting*** by Sue Williams

Shared Reading: Locate and highlight contractions in rhymes such as "What's Your Name" or "Pumpkin Orange" (*Sing a Song of Poetry* contains many other examples.)

Guided Reading: During word work, have the children who have difficulty understanding the concept make three or four contractions with magnetic letters.

Interactive Writing: When composing a text, ask the children to decide whether to use two words or a contraction. Demonstrate (or help the children figure out) how to write contractions.

Independent Writing: Point out contractions when conferring with the children.

assess

- Dictate four or five contractions for the children to write.
- Notice whether the children can locate contractions and state the two words that make up the contraction.
- Notice whether the children are confusing possessives with contractions.

Expand the Learning

Continue to help the children notice contractions during shared reading.

Create a Contraction Lotto game (see *Teaching Resources* for Lotto directions).

Connect with Home

Send home word card sheets (see *Teaching Resources,* Word Card Template) with the words *I'm, I am; she's, she is; he's, he is; that's, that is; here's, here is; there's, there is; where's, where is; I'll, I will; he'll, he will; she'll, she will; they'll, they will* so children can cut them apart and match the two-word phrases with the contractions.

8 Learning about Contractions *with* are *and* not

Contraction Concentration

Consider Your Children

Use this lesson after the children have encountered easy contractions in reading and interactive writing such as those with *am, is,* and *will* (see Lesson WS 7). They should be familiar with the concept and know many contractions, although they will still be learning more about them. The children will probably already know how to read many of the words in this lesson, so they can use them to explore the principle.

Working with English Language Learners

This lesson continues the work with simple contractions so that English language learners can expand their vocabularies. Consider making a cumulative chart so that the set of contractions they know and have worked with will be constantly available. Use contractions in simple sentences that the children can understand and repeat, for example: "You are running. You're running." You may want to write these sentences on a chart and have a small group of English language learners read them and circle or highlight the contractions.

You Need

- Chart, easel, and markers.

From *Teaching Resources:*

- Directions for Concentration.
- Concentration Cards made from Contraction Word Cards and Deck Card Template. Use the cards from Lesson WS 7 and add the following: *aren't, are not; can't, can not; couldn't, could not; didn't, did not; doesn't, does not; don't, do not; isn't, is not; shouldn't, should not.*

Understand the Principle

Knowing how contractions are constructed will help children understand what these words mean when they read them and spell them conventionally when they write them.

Explain the Principle

" To make a contraction, you put two words together and leave out a letter or letters. Write an apostrophe where the letter(s) are left out. "

plan

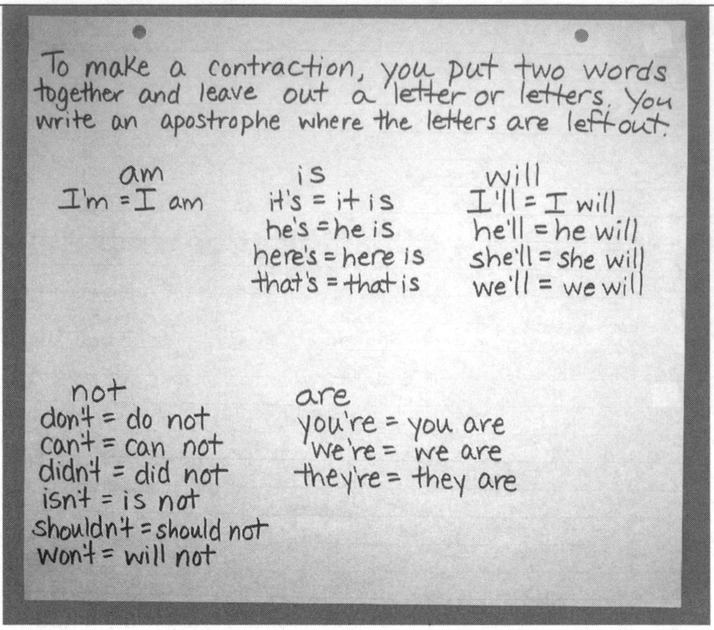

teach

Explain the Principle

“To make a contraction, you put two words together and leave out a letter or letters. Write an apostrophe where the letter(s) are left out.”

① Mention to the children that today they will learn more about contractions.

② Start with a chart on which you have written the principle. The first three columns have been completed in the previous lesson (Lesson WS 7).

③ Begin by stating the principle. Suggested language: “You know that to make a contraction, you put two words together and leave out a letter. You write an apostrophe instead of the letter you leave out.”

④ Invite the children to identify some of the contractions on the chart and say the two words in them. Review as much as necessary, but don’t spend too much time doing so.

⑤ Suggested language: “Today we are going to look at other contractions. [Use the box of “other” contractions when possible.] Previously someone suggested the contraction *don’t.* [Write *don’t* in column 4.] What two words have been put together to make *don’t*? [Children respond.]”

⑥ “That’s right, *do* and *not.* [Write *do not.*] What letter is missing? [Children respond.]”

⑦ Ask the children to generate more examples of contractions that use *not.* For some contractions, more than one letter is left out. In *can’t,* you put the apostrophe in place of the two letters *n* and *o.*

⑧ Show that *won’t* equals *will not* and ask the children what they notice. They can discuss how this contraction is different from the others in this category.

⑨ Repeat the process with examples of contractions that use *are.* Ask the children what they notice about this contraction.

⑩ Summarize by repeating the principle. Have the children play Contraction Concentration by matching two-word phrases with the appropriate contraction.

turn
say
turn
say
match

▸ Have the children play Contraction Concentration with a partner.

Have the children share some of the contractions they learned from the game. They can state the contraction and the two words that were put together.

Link

Interactive Read-Aloud: Children will hear and add to their vocabularies a great variety of contractions in books, such as

- ***Pierre*** by Maurice Sendak
- ***Won't You Come and Play*** by Mary Lee Donovan

Shared Reading: Locate and highlight contractions in poems and chants such as "Baby Rhinoceros," "Grand Old Duke of York," or "I Would If I Could." (*Sing a Song of Poetry* contains many other selections.)

Guided Reading: During word work, have the children who have difficulty understanding the concept make a few simple contractions with magnetic letters.

Interactive Writing: When composing a text, ask the children to decide whether to use two words or a contraction. Demonstrate (or help the children figure out) how to write contractions.

Independent Writing: Point out contractions when conferring with the children.

assess

- Notice whether the children can read the contractions with *am, is, will, are, not*.
- Notice whether the children can locate contractions and state the two words that make up the contraction.
- Notice whether the children are confusing possessives with contractions.

Expand the Learning

Continue to help the children notice contractions during shared reading.

Create a Contraction Lotto game (see *Teaching Resources* for Lotto directions).

Connect with Home

Photocopy word card sheets (see *Teaching Resources,* Word Card Template) with the words *aren't, can't, couldn't, didn't, doesn't, don't, isn't, shouldn't,* and the appropriate two-word phrases, for children to take home, cut apart, and match with the appropriate two-word phrases.

9 Summarizing Contractions

Follow the Path

Consider Your Children

Use this lesson after the children have encountered contractions in reading and interactive writing, have learned several categories of contractions, and understand the principle. This lesson summarizes the learning and helps the children generalize their knowledge of contractions.

Working with English Language Learners

Once English language learners understand the idea of contractions and are familiar with many examples and their component words, they will be able to use the examples they know to solve new contractions or to make contractions in writing. If English language learners do not understand the meaning of contractions, use the contrasting forms in simple sentences. Making a summary chart and stating the principle will also help them recognize new contractions and solve them.

You Need

- Chart, easel, and markers.
- Follow the Path Game Boards.

From *Teaching Resources:*

- Directions for Follow the Path.
- Contraction Word Cards.

Understand the Principle

Knowing how contractions are constructed will help children understand what these words mean when they read them and spell them conventionally when they write them. As children build their knowledge of contractions, they will create mental categories that help them understand them.

Explain the Principle

" To make a contraction, you put two words together and leave out a letter or letters. Write an apostrophe where the letter(s) are left out. "

teach

Explain the Principle

"To make a contraction, you put two words together and leave out a letter or letters. Write an apostrophe where the letter(s) are left out."

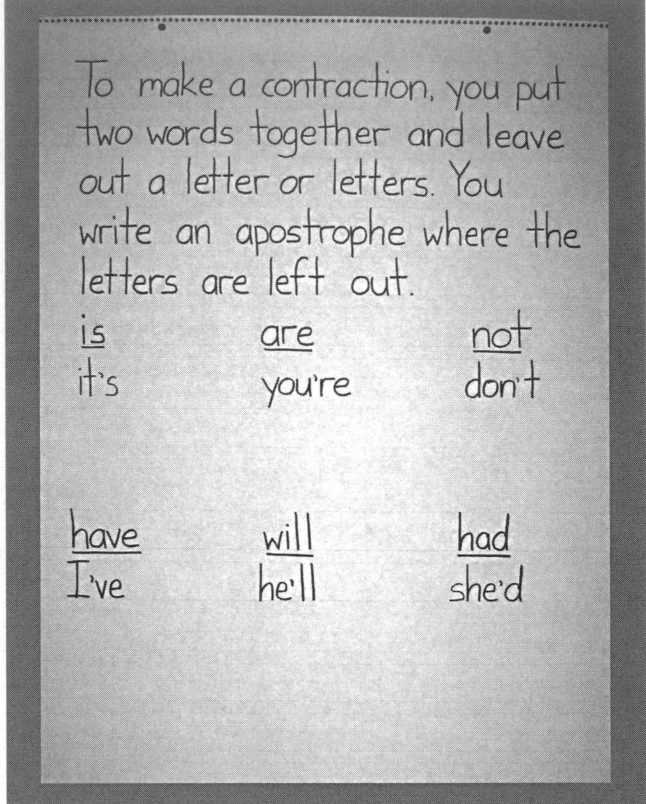
To make a contraction, you put two words together and leave out a letter or letters. You write an apostrophe where the letters are left out.
is
it's
are
you're
not
don't
have
I've
will
he'll
had
she'd

1. Tell children you'll be helping them learn how to think about many different contractions.
2. Start with a chart on which you have written the principle, the words *is, are, not, have, will,* and *had* in columns, and one example of a contraction for each word. Leave the bottom part of each column blank.
3. Begin by stating the principle. Suggested language: "You know that to make a contraction, you put two words together and leave out a letter or letters. You write an apostrophe where the letters are left out."
4. Invite the children to think of contractions in each category and then identify the two words that are contracted. Write the contraction and then the words as they produce them. At this point, the children will be able to produce examples quickly. You can also draw from the list of contractions that did not fit categories in previous lessons.
5. Suggested language: "Today we are going to put examples of all kinds of contractions on this chart. What contractions are made from *is* like *he's*?"
6. Ask the children to summarize what they have learned about contractions.
7. Ask the children to generate more examples of contractions that use *not.*
8. Show them how to play Contraction Follow the Path.

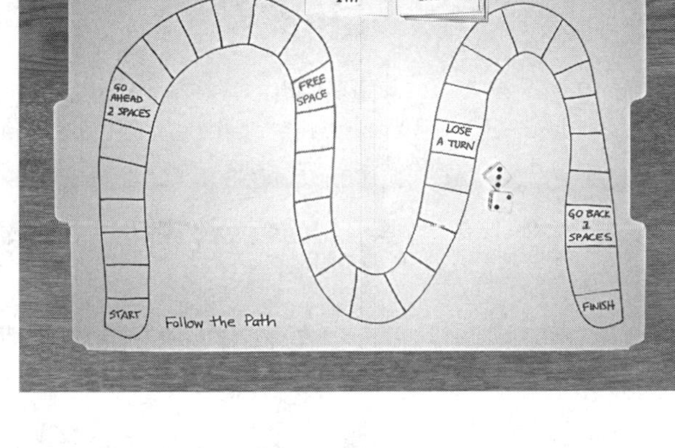

throw
take
read
say
move

▸ Have the children play Contraction Follow the Path with a partner or in groups of three. Cards have two-word phrases (for example, *is not*) or contractions (for example, *isn't*). Students take cards and read the word(s). If the word is a contraction, they say the two words within it. If the card has two words, they say the contraction.

Have children share some of the contractions they learned from the game. They can state the contraction and the two words that were put together.

Encourage the children to challenge themselves by finding more contractions. Place two or three examples of contractions on the word wall.

Link

Interactive Read-Aloud: Children will hear and add to their vocabularies a great variety of contractions in books, such as

- ***Dogs Don't Wear Sneakers*** by Laura Numeroff
- ***Chickens Aren't the Only Ones*** by Ruth Heller

Shared Reading: Locate and highlight contractions in rhymes and songs: "It's Raining, It's Pouring" *('s)*, "Shoo, Fly" *('t)*, "A-hunting We Will Go" *('ll)*; "The Pussycat and the Queen" *('ve)*, "If You're Happy and You Know It" *('re)*, "Fire, Fire, Cried Mrs. McGuire" *('d)*. (*Sing a Song of Poetry* contains many other appropriate selections.)

Guided Reading: After the lesson, have the children locate one or two contractions in the text. During word work, have the children who have difficulty understanding the concept make three or four contractions with magnetic letters.

Interactive Writing: When composing a text, ask the children to decide whether to use two words or a contraction. Use knowledge of contractions to demonstrate (or help the children figure out) how to write words.

Independent Writing: Point out contractions when conferring with the children.

assess

- Notice whether the children can read contractions and write them conventionally.
- Dictate four or five contractions and have the children write them.

Expand the Learning

Create a Contraction Lotto game (see *Teaching Resources* for Lotto directions).

Add words to Contraction Concentration: *aren't, can't, couldn't, didn't, doesn't, don't, isn't, shouldn't, mustn't* (see Lessons WS 7 and 8).

Connect with Home

Give the children a photocopy of a small ($8\frac{1}{2}$" by 11") Follow the Path Game Board and word cards (*Teaching Resources*, Word Card Template) so they can play the game and review all the contractions with family members.

10 Identifying Syllables in Words

Word Sort

Consider Your Children

Children can learn to clap syllables very early in their experiences with literacy. Provide enough practice so that they can quickly and easily identify the number of parts in words. Once they can identify the sounds of the parts, they will have a basis for connecting them to the word parts they see. Provide more examples for children who have difficulty seeing the parts and saying the syllables. Be sure you use words that the children know.

Working with English Language Learners

Once English language learners have internalized the concept of syllable breaks in words, you will want to teach them how to use this information to solve words. Use words that your English language learners know and provide more repetitions and discussion to help them understand word meanings. Unless they understand the words they are using, this lesson will be a meaningless exercise.

You Need

- Chart paper and markers.

From *Teaching Resources:*

- Three-Column Sheets.
- Syllable Word Cards.

Understanding the Principle

Knowing how to break words into syllables helps readers and writers take words apart in order to solve them. Once they have established the concept of syllables and can notice parts of words (such as onsets and rimes, consonant clusters, and word endings), they are better able to break longer words into parts. Spelling is supported because children can deal with one part of a word at a time. Realizing that every syllable has a vowel will help them spell more accurately.

Explain the Principle

“You can hear the syllables in words.”

“You can look at the syllables in a word to read it.”

plan

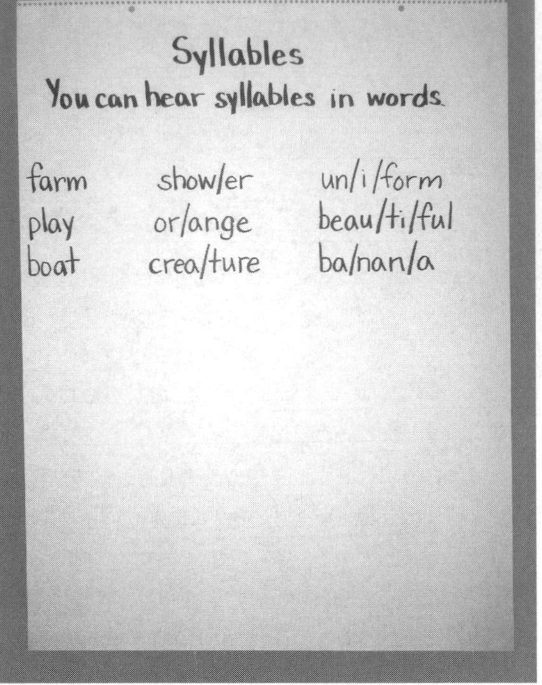

Explain the Principle

"You can hear the syllables in words."

"You can look at the syllables in a word to read it."

① Tell the children they are going to learn to think about the syllables they can hear in words.

② Draw the children's attention to syllables by having them say one-, two-, and three-syllable words. Suggested language: "Listen to the word *hat* [clap once]. Now, listen to the word *mother* [clap twice]. Now, listen to the word *museum* [clap three times]. When you say these words, you can hear the parts, or *syllables*."

③ Ask the children to clap these words: *farm, play, fruit, orange, ship, shower, absent, tomato, beautiful, boat, banana, creature, alphabet, uniform, bread, cricket, butterfly.*

④ Select a few words to write on the chart, making a slash between the syllables, and group them according to the number of parts you can hear.

⑤ Ask the children to discuss what they notice about the words (for example, there is a vowel in every syllable).

⑥ Take three blank cards. Invite the class to select one one-syllable, one two-syllable, and one three-syllable word to place on the word wall. Write the words and place them in the correct column.

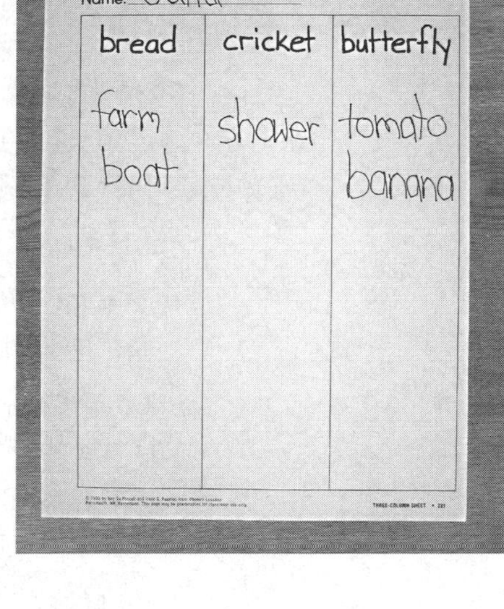

take
sort
clap
write

- Photocopy a three-column sheet that has the words *bread*, *cricket*, and *butterfly* at the top of the columns. Have ready an assortment of twenty or thirty word cards featuring words that have one, two, or three syllables. Place cards face down. The children take one card and say it aloud to themselves or to a partner. The partner claps the word. Each child writes (copies) the word under the appropriate column on the three-column sheet. The children continue until all the words are listed.
- Then the children add one word of their own to each column. (Do not expect conventional spelling for all the words.) The children take turns reading each list to a partner.

Have a few children share a few three-syllable words they added to their list.

Link

Interactive Read-Aloud: Read aloud word play books and have the children clap the syllables of some of the words. Examples are:

- ***The Beastly Feast*** by Bruce Goldstone
- ***Who Took the Cookies from the Cookie Jar?*** by Bonnie Lass

Shared Reading: Invite the children to find and mask one-, two-, and three-syllable words in poems or songs such as "Snowman" or "Two Cats of Kilkenny" (see *Sing a Song of Poetry*). Each time a child finds a word on the chart, have the class clap the parts.

Guided Reading: When the children have difficulty solving a word, show them how to break it apart. Following the lesson, use the whiteboard or magnetic letters to play with one-, two-, and three-syllable words. Write or make the word and ask the children to clap the parts; then draw a slash between the parts or create a space between the letters.

Interactive Writing: Invite the children to clap words before writing them, particularly two- and three-syllable words.

Independent Writing: Before writing a word, show a child how to "tap" the parts. This will help the writer hear the internal sounds.

assess

- Notice whether the children break words into syllables to solve them in reading or writing.

Expand the Learning

Repeat the lesson using the names of the children as the word examples.

Repeat the lesson with other words if needed. Include only two-, three-, and four-syllable words if the children are ready for the challenge.

Teach the lesson using picture cards (see *Teaching Resources*) instead of written words.

Connect with Home

Invite family members and children to play a syllable game. Each takes a turn giving three clues and telling how many parts the word has. For example: It is round. You cut it like a pie. You can put cheese and vegetables on it. The word has two parts. (Answer: *pizza*.)

Word-Solving Actions

Word-solving actions are the strategic moves readers and writers make when they use their knowledge of the language system to solve words. These strategies are "in-the-head" actions that are invisible, although we can infer them from some overt behavior. The principles listed in this section represent children's ability to *use* the principles in all previous sections of the Continuum.

All lessons related to the Continuum provide opportunities for children to apply principles in active ways, for example, through sorting, building, locating, reading, or writing. Lessons related to word-solving actions demonstrate to children how they can problem-solve by working on words in isolation or while reading or writing continuous text. The more children can integrate these strategies into their reading and writing systems, the more flexible they will become in solving words. The reader/writer may use knowledge of letter/sound relationships, for example, either to solve an unfamiliar word or to check that the reading is accurate. Rapid, automatic word solving is a basic component of fluency and important for comprehension because it frees children's attention to focus on the meaning and language of the text.

Connect to Assessment

See related WSA Assessment Tasks in the Assessment Guide in *Teaching Resources:*

- Sorting Names
- Sorting Words
- Using Known Words to Solve New Words
- Solving Unknown Words While Reading Text
- Reading Text—Monitoring, Checking, Word Solving
- Changing Letters to Make New Words

Develop Your Professional Understanding

See *Word Matters: Teaching Phonics and Spelling in the Reading/Writing Classroom* by G.S. Pinnell and I.C. Fountas. 1998. Portsmouth, New Hampshire: Heinemann.

Related pages: 46–47, 63–64, 90–93, 95, 222–228, 237–244.

1 Saying Words Slowly to Predict Letter Sequence

Words in Sentences

Consider Your Children

Use this lesson after the children know that there is a relationship between the letters and sounds in words and after they have learned some letter/sound relationships and a few high frequency words. They should also understand what *first* and *last* letters of a word are. They do not have to know every letter and its related sounds before beginning to use this information to help them read very simple texts. In this lesson, children learn how to relate sounds to letters and letters to sounds and also learn to check the print information with the meaning and language of a text. You can use any kind of enlarged text for this minilesson. Three examples are provided.

Working with English Language Learners

It is very useful for English language learners to say words slowly to hear sounds. This action will not only help them attend to English words and their pronunciation but will help them begin to identify the sequence of sounds they will be connecting with letters. Accept approximate pronunciations. These will improve as they have more experience. Avoid those words that require sounds that are hard for them to hear and say. You are trying to establish a principle rather than teaching a particular letter/sound relationship. Give them plenty of experience in shared reading of the poems that you use.

You Need

- Poem or other text on a chart for shared reading. (*Sing a Song of Poetry* contains many selections in addition to the rhyme provided on the next page.)
- Sentence sheets with blanks to be filled in. For example:
  Here is a __________ house.
  Here is a _________ tree.
  I see a ______ car.
  I see a _____ dog.
  Look at the ______ cat.

Understand the Principle

Children need to understand that connecting the sounds and letters in words is *useful information*. Letter/sound information will help them figure out what the word is so that they can read a story. Knowing about the letters and sounds in words will help them check their reading as they go to be sure it "looks right."

Explain the Principle

" You can use what you know about letters and sounds to check on your reading (and writing). "

plan

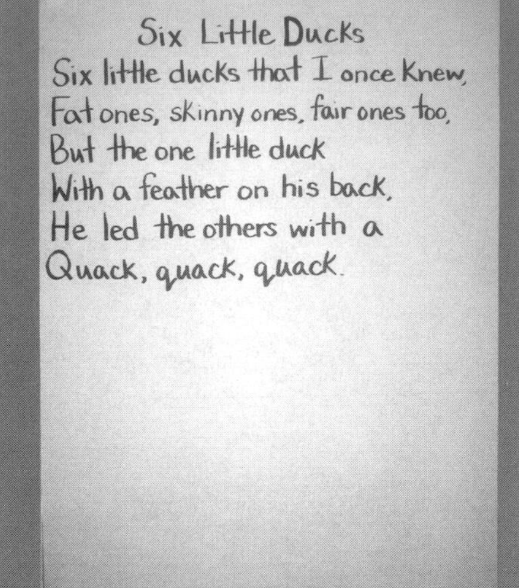

teach

Explain the Principle

"You can use what you know about letters and sounds to check on your reading (and writing)."

① Explain to the children they are going to learn how to think about the sounds in words and how these sounds help them read.

② Select a rhyme such as "Six Little Ducks," or choose a piece of interactive writing you've done. Children should be familiar with the text but not have memorized it.

③ Read the text in a shared way. Then select two or three words and place a stick-on note over them. With the children, read up to the word and have them predict it. Suggested language: "You think the next word is *led*. That might be right. I'm going to show you how to check to see if your reading is right. Say *led*. [Children respond.] Think about the first sound in *led*. What is it? [Children respond.] That's right. It's *l*. What letter will we see if that word is *led*? [Children respond.]"

④ Remove the stick-on note from the first letter of *led*. "Were you right? Yes, it's an *l*, so could this word be *led*? [Children respond.]"

⑤ "Let's check some more. Say *led* again. What will we expect to see at the end of the word? [Children respond.] Let's see if this word ends in *d*." At this point, the children will have said the word slowly, thought about the sounds and letters in the word, and confirmed their predictions by looking at the word.

⑥ Repeat the process with two more words. In the traditional text above, *fat* will be a more difficult word because it is at the beginning of the sentence and there is not as much information from context.

⑦ Then substitute a word children will not know for a word in the text. Be sure it has a predictable spelling pattern. For example, substitute *big* for *fat*. Suggested language: "Now I'm going to change a word and show you how to figure it out by looking at the letters and thinking about the sounds." Change *fat* to *big*. If you think the children cannot see the word clearly in your chart, write it on a whiteboard or dry-erase board.

⑧ "This word has a *b* at the beginning [point to *big*], so I'm going to make the sound of *b*, /b/, and think what the word could be. I'm thinking it could be *but* or *big*. How would I tell which word it is? [Children respond.] I'm going to look at the rest of the letters. There's an *i*, so the first and second letters are *b i*. [At this point, the children will probably not know the vowel sound, so just tell them.] Say /b/, and what's at the end? [Children respond.] A *g*. Could it be *big*?" Run your finger under the word and say it slowly so that the children can think about the letters and sounds. Have them say it with you. "Does it look like *big*? Let's read and see if *big* makes sense and sounds right." Read the whole line together.

⑨ "The letters and sounds help you figure out a word and check to see if what you read looks right."

read
write
read

- Give the children the sentence sheets in which they can write some missing words. This will give them the opportunity to say words slowly and write letters in sequence; not all spelling will be conventional.
- Have the children read each sentence and write a word that fits in the sentences where they see a blank. Then have them read their sentences to a partner.

Have the children read their sentences to a different partner.

Link

Interactive Read-Aloud: Read aloud books that have mostly simple sentences and rhyming text, such as

- ***Mouse Mess*** by Linnea Riley
- ***Sheep Take a Hike*** by Nancy Shaw

Shared Reading: Use poems or songs such as "Six Little Snowmen" or "A Cloud" (see *Sing a Song of Poetry*). Continue to show the children how to figure out words they do not know and to check on their reading by noticing the letters and sounds.

Guided Reading: Prompt the children to use consonant sounds at the beginning and ending of words to solve words in the simple texts they are reading and to check on their reading. Prompt them to use letter/sound information in connection with meaning and structure. Ask: Does it look right? Does it sound right? Does it make sense?

Interactive Writing: Prompt the children to say words slowly and generate beginning and ending consonant sounds. (Unless they know the vowel sounds, fill those in quickly yourself.)

Independent Writing: Prompt the children to say words slowly and represent beginning and ending consonant sounds for themselves. Show them how to say the words more than one time to write more of the letters, but do not insist on accuracy unless they know the words.

assess

- Observe the children's reading behavior and record substitutions.
- Notice whether the children are using the first letter or more letters in the words to monitor their reading, correct themselves, and solve words.
- Notice the letters and sounds the children are using in their writing.

Expand the Learning

Reinforce the learning in this minilesson when the children engage in shared and guided reading.

Repeat the lesson with other texts the children have read in shared reading. Take words out of the text and write them on a whiteboard so children can solve them by using letters and sounds. Then read the word in the text to be sure it makes sense and sounds right.

Connect with Home

When you are sure that the children can read the texts, send home photocopies. You can include your own innovations (changing some words or phrases) to increase the challenge.

2 Changing the First Letter of a Word

Magnetic Letters

Consider Your Children

Use this activity after your children know what a word is, understand the concept of *first* in relation to the sequence of letters in a word, can recognize letters, and have made connections between words during interactive writing. For example, they may have connected *thing* and *sing* or *day, today,* and *may.* This lesson sets up a routine for work with magnetic letters that can be used for many different kinds of word study activities.

Working with English Language Learners

Once English language learners control some basic information about letters, sounds, and spelling patterns, they need to become flexible in their control of words. This lesson deals with making words by changing the first letter. English language learners need to know that learning about words is not just a matter of memorization but of noticing features and connecting words. Have them work with words they know and have used before when you demonstrate the principle for the first time. English language learners will need many experiences with substituting first letters to understand the principles.

You Need

- Magnetic letters.
- Magnetic surface.

From *Teaching Resources:*

- Lined Four-Box Sheets.

Understand the Principle

As the children become more aware of letter/sound relationships within words, they learn that words have parts and that these parts can be changed to make new words. This understanding helps children see relationships among words and to use this knowledge to take words apart while reading and to spell words while writing. Taking away the first letter of a word and substituting another helps children understand a basic principle of how words work.

When you want to show the children the relationship between words, you can show one word and show the new word beneath it or next to it. This way, they still have the first word in view as a reference. A harder task is to show one word and change, add, or remove letters to make a new word from the original word.

Explain the Principle

"You can change the first letter or letters of a word to make a new word."

plan

Explain the Principle

"You can change the first letter or letters of a word to make a new word."

① Let the children know you are going to show them how to use words they know to make new words.

② Show them the word *me*. Suggested language: "When you say a word, you can hear the first sound, can't you? Say *me*. [Children respond.] What's the first sound? [Children respond.] And when you look at the word *me*, you can see the first letter. [Indicate the magnetic letters spelling *me;* point to the *m*.] When I read the word *me*, I can hear the first sound, *m*, and the rest of the word."

③ "Now watch what I am going to do with the word *me*. I'm going to take away the first letter, the *m*, and put a *b* at the beginning of the word. [Demonstrate with magnetic letters.] Now the word is *be*."

④ "Now I'll take away the *b* and put the *m* back in as the first letter. The word is. . . . [Children respond. Demonstrate several times changing from *me* to *be* and back again.] *Me* and *be* sound the same at the end and they look the same at the end. Changing the first letter makes another word."

⑤ "Now I'm going to change the first letter again. I'll take away the *m* and put an *h* at the beginning of the word. Now my word is. . . . [Children respond.]"

⑥ Provide one or two more examples: *to, do; my, by; cat, mat, fat.*

⑦ Have individual children come up to the easel and change the first letter. The rest of the children read the new word each time.

⑧ Suggested language: "Today you are going to make words by changing the first letter, just like we did on the board. You are going to change the first letter of *me, to,* and *cat.*"

⑨ Show the children how to take away the first letter, put in a new letter, and read the word, running a finger under it at first. Later they will be able to check with their eyes only without using a finger to help the eye.

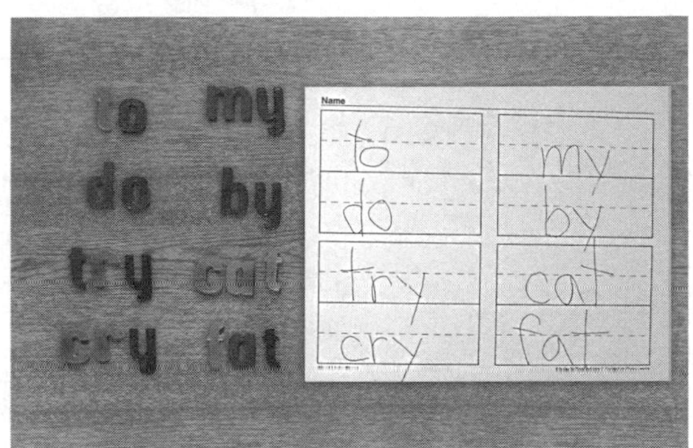

make
say
make
say
write

- Have the children use magnetic letters to build ten simple words they know. At first, to avoid confusion, you may want to limit the choices to the words you have demonstrated. You can raise the challenge by including letters for words you have not demonstrated. For example, you can include an extra *e* so children can discover *see* or you can include *tr* so they can make *try* or *tree*.
- Then have them make ten new words by changing the first letters.
- Have them write four of the pairs they worked with on a Lined Four-Box Sheet.

Have the children share a pair of words they made.

Invite comments on what the children noticed about the words they made. You may get comments like these:

"When you change the first letter, you get a new word."

"You can put two letters in place of a letter at the beginning of a word."

"*See* is like *me* but with *s* and another *e*."

"*See, me,* and *be* rhyme."

Link

Interactive Read-Aloud: Read aloud books that play with changing the first letter of words, such as

- ***The Piggy in the Puddle*** by Charlotte Pomerantz
- ***Fish Wish*** by Bob Barner

Shared Reading: When you read poems and rhymes such as "Five Little Mice" or "Four Seasons" (see *Sing a Song of Poetry*) , point out words that are alike at the end but have different first letters.

Guided Reading: As the children read text and come to new words, prompt them by saying, "Do you know a word like that?" During word work, have the children make four or five words with magnetic letters and change the first letter to make new words.

Interactive Writing: Within the texts the children compose, look for opportunities to connect words by changing the first letter. For example, if they want to write *play* and they know *day,* you can show them on the whiteboard how to go from *day* to *play.*

Independent Writing: Encourage the children to make connections to known words when writing new words.

assess

- Notice whether the children are making connections between words when they are writing and reading.
- Give the children three words. Ask them to change the first letter of each to make a new word.

Expand the Learning

Using magnetic letters, explore other easy, predictable phonogram patterns (*-ad, -ag, -an, -am, -at, -ed, -en, -et, -ig, -in, -it, -ot, -op, –un*), showing how you can change the first letter to make another word.

You may want to repeat the activity with phonograms with silent *e,* such as *-ake, -ate, -ide, -ine, -ike, -oke.*

Connect with Home

Give children a list of five easy words they can make with magnetic letters or letter cards (see *Teaching Resources*) at home with family members. Have them make each word and change the first letter to make a new word.

Changing and Adding Beginning Sounds

Sound Substitution Game

Consider Your Children

Use this activity after your children have had a great deal of experience saying and hearing sounds in words, matching words by first sounds, and associating letters and sounds. Be sure the children know the meaning of *first* in relation to the sequence of sounds in a word, are familiar with some simple high frequency words, and can connect most consonant sounds and letters. Begin the lesson working orally. If the children can manipulate first sounds easily, you may then want to show how it works with letters. You can make connections to the letters by writing on a chart or using magnetic letters on a magnetic chalkboard or whiteboard. This lesson sets up a routine for word play that can be used at any time during the school day. For example, while the class is waiting for another activity to begin, you can make a game of one or two quick examples.

Working with English Language Learners

As English language learners become more conscious of the sounds in words, it is helpful to learn to manipulate them. Use words that are in their speaking vocabularies or that they have encountered many times in shared reading. Provide many demonstrations of how to change words by substituting sounds. English language learners may find it helpful to see the words formed with magnetic letters at the same time they say the words they are making.

You Need

- Magnetic letters.

From *Teaching Resources*:

- Cards for *-an* and *-and* (Word Card Template).
- Letter Cards: *l, m, s, d, f, c, b, h, st, br, pl.*
- Two-Column Sheets.

Understand the Principle

As children become more aware of the sounds in words, they learn to isolate and identify the first sound they hear and connect it to a letter or letter cluster. Identifying this first sound and learning to manipulate the sounds in words helps them understand how to use knowledge of one word to write or read another.

Explain the Principle

“You can change the first letter or letters of a word to make a new word.”

“You can add letters to the beginning of a word to make a new word.”

plan

Explain the Principle

“You can change the first letter or letters of a word to make a new word.”

“You can add letters to the beginning of a word to make a new word.”

① Tell your children you're going to teach them a way to learn new words.

② Suggested language:
"We're going to play a game today. When you say a word, you can hear the first sound, can't you? Say *sand.* [Children respond.] What's the first sound? [Children respond.] Say the first sound by itself. [Demonstrate if needed; children respond.] Now I'm going to say the word *land;* I'm going to change the first sound to an *l.* Say the sound of *l* as in *like* or *learn.* [Demonstrate; children respond.] Listen while I change the first sound of *sand. Sand—land* What did I change? [Children respond.]"

③ "Let's try another one. Say *land.* [Children respond.] The first sound is. . . . [Children respond.] Now change the first sound to *h—hand. Land—hand.*"

④ Demonstrate the game with two or three more examples. Use the same language each time so that the children know exactly what it means to change the first sound: "Say *can.* Change the first sound to *r.* [Children respond.] Say *rug.* Change the first sound to *b.* Say *bug.* Say *room.* Change the first sound to *b.* [Children respond.] Now change the first sound to *z.* [Children respond.]"

⑤ Ask the children to offer examples. Tell them that sometimes when you change the first sound, you don't get a real word.

⑥ [Optional] Suggested language: "Let's look at the spelling of some of these words. [Place *an* on the magnetic board.] You know this word. [Children respond.] Now I'll put a *d* on the end. What is it? [Children respond.] Now, I'll put an *l* at the beginning of the word to make *land.*" Invite comments and/or discussion. Suggested language: "If I want to make the word *sand,* what do I change?" Children respond. Change *land* to *sand.*

⑦ Do two or three more examples to illustrate changing the first sound and letter to make another word. Invite the children to offer examples.

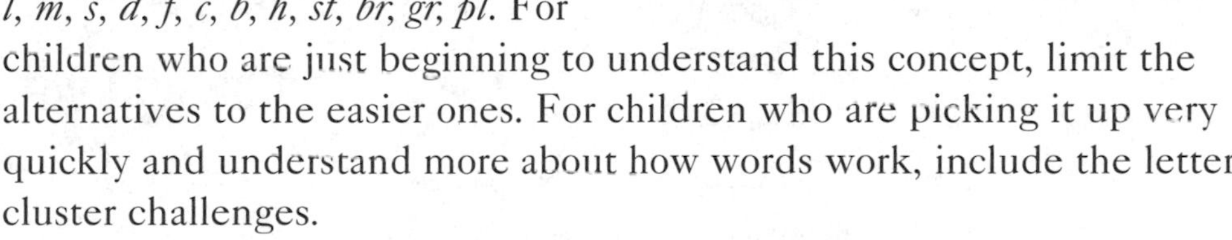

make
read
write
change
read
write

- Prepare a number of cards with the ending patterns *an* and *and* along with the letter or letter cluster cards *l, m, s, d, f, c, b, h, st, br, gr, pl.* For children who are just beginning to understand this concept, limit the alternatives to the easier ones. For children who are picking it up very quickly and understand more about how words work, include the letter cluster challenges.
- Have the children work in pairs. The first child makes a word using a consonant or consonant cluster and a final word part (for example, *st* and *and—stand*), reads it and then writes the word on the left side of the Two-Column Sheet. Now the partner changes the consonant or consonant cluster to make a new word, reads it, and writes it on the column on the right side of the sheet. Each partner makes five words for his partner to change until they have entered ten pairs on the sheet. Have them put both their names at the top of the sheet.
- If the children have made words like *pland* [for *planned*] or *frand* [for *friend*], acknowledge their good thinking and help them to sort it out. Illustrate how *planned* sounds like it should be spelled *pland*, but looks different because you are adding *ed* and doubling the *n*. Demonstrate the spelling of *friend*, pointing out its relationship to the words *end*, *send*, and *bend*.

Have the children share some of the words they made and wrote, and ask them what they noticed about words. Model and encourage comments like these:

> "You can make a new word by changing the first letter."
>
> "You can add letters to make a new word."
>
> "If you put a *t* in *sand* after the *s*, you make a new word."

Link

Interactive Read-Aloud: Read aloud books that contain examples of word play, such as

- ***17 Kings and 42 Elephants*** by Margaret Mahy
- ***My Little Sister Ate One Hare*** by Bill Grossman

Shared Reading: Use poems and nursery rhymes that contain flexible play with words, such as "Jack Sprat," "How Much Dew?," or "Esau" (see *Sing a Song of Poetry*).

Guided Reading: As the children read text, prompt them to use parts of words they know. For example, ask, "Do you see a part that can help?" During word work, have the children use magnetic letters to make four or five new words by changing the first letter.

Interactive Writing: If appropriate examples arise, use the whiteboard to demonstrate quickly making new words by changing the beginning sound. In this case, the children will be changing the first sound and at the same time seeing the letter change.

Independent Writing: Encourage the children to get to words they want to write by using known words and changing the sound or sounds at the beginning.

assess

- Notice the children's ability to substitute first sounds to make new words. A quick check of just two to three examples will tell you whether they understand the principle.
- Notice whether the children can generate appropriate examples for the game.
- Look at the children's written products to determine whether they are applying the principle.

Expand the Learning

Repeat the lesson with other phonogram patterns that are appropriate for your children. See the common phonograms list in *Teaching Resources*.

Connect with Home

Suggest that family members play a word game as they are working in the kitchen or in the yard, driving to school, or going shopping. They take turns saying pairs of words that end the same. For example, the adult may say the word *pan* and the child says *man*. Or the child says the word *stick* and the adult says *pick*.

4 Recognizing Words Quickly

Magnetic Letters

Consider Your Children

Use this lesson when your children have worked with their names and learned many high frequency words through shared reading and interactive writing. They should be able to use visual information (beginning and ending consonants) to locate words and differentiate them. This lesson summarizes the learning of easy high frequency words and makes it more automatic, so that the children can use these known words to monitor the reading of simple texts.

Working with English Language Learners

It is especially helpful for English language learners to develop a repertoire of words they can recognize quickly and easily. You may want to add some simple sentences that have the words in them. Have children read and quickly locate the words in sentences like "Manira is a girl in our class." Or have them locate words in poems that they have read many times. Practice the Follow the Path game with a small group.

You Need

- Magnetic letters.
- Follow the Path Game Boards.

From *Teaching Resources:*

- Directions for Follow the Path.
- High Frequency Word Cards (twenty-five or fifty).

Understand the Principle

Competent readers recognize most words quickly and automatically and can solve any unfamiliar words rapidly by using a range of flexible strategies. Beginning readers gain momentum if they can recognize some words quickly, thus allowing them to give more attention to more challenging word solving. This lesson teaches children the concept of recognizing and locating easy high frequency words with their eyes.

Explain the Principle

"You can read (or write) a word quickly when you know how it looks."

plan

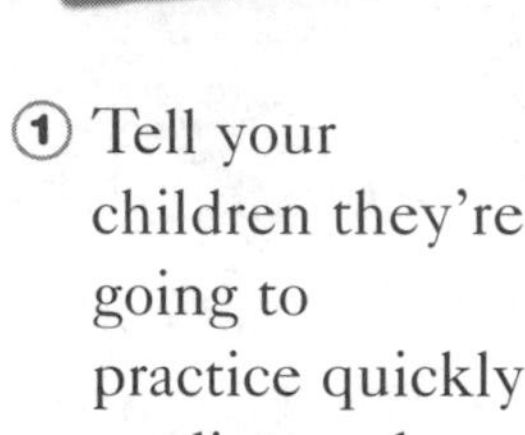

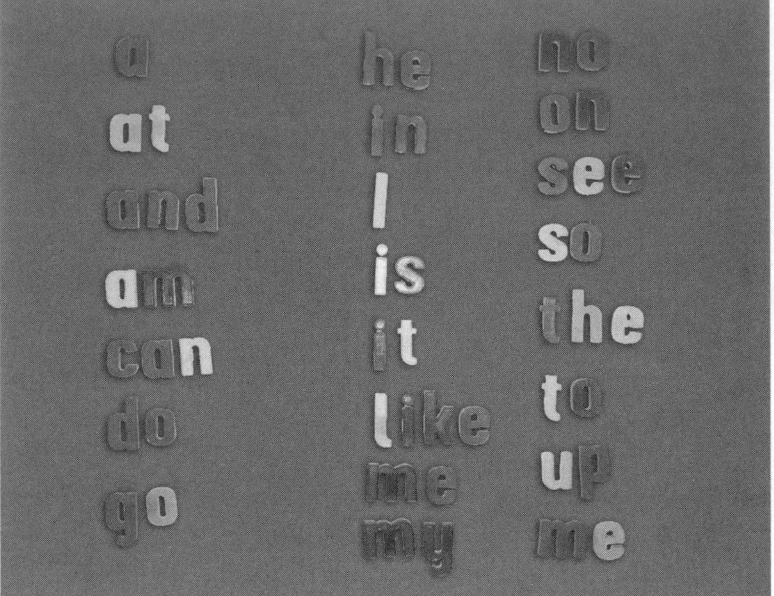

Explain the Principle

“You can read (or write) a word quickly when you know how it looks.”

① Tell your children they're going to practice quickly reading and writing words they know.

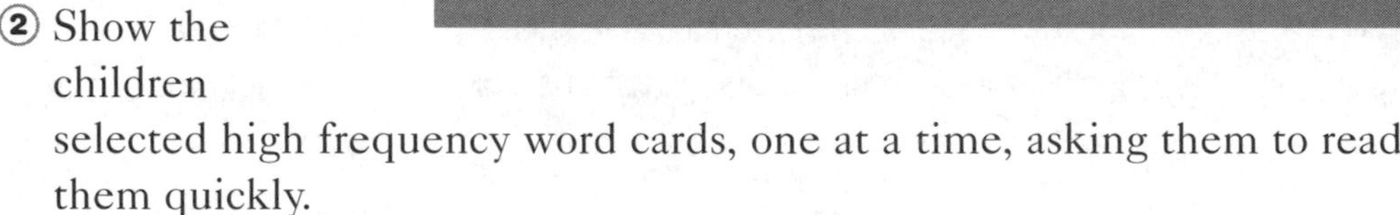

② Show the children selected high frequency word cards, one at a time, asking them to read them quickly.

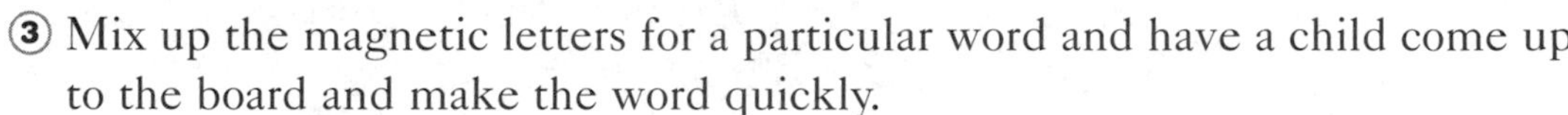

③ Mix up the magnetic letters for a particular word and have a child come up to the board and make the word quickly.

④ Have the children make as many words as they can within a five-minute period.

⑤ Display one or two pieces of enlarged text that the children know well (poems, stories, or interactive writing). Show several high frequency words and have children locate them quickly in the text. One child can point, but others should search with their eyes.

⑥ Tell the children they are going to play Follow the Path. Demonstrate the game with two children.

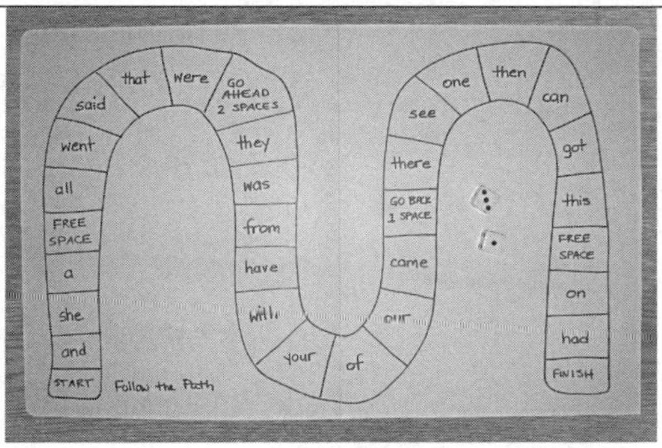

take
read
throw
move

- Have the children play Follow the Path with a partner. They take turns throwing a die, moving the number of spaces indicated, and reading the word quickly. The point of the game is to review a range of high frequency words and ensure the children's quick recognition of them.
- An alternative is to use a game board without words in the spaces and have the children draw a card from a deck of high frequency word cards. The children take a card, read the word quickly, throw a die, and move the correct number of spaces. Remember to add a few "extra turn," "miss a turn," or "go back three" spaces to add fun and enjoyment.

Direct children's attention to the word wall. Then give children "clues" to find the word you are thinking of: "I'm thinking of a word with two letters. It begins with *t*." After you have played this game several times, children may think of and provide clues to find high frequency words.

Link

Interactive Read-Aloud: Point out the high frequency words in books with large print, such as

- ***I Went Walking*** by Sue Williams
- ***This Train*** by Paul Collicutt

Shared Reading: After the children have enjoyed a text such as "The Elephant Who Jumped a Fence" or "I Had a Loose Tooth" (see *Sing a Song of Poetry*), have them locate high frequency words quickly using a masking card or highlighter tape.

Guided Reading: After reading a text, have the children quickly locate two or three specific high frequency words. During word work, have them make a few high frequency words quickly with magnetic letters.

Interactive Writing: Write yourself the easy high frequency words most of the children in the class know well. Point out that when you know words, you just write and read them quickly. Have the children locate specific words they have produced.

Independent Writing: Remind the children to write the words they know quickly. They will not need to say these words slowly and listen for the sounds.

assess

- Notice whether the children are spelling high frequency words accurately in their writing.
- Notice whether the children are reading high frequency words easily in guided and independent reading.
- Notice whether the children are learning more high frequency words.

Expand the Learning

Increase the number of high frequency words by adding words from the list of 100 high frequency words (see *Teaching Resources*).

Once the children have developed a system for learning to read high frequency words, it will not be necessary for them to practice every one with word cards. They may, however, need to work on these words in writing so that they are spelled conventionally.

Connect with Home

Send home a Follow the Path Game Board and high frequency word cards (see *Teaching Resources*) so that children can play the game with family members.

5 Using What You Know about Words

Consider Your Children

Use this lesson after your children have had some experience substituting letters to make words. In this lesson, children will become more aware that they can bring their word knowledge to bear in searching for connections. Ask the children to think about word parts rather than telling them to "find little words inside big words," which can create confusion. Finding the word *me* in *some,* for example, does not help. In this lesson, the children work with a variety of changes, including adding a letter at the beginning of a word and substituting the first letter at the beginning of a word. If you think this task will be too difficult, divide this lesson into three lessons—one on adding a letter to the front of words, one on substituting the first letter of a word, and one on doing both in a flexible way.

Working with English Language Learners

You may want to work with English language learners in a small group first so that you can give them more support. Also observe how they problem-solve. If they have difficulty, try some very simple sentences composed of words they know except for one new word that will be easy. This will set up the expectation that they need to search for what they know to solve problems in reading.

You Need

- Magnetic letters.
- Sentence strips.
- "If you know" chart.
- Index cards.

From *Teaching Resources:*

- "If You Know" Sheet.

Understand the Principle

When good readers and writers solve words, they draw on what they already know. Making connections to what they already know about words helps readers and writers build categories of words and principles for how words work.

Explain the Principle

"You can use parts of words you know to read or write new words."

plan

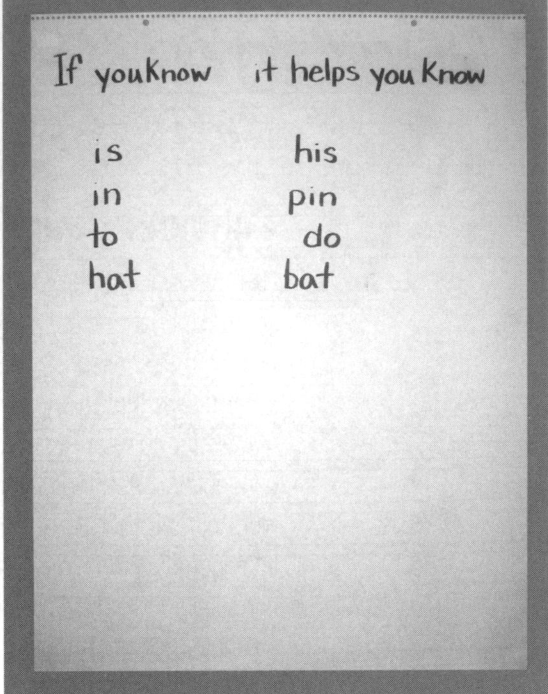

If you know it helps you know
is his
in pin
to do
hat bat

Explain the Principle

" You can use parts of words you know to read or write new words. "

① Tell the children they are going to learn more about using word parts to figure out new words.

② Begin with a blank surface headed "If you know" followed by "it helps you know." Suggested language: "Today we are going to think about how it helps us to find the parts in a word that we know. This says, 'If you know.' That means that when you are looking at a word, you think about what you know. You know this word." Place *is* on the board in magnetic letters.

③ Suggested language: "You know *is*, and if you know *is*, it will help you know another word." Make *his* with magnetic letters. "I have made a word. How is it like *is*?" Children may say, "The last part is the same."

④ Suggested language: "The last part is the same, *is*, *his*. What is different?" Children respond. "There is an *h* at the beginning. So *his* is like *is* except for the *h*. If I know *is* and I know the *h* sound at the beginning, I know this word is *his*."

⑤ Make *in* in the first column. Suggested language: "Here is another word you know, *in*. If I know *in*, it will help me to know this word." Make *pin* and have the children figure it out and discuss it. Explain the process explicitly.

⑥ Continue with *to–do*, *hat–bat*, *can–man*, *and–hand*. Some pairs substitute a first letter and others add a letter at the beginning.

⑦ Explain to the children that they will be using words they know to learn new words. Suggested language: "You are going to work with a partner. You will have a piece of paper just like the big one I have here." Hold up a copy of the "if you know" sheet. "This side says, 'If you know.' On this side you make a word you know. Is everyone thinking of a word you know?" Call on several children to tell the word they have in mind. "On this side it says, 'it helps you know.' On this side your partner is going to change one thing about your word to make a new word. Then you have to read your partner's word. Remember, it has to be a real word, so help each other think about what the word means. Then pick two words that you like, and write them on a card to share with the class." Demonstrate the process with two children. Assign partners within children's work groups.

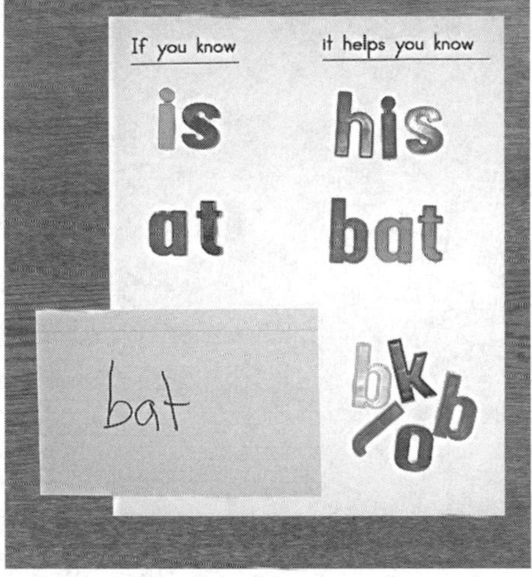

make
read
change
make
read
write

- Have the children work in pairs. Using magnetic letters, the first child makes a word she knows on the left side of the "if you know" sheet. Her partner changes one thing about the word and makes a new word on the right side of the sheet. The first child reads her partner's word.
- After making eight pairs of words, the children choose one pair. They write the first word on one side of an index card and related word on the other side of the index card.

Have children share their word cards. Each child says "if you know," says the word on one side, turns the card over and says "it helps you know," and says the second word. Repeat until all children have tried their cards.

Link

Interactive Read-Aloud: Read aloud books that help children notice how words are related, such as

- ***Green Eggs and Ham*** by Dr. Seuss
- ***There's an Ant in Anthony*** by Bernard Most

Shared Reading: Using a familiar text, play a word game: "I am thinking of a word that is like *it* at the end and like *sun* at the beginning." Use texts such as "The Little Plant" or "Little Bird" (see *Sing a Song of Poetry*).

Guided Reading: Help the children use words they know as a tool in word solving. (Remember, it is not helpful to suggest finding little words in big words.) Suggested language: "What do you know about the word? Can you find a part you know? Do you know a word like that?" You may use the whiteboard to make the point explicit. During word work, have the children use magnetic letters to go from a known word to a new word.

Interactive Writing: When the children are working on a new word, help them connect it to a word they already know.

Independent Writing: Encourage the children to use words they know to help them spell new words.

assess

- Notice whether the children are using words they know to solve words when they are reading.
- Notice whether the children are using words they know to spell words when they are writing.
- Notice whether the children are able to add or substitute letters.

Expand the Learning

Start with easy patterns such as *-an, -at,* and other words with short vowel sounds. Then move to more challenging patterns such as those with silent *e: -ake, -ike, -ite.* Work from a list of words that the children know and expand from there.

Connect with Home

Have the children take home an "if you know" sheet and letter cards (see *Teaching Resources*) and ask them to make three word pairs with family members. (Magnetic letters also work well for this task.)

6 Changing the Last Letter of a Word

Making Words

Consider Your Children

Before being taught this lesson, children should know most of the names of letters and some of their associated sounds. They should understand *first* and *last* in relation to the sequence of letters in words. They should have had experience and practice changing the first letter of a word to make a new word.

Working with English Language Learners

Begin with words that English language learners know very well and have used in reading and writing. Go over the words with them and help them articulate the sounds, especially the last letter, which they will be changing. When they first begin the activity, work with them to be sure they are saying and understanding the words they make. Help them distinguish which words are real English words and to learn what they mean. It will not be helpful to have children simply changing last letters to make meaningless combinations.

You Need

- Magnetic letters.
- List of words (only include the first of each pair): *him–hit, but–bug, leg–let, flag–flat, win–wig, sit–sip, mom–mop, beg–bet, pet–peg, bat–bag, fan–fat, ham–hat, mad–map, fit–fig, fin–fix, pig–pin, top–tot, fox–fog, cut–cup, bus–but.*

From *Teaching Resources:*

- Lined Four-Box Sheets.

Understand the Principle

One of the most powerful ways readers and writers solve words is by making connections to words they know. Learning to manipulate words by changing the last letter will help children understand that words may be alike at the beginning but different at the end. They will learn that the search to connect words gives them valuable information while reading; they will give greater attention to the last letter of a word instead of simply using the first letter in decoding.

Explain the Principle

“You can change the last letter or letters of a word to make a new word.”

plan

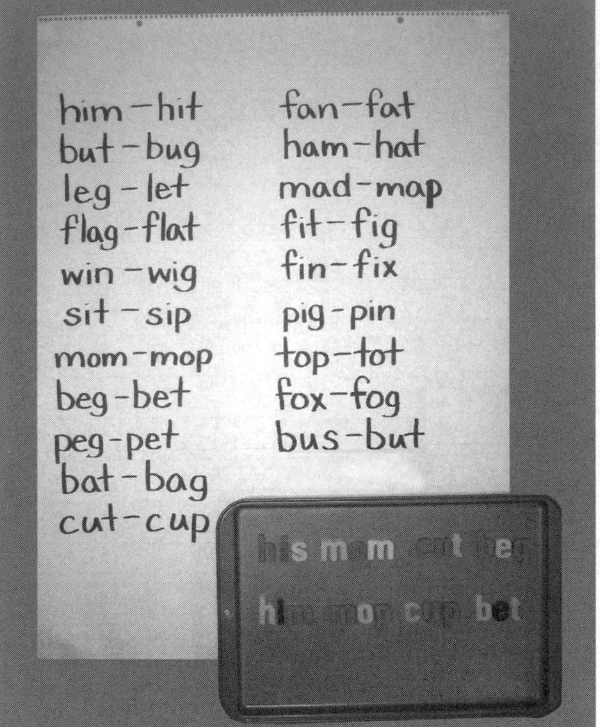

Explain the Principle

“ You can change the last letter or letters of a word to make a new word. ”

① Explain to children that you'll be showing them how to make new words.

② Suggested language: “You know how to change the first letter of a word to make a new word. Watch this. [Make *his* with magnetic letters.] What does this say?” Children respond.

③ Now make the word *him* below it. Suggested language: “What do you notice?” Children respond, explaining that the first part is the same and only the last part is different.

④ Do the same with *mom–mop*, *cut–cup*, *beg–bet*.

⑤ Next show how you can start with *his* and simply change the last letter (remove the *s* and add the *m*). (Remove the *h* and *i* that were part of *him* from the board.)

⑥ Do the same with the other words.

⑦ Explain to the children that today they are going to make a word with magnetic letters, write it in a box on the lined Four-Box Sheet, change the last letter, make a new word, and write it below the first one.

⑧ Post the list of possible words.

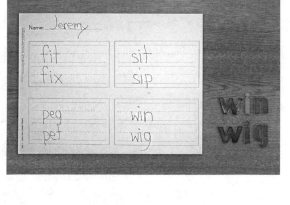

choose
make
write
change
write

▸ Have the children choose four words from the list and make a new word from each one. They make a word, write it, change the last letter to make the new word, and write the new word on the lined Four-Box Sheet. As an additional challenge they can make and write four more pairs on the back of the sheet.

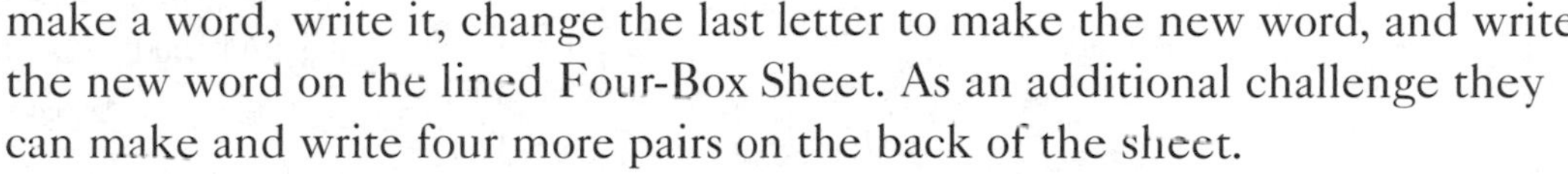

Have the children each read a word pair until all have shared.

Link

Interactive Read-Aloud: Read aloud books that enable children to enjoy language and word play, such as

- ***A Beastly Story*** by Bill Martin, Jr.
- ***Silly Sally*** by Audrey Wood

Shared Reading: After reading and enjoying a text such as "Johnny Appleseed" or "I'm a Little Teapot" (see *Sing a Song of Poetry*), have the children use a masking card or highlighter tape to find a particular word. Write it on the whiteboard and ask if they can change the last letter to make a new word.

Guided Reading: During word work, have the children make three or four words and change the last letter to make a new word. (See *Sing a Song of Poetry.*)

Interactive Writing: As appropriate, show the children how to start with a word they know and change the last letter to make a word they want to write.

Independent Writing: Remind the children to use parts of words they know to figure out new words.

assess

- Observe whether the children use what they know to figure out new words.
- Place three words at the top of three columns (for example, *his, but, mom*). Ask the children to change the last letter to make two new words for each word and write them in the columns. They can find examples on the word wall or check their words with the word wall if you have one. Notice how many conventionally spelled words the children have written.

Expand the Learning

Repeat the lesson with other words that all begin with consonant clusters: *brag–brat, flag–flat, from–frog, plum–plus, slip–slim, skip–skin.*

Connect with Home

Send home letter cards (see *Teaching Resources*) and a list of words from which children can make new words. (They can use magnetic letters instead of letter cards if they have them.)

7 Changing Last Letters of Words

Making New Words

Consider Your Children

Be sure the children understand how to change the first letter of a word before using this lesson. Otherwise, use this lesson first to change beginning letters and then move to changing final letters. (You may need two or three lessons to establish these concepts.) In this lesson you make the first word and keep it on the board while you make the new word below. Later you will want to change the last letter without making the second word below: the task is harder when the children do not have the whole first word as a reference.

Working with English Language Learners

Be sure that your English language learners have worked with and can easily recognize letters and letter clusters and take apart simple words. If they have difficulty with the task, show them known words and have them make connections. By the time you use this lesson, your English language learners will understand *first* and *last* and have experience working with beginning and ending sounds and letters. Alternate changing the first and last letters so that they understand the actions are flexible.

You Need

- Magnetic letters.

From *Teaching Resources:*

- Word Card Template to make word cards chosen from the following list: *bad, bag; bat, bad; bed, beg; bet, bed; big, bit; bud, bun; bus, but; can, cab; can, cap; cap, cat; cup, cub; can, cap; cap, cat; cub, cup; cup, cut; did, dig; dog, dot; fan, fat; fin, fit; fit, fix; fog, fox; had, ham; has, hat; hem, hen; him, hip; his, hit; hog, hop; hop, hot; hug, hum; hum, hut; kid, kit; leg, led; led, let; lid, lip; log, lot; man, map; mat, mad; mom, mop; mud, mug; pad, pan;pen, pet; pig, pin; pin, pit; pop, pot; ran, rag; sat, sad; sit, six; sun, sub; tin, tip.*
- Lined Four-Box Sheets.

Understand the Principle

Children need to recognize parts of words such as beginning and ending parts and to make connections between words. The ability to notice the parts of words quickly and automatically will make word solving easier and free children's attention to think about their reading. Learning how to move from one word to another by changing first and last parts fosters quick word-solving ability.

Explain the Principle

"You can change the last letter or letters of a word to make a new word."

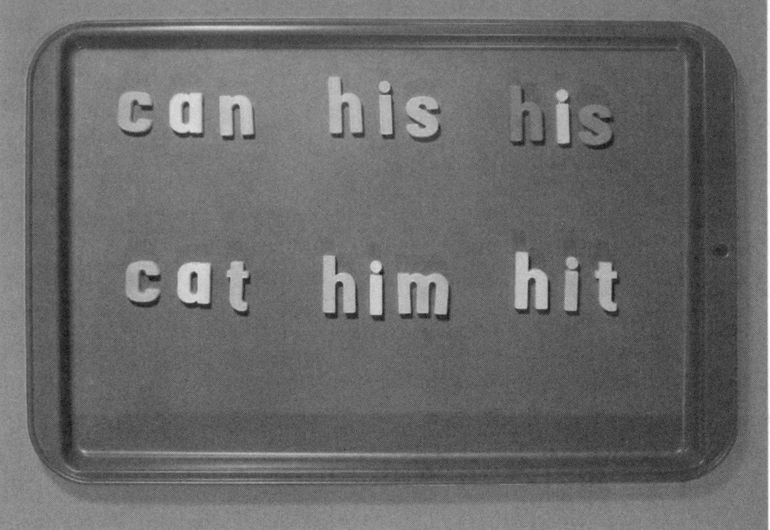

Explain the Principle

"You can change the last letter or letters of a word to make a new word."

① Tell the children they'll be learning how to figure out new words.

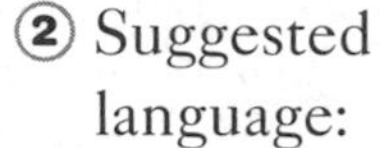

② Suggested language:
"Today you're going to learn how you can change parts of words to make new words. Watch this! This is the word *can* [make it with magnetic letters]. Now I am starting with the word *can* and changing the last letter to make a new word. Now it says. . . . [Children respond, *cat.*]"

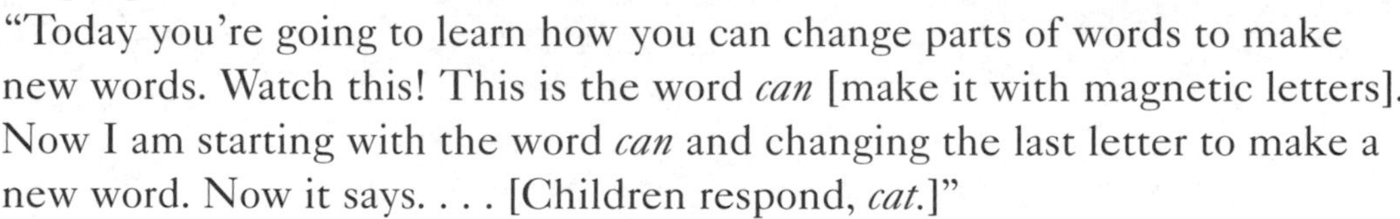

③ Repeat with *his*, *him*, and *his*, *hit*. Make the whole word each time. (Later you can explain that you can change the last part of a word.)

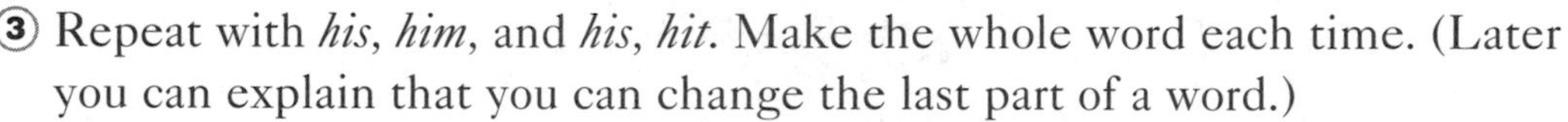

④ Invite the children to give a word and together see if you can change the last letter to make a new word. Remove the last letter and replace it with the new one. The children say the new word quickly.

⑤ Explain the application activity.

choose
make
write
change
write
read

▸ Have the children take a word card, make the word with magnetic letters, and write the word on their Lined Four-Box Sheets. Then they build the word with magnetic letters, change the last letter to make a new word, and write the new word below the first word. They continue the process until they have made six pairs of words. Then they read their words to a partner.

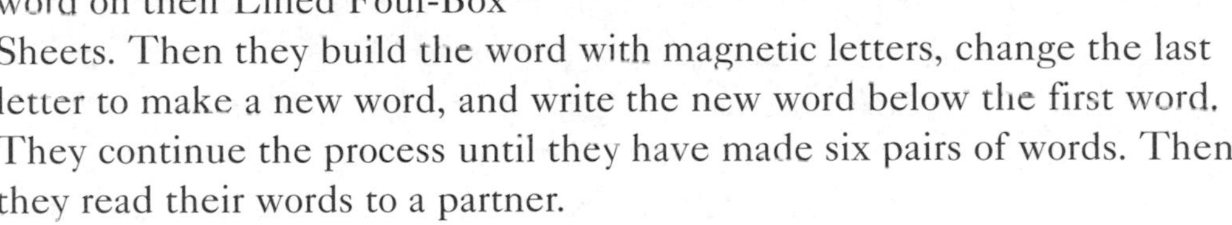

Have the children share pairs of words (a given word and a new one they have made). Have other children say what was changed to make the word.

Link

Interactive Read-Aloud: Invite children to join in during the parts that involve changing letters to make new words when you are reading aloud books, such as

- ***Jamberry*** by Bruce Degen
- ***Pets in Trumpets*** by Bernard Most

Shared Reading: After reading and enjoying a text such as "My Hat, It Has Three Corners" or "The Old Gray Mare" (see *Sing a Song of Poetry*), give some clues for locating words that call for changing the first or last letter: "Find a word in the poem that ends with *it* like *sit.* Find a word that starts with the same first two letters as *his.*"

Guided Reading: Prompt the children to solve new words by saying, "Do you know a word that starts [ends] like that?" During word work, give the children magnetic letters and have them change the first letter to make a new word. Repeat with different words, having them change the first or last letter.

Interactive Writing: When writing a new word, invite the children to think of a word that starts or ends like the word.

Independent Writing: As the children construct words, encourage them to use what they know about words to write new ones. Point out the connections between words that have similar first parts and different letters or letter clusters at the end.

assess

- Notice the connections that the children make between words as they read and write.
- Select five words you have not used in the application activity. Change the last letter and ask the children to read or say the new word. Ask them to change the last letter two ways to make two new words.

Expand the Learning

Have the children use letter tiles, link letters, or letter cards (see *Teaching Resources*) to make and change words. Using different tools will help them attend to letters and word parts in different ways.

Have the children use pictures (see *Teaching Resources,* Picture Cards, Short Vowel Sounds) and write the first word themselves.

Have children make their own three-letter words instead of picking a card.

Connect with Home

Encourage family members and caregivers to play word games with magnetic letters on the refrigerator or on the table (see *Teaching Resources,* Ways to Use Magnetic Letters). Explain at a meeting or in a newsletter how to build a word and change the first or last letter to make a new word.

8 Noticing Word Parts

Magnetic Letters

Consider Your Students

This lesson draws children's attention to the structure of words, both by saying them and by noticing the letters that represent the parts of words. Use this lesson after your children know the names of the letters and most of the associated sounds and have begun to grasp the concept of letter clusters at the beginning of words. Don't use the technical words *onset* and *rime;* rather, you will want them to be able to talk about and recognize the *first* and *last* part of the word. Most first graders will already understand this concept, but a few may need this lesson to help them learn to see parts of words.

Working with English Language Learners

You will want your English language learners to be generally familiar with the text (although not have memorized it), and this may take a few more repetitions than for other children. You may want to work with English language learners in a small group and remind them of words they know that can be connected to the new words they are trying to solve. Be sure that the piece they are reading does not have too many hard words and that it is within the children's understanding.

You Need

- Magnetic letters.
- Highlighter markers.
- Selected words on chart paper (see below).
- Suggested words: *pat, sing, bring, play, clock, hop, pet, make, stay, shop.*

From *Teaching Resources:*

- List Sheets.

Understand the Principle

The easiest sound pattern for children to hear is the whole word; the next easiest is a syllable; then, an individual letter. An intermediary step between hearing syllables and letters is noticing and recognizing the breaks between the first part of the word (the *onset*) and the rest of the word (the *rime*). Noticing these larger parts of words makes it easier for children to break words apart for analysis. It is also a helpful way to learn about the sounds of vowels in letter sequences.

Explain the Principle

“You can notice and use word parts to read (or write) a new word.”

“You can look at the first part and last part to read a word.”

plan

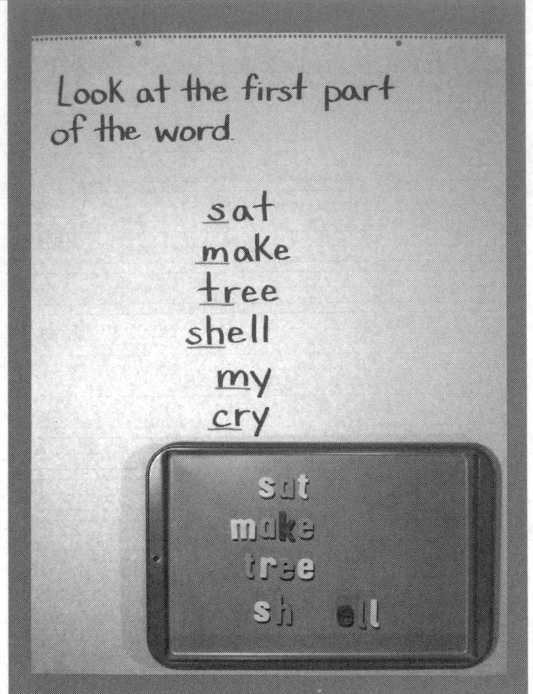

Explain the Principle

“ You can notice and use word parts to read (or write) a new word. ”

“ You can look at the first part and last part to read a word. ”

① Tell children you'll be helping them learn more about word parts.

② Suggested language: “You know a lot of letters, sounds, and words. Today we are going to talk about the parts of words. When you are trying to read or write words, it helps to think about the parts. This word is *sat*.”

③ Make *sat* with magnetic letters. Move the letters as you show the children the first part and the rest of the word. Suggested language: “The first part of *sat* is the first letter—*s*—and the *at* is the rest of the word.”

④ Demonstrate with *make* and *my*. The children may remark that the first and last parts of *my* are just one letter each.

⑤ Suggested language: “This word is *tree. Tree* begins with a consonant cluster. A consonant cluster is a pair (two letters) that you see together a lot at the beginning of words. What is the letter cluster at the beginning of *tree*?” Children respond. “When you have a letter cluster like *tr* at the beginning of the word, the two letters are the first part of the word. So the first part of *tree* is *tr* and the rest of the word is the *ee*.” Demonstrate by moving the letters.

⑥ Suggested language: “This word is *shell. Shell* begins with a consonant cluster that makes one sound. So the first part of *shell* is. . . . ” Children respond.

⑦ Demonstrate with several more words if needed.

⑧ Suggested language: “Let's look at the words on the chart. The first word is *sat*. Who can come up and put a line under [or highlight] the first part of *sat*?”

⑨ Take each word on the chart and have children underline the first part of the word.

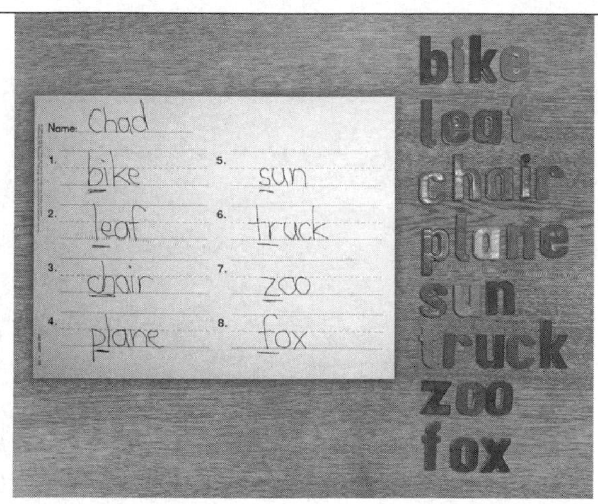

make
write
highlight

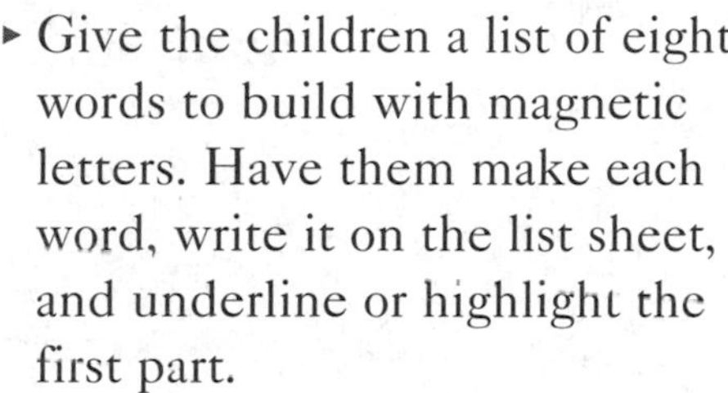

- Give the children a list of eight words to build with magnetic letters. Have them make each word, write it on the list sheet, and underline or highlight the first part.
- As an added challenge, they can make, write, and highlight five extra words of their own choosing.

Invite a few children to make a word with magnetic letters and call on other children to use a masking card to show the first part of the word. Explain to the children that thinking about word parts will help them read and write many words.

Link

Interactive Read-Aloud: Read aloud books that have interesting word combinations in which onsets remain the same but the rimes change and vice versa, such as

- ***In the Tall, Tall Grass*** by Denise Fleming
- ***Sheep Out to Eat*** by Nancy Shaw.

Shared Reading: Have the children use highlighter tape or a highlighter marker to call attention to the first part of words in familiar texts such as "The Old Man and the Cow" or "The Old Woman" (see *Sing a Song of Poetry*).

Guided Reading: After reading a text, draw attention to two or three words and have the children locate onsets. During word work, have the children who need more experience make a few words with magnetic letters and tell the first and last part. Or have them divide the words into the first part and the rest of the word.

Interactive Writing: Have the children say the word they want to write, separating the first part and the rest of the word.

Independent Writing: Encourage the children to think about the parts of words to help them write them.

assess

- Notice whether the children can identify the first part of words.
- Give the children a list of three or four known words and ask them to underline the first part of each.

Expand the Learning

Repeat the lesson using other words until children are very flexible in using parts of words to figure out new words as they read and write.

Connect with Home

Have the children take their list sheets home to read to family members.

Suggest that they make three words with magnetic letters or letter cards and tell the first and last parts.

9 Changing Ending Parts of Words

Building Words

Consider Your Children

This lesson is appropriate when the children have begun to notice the parts of words and can separate first and last parts. They should have some experience changing parts of words to make new words. In this lesson, children work with the rime, or last part of a word. As children explore more complex concepts, consistent language will be helpful; for example, "word parts" for onsets and rimes, "letters" when referring to individual graphic signs, and "syllables" when referring to word breaks.

Working with English Language Learners

When children are just learning words in English, it may be hard for them to change the parts of words. Start by showing them words that have the same phonogram but different first letters. Let them notice and talk about the connections. Then explicitly demonstrate how you can take one word and change the first letter to make the other word. Provide many opportunities for practice. Be sure that the children understand the meaning of the words that you are using as examples. Use pictures if necessary.

You Need

- Chart and easel.

From *Teaching Resources:*

- Onset and Rime Cards. Suggested cards: *with, will; best, bend; stand, stamp; blast, blend; clap, cloth; flag, flash; flat, flap; plan, plug; plus, plump; sled, slip; slip, slide; bring, brush; crash, crab; drip, drum; frog, fresh; grab, grin; trim, trap; trash, trunk; trip, trust; skin, skip; snap, snug; spin, spot; spend, spin; step, stop; stamp, stand; swim, swam; chin, chest; ship, shop; shirt, shelf; this, that; them, then; that, then; when, where; shrink, shrub; place, plane; mice, mile; nice, nine; broke, brown; home, hope; nose, note; tube, tune; stone, stove; hole, house; white, whale; small, smile; hike, hive; pipe, pine; safe, sale; grape, graze; flake, flame; came, come; blame, blast; chair, chop; snap, snail; chair, chest; green, gray; knee, kneel; see, seed; try, tree; stay, stop.*
- Lined Four-Box Sheets (two per child).

Understand the Principle

A powerful strategy for decoding in reading or spelling in writing is to make connections between words. Students learn flexible ways of moving from known words to new words by seeing that they know something about the word in question. They can use the first part or last part they know.

Explain the Principle

"You can change the first part or the last part to make a new word."

plan

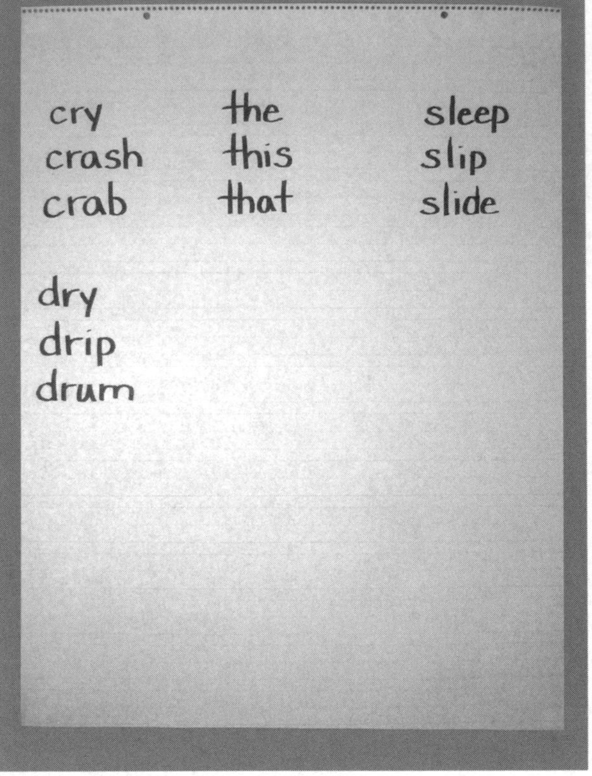

Explain the Principle

"You can change the first part or the last part to make a new word."

① Let children know that today they are going to learn how to change the last part of a word to make a new word.

② Suggested language: "You have learned how to change the first part of words to make new words. Today I will show you how to change the last part of words to make new words."

③ Point to the word *cry*. "What's this word? [Children respond.] Now watch how I keep the *cr*, or first part of the word, and take away the *y* and add *ash*. Now it says. . . . [Children respond.]"

④ "Now I'm going to change the last part again. I'll take away the *ash* and add *ab*. Now it says. . . . [Children respond.]"

⑤ "You can make a new word by changing the ending letters of a word."

⑥ Repeat with other examples: *dry*, *drip*, *drum; the*, *this*, *that; sleep*, *slip*, *slide.* Add more examples if needed.

⑦ Give the children some initial clusters and have them tell one word and then another that starts the same and ends differently.

⑧ Explain that they can use the first part of words they know to help them read or write other words.

⑨ Explain the application activity.

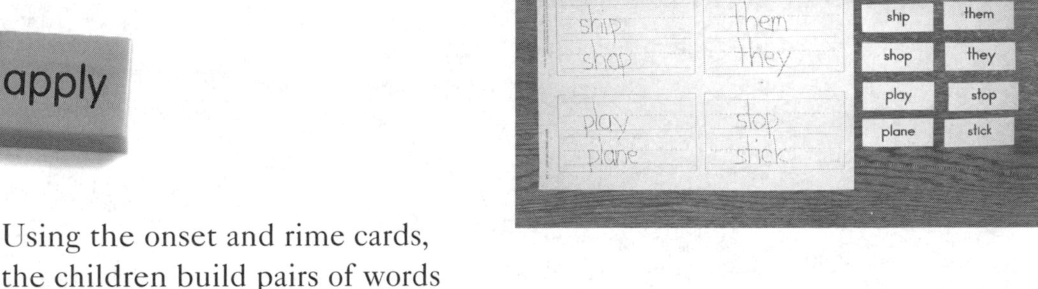

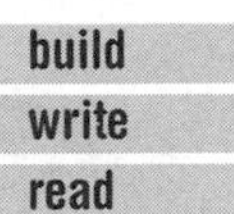

▸ Using the onset and rime cards, the children build pairs of words that start the same and end differently with magnetic letters. They make eight pairs, write them on the Lined Four-Box Sheet (two copies), and then read the words to a partner.

Have the children share their making connections sheets in threes. Ask each group to share an interesting pair. Select two or three to add to the class chart.

Link

Interactive Read-Aloud: Read aloud books that show how you can connect words to make new words or that draw attention to the sound patterns in words, such as

- ***Word Wizard*** by Cathryn Falwell
- ***Counting Crocodiles*** by Judy Sierra

Shared Reading: From a familiar text such as "The Donkey" or "Six Little Snowmen" (see *Sing a Song of Poetry*), select two or three words. Use magnetic letters to show the children how to change the rime (for example, *flight, flag*) and invite them to think of other examples.

Guided Reading: Using the whiteboard, show the children how to solve new words quickly by thinking of a word that starts the same but has a different ending. During word work, have the children use magnetic letters to make words by changing onsets and rimes.

Independent Reading: Prompt the children to use parts of words they know as they try to figure out or analyze new words: "Do you see a part that can help you? What do you know that might help? Do you know a word that ends like that? Starts like that? Do you know a word like that?"

Interactive Writing: As you write new words, ask children to think of words that are similar: "Do you know a word like that?"

Independent Writing: Encourage children to use what they know about words as they write new words.

assess

- Give the children a sheet of ten duplicated words, arranged randomly, that can be connected by the first letter or letter cluster. Include some words they have not previously studied. Have them write the two words that start alike and end differently in columns 1 and 2 of a Three-Column Sheet; they can copy the words as they find them. In the third column, they write another word that starts the same and ends differently.
- Identify the children who need more work on making new words by changing the last part. Work with these children in a small group.

Expand the Learning

Repeat the lesson with other examples of onsets and rimes.

As an alternative or follow-up, have the children take a word card and write another word that starts the same and ends differently.

Connect with Home

Give family members directions for a simple guessing game and encourage them to play it in the car or at the market. Each player tells two words that begin with the same letter or letter cluster but have a different rime. One partner may say *park, police;* the other person then takes a turn: *grass, grill.*

10 Changing the Middle of Words

Magnetic Letters

Consider Your Children

The children should have substantial experience changing beginnings and endings before working on this principle. In this lesson, the children will learn how to think about the middle part of words so they can become more flexible in using word parts. Some children will have begun to change all parts of words quickly and notice connections independently. Others will need more explicit demonstrations, such as this lesson.

Working with English Language Learners

Being able to work flexibly with words they know will help English language learners become familiar with the structure of English words. They need many examples, beginning with words that they can read and understand. If the words in this lesson are too hard for them, here are a few that might be easier: *cap, cup; stop, step; run, ran; cat, cart.* Use simple examples and give children many opportunities to make words with magnetic letters and say them.

You Need

- Magnetic letters.

From *Teaching Resources:*

- Word Cards (use the Word Card Template) for the following suggested pairs of words: *bit–but; cat–cut; run–ran; tip–top; but–bat; fog–fig; stop–step; hip–hop; same–some; came–come; drop–drip; trick–track; pen–pin; pin–pan; get–got; man–men; put–pit; bug–big; pat–pet; click–clack; log–leg; cap–cup; but–bet; shout–shirt; green–grown; feet–foot; stop–steep; store–stare.*
- Lined Four-Box Sheet (two per child).

Understand the Principle

To become truly flexible with word solving, children need to be able to manipulate words by changing the beginning, ending, or middle. Changing the middle of words is the most complex way of manipulating words, but if children learn to perform this operation, they will be able to make powerful connections between words that will help them solve a wide range of words.

Explain the Principle

“You can change the middle letter or letters to make a new word.”

plan

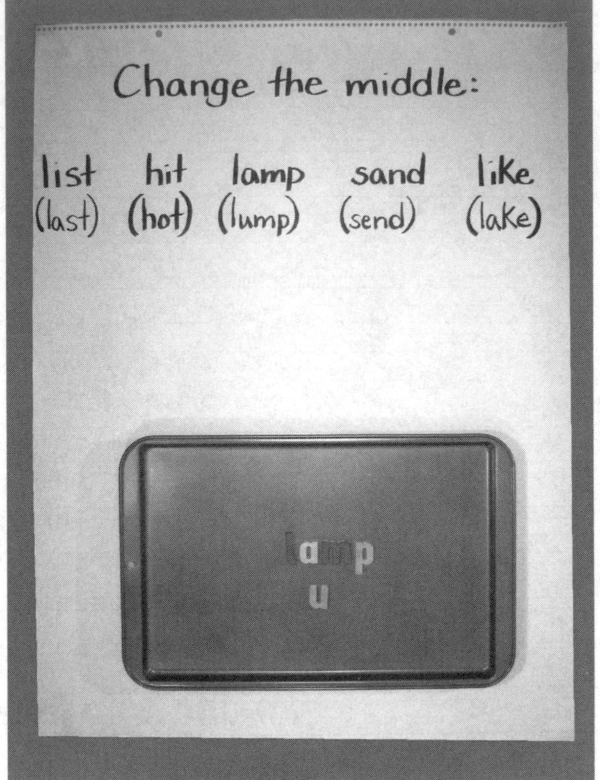

Explain the Principle

"You can change the middle letter or letters to make a new word."

1. Tell your children they are going to learn more about word parts.

2. Using magnetic letters, make the word *list*. Suggested language: "What does the word say? [Children respond.] Watch this! I'm taking the *i* out and putting an *a* in the middle of the word. Now it says. . . . [Children respond.]"

3. Repeat with the other examples: *hit–hot, lamp–lump, sand–send, like–lake*. Each time you build a word, invite the children to change the middle to make a new word.

4. Invite the children to give a few words they know, and call on class members to change the middle.

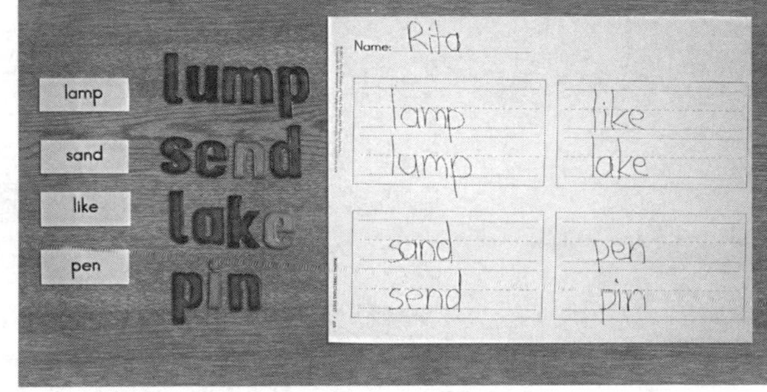

take
build
change
write

- Have the children make eight pairs of words using word cards. You may use pairs from the suggested list or make up your own.
- The children take a card and build the word with magnetic letters. Then they change the middle and write the word pairs on two Lined Four-Box Sheets. Each child makes eight pairs and reads them to a partner.

Have the children share their Making Connections Sheets with a different partner.

Ask the children what they noticed. Look for comments like these:

> "The letter you change is usually a vowel."
>
> "Sometimes you change one letter in the middle and sometimes you change two letters."
>
> "Sometimes the new word sounds different when you change the middle. It doesn't rhyme."

Link

Interactive Read-Aloud: Read aloud books that celebrate the sounds of words, such as

- ***Winter Lullaby*** by Barbara Seuling
- ***The Old Woman Who Named Things*** by Cynthia Rylant

Shared Reading: After enjoying a text such as "Hey Diddle Diddle Dout" or "A Snail" (see *Sing a Song of Poetry*), select two or three words to write on a whiteboard or chart or make with magnetic letters. Write the first word and invite the children to change the middle to make a new word.

Guided Reading: Show the children how they can use a part of a word they know to read a new word and then prompt them to problem-solve when they come to a new word: "Do you know a part that can help?" You might show them how to cover the part they don't know so they can see only what they do know. They say the part they know and uncover the whole word.

Interactive Writing: When the children want to write a new word, quickly write a word they know and show them how to change the middle.

Independent Writing: Provide demonstrations on using parts of words the children know to write new words.

assess

- Give the children a page of words, placed randomly in two columns, that can be connected by both first and last parts of the word. Only the middle is different. Have them draw lines to match the words that are pairs because the middle has changed.
- Have them read the pairs of words aloud to you so you can see how they are processing the words.

Expand the Learning

Repeat the lesson with different examples to help the children become very flexible with word parts. For variety, use letter cards (see *Teaching Resources*), letter tiles, link letters, wood letters, plastic letters.

Connect with Home

Encourage family members to place magnetic letters on the refrigerator or in a large plastic container. As children build words they know, a family member can show them how to change a part of the word to make a new word. (See *Teaching Resources,* Ways to Work with Magnetic Letters, for a sheet of suggestions on working with magnetic letters that you can send home. An alternative to magnetic letters is to send home a set of letter cards.)

11 Adding and Removing Letters to Make Words

Consider Your Children

Use this lesson after children are familiar with some simple high frequency words, know most letters and related sounds, and have had some experience constructing words in interactive and independent writing. They should also have had experience changing letters and word parts to make new words. This lesson helps the children expand the range of connections that will help them in word solving. They will increase their flexibility in working with words.

Working with English Language Learners

In this lesson, children put together different kinds of knowledge and use it in flexible ways. Be sure that English language learners are using high frequency words they know or words they have used in shared reading or writing. If children have difficulty with the concept, you may want to review how to make connections between words. Working with a small group, invite children to select some short words from the word wall and help them change the beginning or ending letter or show them how to add a letter to make a new word.

You Need

- Magnetic letters.
- List of words, perhaps *is, in, an, the, up, to, his, hit, fit, win.*

From *Teaching Resources:*

- Lined Four-Box Sheet.

Understand the Principle

When good readers and writers solve words, they draw on what they already know. They make connections not only to their knowledge of letters and sounds but also to their knowledge of words and word patterns. Connections to known words help children form powerful strategies that will make them fast, flexible word solvers.

Explain the Principle

“You can add letters to the beginning of a word to make a new word.”

“You can add letters to the end of a word to make a new word.”

“You can take away letters from the beginning of a word to make a new word.”

“You can take away letters from the end of a word to make a new word.”

plan

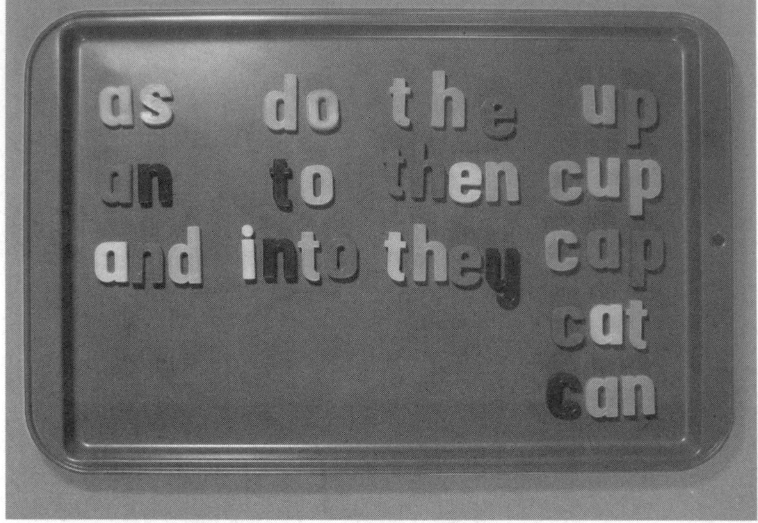

Explain the Principle

“ You can add letters to the beginning of a word to make a new word. ”

“ You can add letters to the end of a word to make a new word. ”

“ You can take away letters from the beginning of a word to make a new word. ”

“ You can take away letters from the end of a word to make a new word. ”

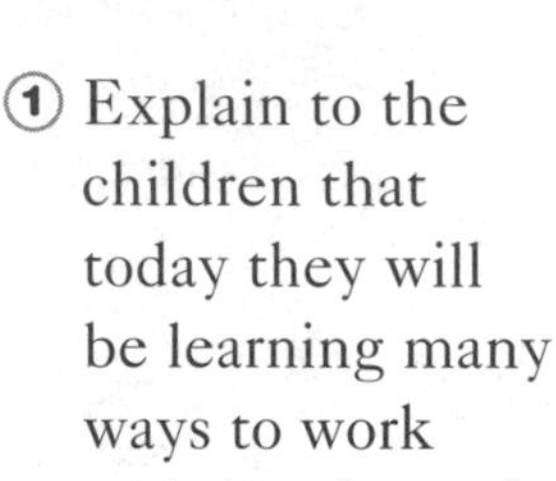

① Explain to the children that today they will be learning many ways to work with word parts.

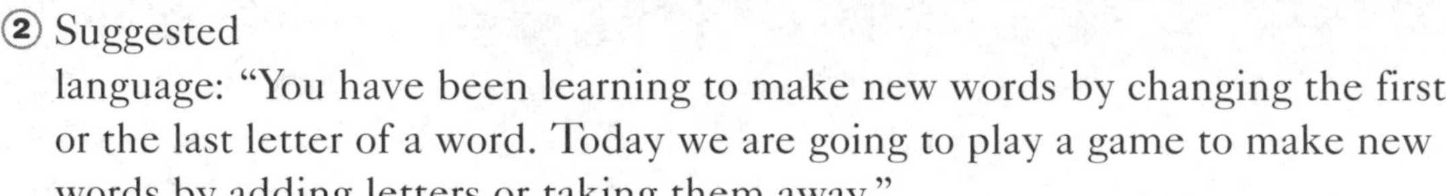

② Suggested language: “You have been learning to make new words by changing the first or the last letter of a word. Today we are going to play a game to make new words by adding letters or taking them away.”

③ Suggested language: “You know *as,* don’t you? I’m going to change the last letter to *n*. Now I have. . . . [Children respond.] Yes that’s *an*. Now I’m going to add a letter at the beginning, *m*. Now I have *man*. Now I’ll take away the *m*, and what do I have again? [Children respond.] Now I’ll add *d* to the end, and I have *and.* You can add letters and make new words, and you can take away letters and make new words.”

④ Demonstrate the same process with *do*, *to*, and *into*. Point out that you added two letters (or the word *in*) to the beginning of *to* to make a new word.

⑤ Demonstrate the process with *the*, *then*, back to *the*, *they*, and back to *the*. Do not be concerned that these words are not phonetically regular. They are high frequency words that the children are learning; simply acknowledge that in these changes, the word sounds different in the middle.

⑥ Repeat the process with *up*, *cup*, *cap*, *cat*, and *can*. You will introduce more complexity here, because *cup* involves changing the middle. If that is too difficult for your group, leave it out.

⑦ Suggested language: “When you are thinking about how to write a word or read a word, think about how the words you know can help you. Just look how many words we made by adding and taking away letters.”

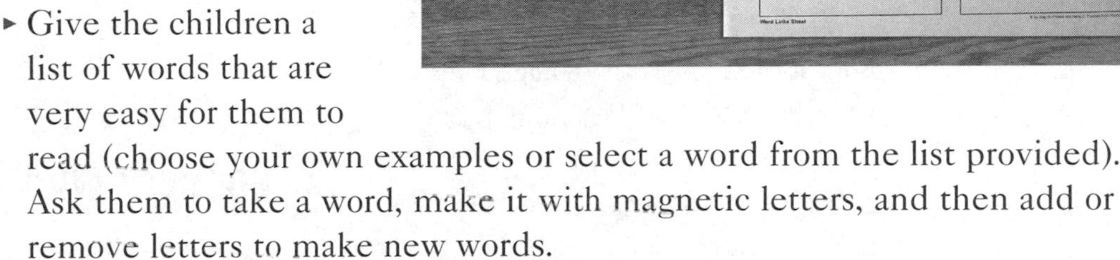

read
make
add/take away
write

- Give the children a list of words that are very easy for them to read (choose your own examples or select a word from the list provided). Ask them to take a word, make it with magnetic letters, and then add or remove letters to make new words.
- On the lined four-box sheet, have the children write four pairs of words they have worked with or others they can think of.

Invite each child to share a word pair while you make a list on a chart so the children can see the many different words that can be made.

Summarize the lesson by explaining that when you know a word, it helps you figure out many other words.

Link

Interactive Read-Aloud: Read aloud books that help children think about connections among words, such as

- ***Before I Go to Sleep*** by Thomas Hood
- ***Monkey Do!*** by Allan Ahlberg

Shared Reading: Using a familiar text such as "A Tiny Seed" or "What Do You See?" (see *Sing a Song of Poetry*), play a game: "I am thinking of a word in the poem that I could make by adding a letter to the beginning of *an* [adding a letter to the end of *an*]." (See *Sing a Song of Poetry* for examples.)

Guided Reading: When the children come to a difficult word, help them use words they know as a tool in word solving. You may want to use the whiteboard to make the point explicit. During word work, do some quick work with magnetic letters on a magnetic board. Start with a simple word and quickly add or remove letters. Have the children use magnetic letters to go from three or four known words to new words.

Interactive Writing: When the children are working on a new word, help them connect it to a word they already know.

Independent Writing: Encourage the children to use words they know to help them spell words.

assess

- Notice whether the children can make a new word by adding or removing letters.
- Notice whether the children are going beyond the lesson to make new words.
- Notice whether the children are using words they know to spell words when they are writing.

Expand the Learning

Repeat this lesson and include changing beginning and ending sounds and adding letters to the beginning and end of words.

Repeat this lesson and include changing the middle of words.

Go on to more complex words, still working from the list of words that the children know.

Connect with Home

Give the children a set of letter cards (see *Teaching Resources*) to take home to make words. Be sure to include a couple of sets of consonant letters and three sets of vowels so that they will have plenty of cards to make words.

Changing First and Last Word Parts

Making New Words

Consider Your Children

This lesson includes some sophisticated ways of connecting and changing words. Be sure that your students have had experience with and understand the concepts of connecting words by letters or parts and of changing word parts to make new words. In the lesson they will actively explore words in enjoyable ways. Encourage experimentation. The children may produce some unconventional spellings, but if they are thinking of real words and the spellings are phonetically accurate, this is not a big problem. Take the time to clear up any spellings you think are confusing.

Working with English Language Learners

English language learners should be working with words that are in their speaking vocabularies. You do not want to encourage meaningless changing of letters. Work with the children on simple examples long enough to learn whether they understand the concept and are searching for connections among real words that they know.

You Need

- Magnetic letters.
- List of words: *plain, mail, grade, swing, stair, shop, spill, scare, flow, bright, dream, reach, split, draw, clear, drip, cheat, slide, fold.*

From *Teaching Resources:*

- Lined Four-Box Sheet.

Understand the Principle

Word solvers are more efficient when they can discern and work with large parts of words. Making connections between words by common patterns (such as rimes) and being able to manipulate word parts increase children's ability to notice patterns and word parts. They become flexible word solvers.

Explain the Principle

“You can change the first part or the last part to make a new word.”

plan

Explain the Principle

“You can change the first part or the last part to make a new word.”

① Mention to children that you are going to show them how to change parts of words.

② Suggested language: “You know how to change the first letter and the last letter in words. Take a look at this part [put *spr* on the board with magnetic letters and ask children to say it] and now this part [put *ing* on the board to the right]. What does this part say? [Children respond.] The word is. . . . [Children respond, *spring*.] *Spr* is the first part and *ing* is the last part. Watch this. [Change *spr* to *br*.] What does it say now? [Children respond. Change *br* to *th*.] Now what does it say?”

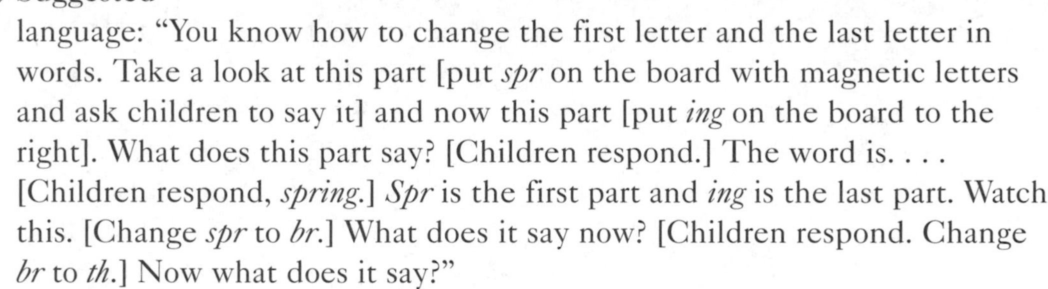

③ Next change the *ing* to *at*. “What does it say now? [Children respond.]” Change the *ing* to *ink*. “What does it say now? [Children respond.]”

④ Repeat with *chair–fair, frame–game, meet–street,* and *store–more.* Suggested language: “So you can change the first part or the last part to make a new word. Today you can choose from the list of words and write the first word on the first line of your Lined Four-Box Sheet. Then make the word with magnetic letters. Change the first or last part and make a new word. A part may be one or two letters or even a rime or an ending. Make four pairs of words on your sheet.”

choose
make
write
change
write

- Have the children choose a word from the list, make it with magnetic letters, write it, change the first or last part to make a new word, and write the new word. Have them write four pairs of words on the Lined Four-Box Sheet.

Have each child share one pair of words they made as you write each pair on a whiteboard.

Have the children tell whether they changed the first or last part.

Link

Interactive Read-Aloud: Read aloud books that show how words are related, such as

- ***Train Leaves the Station*** by Eve Merriam
- ***Cowboy Bunnies*** by Christine Loomis

Shared Reading: After enjoying a text such as "Baby Rhinoceros" or "The Gingerbread Man" (see *Sing a Song of Poetry*), have the children use a masking card or highlighter tape to find words that start or end like a word you say. (See *Sing a Song of Poetry* for many other examples.)

Guided Reading: As the children read, prompt them to use word parts: "Do you see a part you know? What part can help you? Do you know a word like that? Do you know a word that starts [ends] with those letters?"

Interactive Writing: As the children contribute words, ask them to say the first part and the last part.

Independent Writing: Prompt the children to use word parts they know to help with new words: "Do you know a word that starts with those letters?"

assess

- Fold a paper to make four columns and write a word at the top of each: *sand, thin, stay, see,* for example. Invite children to change first parts or end parts to make another word. They can change the original word or work to change parts of each subsequent word they make: *sand, stand, stay, star, car,* for example.
- Notice the children's flexibility in changing word parts. Identify children who need to work with changing word parts in guided reading.

Expand the Learning

Repeat the lesson with different words to develop flexibility.

Connect with Home

Have the children make word pairs at home with magnetic letters or letter cards (see *Teaching Resources*). They write a word and change one part to write another word.

Give each child two index cards. Have them write word pairs, one on each side, and bring the cards back to school to share.

13 Putting Words Together

Building Words

Consider Your Children

Adjust the difficulty of the lesson by choosing easier or more difficult compound words. Usually children find compound words easy to understand and use. Sometimes the meaning of a compound word is clear from the component parts and sometimes it is not. Children will find it interesting to discuss the meaning of compound words.

Working with English Language Learners

Use simple compound words that English language learners understand. Use pictures to help them when possible. Provide many demonstrations. It may be helpful to work with English language learners in a small group as they make words and then write them. If you know any compound words in their language, add them to the list and show how they can be taken apart.

You Need

- Chart and markers.

From *Teaching Resources:*

- Compound Word Cards.
- List Sheet.

Understand the Principle

Children are better able to use and understand compound words if they learn to recognize the words put together to make them. In most compound words, each word contributes some meaning to the whole word (*sidewalk,* for example).

You do not want to teach children to "look for the little word in a bigger word" as a word-solving strategy because this can be confusing (finding the *he* in *mother,* for example, is not helpful). But in the case of compound words, it is very helpful to look at the components as single words.

Explain the Principle

"You can read compound words by finding the two smaller words."

plan

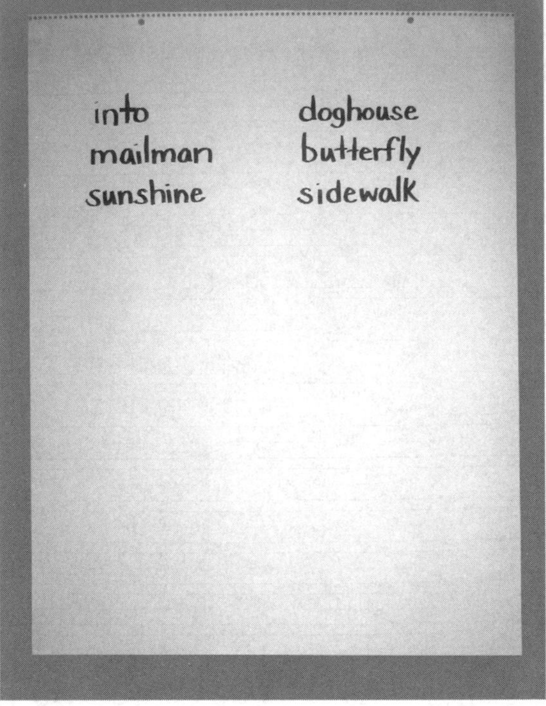

Explain the Principle

"You can read compound words by finding the two smaller words."

1. Mention to your children that today you will help them learn more about words.
2. Suggested language: "Today we are going to learn about another way words work." Ask a child to read the words on the chart. "What do you notice about the words?"
3. If necessary, mask one part of the compound word and then the other to illustrate that there are two (or more) words involved.
4. The children will conclude that each word is made of two words.
5. Explain that each word within the longer word can stand alone and that together they make a compound word. Suggested language: "You can read compound words by finding the two smaller words."
6. Invite the children to suggest a few other compound words to add to the list.
7. Put an example of a compound word on the word wall.

build
write

▸ Have the children use the Compound Word Cards to build ten compound words that contain two words that go together. After making the words, they record the words on a list sheet. Then they read their lists to a partner.

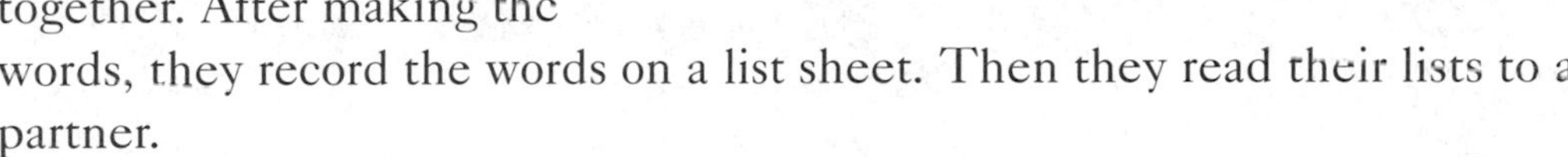

Have the children share their list of compound words with a different partner. Add a few words to the group list.

Link

Interactive Read-Aloud: Read aloud books that use compound words and call a few of the compound words to children's attention. Examples are:

- ***Frozen Noses*** by Jan Carr
- ***Clara Ann Cookie*** by Harriet Ziefert

Shared Reading: After reading and enjoying a text such as "Going to the Fair" or "I Had a Little Rooster" (see *Sing a Song of Poetry*) together, invite the children to use a masking card or highlighter tape to find compound words. (See *Sing a Song of Poetry.*)

Guided Reading: After reading and discussing a text, ask the children to find two or three compound words.

Independent Reading: When the children come to a compound word that is difficult, encourage them to read the first part: "Can you say the first part?" They might cover the last part to isolate the first part and then uncover it to read the whole word.

Interactive Writing: If the children are going to write a compound word in the text you are writing together, remind them that it fits the category—compound words.

Independent Writing: Help the children notice the compound words they are writing.

assess

- Give the children a list of compound words, including some words they have seen before and some new ones. Ask them to circle the words that make up each compound word. Have them read the words to you. Ask them to respond, orally or in writing, with what the word probably means.

Expand the Learning

Have children play Lotto with compound words. Place the first part of the compound word on a square of the game board and the second part on a word card. Children take turns drawing a card, and if it makes a compound word with a word on the game board, they tell the compound word and place the card over the square. (Appendix 19 in *Word Matters: Teaching Phonics and Spelling in the Reading/Writing Classroom* (Pinnell and Fountas 1998) is an extensive list of compound words.)

Ask children to make as many compound words as they can from the same first word. Good words to use are *some (someone, something, somehow, somewhat), in (into, inside), every (everyone, everybody, everything), air (airplane, airport, airline).*

Ask children to make as many compound words as they can from the same last word: *self (itself, myself, yourself), side (inside, outside, beside).*

Connect with Home

Make photocopies of compound word cards for children to cut out (see *Teaching Resources,* Word Card Template). Have them cut the compound words apart and practice putting compound words together at home.

14 Learning How to Learn Words 1

Choose, Write, Build, Mix, Fix, Mix

Consider Your Children

Typically this lesson is used in mid-to-late Grade 1 with children who have had a great deal of hands-on work with spelling principles and are ready to begin a more formal spelling system called Buddy Study (see Pinnell and Fountas 1998). Before presenting this lesson, give the fifty or one hundred high frequency words test to help children build a list of words they need to learn. In addition, teach children how to keep a list of words to learn (see Pinnell and Fountas 1998, Chapter 14). The number of words children choose for the five-day cycle of learning will depend on their skill level. Combine this lesson with a lesson on any particular principle you think children will find easy to understand. You may want to have all the children use the same set of words for the first cycle.

Working with English Language Learners

Through this highly structured and systematic way of learning how to spell, English language learners not only will learn to spell many words but will also add to their English vocabularies. Help them build their Words-to-Learn lists carefully, being sure they know the meaning of the words and are including high frequency words. Work with them in a small group until you are sure that they know the choose, write, build, mix, fix, mix routine.

You Need

- Word study "library" (chart with a pocket for each student).
- Index cards for children's individual word study lists.
- Magnetic letters.

From *Teaching Resources:*

- Words-to-Learn Lists.

Understand the Principle

Good spellers know when a word doesn't "look right" because they recognize the visual sequence of letters that make up a word. If a letter is not there or another letter has been substituted, they know something is wrong. Using magnetic letters to build words in sequence and then checking their accuracy visually helps build the habit of looking closely at and remembering visual features. Ultimately, this process becomes quick and automatic as children develop systems for learning words.

Explain the Principle

"You can make a word several times to learn the sequence of letters."

plan

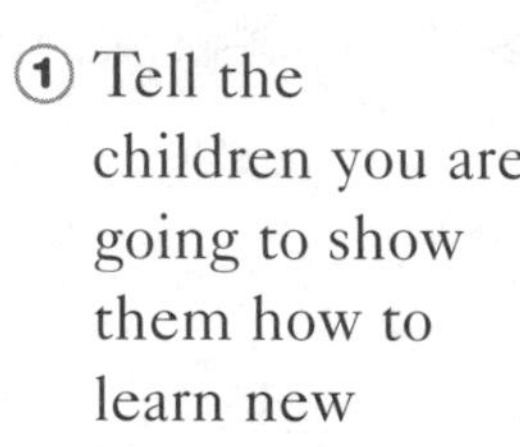

Explain the Principle

“You can make a word several times to learn the sequence of letters.”

1. Tell the children you are going to show them how to learn new words.

2. Suggested language: “Today you are going to select four [or you can choose to start with two or three] words from the minilesson we have just completed (see Consider Your Children). [Children refer to the chart with principle and examples.] You will also choose four words from your Words-to-Learn list in your writing folder. Write the eight words carefully on this index card.” As children choose words from their list, they place a check next to them.

3. Next you will build each word three times with magnetic letters.” Demonstrate mixing, fixing, and mixing with magnetic letters on a cookie tray, magnetic easel, or overhead projector. Show how to check each letter in sequence. Emphasize working carefully but steadily so that the task takes only about five or ten minutes.

choose
write
build
mix
fix
mix

- While the children choose, write, build, mix, fix, and mix their words, review each child's index card and initial the right corner to show you have checked for correct spelling.
- Have the children place their word study cards in their pockets on the word study chart; they will be used again in the next four lessons.

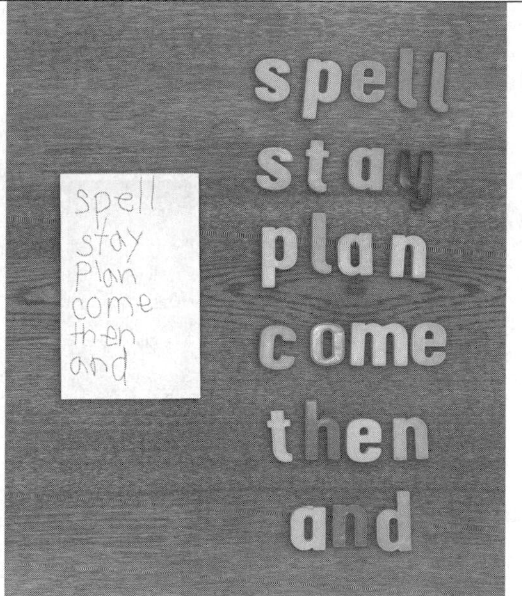

Ask the children to share how building the words is helping them learn the words. Answer any questions. Reinforce the principle in other reading and writing contexts.

Link

Interactive Read-Aloud: As you encounter them, point out examples of words that fit any principle you are working on. Read aloud books such as

- ***How Big Is a Pig?*** by Clare Beaton
- ***A Little Pigeon Toad*** by Fred Gwynne

Shared Reading: As the children are reading familiar texts such as "Hanky Panky" or "Here We Go" (see *Sing a Song of Poetry*), have them locate words that fit any principle you are working on with a masking card, flag, or highlighter tape.

Guided Reading: In word work, give the children more practice in building words quickly and checking them letter by letter.

Interactive Writing: Remind the children that writing words is similar to building words with magnetic letters because they are paying attention to the sequence of letters.

Independent Writing: Help the children learn to notice patterns in words and remind them to spell correctly the words they have learned. Help them transfer what they are learning in word study to their writing.

assess

- Notice if the children are applying the principle they learned in their daily writing.
- Observe the children's ability to recognize these words quickly when they are reading.

Expand the Learning

Repeat the lesson as needed to reinforce the routines of the spelling system.

Connect with Home

Have children make a second index card to take home, where they can practice making the words with magnetic letters or letter cards (see *Teaching Resources*).

15 Learning How to Learn Words 2

Look, Say, Cover, Write, Check

Consider Your Children

This is the second lesson in a series called "Buddy Study." This system is designed to teach children how to learn words. It introduces a more formal way to help children learn and use spelling principles. In this lesson children learn an effective study method for learning words. Teach this lesson in connection with the same principle you used in Lesson WSA 14; that is, the children will be using the same words with a new routine.

Working with English Language Learners

Observe English language learners carefully to be sure that they are using the routines correctly. Demonstrate saying the words to help them pronounce them as accurately as possible. As you confer with them, help them use this word-learning technique and identify words they want to add to their Words-to-Learn list.

You Need

- Word study folders (colored pocket folders with gussets to hold reference pages in the middle).
- Children's word study cards.
- File folders with one side cut in three or four strips (see illustration on page 472).

From *Teaching Resources:*

- Look, Say, Cover, Write, Check Sheet (Use an enlarged version for demonstration purposes.)

Understand the Principle

Children need to look carefully as they say a word, visualizing it, so when they cover it they can remember how it should look. They need to exercise deliberate ways of looking at words so that the visual features remain in the memory.

Children can check whether they remember the word by writing the letters in sequence and visually checking them. This "slowed down" way of considering the word ultimately builds automatic ways of noticing both familiar and new/difficult features of a word.

Explain the Principle

"You can look at a word, say it, cover it, write it, and check it to help you learn to spell it correctly."

plan

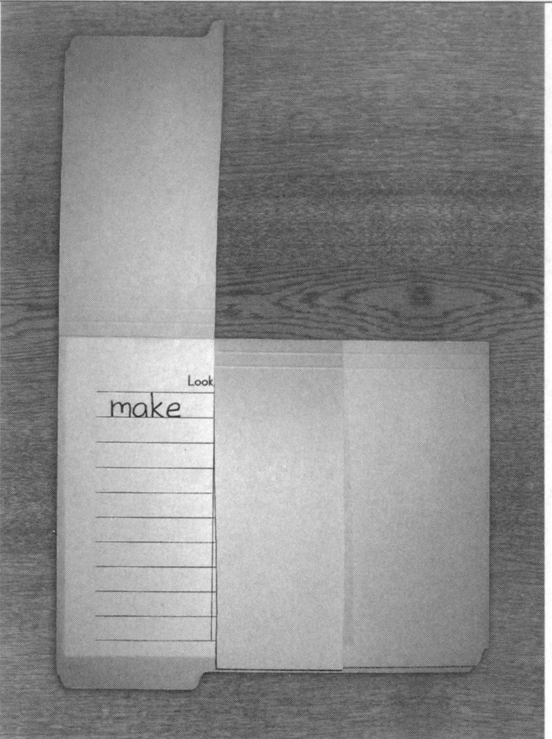

Explain the Principle

"You can look at a word, say it, cover it, write it, and check it to help you learn to spell it correctly."

① Let the children know you will be showing them how to study words so they can learn to write words correctly.

② Place a Look, Say, Cover, Write, Check Sheet in the study folder with all the flaps open.

③ Suggested language: "You'll use your word study cards from yesterday in today's activity."

④ Using an enlarged form of the Look, Say, Cover, Write, Check Sheet, show the children how to write the first word in the left column of the sheet, look carefully at it, cover it with the flap, write it in the second column, and then open the first flap to check it.

⑤ Demonstrate the process with a sample word—*make*. Suggested language: "Put your study sheet in the study folder. Open all the flaps. Copy your first word in the left column. Get a good look and say it. Pull the first flap down to cover the word. Write the word in the second column. Open the first flap and now check letter by letter—*m–m, a–a, k–k, e–e.* Next repeat the process by closing flap 2, looking at the word in column 1, saying it, covering it and writing it in column 3. Open flap 1 to check the word in column 3, letter by letter."

⑥ Tell the children that they will write the next word in column 1 and repeat the process. If they get any words wrong, they should mix and make them three times with magnetic letters.

⑦ Explain that they will be using the study method each week to focus on their words.

apply

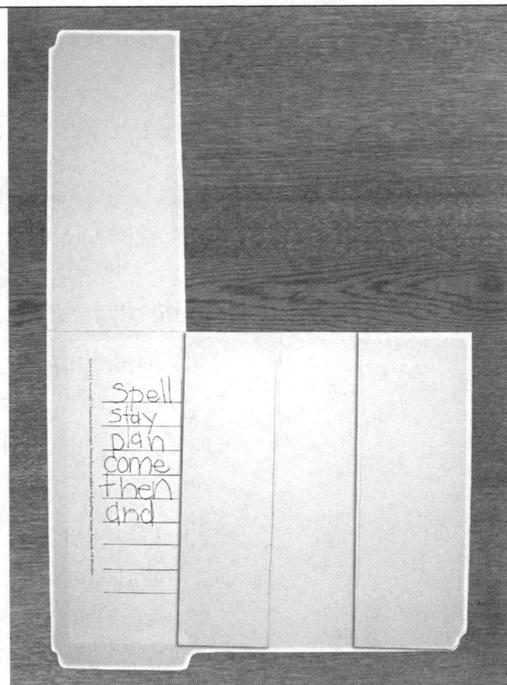

look
say
cover
write
check

- Have the children use the study method with each of the words on their cards.

Remind the children of the principle learned in the cycle. Have them place their cards back in the library pockets.

Link

Interactive Read-Aloud: Read aloud books that expand the children's listening vocabularies, such as

- ***Dinorella*** by Pamela Edwards
- ***Butterfly House*** by Eve Bunting

Shared Reading: Model locating and checking a word in a text that is familiar to the children, such as "Hickory, Dickory, Dock" or "I Don't Suppose" (see *Sing a Song of Poetry*).

Guided Reading: Encourage children to look closely at a word they find difficult and to check it. During word work, have the children look at a word, cover it, build it with magnetic letters, and then check it. Use this time to help children who are having difficulty learn to use the routine smoothly and quickly.

Interactive Writing: For a word the children want to write, model looking carefully at a word in another text or on the word wall, writing it, and checking it. Guide the children to check a word after writing it on the chart.

Independent Writing: When the children are using words from the word wall or their personal word banks, encourage them to use a quick version of "look, say, cover, write, check."

assess

- Notice if the children are applying the principle of the cycle in their daily writing.
- Observe how the children apply the principle to take words apart in reading.

Expand the Learning

Repeat the lesson as needed to reinforce the routines of the spelling system.

Connect with Home

Remind the children to take their word list home and practice words with family members.

16 Learning How to Learn Words 3

Buddy Check

Consider Your Children

This is the third lesson in the series of lessons designed to teach children how to learn words in a formal spelling system incorporating spelling principles and words misspelled in writing. Children learn how to notice and correct spelling errors by checking and "trying it again." Children will need to have a spelling partner. Pair children of similar spelling ability for a period of time (eight to twelve weeks, for example) so they can more easily work with and help each other.

Working with English Language Learners

Be sure that the buddies you put together can read each other's words and also use them in sentences. It is helpful to put a language proficient child with one who needs to learn more English if they can also read each other's words. Demonstrate how to use words in sentences and also how to pronounce them carefully and clearly so that the buddy has the best chance of hearing them. Demonstrate the process again for pairs who have difficulty.

You Need

- List of spelling buddies.
- Highlighter pen.
- Marker.
- Magnetic letters.

From *Teaching Resources:*

- Buddy Check Sheet. (Use an enlarged version for demonstration purposes.)

Understand the Principle

The "try it another way" technique is one adults often use. When we notice a word doesn't look right, we try other letter sequences until the pattern looks right. Children need to learn that looking at the word is a way to search for accurate spelling. Using the looking and checking strategies that build their ability to tell when a word "looks right," they apply this knowledge to solving an unfamiliar word.

Explain the Principle

"You can write a word, look at it, and try again to make it 'look right.'"

"You can notice and think about the parts of words that are tricky for you."

plan

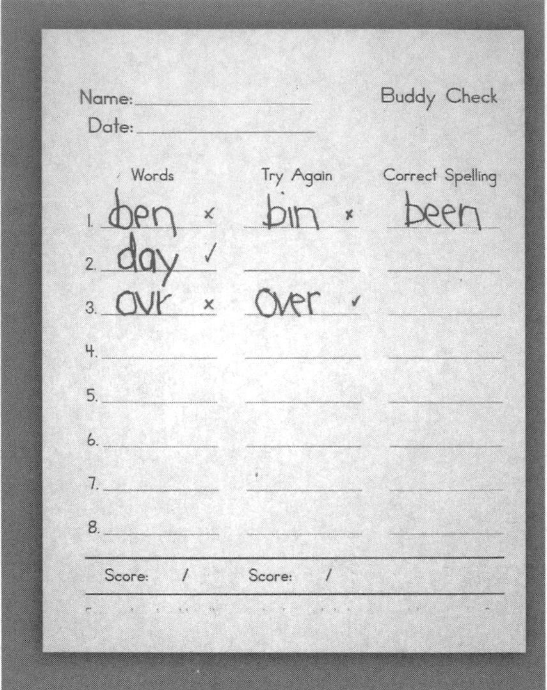

Name: ______ Buddy Check
Date: ______

	Words	Try Again	Correct Spelling
1.	ben ×	bin ×	been
2.	day ✓		
3.	ovr ×	over ✓	
4.			
5.			
6.			
7.			
8.			

Score: / Score: /

Explain the Principle

“You can write a word, look at it, and try again to make it ‘look right.’ ”

“You can notice and think about the parts of words that are tricky for you. ”

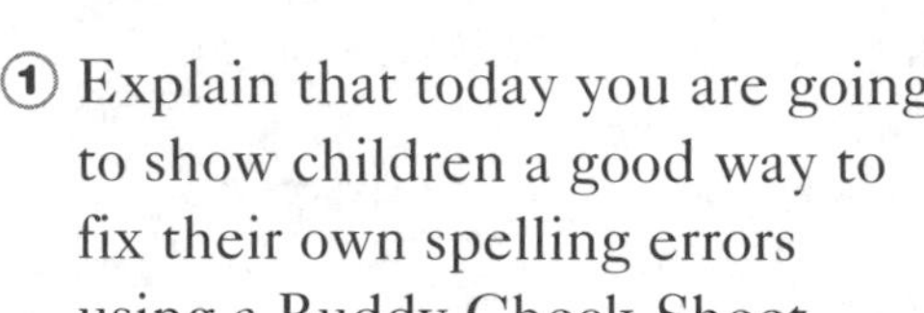

① Explain that today you are going to show children a good way to fix their own spelling errors using a Buddy Check Sheet.

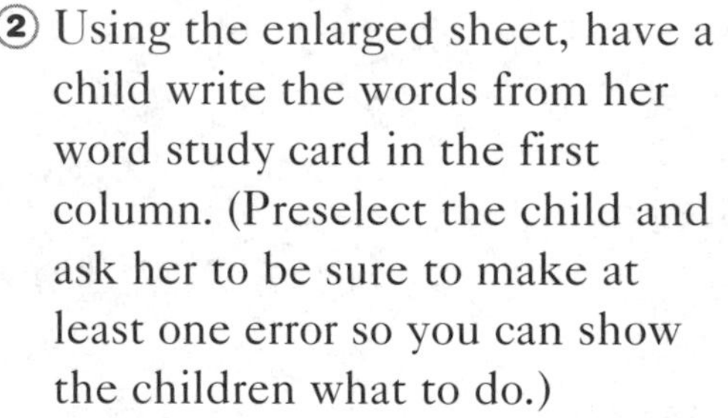

② Using the enlarged sheet, have a child write the words from her word study card in the first column. (Preselect the child and ask her to be sure to make at least one error so you can show the children what to do.)

③ Dictate each word, using it in a sentence as the child writes the word in the first column. When she is finished, put a check mark next to it if it is correct. If it is incorrect, mark it with an X and have the child try it again in the second column. If it is still incorrect, the child writes it correctly from her word card in the last column.

④ Ask the child what she wants to remember about the incorrectly spelled word. Have her write it in the bottom section, make it three times with magnetic letters, and highlight the tricky part with a highlighter pen. She also writes what she wants to remember.

⑤ Explain to the children that they will do buddy check with their partners today.

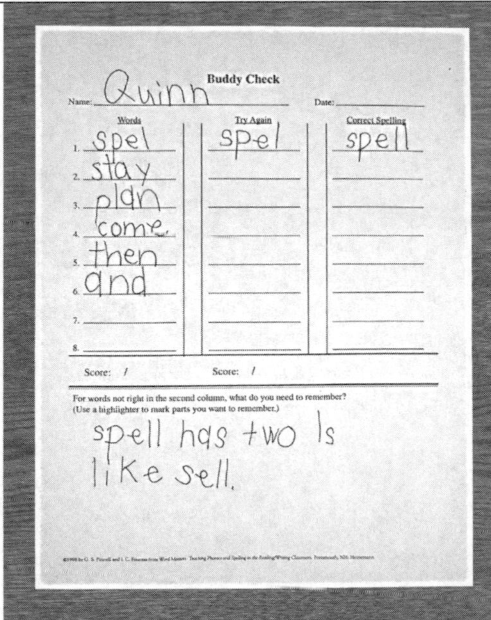

Buddy Check

Name: Quinn   Date:

	Words	Try Again	Correct Spelling
1.	spel	spel	spell
2.	stay		
3.	plan		
4.	come		
5.	then		
6.	and		
7.			
8.			

Score: /   Score: /

For words not right in the second column, what do you need to remember?
(Use a highlighter to mark parts you want to remember.)

spell has two ls like sell.

write
check
try
remember

- Have the children do buddy check with their partners. Observe them to be sure buddies can read each other's words and use them in sentences.
- Work with a small group of children who are having difficulty.

Have the children share some of the statements they made on their sheets about how to remember the tricky words.

Link

Interactive Read-Aloud: Read aloud books that feature the sounds and letter patterns in words, such as

- ***Spider on the Floor*** by Raffi
- ***Bear on a Bike*** by Stella Blackstone

Shared Reading: After reading and enjoying a poem such as "I Have a Little Cough" or "I Went Downtown" (see *Sing a Song of Poetry*), ask the children to locate particular words. Then ask them what they want to remember about writing that word.

Guided Reading: During word work, make a few words that are tricky for the children to read. Ask them what they want to remember about the letter patterns.

Interactive Writing: After constructing a text, have the children locate two or three words and tell what they want to remember about the letters.

Independent Writing: Encourage the children to reread their writing and check the spelling of their words. They may have some words they want to try again.

assess

- Observe the children's self-correction strategies in independent writing.

Expand the Learning

Repeat the process as often as needed to be sure children control the routine.

Connect with Home

Have children take home their Buddy Check Sheets and a copy of their word study cards. Family members can dictate words, and children can repeat the process.

17 Learning How to Learn Words 4

Making Connections

Consider Your Children

This is the fourth in the series of lessons designed to teach children strategies for learning words in a formal spelling system. Children learn how to use what they know about words to learn new words. You will want to repeat this lesson many times, showing children different ways to make connections. You can teach Lessons WSA 14–18 within the same week and repeat them the next week or space the learning of these routines over several weeks, depending on how quickly your children learn them. You will want to start a list of the different conventions you teach, so that your students can refer to it in the future.

Working with English Language Learners

Making connections among words will expand English language learners' vocabularies. Show them how to make connections, demonstrating suggestions if needed. Work with pairs who have difficulty making connections. Encourage children to repeat the sentences that describe their connections. For example: "*Stop* sounds like *rip* at the end."

You Need

- List of spelling buddies.
- List of connections.

From *Teaching Resources:*

- Making Connections Sheets. (Use an enlarged version for demonstration purposes.)

Understand the Principle

Children need to develop a network of knowledge about words. Rather than learning each word in the language, children learn principles, strategies, and patterns that help them use old knowledge to create new knowledge. Establishing the habit of making connections among words by how they look or sound or what they mean will help children form these categories.

Explain the Principle

" You can use what you know about words to read new words. "

plan

Explain the Principle

“ You can use what you know about words to read new words. ”

① Explain to children that knowing a word helps them learn other new words.

② Tell them you are going to show them how they can use what they know about words to think about other words. Suggested language: “You have been learning a lot about words. Today I am going to show you how to use what you know about words to think about other words, or how to make connections.”

③ Make the word *me* with magnetic letters on an easel.

④ Ask if they know another word that starts like *me* and make two or more examples.

⑤ Continue with word examples from the cycle’s spelling chart, inviting the children to give words that connect because they start the same.

⑥ Show the children how they can think of three other words that *start the same*. Write *start the same* on your list of connections.

⑦ Explain that one way of making connections is thinking about words that start the same.

⑧ Tell the children they are going to list their word at the top of the sheet. Then they think of three words that start the same as each of the spelling words on their lists and underline the part that is the same.

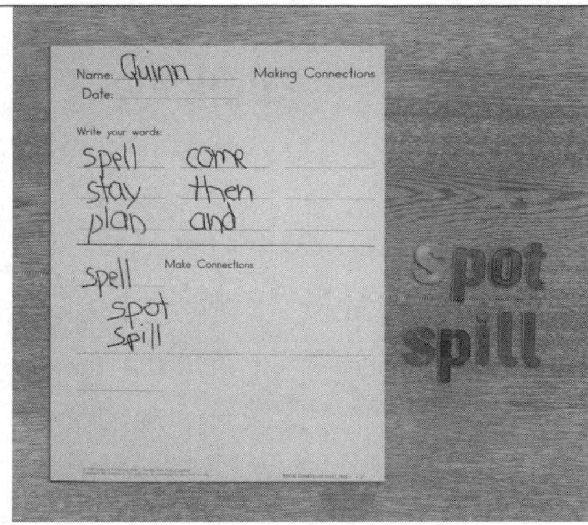

write
connect
underline

▸ Have the children use the words on their word study cards to make connections. First they list their words at the top. They write each word and write more words that start the same. They repeat the process until they have made three connections for each word. Have them underline the part that is the same. Spelling buddies can help each other and read their connections to each other.

Have the children share some of the connections they made.

Link

Interactive Read-Aloud: Model connecting unfamiliar words to words that children know while you are reading aloud books, such as

- ***Hop on Pop*** by Dr. Seuss
- ***Clap Your Hands*** by Lorinda Cauley

Shared Reading: Model connecting new words to known words. After the children become familiar with a text such as "Little Bo Peep" or "The Lion and the Unicorn" (see *Sing a Song of Poetry*), show them a known word on a card and invite them to locate words in the text that are like that word (for example, connect *this, then, them, they,* and *there* to the known word *the*).

Guided Reading: Help the children use known words to solve new words. During word work, use the whiteboard to show the children how to solve new words by making connections to known words.

Interactive Writing: For a new word the children want to write, use the whiteboard to model how to spell a word by using words you already know.

Independent Writing: Encourage the children to use connections to solve words that they are writing. In conversations about words they have written, point out how words are alike (for example, *like* and *likes*).

assess

- Notice whether the children are using what they know about words to write new words.
- Observe the children's ability to solve words when they are reading by connecting them to words they know.

Expand the Learning

Repeat the lesson to show other ways of making connections, and add them to the list of possible connections:

Words that start with the same two letters.

Words that end with the same letter.

Words that end with the same two or three letters.

Words that rhyme.

Words that have the same vowel sound.

Words that mean about the same.

Words that mean about the opposite.

Connect with Home

Making connections is a good activity for homework. When children take their word cards home, they can build their spelling words with magnetic letters and then build other words that are connected to these words in some way.

18 Learning How to Learn Words 5

Test Your Knowledge

Consider Your Children

After four days of learning how to learn words, children take an inventory of their knowledge. Spelling partners or buddies dictate each word and use it in a sentence so their partners can check on their own knowledge. For the next couple of weeks, review the routines each day and observe the children to notice their growing independence. You may want to time the activity and remind them to work carefully but quickly. Decide whether to increase or decrease the number of words each child learns.

Working with English Language Learners

Be sure that English language learners understand the process of the buddy spelling test, including saying words in sentences. One advantage of this system is the children often learn their buddies' words. Work with pairs who have difficulty incorporating the routines. Most of the time, children should be spelling all words accurately because they have had four previous days of study. If they are not, they may be choosing words that are too hard or that they do not understand. Notice the errors children make and guide them in choosing words for the next week.

You Need

- List of spelling buddies.
- Word study notebook.
- Individual word study cards.

Understand the Principle

Ultimately spellers must call to mind the features of a word and produce it in writing. This process must be fluent, automatic, and largely unconscious, so that the writer can keep the meaning of the message in mind as well as continually construct and reconstruct it. It is useful for spellers trying new words to test their knowledge so that they can get an idea of what parts of the word they control and what they still need to learn and remember.

Explain the Principle

“You can write words to see if you know them.”

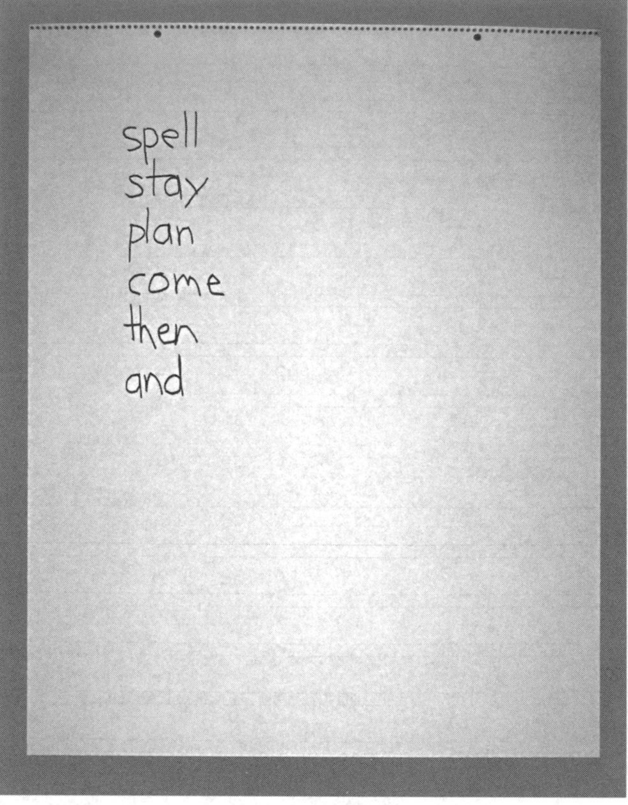

Explain the Principle

“You can write words to see if you know them.”

1. Explain to the children that today they will give each other a spelling test to see how well they can spell their words. Select a child and demonstrate the process on chart paper. Suggested language: “You have been working hard to learn your spelling words. You have built them with letters, studied them with look, say, cover, write, check, checked them with buddy check, made connections with other words, and today you are going to see how well you know them by taking a buddy spelling test.”
2. After dictating your child partner’s list, check it. Children do not check each other’s tests. Explain to the children they will hand in their notebooks after the test so you can check them. (You will be able to learn how effective their learning has been by checking their work.)
3. When you return the notebook, have the children make any words they misspelled with magnetic letters.
4. On children’s Words to Learn lists, circle the checks next to accurate words to show they have learned them.
5. They can select any misspelled words again in a later week.

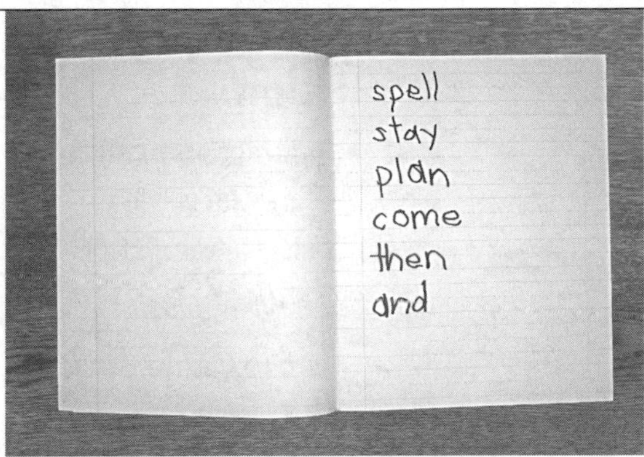

write
check

- Have spelling buddies give the buddy spelling test to each other.

Have the children show how well they completed the routine and ask any questions.

Have a few children share something they learned about their words during the cycle.

Link

Interactive Read-Aloud: Read aloud books that invite children's curiosity and expand their listening vocabularies, such as

- ***Water Music*** by Jane Yolen
- ***Eyes, Nose, Fingers, and Toes*** by Judy Hindley

Shared Reading: After reading and enjoying a text such as "My Love for You" or "The More We Get Together" (see *Sing a Song of Poetry*), invite the children to share what they notice about words. Model some interesting patterns that you know, such as, "I see *y* at the end of *my* and it sounds like *i;* I see *y* at the end of *happy* and it sounds like *e.*"

Guided Reading: Have the children check words for accuracy using visual features as well as whether words make sense. Provide word work for children who need to give greater attention to features of words; write a word on the whiteboard and then have the children build the word with magnetic letters and check it against the word on the whiteboard.

Interactive Writing: Have the children check the accuracy of a word in the message by checking it with the word wall or a word card.

Independent Writing: Require the children to reread what they have written to be sure they have correctly spelled the words they know. Have them circle other words they think may not be correct.

assess

- Observe the children's accurate spelling when they are writing independently, as this is the real measure of their successful use of the spelling system. Hold them accountable for the words they have learned: they must spell them correctly in any writing they do.
- Observe whether the children are able to quickly recognize the words they know when they are reading.

Expand the Learning

Repeat the lesson as often as needed to be sure children follow the routines effectively.

Connect with Home

Invite the children to take their word cards home and share them with family members.

Glossary

Affix A part added to the beginning or ending of a base or root word to change its meaning or function (a *prefix* or *suffix*).

Alphabet book A book for helping children develop the concept and sequence of the alphabet by showing the letters and people, animals, or objects that have labels related to the letters (usually the labels begin with the letters).

Alphabetic principle The concept that there is a relationship between the spoken sounds in oral language and the graphic forms in written language.

Analogy The resemblance of a known word to an unknown word that helps you solve the unknown word.

Antonym A word that has a different sound and opposite meaning from another word (*cold* vs. *hot*).

Assessment A means for gathering information or data that reveals what learners control, partially control, or do not yet control consistently.

Automaticity Rapid, accurate, fluent word decoding without conscious effort or attention.

Base word A whole word to which you can add affixes, creating new word forms *(washing)*.

Blend To combine sounds or word parts.

Buddy study A word study system for learning conventional spelling strategies.

Closed syllable A syllable that ends in one or more consonants *(lem-on)*.

Comparative form A word that describes a person or thing in relation to another person or thing (for example, *more, less; taller, shorter*).

Compound word A word made up of two or more other words or morphemes *(playground)*. The meaning of a compound word can be a combination of the meanings of the words it comprises or can be unrelated to the meanings of the combined units.

Concept book A book organized to develop an understanding of an abstract or generic idea or categorization.

Connecting strategies Ways of solving words that use connections or *analogies* with similar known words (knowing *she* and *out* helps with *shout*).

Consonant A speech sound made by partial or complete closure of the airflow that causes friction at one or more points in the breath channel. The consonant sounds are represented by the letters *b, c, d, f, g, h, j, k, l, m, n, p, q, r, s, t, v, w* (in most of its uses), *x, y* (in most of its uses), and *z*.

Consonant blend Two or more consonant letters that often appear together in words and represent sounds that are smoothly joined, although each of the sounds can be heard in the word *(trim)*.

Consonant cluster A sequence of two or three consonant letters that appear together in words *(trim, chair)*.

Consonant digraph Two consonant letters that appear together and represent a single sound that is different from the sound of either letter *(shell)*.

Consonant-vowel-consonant A common sequence of sounds in a single syllable (*hat*, for example).

Contraction A shortening of a syllable, word, or word group usually by the omission of a sound or letters *(didn't)*.

Decoding Using letter/sound relationships to translate a word from a series of symbols to a unit of meaning.

Dialect A regional variety of a language. In most languages, including English and Spanish, dialects are mutually intelligible; the differences are actually minor.

Directionality The orientation of print (in the English language, from left to right).

Distinctive letter features Visual features that make every letter of the alphabet different from every other letter.

Early literacy concepts Very early understandings related to how print works.

English language learners People whose native language is not English and who are acquiring English as an additional language.

Fluency Speed, accuracy, and flexibility in solving words.

Grammar Complex rules by which people can generate an unlimited number of phrases, sentences, and longer texts in that language. *Conventional grammar* refers to the accepted conventions in a society.

Grapheme A letter or cluster of letters representing a single sound, or phoneme *(a, eigh, ay).*

Graphophonic relationship The relationship between the oral sounds of the language and the written letters or clusters of letters.

Have a try To write a word, notice that it doesn't look quite right, try it two or three other ways, and decide which construction looks right; to make an attempt and check oneself.

High frequency words Words that occur often in the spoken and written language *(the).*

Homograph One of two or more words spelled alike but different in meaning, derivation, or pronunciation (the *bat* flew away, he swung the *bat;* take a *bow, bow* and arrow).

Homonym (a type of *homograph*) One of two or more words spelled *and* pronounced alike but different in meaning (we had *quail* for dinner; I would *quail* in fear).

Homophone One of two or more words pronounced alike but different in spelling and meaning (*meat* vs. *meet, bear* vs. *bare*).

Idiom A phrase with meaning that cannot be derived from the conjoined meanings of its elements *(raining cats and dogs).*

Inflectional ending A suffix added to a base word to show tense, plurality, possession, or comparison *(darker).*

Letter knowledge The ability to recognize and label the graphic symbols of language.

Letters Graphic symbols representing the sounds in a language. Each letter has particular distinctive features and may be identified by letter name or sound.

Lexicon Words in a language.

Long vowel The elongated vowel sound that is the same as the name of the vowel. It is sometimes represented by two or more letters *(cake, eight, mail).*

Lowercase letter A small letter form that is usually different from its corresponding capital or uppercase form.

Morpheme The smallest unit of meaning in a language. Morphemes may be *free* or *bound.* For example, *run* is a unit of meaning that can stand alone. It is a *free morpheme.* In *runs* and *running*, the added *s* and *ing* are also units of meaning. They cannot stand alone but add meaning to the free morpheme. *S* and *ing* are examples of *bound morphemes.*

Morphemic strategies Ways of solving words by discovering *meaning* through the combination of significant word parts or morphemes *(happy, happiest; run, runner, running).*

Morphological system Rules by which morphemes (building blocks of vocabulary) fit together into meaningful words, phrases, and sentences.

Morphology The combination of morphemes (building blocks of meaning) to form words; the rules by which words are formed from free and bound morphemes—for example, root words, prefixes, suffixes.

Multiple-meaning words Words that mean something different depending on the ways they are used (*run*—home run, run in your stocking, run down the street, a run of bad luck).

Onset In a syllable, the part (consonant, consonant cluster, or consonant digraph) that comes before the vowel *(cr-eam).*

Onset-rime segmentation The identification and separation of onsets (first part) and rimes (last part, containing the vowel) in words *(dr-ip).*

Open syllable A syllable that ends in a vowel sound *(ho-tel).*

Orthographic awareness The knowledge of the visual features of written language, including distinctive features of letters as well as spelling patterns in words.

Orthography The representation of the sounds of a language with the proper letters according to standard usage (spelling).

Phoneme The smallest unit of sound in spoken language. There are approximately forty-four categories of speech sounds in English.

Phoneme addition Adding a beginning, middle, or ending sound to a word *(h + and, an + t).*

Phoneme blending Identifying individual sounds and then putting them together smoothly to make a word *(c-a-t = cat).*

Phoneme deletion Omitting a beginning, middle, or ending sound of a word *(cart – c = art).*

Phoneme-grapheme correspondence The relationship between the sounds (phonemes) and letters (graphemes) of a language.

Phoneme isolation The identification of an individual sound—beginning, middle, or end—in a word.

Phoneme manipulation The movement of sounds from one place to another.

Phoneme reversal The exchange of the first and last sounds of a word to make a different word.

Phoneme substitution The replacement of the beginning, middle, or ending sound of a word with a new sound.

Phonemic (or *phoneme*) awareness The ability to hear individual sounds in words and to identify particular sounds.

Phonemic strategies Ways of solving words that use how words *sound* and relationships between letters and letter clusters and phonemes in those words *(cat, make).*

Phonetics The scientific study of speech sounds—how the sounds are made vocally and the relation of speech sounds to the total language process.

Phonics The knowledge of letter/sound relationships and how they are used in reading and writing. Teaching phonics refers to helping children acquire this body of knowledge about the oral and written language systems; additionally, teaching phonics helps children use phonics knowledge as part of a reading and writing process. Phonics instruction uses a small portion of the body of knowledge that makes up *phonetics*.

Phonogram A phonetic element represented by graphic characters or symbols. In word recognition, a graphic sequence composed of a vowel grapheme and an ending consonant grapheme (such as *an* or *it*) is sometimes called a *word family*.

Phonological awareness The awareness of words, rhyming words, onsets and rimes, syllables, and individual sounds (phonemes).

Phonological system The sounds of the language and how they work together in ways that are meaningful to the speakers of the language.

Plural Of, relating to, or constituting more than one.

Prefix A group of letters that can be placed in front of a base word to change its meaning *(preplan)*.

Principle In phonics, a generalization or a sound/spelling relationship that is predictable.

R-controlled vowel sound The modified sound of a vowel when it is followed by *r* in a syllable *(hurt)*.

Rhyme The ending part (rime) of a word that sounds like the ending part (rime) of another word *(mail, tale)*.

Rime The ending part of a word containing the vowel; the letters that represent the vowel sound and the consonant letters that follow it in a syllable *(dr-eam)*.

Root The part of a word that contains the main meaning component.

Schwa The sound of the middle vowel in an unstressed syllable (for example, the *o* in *done* and the sound between the *k* and *l* in *freckle*).

Segment To divide into parts *(to-ma-to)*.

Semantic system The system by which speakers of a language communicate meaning through language.

Short vowel A brief-duration sound represented by a vowel letter *(cat)*.

Silent *e* The final *e* in a spelling pattern that usually signals a long vowel sound in the word and does not represent a sound itself (*make,* for example).

Suffix An affix or group of letters added to a base or root word to change its function or meaning *(replace, handful)*.

Syllabication The division of words into syllables *(pen-cil)*.

Syllable A minimal unit of sequential speech sounds composed of a vowel sound or a consonant-vowel combination. A syllable always contains a vowel or vowel-like speech sound *(to-ma-to)*.

Synonym One of two or more words that have different sounds but the same meaning *(chair, seat)*.

Syntactic awareness The knowledge of grammatical patterns or structures.

Syntactic system Rules that govern the ways in which morphemes and words work together in sentence patterns. Not the same as *proper grammar,* which refers to the accepted grammatical conventions.

Syntax The study of how sentences are formed and of the grammatical rules that govern their formation.

Visual strategies Ways of solving words that use knowledge of how words *look*, including the clusters and patterns of the letters in words *(bear, light)*.

Vowel A speech sound or phoneme made without stoppage of or friction in the airflow. The vowel sounds are represented by *a, e, i, o, u,* and sometimes *w* and *y.*

Vowel combinations Two vowels that appear together in words *(meat)*.

Vowel digraph Two successive vowel letters that represent a single vowel sound *(boat)*, a vowel combination.

Word A unit of meaning in language.

Word analysis The breaking apart of words into parts or individual sounds in order to parse them.

Word family A term often used to designate words that are connected by phonograms or rimes (for example, *hot, not, pot, shot*). A *word family* can also be a series of words connected by meaning (affixes added to a base word; for example: *base, baseball, basement, baseman, basal, basis, baseless, baseline, baseboard, abase, abasement, off base, home base; precise, précis, precisely, precision*).

References

Adams, J.J. (1990). *Beginning to Read: Thinking and Learning about Print.* Cambridge, MA: MIT Press.

Allington, R. (1991). Children who find learning to read difficult: School responses to diversity. In E.H. Hiebert (ed.). *Literacy for a Diverse Society.* New York: Teachers College Press.

Armbruster, B.B., Lehr, F., and Osborn, J. (2001). *Put Reading First: The Research Building Blocks for Teaching Children to Read: Kindergarten Through Grade 1.* Jessup, MD: National Institute for Literacy.

Ball, E.W., and Blachman, B.A. (1991). Does phoneme awareness training in kindergarten make a difference in early word recognition and developmental spelling? *Reading Research Quarterly* 26 (1): 49-66.

Biemiller, A. (1970). The development of the use of graphic and contextual information as children learn to read. *Reading Research Quarterly* 6: 75-96.

Blachman, B. (1984). The relationships of rapid naming ability and language analysis skills to kindergarten and first grade reading achievement. *Journal of Educational Psychology* 76: 614-622.

Blanchard, J.S. (1980). Preliminary investigation of transfer between single-word decoding ability and contextual reading comprehension of poor readers in grade six. *Perceptual and Motor Skills* 51: 1271-1281.

Bradley, L., and Bryant, P.E. (1983). Categorizing sounds and learning to read—a causal connection. *Nature* 301: 419-421.

Bryant, P.E., Bradley, L., Camlean, M., and Crossland, J. (1989). Nursery rhymes, phonological skills and reading. *Journal of Child Language* 16: 407-428.

Bryant, P.E., MacLean, M., Bradley, L.L., and Crossland, J. (1990). Rhyme and alliteration, phoneme detection, and learning to read. *Developmental Psychology* 26 (3): 429-438.

Ceprano, M.A. (1980). A review of selected research on methods of teaching sight words. *The Reading Teacher* 35: 314-322.

Chall, J.S. (1989). Learning to read: The great debate. 20 years later. *Phi Delta Kappan* 70: 521-538.

Clay, M.M. (1991). *Becoming Literate: The Construction of Inner Control.* Portsmouth, NH: Heinemann.

Clay, M.M. (1998). *By Different Paths to Common Outcomes.* York, ME: Stenhouse Publishers.

Clay, M.M. (2001). *Change over Time in Children's Literacy Development.* Portsmouth, NH: Heinemann.

Daneman, M. (1991). Individual difference in reading skills. In R. Barr, M.L. Kamil, P. Mosenthal, and P.D. Pearson (eds.). *Handbook of Reading Research* (Vol. II, pp. 512-538). New York: Longman.

Ehri, L.C. (1991). Development of the ability to read words. In R. Barr, M.L. Kamil, P. Mosenthal, and P.D. Pearson (eds.). *Handbook of Reading Research* (Vol. II, pp. 383-417). New York: Longman.

Ehri, L.C., and McCormick, S. (1998). Phases of word learning: Implications for instruction with delayed and disabled readers. *Reading and Writing Quarterly* 20: 163-179.

Fountas, I.C., and Pinnell, G.S. (1996). *Guided Reading: Good First Teaching for All Children.* Portsmouth, NH: Heinemann.

Fountas, I.C., and Pinnell, G.S. (eds.) (1999). *Voices on Word Matters: Learning about Phonics and Spelling in the Literacy Classroom.* Portsmouth, NH: Heinemann.

Fox, B., and Routh, K.D. (1984). Phonemic analysis and synthesis as word-attack skills: Revisited. *Journal of Educational Psychology* 76: 1059-1064.

Hohn, W., and Ehri, L. (1983). Do alphabet letters help prereaders acquire phonemic segmentation skill? *Journal of Educational Psychology* 75: 752-762.

Holdaway, D. (1987). *The Foundations of Literacy.* Portsmouth, NH: Heinemann.

Hundley, S., and Powell, D. (1999). In I.C. Fountas and G.S. Pinnell (eds.). *Voices on Word Matters* (pp. 159-164). Portsmouth, NH: Heinemann.

Juel, C. (1988). Learning to read and write: A longitudinal study of 54 children from first through fourth grades. *Journal of Educational Psychology* 80: 437-447.

Juel, C., Griffith, P.L., and Gough, P.B. (1986). Acquisition of literacy: A longitudinal study of children in first and second grade. *Journal of Educational Psychology* 78: 243-255.

Lesgold, A.M., Resnick, L.B., and Hammond, K. (1985). Learning to read: A longitudinal study of word skill development in two curricula. In G.E. MacKinnon and T.G. Walker (eds.). *Reading Research: Advances in Theory and Practice* (Vol. 4, pp. 107-138). New York: Academic Press.

Liberman, I., Shankweiler, D., and Liberman, A. (1985). The Alphabetic Principle and Learning to Read. U.S. Department of Health and Human Services. Reprinted with permission from the University of Michigan Press by the National Institute of Child Health and Human Development. Adapted from Phonology and the problems of learning to read and write. *Remedial and Special Education* 6: 8-17.

Liberman, I.Y., Shankweiler, D., Fischer, F.W., and Carter, B. (1974). Explicit syllable and phoneme segmentation in the young child. *Journal of Experimental Child Psychology* 18: 201-212.

Lundberg, I., Frost, J., and Petersen, O.P. (1988). Effects of an extensive program for stimulating phonological awareness in preschool children. *Reading Research Quarterly* 23: 264-284.

McCarrier, A.M., Pinnell, G.S., and Fountas, I.C. (2000). *Interactive Writing: How Language and Literacy Come Together.* Portsmouth, NH: Heinemann.

Moats, L.C. (2000). *Speech to Print: Language Essentials for Teachers.* Baltimore: Paul H. Brookes.

Nagy, W.E., Anderson, R.C., Schommer, M., Scott, J., and Stallman, A. (1989). Morphological families in the internal lexicon. *Reading Research Quarterly* 24: 262-282.

National Institute of Child Health and Human Development (2001). *Report of the National Reading Panel: Teaching Children to Read: An Evidence-Based Assessment of the Scientific Research Literature on Reading and Its Implications for Reading Instruction. Reports of the Subgroups.* Washington, DC: National Institutes of Health.

New Standards Primary Literacy Committee (1999). *Reading and Writing: Grade by Grade.* Washington, DC: National Center on Education and the Economy and the University of Pittsburgh.

Perfetti, C.A., Beck, I., Bell, L., and Hughes, C. (1987). Children's reading and the development of phonological awareness. *Merrill Palmer Quarterly* 33: 39-75.

Pinnell, G.S., and Fountas, I.C. (1998). *Word Matters: Teaching Phonics and Spelling in the Reading/Writing Classroom.* Portsmouth, NH: Heinemann.

Pinnell, G.S., Pikulski, J., Wixson, K.K., et al. (1995). *Listening to Children Read Aloud: Data from NAEP's Integrated Reading Performance Record (IRPR) at Grade 4.* Report No. 23-FR-04, prepared by the Educational Testing Service. Washington, DC: Office of Educational Research and Improvement, U.S. Department of Education.

Pressley, M. (1998). *Reading Instruction That Works: The Case for Balanced Teaching.* New York: The Guilford Press.

Read, C. (1971). Pre-school children's knowledge of English phonology. *Harvard Educational Review* 41: 1-34.

Snow, C.E., Burns, M.S., and Griffin, P. (eds.). *Preventing Reading Difficulties in Young Children.* Washington, DC: Committee on the Prevention of Reading Difficulties in Young Children, Commission on Behavioral and Social Sciences and Education, National Research Council.

Treiman, R. (1985). Onsets and rimes as units of spoken syllables: Evidence from children. *Journal of Experimental Child Psychology* 39: 161-181.

Vellutino, F.R., and Denckla, M.B. (1991). Cognitive and neuropsychological foundations of word identification in poor and normally developing readers. In R. Barr, M.L. Kamil, P. Mosenthal, and P.D. Pearson (eds.). *Handbook of Reading Research* (Vol. II, pp. 571-608). New York: Longman.

Vellutino, F.R., and Scanlon, D.B. (1987). Phonological coding, phonological awareness, and reading ability: Evidence from longitudinal and experimental study. *Merrill Palmer Quarterly* 33: 321-363.

Vellutino, F.R., Scanlon, D.M., Sipay, E.R., et al. (1996). Cognitive profiles of difficult-to-remediate and readily remediated poor readers: Early intervention as a vehicle for distinguishing between cognitive and experiential deficits as basic causes of specific reading disability. *Journal of Educational Psychology* 88: 601-638.